On Law and Justice

On Law and Justice

ALF ROSS

Edited and with an Introduction by
JAKOB v. H. HOLTERMANN

Translated by
UTA BINDREITER

OXFORD
UNIVERSITY PRESS

OXFORD
UNIVERSITY PRESS

Great Clarendon Street, Oxford, OX2 6DP,
United Kingdom

Oxford University Press is a department of the University of Oxford.
It furthers the University's objective of excellence in research, scholarship,
and education by publishing worldwide. Oxford is a registered trade mark of
Oxford University Press in the UK and in certain other countries

First Edition published in 2019

Published in the United States of America by Oxford University Press
198 Madison Avenue, New York, NY 10016, United States of America

British Library Cataloguing in Publication Data
Data available

Library of Congress Control Number: 2019942846

ISBN 978–0–19–871610–5

Editor's preface

The present volume constitutes a full new English translation of Alf Ross's major work originally published in Danish as *Om ret og retfærdighed* in 1953. This is not the first time the book has been translated into English. Shortly after its publication in Danish, Ross himself carried out a translation in collaboration with Margaret Dutton. That work was published in 1958 and immediately reached a wide readership.

Considering that the book has previously been published in English and in a translation authorized by the author, the editorial decision to publish this new full translation instead of merely reprinting the old one may require an explanation. The primary reason is that, regardless of Ross's own contribution, the first translation nevertheless suffers from a number of defects, even to the extent where scholars have been warned against basing their understanding of his version of Scandinavian legal realism on it. Considering the sustained, and in recent years increasing, interest in Ross's work in the Anglophone legal *academe*, this is of course unfortunate.

One specific problem that has attracted considerable attention relates to the English translation of the two key terms in Ross's legal theory *gyldig ret* and *gældende ret*. These terms have no immediate equivalent in English so, in the 1958 edition, Ross chose to translate both terms indiscriminately as *valid law*. Unfortunately, this has led English-language readers, H. L. A. Hart most prominently among them, to overlook the fact that Ross's legal realism relies on a distinction between two *kinds* of valid law expressed in Danish precisely with the two terms *gyldig ret* and *gældende ret*.

Another, apparently less noticed but equally important problem with the 1958 translation is the fact that it is a significantly abridged version containing numerous, seemingly inexplicable omissions. A systematic comparison reveals that there are omissions both within sentences and of entire text passages, sometimes of considerable length. The combined effect of these defects is that the 1958 edition has failed: (i) to state correctly the character and scope of Ross's central philosophical project; and (ii) to adequately represent the core thesis behind Ross's bipartite analysis of valid law. In turn, this has significantly derailed scholarly discussion of Alf Ross's legal theory. By providing a full new translation from scratch, it is our hope to help this scholarly debate back on track by making sure that in the future it will be based on the actual merits and demerits of Ross's realistic theory.

While the translator has essentially provided the full translation, the primary role for me as editor has been to secure philosophical consistency throughout, and in exegetical questions raising dilemmas of theoretical importance to decide on the way forward. This is particularly relevant with regard to the difficult issue already mentioned at the heart of Ross's legal theory, i.e. regarding his distinction between *gyldig* and *gældende ret*. In the separate section, 'A note on the translation of "gyldig" and "gældende ret" as "valid" and "scientifically valid law"', the translational dilemma is outlined and reasons are provided for the solution that has been chosen.

Furthermore, I have provided a general philosophical introduction to *On Law and Justice*. In spite of the general clarity of his writings, Alf Ross is not always an easy philosopher. This is perhaps especially true for readers in the Anglophone tradition in legal philosophy, which generally seems to place less emphasis than Ross on epistemological issues and general issues of philosophy of science. Accordingly, the introduction focuses on explaining Ross's philosophical project and situating it in the context of problems, which will presumably appear more familiar to the average English-language reader. I should also add that the page numbers of the second Danish edition of *On Law and Justice (Om ret og retfærdighed*, 2013) are given throughout, in the margins.

I would like to extend my warm gratitude to those who have supported me in the process of undertaking this project and carrying it to completion.

First and foremost, I would like to express my most heartfelt gratitude to Professor Uta Bindreiter for her untiring, conscientious, and in every way truly excellent work.

I am sincerely grateful to Professors Brian Leiter and Stanley L. Paulson for supporting the project at crucial points, each in their own way.

Several years ago, I read an interview with Brian Leiter, where, in reply to the question 'to which issue of legal philosophy would you most like to see more attention paid in the future?' he said, 'Scandinavian realism deserves a sympathetic reconsideration'. Apart from speeding up my own ongoing research to this end, reading his answer first sowed the idea in my mind that there might be an audience for a new English translation of Ross's major work. Later, upon meeting in person, Brian Leiter expressly supported the idea, he wholeheartedly encouraged me to undertake the task with Oxford University Press, and he has continuously given invaluable advice in the process.

Of equal importance was a meeting with Stanley L. Paulson at the Hans Kelsen conference 'Legal Science and Legal Theory' at the University of Oxford in September 2010; a meeting after which the first concrete plans towards a new translation began to materialize. First, it was Stanley L. Paulson's inspired suggestion to approach the translator Uta Bindreiter, the *sine qua non* of this book. Second, he once wrote to me that a new translation 'would be a major contribution. *Something fundamental*, by contrast to the little articles we all write'. These wise words have continuously helped keep things in perspective.

Also, I would like to extend my sincere thanks to three colleagues at the Law Faculty at the University of Copenhagen—namely, Professor Henrik Palmer Olsen for his early active contribution to and continued warm support of this project; Professor Mikael Rask Madsen for, as the director of iCourts where I am employed, not only allowing but even seeing the contemporary value of old realist thoughts for a centre that studies international courts; and Associate Professor Shai Dothan for his supernatural scholarly generosity, also with this project.

I owe a special debt of gratitude to Alf Ross's son Strange Ross who, on behalf of the family, has kindly granted permission and support not only to this publication in English of *On Law and Justice* but also to the publication in 2013 of a new edition of the original Danish manuscript *Om ret og retfærdighed.*

Finally, I would like to extend my warm gratitude to the commissioning law editors at Oxford University Press, Alex Flach and Jamie Berezin, for their generous encouragement and unwavering support for the project of publishing this new translation.

This research is funded by the Danish National Research Foundation Grant No. DNRF105 and conducted under the auspices of the Danish National Research Foundation's Centre of Excellence for International Courts (iCourts).

Jakob v. H. Holtermann
Copenhagen, January 2019

Translator's preface

Following closely upon the 2013 edition of Alf Ross's major work in Danish, *Om ret og retfærdighed* [On Law and Justice, 1953], this new English translation has a twofold purpose: first, to render Ross's jurisprudential aims as faithfully as possible; and second, to do justice to his characteristic way of expressing himself. Pursuing this purpose, we endeavoured to observe the utmost loyalty to Ross's original text.

Thus, rather than opting for a strictly idiomatic translation, we followed the text as closely as possible: getting Ross's precise meaning in addressing specific legal issues was far more important to us than strictly adhering to the rules of grammar and syntax. At the same time, we not only wished to render Ross's exact meaning, but also his style of speaking and manner of expression without negatively affecting the reading experience.

The fact that the Danish terms *gældende ret* and *gyldig ret* (pivotal in Ross's legal philosophy) have no equivalent in the English language has already attracted considerable attention, the crux of the matter being the question how one might render, in English, Ross's differentiating between these crucial terms. Since this issue is at the heart of Ross's legal theory, it has been given special treatment in a separate section, namely, the editor's 'A note on the translation of "gyldig" and "gældende ret" as "valid" and "scientifically valid law" '; the issue is also extensively discussed in the editor's introduction.

Anxious to express himself as clearly as possible, Ross frequently offers unusual—and, in his view, more precise—compounds, which, however, pose almost insurmountable problems for any translator. In this respect we tried to adhere to the text as much as possible, frequently settling on a new (and perhaps somewhat non-English) compound.

Square brackets used in the body text, in the footnotes, and in Appendix C indicate that additional information has been supplied by the translator or editor. This information may concern obsolete words or phrases, or laws and legal institutions which do not exist anymore and therefore need an explanation.

I would like to extend my sincerest thanks to those who have supported me in the translation process.

First and foremost, I am indebted to those scholars who, well aware of the importance and urgency of providing a new English translation of Ross's major work, have wholeheartedly encouraged me to undertake this task—namely, Professors Jakob von H. Holtermann, University of Copenhagen; Brian Leiter, University of Chicago; Henrik Palmer Olsen, University of Copenhagen; and

Stanley L. Paulson, University of St. Louis/Kiel. In this context, I would like to express my deepest gratitude to Professor Jakob von H. Holtermann, who did not shirk from undertaking numerous trips over the Øresund Bridge in order to give me the benefit of his opinion on Ross's legal philosophy and the intricacies of his terminology.

Special thanks go to Lloyd Cameron, LLM, Policy Adviser at the UK Department for International Development (DFID), who, in the initial stages of the translation, undertook to scrutinize parts of the text and give me excellent advice on English syntax.

Also, I would like to extend my sincere thanks to two colleagues at the Law Faculty of Copenhagen University for their valuable advice—Louise Thiil Parker, BPhil (Oxon), who undertook to check Ross's rendition of Hohfeld's concepts, and Associate Professor Shai Dothan who scrutinized §§ 1–60 of Ross's work with the utmost obligingness.

Last, but certainly not least, I am truly grateful to Oxford University Press for its generous, gracious, and encouraging attitude towards the project of a new English translation of Alf Ross's major work.

Uta Bindreiter
Lund, January 2019

Contents

Introduction

JAKOB v. H. HOLTERMANN[1]

> His greatest philosophical contribution has probably been to develop, in a consistent and rigorous fashion, the consequences of a set of assumptions whose appeal cannot be denied even by those philosophers who reject them.[2]

1. Background

The Danish legal philosopher Alf Ross (1899–1979) and the school of Scandinavian legal realism to which he belonged seem to be witnessing a revival. The present publication of a new full English translation of Ross's main work sixty years after its first translation is but one sign of this renewed interest.[3] This is not to say that the Scandinavian realists have ever been completely off the map since the school was first established around the time of World War I in Uppsala, a small Swedish university town north of Stockholm. But there has undeniably been a period during the final decades of the twentieth century where the group's particular version of legal realism has attracted less interest, and the recent increase in attention should be seen against this background.

(i) 'A whole school of legal theory in Scandinavia'

Scandinavian legal realism consisted of a group of outstanding philosophers and jurists centred on the charismatic Swedish professor of philosophy Axel Hägerström (1868–1939). Besides Hägerström and Ross, the group counted prominent thinkers such as Anders Vilhelm Lundstedt (1882–1955) and Karl Olivecrona (1897–1980). Through their academic activities, the group members managed to establish Scandinavian legal realism as renowned well beyond their small, sparsely populated corner of the world. The Oxford philosopher J. W. Harris once described the Scandinavian Realists as 'wild prophetic figures riding in from the hills with a message for legal philosophers'.[4] Indeed, it seems that this message was powerful enough to secure the riders a lasting place in the

[1] This introduction builds on and integrates parts of previously published work, notably Holtermann (2013, 2014, 2015, 2016, 2017); Holtermann & Madsen (2015).

[2] Originally stated about American philosopher Willard Van Orman Quine (Hookway, 1988, 3).

[3] The first English edition of *On Law and Justice* was published in 1958 as a translation of the original Danish edition *Om ret og retfærdighed*, first published in 1953.

[4] Harris as quoted in Swaminathan (2016), 254.

intellectual history of legal theory. For instance, as an imperfect quantitative measure, the chapter on Scandinavian legal realism in the reference work *Lloyd's Introduction to Jurisprudence* comprises 42 pages—which is only eight pages less than the chapter on American realism.

The specific message of the only member of the Scandinavian school who came riding in from notoriously unhilly Denmark was particularly strong. In 1983, H. L. A. Hart called Alf Ross 'the most acute and well-equipped philosopher of this school',[5] and it is a fact that Ross's work and his particular version of Scandinavian realism remain to this day the most influential and widely discussed.

Ross was an exceptionally prolific writer. Well before internationalization became the mantra of the Academy, he published regularly in the most highly esteemed international journals, and he had his central works translated into several languages, including English, German, Italian, and Spanish. Ross travelled to the most prestigious international universities and met with and kept an extensive personal correspondence with some of the most outstanding intellectuals of his time, both inside and outside the legal field. Right up to the present day, Ross's work remains widely read and studied both inside and outside Scandinavia. Apart from his impact in the Anglophone world, to which we shall return shortly, Ross has been particularly influential in Southern Europe, notably in Italy, Spain, and Portugal, and also in South America, notably, it seems, in Argentina and Chile.[6]

(ii) Some time out of the limelight

In spite of these solid foundations, it remains the case that Alf Ross, and Scandinavian realism more generally, have come upon hard times, especially during the last two or three decades of the twentieth century. Limiting ourselves for present purposes to the Anglophone world, two factors seem to have contributed to this state of affairs. First, the Scandinavian realists seem to have paid a price for their general philosophical alignments. Unlike their distant cousins in American realism, the Scandinavians are known for taking general philosophical questions very seriously. Thus, the school that came to be known as *Scandinavian realism* is most appropriately seen as the specific jurisprudential branch of the more general philosophical movement known as the Uppsala School. Besides Axel Hägerström, the Uppsala School is especially associated with the work of Swedish philosopher Adolf Phalén (1884–1931), and it is known for propounding

[5] Hart (1983), 13.

[6] From the point of view of intellectual history, Ross's lasting influence in Italian- and Spanish-speaking countries is an interesting phenomenon, especially when contrasted with his quite limited influence in countries that are geographically and culturally closer to Scandinavia, like Germany and Austria. One possibility is to see this as a result of Ross's strong anti-metaphysical sentiments and irreconcilable critique of natural law, which seem to have found a more sympathetic audience in the oftentimes anticlerical academic circles that oppose the massive influence of the Catholic church in the aforementioned countries.

a strong empiricist philosophy, which in many ways foreshadowed the views later associated on the international scene with logical empiricism and the so-called Vienna Circle.

On the one hand, this general philosophical orientation towards the Uppsala School probably played a positive role in shaping the Scandinavians' version of legal realism as a consistently empiricist legal theory, and thereby also in placing it on the general jurisprudential map as a distinct and easily recognizable position. On the other hand, however, this philosophical allegiance may also have limited the movement's impact in the long run. To illustrate, Hart at one point accused Hägerström of being 'tortuous and obscure'.[7] This may be taking it a bit too far, but it is probably fair to say that in terms of philosophical temperament, neither Hägerström nor Phalén are known for being particularly forthcoming. To a wider jurisprudential audience, it may not after all have seemed worth the considerable trouble it would take to familiarize oneself intimately with that particular philosophical message of the 'wild prophetic figures'.

Always the opportunist, Ross seems intuitively to have grasped this 'outreach problem' connected with Scandinavian legal realism's reliance on the Uppsala School's somewhat exotic version of empiricism. After becoming acquainted with the deep congenialities between Uppsala and Vienna, Ross therefore decided, well in advance of writing *On Law and Justice*, to shift his ground and simply replace the entire underlying philosophical framework. Instead of relying on the general philosophy of the Uppsala School, Ross decided to build his version of legal realism on the apparently less exotic tenets of logical empiricism; tenets which Ross, on his travels outside Scandinavia, had learned were much more influential and widely understood.

This was not merely a strategic move driven by opportunism or eclecticism. The ingenuity and general consistency with which Ross manages to harmonize his legal realism with the views of logical empiricism make it difficult to doubt that his commitment to its philosophical programme is not genuine and deeply rooted. In any event, it seems plausible that the combination of strategic wit and forceful execution helps explain why Ross has become the most widely known member of Scandinavian realism.

From a wider perspective, however, Ross's philosophical realignment seems to have brought only a short respite. For though logical empiricism was undoubtedly very influential during the early and mid twentieth century, it soon came to lose its momentous influence. In fact, the movement was already waning internationally around the time Ross was writing *On Law and Justice*. Although the process was never as swift and decisive as is often presented, it is a fact that logical empiricism gradually lost its influence during the second half of the twentieth century, and that it has for some time been considered largely moribund.

[7] Hart (1959), 233.

The second reason why Ross and the other Scandinavians appear to have fallen on hard times, at least in the Anglophone world, is related to the first, but it has to do more directly with their *legal* theory. This aspect concerns a line of critique, originally propounded by H. L. A. Hart, which has been hugely detrimental to the long-term reception of Scandinavian legal realism, and especially of Ross's work. Hart's critique is two-pronged, consisting, on one hand, of a generic argument directed, it seems, against empirical theories of law as such (including not only Scandinavian but also American legal realism, and even Austin's version of legal positivism), and on the other hand, of a more specific argument targeting Alf Ross's version of Scandinavian realism.[8] Focusing for present purposes only on their relation to Ross, the soundness of both arguments is, as we shall see, challengeable. However, as a mere matter of intellectual history, it is undeniable that Hart's arguments have been greatly influential, and that, in combination with the widespread scepticism regarding the general philosophical orientation, these arguments have been responsible for the more marginalized role assigned for a time by many to Ross, and to Scandinavian realism along with him.

(iii) The recent return of Scandinavian legal realism

However, this general sentiment of reserve and scepticism has gradually been shifting in recent years. Increasingly, a number of legal theorists have realized there might be a need to reconsider the arguments against Ross and Scandinavian legal realism that have for so long been considered conclusive. Later in this introduction, we shall look more closely into the reasons underlying this development, but in rough outline the following two factors seem to have been driving the change of sentiment.

First, and focusing here exclusively on Alf Ross, scholars, primarily with the ability to read Ross's original Danish manuscript of *On Law and Justice*, *Om ret og retfærdighed*, have increasingly directed attention to the fact that Hart's critique seems to be fundamentally mistaken and that these mistakes are due, at least in part, to relatively simple errors in the first English translation. Thus, closer scrutiny of Ross's writings in Danish has revealed that his realism has sufficient resources to counter those Hartian arguments that have so widely been considered fatal.[9]

Second, something similar has happened as regards the question of Ross's general philosophical alignments, though the case here is slightly more complicated, seeming as it does to rely on some measure of rational reconstruction. Increasingly, scholars have pointed to the fact that in spite of Ross himself

[8] This latter argument was presented in Hart's review of *On Law and Justice*, which he, somewhat misleadingly, called 'Scandinavian Realism', thereby conveying the impression that the critique was, *pars pro toto*, suited to the Scandinavian school in its entirety, cf. Hart (1959).

[9] For two recent examples, cf. Eng (2011) and Holtermann (2017).

explicitly building his legal realism on logical empiricism, his legal theory is perhaps not as inextricably tied to this general philosophical programme as commonly thought. Thus, studies have shown that it may in fact be possible, with only relatively minor changes to Ross's legal theory proper, to realign it with a quite different present-day philosophical movement. More specifically, it seems that it is possible to realign Ross's legal realism with so-called *philosophical naturalism*, which is often seen as the theory that has most directly replaced logical empiricism, and which is considered by many to be one of the most viable schools of contemporary philosophy.[10]

Interestingly, pursuing this track has simultaneously reaffirmed the kinship between the Scandinavian realists and their transatlantic cousins; more specifically because this whole manoeuvre closely parallels the very fruitful exercise known as *naturalizing jurisprudence*, which was initiated approximately a decade earlier in relation to *American* legal realism.[11] Moreover, the prospects of thus combining legal realism with naturalism in general philosophy has been associated, on both sides of the Atlantic, with recent attempts to combine legal realism with the ongoing empirical turn in legal scholarship under the banner *New Legal Realism*.[12]

(iv) The structure of this introduction

These developments form part of the background for this new publication of Ross's *magnum opus*. *On Law and Justice* is a milestone in twentieth-century legal philosophy, and the viability of the legal theory propounded in it makes it natural to ensure the book is available in its entirety to new generations of English-language legal scholars and philosophers. But even in a new and improved translation, Ross is not always an easy philosopher. In spite of the general clarity of his writing, Ross's comprehensive text contains tensions and in some places even apparent contradictions. Consequently, and judging from the large commentary on his work, Ross seems to invite diverging and at times even mutually contradictory readings. Before proceeding to introduce and explain in detail the contents of *On Law and Justice*, it seems prudent to add a few words on the fundamental views that permeate this introduction and structure its argument.

[10] Cf. e.g. Holtermann (2014); Spaak (2009). As we shall see later in this introduction, philosophical naturalism in the meaning referred to here is especially associated with the work of American philosopher Willard Van Orman Quine, and his call for a naturalizing of epistemology; cf. notably Quine (1969).

[11] The project of naturalizing American legal realism is associated in particular with the pioneering work of Brian Leiter (for an overview, cf. Leiter, 2007b). Interestingly, around the time when the first steps had just been taken to naturalize Scandinavian realism, Leiter independently saw the prospects of exploring possible parallels, remarking that 'Scandinavian Realism deserves a sympathetic reconsideration, along the lines of what I have tried to do for its (distant!) American cousin' (Leiter, 2007a).

[12] With regard to American realism, cf. e.g. Nourse & Shaffer (2009). With regard to Scandinavian realism, the push towards a new legal realism has been combined with an attempt to broaden out the inspirational heritage both geographically to continental Europe and from a disciplinary perspective to include famous legal sociologists Max Weber and Pierre Bourdieu; cf. e.g. Holtermann & Madsen (2015).

First, the present introduction is based on a reading of Alf Ross's legal realism as a position in legal theory that is fundamentally distinct from *both* traditional contenders in the game, i.e. natural law and legal positivism. Importantly, the view is propounded that, on the most consistent reading, Ross's legal realism is categorically distinct not only from the legal positivism of his early inspiration, Hans Kelsen, but also from that of H. L. A. Hart. While distinguishing thus between Ross and Kelsen is widely accepted, it is more controversial to assert a deep difference between Ross and Hart. But as we will see—both in the remaining parts of the introduction and in Ross's own text—there are nevertheless good reasons for so doing. Still, the reader should be aware that this view is not uncontested in the scholarly debate.[13]

Second, although Hans Kelsen will naturally play some role in the following pages, Hart has been assigned a more prominent role, primarily because of his influential critique of Ross's legal theory. Even if, ultimately, there are good reasons for finding this critique mistaken, it would be facile and misleading to blame this mistake entirely on Ross's good sense simply being lost in translation. It cannot be denied that Hart's critique rests on a number of well-considered understandable concerns and objections that are invited by Ross's theory. Heuristically, going through Hart's well-known objections provides a framework against which it is helpful steadily to refine the articulation of Ross's actual theory by seeing the convincing and consistent way in which he anticipated such a line of critique. Furthermore, for the majority of readers this approach will presumably have the benefit of honouring Thomas Aquinas's dictum of moving from the more known to the less known. Finally, keeping a keen eye on the points of contact between Ross's legal realism and Hart's legal positivism is also helpful with a view to better assessing the controversial question regarding the theoretical relation between the two.

2. The contents—Alf Ross's legal realism

(i) The philosophical project

In order to get the full benefit from reading *On Law and Justice*, the first question we should ask ourselves is: what is Ross's philosophical project? What is it that ties this work, and more generally his entire oeuvre, together? What is the essential philosophical challenge that Ross is trying to address? We find the general answer to this question in the philosophy of science—the branch of philosophy that takes science itself as the object of theoretical enquiry. Within

[13] Most importantly, Ross himself claimed—in his review of Hart's *The Concept of Law*—that Hart's perception of Ross's position was mistaken and that, once correctly perceived, it would be clear that there was really no disagreement between them. The case was merely that, for the most part, they were talking about different things (Ross, 1962). Cf. also Svein Eng (2011) for an interesting and thorough argument to the effect that Ross and Hart are essentially in agreement.

this broad field, Ross studies the subfield that one might call the philosophy of *legal* science, the term legal science primarily (though not exclusively) referring to the doctrinal study of valid law.[14] For Ross, the central problem for the philosophy of legal science—the academic discipline whose aim is to describe, interpret, and systematize valid law—is to justify its status as a *science*. This is primarily an epistemological concern. Ross wants to make certain that the scholarly determination of the legal rights and duties in given jurisdictions, which is the task of the doctrinal study of law, actually represents *knowledge* and is not merely the expression of the whims of individual jurists, or of those in power. Phrased in philosophical jargon, we can say that Ross tries to answer the question: *how is the doctrinal study of law possible as a science?*

In focusing on this issue, Ross is in close accordance with his teacher, and the main inspiration of his youth, Hans Kelsen. Kelsen also aimed to justify the doctrinal study of valid law as a science.[15] But Ross's approach to this question is more systematic than Kelsen's. First, Ross does not approach his project as an ad hoc task specific to the doctrinal study of law and calling for an answer relevant only to this discipline. Instead, Ross sees the problem from a much broader philosophical perspective. He sees the challenge to legal science merely as one special case of what in the philosophy of science is known more generally as the *demarcation problem*: that is, the problem of how we can generally distinguish between science and non-science—or, more accurately, between science and *pseudo*-science.

Nowadays, we see this question in, for instance, the heated debates about movements such as creationism and intelligent design, movements which challenge evolutionary biology on religious grounds; or in relation to so-called climate change sceptics, who challenge scientific consensus on the existence of man-made climate change. In both cases, the key issue of controversy can be boiled down to a special version of the demarcation problem: are the assertions and theories of this or that movement really science, or are they merely pseudo-science? In Ross's day, the demarcation problem was also a pressing topic, but the fight was fought over different theories and issues. Discussions focused, for example, on whether specific theories such as Freud's psychoanalysis or Marx's theory of history were really scientific. Or they focused, more generally, on

[14] It should be emphasized that in this introduction, and generally in Ross's *On Law and Justice*, the word 'science' is used in a broader sense than may be standard to most English-language readers. In English, 'science' is primarily used to denote the natural sciences and sometimes also fields of research that are considered relevantly similar to them, notably through the application of quantitative methods. Hence, economics and sociology are usually counted as *sciences*, whereas literature studies and history are not. Sometimes, however, 'science' is used more broadly, corresponding to the German word 'Wissenschaft' (and its equivalents in other Germanic languages, e.g. 'videnskab' in Danish). This is taken to include all the academic scholarly disciplines, including the humanities. The German term has the advantage of more adequately delimiting the kind of systematic and critical search for knowledge that usually takes place in an academic setting. As the next pages will show, this extended sense is also the one most fitting to convey Ross's thoughts.

[15] Cf., in particular, Kelsen (1967). As we shall see below, Kelsen was fundamentally *unlike* the other great legal positivist of the twentieth century, H. L. A. Hart, on this issue.

whether entire academic disciplines such as theology or, of relevance here, the doctrinal study of law deserved to be counted among the sciences—*die Wissenschaften*.

Second, Ross's approach is also more systematic than Kelsen's in terms of the answer he provides. Ross maintains that any workable solution to the specific challenge relating to the disputed scientific character of the doctrinal study of law has to build on a general unified theory about science: about what generally distinguishes science from pseudo-science. At the time of writing *On Law and Justice*, Ross thinks that this general theory is provided by the then influential philosophical movement known as logical empiricism.[16] Logical empiricism is known precisely for its fierce advocacy of a strong, universal criterion that makes it possible to distinguish categorically between science and pseudo-science. In the next section we shall take a closer look at this criterion, and also unfold in detail how Ross applies it in relation to the doctrinal study of law. For now, it should just be emphasized that the significance of this theoretical allegiance can hardly be overestimated if one is to fully appreciate *On Law and Justice*. The book as a whole is simply best read as a manifesto for an epistemologically sound doctrinal legal science developed on the basis of the criteria for science asserted by logical empiricism.

Logical empiricism is also sometimes referred to as logical *positivism* and, accordingly, Ross is also often described as a logical *positivist*. Most commentators agree that there is no principled boundary between these two –isms, and it should not be problematic to speak of Ross in that way. Still, there might be a reason for caution. Ross is also sometimes described as a *legal* positivist, but this is unfortunate, and it is not unlikely that the partial homonymy plays a role here. First, the term positivism is, as Ross also reminds us, 'ambiguous. It can mean both "what is building on experience" and "what has formally been enacted"'.[17] Correspondingly, logical positivism and legal positivism in fact refer to two very different theoretical traditions and positions. Second, as seen from Ross's case, logical empiricism's general philosophical programme has implications that in key areas contradict the legal positivist interpretation of the doctrinal study of law, at least as this position is most often stated. It is probably no coincidence that two of the best-known legal positivists, Kelsen and Hart, were not logical empiricists (or even empiricists for that matter). Therefore, even if Ross

[16] 'The *leitmotif* of jurisprudential *realism* is the desire to understand legal science in conformity with the idea of the nature, tasks, and method of science which has been developed by modern, scientific philosophy. Several schools of philosophy—logical empiricism, the philosophy of the Uppsala school, the Cambridge school of philosophy, and others—find common ground in rejecting all speculative knowledge grounded in *a priori* reasoning; in short, in rejecting so-called metaphysics. There is only one world and one type of knowledge. Ultimately, all science is concerned with the same body of facts, and all scientific statements about reality—that is to say, all those statements which are not purely logical-mathematical—are subject to empirical test.' (See below, pp. 80–1.)

[17] See below, p. 118.

at times contributed to the confusion,[18] there is good reason to stick strictly to the term he chose for his own theory in the preface to *On Law and Justice*, i.e. *the realistic theory of law*.

(ii) The central tenets of logical empiricism

Considering the central role assigned by Ross to logical empiricism, we should first provide a brief account of the fundamental perception of science articulated in this philosophical programme. At the most general level, logical empiricism belongs to the empiricist tradition in philosophy according to which sense perceptions provide the ultimate foundations for knowledge and science. At the same time, however, logical empiricism aligns itself in one crucial regard with René Descartes (1596–1650) who, as a central figure in rationalism, is otherwise traditionally perceived as being starkly opposed to empiricism. The fundamental parallel has to do with the fact that Descartes saw it as the most essential task of philosophy to provide indubitable foundations for knowledge and science. Referring to Archimedes' saying he needed 'just one firm and immovable point in order to shift the entire earth',[19] Descartes was searching for 'just one thing, however slight, that is certain and unshakeable'.[20] Descartes famously thought he found such an Archimedean point in his proposition *cogito ergo sum*, I think therefore I am. This sentence, claimed Descartes, 'is necessarily true whenever it is put forward by me or conceived in my mind'.[21]

Proponents of logical empiricism were not particularly impressed with Descartes's answer. *Qua* empiricists, they had both semantic and epistemological issues with his rationalistic strategy of constructing knowledge and science from a foundation of self-evident truths of reason. However, they did not disagree with Descartes's basic idea that knowledge should be certain and indubitable, and that it should therefore rest on rock-solid foundations. They only maintained that these foundations should instead be provided by elementary sense perceptions.

Against this background, the logical empiricists established the so-called verification principle according to which any given proposition—unless an analytical truth—can only be meaningful if it can be proven (*verified*) empirically, that is, by reference to elementary sense perceptions, either directly or indirectly by

[18] Thus in, e.g., Ross (1961), where Ross seems to argue that we should consider *legal positivism* to harbour the same ambiguity as the term *positivism* does. However, for the reasons generally propounded in this work regarding the categorical differences between traditional legal positivism and Ross's own logical positivism-cum-empiricism-based legal theory, it seems more fitting to say that legal positivism harbours only one of the meanings of positivism, i.e. 'what has formally been enacted'.

[19] Descartes (2013), Second Meditation: The nature of the human mind, and how it is better known than the body.

[20] Descartes (2013), Second Meditation: The nature of the human mind, and how it is better known than the body.

[21] Descartes (2013), Second Meditation: The nature of the human mind, and how it is better known than the body.

inference from such perceptions via the application of logic. This principle played an immensely important role in relation to the movement's approach to the demarcation problem. The members of the Vienna Circle came to see the verification principle as *the* criterion to determine whether something can potentially count as belonging to science or not. Any given proposition—or, more generally, any given theory—can only count as science if it can be verified empirically. If the propositions of a given theory cannot accommodate this particular criterion they will, according to the logical empiricists, be meaningless. The theory will be deprived of its claim to being scientific, and categorized instead as *pseudo*-science—or *metaphysics*, to use the favourite pejorative term of the logical empiricists.

This outline of logical empiricism is sufficient for now, but, as we shall see below, there is more to say about both the verification principle—in particular in relation to the strictness with which the demand for verifiability is interpreted—and the logical empiricists' perception of discourse that cannot satisfy the verification principle.

(iii) Turning to legal science: the epistemological challenge outlined

The ability to satisfy the verification principle is the generic notion of science that Ross brings to the table when he turns to legal science to solve his main problem in *On Law and Justice*: how the specific study *of law* is possible as a science.

Ross outlines the challenge as follows. Like most other legal theorists, he considers law to consist of a body of rules, that is, of norms prescribing behaviour. Linguistically, Ross categorizes such norms as so-called *directives*. Directives are usually (though not always) identifiable by normative words like 'ought', 'shall be', 'may', 'must', etc. Furthermore, Ross observes that from a linguistic point of view, sentences commonly found in traditional scholarly legal doctrinal work appear to be no different from the directives of legal rules: they apparently prescribe behaviour using the same kind of deontic markers. Thus, virtually all textbooks and research articles in law speak straightforwardly of normative phenomena like rights and duties.

For purposes of illustration, Ross picks a random sentence from a random Danish textbook in law, the following sentence from *Enkelte Kontrakter* (*Individual Contracts*) by Professor Henry Ussing, p. 116: 'The acceptor is obligated to pay the bill of exchange on the due day for payment, cf. § 28 (1) Danish Bill of Exchange Act.'[22] From an epistemological perspective, the problem with a completely ordinary legal doctrinal proposition like this one is that it is not immediately obvious how the existence of a normative phenomenon like an *obligation* can possibly be reduced to solid sense data:

> But what is an 'obligation' and how can one empirically determine if it has arisen? The acceptance as such, accomplished by drawing some ink

[22] See below, p. 14.

> lines on a piece of paper, does not, among its observable consequences, seem to have one that can be called 'obligation'. (cf. p. 14.)

It is difficult to imagine how *any* sense data could possibly verify such an obligation. Regardless of how one might approach this challenge, one seems invariably to be caught up in a *naturalistic fallacy*—in a logically unwarranted inference from *is* to *ought*.[23]

(iv) Critiquing the tradition

In attempting to overcome this challenge, philosophers of law have traditionally pursued two different tacks, natural law and legal positivism, respectively. Notwithstanding the tangible differences between these two approaches, they share in common the attempt to save the specific *ought* of the scientific study of legal doctrine. Furthermore, as Ross sees it, they both try to save this ought by demonstrating how all the individual theoretical statements about the validity of individual legal rules can be derived, ultimately, from secure and indubitable foundations in the shape of some kind of foundational norm. Natural law and legal positivism only differ with regard to the specific character of these foundations and the method of their identification.

In light of these commonalities, Ross categorizes both approaches as versions of what he calls *legal idealism*—specifically as *substantive* and *formal* idealism, respectively. As we shall see, Ross is profoundly sceptical about the prospects of both approaches. By lumping together natural law and legal positivism as two kinds of idealism, in contradistinction to his own legal *realism*, he is also expressing this scepticism terminologically.

Natural law—or *substantive idealism*—is the first candidate Ross considers. It is also his favourite whipping boy, whose alleged failure he never tires of exposing. In Ross's interpretation, natural law pursues a rationalistic strategy in so far as it tries to derive the validity of the statements made in the doctrinal study of law from a foundation of self-evident truths of reason. More specifically, natural law tries to derive this validity from a basic intuition or idea of justice to which we all, *qua* rational creatures, have access and can assent. Ross outlines this natural law conception of legal science as follows:

> The specific idea manifesting itself in the law is the idea of justice. The idea of justice not only establishes an ideal against which positive law can be measured: it also constitutes the law, that is, it is that principle inherent in the law which endows the law with binding force or validity as law. (See below, p. 79.)

[23] The term 'naturalistic fallacy' was introduced by G. E. Moore (1903) but the underlying problem was first famously addressed by D. Hume (Hume et al., 1978).

In other words, if the acceptor is 'obligated to pay the bill of exchange on the due day' it is *ultimately* because it would violate the idea of justice if this were not the case.

For Ross as a logical empiricist, however, the problem with such intuitions is that they, unlike elementary sense data, are necessarily private. Intuitions can, and patently often do, vary from one person to the next. As Ross puts it in one of his most quoted phrases:

> Like a harlot, natural law is at the disposal of everyone. There is no ideology that cannot be defended by invoking the law of nature. And indeed, how could it be otherwise when the ultimate basis for every natural law is to be found in a private (intra-subjective), direct insight, a self-evident contemplation, an intuition. Cannot my intuition be just as good as yours? Self-evidence as a criterion of truth explains the utterly arbitrary character of metaphysical assertions. It raises them above any form of inter-subjective control and opens the door wide to unbridled fantasy and dogmatics. (See below, p. 338.)

The doctrinal study of law is therefore in deep trouble *qua science* if it were to follow the road suggested by natural lawyers. From the point of view of empiricism, assigning the role of an Archimedian point to an idea of justice, however conceived, will inevitably condemn the entire doctrinal study of law to a fate as *pseudo-science*, or, as Ross and the Vienna Circle would prefer it, as *metaphysics*.

This rather fierce natural law critique is a well-known and oft-cited side of Ross's work. But Ross is in fact equally dismissive of (even if considerably less hostile towards) the parallel attempts of *legal positivism*—or *formal idealism*—to save the doctrinal study of law as a science. To be sure, Ross certainly does appreciate that legal positivism, often with equal fierceness, rejects the attempts of natural law to build legal science from moral foundations. But as Ross sees it, the legal positivists nevertheless end up taking essentially the same flawed foundational strategy. Thus, legal positivism attempts in much the same way as natural law to derive the validity of individual normative doctrinal statements, for instance about the obligations of acceptors of negotiable instruments, through a hierarchy of norms leading back to one foundational norm (in Hans Kelsen's terminology, the *Grundnorm*; in H. L. A. Hart's, the *rule of recognition*). The school only insists that this foundational norm, which provides the ultimate justification for the doctrinal statements of legal science, can only be that norm which, as a historical fact, happens to be efficacious in the jurisdiction under scrutiny—that is, entirely regardless of whether one might find this norm morally reprehensible.[24] It is in this sense that legal positivism is a purely *formal* kind of idealism as opposed to the *substantive* idealism of natural law.

[24] In *On Law and Justice*, Ross is primarily referring to Hans Kelsen's *Grundnorm*. In terms of the basic legal positivist verification procedure for any individual statement of legal validity made in the doctrinal study of law there is, however, no relevant difference between the role of Kelsen's *Grundnorm* and Hart's rule of recognition:

According to Ross, however, this legal positivist attempt to identify an Archimedian point for scientific statements about valid law is also fundamentally flawed—and in much the same way as natural law. The ultimate problem is that the whole exercise necessarily builds on a naturalistic fallacy, an inference from *is* to *ought*, right at the foundations: from the *efficaciousness* of the foundational norm to its *validity*.[25] Absent this fallacious inference, it is possible to construct an infinite number of foundational norms, which in turn justify an infinite number of sets of legal rules. Legal positivism leaves us with no uncontroversial criterion we can use to choose between them. In other words, and extending Ross's infelicitous language, it is not only natural law but also legal positivism that is 'like a harlot, at the disposal of everyone'.

(v) Considering austere behaviourism: Hart's first challenge...

This serves to pose the philosophical challenge that Ross is trying to solve at its most radical: if we are forced, on the general logical empiricist premises adopted by Ross, to disregard the standard solutions proposed by the two traditional contenders in legal philosophy—natural law and legal positivism—is there, then, any hope that a genuine *legal* science is possible at all? What remains of the doctrinal study of valid law if we are barred—whether on the grounds of the evidentiary fragility of intuitive notions of justice, or on the grounds of the naturalistic fallacy—from making any reference to foundational norms?

Against this background, it could seem from Ross's empiricist starting point that the only way forward lies in turning legal science into a strictly behaviourist discipline, one that limits itself exclusively to observations of regularities and subsequent predictions of judicial behaviour. This kind of austere behaviourism

> The sense in which the rule of recognition is the *ultimate* rule of the system is best understood if we pursue a very familiar chain of legal reasoning. If the question is raised whether some suggested rule is legally valid, we must, in order to answer the question use a criterion of validity provided by some other rule. Is *this purported by-law of the Oxfordshire County Council* valid? Yes: because it was made in exercise of the powers conferred, and in accordance with the procedure specified, by *a statutory order made by the Minister of Health*... We may query the validity of the statutory order and assess its validity in terms of *the statute empowering the minister to make such orders*. Finally, when the validity of the statute has been queried and assessed by reference to *the rule that what the Queen in Parliament enacts is law*, we are brought to a stop in enquiries concerning validity: for we have reached a rule which, like the intermediate statutory order and statute, provides criteria for the assessment of the validity of other rules; but it is also unlike them in that there is no rule providing criteria for the assessment of its own legal validity. (Hart, Raz, & Bulloch, 2012, 107, all but first emphasis added.)

[25] Strictly, both Kelsen and Hart deny that they *infer* the validity of the *Grundnorm*/rule of recognition from its efficaciousness. Kelsen famously, though somewhat enigmatically, insists that efficaciousness is a *conditio sine qua non*, not a *conditio per quam* for the validity of the *Grundnorm* (2009), 119. Hart takes a somewhat different tack, dodging the question of validity at the level of the rule of recognition altogether. Instead, he speaks merely of a 'presumption of existence' of this rule and displaces the issue of validity to the level of all the primary rules; i.e. to those rules ultimately verified by the rule of recognition (Hart, Raz, & Bulloch, 2012, 108–10). However, this cuts no ice with Ross, whose epistemological agenda seems only to leave two options: either there is an inference to the first claim of validity, in which case there is a naturalistic fallacy; or there is no inference, in which case the first claim of validity is an arbitrary postulate. Both are equally unsatisfactory from an epistemological point of view.

finds its classic statement in the famous quip by the early American legal realist Oliver Wendell Holmes, Jr., that '[t]he prophecies of what the courts will do in fact, and nothing more pretentious, are what I mean by the law'.[26] It has often been suggested that Ross's adherence to logical empiricism necessarily implies a similar, radically behaviourist theory about the law, a fact that in the broader picture has simultaneously been taken to explain the kinship between American and Scandinavian legal realism.

Many have accused behaviourism-cum-legal realism of irredeemable failure as a theory of *law* and no one probably with greater success than H. L. A. Hart. Hart's celebrated critique of extreme empiricist approaches to law has several facets and although he indubitably did have Ross in mind with some of the arguments, it is more doubtful with others.[27] Regardless of Hart's intentions, it is a fact of intellectual history that his argument has often been read (also) as a critique of Ross, and that, as such, it has had a lasting negative effect on the Anglo-American reception of Ross's work. But as we shall see, even if there may be legal theorists to whom Hart's critique is relevant, there are good reasons for resisting it in relation to Ross's specific theory.

In a nutshell, Hart accuses 'the predictive theory', behaviouristic realism, of ignoring, or at least significantly distorting, the normative aspect so characteristic of law. More specifically, he accuses these approaches to law of being incapable of identifying and explaining the distinction between merely *regular* social behaviour in groups (for instance, when a group has the habit of going to the cinema on Saturday nights) and such behaviour that is also *rule-governed* (for instance, when a group has a rule that a man's head is to be bared on entering a church).[28] According to Hart, these two kinds of social phenomena differ only by the existence exclusively in the latter of what he calls *the internal aspect* of social rules. Unlike *the external aspect* (the regular uniform behaviour), this internal aspect remains empirically unobservable because it has to do with the specific *critical reflective attitude*, which group members exhibit in compliance with or in deviation from the rules exhibited by other members of the group.[29] The legal scholar who confines herself to observations of regularities of behaviour will therefore, according to Hart, necessarily miss out on the very feature that defines the object of inquiry *as law*:

> One of the difficulties facing any legal theory anxious to do justice to the complexity of the facts is to remember the presence of both these points of view [the internal and the external, respectively] and not to define

[26] Holmes (1897), 461.

[27] Hart initially outlined his critique of extreme behaviourism in his review of *On Law and Justice* (Hart, 1959). However, in his main work, *The Concept of Law*, Hart ascribed the allegedly problematic behaviouristic views more diffusely to a position anonymously called the 'predictive theory,' and he even accredited 'a whole school of legal theory in Scandinavia' for having articulated a line of argument against this predictive theory that is very close to Hart's own (Hart, Raz, & Bulloch, 2012), 10–11.

[28] Cf. Hart et al. (2012), 55.

[29] Cf. Hart et al. (2012), 57.

one of them out of existence. Perhaps all our criticisms of the predictive theory of obligation may best be summarised as the accusation that this is what it does to the internal aspect of obligatory rules.[30]

(vi) . . . and Ross's anticipation of it: the necessity of 'an introspective method'

Hart is undoubtedly on to an important truth here—about the character of law and consequently also about the scientific study of it. But at least with regard to Ross's version of legal realism, it is ironic that these considerations have come to be considered a virtual knockdown argument against him. The reader of *On Law and Justice* will quickly learn that Ross is by no means a stranger to this line of thinking. On the contrary, the first two chapters already make it painstakingly clear that rather than embracing such an external perspective, Ross actually warns strongly *against* it, and he considers strict behaviourism a methodological cul-de-sac for legal science.

In fact, in so arguing, Ross even uses the very same analogy of an outside observer of a game that Hart later adopts as his own. Thus, with the example of chess, Ross describes the inaptitude of behaviourism in grasping the rule-governed character of a game in the following way:

> One could perhaps think of proceeding in a behaviourist manner, that is, restricting oneself to what can be determined by external observation of the actions in order to find certain regularities. However, in this way we would never gain an insight into the rules of the game since we would not be able to distinguish actual custom, or even regularities conditioned by chess theory, from the actual rules of chess. Even after having watched a thousand games it would still be possible to think that it was against the rules to open with a rook's pawn.[31]

The unmistakable conclusion that Ross draws from this is that the scientific study of law has to 'adopt an introspective method',[32] it has to refer to the communal psychological processes, thoughts, and ideas of the judicial actors in the legal field:

> A behaviouristic interpretation, then, is bound to fail. To understand and predict judicial behaviour can only be achieved through ideological interpretation, that is, by means of the hypothesis about a certain ideology which animates the judge and motivates his actions... To express the same idea in another way: the law presupposes not only regularity in the judge's pattern of behaviour, but also its being rule-governed. The concept of scientific validity contains two elements: partly the outwardly observable and regular compliance with a certain

[30] Hart et al. (2012), 91. [31] See below, p. 23. [32] Ibid.

> pattern of behaviour, partly the experiencing of this pattern as a socially binding norm.[33]

In other words, rather than formulating a critique of Ross, it seems that on this point Hart is in fact only repeating (and by an irony of intellectual history getting the credit for) a warning against behaviouristic excesses, which a few years earlier Ross had already carefully articulated in his own attempt to develop a sufficiently sophisticated and nuanced version of legal realism.

(vii) A betrayal of empiricism? Remembering the left wing of Old Vienna

In spite of these (and several similar) passages in *On Law and Justice*, it is nevertheless understandable that Hart and others arrived at the conclusion that Ross overlooks the internal aspect of legal rules. It is tempting in particular to disregard or downplay the textual evidence to the contrary as one might think that, in thus advocating an introspective method, Ross comes dangerously close to contradicting his own logical empiricist premises. This empiricist programme is after all known for its strong emphasis on the possibility of achieving *intersubjectively available* verification. One might reasonably raise the point that it is not altogether clear how introspection should be able to accommodate this demand.

This in turn raises two concerns. First, whether Ross's embrace of introspection instead makes him emerge as a confused and self-contradictory thinker who as a legal theorist blatantly violates the logical empiricist tenets to which he claims to subscribe in general philosophy. Second, in so far as it is possible to salvage a consistent interpretation of Ross's legal theory, one might ask whether this position does not in effect coincide with Hart's well-known version of legal positivism—in which case, one might ask whether reading Ross brings anything substantially new to the table. (Although, considering chronology, one might in all fairness say that the question should be reversed: we should ask whether reading *Hart* brings anything new to the table.)

As we shall see, both these concerns can in fact be allayed. Still, it is a fine line Ross is trying to walk. The strong exegetic temptation is either to push Ross all the way out into the scientistic camp of austere behaviourism, or to call off the general attack on doctrinal scholarship and pull him back into the familiar surroundings of traditional legal positivism. This is partly Ross's own fault; he does not always express himself with sufficient care and clarity. But, as we shall see, there is indeed room for an interpretation that outlines a consistent position that steers clear of the two extremes. In fact, this is precisely what makes Ross's version of legal realism so interesting.

In order to see this distinct realist position clearly, we should remind ourselves that the Vienna Circle was never completely uniform as a theoretical

[33] See below, pp. 48–9.

school.[34] As part of the popular narrative of resounding and definitive failure, the views of logical empiricism are often both oversimplified and radicalized. But this narrative overlooks the fact that for many years quite substantive nuances and differences existed within the circle between conflicting interpretations of the programme. In particular, the members were strongly divided—from the early 1930s onwards—over competing conceptions of the verification principle. A conservative camp organized around Moritz Schlick insisted on an uncompromising line sticking to a strict empiricist verificationist conception of meaning—literally expelling all that is unverifiable from that realm. A so-called left wing, however, centred around Otto Neurath and Rudolph Carnap, took a more liberal approach. Not only did they relax the verification principle in order also to include as verifiable and meaningful and thus potentially scientific so-called laws of nature (by definition extending beyond empirical observation). The left wing even admitted that 'metaphysical' statements—including, importantly for present purposes, normative statements[35]—may not strictly speaking be *meaningless* even though they notoriously cannot honour even this relaxed version of the verification principle. These moderate logical empiricists maintained that such statements are only *cognitively* or *empirically* meaningless. In other words, the left wing drew a distinction *within* the realm of meaningful discourse between that which is *empirically* or *cognitively* meaningful and other kinds of meaningful discourse. Neurath and Carnap maintained only that statements of the former kind could be called scientific, while preserving the term metaphysics for the latter. (Left wing or not, they were, after all, still logical empiricists.)

Though there is no record of Alf Ross explicitly commenting on this rift in the movement, the content of *On Law and Justice* quite clearly supports aligning him with this left wing of the Vienna Circle.[36] As we shall see, his theory is perfectly consistent both with the described relaxation of the verification principle, and with the perception of atomic normative statements as meaningful even if they are unverifiable and therefore unscientific per se.

(viii) The move to realism: from norm-expressive to norm-descriptive propositions

Ross's key move in walking this tightrope, his Egg of Columbus, is to be found in his advocacy for a subtle yet decisive change of perspective for legal science. Like the case of introspection vs. behaviourism, this change of perspective may also be described in terms of an internal/external distinction. However, it is a

[34] For a first-hand account of this debate, see Carnap (1963).

[35] That is, in Ross's terminology, norm-*expressive* statements, not norm-*descriptive* statements (cf. section (viii)).

[36] Doing so is further justified by the fact that from 1932 onwards Ross had an extensive correspondence with Otto Neurath. The contents of this correspondence confirm that Neurath's specific interpretation of logical empiricism had a very substantive impact on Ross's legal realism (Evald, 2014, chapter 8, 'A modern philosophy of law informed by scientific method').

different kind of internal/external distinction, and this time the change Ross is advocating moves in the opposite direction: *from* the internal and *to* the external perspective. This second internal/external distinction is between what Ross calls norm-*expressive* and norm-*descriptive* propositions, respectively (or, as he sometimes also calls it, between propositions *in* norms and *about* norms, respectively).

The significance of this distinction can hardly be overestimated. It is Ross's acute awareness of this distinction that makes his legal realism categorically different not only from the substantive idealism of natural law but also from the formal idealism of legal positivists like Kelsen and Hart. Furthermore, as we shall see below, the distinction between norm-expressive and norm-descriptive propositions also holds the key to fully understanding Ross's distinct concept of so-called *scientific validity* of legal rules, and to seeing how this concept differs from traditional legal validity.

In a key passage, Ross outlines the basic idea of the distinction between norm-expression and norm-description as follows:

> Since the doctrinal study of law is concerned with norms, it can be called normative. This expression must not be misunderstood, however... [S]cientific sentences naturally cannot consist of norms (directives). They have to consist of assertions—assertions concerning norms; and this means assertions to the effect that certain norms have the character of 'scientifically valid (Danish) law'. To say that the doctrinal study of law has normative character means, then, that it is a study *about* norms, not *in* norms. It does not aim to 'lay down' or express norms but, rather, to establish their character of 'scientifically valid (Danish) law'. The doctrinal study of law is normative in the sense of *norm-descriptive*, not in the sense of *norm-expressive*.[37]

What is captured by the distinction between two such modes of normativity-talk may not be immediately clear, nor how the propositions of legal science should suddenly be transformed into epistemologically safe assertions if they only remain external in the sense of staying on the 'norm-descriptive' side of the gap.

As an illustration, imagine six-year-old Ellen who has been exposed to Norse folklore from early childhood. One day, shortly before Christmas, Ellen says to her father: 'We *ought* to leave some rice pudding in the attic for the pixie.' In spite of Ellen's sincerity, we may safely assume that her claim is not true. We do not as a matter of fact have any duties towards imaginary creatures like pixies. However, imagine that later the same day Ellen's father says almost the same sentence to his wife, adding only that: '*Ellen believes that* we ought to leave some rice pudding in the attic for the pixie.' Interestingly, by virtue of this small addition, the case is now completely changed. This is so because in contrast to

[37] See below, p. 27.

the first statement, the truth-value of this latter statement is entirely independent of the existence or not of duties towards imaginary creatures. The latter statement's truth-value depends solely upon whether or not Ellen *actually believes* in the existence of such a duty. And this is ultimately a psychological question regarding her beliefs, not a normative (that is, norm-expressive) question about the existence of duties towards pixies.

This analogy illustrates an old insight from the philosophy of language traditionally attributed to Gottlob Frege:[38] if a given proposition P (where P can be both an assertion and a directive) is embedded in a so-called *propositional attitude report* (a sentence stating that an agent A *believes*, *claims*, *feels*, etc. that P), then the truth-value of the particular proposition P has no bearing on the truth-value of the compound proposition, that is, of the propositional attitude report in its entirety. Whether or not things actually *are* the way A believes, claims, feels, etc., is irrelevant to the truth of the full propositional attitude report. In such *propositional attitude contexts*, the truth-value depends solely on whether or not A in fact holds the kind of attitude towards P that is asserted in the report, that is, whether or not A actually *believes*, *claims*, *feels*, etc. that things are/ought to be in the way stated in P.

Ross refers to precisely this shift in truth-value pursuant to the introduction of a propositional attitude context when he maintains that legal science should be a norm-*descriptive* and not a norm-*expressive* discipline.[39] Accordingly, a norm-expressive statement is an atomic normative statement whose utterance directly expresses acceptance or endorsement (if only *hypothetically* or *legally*, and not *morally*) of a given legal norm. A norm-descriptive statement, by contrast, inserts a propositional attitude context *around* the atomic normative (norm-expressive) statement and thus renders the truth-value of the latter (or lack thereof) immaterial to the truth-value of the compound norm-descriptive proposition. To use Ross's linguistic categories: the norm-expressive statement of the legal norm is a *directive*, while the norm-descriptive statement is an *assertion*, that is, an assertion to the effect that a particular attitudinal relation (the attitude of *believing in the truth or legal validity of*) exists between an agent or a group of agents and a given directive/legal norm.

With this crucial distinction in place, we can now make sense of what Ross is advocating when he says 'the doctrinal study of law is normative in the sense of *norm-descriptive*, not in the sense of *norm-expressive*'. The quite radical idea behind these seemingly innocuous words is that the doctrinal study of law shall henceforth refrain completely from being internal, in the sense that it shall no longer say *anything* about the existence of this or that legal right or obligation. It shall refrain altogether from making norm-expressive statements. Instead, legal science shall adopt an exclusively external point of view in the specific sense that it shall restrict itself to the making of norm-descriptive assertions,

[38] See Frege (1994 [1892]), at 149.

[39] See below, p. 27.

assertions about propositional attitudes towards norm-expressive statements about, for instance, the obligations of acceptors of bills of exchange.

Put differently, the doctrinal study of law shall, according to Ross, no longer be a study of how *we ought* to behave, legally speaking; of what legal rights and obligations *we have*. Instead, it shall be a study exclusively of how *judges think* we ought to behave legally speaking; of what legal rights and obligations *they think* we have. Or, more accurately, since Ross adopts the Kelsenian notion that legal rules are essentially directives to courts to apply sanctions under certain conditions: the doctrinal study of law becomes a study of what rights and obligations *judges think* they have *qua* judges. In Ross's words:

> Consequently, scientifically valid Danish law can be defined as the normative ideology which is actually operative, or must be thought operative, in the mind of the judge, because it is felt by him to be socially binding and is, therefore, complied with efficaciously.[40]

Ross is consistently careful in his examples to emphasize the paraphrasing from norm-expression to norm-description terminologically. Thus, he stresses that 'the concept "scientifically valid Danish law" is an element within every juridico-scientific sentence'.[41] In this way, Ross emphasizes that propositions of legal science must consistently be *ascribed to an attitudinal subject*: that is, they must always be propositions about the beliefs of a *particular group of people* regarding *a particular set of legal rules*—about the beliefs of, say, Danish (Swedish, etc.) judges regarding Danish (Swedish, etc.) law. According to circumstances, the addition '*is scientifically valid Danish (Swedish, etc.) law*' denoting for any given doctrinal study who the relevant holders of the propositional attitude are, may be tacitly implied. However, it can never be thought away entirely, lest the propositional attitude context and hence the actual condition of possibility of legal knowledge disappear entirely. In other words, adding 'is scientifically valid Danish (Swedish, etc.) law' is a way for the legal scholar to say 'not my words' about the epistemologically problematic directives. Instead, these words (plus adhering beliefs/feelings) are carefully placed in the mouths (and minds) of judges.

(ix) A(nother) betrayal of empiricism? Hypothesizing about judges' beliefs

Thus far, the account has served to illustrate the fundamental logical relationship in Ross's theory between the external, norm-descriptive statements of legal science and the internal, norm-expressive statements of the judges. But this occasions a new set of worries—or, rather, an old set of worries in a new form. As we've seen, Ross is trying to walk a thin line between traditional legal positivism and extreme behaviourism. In order to perceive the distinctness of his realist position clearly, we are therefore forced to move, as it were, in a pendular

[40] See below, p. 46. [41] See below, p. 19.

fashion, back and forth, reinforcing the boundaries against the two positions encroaching on his realism from either side.

Accordingly, the first of these worries returns to the issue of the internal consistency of Ross's theory and his possible betrayal of logical empiricism, but it does so from a new angle. On the one hand, by paraphrasing the statements of legal science as propositional attitude reports, Ross has cleverly shown how legal science can avoid propounding the notoriously problematic ought-propositions entirely. On the other hand, when it comes to honouring the epistemological commitments of logical empiricism, this could seem like a Pyrrhic victory. Propositional attitude reports about judges' convictions about rights and duties could seem to run into exactly the same kind of epistemological difficulties that according to Ross overthrew natural law. After all, how do we know what judges actually feel or believe? This, it seems, is private too.

Ross does not deny that paraphrasing statements of the doctrinal study of law gives rise to epistemological challenges of its own. But unlike the challenges that brought down natural law, Ross does not consider these new challenges facing norm-descriptive propositional attitude reports to be fatal. The reasons he gives bear witness to the balanced and moderate version of empiricism he subscribes to, which justifies placing him firmly in the 'left wing' of the Vienna Circle. Thus, Ross writes:

> Since prediction [of judicial decisions] is nevertheless possible, it must have to do with the fact that the mental process through which the judge arrives at a stage where he can base his decision on one rule rather than another, does not take place in a capricious and arbitrary way (varying from judge Peter to judge Paul), but is determined by attitudes and notions—by a common normative ideology which is present and operative in a uniform way within the minds of Danish judges when acting in their vocation as judges. *It is true that we cannot directly observe what takes place within the judge's mind, but we can make hypotheses thereon, and their value can be tested exactly because they enable us to make predictions.*[42]

Returning to the analogy above, if Ellen believes in the existence of obligations towards Christmas pixies, she will presumably behave accordingly around Christmas: she will remind her father to buy rice in the supermarket, to prepare it when they get home, etc. And if a Danish judge believes that § 28 of the Danish Bill of Exchange Act is valid law, she will behave accordingly if a case fulfilling the conditions specified in that article is brought before her court: she will order the acceptor to pay.

It is in view of these considerations that Ross's theory of scientifically valid law becomes a predictive theory, even if it immediately 'rests upon hypotheses concerning the inner life, or the thought processes, of the judge'. It becomes a

[42] See below, p. 89, emphasis added.

set of predictions of judges' behaviour under certain specified conditions *based on hypotheses about their beliefs about rules*. In Ross's final analysis, an assertion A made in the doctrinal study of law that a given directive D is scientifically valid Danish (Swedish, etc.) law, becomes:

> a prediction that *if an action in which the conditioning facts, given in § 28 of the Danish Bill of Exchange Act, are considered to exist, is brought before a court; and if in the meanwhile there have been no alterations in the circumstances which motivate A, the directive to the judge contained in § 28 of the Danish Bill of Exchange Act will form an integral part of the reasons for the court's decision.*[43]

On the most general level, the entire doctrinal study of law becomes a theory about '*the sum total of the factors exercising influence* on the judge's formulation of the rule on which he bases his decision'.[44] Ultimately, these factors can be subsumed under four sources of law: legislation; precedent; custom; and cultural tradition ('the nature of the matter').[45]

In accordance with this analysis, Ross submits that scientific validity becomes a matter of degree, varying with the degree of probability that a given directive, and more generally a given source of law, will influence the judge's reasoning process and hence (co)determine her decision.[46] As an illustration of the consistency of Ross's moderate empiricism across different scientific fields, he further reminds the reader that this is no different from the situation in other natural and social sciences, where uncertainty and probability are just the run-of-the-mill modalities of scientific discourse.

(x) 'This cannot be its meaning in the mouth of a judge': Hart's second challenge

Based on these considerations, it seems reasonable to conclude that the norm-descriptive doctrinal study envisioned by Ross is not a sign that he has succumbed to any of the usual jurisprudential 'ad hockery' for law. On the contrary, Ross's realistic study remains in compliance with the generic epistemological tenets of logical empiricism, at least as conceived by the movement's moderate left wing. At the same time, however, these considerations seem to push us back in our pendular movement, now prompting us to reconsider an argument against Ross's theory, which, in a slightly different form, we have also already addressed and rejected once.

Again, we turn to Hart for an exemplary formulation—and this time we know for certain that the Oxford philosopher did in fact intend the critique specifically against Ross. Thus, in an often-cited passage from his review of *On Law and Justice*, Hart objects to Ross's analysis that 'even if in the mouth of the

[43] See below, p. 54, original emphasis. [44] See below, p. 91, original emphasis. [45] Cf. Chapter 3.

[46] This is unlike Kelsen, who found Ross's notion of degrees of legal validity preposterous, cf. Kelsen (1959–60).

ordinary citizen or lawyer "this is a valid rule of English law" is a prediction of what a judge will do, say, and/or feel, *this cannot be its meaning in the mouth of a judge who is not engaged in predicting his own or others' behaviour or feelings*'.[47] By the same token, Hart accuses Ross of creating 'the impression that what Kelsen terms "ought-propositions" may be dispensed with in the analysis of legal thinking'.[48] From this point of view, then, the concern is that *in spite of* Ross's explicit pledge to apply an introspective method, he nevertheless de facto ends up 'defining out of existence the internal aspect of obligatory rules'.

(xi) Indeed it cannot—Ross's distinction between valid law and scientifically valid law

This line of critique is both right and wrong. It is correct that judges who pronounce 'that this is a valid rule of law' are generally engaged in an act of recognition and in that sense directly make norm-expressive statements, not norm-descriptive propositional attitude reports. It is wrong, however, to assume that this fact, in and of itself, should somehow refute Ross's analysis. To see this we should first remind ourselves how Ross's philosophical project as described above differs crucially from that of Hart's.

Unlike Ross, Hart was never a logical empiricist. Hart's main philosophical inspiration was the so-called *linguistic philosophy* or *ordinary language philosophy* associated with J. L. Austin and the later Ludwig Wittgenstein. By the 1950s and 60s ordinary language philosophy had largely replaced logical empiricism as the fashionable philosophy of the day, and it is no understatement to say that, unlike its predecessors, this new philosophical school never really took an interest in the epistemological foundations of science.[49] Instead, ordinary language philosophers, especially proponents of the Austinian approach to which Hart adhered, saw the crucial task of philosophy as providing comprehensive conceptual analysis based on a study of *the actual uses of language*. In this sense, Hart saw the task of philosophy as engaging in a descriptive exercise—a kind of lexicography. In terms of his critique of Ross, it is therefore not surprising that Hart, as an ordinary language *legal* philosopher, would expect a definition of a key legal term like *valid* to be able to capture accurately the actual meaning of the word 'in the mouth of a judge'.

At the same time, this is precisely what makes this line of critique misfire—and in much the same way as someone who criticizes a cat for not being a good dog. What the argument overlooks is that, unlike the descriptive lexicographic ambition of Hart, Ross simply does not aim, with the definition provided above, to capture the ordinary meaning of 'valid law' in the mouth of a judge. It is not that he is blind to the independent value of such ordinary language analysis. The

[47] Hart (1959), 237 (emphasis added). [48] Hart (1959), 237.

[49] W. V. O. Quine dryly expressed this change in sentiment when remarking that the ordinary language philosophers 'found a residual philosophical vocation in therapy: in curing philosophers of the delusion that there were epistemological problems' (Quine, 1969, 82).

problem is that for Ross's epistemological purposes and for his ambition to establish the conditions of possibility of legal science, the soundness of ordinary language, and hence its ultimate usefulness, simply cannot be taken for granted. On the contrary, for such philosophical purposes it may well be necessary, in the final analysis, to reject ordinary language or at least to reform it fundamentally.[50] At any rate, this is the conclusion Ross draws after having reviewed and rejected the most prominent traditional attempts to answer the epistemological challenge on the basis of ordinary language: natural law and legal positivism.

When providing his definition above, Ross is therefore no longer engaged in the lexicographic exercise of *describing* the ordinary meaning of 'valid law' *in the mouth of a judge*. Instead, he is talking precisely about *scientific* validity. He is engaged in *prescribing* the ideal meaning of 'validity-talk' *in the mouth of a legal scientist*. In this sense, Ross's definition of scientific validity is not a descriptive definition but rather a *stipulative*, or better yet, an *explicative* definition, as this notion is defined by Rudolph Carnap; that is, as '[t]he task of making more exact a vague or not quite exact concept used in everyday life or in an earlier stage of scientific or logical development, or rather of replacing it by a newly constructed, more exact concept'.[51]

Even if this is granted, and we admit that Ross's definition of scientific validity does not aim to capture 'meaning in the mouth of a judge', one might still object, with Hart, that Ross is nevertheless creating 'the impression that what Kelsen terms "ought-propositions" may be dispensed with in the analysis of legal thinking'.[52] Along these same lines, one might further say, again with Hart, that Ross is not 'allow[ing] for the internal, non-factual, non-predictive uses of

[50] Ross is very clear on this point in a parallel critique of Kelsen who, in terms of the descriptive ambition analogous to Hart's 'meanings in the mouths of judges', suggests basing philosophical analysis of validity on what he calls 'juristic thinking':

> 'Juristic thinking' refers, I suppose, to ideas and beliefs commonly held by lawyers. 'Juristic thinking', however, is no trustworthy guide for a logical analysis. It may be, and it is highly probable in the field of law and morals, that the common way of 'thinking' is saturated by ideological ideas reflecting emotional experiences but without any function in the description of reality, *the task of legal science. In that case, the job of the analyst is to reject, not to accept, the idea of 'validity'.* (Ross, 1957, 568, emphasis addded.)

[51] Carnap (1947), 7–8. It should be emphasized that the responsibility for thus mistaking Ross's prescriptive exercise for a piece of (bad) descriptive lexicography does not rest exclusively with his readers from Hart onwards. First, Ross could generally have been more careful in spelling out when he is engaged in describing ordinary use and when prescribing ideal scientific use. Second, and as mentioned above, Ross must assume a greater part of the responsibility for the mistake specifically vis-à-vis his Anglophone audience because he made some very unfortunate translation choices in the 1958 English language edition of *On Law and Justice*. Thus, a comparison reveals the first English edition to be a quite heavily truncated or redacted version of the full original Danish manuscript (cf. Holtermann, 2015). Furthermore, in the 1958 English edition Ross uses the same term, i.e. *valid* (*law*) both when he is talking about validity in ordinary use and when he is talking about validity in ideal scientific use. In the Danish original, Ross consistently distinguishes these on the terminological level (between *gyldig* and *gældende ret* respectively). In this translation, we have also chosen to distinguish terminologically using the terms *valid law* and *scientifically valid law* respectively. For an account of the reasons for this choice, cf. the section 'A note on the translation of "gyldig" and "gældende ret" with "valid" and "scientifically valid law" ' following this introduction (p. l).

[52] Hart (1959), 237.

language inseparable from the use of rules'[53] and therefore de facto ends up '[defining] the internal point of view out of existence'.

But this way of phrasing the objection is also misleading. For, on closer inspection, we see that Ross is not literally dispensing with such normative uses of language, nor is he defining the internal point of view out of existence. On the contrary, such uses of language survive perfectly intact in Ross's analysis of scientifically valid law. In fact, 'ought-propositions' are literally *indispensable* in this analysis because, without them, there would simply be no propositional attitude report at all. Such a report presupposes full awareness of the existence and meaningfulness of 'the internal, non-factual, non-predictive uses of language inseparable from the use of rules', *viz. in the minds and mouths of the judges*. As a legal scientist, you simply cannot say that Danish judges believe that 'the acceptor is obligated to pay the bill of exchange on the due day' without *eo ipso* considering this latter statement meaningful. In this way, norm-descriptive statements by definition presuppose norm-expressive statements. What Ross *is* saying, on the other hand, is just that such norm-expressive statements are not *cognitively* meaningful—that they do not have a truth-value—and that therefore they can only appear in scientific discourse when embedded in a propositional attitude context.

(xii) The boundary redrawn: why 'ought-propositions with a merely descriptive import' and 'detached normative statements' are not norm-descriptive statements

This, finally, brings us to the point where we can see, in a clear and principled way, why Alf Ross's legal realism remains categorically distinct from the legal positivism not only of Hans Kelsen but also of H. L. A. Hart: expressed in Ross's terms, the crucial difference is that, for both Kelsen and Hart, any scientific assertion made in the doctrinal study of law about the validity of any given legal rule (other than the *Grundnorm*/rule of recognition) is a norm-*expressive* statement. For Ross, by contrast, it is a norm-*descriptive* statement.

On its face, this may sound counterintuitive. We are used to thinking that legal positivism differs from natural law precisely by virtue of its not being normative but descriptive. In an oft-quoted passage, Kelsen expresses this core idea as follows: 'The ought-statements in which the theorist of law represents the norms have a merely descriptive import; that, as it were, descriptively reproduce the "ought" of the norms.'[54] Joseph Raz later helpfully introduced the distinction between committed and detached normative statements to explain Kelsen's point: '[A] detached normative statement does not carry the full normative force of an ordinary normative statement. Its utterance does not commit the speaker to the normative view it expresses.'[55] Hart, who initially struggled with Kelsen's notion of 'ought-propositions with a merely descriptive import',

[53] Hart (1959), 238. [54] Kelsen (2009), 163. [55] Raz (1979), 153.

was later convinced by Raz's explanation, praising the category of detached normative statements for creating the necessary logical space for making sense of the difference between legal positivism and natural law.[56]

Judging from this brief description, one might initially think that Kelsen's *ought-statements having a merely descriptive import* and Raz's *detached normative statements* could be the equivalents of Ross's *norm-descriptive statements*. However, this would be wrong, and for the simple reason that, in spite of the detached character, these legal positivist statements are *not* propositional attitude reports. This follows from Kelsen's analysis, and it is expressly stated by Raz: 'It is important not to confuse such statements from a point of view [that is, detached normative statements] with statements about other people's beliefs.'[57] Instead, the distinction between committed and detached normative statements is, in Ross's vocabulary, a distinction between two kinds of norm-expressive statements and, as such, they both stand in contrast to norm-descriptive statements. Corresponding to these distinctions, therefore, we find the difference between the two kinds of legal idealism—substantive and formal idealism, respectively—which both stand in contrast to Ross's legal realism.

3. Life after logical empiricism

(i) 'An important group of modern philosophers' gone out of fashion

As we saw at the beginning of this introduction, it seems plausible that Ross's alliance with logical empiricism helps explain why he eventually became the most widely known and studied member of Scandinavian legal realism. As also touched upon, this effect has in all likelihood been reinforced significantly by the fact that Ross so elegantly and consistently manages to build a legal theory on the basis of the central tenets of logical empiricism.

Evidently, this strategy of 'standing on the shoulders of giants' implies a sort of division of labour between general philosophy and legal philosophy. Ross was conscious about this and embraced it openly:

> Getting involved in a profound discussion on fundamental philosophical problems must fall outside the scope of a juridico-philosophical presentation. Surely, it is permitted to state one's position and point out that it is shared by an important group of modern philosophers as well as professionals interested in philosophy...[58]

This generally seems like a sensible approach to legal philosophy, and indeed Kelsen and Hart in each their own way did much the same when they were relying on neo-Kantianism and ordinary language philosophy, respectively. However,

[56] Cf. e.g. Hart (1983), 14–15. [57] Raz (1979), 156–7. [58] See below, p. 382.

the strategy of referring to 'an important group of modern philosophers as well as professionals interested in philosophy' may also cause repercussions. After all, philosophical fashions can and often do change. And it is a fact that today logical empiricism no longer enjoys the same prestige and renown as it did around the middle of the twentieth century. Quite the contrary, the intervening years seem to have turned the previous winning strategy of teaming up with logical empiricism into something much closer to the academic equivalent of an own-goal.

Though the narrative of the definitive failure of logical empiricism may be somewhat exaggerated, and it often seems to rest on a narrow identification of the movement with the version propounded by its most conservative and irreconcilable members, it remains a fact that a number of sustained challenges have been articulated at a principled level, and that consequently it is difficult to find serious proponents of the school in contemporary philosophy. The pressing question for our purposes is where this leaves Ross's legal theory today. What remains of Ross's characteristic version of legal realism if its philosophical premises are no longer tenable?

(ii) Turning to naturalism

At first glance, one might be tempted to reverse Ross's own manoeuvre and put his realism back into its original philosophical framework as provided by the Uppsala School. But this hardly solves the problem—in the eyes of many, the Uppsala School is simply a more esoteric version of logical positivism. Instead of going back to basics, therefore, scholars sympathetic to Scandinavian legal realism have in recent years tried a different, more offensive strategy, finding grounds for (cautious) optimism in the phenomenon known as 'naturalism'. Naturalism has been high on the agenda in general philosophy for the last three or four decades, following American philosopher Willard Van Orman Quine's seminal article 'Epistemology Naturalized' from 1969. With roughly the usual delay, this trend in general philosophy has percolated down into legal philosophy. Here, the pioneering work was done by Brian Leiter with his naturalistic reconstruction of the American realists,[59] but in recent years parallel attempts have also been made to look at Scandinavian realism through this new philosophical prism.[60]

The result of these exercises depends of course on what exactly one means by *naturalism*. The term has received considerable hype and, as is often the case with such intellectual fashions, the term itself has in this process come to mean quite different things to different people and in different contexts. In an attempt to minimize potential confusion we shall therefore initially distinguish between

[59] For a collection of the central texts, cf. Leiter (2007b).

[60] Cf. notably Holtermann (2006, 2014); Mautner (2010); Spaak (2009).

three main ways of using the term: (i) ontological naturalism; (ii) semantic naturalism; and (iii) epistemological (or replacement) naturalism.[61] In the subsequent discussion, we will focus only on the latter epistemological kind of naturalism—for reasons we will see shortly.

Ontological naturalism is concerned with the contents of reality. It is the rejection of the existence of 'supernatural' things and the view that there are only natural or physical things with natural properties. *Semantic naturalism* is the claim that conceptual analysis is philosophically acceptable only if the concepts are analysable in terms of natural properties or entities. *Epistemological*, or *replacement naturalism*, is the rejection of traditional *a priori* or 'armchair' approaches to epistemology in favour of methods that are continuous with the empirical sciences. It is a *replacement* approach because it advocates replacing traditional justification-centred *a priori* approaches to epistemology with empirical descriptive studies of human cognition.

Although these three general conceptions of naturalism are interrelated, they can be distinguished in abstract analysis, and although they often occur together in philosophical practice, this need not be the case. This is illustrated by the case of logical empiricism. On the one hand, the verification principle—this centrepiece of the Vienna Circle—is carefully designed both to provide a naturalistically respectable account of the otherwise flimsy notion of meaning, and at the same time to provide a tool for a complete physicalistic sanitizing of our ontology, by denouncing all non-naturalistic things or properties as *metaphysics*. On the other hand, logical empiricism is quite clearly *not* an example of replacement naturalism in the epistemological sense. On the contrary, its dedication to the demarcation problem is clearly motivated by the ambition to find a general way to provide justifications for science. In this sense, logical empiricism sees its own practice as classical first philosophy or armchair philosophy. Naturalized epistemology is conceived in direct response to the perceived failure of this logical empiricist project, proceeding almost *ex negativo* as the careful repudiation of their project precisely *qua a priori*, Cartesian, foundationalist and centred on justification. Hence, the movement's evocative motto: 'Out of the armchair and into the field!'[62]

This simultaneously explains why, for our purposes, it is preferable to focus on the third rather than first or second kinds of naturalism. Considering the immediate affinity between logical empiricism and both ontological and semantic naturalism, it is simply not likely to be very philosophically interesting or fruitful to naturalize Ross's theory in either of these meanings of the word. First, an ontological and semantic naturalizing of Ross is likely to be *uninformative* because it, de facto, does little more than add a new and topical label to his theory. Second, this approach in effect does nothing to address Ross's

[61] This way of partitioning the field is inspired by Brian Leiter and Matthew X. Etchemendy (2017).
[62] Dennett (1988).

'publicity crisis', caused by the ostracism of logical empiricism in contemporary philosophy. Showing that Ross's version of Scandinavian realism can be considered naturalistic by virtue of those very features that signify its commitment to logical empiricism therefore does little to address *this* challenge.

Instead, a different and more promising avenue is to try to naturalize Ross's theory in the genuinely novel and topical sense of epistemological replacement. Considering Ross's own explicit allegiance to logical empiricism we should expect this exercise to be more demanding and to involve a greater element of philosophical reconstruction. But, as already remarked, it seems that it can in fact be done. It seems possible to disentangle Ross's realist legal theory almost intact from its commitment to logical empiricism—or, more precisely, from its commitments to those particular tenets of logical empiricism that have today been abandoned—and to reinsert this remaining theory into a Quinean replacement framework.

(iii) The basic tenets of epistemological replacement naturalism

In order to see this more clearly, let us take a closer look at the two basic tenets of Quine's replacement naturalism. First, Quine explicitly denies the feasibility of so-called Cartesian foundationalism. That is, Quine denies the feasibility of *any* attempt to derive our scientific beliefs from indubitable foundations—whether rationalistically conceived of as truths of reason, or empiricistically conceived of as sense data. Quine's bleak statement of this underdetermination is already a modern classic: 'Any statement can be held true come what may, if we make drastic enough adjustments elsewhere in the system.'[63] Second, Quine asserts that this normative justificatory project should be replaced by a descriptive empirical study of how we actually form our scientific beliefs. In Quine's words: 'But why all this reconstruction, all this make-believe? The stimulation of his sensory receptors is all the evidence anybody has had to go on, ultimately, in arriving at his picture of the world. *Why not just see how this construction really proceeds?*'[64]

Before proceeding, it should be emphasized that, while the conception of replacement considered here is essentially Quinean, it differs on one particular point. Following most modern replacement naturalists, the present account rejects Quine's narrow scientistic conception of the outlined empirical study of knowledge production and of the construction of our picture of the world. Quine construes this study as a strictly behaviouristic natural scientific project. But this just sounds like the old empiricist habits of the right wing of the Vienna Circle. If in replacement naturalism we are, as Quine maintains, 'well advised to use any available information',[65] then this should surely include any successful contemporary empirical science, natural or social, as long as it promises

[63] Quine (1980 [1951]), 43. [64] Quine (1969), 75 (emphasis added). [65] Quine (1969), 76.

to give us reliable information about the factors that actually shape our beliefs about the world.[66]

Thus suitably expanded, Quinean naturalism simultaneously connects more broadly to a general movement sometimes referred to as the *empirical turn* in epistemology and the philosophy of science, and which in particular covers sociology of science and knowledge. This tendency goes back to Thomas Kuhn's groundbreaking work, *The Structure of Scientific Revolutions*,[67] from 1962, and it includes a broad spectrum of diverging and sometimes mutually contradictory tendencies in the sociology of knowledge and science, such as the Edinburgh School associated with David Bloor and Barry Barnes,[68] social epistemology as propounded by Alvin Goldman,[69] and Pierre Bourdieu's reflexive sociology[70]—to name just a few.

(iv) Naturalizing Alf Ross's legal realism

As studies have shown,[71] Ross's programme for a realistic legal science outlined in *On Law and Justice* fits this expanded replacement programme surprisingly well. First, Ross's legal theory consists of the parallel rejection of two of the most prominent attempts to provide principled epistemological foundations for doctrinal legal science. As we have seen, Ross rejects both substantive and formal idealism (natural law and legal positivism), concluding that both theories are underdetermined because they are 'like harlots, at the disposal of everyone'—a conclusion that strongly echoes Quine's conclusion of underdetermination above.

Second, from this foundational failure, Ross draws a perfectly analogous replacement conclusion. He simply gives up on the traditional project of providing principled foundations for traditional normative (norm-expressive) statements about valid law. Instead, he changes the fundamental perspective from being justificatory and normative to being empirical and descriptive. Just like Quine turns towards science as an empirical phenomenon, as the body of beliefs actually held by scientists, Ross in the same way turns towards legal doctrine as an empirical phenomenon, as the body of beliefs about valid law actually held by judges. This is what is implied in Ross's change of perspective from the internal, norm-expressive to the external, norm-descriptive point of view. Instead of the usual complex exercise in deontic reasoning of deriving valid legal norms from a presupposed (formal or substantive) Archimedean point, the primary task of doctrinal studies now becomes the task of determining as accurately as possible which legal norms are actually *held to be valid by judges*. In Ross's words: '[S]cientifically

[66] In this sense, *naturalism* is, strictly, a misnomer. It would be more fitting to speak simply of an *empirical turn* since what we are dealing with is a broad turn to successful empirical science *en bloc* in the epistemological study of science.

[67] Kuhn (1996). [68] Cf. e.g. Bloor (1991). [69] Cf. e.g. Goldman (1999).

[70] Cf. e.g. Bourdieu (2004). [71] Cf. Holtermann (2006, 2014, 2016).

valid Danish law can be defined as the normative ideology which is actually operative, or must be thought operative, in the mind of the judge.'[72]

How this study qualifies as replacement naturalism follows straightforwardly from this: legal scholarship is turned into an empirical study that aims to identify as correctly as possible the legal beliefs actually held by judges, to determine their causes and their impact in legal practice. As Ross writes:

> [T]he hypothesis of this [normative] ideology, used as a scheme of interpretation, enables us to understand the judge's (verbal) behaviour, his judicial decision, as being linked, within a coherent whole of meaning and motivation, with other social actions which, according to the contents of the normative ideology, are conditioning the judge's reaction (legislative acts, other public and private legal acts, and factual actions).[73]

In other words, Ross too abandons 'all this creative reconstruction, all this make-believe', and he does so in favour of a sober empirical study of how 'the construction of the judge's picture of the legal world really proceeds'. And this is conceived as a (specialized branch of) social or socio-psychological science.

We can see on the basis of this philosophical reconstruction how Ross can still, or again today, satisfy the desideratum that he himself set up for a viable position in legal philosophy: that it should be 'shared by an important group of modern philosophers as well as professionals interested in philosophy'. Interestingly, however, and expanding Ross's own *desideratum*, it also puts him in accord with 'an important group of legal scholars and scholars interested in law'. Thus, corresponding to the empirical turn in philosophy of science described above, it seems that the last couple of decades have seen the parallel advent of an empirical turn *in legal studies*. To mention only the most conspicuous trends, law and economics, the empirical legal studies movement, political science, and sociology of law have in each their different ways made inroads into the traditional doctrinal (armchair) study of law.[74]

(v) The empirical turn in contemporary legal scholarship: from Scandinavian legal realism to European New Legal Realism

It seems plausible that this empirical turn can, in much the same way, be described as a selection of different attempts to naturalize jurisprudence. By the same token, Ross's version of legal realism can therefore be said to be as modern as ever, not only in terms of philosophical foundations but also in terms of the realistic legal research programme he outlines.

Even more suggestive, seeing Ross's realism in light of these developments does not only serve to demonstrate the continued timeliness of his thought on the

[72] See below, p. 46. [73] Ibid.

[74] Thus, e.g., Lee Epstein and Andrew D. Martin: 'To claim that research based on data—that is, empirical work—has infiltrated the legal community borders on the boring' (Epstein & Martin, 2014, vii).

character of legal science. Mindful of the conceptual sophistication and nuance in Ross's moderate empiricism, seeing him in this light also holds the promise of actively qualifying ongoing debates about the empirical turn in contemporary legal scholarship. One of the hotly debated issues here relates to the alleged significance of the many results of the various empirical studies of law. Of course, traditional legal doctrinal scholars generally seem sceptical about the implications of these empirical studies vis-à-vis traditional doctrinal studies of law. This concern has been expressed concisely by K. A. Armstrong in specific relation to political scientists making inroads into the field of European Union law: 'Political science has discovered the European Court of Justice (ECJ). But has it discovered law?'[75]

It is plain that Armstrong's concern is in essence a modern replay of Hart's warning that empirical approaches run the risk of overlooking and ultimately 'defining out of existence the internal aspect of obligatory rules'. For this reason, it seems helpful to turn to Ross's legal theory. For though it might be the case that there are political scientists—and other empirical legal scholars along with them—who have not indeed 'discovered law', the same cannot be said about Ross's approach, in spite of his consistent commitment to empiricism. The conceptual richness of Ross's realism—especially his characteristic internal-cum-external *norm-descriptive* perspective and the associated concept of *scientifically valid* law—shows a feasible way to turn law into a consistently empirical object of study without simultaneously 'defining it out of existence'. Indeed, the potential of so using Ross to carve out and secure the conceptual space that allows the empirical study of law without forgetting about law itself has already inspired attempts to see influential contemporary socio-empirical studies of the legal field as manifestations of what has been called European New Legal Realism.[76]

Of course, nothing in this introduction should be taken to imply that Alf Ross (let alone the contemporary empirical turn as such) is necessarily right that legal studies should either go empirical or be closed down. What Ross does show, though, and show very convincingly, is *just how far* in the direction of law empirical science can go without resorting to any of the usual epistemological exceptionalism for the doctrinal study of law.

[75] Armstrong (1998), 155.

[76] Cf. e.g. Holtermann & Madsen (2015). The expansion of the geographical denominator beyond Scandinavia is due to the identification of a deep congeniality hitherto largely unrecognized between Rossian realism and leading European sociologists (of law), sociologists who have not previously been associated with realism but whose thoughts on the study of law have nevertheless been found to be profoundly realist in spirit. This is particularly true of Max Weber, whose thoughts on the empirical study of law as a normative phenomenon, especially as presented in the somewhat neglected work *Critique of Stammler* (Weber, 1977), bear a striking resemblance to the core ideas in Alf Ross's legal realism in *On Law and Justice*. First, Weber operates with a distinction between so-called *axiologically* and *empirically valid law*, which is, for all practical purposes, identical with Ross's distinction between *valid* and *scientifically valid law* (Weber, 1977, 128–9). Second, Weber essentially anticipates the role which Ross assigns to the judge ideology when saying that 'a "legal order" may be analysed as a complex of maxims in the minds of certain men who really exist' (Weber, 1977, 130).

Ross demonstrates, against the usual objections launched by legal positivists like Hans Kelsen and H. L. A. Hart, that it is perfectly possible for empirical science to produce a phenomenologically accurate account of law *without* leaving unexplained any significant aspect that makes it a distinct social phenomenon among other social phenomena. Ross's empirical perspective does not in any way overlook or define out of existence the internal aspect of law, including the characteristic normativity of legal rules. He does not overlook the phenomenological distinctiveness of rule-governed behaviour, or the widespread occurrence of ought-propositions in legal language. Nor does Ross overlook the equally widespread belief in the epistemological justifiability and consequently potentially scientific character of such language. Ross grants all of that. He only denies that these widespread beliefs are in fact also correct. And it is this challenge that should be countered if the traditional doctrinal study of law is to preserve its status as a science suitably placed within the walls of the academy.

It is because of this that Alf Ross fits the description quoted at the beginning of this introduction: 'His greatest philosophical contribution has probably been to develop, in a consistent and rigorous fashion, the consequences of a set of assumptions whose appeal cannot be denied even by those philosophers who reject them.'[77]

References

Armstrong, K. A. (1998). Legal Integration: Theorizing the Legal Dimension of European Integration. *Journal of Common Market Studies, 36* (2. June), 155–74.

Bloor, D. (1991). *Knowledge and Social Imagery* (2nd edn). Chicago, IL; London: University of Chicago Press.

Bourdieu, P. (2004). *Science of Science and Reflexivity* (R. Nice, trans.). Cambridge: Polity Press.

Carnap, R. (1947). *Meaning and Necessity: A Study in Semantics and Modal Logic*. Chicago, IL: The University of Chicago Press.

Carnap, R. (1963). Intellectual Biography. In P. A. Schilpp (ed.), *The Philosophy of Rudolf Carnap* (pp. 3–84). La Salle, IL: Open Court.

Dennett, D. C. (1988). Out of the Armchair and into the Field. *Poetics Today, 9*(1), 205–222.

Descartes, R. (2013). *Meditations on First Philosophy: With Selections from the Objections and Replies*. In J. Cottingham (ed.). doi:10.1017/CBO9781139042895

Eng, S. (2011). Lost in the System or Lost in Translation? The Exchanges between Hart and Ross. *Ratio Juris, 24*(2 June), 194–246. doi:10.1111/j.1467-9337.2011.00482.x.

Epstein, L., & Martin, A. D. (2014). *An Introduction to Empirical Legal Research*. Oxford: Oxford University Press.

Evald, J. (2014). *Alf Ross—a Life*. Copenhagen: DJØF Publishing.

Frege, G. (1994 [1892]). On Sense and Reference. In R. M. Harnish (ed.), *Basic Topics in the Philosophy of Language* (pp. 142–160). New York: Harvester/WheatSheaf.

77 Hookway (1988).

Goldman, A. I. (1999). *Knowledge in a Social World.* Oxford: Clarendon.

Hart, H. L. A. (1959). Scandinavian Realism. *The Cambridge Law Journal, 17*, 233–40.

Hart, H. L. A. (1983). *Essays in Jurisprudence and Philosophy*. Oxford: Clarendon.

Hart, H. L. A., Raz, J., & Bulloch, P. A. (2012). *The concept of law* (3rd edn/introduction by Leslie Green (ed.)). Oxford: Oxford University Press.

Holmes, O. W. (1897). The Path of the Law. *Harvard Law Review, 10*(8).

Holtermann, J. v. H. (2006). Ross og erkendelsesteorien. In J. v. H. Holtermann & J. Ryberg (eds.), *Alf Ross—kritiske gensyn* (pp. 37–62). Copenhagen: Jurist- og Økonomforbundet.

Holtermann, J. v. H. (2013). Introduktion. In A. Ross & J. v. H. Holtermann, *Om ret og retfærdighed: En indførelse i den analytiske retsfilosofi, med introduktion af Jakob v. H. Holtermann* (pp. 9–42). Copenhagen: Hans Reitzels Forlag.

Holtermann, J. v. H. (2014). Naturalizing Alf Ross's Legal Realism: A Philosophical Reconstruction. *Revus. Journal for Constitutional Theory and Philosophy of Law* (24), 165–86.

Holtermann, J. v. H. (2015). 'This Cannot be its Meaning in the Mouth of the Judge': The Case for the New English Language Translation of Alf Ross's On Law and Justice, forthcoming on Oxford University Press. *Utopía y praxis latinoamericana: revista internacional de filosofía iberoamericana y teoría social, 20*(71), 19–30.

Holtermann, J. v. H. (2016). Getting Real or Staying Positive—Legal Realism(s), Legal Positivism and the Prospects of Naturalism in Jurisprudence. *Ratio Juris—An International Journal of Jurisprudence and Philosophy of Law, 29* (4 (December)), 535–55. doi:1111/raju.12071

Holtermann, J. v. H. (2017). A Straw Man Revisited—Resettling the Score Between H. L. A. Hart and Scandinavian Legal Realism. *Santa Clara Law Review, 57*(1), 101–41.

Holtermann, J. v. H., & Madsen, M. R. (2015). European New Legal Realism and International Law: How to Make International Law Intelligible. *Leiden Journal of International Law, 28*(2), 211–30.

Hookway, C. (1988). *Quine: Language, Experience and Reality*. Cambridge: Polity.

Hume, D., Selby-Bigge, L. A., & Nidditch, P. A. (1978). *A Treatise of Human Nature* (2nd edn). Oxford: Oxford University Press.

Kelsen, H. (1959–60). Eine 'Realistische' und die Reine Rechtslehre. Bemerkungen zu Alf Ross: On Law and Justice. *Österreichische Zeitschrift für Öffentliches Recht, 10*, 1–25.

Kelsen, H. (1967). *Pure Theory of Law*. Berkeley, CA: University of California Press.

Kelsen, H. (2009). *General Theory of Law and State*. Union, NJ: Lawbook Exchange.

Kuhn, T. S. (1996). *The Structure of Scientific Revolutions* (3rd edn). Chicago, IL; London: University of Chicago Press.

Leiter, B. (2007a). Brian Leiter: Interview about legal philosophy. In M. E. J. Nielsen (ed.), *Legal Philosophy: 5 Questions* (pp. 143–51): Automatic Press/VIP.

Leiter, B. (2007b). *Naturalizing Jurisprudence: Essays on American Legal Realism and Naturalism in Legal Philosophy*. Oxford: Oxford University Press.

Leiter, B., & Etchemendy, M. X. (2017). Naturalism in Legal Philosophy. In E. N. Zalta (ed.), The Stanford Encyclopedia of Philosophy (Summer 2017 edn): Metaphysics Research Lab, Stanford University. Retrieved from <https://plato.stanford.edu/archives/sum2017/entries/lawphil-naturalism/>.

Mautner, T. (2010). Some Myth about Realism. *Ratio Juris, 23*(3), 411–27.

Moore, G. E. (1903). *Principia Ethica*. New York: Cambridge University Press.

Nourse, V., & Shaffer, G. (2009). Varieties of New Legal Realism: Can a New World Order Prompt a New Legal Theory? *Cornell Law Review, 95*(1), 61–137.

Quine, W. V. O. (1969). Epistemology Naturalized. In W. V. O. Quine (ed.), *Ontological Relativity and Other Essays* (pp. 69–90). New York: Columbia University Press.

Quine, W. V. O. (1980 [1951]). Two Dogmas of Empiricism. In W. V. O. Quine (ed.), *From a Logical Point of View: 9 Logico-Philosophical Essays* (pp. 20–46). Cambridge, MA: Harvard University Press.

Raz, J. (1979). *The Authority of Law: Essays on Law and Morality*. Oxford: Oxford University Press.

Ross, A. (1953). *Om ret og retfærdighed. En indførelse i den analytiske retsfilosofi*. Copenhagen: Nyt Nordisk Forlag. Arnold Busck.

Ross, A. (1957). Review of Kelsen, Hans. 'What is Justice? Justice, Law and Politics in the Mirror of Science. Collected Essays'. *California Law Review, 45*(4), 564–570.

Ross, A. (1958). *On Law and Justice*. London: Stevens & Sons Limited.

Ross, A. (1961). Validity and the Conflict Between Legal Positivism and Natural Law. *Revista Juridica de Buenos Aires*, 46–93.

Ross, A. (1962). Review of *The Concept of Law* by H. L. A. Hart. *The Yale Law Journal, 71*(6), 1185–90.

Ross, A. & Holtermann, J. v. H. (2013). *Om ret og retfærdighed: En indførelse i den analytiske retsfilosofi, med introduktion af Jakob v. H. Holtermann*. Copenhagen: Hans Reitzels Forlag.

Spaak, T. (2009). Naturalism in Scandinavian and American Realism: Similarities and Differences. In M. Dahlberg (ed.), *De lege. Uppsala-Minnesota Colloquium: Law, Culture and Values* (pp. 33–83). Uppsala: Iustus förlag.

Swaminathan, S. (2016). Projectivism and the Metaethical Foundations of the Normativity of Law. *Jurisprudence: An International Journal of Legal and Political Thought, 7*(2), 231–66.

Weber, M. (1977). *Critique of Stammler*. New York: Free Press.

A note on the translation of 'gyldig' and 'gældende ret' as 'valid' and 'scientifically valid law'

This section addresses a thorny translation issue that has attracted almost separate attention and controversy since the publication of the first English edition of *On Law and Justice* in 1958, even to the degree of leading to warnings against using that edition as a basis for serious scholarly debate about Alf Ross's legal philosophy.

One central element of Ross's legal realism as propounded in the present work relates to his concept of legal validity. Or rather, to Ross's *concepts* of legal validity, since two distinct (though interrelated) concepts relating to this key jurisprudential term are at play in his legal theory. On the one hand, Ross pays close attention to the concept of legal validity as it is commonly used and understood by legal scholars and practising jurists, including judges (and, by extension, though in a less developed way, the concept of legal validity as commonly used by ordinary citizens). In definitional terms, this concept of validity is based on a *descriptive* definition: a piece of lexicography, in so far as Ross is here aiming to capture as precisely as possible actual uses of language. On the other hand, however, Ross also introduces and places central emphasis on quite a different concept of legal validity, and one that does not involve the same commitment to agreement with prior uses of the term, neither among professional lawyers, nor among lay people. Instead, this second usage is a technical concept, which Ross has created and designed specifically for the ideal use by the legal doctrinal scientist in accordance with the overall philosophical project, which Ross is pursuing in *On Law and Justice*. In definitional terms, therefore, this concept of validity is based on a *stipulative* definition, or, more accurately, on what Rudolf Carnap has called an *explicative* definition, since this concept is not a completely new creation but builds in certain ways on the concept of validity in ordinary use.[78]

In the editor's introduction, the legal-philosophical contents of these two concepts of legal validity and the role they each play in Ross's theory is explained in greater detail. From the specific point of view of translation, however, these two kinds of legal validity present an independent challenge, which has attracted considerable attention in the reception of Ross's work, and which therefore merits separate treatment in this note.

[78] The concept of *explication* is explained in the introduction, cf. p. xxxviii.

In the original Danish-language edition of *On Law and Justice, Om ret og retfærdighed* (1953), Ross uses the two terms *gyldig* and *gældende* (*ret*) to denote the descriptive and the explicative notions of valid (law) respectively. Linguistically, the specific Danish distinction between *gyldig* and *gældende* has no immediate parallel in the English language. The Danish terms *gyldig* and *gældende* are etymologically connected in the sense that *gyldig* is a proper adjective whereas *gældende* is the adjectival present participle form of the verb *gælde*, which has the same root as *gyldig*. In ordinary Danish, *gyldig* and *gældende* are oftentimes used synonymously, but there are nuances of meaning. Thus, the term *gældende*, the term for which Ross provides his explicative definition, is predominantly used among legal professionals in the context of legal rules currently in force in a given jurisdiction. By contrast, *gyldig* is more commonly used by laypeople and its use also extends to other contexts such as morality and logic.

Given that Danish is a member of the Germanic language family, it is not surprising that the two terms *gyldig* and *gældende ret* are perfectly translatable into German—as *gültiges* and *geltendes Recht*, respectively. But this particular distinction seems not to have entered the English language—in spite of the solid and lasting imprint of Old Norse during the Viking Age. To be sure, the adjective *valid* in English works well as a translation of the Danish *gyldig* in almost all contexts. However, English remains deprived of an etymologically related but distinct adjectival form like *gældende* to cover professional lawyers' talk about legal rules. Instead, it seems valid is used here as well.

Faced with this factual limitation of language, in the 1958 English translation of *On Law and Justice* Ross chose not to distinguish these terms linguistically, but to use *valid* (*law*) across the board, relying on context alone to convey to the reader that two different concepts are at play in the text. Today, it is widely agreed that this was an unfortunate decision. In particular, the lack of an explicit terminological distinction seems to have led H. L. A. Hart to articulate one of his best-known arguments against Ross's analysis of legal validity—an argument that has widely been considered fatal to Ross's theory and has, as such, had a severe impact on the reception of his work in the Anglophone world. But Hart's argument is fundamentally mistaken, for the simple reason that it is based on a confusion of the two kinds of valid law at play in Ross's work: *gyldig* and *gældende*.[79]

A central reason for devising this new full English translation from scratch has been the wish to remedy this particular misreading, and to ensure that discussion of Ross's legal realism is based on the actual merits and demerits of his thought. It has been high on the agenda to try to find a more suitable solution to the translation of *gyldig* and *gældende ret* than the one Ross chose.

[79] Briefly, with regard to Ross's analysis of valid law Hart objects that 'this cannot be its meaning in the mouth of a judge' (Hart, 1959, 237). What Hart does not see is that Ross is not, in that context, talking *descriptively* about ordinary meaning among judges (i.e. about *gyldig*) but prescriptively about ideal meaning among legal scientists (i.e. about *gældende*). For a more extensive explanation, see the introduction.

This has not been an easy task. At first glance, it could seem that a natural option would be to abandon the word *valid* altogether as a translation of *gældende ret* and to opt for a translation more along the lines of *law in force*, or of *existing* or *efficacious law*. As explained in detail in the introduction, Ross's central philosophical project is to demonstrate that the doctrinal study of law is possible as a genuine science in accordance with the general empiricist philosophy propounded by the Vienna Circle. Accordingly, the technical or artificial concept of validity developed by Ross places considerable emphasis on the identification of those legal rules that are actually enforced by legal authorities, and whose status as valid (in the sense of *gældende*) can therefore be observed empirically in the behaviour of the judiciary.

The problem with using *law in force* or *existing* or *efficacious law* is that these alternatives invite too crude or rigidly empiristic a reading of Ross's realism. As explained in the introduction, one attraction of Ross's theory is precisely that he manages to devise a consistent programme for an empiristic legal theory without succumbing to simplistic reductionism, and, in particular, without ignoring what Hart has called the internal aspect of law. Even if judicial behaviour is indeed a central element of Ross's scientific concept of valid law, he demonstratively does not commit the empiristic fallacy of directly *reducing* law to such behaviour. On the contrary, Ross is keenly aware that law is a normative phenomenon and that any workable scientific concept of validity, even one based on an explication, must reflect that fact. By choosing, as a translation of *gældende ret*, words like *law in force*, or *existing* or *efficacious law*, which point only to outwardly observable facts, and which unlike *gældende* do not have the same root as the ordinary word for valid (*gyldig*), it would be easier to overlook this important element of moderation and sensitivity toward the normative in Ross's theory.

For these reasons it seems most fitting to maintain the word *valid* as at least *part* of the translation not only of *gyldig* but also of *gældende* (*ret*). In turn, this has led to the consideration of quite a different strategy: to convey the conceptual distinction between the two terms only with the use of a purely notational marker, either abstractly ($valid_1$ and $valid_2$); or with a reference to the original Danish words ($valid_{gyldig}$ and $valid_{gældende}$). This could then be supplemented with a reference to the introduction, which would detail the difference between the two concepts.

This solution would have the merits of simplicity and consistency, and also of transparency and neutrality in so far as it implies no controversial interpretational choices. For these reasons, it might be preferable from a purely philological point of view. But the publication of this book is not first and foremost intended as a philological exercise. The ambition is to circulate and facilitate a discussion of Ross's ideas to the widest possible English-language audience with no prior knowledge of or particular interest in the subtleties of the Danish language. The problem with the suggested purely notational solution is that it is simply not very reader friendly. In fact, it might even imply a surrender on the part of the translator. In and of themselves, neither abstract numbers nor the original Danish words for *valid* evoke any meaningful connotations in the mind of the average English-language reader. A purely notational solution would have to rely entirely on an explanation provided elsewhere, forcing the reader away from the text in order to understand which of the two kinds of validity Ross is talking about at any given time. This problem is only magnified when the material is used outside its original context (for instance, in quotation in research).

To avoid these pitfalls, we have chosen a different solution, one that tries to use the resources of the target language to help produce the right kind of connotations in the mind of the reader, and so make the text as readable and meaningful as possible in its own right. To this end, we have chosen, first, to retain *valid* (*law*) as the translation of *gyldig* (*ret*) throughout.[80] As mentioned, this does not constitute a translation problem since using *valid* for *gyldig* consistently conveys the right meaning in English. Second, and perhaps more controversially, we have chosen to translate Ross's explicative notion of *gældende* (*ret*) with the neologism *scientifically valid* (*law*).[81] This combined term is preferable for two reasons. First, because it is not ordinarily used in English and so alerts the reader to the fact that we are dealing here with a technical term (in this case, a term based on an explicative definition). Second, this combined term is almost self-explanatory, and it makes intuitive sense to the reader without prior explanation. Stating that a given rule is *scientifically valid law* naturally implies that it is a property of the rule *in the eyes of science*, or *as described by science*. Furthermore, by explicitly mentioning this relation to science, the term invites the implication that the rule in question is not (necessarily) valid in the eyes of other institutions or groups, be they laypeople, practising lawyers, or even judges. In other words, it would be very difficult to criticize Ross's analysis, as Hart did, on the grounds that 'this cannot be its meaning in the mouth of a judge'. Indeed, it cannot. That is the whole idea.

In spite of these virtues, this solution is not unproblematic. First, using the two terms *valid* and *scientifically valid* for *gyldig* and *gældende* respectively is a less neutral and potentially more controversial translation than, say, $valid_1$ and $valid_2$ because it rests on a higher degree of interpretation of Ross's legal theory. It rests, as just mentioned, on the substantive interpretation that Ross's concept of *gældende ret* is indeed an explication devised by him primarily for scientific purposes, and that it is therefore not, for instance, an attempt at capturing the

80 Correspondingly, we use *validity* as the translation of *gyldighed*.

81 Correspondingly, we use *scientific validity* as the translation of *gælden*. As emphasized in the introduction, the term science is used here in a broader sense than usual in English, and more along the lines of the corresponding German word, *Wissenschaft*. In this broader sense, science extends beyond the natural sciences to all academic specialities, including the social sciences and the humanities—and, of particular importance, the doctrinal study of law.

ordinary 'meaning in the mouth a judge'. It must in all fairness be emphasized (as in the introduction) that this interpretation can be reasonably challenged. Ross is not perfectly consistent throughout the several hundred pages of *On Law and Justice* (let alone across his entire oeuvre). Even though the textual evidence overwhelmingly supports the reading presented here, there are admittedly passages where it is difficult to see that when using the term *gældende ret* Ross should really be talking about ideal scientific use and not about ordinary use among, for instance, judges.

But translation is never entirely neutral. Representing a work as voluminous and complex as *On Law and Justice* in another language inevitably involves *some* measure of rational reconstruction. We have therefore seen it as our task: (i) to make certain, within reasonable limits, that the text itself is as consistent and makes as much sense to an ordinary English-language reader as possible; and (ii) for scholars who wish to go deeper, to state clearly in this note the (potentially controversial) choices that have been made to that end and the reasons for making them.

One such potentially controversial choice relates precisely to the fact that, as mentioned, there are a few passages in the Danish edition where Ross uses *gældende* (*ret*) but where he is clearly not referring to ideal scientific use but rather to ordinary use among professional jurists, including judges. On such occasions, it would clearly be misleading to use *scientifically valid* (*law*), and we have therefore chosen simply to use *valid*. To some, this could seem like excessive charity, as if we are ironing out tensions and contradictions in the text so as to make Ross more meaningful and consistent than he really is. This is the balancing act between meeting the responsibilities of a translator and not overstepping the role and imposing oneself as a co-author of the text. We nevertheless believe for the following reasons that this particular choice remains faithful both to Ross's text and to his intentions.

Ross's definition of *gældende ret* (*scientifically valid law*) can be described as a kind of *explicative* definition. As explained in the introduction, an explicative definition differs from a purely stipulative definition in so far as it does not constitute a completely new linguistic creation. Instead, it builds, as emphasized by Carnap, on an already existing but in some sense problematic concept 'used in everyday life or in an earlier stage of scientific... development'.[82] *Gældende ret* is already used in Danish among jurists as their preferred professional term for *valid law* (although not entirely to the exclusion of *gyldig*, which is also used by professionals to roughly the same effect). It is therefore likely that in the passages where Ross is using *gældende ret* but is clearly not talking about ideal scientific use he is simply falling back into ordinary professional use of that term—that is, he is using it in its pre-explicative meaning. This may be unfortunate but also to some degree understandable considering that Ross is

[82] Carnap (1947), 7–8.

himself trained as a jurist and he is communicating to an audience of trained jurists.

To recapitulate the considerations in this separate section, in the original Danish manuscript of *Om ret og retfærdighed* Alf Ross uses the two Danish words *gyldig* and *gældende* (*ret*) for his two concepts of *valid* (*law*). *Gyldig* (*ret*) is unambigu ous and is translated throughout with *valid* (*law*). *Gældende* (*ret*), on the other hand, is ambiguous as used by Ross in the book. It is (on rare occasions) used *pre-explicatively* corresponding to the ordinary professional meaning among jurists. In these cases, we have translated it in the same way as *gyldig* (*ret*): as *valid* (*law*). However, *gældende* (*ret*) is (predominantly) used *explicatively*, corresponding to the ideal concept, which Ross coins in the hope that it will replace the pre-explicated concept. In these cases, we have translated *gældende* (*ret*) with *scientifically valid* (*law*).

Jakob v. H. Holtermann

References

Carnap, R. (1947). *Meaning and Necessity: A Study in Semantics and Modal Logic.* Chicago, IL: The University of Chicago Press.

Hart, H. L. A. (1959). Scandinavian Realism. *The Cambridge Law Journal, 17*, 233–40.

Ross, A. (1953). *Om ret og retfærdighed. En indførelse i den analytiske retsfilosofi.* Copenhagen: Nyt Nordisk Forlag. Arnold Busck.

Ross, A. (1958). *On Law and Justice.* London: Stevens & Sons Limited.

Ross, A. & Holtermann, J. v. H. (2013). *Om ret og retfærdighed: En indførelse i den analytiske retsfilosofi, med introduktion af Jakob v. H. Holtermann.* Copenhagen: Hans Reitzels Forlag.

List of abbreviations

JFT	*Tidsskrift utgiven av Juridiska Föreningen i Finland* [Journal published by the Lawyers' Association of Finland]
Jus Gentium	Jus Gentium. *Nordisk Tidsskrift for Folkeret og international Privatret* [*Jus Gentium*. A Nordic journal of International Law and International Private Law], ed. by Alf Ross
NIR	*Nordisk industrielt rättsskydd* [Nordic industrial legal protection]
NTIRJG	*Nordisk Tidsskrift for International Ret og* Jus Gentium [Nordic Journal of International Law and *Jus Gentium*]
ÖZöR	*Österreichische Zeitschrift für öffentliches Recht* [Austrian Journal of Public Law]
StvT	*Statsvetenskaplig Tidskrift för politik—statistik – ekonomi* [Journal of Political Science concerning politics, statistics, economics]
SvJT	*Svensk Juristtidning* [Swedish Law Journal]
TfR	*Tidsskrift for Rettsvitenskap* [Journal of Legal Science]
UfR	*Ugeskrift for Retsvæsen* [The Danish Lawyers Weekly]

ON LAW AND JUSTICE

Preface

The general study of law—or as I prefer to call it, legal philosophy—has long played a comparatively pitiful role in the field of Danish legal education. However, a new curriculum, according to which this particular branch of study is given a more prominent place, is currently under consideration. This book has been written especially to provide students with a textbook on the subject.

A textbook of this type is problematic in several respects. First of all, there is *the choice of subject*. As further explained below (§ 5), analytical legal philosophy does not constitute a systematically delineated field of inquiry. The borderline between analytical legal philosophy and the doctrinal study of law is vague. The choice of subject will therefore always be arbitrary, depending on the individual researcher's personal interests and the extent to which analytical problems have already arisen within current doctrine. Analytical legal philosophy can never be completely exhaustive, and it goes without saying that one can easily point out a number of issues that interest the current front line of legal science in the Nordic region but nevertheless are not included in this book. Due to sheer lack of space, it has been necessary to make a selection. The determining factor has been partly my desire to cover the most important traditional issues of a more general nature (e.g. the scientific concept of 'legal validity', the sources of law, legal method, the concept of rights)—issues whose significance must principally be sought in the general attitude towards methodology they are suited to convey to the students; and partly my desire to go into further detail regarding individual fields concerning the problematics surrounding doctrinal legal science, in order to demonstrate the fruitfulness of the analytical method (e.g. the problem of unlawfulness, the distinction between rights *in personam* and rights *in rem*, and the principle of free disposition).

Further, the problem of how to *approach* the issues chosen by himself made the author face a difficult choice. Should these issues be presented in an introductory textbook in such a way as to express, for the most part, the author's personal views, or should the presentation give a historical account of the different doctrines developed over time? It is not unusual to choose the latter method. If so, the introduction to legal philosophy almost becomes a piece of intellectual or cultural history which provides a panoramic view of the various legal philo- [44]
sophical schools and trends, and which characterizes the individual authors in relation to them. There is no doubt that this method has its advantages, but it is not the method I have chosen. Legal philosophical tradition and doctrine are so permeated by metaphysics, and there is such a gap between metaphysics and scientifically orientated schools that, in the light of my own experiences, there

was no point in employing a 'neutral' method. In my opinion, studies in legal philosophy can hardly purport to give students a so-called neutral 'education' in intellectual history but, rather, to train them in arguing from a tenable and scientific legal standpoint. Consequently, I largely adopted the following scheme: first, to present a certain topic in a reasonable way; and secondly—and rather summarily—to contrast this theory with fundamentally different views in a subsequent 'confrontation'. It is only in the legal politics section, and owing to the intrinsic power which ideas of justice and public utility have over our thinking, that I found it expedient to let my presentation begin with a description and critique of natural law doctrines and utilitarian doctrines.

It goes without saying that in a comprehensive introductory textbook, individual subjects cannot be treated with the same exhaustive thoroughness as they are treated in a monograph. Therefore, I may be permitted to refer the interested reader (who wishes to enter more closely into my views, or looks for more extensive documentation) to my earlier books and articles in legal philosophy, where I have treated—in more detail, and with a display of a larger scientific apparatus—many of the subjects presented here.[1] This book, however, is more than a summary of earlier work. Apart from including completely new fields of study, this comprehensive account purports to bring to light a fundamental position and a unified view which do not emerge, or at least not with the same clarity, from my specialized studies.

This fundamental position is an *anti-metaphysical* one. It expresses the programmatic demand for legal science to be established and constructed as an empirical science, in the same relativistic spirit and after the same methodological pattern that applies to all modern science which is not purely formal-
[45] logical in nature. Therefore, I reject the idea of a specific *a priori* 'validity' and interpret the scientific concept of 'legal validity' in terms of social facts.

[1] See especially: *Theorie der Rechtsquellen* [The Theory of the Sources of Law] (1929); 'Realismen i Retsvidenskaben og Samfundsnyttekimæren' [Realism in legal science and the chimera of public utility], *SvJT* 1932, 324; 'Samfundsnytteprincippet' [The principle of public utility], *SvJT* 1933, 115 f.; *Kritik der sogenannten praktischen Erkenntnis* [Critique of the So-called Practical Reason] (1933); *Virkelighed og Gyldighed i Retslæren* [Reality and Validity in Jurisprudence] (1934), rewritten under the title *Towards a Realistic Jurisprudence* (1946); *Ejendomsret og Ejendomsovergang* [On Property Rights and the Passing of Property] (1935) Ch. I; 'Sondringen mellem privat og offentlig Ret' [The division between private law and public law], *TfR* 1936, 109 f.; 'Den rene Retslæres 25-Aars Jubilæum' [The 25th Anniversary of the Pure Theory of Law], *TfR* 1936, 304 f. [translated into English by Henrik Palmer Olsen and published in *Oxford Journal of Legal Studies*, Vol. 31, No. 2 (2011), 243–72, at 243–64]; 'Vinding Kruses Bidrag til Retskildelæren' [Vinding Kruse's contribution to the doctrine of the sources of law], *UfR* 1940 B 149 f.; 'Rettens Grundproblemer' [The fundamental problems of law], *TfR* 1940, 281 f.; 'Imperatives and Logic', *Theoria* 1941, 46 f.; 'Ophavsrettens Grundbegreber' [The basic concepts of intellectual property law], *TfR* 1946, 321 f.; 'Sociolog som Retsfilosof' [A sociologist as a philosopher of law], *Juristen* 1946, 259 f. as compared to 319; 'Om Begrebet 'gældende Ret' hos Theodor Geiger' [On the concept of 'valid law' in the work of Theodor Geiger], *TfR* 1950, 242 f.; 'Opgør med Retstridighedslæren' [Refuting the theory of unlawfulness], *TfR* 1951, 205 f.; Tû-tû, *Festskrift til Henry Ussing* [A Tribute to Henry Ussing] (1951), 468–84 [English translation published in *Harvard Law Review*, vol. 70, Issue 5, March 1957, 812–825]. Of course, these references do not mean that the present book lends itself at all points to an interpretation in conformity with earlier works.

Therefore, I reject the notion of an *a priori* idea of law, the principle of justice, as being 'constitutive' of the 'concept' of law and 'regulative' with respect to legal-political evaluation, and I establish legal politics without any thought of 'correctness' as an empirical technique purporting to guide the legislator via scientific argumentation, and on the basis of hypothetically accepted evaluation criteria. Hence, I finally reject the idea of a specific normative knowledge of the ought *qua* formal-logical presupposition of legal science, and I interpret legal thinking in terms of the same logic as that upon which all scientific knowledge is based. As a label for the legal philosophy based on this position, I have chosen the term 'Realistic theory of law'.

These programmatic demands may seem commonplace at first sight, but actually they are not commonplace at all. There is no denying that, today, legal philosophical tradition, as well as the prevailing legal philosophy, bear all the marks of metaphysics. However, one might argue that metaphysical speculation is irrelevant to modern doctrinal lawyers. Without going to such lengths as certain realists who tend to condemn the whole of modern legal doctrine as sheer superstition and scholasticism, we nonetheless have to admit that even today, our conceptual, legal, and moral system is characterized as originating in primitive, magical-metaphysical ideas, and that critical self-reflection in a realistic spirit is therefore perfectly appropriate for the doctrinal lawyer as well.

This is not the first time that an attempt has been made to develop a legal philosophy based on realistic premises. The entirety of modern Scandinavian legal philosophy (influenced by Axel Hägerström's philosophy) is pervaded by the same spirit. A special mention goes here to Vilhelm Lundstedt's enormous production, characterized by passionate commitment. Similarly, the movement known as realism in America also rests upon an anti-metaphysical attitude. However, there is no denying, I think, that until now, realism has shown a rather naive tendency to equate law with adjudication, without realizing that the social act in question gets its character of 'law-application' by 'law-applying authorities' only by relating it to a normative ideology. One has thereby ended up in an untenable sociologism which diminishes the unique nature of the doctrinal study of law as something distinct from sociology—something which is frequently pointed out and has helped discredit realism. Through the synthesis of ideological and behaviouristic views defended in this book I hope to have succeeded in removing this stumbling-block and conquered the problems which realism will encounter if it is drawn up either purely ideologically or purely behaviouristically (§ 14). Equally, I believe that on the level of legal politics, I have overcome the echoes of the moral-metaphysical ideas expressed in the theory of 'public utility', as a beacon for legal politics.

Students ought to be informed at the outset that it is not possible to study and [46]
master the substance of a book such as this in the way they are used to from the

study of the substantive law. According to Kant, we cannot learn philosophy—we can only learn to philosophize. Not everyone feels an urge to do so; nonetheless, the spirit permeating the study of legal philosophy has to be directed specifically towards personal learning. It would be meaningless to require students to be 'in command' of the subject of the book. Their becoming familiar with the kind of reasoning peculiar to legal philosophy must be our aim. The best way to put this view into practice is, I believe, the following: the entire book is to be read only cursorily, whereas individual sections (at the reader's discretion) are to be studied more closely, alongside complementary studies on the same topic in other legal philosophical works.

This book is the result of studies in legal philosophy pursued over a period of approximately thirty years. It goes without saying that during those years, I have undergone a certain development and I have received enriching impulses from many quarters. Science is never an individual achievement. The goods are seized wherever they are found, and the debt is forgotten all too often. I cannot settle my debt now, but I would like to mention three scholars to whom I am particularly indebted. The first scholar is Hans Kelsen, the teacher of my youth. I am indebted to him more than to anybody else for giving me an insight into the importance of logical consistency in scientific theories. The second scholar is Axel Hägerström, who opened my eyes to the emptiness of moral metaphysics and who was a source of inspiration to me with respect to a realistic conception of law. The third scholar is Viggo Bentzon. It is perhaps only in the last few years that it has dawned on me how sound was the spirit in Bentzon's legal-philosophical ideas, how realistic his legal method, and how many threads unite my own legal thinking with Bentzon's. Logical stringency was not his strong point, nor did he know very much about philosophy; but on the other hand, he was—much more than my other two teachers—in touch with the practical application of legal science. I shall only be too happy if this book were to contain values which can be traced back to these three scholars.

Copenhagen, April 1953 Alf Ross

CHAPTER I [47]

The Problems of Legal Philosophy

§ 1. Terminology and Tradition

The central problem of legal philosophy is legal philosophy itself: how does it differ from other legal disciplines, what kind of problems is it concerned with, what is its task and what is its method?

The various branches of science are often deeply rooted in tradition. Through the work of generations, the problems appertaining to a certain branch have already been laid down. Perhaps the delimitation principles applying to this particular branch, or its relation to other branches, are still under discussion. However, this becomes less important in view of the fact that there exist a series of problematic issues as well as a theory that serves as the stable point of departure for the individual researcher turning to this subject area.

This is not the case with legal philosophy. Certainly, an overwhelming amount of literature has appeared on the subject, and common to all of it is the approach to law from perspectives and problems other than those characterizing legal science in the narrower sense. Beyond that, however, it seems hard to find something which is common to all types of inquiry and which, from a guidance perspective, would arrange these studies like twigs growing from the same branch of science. They are to some extent concerned with different subjects, or they approach these same subjects by taking, as their point of departure, philosophical assumptions so different that the problem and the approach to it do not actually have much in common. There is not even consensus on the terminology denoting systematic expositions of this kind. In the Anglo-Saxon world, the term *jurisprudence* has prevailed. On the continent, terms such as *legal philosophy*, [48] *general study of law*, *legal theory*, *encyclopaedia of law*, and *general theory of law* are used. Each of these terms carries its own nuance of meaning, reflecting the traditional approach of a certain school or trend to the problems.

Given these circumstances, a survey of the problems approached by a type of literature that lies beyond legal science in the narrower sense can only be offered in a grossly simplified shape. On the whole, one can discern three different problem groups. The different schools or trends are characterized by the fact that they focus, to a greater or lesser extent, on one of these problem groups and touch on the others only peripherally, and only in so far as their treatment is implicitly of importance to the main subject. The three problem groups[1] are as follows:

(1) Problems concerning the *'concept' or 'nature' of law*; concerning a series of other fundamental concepts conceived as necessarily[2] implied in the very concept of law itself—for example, the concepts source of law, legal subject, legal duty, legal norm, legal sanction, and so on; possibly, also concerning a series of other legal concepts of general interest, regardless of whether or not they are considered 'necessary'—for example, concepts such as (subjective) right, property, rights *in rem* and rights *in personam*, punishment, intent, guilt, and so on.

This school of 'legal philosophy'[3] (to use, just for the time being, this term as an umbrella term for the type of literature under discussion), which chiefly concerns itself with this group of problems, is known as the *analytical* school because it conceives of its task as that of analysing and clarifying the concepts in question. The trend was initiated by the Englishman John Austin, who held a series of lectures at University College London in the years 1828 to 1832, lectures subsequently published under the title *The Province of Jurisprudence Determined.*[4] Austin himself did not achieve much fame during his lifetime. For financial reasons, he was obliged to give up his career as a lecturer, and his death in 1859 went unnoticed. However, shortly afterwards the tide turned. In the years 1861 to 1863 Austin's widow published a new and complete edition of his lectures which subsequently went through numerous reprints. Austin's analytical method has left its mark on a number of English and American writers up to the present day—including names such as Sir William Markby,[5] Sheldon Amos,[6] Sir
[49] Thomas Erskine Holland,[7] Edwin Charles Clark,[8] William Edward Hearn,[9] Sir John William Salmond,[10] John Chipman Gray,[11] and Sir George Whitecross Paton,[12] so that one can speak of an analytical school.

[1] One usually distinguishes between an analytic approach, a value-philosophical approach and a historical-sociological approach to legal philosophy in a wider sense—a distinction underlying, for example, Josef L. Kunz's survey article 'Zur Problematik der Rechtsphilosophie um die Mitte des zwanzigsten Jahrhunderts' [On the problematics of legal philosophy in the mid twentieth century], *Österreichische Zeitschrift für öffentliches Recht* [*ÖZöR*] 1951, 1 *et seq* – see Bibliography.

[2] Cf. § 6 (3).

[3] The word is enclosed in inverted commas because it must remain undecided, for the time being, whether or not it ought to be retained and, if it is retained, in what sense.

[4] For an account of Austin and his theory and influence, see Alf Ross, *Theorie der Rechtsquellen* [Theory of the Sources of Law] (1929), ch. IV, including digression A, especially 83–87.

[5] *Elements of Law* (1871).

[6] *A Systematic View of the Science of Jurisprudence* (1872).

[7] *The Elements of Jurisprudence* (1880).

[8] *Practical Jurisprudence* (1883).

[9] *The Theory of Legal Duties and Rights* (1883).

[10] *Jurisprudence* (1902).

[11] *The Nature and Sources of the Law* (1909).

[12] *A Text-Book of Jurisprudence* (1946).

It was not until the twentieth century that Austin came to exert influence on the Continental philosophy of law, notably on the Hungarian scholar Felix Somló[13] and the Swiss scholar Ernest Roguin.[14]

Hans Kelsen's *Pure Theory of Law*, the most influential achievement in legal philosophy of the present century, also forms part of the analytical movement.[15] From a historical perspective, however, there is no connection between the Pure Theory of Law and Austin's school.

The analytical school in its entirety is characterized by a methodological formalism. The law is seen as a system of positive, that is to say, actually efficacious norms. The only task of legal knowledge is to establish the existence of these norms as scientifically valid law without involving either issues concerning their value, as measured against given moral or political ideals; or issues concerning the actual social context of which law forms part: in other words, the social factors determinative of the creation and development of the law and the social effects that were caused, or were intended to be caused, by the legal rules. This formalism is strikingly expressed particularly in Kelsen's work. The 'purity' which he demands from the doctrinal study of law has precisely this twofold aim: on the one hand, to liberate the doctrinal study of law from every kind of moral and political ideology; on the other, to liberate it from all traces of sociology, that is, from reflections referring to actual sequences of events. According to Kelsen, legal knowledge is neither moral philosophy nor social theory but, rather, knowledge of norms, dogmatics.

(2) Problems concerning *the 'objective' or 'idea' of law*, that is to say, the rational principle that endows the law with its specific 'validity' or 'binding force' and serves as a yardstick for the value or 'correctness' of legal rules. The idea of law is generally taken to mean justice, which leads to questions concerning the content and basis of the principle of justice; concerning the relation between justice and positive law; the role of the principle of justice as regards legislation, the application of law, and so on.

The school of 'legal philosophy' which is chiefly concerned with issues of this kind is called *Philosophy of Values* or *Natural Law*. In modern times, the term 'legal philosophy' is often limited to this type of philosophy.

This particular school—closely connected, as it is, with religious or meta- [50] physical-philosophical ideas—has a long history. Natural law philosophy stretches back to the times of the first Greek philosophers and extends

[13] *Juristische Grundlehre* [The Basic Features of the Study of Law] (1917).

[14] *La science juridique pure* [The Pure Legal Science] (1923).

[15] The latest complete exposition of Kelsen's views is his work *General Theory of Law and State* (1945). A brief, highly readable survey of the basic ideas underlying his system can be found in his work *Reine Rechtslehre* (1934). By way of introduction, see my essay 'Den rene Retslæres 25-Aars Jubilæum' [The 25th Anniversary of the Pure Theory of Law], *TfR* (1936), 304–31 [translated into English by Henrik Palmer Olsen and published in *Oxford Journal of Legal Studies*, Vol. 31, No. 2 – see Bibliography (2011), 243–72, at 243–64].

to the present day. This philosophy reached its classical peak with the great rationalistic systems arising in the seventeenth and eighteenth centuries. Following a historic and positivistic reaction during the nineteenth century, the philosophy of natural law has once again gained ground during the present century. Indeed, it is very common nowadays to speak of a 'renaissance of natural law'. Its philosophical foundation consists above all in Catholic scholastic philosophy, living on in Thomist natural law, as well as in various offshoots of Kant's and Hegel's systems, adherents of which can be found particularly in Germany and Italy. However, other schools of philosophy have also provided foundations for natural law speculation (utilitarianism, solidarism, Bergson's intuitionism, Husserl's phenomenology etc.).

To avoid repetition, reference is made to chapter X below for an overview of the history of natural law.

(3) Problems concerning *the interaction between law and society* include: the historical origin and development of the law; the social factors which condition the changeable content of the law nowadays; the law's dependence on, and influence upon, economics and the sense of justice; the social effects of individual legal rules or institutions; the legislator's power to direct social development; the relation between the 'living' law (that is, the law as it actually shapes itself within a community) and the law in books; and the forces that actually motivate judicial decisions, in contrast to the rationalized justifications figuring in the premises, and so on.

The school of 'legal philosophy' which has concerned itself chiefly with issues of this type is called the *historico-sociological* school which, in turn, can be subdivided into a predominantly historical and a predominantly sociological branching. Just like analytical 'legal philosophy', this branch is of a comparatively recent date. After a few precursors in the eighteenth century (Giambattista Vico, Charles-Louis de Secondat Montesquieu), the historical approach to law had a breakthrough with the German romantic school (Friedrich Carl von Savigny and Georg Friedrich Puchta); on this issue, see §§ 61 and 86 below.

In England, Sir Henry James Sumner Maine[16] laid the foundation for a 'historical jurisprudence', which studies the correlation between legal and social types in ancient times. He was succeeded by James Bryce, 1st Viscount Bryce,[17] Sir Paul Vinogradoff,[18] Sir Carleton Kemp Allen,[19] and others. The sociological approach is especially well represented in France and the US, where correlation problems relating to the present have been particularly

[16] *Ancient Law* (1861), and *Lectures on the Early History of Institutions* (1875).

[17] *Studies in History and Jurisprudence* (1901).

[18] *Historical Jurisprudence* (1923).

[19] *Law in the Making* (1927).

addressed by Émile Durkheim,[20] Léon Duguit,[21] and Nathan Roscoe Pound.[22] [51]

There are a large number of specialized studies in legal sociology—especially in the field of criminology—which are of considerable interest. Also, commission reports and similar practical studies frequently contain valuable contributions towards clarifying the facts of legal life and their interplay in practice. On the other hand, those publications of a more general character which fall under the rubric of 'legal sociology'[23] seem to have a deplorable tendency to either content themselves with general policy statements or to reveal themselves as natural law philosophies in disguise. The latter is owing to the circumstance that sociology was originally political philosophy in disguise (§ 61). A particularly frightening example is Georges Gurvitch, whose sociology of law has nothing to do with empirical science, but might be likened to a metaphysical-spiritualistic interpretation of the concepts of law and justice, with its roots in Bergson's intuitionism and in Husserl's phenomenology.[24]

Following this exceedingly brief survey of the themes and trends in current 'legal philosophical' literature, the question then arises as to how, in our opinion, the object of inquiry ought to be defined. It seems as if this question could only be tackled if it can be made clear how different the issues can be from which a scientific investigation into legal phenomena may be built up, in order to distinguish an approach that can reasonably be termed 'legal philosophy'.

Here, however, a certain difficulty arises. On the one hand, it is not possible to form a well-founded opinion on the various ramifications of the whole of the science of law unless one has developed more accurate conceptions of the 'nature' of the legal phenomena. On the other hand, the problem of the 'concept' or 'nature' of law is undoubtedly one of the central problems of 'legal philosophy'. All schools of thought are unanimous on this point. Even those that direct their attention mainly towards the ideal validity of the law and its social existence, respectively, must necessarily base their theories upon an understanding of the

[20] *De la division du travail social* [The Division of Labour in Society] (1893).

[21] *Les transformations générales du droit privé depuis le Code Napoléon* [The General Transformations of Private Law since the Napoleonic Code] (1912); *Les transformations du droit public* [The Transformations of Public Law] (1913).

[22] A synopsis of Pound's theory of social lines of development in modern English and American law (with extensive bibliographic references) can be found in his work *Outlines of Lectures on Jurisprudence* (5th edn 1943), 43–49. See also Pound, *Social Control through Law* (1942); *Interpretations of Legal History* (1923); 'Scope and Purpose of Sociological Jurisprudence' (1911), 24 *Harvard Law Review* 591.

[23] One of the most well-known works is E. Ehrlich, *Grundlegung der Soziologie des Rechts* [Fundamental Principles of the Sociology of Law] (1913). In addition, the following works deserve mention: N. S. Timasheff, *An Introduction to the Sociology of Law* (1939); B. Horváth, *Rechtssoziologie* [Sociology of Law] (1934); G. Gurvitch, *Sociology of Law* (1942); H. Cairns, *The Theory of Legal Science* (1941).

[24] See note above and cf. my critique of Gurvitch in *Towards a Realistic Jurisprudence* (1946), ch. II, 8.

general 'nature' of law. Thus, it would seem as if the object of 'legal philosophy' cannot be defined unless one of its main problems has been solved.

This difficulty can be overcome by giving, in this context, merely a preliminary orientation concerning the 'nature' of the legal phenomena—an orientation merely as detailed as our purpose demands. Thus, an in-depth discussion must be postponed until a later chapter.

§ 2. *The Problem of the 'Nature' of Law: What Exactly Does it Consist of?*

The issue of the 'nature' of law poses a constant and fundamental problem to 'legal philosophy' in its entirety. Curiously enough, however, it seems that nobody has ever been surprised that such a problem arises in the first place, nor pondered its cause and import. Yet this question is actually rather curious. For example, who would consider referring, for special treatment, the issue of the 'nature' of mental phenomena to any science other than psychology? Or who would consider referring the issue of the 'nature' of Nature to any science other than the natural sciences? What more could possibly be said about the 'nature' of mental phenomena, apart from what emerges from the description and explanation of them given in psychology? Or about the phenomena of Nature, apart from what emerges from the various natural sciences? A psychology book would perhaps begin with establishing the meaning of the term 'mental phenomena' as being the object of the study of psychology, while a chemistry book might begin with explaining the term 'chemical process'. In both cases, however, the point of doing so is merely to delimit the research area to certain phenomena, not to describe the 'nature' of these phenomena. [52]

Why are things different with respect to law and legal science? Why is the 'nature' of law a problem outside the realm of legal science proper? What can possibly be said about the 'nature' of legal phenomena, apart from what emerges from the science—legal science in the narrower sense—whose object of study are these very phenomena?

In order to answer these questions one might, by way of a starting point, compare typical sentences belonging to the realms of legal science with those of the sciences named above.

For example, let us look at the following sentence, belonging to the realm of physics:

> *Pressure and volume of a given mass of confined gas are inversely proportional.*

Or let us look at the following sentence, belonging to the realm of psychology:

> *The memorizing of certain material through a number of readings achieves the best results when the material is perused at suitable intervals.*

We need not know anything about the 'nature' of these physical or psychical phenomena in order to understand the scientific meaning of these statements.

The fact is that we are aware of what experiences these sentences are referring to, that is, how we should proceed in order to verify their truth.

The situation is different as regards a typical juridico-scientific sentence, such as, for example, this sentence from Ussing's book *Individual Contracts* [in Danish: *Enkelte Kontrakter*], at p. 116:

[53] *The acceptor is obligated to pay the bill of exchange on the due day for payment, cf. § 28 (1) Danish Bill of Exchange Act.*

First, let us take a closer look at the reference, namely at § 28 (1) Danish Bill of Exchange Act. There, we find the following sentence:

> *By accepting, the drawee becomes obligated to pay the bill of exchange on the due day for payment.*

This is almost of the same tenor as the sentence in Ussing's book. Another formulation, synonymous with it and frequently used, is the following:

> *Acceptance obligates the drawee to pay the bill of exchange on the due day for payment.*

Thus, the sentence expressing the legal rule seems to comprise a descriptive assertion about what is happening under certain circumstances: the acceptance of the bill causes the effect that the drawee becomes obligated to a certain course of action. Apparently, this is an assertion that says something about a process in reality in much the same way as, for example, a chemistry sentence stating that sulphur dioxide is created in the process of decomposition. However, while the verification of the chemistry sentence does not present a problem, it is far from clear how to verify the apparent assertion of the law. Perhaps one could arrange experiments, letting people accept bills of exchange and then see what happens. But what is an 'obligation' and how can one empirically determine if it has arisen? The acceptance as such, accomplished by drawing some ink lines on a piece of paper, does not, among its observable consequences, seem to have one that can be called 'obligation'. If one were to say that the 'obligation' effect implies that now there is a chance that the drawee, under certain specified conditions, will be required to pay the bill of exchange, then curious consequences arise. Apparently, this 'effect' is conditional on the fact that § 28 (1) Danish Bill of Exchange Act exists precisely as it does. The 'assertion' included therein will thus be true, precisely because it was uttered in a sentence. Obviously, this does not make sense. An assertion must refer to a state of affairs outside itself and the truth of the assertion must be independent of whether the assertion is put forward in a sentence or not. For otherwise it would be a question of sheer magic: words creating their own object and, thereby, their own truth.

These difficulties and absurdities disappear as soon as one realizes that § 28 (1) Danish Bill of Exchange Act, according to its meaning and function, is not an assertion about anything whatsoever; it is not a statement which can be true or false. § 28 (1) Danish Bill of Exchange Act does not seek to disclose information about reality, it does not have what is called logical meaning.

In order to understand this, it seems appropriate here to adduce, even if only briefly, a few basic linguistic considerations.[1]

By *linguistic utterance*, I understand all sorts of actually occurring linguistic formulations, delivered in either oral or written form.

Distinct from the utterance itself *qua* linguistic phenomenon is its *meaning.* [54] This distinction must be made since different utterances can have the same meaning, just as one and the same utterance, according to circumstances, can have different meanings.

There are two types of meaning: on the one hand, *expressive* or *symptomatic* meaning; while on the other, *representative* or *semantic* meaning.

Every linguistic utterance carries expressive meaning; it is an expression of something, or a symptom of something. This means that the linguistic utterance, being a link in a psycho-physical whole, points back to that experience which has prompted the utterance in the first place. No matter what I am saying, the act of uttering must have been caused by emotional-volitional circumstances that have made me speak, by an urge to open my heart, or an emotion demanding spontaneous expression.

Certain linguistic utterances carry representative meaning as well, which means that the utterance 'indicates', 'symbolizes', or 'stands for' a state of affairs. This is no causal relation but a logical one. For instance, if I say: 'My father is dead', then this utterance indicates the fact that my father passed away at a certain time.

Upon this basis I shall now put forward the following distinctions and concepts:

(a) *Utterances carrying both expressive and representative meaning*, such as, for example, the utterance: 'My father is dead'. The expressive meaning thereof will normally be (the utterance is normally an expression of) an urge to communicate this fact to another person. Its representative meaning is called an *assertion*—the assertion that it is the case that my father is dead. This assertion can be viewed in abstraction from the utterance and the context of experience in which it was given. It can be tested for its truth value, as being either true or false, inasmuch as verification results in proving that what has been asserted really is the case.

(b) *Utterances with merely expressive meaning.* For instance, if I shout: 'Ouch!' because I have burnt myself, or if I say to another person: 'Close the door!',

[1] Cf. Jørgen Jørgensen, *Psykologi paa biologisk Grundlag* [Psychology on a Biological Basis] (1942–46), 455 f.

> then these utterances do not assert that I am in pain, or that I am in a state that can be described as a desire that the other person shall close the door. These utterances do not symbolize anything, they have no representative meaning but are direct bearers of an emotional or volitional 'load'. They express an experience but do not represent anything. Their expressive meaning cannot be separated from the concrete context of experience.

Frequently—for example, when I am shouting: 'Ouch!'—the utterance is not borne by intention, is not an expression of a volitional attitude, but is an automatic reflex. Such utterances are called *exclamations*. Frequently—for example, when I say to somebody: 'Close the door!'—the utterance is made with the intention (expressed by the utterance itself) to directly influence the other person in a certain way, to induce him to close the door. The distinctive feature is the directness of the influence, that is to say, that the influence is exercised by the suggestive 'force' and pressure within the utterance itself, not conveyed through the communication of an assertion. It is obvious that one can also excite
[55] impulses to action by the latter method, for example, by informing another person that his house is on fire. Our language lacks a general term for intention-borne, emotive-volitional expressions. Among these, there are phenomena as heterogeneous as commanding, directing, suggesting, wishing, admonishing, entreating, requesting, etc. Since it is practical to work with a general term, I propose using the term *directive* for this purpose.

Accordingly, three types of linguistic utterances can be distinguished:[2]

(1) *utterances of assertion* (or briefly *assertions*, whereby this word becomes ambiguous, however, since it denotes both the utterance and its representative meaning): that is, utterances carrying representative meaning;

(2) *exclamations*: that is, utterances with no representative meaning and with no intent to exert influence; and

(3) *directives*: that is, utterances with no representative meaning but with the intent to exert influence.

To some extent, these three types correspond to the following grammatical conceptions: indicative sentences; interjections; and imperative sentences. However, it is only to some extent that they correspond. In particular, it should be noted that a linguistic utterance, which grammatically appears as a sentence in the indicative form, can well be a directive and not an assertion. The sentence: 'You will close this door now' may well be, according to circumstances, an assertion, a piece of information about what is happening. Normally, it will be understood as a directive (a command), indicated in written form by a subsequent exclamation mark.

[2] I can see no reason to enter into the issue of whether the distinction can be upheld as exhaustive: whether, for example, interrogative utterances can be reduced to a combination of (1) and either (2) or (3).

If we now, after this linguistic digression, return to § 28 (1) Danish Bill of Exchange Act, it will probably not be difficult to see that this utterance is no assertion but a directive.[3] The law is not written in order to impart theoretical truths but, rather, to influence people—judges and citizens alike—to act in a certain way, that is, to direct them. Parliament is not an information bureau but [56] a central office for social direction.[4] Obviously, the meaning behind the particular legal imperative in question is to prompt drawees who have accepted a bill of exchange to pay it on the due day for payment and, if this should not happen (and if various other conditions have been fulfilled), to prompt the judges of the country to sentence the drawee (acceptor) for non-payment. Why, exactly, § 28 (1) Danish Bill of Exchange Act is capable of actually directing people to behave in conformity with it is an issue we need not discuss in the present context.

Enough about the sentence expressing the legal rule. Let us now turn to the corresponding scientific sentence which, after all, is what immediately interests us in connection with the issue of why the 'nature' of the law constitutes a problem.

We have seen:

(1) that the sentence expressing the legal rule is a directive and not an assertion;

(2) that the scientific sentence in Ussing's book apparently has the same content and structure as the sentence expressing the legal rule;

whereof it seems to follow:

(3) that the juridico-scientific sentence is a directive, too, and no assertion.

[3] The preceding analysis has assumed the simple circumstance that the utterance emanates from an individual author. There is no such author behind the law. This makes no difference, however. What is decisive is that the law functions in the same way as directives issued by an individual author, and that legislation is borne by a 'social intention' that can be regarded as analogous to individual intention. Karl Olivecrona has expressed this idea by calling the legal rules '*independent imperatives*', see *Om lagen och staten* [On Law and the State] (1940), 35 *et seq.* and *Lagens imperativ* [The Imperative of the Law] (1942). I have chosen the more general and neutral term 'directive' since the word 'command' ('imperative') is associated with ideas hardly appropriate to the law, especially in its relation to the judges and other law-applying authorities who undoubtedly experience the law rather as a 'directive' than a 'command'. None of the current, actual terms for utterances without representative meaning, but with the intent to influence, seem to me to be fully adequate for denoting the content of the law. The terminology used here avoids these difficulties by creating a general term for utterances of this type. To all intents and purposes, I do not disagree with Olivecrona.

[4] In addition, one might point out that the meaning of the legal rule, unlike the representative meaning of an assertive utterance, cannot be detached from the actual context in which it occurs. That 2 plus 2 makes 4 holds good, irrespective of the context in which this is asserted. The legal imperative, on the other hand, is valid exactly because it is being issued by the legislator. On this issue, see Alf Ross, 'Den rene Retslæres 25-Aars Jubilæum' [The 25th Anniversary of the Pure Theory of Law], *TfR* 1936, 312 and 325 *et seq.*, as well as *Towards a Realistic Jurisprudence* (1946), ch. IV, 7, where, however, a somewhat different terminology has been used.[Editor's note: The passage in this footnote does not really square with Ross's general view on the possibility of considering the meaning of a directive in abstraction from the context in which it is conceived (see in particular below, § 3, pp. 23–4, where Ross expressly states that 'it is possible to abstract the meaning of a directive ("the King can move one square in any direction") from the concrete experience of the directive'). Indeed, it seems that Ross's whole analysis developed in Chapters I and II of statements about scientifically valid law as propositional attitude reports depends on the existence of such a possibility (see Introduction, pp. xxxi–xxxiv). In the 1958 English edition this footnote was left out, and one is left wondering if Ross noticed the inconsistency and deliberately left out the footnote for that reason.]

However, it seems clear that if one conceives of science—as one usually does—as something in line with systematically ordered knowledge, then scientific sentences cannot be directives, that is to say, emotional expressions directly serving as means of exerting pressure. Science claims to possess the quality of truth and assertions alone can possess this quality. Scientific sentences must possess representative meaning. Consequently, we are bound to conclude that, if there is to be a legal science at all, if the prevailing doctrine can claim at all to consist of true statements about the law,[5] there must be something wrong in the above reasoning in points (1), (2) and (3). The error lies with (2). Notwithstanding an apparent similarity, there must be a decisive difference between the sentences expressing the legal rule and the doctrinal sentences.

Which is exactly the case. The sentence concerning the drawee's obligation to make payment, which we had chosen by way of example, is taken from Ussing's
[57] work *Individual Contracts*, the main title of which is *The Danish Law of Obligations. Special Part* [in Danish: *Dansk Obligationsret. Speciel Del*]. Thereby, it is implied that the author has announced, once and for all, that what is set forth in this work is scientifically valid Danish law. Every single sentence in the book setting forth a legal matter has therefore to be understood in a paraphrased version, namely, that a directive with given content is scientifically valid Danish law. Thus the directly existing doctrinal sentence which has the character of a directive (D), must be paraphrased into a juridico-scientific sentence which has the character of an assertion:

(D) is scientifically valid Danish law.[6]

[5] Thereby, one does not take stand on the controversial issue concerning the character of the doctrinal study of law in its entirety. It is merely assumed that it is possible, at least to a certain extent, to produce true assertions on what is scientifically valid Danish law.

[6] Thereby, the radical diversity between the sentences expressing the legal rule and the juridico-scientific sentences has been distinctly worked out. The former are (alogical) directives; the latter are (logical) assertions (to the effect that certain directives are scientifically valid law). If this diversity is not clearly borne in mind, and if the *directives of the law* are set on equal footing with the scientific sentences concerning them, a distorted view of both will be an inevitable consequence. On the *one hand*, there arises a tendency to imagine that the sentences of legal science also consist of directives or norms. This is illustrated by the conception of legal science *as a normative science*. By this, one can mean different things, either: (1) that it is a science aiming at *producing* (*issuing*) *norms*; or (2) that it is a science which expresses itself *in norms*, albeit without producing them, since the norms stated are those existing as 'positively given'; or finally (3) that legal science is a science *about norms*. This last meaning alone is tenable. However, the term 'normative', when used in this sense, is linguistically less appropriate since it naturally suggests the meaning of (1) or (2). The former expresses the postulate of natural law of a knowledge which is at once insight and claim, cf. § 75. The latter corresponds to Kelsen's view, at least as presented in his earlier work. There (see especially *Reine Rechtslehre* (1934), 21 *et seq.*), 'Rechtsnorm' and 'Rechtssatz' came to the same thing. 'Das Sollen' was the categorial form of both the law itself and scientific sentences about the law, and legal science was, thus, dogmatics in the true sense of the term; it was norm-expressive, not norm-descriptive, as the direct expression of norms with 'validity intent'. (On this issue, see my critique in *TfR* (1936), 304 *et seq.*) In a later work (*General Theory of Law and State*, 1945, 45, *cf.* 167), the author clearly aims at a distinction between *the legal norm* (the sentence expressing the legal rule) as being *prescriptive* and *the legal rule* (the sentence of legal science) as being *descriptive*. However, the distinction is not clearly drawn. From a purely linguistic point of view, it seems misleading to call a descriptive sentence (an assertion) a 'rule'. Also, the scientific sentence is still assumed to be a 'Sollens'-statement, not a 'Seins'-statement and is constantly referred to as a norm (in the descriptive sense of the word), see p. 46 in contrast to p. 167, where it is denied that the scientific sentences are norms. This is not clear to me. I do not

Thereby, we have reached the point which offers an explanation of why 'the [58]
nature of the law' constitutes a problem and which, in addition, indicates wherein this problem actually lies. We have seen that *all juridico-scientific sentences, such as exist in the usual doctrinal legal science, contain within themselves, as an integral element, the concept 'scientifically valid Danish law'*. Indeed, this is something quite extraordinary. There is nothing similar that would apply to, say, psychological sentences and the sentences of natural science. The assertions contained therein refer directly to the phenomena described and there is no reason to paraphrase them with the addition that phenomena such as have been described are psychological or physical, respectively.

Since the concept 'scientifically valid Danish law' is an element within every juridico-scientific sentence, it is impossible to state, accurately and exhaustively, the representative meaning of any such sentence prior to an explanation of what the concept 'scientifically valid Danish law' means. Much apparent disagreement between legal writers can be attributed to each of them tacitly taking their point of departure from different assumptions as to the meaning of 'scientifically valid Danish law'.

Therefore, it is important to clarify this point. *Divested of its metaphysical formulation, the problem of 'the nature of law' is the problem of how to interpret the concept 'scientifically valid (Danish, Swedish etc.) law' as an integral element of every juridico-scientific sentence.* What, then, is the representative meaning of this concept? This is a task which lies beyond the scope and interest of the professional lawyer and which, therefore, is naturally assigned to 'legal philosophy'.

know what is meant by a norm in the descriptive sense. Like all other descriptive sentences, the sentences of legal science must state what 'is', not what 'ought to be'—they must be assertions, not directives (norms). In describing certain norms as scientifically valid law, legal science describes certain social realities: a certain normative meaning content which is actually experienced, and which is efficacious. If this is admitted, however, then Kelsen's radical distinction between natural ('Seins'-) science and norm- ('Sollens'-) science collapses. [In the 1958 publication, Ross added the following: 'For a more elaborated presentation of this criticism, see my review of Hans Kelsen, *What is Justice?*, *California Law Review* 45 (1957) 564 *et seq.*'] On the *other hand*, the fusion of the sentences of the law and of legal science can lead to one's regarding the former like the latter, that is to say, as being assertions, expressions of an insight or a knowledge, not of an intention. Kelsen's doctrine on this issue is not completely clear and this has brought its own difficulties for those of his successors who were endowed with speculative propensities rather than common sense. Thus Carlos Cossio, the founder of the so-called 'egologic' theory of law, maintains in all seriousness that a statute book, no less than a scientific representation of the law, is knowledge, is science ('Egologische Theorie und Reine Rechtslehre' [The Theory of Egologics and the Pure Theory of Law], *ÖZöR* (1952), 15 *et seq.*, especially 46–61; 'Jurisprudence and the Sociology of Law', 52 *Columbia Law Review* (1952), 356 *et seq.*, especially 499). Not in the sense that legislation is based on scientific knowledge of a certain kind. Rather, that the legal rule as such, the norm, is in itself an insight, is knowledge, legislation is in itself a scientific act. The legal rule is the community's legal knowledge of itself. Understand that, if you can!

§ 3. *Preliminary Account of 'the Nature of Law' (Analysis of the Concept 'Scientifically Valid Danish Law')*

Let us imagine that two people are playing chess, while a third person is merely watching.

If the onlooker knows nothing at all about chess, he will not understand what is going on. Presumably, his knowledge of other games will make him realize that it is a question of some sort of game. However, he will not be able to
[59] understand the individual moves, nor discern any connection between them. Still less will he have any notion of the problems presented by a specific chess composition.

If the onlooker knows the rules of chess but otherwise does not know much about the theory of the game, his experience of the others' play changes character. He will understand that the 'irregular' movement of the horse is the prescribed knight's move. He will be able to read the alternating movements of the pieces as rule-governed moves. Within certain wide limits, he will even be able to predict what will happen. For he knows that the players take turns to make their moves, and that each move must fall within the sum total of all possibilities allowed by the rules in any given configuration of the chess pieces. Apart from that, however, a great deal will appear puzzling to him—especially if the players are above beginner level. He does not understand the players' strategies, and he has no eye for the tactical problems of the situation. For instance, why does White not take the bishop? In order to fully understand what is going on, one must know not only the rules of chess, but also the essentials of chess theory. The possibility of predicting the next move is enhanced if one takes into account not only the rules of the game, but also the theory of the game and the individual player's insight into it. Finally, one must take into account the purpose governing the game of the individual player. It is normally assumed that he plays in order to win. But there are also other possibilities (for instance, he plays in order to let the opponent win, or to test, experimentally, the value of a certain move).

There is a peculiar and interesting lesson to be learned from these reflections on chess. A series of human actions is unfolding before our very eyes (the movements of the hands causing certain objects in space to alter their position) and we might think that these actions, together with other bodily processes (breathing, psycho-physical processes etc.), constitute a course of events which follow certain biological and physiological laws. It is, nevertheless, obvious that it is beyond the limit of all conceivable possibilities to give an account of this course of events in such a way as would explain the individual chess moves and predict them on a biological and physiological basis.

The problem presents itself differently if we move to another level of observation and 'interpret' the course of events in light of the rules of chess and chess theory. If we do so, certain elements in the entire series of events, namely, the moving of the pieces, stand out as being 'chess-relevant' or 'chess-meaningful' actions. Moving the pieces is not seen as merely altering the position of objects in space but, rather, as moves in the game, and the game turns into a meaningful and coherent whole because the moves mutually motivate each other and are interpreted as attack and defence, in accordance with the theoretical principles of the game. If we look at the players, we understand the individual moves made by each player from the point of view of his being conscious of the rules of chess, together with the knowledge which he is presumed to have of the theory of the game, as well as the goal he has set for himself. Incidentally, one may also ignore the players altogether and simply understand the game in its abstract meaningfulness (as a game in a chess book).

It should be noted that the 'understanding' as it is used in the present context is of another kind than causal understanding. We are not operating here with [60] the laws of causality. There is no mutually causal relationship between the moves. The connection between them is established through the rules of chess and chess theory. This connection is a connection of meaning.

Furthermore, it should be emphasized that the notion of community is constitutive of what we experience in a game of chess. This means that the goals and interests pursued, and the actions conditioned by these goals and interests, can only be understood as links within a larger context which also includes the actions of another person. When two men working together are digging a ditch, they are doing nothing but what each of them also could do individually. With chess it is otherwise. A single person cannot pursue the goal 'to win at chess'. The actions which are included in 'playing chess' can only be performed in interaction with another person. Each player has his part to play, but this part has meaning only on the condition that the second player also plays his part.[1]

The notion of community generated by playing together also manifests itself in the supra-individual character of the rules of chess. They must necessarily be interpreted in the same way, at least by the two players playing a certain game. Otherwise, there would be no game, and the individual moves would remain isolated without any coherence of meaning.

All of this indicates that the game of chess can function as a simple model of what is called a *social phenomenon*. Human social life in a community is not merely a cacophony of mutually isolated, individual actions. It acquires the

[1] In his work *Schachnovelle* [frequently translated as *The Royal Game*], Stefan Zweig gives an interesting description of a person who is able to play chess against himself. However, this is explained by his having cultivated a pathological splitting of consciousness, thus being able to function as two persons.

character of community life from the very fact that a large number (not all!) of individual actions are relevant, or have meaning, in light of a set of common ideas about rules. They constitute a coherent whole of meaning by referring to each other, just like move and counter-move. Here, too, there is mutual interplay motivated by, and acquiring its meaning from, the common rules of the social 'game'. It is the consciousness of these rules which enables us to understand, and in some measure to predict, the course of events.

In what follows, I shall examine more closely what a rule of chess 'actually is', and how it is possible to establish scientifically what the valid rules of chess are.

Here, I am thinking of the rules of chess proper, that is, the rules determining the arrangement of the pieces, the moves, the 'taking' etc.—not of the norms of chess theory.

With respect to the latter, it will suffice to mention briefly that they, just like other technical rules, are obviously of the same nature as hypothetical theoretical statements. They presuppose the actual rules of chess and point out the consequences for the game which the various openings and ways of playing have, weighed against the chance of winning. Just like other technical rules, their guiding force [61] is determined by an interest, namely, to win the game. To a player who is not interested in winning the game, the theory does not carry any meaning.

The rules of chess proper, on the other hand, are directives. Irrespective of the fact that they can be formulated as assertions concerning the chessmen's 'abilities' or 'power' to make moves and take other pieces, it is clear that their meaning is to specify how to play the game. They aim directly—that is, irrespective of any underlying purpose—at motivating the player: This is playing chess!

These directives are felt by each player to be *socially binding*, which is to say that the player not only feels spontaneously motivated ('bound') to pursue a certain course of action but, in addition, realizes that breaking the rules will prompt a reaction (a protest) on the part of his opponent. The rules of chess thus distinguish themselves from the rules of skill contained in chess theory. A stupid move may arouse surprise but would hardly call forth any protests.

On the other hand, the rules of chess are not tinged with morality, owing to the fact that, normally, nobody is inclined to break them (cf. § 90 below). A desire to cheat presupposes that one is playing with a purpose other than merely to win according to the rules of the game; for example, in order to win admiration, or to win the sum of money at stake. The last named purpose is frequently pursued in card games, and it is well known that the demand for a fair game thus acquires a moral value.

How is it possible, then, to establish which rules (directives) are the scientifically valid rules of chess?

One could perhaps think of proceeding in a behaviourist manner, that is, restricting oneself to what can be determined by external observation of the actions in order to find certain regularities. However, in this way we would never gain an insight into the rules of the game, since we would not be able to distinguish actual custom, or even regularities conditioned by chess theory, from the actual rules of chess. Even after having watched a thousand games it would still be possible to think that it was against the rules to open with a rook's pawn.

Perhaps the easiest way would be to follow certain authoritative regulations, such as, for example, the decisions taken by chess congresses, or the information provided in authoritative textbooks on chess. But this is not sufficient either because it is not certain that such declarations are adhered to in practice. It is a well-known fact that, in many games, there are a large number of possible variations. Even in a classic game like chess there are variations (for example, the rule called '*en passant*' is not always followed). The question, 'What are the scientifically valid rules of "chess"?' must, therefore—strictly speaking—be understood to mean: 'What are the scientifically valid rules of an actual game played by two specific players?' It is their actions, and their actions alone, which are bound up with each other within a coherent whole of meaning derived from rules.

Therefore, we cannot but adopt an introspective method. Our task is to discover which rules are actually perceived by the players themselves as socially binding—that is, to discover the fact of their being bound by rules. The first criterion applying here is that they are actually efficacious in the game—something which can be observed from the outside. But in order to decide whether observed regu- [62] larities are distinct from, and more than, actual custom or conditions dictated by technical details, it is necessary to ask the players what rules they feel bound by.

Thus, we can state the following: that a rule of chess *is scientifically valid* means that, within a given community (which, in principle, comprises the two players playing an actual game), this rule is actually adhered to *because the participants feel socially bound by the directives contained in the rule.* The concept of scientific validity (in so far as it relates to chess) thus comprises two elements. One refers to the actual efficacy of the rule, which can be established through external observation. The second refers to the way in which the rule is experienced as motivating, namely, as being socially binding.

There is a certain ambiguity in the concept 'rules of chess'. In actual fact, the rules of chess only exist as a content of the players' experience: namely, their ideas of certain patterns of action, and the emotional experience of bindingness tied to them. But, just as it is possible to consider the meaning of an assertion as a pure thought content ('2 plus 2 makes 4') in abstraction from the experience of it by a particular person at a particular time, it is possible to abstract the meaning of a directive ('the King can move one square in any direction') from the concrete experience of the directive. In any accurate analysis, the concept 'rules of chess' must, therefore, be divided into two components, namely: into certain ideas of patterns of action experienced by the players (with the accompanying emotion), and the abstract norm.

Thus, the *norms of chess* constitute the abstract idea content (of a directive nature) which the players have in common and which makes it possible, *qua* scheme of interpretation, to understand the *phenomena of chess* (the chess moves and the experienced ideas of patterns of action) as a coherent whole of meaning and motivation—as a game of chess; and, in conjunction with other factors, to predict the result of the game to some extent.

It should be noted that the phenomena of chess and the norms of chess are not different types of phenomena existing independently of each other; rather, they are only two *abstract aspects of the same thing*. No biologico-physical action in itself is considered a chess move. The action acquires this quality through interpretation alone, the norms of chess serving as a scheme of interpretation. And *vice versa*: no directive idea content in itself has the character of a scientifically valid norm of chess. The directive acquires this character only through the fact that it can (along with other directives) be used effectively as a scheme of interpretation for the phenomena of chess, in the way indicated above. The phenomena of chess first become phenomena of chess in relation to the norms of chess, and *vice versa*.

Presumably, it has now become clear to the reader what all this talk of chess is about. It provides a clue to the assertion that the concept 'scientifically valid norm of chess' can serve as a simple model for the concept 'scientifically valid (Danish) law', which is, after all, the object of our preliminary considerations.

[63] The law can also be regarded as partly *legal phenomena*, partly *legal norms*, in mutual correlation.

In the same way, when looking at law working in the real world, we find that a large number of human actions are interpreted as a coherent whole of meaning and motivation through a legal norm ('scientifically valid (Danish) law') *qua* scheme of interpretation. For example, A purchases a house from B. It turns out that the house is full of longhorn beetles. A demands from B a reduction of the purchase price but B refuses. A sues B, and the judge orders B to pay a sum of money to A within a certain time, in accordance with the Sale of Goods Act. B does not do this. A applies to the bailiff who levies execution against B's property and puts it up for auction. This sequence of events comprises a whole series of human actions, from the passing of the Sale of Goods Act, in the year 1906, down to the auction. Considering these events from a biologico-physiological perspective will not reveal any causal connection between them. These chains of causation are to be found within each individual. However, by means of the scheme of reference and interpretation of 'scientifically valid Danish law' we interpret them as legal phenomena, constituting a coherent whole of meaning and motivation. Each of them acquires its legal character only in this way. A's purchase of the house is being done either orally or in writing. However, it becomes a 'purchase' first when seen in relation to the legal norms. The different actions are reciprocally motivated, just like chess moves. The judge, for example, is motivated by the sales agreement between A and B (and the further circumstances in connection with it, namely, the condition of the house), as well as by the act of legislation of 1906. The whole thing resembles 'a game', the only difference being that it is a game according to norms which are far more complicated than the norms of the game of chess.

On the basis of the above considerations, I am asserting the following: *There seems to be no reason to think that the concept 'scientifically valid (Danish) law' (legal norm) cannot be explained and defined in basically the same way as the concept 'scientifically valid (for any pair of players) norm of chess'.* That is to say that 'scientifically valid (Danish) law' means an abstracted set of normative ideas which serve as a scheme of interpretation for the phenomena of law in Danish society—which, again, means that these norms are actually followed[2] because they are experienced as socially binding.

One might think that the above conclusion is trivial, and that an overly large thinking apparatus has been employed for the purpose. This may have been rightly judged by someone who approaches these problems without preconceived notions. It does not hold good for a historical perspective, however. By far the greatest number of all legal philosophers until the present day have argued that the concept 'scientifically valid (Danish) law' is something that cannot be explained without recourse to the supernatural. Consequently, the law is not merely an empirical phenomenon. Saying that the law is 'scientifically valid' does not only refer to something factual and observable, but also to a 'validity' which is of a supernatural and non-sensual kind; to an idea of pure reason, of divine origin or given *a priori* (that is, independent of experience) in [64]
the supernatural and rational nature of man; to the idea of law. Eminent legal philosophers who deny such spiritual metaphysics have nevertheless held the view that the 'scientific validity' of the law has nothing to do with real-life social phenomena, but can be explained only with the help of specific postulates.

Viewed in this light, our preliminary analysis can hardly be called trivial, I think. Even if the idea as such requires further elaboration, this analysis of a simple model is nonetheless calculated to raise doubts as to the necessity of metaphysical ideas in order to explain the concept of law. Who would ever think of tracing the scientifically valid norms of chess back to an *a priori* validity, to a pure idea of chess, given to Man by God, or deduced from his eternal reason? The very idea is ridiculous. Why? Because we do not take chess as

[2] By the judge and other law-applying authorities, cf. § 8.

seriously as law. Because stronger feelings are bound up with legal notions. But this is not reason enough to believe that a logical analysis would adopt a fundamentally different attitude in the two instances.

Of course, a great many problems remain to be solved before the concept 'scientifically valid (Danish) law' has been analysed satisfactorily. At present, there is no need to proceed, however. This preliminary account is adequate to serve as a basis for a survey of the various branches of legal science as such and, thereby, as a basis for assigning the proper place to 'legal philosophy'.

§ 4. Overview of the Branches of Legal Science

The distinction (explained in the previous section) between the phenomena of law—or, as I prefer to put it, law working in the real world—and the norms of law, forms the basis for the corresponding distinction between the two main branches of legal science. The branch concerned with law working in the real world is called *sociology of law*,[1] while that concerned with the norms of law is called *the doctrinal study of law or legal science in the narrower sense.*

Here we should remember that real life and norms are not two independent spheres of existence but, rather, abstract aspects of the same reality. Thus, it is a matter of two viewpoints which presuppose each other reciprocally.

The doctrinal study of law is directed towards legal norms, that is, the abstract idea of the content of directives, and ignores the realities of law working in the real world. It is the task of the doctrinal study of law to discover the idea [65] content—or we might say, the ideology—which functions as a scheme of interpretation for law working in the real world, and to present it coherently and systematically according to its inherent structure and meaning. Since the doctrinal study of law is concerned with norms, it can be called normative. This expression must not be misunderstood, however. As has been emphasized in § 2, scientific sentences naturally cannot consist of norms (directives). They have to consist of assertions—assertions concerning norms; and this means assertions to the effect that certain norms have the character of 'scientifically valid (Danish) law'. To say that the doctrinal study of law has normative character means, then, that it is a study *about* norms, not *in* norms. It does not aim to 'lay down' or express norms but, rather, to establish their character of 'scientifically valid (Danish) law'. The doctrinal study of law is normative in the sense of *norm-descriptive*, not in the sense of *norm-expressive.*

The doctrinal study of law can never be detached from the sociology of law, however. Even though the interest of the former inclines towards ideology, it will always be an abstraction from social reality. Even if the jurist is not professionally interested in the link between legal doctrine and real life, the link nevertheless exists. It lies embedded within the concept 'scientifically valid (Danish) law' which—as shown above—is an integral part of every doctrinal sentence. For this concept refers back to the realities of life: to social efficacy and the experience of being socially bound.

[1] It should be noted that for the sake of convenience, this term is used as a *pars pro toto* to refer to psychological as well as historical studies of the law working in the real world.

In addition, a doctrinal study of law which closes its eyes to the social function of the law may appear unsatisfactory when measured against the interest that lies in being able to make predictions about judicial decisions. As we have seen, a knowledge of the proper norms of chess will only make it possible to predict the course of a game of chess within a larger context. This is so because the players are motivated, not only by the norms of chess but by other things as well, namely, by their aim in playing and by the propositions of chess theory concerning the consequences of the moves. The same is true with respect to the law. The judge is not motivated exclusively by legal norms, but also by social purposes and theoretical insight into social contexts, which are of operational relevance to the furtherance of these purposes. For that reason, and especially in modern times, there has been a programmatic demand for the doctrinal study of law to orient itself towards the realities of social life as well, to the extent prompted by the aforementioned interest. This is a further indication of the fact that the borderline between the doctrinal study of law and sociology is not clear-cut but, rather, depends upon a relative difference in perspective and interest.

Sociology of law, on the other hand, is directed towards law working in the real world, legal transactions and various conceptions of law, and can no more be detached from the doctrinal study of law than the doctrinal study of law from sociology. The social phenomena which are the subject of the sociology of law acquire their specifically legal character only in relation to the norms of law, to scientifically valid law.

[66] This branch of science is still so new and undeveloped that it is difficult to name the issues it is concerned with.[2] Speaking in general terms, this branch describes, and attempts to discover, regular connections between the law and how it works in real life, and it does so from an individualistic psychological, a socio-psychological, a historical, and a sociological viewpoint (in the narrower sense). Once again, one should remember that the legal norms only indicate the frame within which the law working in real life is developing, influenced by custom, economic and ideological factors, social aims, and socio-theoretical insight. A given set of legal norms (such as, for example, the set governing divorce, or that governing contracts) can develop—I would like to say: can 'be played out'—in a variety of ways when it comes to law working in real life. Anyone knowing only the norms does not know much about the corresponding social reality. What are the grounds for divorce that are actually invoked by the various sections of the population? What are the possibilities of evading the rules in fabricating evidence, and what kind of customs have emerged in this

[2] On this issue, cf. Vilhelm Aubert, 'Noen problemområder i rettssociologien' [Problematic issues in the sociology of law], *TfR* (1948), 432 *et seq.*, where the problems of a sociology of law are arranged under the following three major headings: (1) The sociological origin and development of legal rules; (2) The sociological causes of actual conflicts of juristic relevance; and (3) The social effects of law.

respect? With what favour or disfavour do the courts look upon the various grounds for divorce, especially as regards evidence? What types of contract have evolved? What role does collective bargaining play as compared to that of individual contracts? Furthermore, how does one consider effective taxation in relation to the tax laws? What about the legal consciousness of the population towards tax avoidance, and what role does legal consciousness play in actual behaviour? etc. etc. Questions like these—questions aiming at the concrete, living, social, legal reality—are raised and dealt with by sociology of law.

A field of inquiry within sociology of law which is of particular interest is the interplay between law and society. How can it be explained that legal notions are able to motivate people? What causes—individually and socially—the attitude of respect and obedience to valid law which enables the legislator to direct social life? What other factors come into play and restrict the power of the legislator? What reactions may an intended legislative measure be expected to call forth? And conversely: What social forces are determining the content and further development of the law? What role is played in this respect by economic power relations and the citizens' convictions of law and justice? Is the evolution of the law the product of blind forces, or do planning and rational insight also have a role to play?

The two main branches of legal science, in turn, fall into different subdivisions.

The doctrinal study of law in the narrower sense is concerned with an actual legal system within a given society—such as, for example, currently scientifically valid Danish law. Danish law is, in turn, traditionally subdivided into several disciplines according to how the legal material is divided. On this issue, see chapter VIII below.

The history of law describes previously scientifically valid law and its historical [67]
development. However, this must not be understood to mean that the difference between this discipline and the doctrinal study of present-day law merely lies in a difference in the point in time of the legal rules. In addition to this temporal aspect, there are two points through which one can discern a difference with respect to the fields of inquiry dealt with by the two disciplines.

Firstly, the present moment is not merely a point in time arranged alongside all other points in time. It is a moment distinguished from all other moments in that it is that point in time at which the course of reality has arrived and is about to enter the still unknown future. Also the law is part of this ongoing process. Any presentation of scientifically valid law dated at a given moment is a snapshot which captures a cross-section of this stream. But such a cross-section through the present 'now' is characterized by open questions for the future. What is law today is, as we shall see later on (§ 9), always a question of what will happen tomorrow. A merely co-determining factor in this calculation is what happened yesterday. Scientifically valid law is never a historical fact but, rather, a calculation with regard to the future. This endows the sentences of present-day legal science with a fundamental element of uncertainty and has the effect that questions about scientifically valid law, as the certainty of the calculation diminishes, are in a peculiar way fused with questions about legal politics on the issue of the creation of new law. There is no equivalent to this in legal history. Those questions which were open when seen with the eyes of the past have been answered now. Therefore, the history of law is concerned only with facts.

Secondly, even if the history of law does not affect legal politics it is, on the other hand, related to the sociology of law.[3] It does not merely aim at presenting a series of snapshots but, rather, at describing and explaining a development. It studies the development of law in relation to other social developments, and this has been shown to be a task for sociology of law.

Similarly, *comparative legal science*[4] is more than a mere presentation of scientifically valid law with different national characteristics. Comparative legal science may be either contemporary or historical in nature. The former applies whenever it investigates the social effects connected with different legal orders. In this case it is an instrument of legal politics. The latter applies whenever it aims to investigate the social circumstances which might explain why law has developed differently in different countries. In both cases, comparative legal [68] science has powerful sociological traits, in so far as it investigates the relationship between law and society as viewed from either side.

This shows that legal sociological considerations play such an important part in the history of law, as well as in comparative legal science, that it is almost a matter of taste whether to regard them as subjects of doctrinal legal studies or of legal sociology.

Sociology of law can be divided into a basic science and an applied science.

The basic science falls into a general part and a number of specialized branches.

The general part concerns itself—without any reference to the actual content of the law—with the general features of law working in the real world, its structure and dynamics. The investigation may either aim at a certain type of society—such as, for example, modern democratic society—in order to inquire into the typical features of the structure and function of the law working in

[3] The apparent lack of clarity that ensues if one maintains, as we shall see in the following, that legal politics is applied sociology of law, disappears as soon as we perceive that the sociology which is of interest to the legal politician and, thus, to the doctrinal legal scholar, deals with problems concerning the social effects of law, whereas the sociology which is of interest to the legal historian deals with the social factors that influence the development of law.

[4] See Folke Schmidt, 'Komparativt rättsstudium' [Comparative legal studies], *TfR* (1951), 473.

the real world within this particular society, especially the mechanics of legal motivation and the interplay of the law with other social forces (*static sociology of law*); or it may aim at the historical development of the law, in order to discover general laws for the social forces which form the law; or for its correlation with societal development (*dynamic sociology of law*). The various *specialized branches* correspond to the respective specialized areas of law. *Criminology*, which investigates criminal behaviour and the individual and social factors which condition it, corresponds to criminal law. *Political science*, investigating political life (in particular political ideologies and institutions), corresponds to constitutional law. *International relations* corresponds to international law. At present, other specialized branches within sociology of law do not seem to have established themselves, but it seems quite possible to envisage such branches as corresponding to, respectively, property law,[5] the law of persons, family law, etc.

Like the branches of applied natural science, *applied sociology of law* is concerned with a field of study chosen and arranged according to its relevance to certain practical purposes. For example, just as the construction of bridges is concerned with the circumstances and problems relevant to the desire to be able to build bridges, applied sociology of law is concerned with the facts and contexts which are important for the practical purposes of legislation. In view of a certain legislative reform, the task of applied sociology of law involves describing the social conditions within a given society and analysing the changes in these conditions which different legislative measures may be assumed to bring about. Thereby, one arrives at an insight which provides invaluable guidance to the legislator or to him who ponders the problems from the legislator's perspective (the legal politician). Legal-sociological inquiries of this kind are most often pursued (in any case as yet), not as independent scientific studies but, [69]
rather, as part of the official spade-work for legislative reform (commission reports and the like).[6]

Legal politics (*legal science de lege ferenda*) is not a new, independent branch of legal science; rather, it is applied sociology of law. In so far as the activity labelled 'legal politics' is genuinely scientific, it consists in legal-sociological knowledge. The 'application' of the legal sociological insight, on the other hand, is a mental activity of a non-scientific nature. These issues will be thoroughly examined in later sections of this work (§§ 78 and 84).

[5] See, e.g., Karl Renner, *The Institutions of Private Law and their Social Functions* (1949).

[6] On this issue, cf. Vilhelm Aubert, Torstein Eckhoff, and Knut Sveri, *En lov i søkelyset* [Spotlight on a Statute] (1952); Verner Goldschmidt, 'Retssociologiens praktiske Muligheder' [The Practical Possibilities of Legal Sociology], *UfR* (1952), B 261.

§ 5. Not 'Legal Philosophy' but 'Juridico-Philosophical Problems'

Yet, where does one find 'legal philosophy' in the overview of all the branches of legal science, presented in the preceding section? How strange that there should be no place for a special branch of science which might properly be called 'legal philosophy'.

If we compare the overview in § 4 with that in § 1 concerning the problems which traditionally have been regarded as 'juridico-philosophical' problems, we shall see:

(1) that what has been called 'historical jurisprudence' or 'sociological jurisprudence' (§ 1) clearly falls within the purview of the sociology of law as defined in § 4. As such, the term is, of course, of secondary importance. But objectively there is no reason why the sociology of law should be lumped with the analytical movement under the umbrella term 'jurisprudence', 'legal philosophy' or the like. If pursued as an empirical science, sociology of law has nothing in common with philosophical science but clearly bears the stamp of a specialized branch of science among other branches. Therefore, sociology of law cannot be the science we are seeking;

(2) that what has been called legal philosophy in the narrower sense, the doctrine of the idea of law (justice) or the natural (correct) law, does not appear at all in the overview in § 4. This is due to the fact—and the reason for it will be disclosed at a later stage—that what goes by this name is merely empty, metaphysical speculation and imagination without any scientific value. From the point of view of legal realism, legal politics is applied legal sociology, nothing else;

[70] (3) that of the traditional fields of inquiry, the only one that remains as a possible object of 'legal philosophy' is that which the analytical school is concerned with. But how is there room for such a specialized discipline as this within the overview in § 4?

The answer to the above question must be looked for among more general views on the relationship between philosophy and specialized branches of science. The general opinion within modern, scientifically oriented philosophy (to which I subscribe) is to the effect that philosophy has no specific subject field coordinated with, and distinct from, that of the various specialized branches of science. Philosophy is not a deduction from basic principles of reason through which another, and higher, reality than sensible reality is revealed to us. Nor is philosophy an extension of the specialized branches of science designed to investigate the uttermost components of reality. Philosophy is not a theory at all, but a method. This method is logical analysis. Philosophy is the logic of science, and its subject is the meaning of scientific language.

Accordingly, legal philosophy has no specific subject coordinated with, and distinct from, the subject of legal science in its various forms. In its relation to legal science it is reflexive, turning towards the latter's logical apparatus, in particular its conceptual apparatus, in order to make it the object of a more detailed logical analysis than is done within legal science itself. Legal philosophy is focused on that which, to the jurist, frequently constitutes a premise 'taken for granted'. It is largely a question of fundamental and more general concepts—such as, for example, the concept 'scientifically valid (Danish) law' which, for that reason, is not assigned as a special task to any of the many specialists within the wide realm of the law.

The subject of legal philosophy is not law, nor any part or aspect of it, but legal science. Legal philosophy dwells, so to speak, one storey higher than legal science and looks down upon it 'from above'.[1]

The boundaries between legal science and legal philosophy are fluctuating. Logical analysis is also widely used within the traditional doctrinal study of law. There are no internal criteria to determine where legal science ends and 'legal philosophy' begins. A reasonable delimitation of the problems of 'legal philosophy' may be provided by considering what legal science itself has provided. This would explain why current English 'jurisprudence' includes a number of concepts and problems, such as: *dolus*, *dolus eventualis*, *culpa*, intent, the purpose and theories of punishment, ownership, possession, contract, evidence, burden of proof, and so on; concepts and problems which in our own legal tradition[*] currently form the components of various legal disciplines. This can be explained by the slow development of scientific analysis and adaptation of scientifically valid law in England. Therefore, 'jurisprudence' has more or less [71] become an assembly point for any and all investigations of a more fundamental nature. In our own legal tradition, a correspondingly broad definition of the field of 'legal philosophy' would be absurd since it leads to repetition. It can only make sense to take up such problems which have not been treated at all within the current doctrine, or which are thought to have been treated unsatisfactorily.

This relativism also demonstrates that it is not appropriate to speak of 'legal philosophy' because this term involuntarily suggests a vision of an objectively

* In the first English translation (on p. 26), Ross contrasts not only 'our own' (that is, the Danish) tradition but also the American and Continental tradition with the English tradition.

1 The sentences in this section of the text which are concerned with 'legal philosophy' are, in turn, lodged at a still higher level. The first sentence in this footnote, concerning sentences on legal philosophy, is lodged at a still higher level. In this way, one could go on *ad infinitum*. The idea defended by K. Grue-Sørensen, *Studier over refleksivitet* [Inquiries into Reflexivity] (1950), namely, that the series can be brought to an end through a self-referring sentence, is absurd.

delimited field of research. Therefore, I prefer to speak of *juridico-philosophical problems*. What problems are brought forward to philosophical analysis will have to do partly with the discretion and selection dependent upon the individual researcher's interests, studies, and taste; partly with the development of legal science at any given time.

Juridico-philosophical analysis may be directed either towards the concepts and problems of the doctrinal study of law or towards those of sociology of law. However, since the logical apparatus of sociology of law is in the main the same as that employed in other branches of sociology (and history), it would seem reasonable to confine the specifically juridico-philosophical problems to dealing with the realm of the doctrinal study of law. This outcome is also prompted on pedagogic grounds, since a philosophical analysis of the sociology of law would be valueless as an element in traditional legal education. Within the sociology of law, however, a special position is held by applied sociology of law, or legal politics, owing to its close connection with the doctrinal study of law, which makes it a component of the jurist's traditional field of activity.

Accordingly, the following presentation falls into two main parts: juridico-philosophical problems in relation to the doctrinal study of law (chapters II–IX); and juridico-philosophical problems in relation to legal politics (chapters X–XVIII).

§ 6. *Confrontation*

The relation between my own interpretation of the nature and task of legal philosophy and other current views will already have emerged, at least in part, from the overview, in § 1, of the various movements in the legal literature. Here are a few additional remarks.

(1) For time immemorial, legal philosophy has chiefly been regarded as a *value philosophical* interpretation of the very idea of law. That is, of the ethical principle of reason which explains the 'binding force' of scientifically valid law and serves, at the same time, as a yardstick of the ideal 'correctness' of the law. In this presentation, such speculations have been dismissed as [72] metaphysical from the area of scientific thinking.

In Denmark, legal philosophy has traditionally been regarded in the same way. Leaving aside the older, classical natural law literature, we can observe the following.

To my knowledge Anders Sandøe Ørsted, after having freed himself from natural law, has not come up with any explicit definition of the task of legal philosophy. Although he overcame his youthful dependence upon natural law, he nonetheless retained the idea, grounded in the philosophy of value, that law, essentially, is a valid order—an order which (in contrast to violence and tyranny) has the character of legal order only in so far as it is a (more or less perfect) realization of the moral law of reason within the state. Accordingly, the state is called the organ of legal science, and the vocation of legal science—or so it is alleged—consists in further developing the commands of reason according to which external legislation must form the mutual, external relationships between human beings.[1] Therefore, there can hardly be any doubt that Ørsted, even if he renounced his belief in an independent juristic law from which a natural law can be deduced, nonetheless continued to regard legal philosophy as a branch of moral philosophy.

The same applies to Frederik Christian Bornemann. According to him, a legal order is 'certainly a secular realm but nonetheless a manifestation of divine reason . . . a realm of morality—a realm of objective, secular morality'. The task of legal philosophy—or, as Bornemann himself puts it—of the general study of law, consists of investigations into the general and unchangeable nature of legal norms and institutions—which is to say: into the transcendent, moral principles as revealed through the legal order.[2]

[1] Anders Sandøe Ørsted, *Eunomia*, vol. I (1815), 51, cf. Alf Ross, *Virkelighed og Gyldighed i Retslæren* [Reality and Validity in Jurisprudence] (1934), ch. II, 4.

[2] Frederik Christian Bornemann, *Foredrag over den almindelige Rets- og Statslære* [Lectures on the General Theory of Law and State] (1863), 25–6 cf. 2; on this issue, examine in more detail Ross, *loc. cit.*, Ch. II, 5.

Carl Goos maintained the same outlook. According to him, the general study of law includes, on the one hand, 'the philosophy of positive law' which is concerned with the psychological basis of the law—with those factors which have determined the origins and development of the law; and, on the other hand, 'ethical jurisprudence' which is concerned with morality's demands upon the law and which 'teaches the doctrine of an ideal law, which ought to be'. Goos himself confines the general study of law to the latter task—observing that a thorough investigation into the true nature of individual legal relationships is a necessary precondition for demonstrating the maxims (derived from the idea of law) which govern them.[3]

It was Viggo Bentzon who first objected to a philosophical-ethical interpretation of legal philosophy. He claimed that 'it should not be the task of a general study of law to transcend positive law but, rather, to deal [73] with the most common problems surrounding our domestic positive law as well as the positive law of other countries'.[4] His attitude is purely analytical, even though he did not fully succeed in consistently maintaining, and enforcing, this attitude.[5]

Unfortunately, this change in perspective was not upheld and further pursued after Bentzon. Frederik Vinding Kruse goes back to Goos. According to Vinding Kruse, the task of the general study of law consists, in the first place, of finding out 'those rules which lawyers call the nature of the matter, or natural law'. In the second place, it consists of dealing with the basic concepts and fundamental problems of legal orders.[6] In their presentation, however, these two tasks have not been accorded equal importance. Except for the doctrine of the sources of law and the concept of unlawfulness, few words are wasted on fundamental concepts. Moreover, these are dealt with in a superficial and traditional way. Therefore, it may be said that the general study of law, in Vinding Kruse's version, is chiefly a theory of 'scientifically' established 'natural law'; that is, a series of loose postulates on what, in the author's eyes, is the 'most wholesome' or the 'most reasonable' arrangement of various legal matters. What the author offers is to a large extent a diluted version of what is better and more profoundly treated by the individual legal disciplines.[7]

The term '*general study of law*'—a term that has been used in Denmark since Bornemann's time—is unfortunate since it prompts the view that

[3] Carl Goos, *Forelæsninger over den almindelige Retslære* [Lectures on the General Study of Law], vol. I (1885), § 1, cf. Ross, *loc. cit.*, Ch. II, 6.

[4] Viggo Bentzon, *Retskilderne* [The Sources of Law] (1900–1907), 2.

[5] On the issue of his doctrine of the sources of law, see Alf Ross, *Virkelighed og Gyldighed i Retslæren* [Reality and Validity in Jurisprudence] (1934], Ch. VII, 6.

[6] Vinding Kruse, *Retslæren* [Jurisprudence], vol. I (1934), 87.

[7] On this issue, examine in more detail my article 'En Retslære fra det 19. Aarhundrede' [A jurisprudence dating from the nineteenth century], *TfR* 1945, 273–92.

legal philosophy is the most general part, but nonetheless a part, of doctrinal legal science. Thus, both Bentzon and Vinding Kruse mention, among the tasks of legal philosophy, the treatment of the most common problems (the fundamental problems) of the doctrinal study of law. This view is untenable. There is no plausible reason why legal philosophy should compete with the doctrinal study of law as regards the presentation of scientifically valid law or discussions *de lege ferenda.* Legal philosophy shall not be turned into a scientific Supreme Court (as Vinding Kruse would like to have it), before which the individual disciplines can be summoned. One might say that legal philosophy is, in a certain sense, concerned with jurisprudential problems but in a manner that is different from the concerns of jurisprudence itself. Legal philosophy does not aspire towards 'solving' these problems in the same manner as jurisprudence, but merely towards analysing them with reference to implicit logical premises. That such an analysis may be valuable to a doctrinal presentation is quite another thing. Legal philosophy is not part of positive legal science but, rather, a discipline which is independent from it, and with specific problems and a specific method.

(2) Legal philosophy has subsequently been regarded as *sociology of law.* If I reject this interpretation, it is not because I have objections to legal-sociological studies as such (provided they are pursued according to empir- [74] ical science and are not speculative metaphysics in disguise). My position is motivated solely by the view that sociology of law, showing all the characteristics of a specialized science, consequently should not be mixed up with conceptual analysis. Moreover, the personal interests and abilities necessary for usefully studying the two fields differ widely.

In Denmark, highly meritorious contributions to historic-sociological research on the origins of law have been made by Carl Wium Westrup.[8] Theodor Geiger's interesting book *Vorstudien zu einer Soziologie des Rechts* [Preliminary Studies on the Sociology of Law] (1947) is largely concerned with the fundamental problems of legal philosophy (from the perspective of a sociologist) and is, in this respect, more legal-philosophical than sociological.[9]

Even though sociology of law is distinct from legal philosophy, legal sociological insight is of great importance for conceptual analysis, provided that one proceeds, as I do, from the assumption that all juridico-scientific sentences in the last analysis refer to social reality. *Legal philosophy must be sociologically oriented.* Such sociological orientation is characteristic of modern

[8] C. W. Westrup, *Introduction to Early Roman Law,* vols. I–IV (1944–50); *Rettens Opstaaen* [The Origin of Law] (1940).

[9] On this issue, see my review in *TfR* 1950, 215 and my article 'Om begrebet "gældende Ret" hos Theodor Geiger' [On Theodor Geiger's concept of 'valid law'], *loc. cit.* 242.

Swedish legal philosophy, which more or less originates in Axel Hägerström's philosophy.[10]

(3) Legal philosophy as defined here is nearly in keeping with *analytical 'jurisprudence'* and corresponding trends on the Continent.

Felix Somló means to delimit '*die juristische Grundlehre*' [the basic features of the study of law] in so far as to concern only the form of the law, that is, the very concept of law and the *necessary concepts* implied therein—which, in turn, means the concepts which are necessarily presupposed intellectually in all statements about scientifically valid law, regardless of their content, such as, for example, the concepts of legal norm, legal duty, and legal source. The doctrinal study of law, on the other hand, is a science concerned with the content of the law.[11] Regardless of what one may think of the possibility of such a distinction—it seems to be grounded in the metaphysical assumption that there 'exists' a concept of law of a certain structure, as an *a priori* form of thought in Kant's sense, or as a platonic idea—it is inappropriate to delimit
[75] the problematics of legal philosophy in this manner. The results are as follows: while the concept of legal duty belongs to the domain of legal philosophy, the concept of subjective rights and its classification falls outside of this domain, since one can logically envisage a legal order without any right to file a lawsuit which is typical of subjective rights. Such fragmentation in the approach to problems of the same nature is unreasonable.

(4) An *eclectic* definition of the task of legal science (i.e. in the sense of including both logical-analytical and moral philosophical as well as sociological problems) is provided by Julius Stone.[12] According to the common guiding principle, legal philosophy—jurisprudence—approaches the law in the light of other sciences: logics, ethics, and sociology. The principle itself is not clear and results in a heterogeneous set of components without organic

[10] See especially Axel Hägerström, *Till frågan om den objectiva rättens begrepp* [On the Concept of Objective Law] (1917); *Der römische Obligationsbegriff* [The Roman Notion of Obligation] (1927); V. Lundstedt, *Föreläsningar över valda delar av obligationsrätten* [Lectures on Selected Parts of the Law of Obligation], vols. I–IV (1920–44); *Superstition or Rationality in Action for Peace?* (1925); Karl Olivecrona, *Om lagen och staten* [On Law and the State] (1940); Ingemar Hedenius, *Om rätt och moral* [On Law and Morality] (1941); Per Olof Ekelöf, *Straffet, skadeståndet och vitet* [Punishment, Damages and Penalty] (1942); *Är den juridiska doktrinen en teknik eller en vetenskap?* [Is the Doctrinal Study of Law a Technique or a Science?] (1951); Björn Ahlander, *Är juridiken en vetenskap?* [Is the Study of Law a Science?] (1950); *Om rätt och rättstillämpning* [On Law and the Application of Law] (1952). (Only the most important monographs have been mentioned. Moreover, there is a large number of articles written by the authors mentioned above, as well as by other authors.)

[11] Felix Somló, *Juristische Grundlehre* [The Basic Features of the Study of Law] (1917), § 3 as compared with § 10.

[12] *The Province and Function of Law* (1946/50), Ch. I, §§ 11–13. Similar eclectic definitions can be found in the works of many Anglo-American authors: Vinogradoff, Pound, Keeton, Kocourek, Hohfeld, Wigmore, Timasheff and others, sometimes—as in Stone—camouflaged by a supposedly rational scheme of classification. On this issue, see Stone, *loc. cit.*, Ch. I, §§ 8 and 9. Also Josef L. Kunz (§ 1, note 1 *loc. cit.*) holds that all three lines of inquiry are branches of one and the same science—legal philosophy or jurisprudence—enjoying equal status.

cohesion. Stone's giant book evinces tremendous industry and scholarship but has not produced any coherent theory. Within each of its three parts, loosely tied together, the work consists mainly of a number of summaries of the writings of other authors, concerning many different problems and starting from many different premises. The book is a spineless and brainless colossus—a book about books, not about legal science. [76]

[76]

CHAPTER II

The Concept 'Scientifically Valid (Danish) Law'

§ 7. 'Danish Law': Rules about the Monopolized Use of Physical Force through Public Authorities

On the basis of the analysis of the game of chess and chess rules, I proposed, in the preceding chapter, the working hypothesis that, in principle, it must be possible to define and explain the concept 'scientifically valid (Danish) law' along the same lines as the concept of a 'scientifically valid norm of chess'. My task now is to try to develop this working hypothesis into a comprehensive theory about what the concept 'scientifically valid (Danish) law' actually means.

My working hypothesis implies that the law, like the rules of chess, is a supra-individual, social phenomenon, in the sense that the legal notions of action give rise to a common ideology which is active in most people's minds, thereby creating *an interpersonal context of meaning and motivation.* The law is, at the same time, legal norm and legal phenomenon (the law working in the real
[77] world).[1] The legal norms are the abstract normative ideas which, employed as a scheme of interpretation, make it possible to comprehend the legal phenomena (the law working in the real world) as a meaningful network of legal transactions and to make predictions, within certain limits, about the course which the law is going to take when it is operating in a real world context. It is to the norms, not to the phenomena,[2] that the property of 'being scientifically valid'

[1] In my earlier work, in particular *Virkelighed og Gyldighed i Retslæren* [Reality and Validity in Jurisprudence] (1933) and 'Den rene Retslæres 25-Aars Jubilæum' [The 25th Anniversary of the Pure Theory of Law], *TfR* 1936, I have defined the law in a one-sided way: as a real-world phenomenon. In contrast, I am emphasizing now that the law is both idea and phenomenon. Harald Ofstad has quite rightly pointed out this flaw in my former writings; see 'Om descriptive definisjoner af begrepet "rettsregel"' [On descriptive definitions of the 'legal rule' concept], *TfR* 1952, 38 f., 58. He is wrong, however, when he identifies the contrast between phenomenon and idea content with the dualism between reality and validity which I have been fighting against (*op. cit.* 66). This dualism refers to the contrast between empirical knowledge of reality and *a priori* knowledge of a specific validity beyond all reality. I must persevere in fighting against this dualism, and as vigorously as possible, cf. § 13.

[2] T. Geiger is therefore on the wrong track when he attempts to tie the concept of scientific validity to the actual course of events ('the real norm'); for details, see Alf Ross, 'Om Begrebet "gældende Ret" hos Theodor Geiger' [On the concept 'valid law' in the work of Theodor Geiger], in *TfR* 1950, 251.

is being ascribed, and this means that the norms can function as a scheme of interpretation in the way indicated—which, in turn, is due to the fact that the corresponding notions of action are experienced as binding in people's minds and effectively guide their actions.

However, all that has been said until now is that the law, just like chess, represents an interpersonal context—but not what context. Therefore, my next task must primarily purport to establish which set of social norms, operating under the name of 'Danish law', are the object of legal science. Once this has been established, what this means and how one decides that these norms 'are scientifically valid' needs to be developed, both in more detail and according to the stated fundamental viewpoint.

Given these preconditions, the analysis of the concept 'scientifically valid (Danish) law' can be divided into two question areas:

(a) What norms are treated by legal science under the name of 'Danish law'? How do they distinguish themselves from other social norms, such as, for example, the norms of chess, courtesy and good manners?

(b) How is the quality of these norms as 'being scientifically valid' (which is presumed to indicate a certain social efficaciousness) to be defined more precisely, and how can it be established whether or not a certain legal norm is scientifically valid?

The first question will be discussed in the present section; the second in §§ 8–10.

Once again, let us return for a moment to chess. Obviously, there is no point in attempting to define the rules of chess by distinguishing them, for example, from the rules of tennis, football, or bridge. 'The rules of chess' is the name for an individual set of norms constituting a coherent whole of meaning. Just as Nikolaj Petersen is the name of an individual who is not defined but shown, so 'the rules of chess' is the name for an individual set of norms which are not defined but pointed out: these are the rules of chess. Nor is it problematic, in practice, to keep the rules of chess distinct from the rules of tennis, football, bridge, or from any other type of social norms. The problem of definition would only arise if the rules of chess were classed together with the rules of football and bridge under the heading 'rules of games'. We would then have to ask in [78]
the usual manner what characteristic it is in any individual system of norms that is the decisive factor in determining whether or not it falls under this heading. I shall not enter more closely into the definition problem but merely point out that it is a matter of no interest to anyone who merely wants to describe the rules of chess. For in order to do so, it is not necessary to know anything about what the rules of chess have in common with other individual rule systems which can be grouped together under the heading 'rules of games'.

In the law it is exactly the same. 'Danish law' is the name for an individual set of norms which constitute a coherent whole of meaning and which, therefore, are not defined but pointed out. 'Danish law', 'Norwegian Law', 'Swedish Law', etc., correspond to the various individual sets of rules of games. The problem of definition arises only if we class these various individual systems under the heading 'law' or 'legal system'. Yet here, too, it holds true that this definition problem is of no interest to anyone who merely wants to describe scientifically valid Danish law. This is because here, once again, it is not necessary to know anything about what this norm system has in common with other norm systems, grouped together under the heading 'law' or 'legal system'.

In so far as one intends, consistently, to develop legal philosophy so as to encompass only those concepts which are presupposed in the doctrinal study of law, the question of a plausible definition of the concept 'law' ('legal system') is consequently not a task for legal philosophy. This has hitherto not been realized. Legal philosophers have believed that, in order to delimit the jurist's field of activity, it was necessary to produce a definition of the concept 'legal rule' so as to distinguish law from other kinds of social norms. This misunderstanding was caused by our failure to realize that scientifically valid Danish law constituted an individual whole. What is included in it depends on the context of meaning. The concept 'law' is not an umbrella term for a class of legal rules but, rather, for a class of individual legal systems. This is also borne out by experience, for in practice, it is usually[3] not difficult for the jurist to determine whether a certain rule is a part of Danish law or whether it belongs to a different norm system—such as, for example, Norwegian law, the rules of chess, or the rules of morality. On the other hand, what may raise doubts and difficulties is the issue of whether or not a given rule can be considered scientifically valid, but this issue is not addressed in the present context.

Yet even if the problem of how to define the concept of 'law' or 'legal system' falls, strictly speaking, outside the province of legal philosophy (as delineated in this book), it would nonetheless be natural, as regards both tradition and a complete survey, to offer some views on the subject. I shall return to this issue in § 12. For the moment, I merely wish to put forward the fundamental point
[79] of view that *no particular interest attaches to how the concept is defined.* The endless philosophical discussions on the 'nature' of law are based on the assumption that the law derives its specific 'validity' *qua* law from an *a priori* idea, and that the definition of law is therefore decisive in determining whether a given normative order can lay claim to the 'honorary title' of law. If one renounces these metaphysical assumptions and the emotional attitudes associated with them, then the problem of definition will no longer be interesting. It is the task

[3] In some exceptional cases doubts may arise; for details, see § 10.

for Danish legal science to present the individual system of norms called 'Danish law'—that much is certain. There are various other individual systems which, to a greater or lesser extent, resemble it—such as, for example, 'Norwegian law', 'Swedish law', 'International law', the social order in primitive communities where there is no organization to establish or enforce the law, the order of an association or of a band of gangsters, the order maintained by the occupying power in an occupied country, and so on. In all of these cases, the norm system can be said to be 'scientifically valid', and given this social fact, it may be of both practical and theoretical interest to know and to present the content of the system in question. Whether or not one wants to call such a system (as, for example, the order of a band of gangsters) a 'legal system' (the band) is, from a scientific point of view—that is, if the word 'law' is freed from its emotional-moral connotations—an arbitrary and completely uninteresting question of definition. It has been claimed that Hitler's régime was no legal order, and juridical 'positivism' has been accused of moral treason for uncritically recognizing such an order as law.[4] However, descriptive terminology has nothing to do with moral approval or condemnation. When labelling a given order as 'a legal order', I may, at the same time, believe that it is my utmost moral task to overthrow that order. The mixture of descriptive views and moral attitudes of appraisal that characterizes the discussions on the concept of law is a good example of what Stevenson calls a *persuasive definition*.[5]

But enough has been said on the unnecessary problem of how to define the concept of 'law' or 'legal order'. I can now turn to the problem of how to characterize the individual system of norms called 'Danish law'.

As mentioned earlier, 'Danish law', like the norms of chess, constitutes an individual system determined by an inner coherence of meaning. Our task must be to point out what this coherence of meaning consists of. With respect to the rules of chess, this is easy. Coherence of meaning is provided by the fact that all these rules, directly or indirectly, have reference to the moves made by the chess players. If the legal rules likewise are to constitute a system, they must likewise have reference to *definite actions performed by definite persons*. But what sort of [80]
actions, and what sort of persons? This question can only be answered by doing an analysis of the rules usually presented as 'Danish law' and finding out to whom they are directed, and what the purpose is of these rules.

According to their *prima facie* content, the norms of law may be divided into two groups: norms of conduct; and norms of competence (or procedure). The former prescribe a certain course of action—such as, for example, § 28 of the Danish Bill of Exchange Act. The latter create a competence (power, authority) which, in turn, means that they are directives to the effect that norms created

[4] Gustav Radbruch, *Vorschule der Rechtsphilosophie* [Introduction to Legal Philosophy] (1947).
[5] Charles L. Stevenson, *Ethics and Language* (1944), 206 *et seq.*

in conformity with a given mode of procedure shall be considered norms of conduct. Thus, a norm of competence is an indirectly expressed norm of conduct. The norms of the constitution concerning legislative power, for example, are norms of conduct prescribing behaviour in conformity with the further norms of conduct, created by legislation.

To whom, then, are *the norms of conduct* addressed? § 28 of the Danish Bill of Exchange Act, for instance, seems to prescribe how a person who has accepted a bill of exchange shall act. Yet this is by no means an exhaustive description of the normative meaning of the provision—indeed, it completely fails to capture what is really relevant. At the same time, § 28 of the Danish Bill of Exchange Act is a directive to the judge, telling him how, should the occasion arise, he should exercise his judicial authority. This alone would appear to be of interest to the jurist. If it must be assumed with respect to any statutory provision—such as, for example, Chapter II § 1 of the Danish Marriage Act—that it does not contain any directive to the judge, it is for that reason regarded as a mere moral-ideological pronouncement without any legal relevance. Conversely, if it is certain that a provision does contain a directive to the judge, then there is no need to give the private individual any further instruction as to how he should act. These things are two sides of the same coin. The instruction to the private individual implies that he knows what reactions on the part of the judge he can expect under certain conditions. If he wants to avoid these reactions, this knowledge constitutes a challenge to him to adjust his conduct accordingly. The rules of the Danish Penal Code are drafted in this way. They do not say anything about the citizens being forbidden to commit homicide; rather, they merely give an instruction to the judge on how to decide such a case. In principle, there is nothing to prevent § 28 of the Danish Bill of Exchange Act, or any other norms of conduct, from being drafted according to the same pattern. This shows that *the legal norm proper*, in so far as the norms of conduct are concerned, is a *directive to the judge*, whereas the instruction to the private individual is merely a non-proper legal norm, deduced from the directive and conditioned by the private individual's wish to avoid certain reactions on the part of the judge.[6]

[81] As has already been mentioned, § 28 of the Danish Bill of Exchange Act contains a directive to 'the judge'. But who is a judge, and under what conditions does he enter upon his duties? These questions can be answered only by referring to the rules of court organization and court procedure. In this way, the rules of private law are linked to those of public law in one indivisible complex of meaning.

[6] § 11 notes that the non-proper legal norms also have an ideologically motivating function, independent of the fear of sanctions.

The rules of the constitution on the organization and exercise of legislative power may serve as an example of rules belonging to the second aforementioned group, namely, the *norms of competence*. The true meaning of these rules, too, is an instruction to the judge (and other law-applying authorities), namely, to make a decision in accordance with the detailed instructions issued by the legislation.

It emerges from the above that what is called 'Danish law' constitutes an indivisible context of meaning where any single integral rule—be it (viewed in isolation) a norm of conduct or a norm of competence—is, ultimately, a norm of conduct concerning the exercise of public authority, in the form of concrete judgments or administrative acts.

The judgment, in turn, is the basis for a writ of execution. Whatever form the execution may take, it will, in the end, be a question of exercising physical force against a certain person if the person in question attempts to resist execution. As a rule, administrative acts are enforced only on the basis of a judgment; to a certain extent, however, the immediate use of force is possible.

Summing up and generalizing these considerations, one must conclude that law consists of a coherence of rules, all of which—directly or indirectly—have to do with the exercise of *physical force against a person, warranted through a designated public authority*. Leaving out the comparatively few cases where administrative agencies have direct access to the use of force, we can say that law consists of directives for *organizing the exercise of specific coercion through the courts*.

It is worth noting that the law, in itself,[7] establishes who, as 'a public authority', has the competence to arrange, and the duty to exercise, physical force. Thus, 'Danish law' is a system which establishes who, *qua* public authority, shall order and exercise coercion and, at the same time, establishes the conditions under which this shall be done.

The natural counterpart to this, and what gives the public exercise of force its special meaning and effect, is the fact that the exercise of physical force is essentially *monopolized* by public authorities. Thus, where there is a machinery for exercising the monopoly of force, we speak of a *state*. Law, then, can be said to be rules for the organization and function of the state machinery of force; or [82] rules for the monopoly of physical force, exercised through the respective public authorities.

[7] Thus, the expression 'public authority' refers to a person possessing a certain legal competence, and therein lies no further ideological qualification conditioned by the circumstance that the exercise of force is experienced as 'valid', cf. § 11.

§ 8. *The Scientific Validity of the Legal System*

Our point of departure is the hypothesis that the scientific validity of a system of norms derives from its ability to function as a scheme of interpretation for a corresponding set of social actions—for the actual substratum of normative ideas—in such a way that we can comprehend this set of actions as a coherent whole of meaning and motivation and, within certain limits, make predictions about these actions. This capacity within the system is due to the fact that the norms are effectively complied with because they are felt to be socially binding.

But what are those social actions which, as legal phenomena, constitute the social substratum of the legal norms? We have seen that legal norms are, in the last analysis, norms about the exercise of force through public authorities or—in a slightly simplified way—norms for the ordering of the specific exercise of force through the courts. It follows that the *legal phenomena, as the real counterparts of the norms, must be the administration of justice through the courts.* It is there, then, that we must look for the efficaciousness defining the scientific validity of law.

Consequently, scientifically valid Danish law can be defined as the normative ideology which is actually operative, or must be thought operative, in the mind of the judge, because it is felt by him to be socially binding and is, therefore, complied with efficaciously. What is characteristic of this efficaciousness is that the hypothesis of this ideology, used as a scheme of interpretation, enables us to understand the judge's (verbal) behaviour, his judicial decision, as being linked, within a coherent whole of meaning and motivation, with other social actions which, according to the contents of the normative ideology, are conditioning the judge's reaction (legislative acts, other public and private legal acts, and factual actions).

All of these actions—the application of the law through the courts plus other actions which are presumed to condition the application of the law (legislative acts, administrative acts, the citizens' legal acts and breach of the law, and so on) could be called *legal phenomena in the wider sense,* or *law working in the real world*, because they all get their specifically legal meaning and relevance by being interpreted in light of the ideology of the legal norms, *qua* motivating precondition for the application of the law.

We must nevertheless unconditionally maintain that it is solely the legal phenomena proper—the application of the law through the courts—which are decisive in determining the scientific validity of the legal norms. Contrary
[83] to generally accepted ideas on that head, we must insist that the law regulates

the behaviour of the courts, not that of the citizens. The efficaciousness which conditions the scientific validity of the norms can, therefore, solely be sought in the judicial application of the law, not in the law working in the real legal life of the citizens. If abortion is prohibited, for example, the true content of the law consists in a directive to the judge to the effect that, under certain conditions, he shall impose a penalty for abortion. The decisive factor determining the scientific validity of the prohibition is solely the fact that it is effectively upheld by the courts whenever breaches of the law are discovered and prosecuted.[1] On the other hand, it makes no difference whether the prohibition is actually being complied with by the citizens or whether it is frequently ignored. From this follows the apparent paradox that the more efficaciously a rule is complied with in extra-judicial legal life, the more difficult it is to ascertain the scientific validity of the rule, because the courts do not have the opportunity to display their reaction.[2]

In the previous sections we have sometimes used the word 'judge', sometimes the word 'courts'. A precondition for using the concept 'Danish law' for a system which is identical with, and common to, the legal community in its entirety is that the judges, albeit individually different, are animated by a common, supra-individual ideology. Consequently it makes no difference whether we refer to 'the judge' or to 'the courts'. Law is a social, that is, supra-individual phenomenon. To the extent that the individual judge is motivated by any particular idiosyncrasy, it will not count as 'Danish law'—even though it is a factor that must be taken into consideration by anyone who is interested in predicting any concrete judicial decision.

When the basis for the scientific validity of law is sought for in the judicial decisions of the courts, it may seem that the chain of reasoning is moving in a circle: one might point out that being qualified as a judge is no mere factual quality but, rather, can only be assessed by referring to scientifically valid law, in particular to the rules of public law, governing the organization of the courts and the appointment of judges. Before I can state that, for example, § 28 of the Danish Bill of Exchange Act is scientifically valid law, I must have established what is scientifically valid law in those other respects. But what is the proper criterion?

The answer to this problem is this. In principle, it is the entire legal system *qua* coherence of meaning, encompassing the rules of public law and private

[1] The word 'courts' is here understood as a comprehensive term, referring to the authorities which together commence criminal prosecutions—the police, the prosecution, and the courts. If the police regularly omit to investigate certain breaches of the law, or if prosecutors regularly decide not to prosecute, the penal law will lose its character of scientifically valid law, irrespective of whether it is intermittently applied by the courts or not.

[2] On the application of this point of view in international law, see Alf Ross, *Lærebog i Folkeret* [A Textbook of International Law], § 24, § 28 IV *et passim*.

law, which is being verified as a corporate body. The behaviour of the people prescribing coercion becomes intelligible as being based upon an ideology which explains *that* they act as 'judges' and, at the same time, *how* they act as
[84] judges. There is no Archimedean point for verification, no part of the law which is verified before any other part. Verification simply takes place in such a way that a certain concrete, wholly normative pattern—namely, the pattern which is expressed in the constitution concerning a set of public authorities and the legislation emanating from them[3]—can actually be used as a scheme of interpretation regarding social reality. The behaviour of the judge is an actual realization of those parts of the pattern which make him a judge, as well as of those which instruct him how to act as a judge.[4]

The fact that it is, in principle, the entire legal system that is being verified, does not exclude the possibility of investigating whether or not a particular given rule is scientifically valid law. It only means that the problem cannot be solved without reference to the assumptions concerning what is otherwise thought to be scientifically valid law. These more specific problems of verification will be discussed in §§ 9 and 10 below.

According to the explanation given in this section, the concept of the scientific validity of law rests upon hypotheses concerning the inner life, or the thought processes, of the judge. What is scientifically valid law *cannot be determined purely behaviouristically*, that is, through external observation of regularities in the reactions (practice) of the judges. Over a long period of time, the judge may have exhibited a certain typical reaction—he may, for example, have imposed sanctions on abortion. Suddenly, this reaction changes because a new law has been promulgated. It is not possible to fall back on a more general, externally observable custom, namely, the custom of 'obeying the legislator', for it is not possible to observe, from the outside, who is 'the legislator' that is being obeyed. Purely external observation will lead to the conclusion that the attitude of obedience is directed towards a certain circle of individuals, mentioned by name, who, at the time of observation, meet at Christiansborg* as members of the legislature. Yet this, too, will change one day. One can continue in this way right up to the constitution, but not even the constitution is unchangeable. A behaviouristic interpretation, then, is bound to fail. To understand and predict judicial behaviour can only be achieved through ideological interpretation,

* Translator's note: Christiansborg Slot [Christiansborg Castle] is the seat of the Danish Parliament.

[3] In the next chapter, it will be shown that this ideology is, in fact, slightly more complicated, and encompasses other legal sources as well. There is no need to go into details for the time being.

[4] There is nothing odd about the fact that, in principle, it is the entire system that is being verified. The same applies to the natural sciences. Verification of an individual law of nature takes place on the assumption that a number of other laws are true. The question is whether the individual law is compatible with the system that has been hitherto assumed. However, nothing is established in advance. As such, there is nothing to prevent new experiences from forcing us to revise the standpoints we have hitherto assumed. It is always the entire systematic whole that remains the ultimate criterion for what is held to be true.

that is, by means of the hypothesis about a certain ideology which animates the judge and motivates his actions. Fundamental epistemological[**)] objections which might be raised against operating with hardly accessible mental phenomena simply do not apply. This is because the components of the experience are not being introduced on the basis of uncertain inferences but, rather, as merely hypothetical factors, which alone render possible the meaningful understanding and effective prediction of the course of events. Verification is objective and [85] pragmatic: it lies in the comprehension and the predictability which is made possible by the hypothesis.

To express the same idea in another way: the law presupposes not only regularity in the judge's pattern of behaviour, but also its being *rule-governed.* The concept of scientific validity contains two elements: partly the outwardly observable and regular compliance with a certain pattern of behaviour; partly the experiencing of this pattern as a socially binding norm. Not every outwardly observable custom in the game of chess—such as, for example, not opening with a rook's pawn—is an expression of a scientifically valid norm of chess. Similarly, not every outwardly observable regularity in the judge's reactions is an expression of a scientifically valid legal norm. Thus, for example, a custom may have arisen to impose only fines on certain offences, although imprisonment is authorized as well. To be sure, one should add here that the habitual behaviour of judges is apt to develop into binding norms, and that a habit will, in that case, be considered as an expression of scientifically valid law. But as long as it remains merely a habit, this is not the case.

This dual element contained within the concept of scientific validity can thus explain the dualism that has always been a characteristic of this concept in current metaphysical theory of law. According to this theory, the expression 'scientifically valid law' refers to both an order which is actually efficacious and an order which is valid by virtue of *a priori* principles. Law is at the same time something factual within the realm of reality, and something valid within the realm of ideas (§ 13). It is easy to see that this dualism in outlook must lead to logical and epistemological complications, reflected in a series of antinomies in legal theory.[5] It consistently leads to the metaphysical assertion that existence itself, in its innermost being, is what is valid (Hegel).[6] Like most metaphysical constructions, the construction of the immanent validity of positive law rests

**) Editor's note: In Danish, Ross is here using an adjectival inflection [*videnskabsteoretisk*] of a noun [*videnskabsteori*] which in English literally means *theory of science*, i.e. roughly *philosophy of science*. As philosophy of science does not have a corresponding adjectival inflection in English, we shall use the adjective *epistemological* throughout, as this, we presume, conveys Ross's meaning. However, please observe that Ross's focus is specifically on the philosophy of science, rather than on epistemology in general. For clarification, see editor's introduction.

[5] This is the main theme of my book *Virkelighed og Gyldighed i Retslæren* [Reality and Validity in Jurisprudence] (1934).

[6] Ibid. 67.

upon a misinterpretation of certain experiences, in this case the experience that the law is not a merely factual, habitual order, but an order experienced as socially binding. Therefore, the traditional view, once deprived of its metaphysical garb, can be seen as my own view, in its opposition to a purely behaviourist interpretation of the scientific validity of law.

§ 9. Verification of the Sentences of Legal Science concerning Norms of Conduct [86]

Let us recall the following major issues:

In § 2 we explained the difference between the meaning content of the legal norms and that of the sentences of legal science. Legal norms are directives, whereas the sentences of legal science are assertions referring to these directives, according to the pattern below:

A = (D) is scientifically valid (Danish) law

where, for example:

D = § 28 Danish Bill of Exchange Act

In § 7 it was shown that 'Danish law' constitutes an individual system of norms, whose unity must be sought in the fact that all of them are, directly or indirectly, directives concerning the exercise of physical coercion by public authorities. In § 7 we were concerned, therefore, with the 'D' in the formula above.

In § 8 we turned our attention to that part of 'A' in which 'D' is described as 'scientifically valid (Danish) law'. We could show that this assertion referred to such a correspondence between the norm system to which 'D' belongs and a social reality (namely, the application of law by the courts) that we, by using the norm system as a scheme of interpretation, can comprehend the application of law within a context of meaning and motivation with the law working in real life, and can predict, within certain limits, the judge's reactions.

In this section and the following one, we shall inquire more closely into the method of testing whether a given norm is scientifically valid (Danish) law, which is the same thing as testing the truth of the corresponding assertion of legal science. Circumstances may vary somewhat, depending on whether we are talking about immediate norms of conduct or norms of competence, respectively. Accordingly, the inquiry will be divided into two parts: while the present section focuses on *immediate norms of conduct*, the subsequent section will focus on norms of competence.

Our present task touches upon the core of the problem of the empirical content of legal science. If the sentences of legal science are to be understood as empirico-scientific assertions about social reality, not as metaphysical postulates concerning a validity beyond the horizon of experience, then the same holds true for them as for all statements about reality, namely, that their logical meaning content is identical with the immediate experience through which the truth of the statement is tested.

[87] It is a principle of the modern, empirically orientated logic of science that an assertion claiming to be a statement about reality (and not a mere logical-mathematical, analytical sentence) implies, directly or indirectly, that when following a certain procedure one will, under certain conditions, have certain direct experiences. This procedure is called verification: it is concerned with the method of testing the truth of a statement and, at the same time, defines its meaning content. If it is not possible to indicate such a procedure—such as, for example, with regard to the assertion that the world is governed by an invisible demon—then we feel totally helpless vis-à-vis the question whether the statement is true or false. Such statements are said to lack (logical) meaning and are called metaphysical.

Thus, any meaningful assertion about reality may directly concern or imply fundamental, immediate experiences. If I say, for example: 'This object is made of chalk', then my assertion—together with a set of other assertions—implies, *inter alia*, that if I hold the object under a microscope, I shall make certain observations; if I pour acid over it, I shall observe certain chemical reactions; if I draw it on a blackboard, I shall see that a line shows, and so on. All these verifiable implications constitute the logical meaning or the *real content* of the assertion.[1]

In the same way, juridico-scientific assertions—such as, for example:

A = (§ 28 Danish Bill of Exchange Act) is scientifically valid Danish law

must also, if they are to be interpreted as meaningful statements about reality, imply assertions about certain basic, direct experiences which can be tested through a verification procedure, and which define the real content of the juridico-scientific sentence.

On the basis of what has been discussed in the previous section, we have to assume that the real content of A refers to the courts' pattern of behaviour under certain conditions. Since 'being a judge' is a legal qualification, we can also say that A, together with other juridico-scientific assertions about rules of public law supposed to apply within this context, implies a certain behaviour on the part of individually specified persons, namely those persons who, in conformity with certain pre-established rules of public law, are qualified to be 'judges'.

[1] See, e.g., Eino Kaila, *Den mänskliga kunskapen* [Human Knowledge](1939), 209 *et seq.*; G. H. von Wright, *Den logiska empirismen* [Logical Empiricism] (1943), 56 *et seq.*; Victor Kraft, *Einführung in die Philosophie* [Introduction to Philosophy] (1950), 68 *et seq.* These three works offer a good introduction to the fundamental ideas of modern, scientific philosophy.—For the sake of convenience I have, in the text above, used the term 'verification'. Since it is not possible to confirm, in a conclusive way, the truth of a sentence about reality, it is more accurate to speak of 'testing'.

But what kind of behaviour? Once again we must assume (according to the general view expressed in § 8) that this refers to the pattern of behaviour [88] complying with the normative content of the statutory provision in question; which, in turn, is a directive to the judge to sentence the drawee (under certain conditions) to pay the bill of exchange he has accepted but failed to pay when it became due.

Accordingly, people often say that a rule is scientifically valid law when it *is applied by the courts in legal practice*. This is a rather rough formulation, however, and it requires precision in several respects.

(1) Firstly, it is unclear what is meant by the neutral present-tense form 'is applied'. Does it refer to judicial decisions in the past, present, or future?

If anyone wants to know what is scientifically valid law at the present moment with respect to a certain matter, then this question undoubtedly refers to how a potential dispute would be decided if it were brought before a court. Obviously, it does not matter in this case what rules the courts have followed in their previous decisions, unless there is reason to believe that they will continue along the same line. Conversely, there is nothing that prevents a rule from being considered scientifically valid despite the fact that this rule—a recently promulgated law, for example—has not yet been applied by a court. It is considered scientifically valid if there is reason to assume—on a basis other than the previous practice of the courts—that the rule will be applied in future judicial decisions.

Therefore, statements about law that is scientifically valid at the present time do not refer to the past. Yet on the other hand, they do not seem to refer to the future, either. Stating what scientifically valid law is at the present time cannot purport to predict how the courts will react in twenty years' time (that is, if an action on the issue in question should not have been brought before court before that). After all, the state of the law may change in the meantime. And in principle, the same must be true of judicial decisions made somewhat earlier.

Finally, it should be noted that we do not know whether the issue in question will be decided at all in a future judicial decision.

These considerations must lead to the conclusion that statements about currently scientifically valid law must be understood as referring to hypothetical future decisions under certain conditions. If an action which falls under the legal rule in question should be brought before the court, and if, in the meantime, there has been no change in the law (that is, concerning the circumstances conditioning our assertion that the rule is scientifically valid law), the rule will be applied by the courts in deciding the case.

The above-mentioned conditions determine at the same time the verification procedure. A = '(§ 28 of the Danish Bill of Exchange Act) is scientifically valid Danish law' is verified by fulfilling the prescribed conditions and by observing the decision. The circumstance that I personally may not be able to carry out this procedure is of no importance whatsoever. The [89] meaning of an assertion is adequately defined if it is specified how, in principle—that is, apart from technical difficulties or obstacles—it can be verified. For example, the assertion that the hidden side of the moon is covered by forests is thus perfectly meaningful, although we have not yet been able to bring about the necessary conditions for observing that side of the moon. Moreover, we have every reason to believe the assertion to be untrue because it is not compatible with a number of well-verified assumptions concerning the conditions on that planet. The same holds true for the assertion that a statutory provision, which has been in force only for a short time and has never been applied, has been scientifically valid law during the period in question. We have not been able to verify this assertion through direct observation, but we nevertheless have good reason to consider the assertion true, namely on the basis of a number of other, well-verified assumptions concerning the inner life of Danish judges.

(2) Secondly, it must be clarified what is meant by saying that § 28 of the Danish Bill of Exchange Act '*is applied*' by the courts under the aforesaid conditions. 'Being applied' cannot be intended to refer to the court's conclusion—namely, that the drawee is ordered to pay the bill—because it is possible that the drawee, in conformity with other regulations, raises sound objections. For example, it may be the case that he was a minor, or that the holder of the bill agreed later on to receive goods instead of money.[2] Obviously, § 28 of the Danish Bill of Exchange Act belongs to a coherent whole of meaning, together with several other legal rules. Therefore, its 'being applied' in legal practice can only mean that in decisions in which its conditioning facts are assumed to exist, it forms an integral part of the reasons for the court's decision, and has thus been a decisive factor in determining the court's conclusion.

The specifications put forth under (1) and (2) can be combined in the following formulation:

> The real content of A = (§ 28 of the Danish Bill of Exchange Act)
> is currently scientifically valid Danish law

is a prediction that *if an action in which the conditioning facts, given in § 28 of the Danish Bill of Exchange Act, are considered to exist, is brought before a court; and if in the meanwhile there have been no alterations in the circumstances which motivate A, the directive to the judge contained in § 28 of the Danish Bill of Exchange Act will form an integral part of the reasons for the court's decision.*

[2] The procedural rules governing the temporary exclusion of certain objections in a case concerning bills of exchange are not taken into account here.

A is considered true, if we have good reason to assume that this prediction will be fulfilled.

It is worth noting that even if there are several decisions verifying A, A never- [90]
theless continues to be a fundamentally uncertain prediction concerning future decisions. The question of the truth of A is by no means definitely settled thereby. Let A_t represent the assertion A put forth at the time t: A subsequent judicial decision at the time t_I may verify A_t, but not A_{tI}. The decision merely provides further support to the assertion that § 28 Danish Bill of Exchange Act is still—that is, at the time t—scientifically valid Danish law. No matter what has happened or happens: the statement about currently scientifically valid law always refers to the future, because the present is continuously being postponed forward in time.

It is also worth noting that the truth of A does not presuppose that we are able to predict, with any reasonable certainty, the outcome of an actual future court case, even if we are in full possession of the relevant facts. To begin with, the outcome will depend on the evidence produced, and on the weighing of evidence. For example, how will the witnesses behave and express themselves in court, and what impression concerning reliability will they make on the judge? The weighing of evidence is subjectively conditioned to such an extent that this reason alone excludes all possibility of calculating, with any certainty, the outcome in cases where legal facts are in dispute.[3] Moreover, the interpretation of the legal rules—in their mutual interaction, and in relation to their application to specific cases—offers considerable scope for uncertainty which will be discussed thoroughly in a subsequent chapter. Finally, the judge's own notion of what is valid law is not the only factor motivating him.

This final point is of particular interest because the extent to which the judge is motivated by other than juridico-ideological factors is decisive for the practical value of legal science. Legal science concerns itself with the normative ideology inspiring the judge. A knowledge of this ideology (and its interpretation) enables us, therefore, to precalculate, with considerable certainty, the legal basis on which subsequent decisions will be made, and which will therefore figure in the judge's reasoning. But what is the relation between reasoning and what we really want to predict, namely, the conclusion?

[3] This view has been emphatically put forward by Jerome Frank; see, for example, his work *Courts on Trial* (1949) where he stresses the elements of uncertainty which are inherent in the witness's observation and account as well as those which are a consequence of the judge's personal bias when weighing the evidence. With respect to the latter, the following statement is characteristic: 'The judge's sympathies and antipathies are likely to be active with respect to the witnesses. His own past may have created plus or minus reactions to women, or blond women, or men with beards, or Southerners, or Italians, or Englishmen, or plumbers, or ministers, or college-graduates or Democrats. A certain facial twitch or cough or gesture may start up memories, painful or pleasant. Those memories of the judge, while he is listening to a witness with such a facial twitch or cough or gesture, may affect the judge's initial hearing, or subsequent recollection, of what the witness said, or the weight and credibility which the judge will attach to the witness' testimony' (*op. cit.*, 151).

There have been widely differing views on this subject. Traditional juristic
[91] opinion has no doubt that it is the reasoning which really decides the conclusion. The decision is a 'syllogism', unequivocally established according to the judge's opinion of what is valid law, such as has been set out in the reasoning. In stark contrast to this view, some scholars have recently maintained that the reasoning is nothing but a subsequent rationalization, expressing good, but not the genuine, reasons for the decision. In reality, they maintain, the judge makes his decision partly according to emotional impulses, partly out of practical purposes and considerations. The conclusion once established, he will subsequently find a suitable juridico-ideological argumentation in order to justify his decision. Usually he will not find this difficult. The variety of the rules, the uncertainty of their interpretation, and the possibility of constructing the issue in question in more ways than one, will usually enable the judge to find a suitable juristic garment in which to clothe his decision. The juristic argumentation of the reasoning is but a facade, designed to support belief in the objectivity of the decision.[4]

I shall not attempt here to assess the merits of these conflicting theories on the genesis of the court's conclusion; rather, I shall merely point out their relevance to the practical value of legal science. It is obvious that if the traditional view is tenable, then scientific insights into scientifically valid law and its interpretation offer the best possible basis—except for questions of evidence—for predicting the outcome of future judicial decisions. If we can predict the legal premises, we can also predict the conclusion. Conversely, if the opposing theory is tenable, then insight into legal ideology is not really useful because, in reality, it is not this ideology that motivates the judge. If it is at all possible to arrive at a true understanding of what is happening and at a prediction of the outcomes of lawsuits, then this would require studies of a rather different kind than studies in legal science.

If the assertion of legal science that a certain rule is scientifically valid Danish law is, according to its real content (as has been demonstrated), a prediction
[92] that the rule will be applied in future judicial decisions, then it follows that assertions of this kind can never claim absolute certainty, but can only be made

[4] Such views have been put forth in particular by the group of American jurists known as *legal realists*, and especially by the subgroup which is called, by Frank, *op. cit.*, 73, *rule-sceptics,* in contrast to *fact-sceptics.* For examples to illustrate these views, see Frank's own earlier works, especially *Law and the Modern Mind* (1930), 100 *et seq.* and 'What Courts do in Fact', 26, *Illinois Law Review* (1932), 645 *et seq.* See also Felix S. Cohen, 'Transcendental Nonsense and the Functional Approach', 35 *Columbia Law Review* (1935), 809 *et seq.*; Karl N. Llewellyn, 'A Realistic Jurisprudence—the Next Step', 30 *Columbia Law Review* (1930), 431 et seq.; John Dickinson, 'Legal Rules: Their Function in the Process of Decision', *University of Pennsylvania Law Review* 79 (1931), 833 *et seq.* B. N. Cardozo has in various writing put forth a balanced criticism of the exaggerations of realism, pointing out in particular the difference between 'current cases' and 'exceptional cases'. On this issue, see *Selected Writings* (1947), 7 *et seq.*, 20, 160, 177, 212. In the same spirit, see also Lon L. Fuller's valuable article 'American Legal Realism', *Proceedings of the American Philosophical Society,* vol. 76 (1936), 191 *et seq.*

with *a higher or lesser degree of probability*, depending on the strength of the basis upon which the calculations concerning the future rest. The probability value may vary considerably, from virtual certainty down to values around 0.5. Hereby, an element of relativity enters the sentences of legal science—something that is important to remember but is all too frequently overlooked.

For a philosophy of law purporting to derive the scientific validity of the law from an irreducible validity, either given *a priori* or hypothetically presupposed, purporting to justify the scientific validity of the individual norm deductively, through the norm's coming into being in conformity with higher norms and, ultimately, in conformity with natural law or a presupposed basic norm:[5] for this philosophy of law, the concept of scientific validity must become an absolute concept. Consequently, a legal rule is either scientifically valid, or it is not scientifically valid. It would appear that juridico-scientific treatises are still based chiefly on similar assumptions. In reality, however, the assertion that a rule is scientifically valid law is indeed something relative. One can also say that a *rule can be scientifically valid law to a greater or lesser degree, depending on the degree of probability with which it can be predicted that the rule will be applied.*[6] This degree of probability, in turn, depends on the empirical material the prediction is based upon (the sources of law). There is a great difference between the situation where the assertion concerns a statutory provision whose interpretation has been established in long and consistent practice, and the situation where the rule claimed to be scientifically valid law is justified neither through legislation nor through legal practice, but is only based upon 'theories', that is, principles, evaluations, and policy considerations held to be of decisive weight for the court. Between these two extremes there is a sliding scale of variations. Therefore, it is misleading to treat the various sources of law as if they were on a par, just as if all of them, 'the nature of the matter'[*] as well as 'the law', to the same degree provide solid grounds for assertions about what is scientifically valid law. An honest account requires differentiation in the sense that it is indicated in which areas we can, with a high degree of probability, express an opinion on what is scientifically valid law, and in which areas our views on this issue will remain a matter of guesswork.

* Editor's note: *The nature of the matter* is a verbatim translation of the set phrase in Danish legal theory 'forholdets natur', which is unknown in English but is known in German as 'die Natur der Sache'. 'Forholdets natur'/the nature of the matter is a separate category of legal sources, resembling to some extent Dworkin's principles. For Ross's extensive treatment, see § 19.

5 See § 13 below.

6 Cf. Björn Ahlander, *Är juridiken en vetenskap?* [Is the Study of Law a Science?] (1950), who uses the expression 'plausible legal rules' in connection with those rules whose character as scientifically valid law cannot be verified satisfactorily.

Our analysis of the concept 'scientifically valid Danish law' has purported to interpret the real content of sentences which, according to their meaning and intention, have the character of scientific assertions that a certain rule is valid Danish law.

[93] Whether the doctrinal study of law, in the form in which it actually exists in current scholarly work concerning Danish law, actually purports (according to its own meaning and intention) to present and explain assertions of this kind is quite another question. It is the *question whether the doctrinal study of law is, and wants to be, a science* about scientifically valid law in the sense previously defined.[7]

There can hardly be any doubt that all juristic writings which do not limit themselves to purely political considerations *de lege ferenda* are aiming (according to their meaning and intention and at least partially) to state, objectively and scientifically, what must be considered (with greater or lesser probability) valid Danish law.

On the other hand, it is presumably just as certain that only very few writings stop there. Whenever rules and principles are at stake where it is not possible to predict, with high probability, how the courts will react—that is, in areas where the state of the law has not been definitely established but in part still lies in the future—most jurists will not content themselves with making calculations of the most likely outcome; rather, they will try to affect the outcome by influencing the judge's decision. Appealing to a sense of justice or to policy considerations, the jurist will support a certain interpretation of the law, in the hope that his pronouncements will prove to be well suited to influence future judicial decisions. To this extent, therefore, his utterances are not assertions but directives (§2) in the form of advice, suggestions, and recommendations to the judge as to how he should decide in the case before him; they are directives *de sententia ferenda*.

Consequently, the typical content of doctrinal works may be classified as follows:

(1) scientific assertions about valid law of a higher or lesser degree of probability;
(2) non-scientific directives; and
(3) scientific assertions about historical, economic, and social facts and contexts serving to explain either (1) or (2).

The relative role of points (1) + (3) and (2) + (3), respectively—that is, of the juridico-scientific and the legal-political content of the doctrinal study of

[7] Cf. Björn Ahlander, *Är juridiken en vetenskap?* [Is the Study of Law a Science?] (1950); Per Olof Ekelöf, *Är den juridiska doktrinen en teknik eller en vetenskap?* [Is the Doctrinal Study of Law a Technique or a Science?] (1951); and Carl Jacob Arnholm, 'Noen metodologiske betragtningar' [Some reflections on methodology], *SvJT* 1952, 505 *et seq.*

law—will vary according to the practical purpose of the treatise and the personality of the author. It is hardly too much to say, however, that the majority of today's jurists in Scandinavia regard the political side of the doctrinal study of law, the directives *de sententia ferenda* (not to be confused with directives *de lege* [94]
ferenda), as the jurist's main essential task: it appeals to his interest and acts as a driving force for his work.[8] The jurist's main interest is practical, not theoretical. Indeed, one might say that jurists look upon themselves as politicians (in the widest sense of the word) rather than as legal scholars—although one must keep in mind, of course, that their policy is based on scientific observations; cf. point (3) in the classification of the content of legal doctrine.

I shall not, in this context, touch upon the programmatic debate on whether the doctrinal study of law should refrain from expressing directives, or at any rate account for its practical evaluations and the preconditions underlying them (on this issue, see §§ 78 and 84 below). However, I shall mention, here, an issue of considerable epistemological interest, namely the difficulty of drawing a sharp dividing line between statements of legal science and statements of legal politics; a difficulty rooted in a peculiarity characterizing all social sciences, as distinct from the natural sciences.

If an astronomer predicts an eclipse of the sun, this prediction does not affect the course of astronomical events to which it refers. There is no causal connection between, on the one hand, the mental phenomena constituting the prediction and the belief in its truth and, on the other, the movements of the sun and the moon. The prediction is either true or false, depending on whether the eclipse really takes place as predicted or not.

In 1950 it was predicted that the Communists would march towards West Berlin at Whitsuntide. It is possible that this prediction was true in the sense that a march of this kind had been decided on, and that we can reasonably assume that it would have taken place—had not the very prediction called forth countermeasures on the part of the Western Powers through which the 'actually' true prediction rendered itself false. Conversely, it is possible to imagine that an economist predicts price rises under circumstances which most certainly do not warrant this assumption; and that the prediction must therefore be classified as false. It is possible, however, that the very voicing of a prediction of this nature, in combination with the peoples' usual confidence in it, might cause prices to

[8] The following statement was made by Phillips Hult, 'Lagens bokstav och lagens andemening' [The letter and spirit of the law], in *SvJT* 1952, 580 and can probably be regarded as typical: 'Speaking for myself, I could hardly feel sufficient interest in my task as a legal scholar if I were to limit myself to registering what the legislator expressly and clearly has pronounced, and what the courts have decided in various legal disputes; and if I, apart from that, were to draw attention to what may appear opaque and ambiguous as to content. That which gives life to the study of law is investigating into the issue how legal rules and judicial decisions should be judged from a general social perspective, and how the different solutions in practical issues relate to the specific purposes which the rules issued by the legislator (or developed independently of the legislator) are meant to realize.'

[95] rise (since consumers try to provide against such a contingency) and thus turn the false prediction into a true one.

These peculiar circumstances are obviously due to the fact that the prediction, its pronouncement, and other people's confidence in it are mental phenomena which in themselves are elements of the social context the prediction is referring to. Social life cannot be studied independently of the study itself, in the way that the movements of the planets, or a landscape seen from the air can be.

This means that 'history'—the evolution of social life—is, in principle, indeterminate. At best, it is possible to predict probable tendencies. However, each prediction of a tendency is, at the same time, a factor that lends itself either to the furtherance of this tendency or to opposing it, and is thus a political factor; which in turn means that *in the social sciences it is, in principle, impossible to make a sharp distinction between theory and political intervention.*

In light of the above, it is obvious that it is not possible to draw a sharp and radical dividing line between scientific statements about valid law and legal political activity.

First, it is worth noting that it is difficult to draw a dividing line even according to intention. When it is about legal problems where it is possible to predict the reaction of the courts only with a low degree of probability—because there are no clear directives and the decision, consequently, is made on the basis of more general evaluations, the sense of justice, and policy considerations based upon legal-sociological calculations concerning the social effects of various rules—the doctrinal lawyer can adopt one of two possible attitudes. He can either identify himself with the courts, because he knows how to adopt, hypothetically, the evaluations and views which actually must be supposed to dominate the judiciary; because he tries to arrive at a solution which best harmonizes with them and, therefore, must be considered the most probable one.[9] Or, he can pursue his own evaluations and views in order to find the solution which he himself would arrive at, if he were in the judge's place. In the first case he adopts a scientific attitude, and his statement is a theoretical statement—albeit of low probability value—about what is scientifically valid law. In the second case he adopts a political attitude, and his statement is a directive calculated to influence the judge as to what ought to be valid law. This difference of attitude is not often clearly expressed in practice, however, since the jurist—rightly or

[9] On this issue, cf. Julius Lassen's words in his farewell lecture ['Afskedsforelæsning], published in *UfR* 1918 B. 17: 'It was perfectly clear to me that it could not be my task to instruct the students on Professor Jul. Lassen's opinions on Danish law, on what was valid law, and on what ought to be valid law. Under the circumstances, I had to see it as my foremost task to present an exposition of valid Danish law, to give information (as reliable as possible) on the legal rules which were really followed in the Danish legal community, which were applied by the respective authorities, and which legal life has established and is adapting to. The task was almost one of history.'

wrongly—identifies his own evaluations and views with those of the court. Frequently, he is completely unaware of the conditional and problematic nature [96] of these assumptions; he does not attribute them either to himself or to the courts but, rather, operates with them as something to be taken for granted, as some sort of cultural atmosphere surrounding both himself and the courts. Under these circumstances the practical result will be the same, regardless of the attitude being theoretical or political, and it will be a matter of temperament which of the two interpretations of his work the jurist himself (if pressed) will accept. Some jurists will give priority to evaluation: they will feel like pontifical mouthpieces of an ideology and consistently admit that their activity, in the last analysis, is not a scientific one (apart from the knowledge of facts and circumstances constituting the precondition for their evaluations).[10] According to others, the theoretical factor will predominate, and they will look upon their evaluating interpretations as the least certain parts of their calculations of what is scientifically valid law; a calculation which—as long as more solid reference points are lacking—must be based upon the supposition that the same reasonable considerations as those in which the interpretation is grounded will also determine the courts' behaviour in future judicial decisions.[11]

Secondly—and this is the essential point, a paradox in all social sciences[12]—we also have to consider that even if the intention is purely theoretical, even if the interpretation merely purports to predict, with some probability, which rule will be accepted by the courts, the interpretation (like any other socio-scientific prediction) is nevertheless in itself a legal and political factor. The argumentation upon which the interpretation is based and which, hypothetically, is the one the courts will put forth, is liable to influence the courts and thereby turn itself into a true one even though the hypothesis was initially false.

Conclusion: The assertions of legal science concerning scientifically valid law are, according to their real content, predictions of future social events. These events are, in principle, indeterminate and impossible to predict unequivocally. Every prediction is at the same time a real factor which can influence the course of events and is, as such, a political act. *Therefore, in principle, legal science cannot be separated from legal politics.*

It would be a serious mistake, however, to interpret this insight as a methodological *carte blanche*, justifying a complete blurring of science and politics; particularly if an evaluating interpretation, grounded in 'the nature of the matter',

[10] Thus, for example, Knud Illum, *Lov og Ret* [Law and Justice] (1945), 150 *et seq.*

[11] This is how I, for one, prefer to look at it.

[12] In the field of nuclear physics, it is a well-known fact that observation and intervention in what has been observed cannot be sharply separated. However, this circumstance and its consequences are fundamentally different from what applies to the social sciences. In nuclear physics, the observation itself influences its object, whereas in the social sciences, the insight achieved through observation, and the proclamation of this insight, bring about this effect.

is shamelessly presented as scientifically valid law on a par with statutory law, [97] so as to hypnotize the courts into compliance. What is decisive for good legal method is not so much whether the interpretation is offered as subjective counsel or as an objective assertion. What is decisive, on the other hand, is that the jurist is fully aware of the situation and declares openly that his interpretations cannot be presented as scientifically valid law with the same certainty as if it were a question of well-established rules; and that in many cases, the degree of certainty can be so small that it would be more natural not to mention scientifically valid law at all but simply speak of counsel and proposals to the judges. What is decisive is that the jurist, at this stage, does not attempt to deceive both himself and others by obscuring the differences as to the degree of certainty. This is frequently omitted, and the pedagogical and scientific value of a well-developed theory of the concept of 'scientifically valid law' lies in drawing attention to the sliding scale of probability and thereby inculcates the requirements of carefulness and probity in this respect.

One objection to my interpretation of the concept 'scientifically valid (Danish) law' might be *that it makes theory the slave of practice* and excludes the possibility of criticizing a judicial decision as incorrect. This is contrary to custom and current views and must, therefore, be a sign that the interpretation is not an adequate reading of the concept of scientifically valid law that jurists are actually operating with.

This objection rests on a misunderstanding. The ideas developed here are no hindrance to calling a judicial decision incorrect. A judicial decision is consequently incorrect, that is, at variance with scientifically valid law if—all things considered, including the decision and the criticism it might evoke—there seems to be every probability that the courts, in future, will not follow the decision. Such a verdict over the verdict is frequently, and with great precision, given by expert jurists.

This misunderstanding is obviously rooted in the idea that as soon as a decision has been made, the problem of the scientific validity of a rule has been definitely settled. This is not correct (as mentioned above). The problem of what is scientifically valid law never refers to past history but always to the future, because the present is continuously being postponed forward in time.

In principle, the same must hold true even if the incorrect decision is followed by one or more decisions supporting it. It goes without saying, however, that the more judicial decisions there are (especially if they stem from the respective country's supreme court), the less reason there is for asserting that it is unlikely that the courts in future will follow that line.

In view of firmly established case law, theory must capitulate—just as in view of a new law. It is nothing but empty rhetoric if the doctrinal study of law wishes to adhere to a certain rule as being 'scientifically valid law' and, at the same time, informs us, in a footnote, that legal practice 'erroneously' adheres to a different rule (as was done, for example, by the French exegetic school around [98] the middle of the nineteenth century).[13]

[13] On this issue, see Alf Ross, *Theorie der Rechtsquellen* [Theory of the Sources of Law] (1929), ch. III.3 and 4. As late as 1934, Ancel (*Journal of the Society of Comparative Legislation*, February 1934. 1) writes as follows: 'Writers are in the habit of giving their own interpretations of the law, which are sometimes contrary to the solutions of the courts, but which they nevertheless consider as the only real expression of French law. On many important points . . . there exists a doctrine of the courts and a doctrine of law writers. So you can find in France a law which is printed in books and taught in universities, and which yet differs much from, even when not contrary to, the law applied by the courts of justice. Writers nowadays take care to state not only their own opinion, but also the opinion of the *jurisprudence*, but yet they put forward their solution as the only legal one.' (Quoted from C. K. Allen, *Law in the Making*, 4th edn, 1946, 167–68.)

§ 10. *Verification of the Sentences of Legal Science concerning Competence Norms*

Since competence norms are indirectly formulated norms of conduct, their verification as scientifically valid (Danish) law must, in principle, be done as shown in the preceding section. Thus, the real content of the assertion that the rules of the constitution governing the organization of the legislature and the exercise of power are scientifically valid Danish law, is a prediction that the norms of conduct created through legislation will be applied by the courts, cf. § 9.

The construction above is based on the assumption that competence norms entail *voidability*. This means that the courts examine whether the prescribed procedure has been followed, and that they follow the norm of conduct in question only if this is the case. That the court has the right of judicial review regarding most competence norms—those concerning the competence of private individuals to conclude contracts, the competences of the administration, and the central formal rules concerning legislative competence—is certain. On the other hand, it is just as certain that in connection with legislative competence, there are certain formal rules—for example, the requirement in § 51 of the Constitution[*] of three readings in each of the Houses of Parliament—which will not be reviewed by the courts and, therefore, lack voidability. Also, it may be doubtful if the courts have the right of judicial review with regard to the substantive limitations on legislative competence, embodied in the Constitution, particularly with regard to various civil rights as a guarantee to the citizens. The
[99] situation varies from country to country. Without touching upon the present state of the law here in Denmark, we shall now discuss the problems that arise if the courts do not have the right of judicial review.

Formal or substantive norms of competence which do not entail voidability (which is dealt with by the courts) consequently cannot be interpreted as directives to the courts, telling them which norms of conduct they should apply.

The next question is whether they can be understood as direct norms of conduct, ordering the judge to impose sanctions (exercise of coercion) against certain individuals, if competence is exercised in defiance of the aforementioned norms. In certain cases—namely, if a minister has been an accessory to an excess of competence—the minister in question can, in principle, be made responsible before the impeachment court. It is only of minor practical importance, to

* Translator's note: Which, at that time, was the Danish Constitution of 1920.

be sure, but on this basis it is nonetheless possible, in principle, to confer the character of law to the competence norms in question, in conformity with the criterion set forth in § 7.

The remaining rules are rules such as the regulation in § 51 of the Constitution, concerning three readings in each of the Houses of Parliament; that is, rules entailing neither voidability nor responsibility. Are these rules 'scientifically valid Danish law'? As soon as one is aware of the special position occupied by these rules, this question is of no real interest. On the one hand, these rules do not have any legal effect whatsoever, and thus do not provide any basis for predictions of future judicial decisions. In this respect they fall outside the concept 'scientifically valid Danish law' (as previously explained). On the other hand, they exercise the same moral and ideological force which otherwise is linked to the rules of scientifically valid law, cf. § 11. If one should wish to include them in the category 'scientifically valid Danish law' for that reason, one ought to remember that they differ in one respect from what we usually call Danish law: they are not directives concerning the exercise of coercion through public authorities.

§ 11. Law—Force—Validity

In the preceding section we assumed that 'Danish law' consists of rules *about* the exercise of physical force. It is widely held, however, that the relation between law and force is defined in a different way: The law—or so it is believed—consists of rules *upheld* by force.

It is apparent that this belief stems from a consideration of those norms which in § 7 are called non-proper norms of conduct; such as, for example, § 28 Danish Bill of Exchange Act which is understood, according to its content, as
[100] a directive to the acceptor of a bill. These norms can justly be said to be upheld by force: if the acceptor does not pay on the day payment is due, he runs the risk of a sentence and its enforcement.

This interpretation of the legal norms cannot be accepted because it rests on false assumptions and leads to unacceptable results.

The interpretation rests on the assumption that the directive in § 28 Danish Bill of Exchange Act, addressed to the acceptor, is one thing, and that the directive to the judge to uphold this rule by force is quite another. This is incorrect. It is not a question of two different norms but, rather, of two aspects of the same norm. There is only *one* norm. It is directed to the judge, because it makes the ordering of coercive measures on his part conditional on a certain behaviour on the part of the acceptor. This evokes a reflex, namely, a motive for the acceptor to avoid behaviour that conditions the use of force; that is, it evokes a motive to pay.

In addition, this interpretation would result in essential parts being excluded from the realm of law—parts which are inseparably connected with the non-proper norms of conduct upheld by force, and with which they form a coherent whole of meaning.

First, this interpretation would exclude all competence norms because they are not upheld by force. From the point of view we are criticizing, it has always been a problem of how large parts of constitutional and administrative law, composed of such norms, can be recognized as law. Consistent adherents of this kind of view have deprived these parts of the law of their legal character. This is unreasonable, not so much because it contradicts the prevailing view but, rather, because these norms—indirectly formulated norms of conduct—are indissolubly connected with the direct norms of conduct with which they form a coherent whole of meaning.

Secondly, this interpretation would exclude the very norms concerning law enforcement, namely, the secondary norms supposed to guarantee the primary norms of conduct. It is not possible to avoid this conclusion by pointing out that these secondary norms, as such, are upheld by force by means of a set of tertiary norms. For one thing, there will usually be no social reality corresponding to this construction; and then, the problem will only be postponed because in this way, we could go on *ad infinitum*, with norms behind norms.

Thus, we can state that the relation between legal norms and force expresses the fact that the legal norms *concern the application of force, not their being upheld by force.*[1]

A question intimately connected with the analytical problem discussed above is the legal-sociological question, what kind of *motive* actually prompts people to act lawfully? The question falls outside the scope of this book and shall, therefore, only be touched upon in passing.

As will be discussed in greater detail later on (§§ 89 and 90), human motives can be divided into two main groups: impulses based on needs, which arise from a certain biological mechanism and are experienced as 'interests'; and [101] impulses which have been imprinted upon the individual by the social environment and are experienced as categorical demands, 'binding' the individual without reference to his 'interests', indeed in direct conflict with them. Therefore, these impulses are easily interpreted, in metaphysical terms, as a revelation within the 'conscience' of a higher 'validity' which, as a 'duty', is contrasted with the 'sensual nature' of man and the interests arising from it. What part do these different motive experiences play in the law working in real life?

As far as the legal norms proper are concerned—that is, the norms directed to the judge, serving as the standard for his decision—it must definitely be assumed that the judge is motivated, first and foremost, by disinterested impulses, by a pure sense of duty, and not by fear of legal sanctions or by any other interests. Certainly, legal sanctions against a judge, as a consequence of his decision, are not wholly excluded, cf. § 146 Danish Penal Code which warrants punishment if a member of the judiciary commits an act of injustice when deciding a case. However, incorrect application of law as such is not affected thereby, and what is more, the rule is not really practicable owing to evidentiary reasons. As far as I know, it has never yet been applied. The driving force behind the judges' respect for the law can therefore hardly be sought in internal administration of legal justice on members of the judiciary. To judges in subordinate courts, whose decisions can be appealed to higher courts, professional reputation and promotion may well play a role, but hardly a decisive one. When the courts are understood as a collective body, with the Supreme Court

[1] I am indebted to Hans Kelsen for this insight; see, for example, his work *Allgemeine Staatslehre* [General Constitutional Theory] (1925), 17. The same view was expressed by Karl Olivecrona, *Om lagen och staten* [On Law and the State] (1940), 125 *et seq.*

at the head of the court system, no appeal is possible against the course actually pursued by them. In my view, it can be assumed without any doubt (although I must admit that it is difficult to prove) that it would never be possible to create a properly functioning legal order unless there existed, within the judiciary, a strong, disinterested feeling of respect for, and solidarity with, traditional legal ideology. *The legal norms proper must be assumed to be observed just as 'voluntarily' as the norms of chess are observed by chess players.*

The situation is more complicated if we turn to the non-proper norms of conduct, that is, to those norms that can be derived from the norms proper; such as, for example, § 28 Danish Bill of Exchange Act according to its content, as it stands. Clearly, being aware that behaviour conflicting with this regulation entails the risk of lawsuit, sentence, and enforcement is a strong motive for acting lawfully. This is obvious and has been confirmed by the experience of a strong increase in crime in exceptional circumstances, in which the police and the courts have been suspended.[2] One ought to emphasize, however, that this is not all. Most people obey the law—not merely because they are afraid of the police, of going to prison, and of extralegal social sanctions (loss of reputation, of trust, etc.), but also because they have a disinterested respect for law and justice. Even the ordinary citizen is—to a higher or lesser degree—inspired by
[102] an ideological sense of justice, in light of which those in power appear as 'legitimate powers' or 'authorities', the claim of the law appears as a 'valid' norm with a claim to respect, and the force exercised in the name of the law is not mere crude violence but appears as legitimate law enforcement. If there are well-established legal rules, this attitude becomes automatic to such an extent that impulses to act contrary to the law simply do not arise. It may be presumed that only very few people ever felt, and had to suppress, an inclination to commit murder.[3]

This ideological, disinterested element of motivation is often called moral consciousness, produced by the traditional maintenance of the legal system. Owing to the ambiguity of the concept of morality,[4] this description can be called into doubt. Certainly, the attitude we have in mind may have the character of a genuine, conscientious disapproval of the unlawful act, but it need not have that character. Rather, the attitude is typically of a formal character. It is directed towards the established institutions, recognizing their 'validity' as such, irrespective of whether the demands in which they manifest themselves can be accepted as 'morally correct' or 'just'. Law is law, and the law must be obeyed, they say, and one applies this maxim even in those cases where the demands of the law are at variance with an evaluation of the law's content in the name of

[2] See Jørgen Trolle, *Syv Maaneder uden Politi* [Seven Months without Police Force] (1945).

[3] For a detailed description of the ideologically motivating function of the law, see Karl Olivecrona, *Om lagen och staten* [On Law and the State] (1940), 140 *et seq.*

[4] Cf. § 12.

morality or justice. In order to distinguish this attitude from a genuinely moral attitude, I shall call it the *formal or institutional legal consciousness.*

Naturally, there is a limit to the span between formal and substantive legal consciousness.[5] When this limit is reached, the loyal and cooperative attitude vis-à-vis state and law is superseded by a revolutionary consciousness. Whether this subsequently also manifests itself in an open struggle for power will depend on a strategic estimate of the chances of success. If the time for revolution has not come yet, the tactical task will consist in undermining the existing social order through obstruction and the use of propaganda.

It is not always the case that a coercive order actually maintained is experienced, by all subjects, as a valid order (that is, in conformity with the legal consciousness). Seen from a purely scientific and descriptive point of view, this does not make any difference with respect to the character of the given system as a system of scientifically valid law: the norms of the system can still be described in statements about the probable content of future judicial decisions. This differs from ordinary usage where 'the law' is an emotionally charged word, closely tied to the subjective, emotional experience of validity.

In so far as an order actually maintained does not receive ideological approval from its subjects in a formal legal consciousness but is solely obeyed out of fear, the subjects do not experience the order as a 'legal order' but, rather, as a dictate [103] of power or violence.[6] In this case, the ruler is not an 'authority' or a 'lawful power', but a violent criminal, a tyrant, and a dictator. In this way, the population of an occupied country experiences the regime of force resting solely on the military strength of the occupying power, or the individual who has fallen among a gang of robbers and must subject himself to their rule.

When describing the phenomena of life, science cannot employ words whose use is defined by their emotional charge. In such a description, one cannot differentiate between 'legal order' and a 'regime of violence', because the quality of validity distinguishing the law is not an objective quality inherent in the order itself, but only an expression of the way in which it is experienced by the individual. Therefore, one and the same order vis-à-vis one person can be a 'legal order' and vis-à-vis another person a 'regime of violence'. Of course, it is quite possible to restrict the concept of law through an objective, social psychological characteristic, so that an order is called a 'legal order' only if it enjoys the ideological approval of a majority of those subject to it. I fail to see the point of

[5] The problem is discussed in an interesting study by Vilhelm Aubert, 'Kriminalisering og moralpåvirkning i den næringsrettslige lovgivning' [Criminalization and the influence of morality in business law], *Nordisk Tidsskrift for Kriminalvidenskab* 1951, 120 et *seq.*

[6] On the issue of permanent minorities, cf. Alf Ross, *Hvorfor Demokrati?* [Why Democracy?] (1946), 284–85.

doing this, however, whilst on the other hand, I can see the inconvenience of having the concept tied to a criterion that is difficult to work with in practice.

The two motivating elements characteristic of legal experience—namely fear and respect—are not elements contributing independently, but are in a relation of mutual functional cooperation.[7]

The force exercised by the police and the executive authorities is not only based on purely physical factors such as available manpower, its training and arming, but on ideological factors as well. If all private citizens were to gang up they would undoubtedly be stronger than the police. This does not happen, though. The law-abiding citizen does have respect for the police. Police power is mainly grounded in this respect, as well as in an ideologically determined feeling, on the part of the police themselves, that they are exercising their authority 'in the name of the law'. In general, one can say that the outer, physical means of coercion must always be operated by human beings. Control over the means of coercion thus depends on the mastery of the human beings operating these means. This mastery, in turn, may partly, but never entirely, be based upon other types of coercion. Ultimately, there must be norms governing the exercise of coercion which are not themselves upheld by force, but are followed in fearless obedience by virtue of ideological allegiance. A strong man can obtain mastery over a few others through sheer physical force. This is not possible in societies of a certain dimension which presuppose an organized power apparatus, operated by other human beings. No Hitler would be able to terrorize a
[104] population without any ideological allegiance, at least not within the group operating the coercive mechanism. In the last analysis, all power rests upon an authoritative ideological basis.[8]

Thus, the compelling power of the law is a function of its 'validity'. Conversely, the latter is also a function of the force actually exercised. Since attitudes of obedience are strengthened by custom, every order actually upheld (including orders mainly based upon sheer force) shows a tendency to develop into an order that is approved ideologically as well. This phenomenon has been called 'the normative force of the factual'. Whether in recent or more distant times,

[7] This idea has been explored in greater detail in my book *Virkelighed og Gyldighed i Retslæren* [Reality and Validity in Jurisprudence] (1934), ch. V, 3.

[8] Thus also R. M. MacIver, *The Web of Government* (1947), 12 *et seq.*: 'Force alone never holds a group together. A group may dominate by force the rest of the community, but the initial group, already subject to government before it can dominate, is not cemented by force. Conquerors may forcibly impose their will on the conquered, but the conquerors were themselves first united by something other than force . . . In all constituted government authority of some sort lies at the back of force', *a. st.*, 16. On the other hand, Theodor Geiger, *Vorstudien zu einer Soziologie des Rechts* [Preliminary Studies on the Sociology of Law] (1947), 275 f., especially 288 f., asserts the primacy of power over the law. For a critique of this theory, see Karl Olivecrona, 'Viljan bakom rätten' [The will behind the law], *StvT* 1947, 1 f., and Alf Ross, 'Review of Th. Geiger, *Vorstudien zur einer Soziologie des Rechts*', *TfR* 1950, 220–23.

every *de jure* government is a continuation of a *de facto* government. 'Time is a great healer', they say—obviously even in this case.

Fear and respect, physical force, and 'validity' are mutually conditioning each other, and this holds good for a static analysis of legal life at any given moment, as well as for historical and evolutionistic considerations. None of them is the primary factor.

These considerations are apt to throw new light on the age-old problem of *the relation between right and might* which has given rise to a vast amount of metaphysical speculation. According to the traditional metaphysical view, right and might are diametrical opposites. Right is what is ideally valid—it is a system of binding norms, and sovereignty is the power to create law, to bind others. Might is what is socio-factual, it is mastery over people, the power to motivate them to act in accordance with the will of those in power. On this basis, it is possible to engage in endless dialectics concerning the relation between right and might. Right needs might 'behind' it in order to be realized. Yet how can this be done unless right capitulates to might? Is it the case that might is right?[9]

From the perspective of legal realism, right and might are not opposites. If (social) power is understood as the possibility of directing the actions of other human beings, then the law is an instrument of power, and the relation between those who decide what is to be the law, and those who are subject to the law, is a power relation. Power is not something that is 'behind' the law, but something that works through law. The problem which in metaphysical [105]
terms is formulated as a problem concerning the external relation between right and might is, in reality, a problem concerning the relation between physical force and ideological bond *qua* elements of motivation within the power relations of the law itself; it is, in short, the problem we have discussed above.

Depending on the means and the technique employed in the exercise of power, we can distinguish various typical forms of power; for example, power through force, economic power, spiritual power, and the power of personality.[10] Political power, or state power, is the power exercised through legal technique or, in other words, through the state apparatus, which is a mechanism for the exercise of force (physical coercion). However, the function of this apparatus is, as we have seen, conditioned by ideological factors, that is, by formal legal consciousness. The power of those in control over the state apparatus is dependent on

[9] Goos struggled with this problem and believed that he could manage with the following play on words: If one wants to assert the power of the law, then one must recognize the law of power. *Forelæsninger over den almindelige Retslære*. [Lectures on the General Study of Law]. vol. I (1885); cf. Alf Ross, *Virkelighed og Gyldighed i Retslæren* [Reality and Validity in Jurisprudence] (1934), ch. LL., 6, especially 56–7.

[10] See Bertrand Russell, *Power* (1938).

their actually occupying the legal key positions which, according to the constitution, endows them with the necessary competence to hold this power. All political power is legal competence. An 'empty' power, independent of the law and its basis, does not exist.

Moreover, the ideological foundation for a political regime need not extend to the entire population subject to this regime. The tragic experiences of the last generation have shown that it is possible for a relatively small group, inspired by revolutionary urge, to gain control over a functioning state mechanism, replace the staff, and uphold a regime that is experienced as violence and terror by a majority of the population.

§ 12. Law, Morality, and other Normative Phenomena

As pointed out in § 7, from a scientific point of view—that is, if the word 'law' has been liberated from its emotional charge—no particular interest attaches to how the concept of 'law' or 'legal system' is defined. It is not important in itself whether or not we want to attach the term 'legal system' to individual norm systems which are more or less similar to the system we have called 'Danish law'. The legal systems in question will neither gain nor lose by being given a name. What is important here is to be aware of their respective similarities and differences.

Starting from this premise, I prefer to reserve the term 'legal system' for normative orders showing the same essential characteristics as 'Danish law', without, [106] however, affixing any ideological stamp to the term; that is to say, regardless of whether the respective order is experienced as 'a valid order' or as 'a regime of violence' by a greater or lesser part of the subjects.

Accordingly, the concept of 'law' or 'legal system' is characterized by two features.

First, the law consists of rules on the exercise of *physical force*. In relation to the non-proper, derived legal norms, force appears in the shape of a sanction, that is, as a means of exerting pressure for bringing about the desired behaviour. Whenever we say, later on, that legal norms are enforced by physical force while other norms are enforced by other means, then one must understand that this is only a convenient, albeit not entirely correct, way of speaking.

Secondly, the law consists not only of norms of conduct, but also of norms of competence, instituting a set of public authorities for laying down norms of conduct and exercising coercion in conformity with them. Thereby, the law assumes what may be called an *institutional character*. It is at work within a legal machinery for the purpose of legislation, sentencing and enforcement, and thus appears to the individual as something objective and external. It is an expression of a supra-individual community, a social order with its roots in formal legal consciousness.

Other normative phenomena can be classified schematically, according to their corresponding characteristics concerning these two features. They vary, partly as to the nature of the sanction, partly depending on whether they have institutional character or not.

(a) There are normative phenomena with an *institutional structure* similar to the law, but based on sanctions other than physical coercion.

(1) Private *associations* and various types of organizations are frequently based on a system of rules of an institutional character similar to the law. These rules are often called the legal rules of the association (the articles of association, the association statutes). It is possible that there is a legislative authority as well as an executive authority and a judiciary. The rules of association differ from the law (such as we have defined this term, namely, as a name for the normative order of a modern state) in so far as the sanctions do not consist in physical coercion. The exercise of physical coercion is monopolized by the state. An association may impose various kinds of penalties on its members, but it can never enforce these penalties through coercion. The most severe sanction is expulsion from association, and all other sanctions are derived from it. For example, it may happen that a fine can be enforced in the ordinary way, pursuant to the decision of a court: however, the enforcement will take place by virtue of national law, which has received the 'law of associations' into its own legal system.

Various kinds of rules of games are closely related to the rules of association. A game can be seen as a temporary association of two or more [107] persons, assembling for the purpose of amusing themselves by playing games according to certain rules. There is rudimentary legislation, if it is necessary that the players are in agreement, or come to an agreement, as to what rules should be followed. Frequently, there is also an umpire who can impose penalties. Here, too, the most severe sanction is expulsion from the 'association'; that is to say, the game is being discontinued.

(2) *International law*, too, has an institutional character. There are institutional methods of procedure, both for laying down general norms and for deciding legal disputes. On the other hand, neither are there any institutional provisions in international law for sanctions applied by physical force. It is a well-known fact that the international community is not given a monopoly on the use of force. The sanction tied to a judicial decision of international law is merely the expression of public disapproval of the losing party if the latter does not conform to the decision.

(b) In every society, there is a cultural tradition expressed through more or less uniform ideas about how to behave in a given situation. As will be shown in greater detail later on (§ 90), such ideas are inculcated in the individual while growing up, due to the suggestive pressure exerted by the individual's social environment. From its earliest years, the child is bombarded with attitude-forming influences. The child learns how to eat and drink, how to talk, to keep clean, to say 'How do you do?' and to shake hands; he learns to tell the truth, to refrain from swearing, to be industrious, to keep his word, etc. etc. In this way, the child becomes familiar with an extensive set of rules of life which he gradually absorbs, and which manifest themselves in automatic attitudes bearing the stamp of validity tied to a certain practical situation. These rules are perceived as *moral* rules in so far as they are apt to contradict the individual's inclinations. If there is no such conflict, these rules are experienced as a *convention*—such as, for example, the rules of politeness, the rules of dress, and the rules of decorum.

Although these rules originate in society and therefore are more or less the same among people with the same social environment, they are nevertheless *individual phenomena*. They are not linked to the norms of competence, instituting common decision-making authorities which are empowered to lay down general norms and to apply sanctions on behalf of the community. There is no legislator—with respect to either morality or convention—and there is no judge, either. Each individual decides for himself what he thinks is moral or proper. Likewise, the disapproval[1] punishing breaches of morality and convention stems from each single individual, not from any common [108] authority. Therefore, there is no 'scientifically valid Danish' morality or convention; there are only more or less parallel individual attitudes some of which may be called 'prevailing' or 'typical' attitudes within a certain social environment. When the word 'morality' is used to denote the norms of conduct which, by the individual, are approved within his conscience, then it is not possible to speak of 'morality' as an objective phenomenon in the same way as one speaks of 'the law'. There is a science of law (understood as 'Danish (Norwegian, etc.) law'), but there is no science of morality—merely a science concerning psychological and moral phenomena. The current usage according to which 'morality' is called (in analogy with 'the law') an objective system of norms stems from a metaphysical interpretation of the conscience, namely as a revelation of *a priori* principles, self-evident to reason.

As far as the law is concerned, the fear of sanctions and the feeling of being bound by what is 'valid' typically cooperate as integral elements of motivation concerning one and the same action, whereas with respect to morality and convention, the corresponding motives work each in its own way and independently of each other. The interested motive—the fear of sanctions—motivates me to act in such a way as to avoid disapproval from others. The disinterested motive—the feeling of an inner impulse towards what is 'right'—motivates me to act in such a way that I can approve of it myself.

This twofold motivation manifests itself especially in morality. There, it can easily happen that my own moral judgment differs from that of others, and that my conscience therefore demands from me a line of action which, as I know, is disapproved of by the opinion prevailing in my surroundings. This is less clearly visible in the case of convention because individual divergences are less important there. At any rate, in principle, the situation

[1] Reactions manifesting themselves in the exclusion from polite society, in ridicule or the like, are not intended as a means of exerting pressure but, rather, are qualified expressions of disapproval.

must be the same. The reaction to an infringement of convention stems from each single individual and must therefore imply that each individual has his own attitude towards propriety.

[109] The above-mentioned[2] normative phenomena can be listed as follows:

Table 2.1 Normative Phenomena

	Sanction		
	Physical coercion	**Expulsion**	**Disapprobation**
Institutional phenomenon	The law	Association law	International law
Individual phenomenon	E.g. the rules on vendetta: they do not exist in modern states where force is monopolized	Moral convention	

The word 'morality' is frequently understood in a much wider sense than has been described here. There is a tendency to call all disinterested impulses experienced with a stamp of 'validity', or 'bindingness', 'moral' impulses. Understood in this sense, formal legal consciousness is of a moral character, and the moral phenomena form an integral part of the legal phenomena.[3] Reality is thus somewhat more complicated than would appear from the scheme above. Coercive legal responses usually signal public disapproval as well, as an expression that the behaviour conditioning the reaction is socially undesirable. This behaviour is therefore also called 'unlawful' behaviour, and contradictory behaviour is called 'duty'. However, coercive measures do not always have this character. One must distinguish between *reprimanding* and *non-reprimanding* sanctions. Without making such a distinction as to the ideological and moral function of the sanction, it would be impossible to understand the difference between fault-based liability and strict liability, or the difference between, on the one hand, punishment and, on the other, safety measures and fiscal regulations.[4]

Thus, the problem of *the relation between law and morality* cannot be posed in the form of a comparison between two analogous systems of norms. Rather, it

[2] This account does not claim to be exhaustive.

[3] In traditional metaphysical jurisprudence, this is reflected by the law (coordinated with morality) being considered a branch of 'the ethical' or 'the realm of morality'. The same usage occurs when international law is described, by the 'deniers of international law', as a mere moral order. Thereby, one cannot possibly mean to characterize international law as a matter of personal conscience.

[4] On this issue, cf. Alf Ross, *Virkelighed og Gyldighed i Retslæren* [Reality and Validity in Jurisprudence] (1934), ch. VIII, 6 and at § 54. In contrast to the views expressed here, Theodor Geiger, *Debat med Uppsala om Moral og Ret* [Debate with Uppsala about Morality and the Law] (1946), 218 f., maintained that law has nothing to do with morality; on this issue, see further my controversy with Geiger in *Juristen* 1946, cf. Ross, 'Sociolog som Retsfilosof' [A sociologist as a legal philosopher], 299 f. and Geiger, 'Svar til Professor Alf Ross' [Reply to Professor Alf Ross], 309 f. respectively.

must depend upon how the institutional system of the law relates to the individual moral attitudes prevailing in the legal community. Of course there has to be a considerable degree of harmony between them. For one thing, both are rooted in common basic evaluations—in the cultural tradition of the society; for another, the relation between them is one of reciprocal interaction. The institutions of the law are among those environmental factors which shape the [110] moral attitudes of individuals. These, in turn, count among the real factors shaping the development of the law through 'the sense of justice'.

Then again, there are some characteristic dissimilarities, with the effect that comparing law and morality turns out to be problematic. Legal rules tend to become fixed within conceptual categories purporting to ensure certainty and objectivity in the application of law. This is one aspect of the idea of justice (§ 70). Moral attitudes, however, spring up from the individual's reaction in concrete situations. Even if some of these maxims are accepted as moral guides, they are not perceived as binding rules, but only as experimental generalizations, bound to give way to a new reaction in a situation when that situation is being considered in its full specificity. This is the true meaning of the saying that rules are made to be broken. If one reflects on a current moral maxim—such as, for example, the demand for truthfulness—one will soon discover that it cannot be accepted as an 'absolute' maxim (as the moral rearmament movement naively believes). The maxim has to be modified in light of diverse circumstances, which moral feeling neither wants to, nor can, rationalize in conceptually fixed rules. Moral experience always manifests itself most strikingly in the concrete decision, adapted to a particular situation.

The tendency of the law towards conceptual rationalization can, therefore, only be bought at the expense of a conflict with the moral desire for specific adaptation. Thus far, then, law and morality are everlastingly and insuperably in conflict with each other. Extreme law, extreme injustice, as they say. If the law under this pressure relaxes its objectivity in favour of a smooth adaptation 'according to the circumstances', we speak of a moralization of the law, or of equity as opposed to strict law. Such adaptation frequently takes place simply because the legal rules direct the judge to be guided by current moral standards.

In their effect on social life, law and morality differ widely. Since the law is a social phenomenon or a common integral order purporting to monopolize coercion, it is always an order tending to promote society and always an order of peace. One might say that the 'purpose' of the law is, in a certain sense, peace; namely, in so far as every legal order, irrespective of content, is a peacemaking order (even if it is only the peace maintained in a penitentiary). Morality, on the other hand, is an individual phenomenon and may both sow discord and create harmony among people. Indeed, conflicting moral ideals may become a source of strife, and a source of the most profound, the most dangerous, and the most insurmountable kind. [111]

§ 13. Confrontation: Idealism and Realism in Legal Philosophy

The interpretation of the concept 'scientifically valid (Danish) law' that was offered in the foregoing sections differs sharply from the traditional view, which is generally prevailing and especially so in Continental jurisprudence. The interpretation may be characterized as jurisprudential realism and be contrasted with jurisprudential idealism—not so much because it is a particularly enlightening term, but because we would like to use a battle cry.

Jurisprudential idealism rests on the assumption that there are two different worlds, corresponding to two different methods of knowledge acquisition. First, there is 'the world of reality', comprehending all the physical and psychical phenomena in time and space, which we perceive through sense experience. Then, there is 'the world of ideas or of validity', comprehending various clusters of categorically valid normative ideas (the true, the good, and the beautiful), which we directly apprehend through reason. This knowledge is thus independent of sense experience and is, therefore, called *a priori* knowledge.

Furthermore, *jurisprudential idealism* assumes that the law belongs to both worlds. Therefore, legal knowledge is based on both external experience and *a priori* reasoning. The law is a phenomenon of reality in so far as its content is a historical fact varying in time and space, having come into existence through law-creating acts performed by human beings and dependent on external forces. However, the circumstance that this content 'is scientifically valid', or 'has validity' as law, cannot be observed empirically. 'Validity' does not lend itself to further description. It is an irreducible *a priori* concept, arising from direct apprehension through reason. However, validity is not merely a perceived quality; it is also a claim that is absolutely binding upon human action and human volition. Only those who fulfil a valid claim act 'correctly.' This 'correctness' can no more be explained or motivated than validity proper. It is merely another aspect of the very concept of validity.

The law is distinct from morality with respect to the following. While the moral norm stems from pure reason even as to content, the validity of the law is tied to a worldly and temporal content—the 'positive' law with its historically determined content. Morality is pure validity, whereas the law is phenomenon and validity at the same time: it is a fusion of reality and idea, or a revelation of the
[112] *a priori* validity of reason in the real world.[1]

[1] For documentation, see Alf Ross, *Virkelighed og Gyldighed i Retslæren* [Reality and Validity in Jurisprudence] (1934), chs. II and III. For present purposes, a simple and illustrative quotation should suffice: 'Thus, in order to arrive at an understanding of the concept of law, we must first establish that a given

There are two main versions of idealism, and they could be called the 'substantive version' and the 'formal version', respectively.

The *substantive version* takes idealism seriously, one might say. The specific idea manifesting itself in the law is the idea of justice. The idea of justice not only establishes an ideal against which positive law can be measured: it also constitutes the law, that is, it is that principle inherent in the law which endows the law with binding force or validity as law. Therefore, the idea of justice also draws up the limits of what can be recognized as law. Any order which is actually upheld and does not fulfil certain minimum demands derived from the idea of justice; or which does not even constitute an attempt to realize justice—such an order is deprived of its legal character and is labelled a mere factual phenomenon, a regime of violence. Views like these have dominated natural law philosophy from the earliest ages to our own times (ch. X).

The *formal version*, developed to perfection in Hans Kelsen's system, dissociates itself sharply from the idea of positive law being subjected to the ethical censorship of natural law. According to this version, any order actually upheld, is unreservedly accepted as law. Nevertheless, this version insists that the law, according to its own inherent meaning, does not aim to convey anything factual but, rather, to establish that something is normatively required or valid. To recognize the existence of a norm is the same as to recognize its validity. The validity of a norm, however, can never derive from a natural fact, only from another, higher norm from which the first norm is derived. A royal decree, for example, is not valid because it has been issued by the king—it is valid because it has been issued in conformity with a statute establishing that such decrees are valid. Thus, one is compelled to motivate the validity of the sentences of law by climbing from norm to norm. The validity of the statute is grounded in the validity of the constitution. To explain the validity of the constitution it is necessary to postulate a still higher, presupposed norm—the basic norm, whose sole function is to endow the constitution with validity. Therefore, legal knowledge moves in every stage in normative statements of what validly ought to be—not in statements of what actually is. Juristic thinking is thinking in terms of 'sollen', not in terms of 'sein':* legal science is the doctrinal study of law, not social theory. In this version of idealism, validity has been watered down (as will be shown later) to a formal category of thought, without any claim as to the content of the material which is perceived in this

* Translator's note: in German, *sollen* means 'ought'; *sein* means 'is'.

content—norms with a real foundation—can doubtlessly be considered "law". The definition of the concept of law presupposes a generalizing consideration of these simple spiritual phenomena. However, the very jump from the observation of the psycho-physical realities—legislation, legal beliefs, obedience—to the assumption of a "valid legal rule" implies an a priori element. *That the norm "is scientifically valid"*—that it has "validity"—*is not something we can observe in the real world . . . The idea of validity is the a priori element of the concept of law*', Frede Castberg, *Rettsfilosofiske grunnspörsmål* [Fundamental Issues in Jurisprudence] (1939), 38–39.

categorical form. The basic norm is devoid of any moral tinge. It is adapted to fit an actually efficacious order, and is no more than a postulate to the effect that this order does possess validity.[2]

[113] Kelsen's *Reine Rechtslehre* [The Pure Theory of Law] is a unique achievement within the field of modern legal philosophy. Distinguished by remarkable perspicacity, brilliant dialectics and inexorable logic, Kelsen's theory has created a school of thought and has, in recent years, influenced jurisprudential thinking more than any other individual achievement. Nowadays, there are not many legal philosophers who are not indebted to Kelsen—directly or indirectly, consciously or unconsciously. The inspiring potential of his work is not owing to any revolutionary ideas but, rather, to the logic with which he develops the preconditions for juristic positivism. These can be formulated in two fundamental principles: (1) The law is a normative idea content, created through historical acts but in itself different from these acts; (2) The law possesses validity in its own right, that is, regardless of whether its content is in conformity with ethical postulates or not. On this basis, Kelsen developed his theory of the purity of the doctrinal study of law, that is, its independence of the social sciences as well as ethics and politics. Legal science is the doctrinal study of law and is neither knowledge of reality nor natural law.

Kelsen's major works are *Hauptprobleme der Staatsrechtslehre* [Main problems in the theory of public law] (1911); *Allgemeine Staatslehre* [General constitutional theory] (1925) and *General Theory of Law and State* (1945). The last-mentioned work also offers a detailed bibliography of Kelsen's numerous other writings and of literature in connection with the Pure Theory of Law. A concise survey of the theory's main points is given by Kelsen himself, in his work *Reine Rechtslehre* [The Pure Theory of Law] (1934), the most important parts of which have been published in the journal *Statsvetenskaplig Tidsskrift* 1933, under the title *Den rena rättsläran* [The Pure Theory of Law]. For an introduction, see the opening sections in Jan-Magnus Jansson, *Hans Kelsens statsteori mot bakgrunden av hans rättsfilosofiska åskådning* [Hans Kelsen's theory of the state against the background of his system of legal philosophy] (1950). This work also offers a reliable in-depth analysis as well as a critique of Kelsen's theory.

The *leitmotif* of jurisprudential *realism* is the desire to understand legal science in conformity with the idea of the nature, tasks, and method of science which

[2] For a fuller account of Kelsen's way of thinking, see my book *Theorie der Rechtsquellen* [Theory of the Sources of Law] (1929), chs. 1 and 9, as well as my book *Virkelighed og Gyldighed i Retslæren* [Reality and Validity in Jurisprudence] (1934), ch. III. 4, to which the reader is referred. See also Jan-Magnus Jansson, *Hans Kelsens statsteori mot bakgrunden av hans rättsfilosofiska åskådning* [Hans Kelsen's Theory of the State against the Background of his System of Legal Philosophy] (1950), 238 f. and § 2 note 6 above.

has been developed by modern, scientific philosophy. Several schools of philosophy—logical empiricism, the philosophy of the Uppsala school, the Cambridge school of philosophy, and others—find common ground in rejecting all speculative knowledge grounded in *a priori* reasoning; in short, in rejecting so-called metaphysics. There is only one world and one type of knowledge. Ultimately, all science is concerned with the same body of facts, and all scientific statements about reality—that is to say, all those statements which are not purely logico-mathematical—are subject to empirical test.

In light of these assumptions, a specific 'validity' cannot be acknowledged, either as a substantive, *a priori* idea of justice, nor as a formal category. Ideas of validity are metaphysical constructions, based on the experience in moral consciousness of the gradually evoked attitudes and their peculiar, automatically motivating force. In the final analysis legal science, like all other social sciences, must be a study of social phenomena, a study of human society; and it must be [114] the task of legal philosophy to interpret the 'scientific validity' of the law in terms of social efficaciousness, that is, of a certain correspondence between a normative idea content and the social phenomena. In the present chapter, I have attempted to show how this task can be fulfilled.

In the Nordic countries, realism prevails in modern legal philosophy—a fact which for the most part can be traced back to Axel Hägerström's influence upon moral and legal philosophy. In Sweden, the following authors deserve particular mention (for their major works, see § 6 note 10 above): V. Lundstedt, Karl Olivecrona, Ingemar Hedenius, Per Olof Ekelöf and Björn Ahlander. In Norway: G. Astrup Hoel (*Den modern retsmetode* [Modern Legal Method], 1925) and Vilhelm Aubert ('Om rettsvitenskapens logiske grunnlag' ['On the logical foundation of legal science'], *TfR* 1943, 174). In Denmark: Viggo Bentzon (*Retskilderne* [The Sources of Law], 1900–1907), Knud Illum (*Lov og Ret* [Law and Justice], 1945), Theodor Geiger (*Debat med Uppsala om Moral og Ret* [Debate with Uppsala about Morality and Law] (1946) and *Vorstudien zu einer Soziologie des Rechts* [Preliminary Studies on the Sociology of Law], 1947) and Henry Ussing (*Retsstridighed* [Unlawfulness], 1949). In Finland: Otto Brusiin (*Über die Objektivität der Rechtsprechung* [On Objectivity in the Administration of Justice], 1949; *Über das juristische Denken* [On Juristic Thinking], 1951) who, however, acknowledges metaphysical experiences, if not metaphysical knowledge; Osci Lahtinen (*Zum Aufbau der rechtlichen Grundlagen* [On the foundations of law], 1951) and Jan-Magnus Jansson (*Hans Kelsens statsteori mot bakgrunden av hans rättsfilosofiska åskådning* [Hans Kelsen's theory of the state against the background of his legal philosophy], 1950).

Also in American legal philosophy there is a school which calls itself realistic. In this case, however, the term 'realism' is used primarily in a sense different from the present one, namely, as an expression of scepticism vis-à-vis legal concepts and rules and the part they are playing in adjudication, cf. § 9, note 4 above. At the same time, however, this school is nonetheless 'realistic' also in the sense in which it has been used here, namely in so far as it looks upon the law as a social phenomenon, determined by the application of law by the courts. In the vanguard of American realism was Oliver Wendell Holmes ('The Path of the Law', 10 *Harvard Law Review* (1897), 457 F., reprinted in Collected Papers, 1920) and John Chipman Gray (*The Nature and Sources of the Law,* 1909). Among the best-known representatives of this school are Jerome Frank (*Law and the Modern Mind,* 1930; *Courts on Trial,* 1949), K. N. Llewellyn ('Some Realism about Realism', 44 *Harvard Law Review* (1931) 1222; (with E. A. Hoebel), *The Cheyenne Way,* 1942) and Underhill Moore ('Rational Basis of Legal Institutions', 23 *Columbia Law Review* (1923) 609; 'An Institutional Approach to the Law of Commercial Banking', 38 *Yale Law Review* (1929) 703). A bibliographical survey will be found in E. N. Garlan, *Legal Realism and Justice* (1941). For an introduction, see, e.g., W. Friedmann, *Legal Theory* (2nd ed., 1949) 189 f. For a critical study, see, e.g., Cardozo, *Selected Writings* (1947) 7 f.; Lon L. Fuller, 'American Legal Realism', *Proceedings of the American Philosophical Society,* vol. 76 (1936) 191 f. and Ross, *Towards a Realistic Jurisprudence* (1946), 59 f.

[115] The trend in jurisprudence that calls itself sociological jurisprudence is mainly idealism in disguise, cf. § 1, at notes 23 and 24.

The two main schools of jurisprudence, metaphysical idealism and scientific realism, are thus opposed to each other. The ultimate struggle between them cannot be carried out within the realm of legal philosophy itself, but must be fought out on the battlefield of general philosophy. The debate between idealism and realism in legal philosophy is bound to get lost in fundamental problems of epistemology. Considering these, a legal philosopher cannot be expected to do more than outline the main features of the philosophical basis he is building upon. Moreover, I am convinced that legal metaphysics will gradually disappear, just as it has all but disappeared as far as the natural sciences are concerned: 'disappeared' not so much because of the logical arguments that have been put forth against its defensibility, but because interest in metaphysical constructions is fading away; whilst, on the other hand, a regular science has developed which is able to prove its usefulness. Nowadays, who would dream of 'disproving' the belief in the philosopher's stone? Let the dead bury their dead.

On the other hand, it falls within the realm of legal philosophy to put forward a *criticism of idealism* in its application to the problems of legal theory. It has always been a serious problem for idealistic legal philosophy to explain how it is possible that the act of legislating, an actual social phenomenon, can produce anything other than actual social effects, namely, valid obligations of an *a priori* character. If idealism is taken *seriously*, and if certain actually maintained rules or systems are denied the character of law because they do not harmonize with a presupposed ideal of justice—then this leads to an inappropriate demarcation of the concept of law. An elementary scientific principle says that an object must be defined according to the objective qualities of the facts, not according to evaluative views. It is irrelevant, for example, whether Hitler's racial laws, or certain more exotic laws permitting polygamy, are held to contradict the idea of law: it still remains an inescapable, practical task to describe these actually efficacious rules within the context of their respective system. It would be unreasonable to express moral disapproval by excluding these topics from the realm of legal science. The idea of law—that is, if it is at all possible to acknowledge such an idea—can therefore be no more than a regulative legal-political idea which is not constitutive of the concept of law. If one tries to mitigate the ideal demand by saying that positive law at any rate has to be an *attempt* to realize justice, then this introduces among the objective facts of the law a subjective, intentional factor which is difficult to explain. After all, an attempt can be successful or it can fail. Is the unsuccessful attempt also 'law'? If so, the construction would appear to be just as arbitrary as if one were to maintain that a dog constitutes an unsuccessful attempt to create a cat.

Finally, if one radically *rejects all moral censure*, as Kelsen does, and simply [116] accepts an order which is actually upheld as scientifically valid law, then the specific validity as a categorical form becomes a superfluous drapery. The impossibility of Kelsen's attempt to ignore psychological and social reality when determining the nature of positive law becomes apparent as soon as we reach the basic norm and shall define it. As long as we remain on the lower steps of the legal system, it is possible to postpone the problem of the scientific validity of the norm by referring to a higher norm. However, this procedure cannot be used in connection with the basic norm itself: there, the problem of the relation between norm and reality can no longer be avoided. It goes without saying that the basic norm cannot be chosen arbitrarily if the system is to make sense. Kelsen himself says that it must be chosen in such a way as to correspond to an efficacious system. It is obvious, though, that in reality, the criterion of positive law is its efficaciousness; and in reality—once we know what is positive law—the only function of the basic norm consists in endowing it with that kind of 'validity' which the metaphysical interpretation of the legal consciousness demands, but which nobody is able to define. The basic norm is the ultimate source from which validity wells forth and branches off throughout the entire system. One might overlook this as a superfluous but harmless construction, were it not that it makes one shut one's eyes to a deeper analysis of the criterion of efficaciousness. By turning validity into an inter-normative relation (the validity of a norm derives from the validity of another norm), Kelsen has precluded himself, and from the outset, from dealing with the heart of the problem of the scientific validity of law, namely, the relation between normative idea content and social reality.[3]

[3] On this issue, see Alf Ross, *Virkelighed og Gyldighed i Retslæren* [Reality and Validity in Jurisprudence] (1934), ch. III. 4.

§ 14. *Confrontation: Ideological and Behaviouristic Realism and their Synthesis*

All realistic theories agree in interpreting the scientific validity of legal norms as expressing a certain social efficacy. What differentiates a scientifically valid law from a mere draft statute or a demand for reform is that the normative idea content of the former is efficacious in legal life. Our task, then, is to study the close correspondence between the legal norms (*qua* abstract ideas) and the legal [117] phenomena they have been abstracted from. Since legal phenomena (cf. § 3) include both legal notions and legal actions, there are two possible approaches for establishing the actual correlate of the norms. Accordingly, there are two branches of realism, which could be called the ideological and the behaviouristic branch, respectively.

Ideological realism finds the reality of law in those ideas and impulses of action which actually inspire people. A norm is scientifically valid in so far as it is part of the ideology which is actually experienced, and which can be called the legal consciousness. These experiences are psychical facts, and they constitute the content proper of the assertions of legal science about scientifically valid law. Consequently, verification consists in proving that a certain rule is included in the general legal consciousness. According to this view, the fact that such a rule is also upheld by the courts is something derived and of secondary importance; it is a normal consequence of the general legal consciousness which also determines the reactions of the judge. The actual criterion is not the rule being upheld as such but, rather, the cause for its being upheld.

In order to test whether a given rule—for example, § 28 Danish Bill of Exchange Act—is scientifically valid law, we must carry out certain social psychological investigations. We shall examine whether the rule is accepted by the general legal consciousness. In a case like this the examination is said to be an easy one. The fact is that the rule can be found in the Bill of Exchange Act, which has been enacted by the King and the Parliament according to the Constitution, and the (indirect and formalized) content of the general legal consciousness is, first of all, that law is law, and that the law must be obeyed. There is a prevailing attitude among the population in general that anything established in conformity with the constitution has the right to be respected as law.[1]

[1] For further details, see Karl Olivecrona, *Om lagen och staten* [On Law and the State] (1940), 64 f. To a certain extent, ideological realism resembles Kelsen's formal idealism, according to which the validity of the law is deductively derived from the constitution (and the basic norm). The only difference seems to be that while Kelsen looks upon constitutional ideology as an autonomous normative hypothesis abstracted from the social reality, Olivecrona points out that it is the content of real psychological acts, of attitudes which exist in 'the general consciousness'. Knud Illum does not lay so much stress on the deductive aspect. What is important

The general legal consciousness is not tied to the statute, however. It is quite possible that a statute does not become scientifically valid law because it is not accepted by the general legal consciousness. Similarly, a precedent which for the first time lays down a rule as a basis for the decision is no more than an attempt to create law. The important thing is whether the rule is accepted by the legal consciousness. 'The only possible touchstone for the existence of a legal rule is
[118] its being confronted with the general legal consciousness.' Admittedly, the legal consciousness of the man in the street is usually far too scanty to be taken into consideration as a criterion. Therefore, due weight must be given to the legal consciousness of the country's professional lawyers— the true experts, familiar with the traditional legal culture. Within this context, the legal scholars in the academy ought to be mentioned in the first place. They are the nation's guardians of our legal culture, and it must be their opinion which, in case of doubt, is the criterion of what is scientifically valid law.[2]

Views along similar lines[3] already inspired the romantic, historical school of law (Friedrich Carl von Savigny, Georg Friedrich Puchta, cf. § 86 below) and were recently defended energetically by Knud Illum. Similar ideas, although less fully elaborated, may also be found in the work of Karl Olivecrona.[4]

The main objection to ideological realism is that the legal consciousness is an individualistic psychological concept. By linking the concept of scientifically valid law to individual legal consciousness, the law—just like morality—is converted into an individual phenomenon. Let us just think of problems such as abortion, the trials against traitors,* the taxation of cooperative societies, the freedom of trade, and so forth, to see how diversified legal consciousness can be even among lawyers. Illum himself does not draw back from the consequence that, in principle, the law exists in just as many varieties as there are people acquainted with the content of legal notions.[5] Consequently, one cannot speak of 'Danish law'—nor can one speak of 'Danish morality'. One can only speak of a prevailing conception of law.

Such a definition cannot be accepted: it obviously contradicts the assumptions of legal science according to which 'scientifically valid law' is the same as 'scientifically valid Danish law'—a social phenomenon ascribed to Danish society,

to him is that a legal rule shows, in fact, a mark of validity in our legal imagination, quite irrespective of how it harmonizes with the constitution (which, in turn, can be modified to a greater or lesser degree without legitimate foundation). As far as I can see, however, Illum does not mean to deny that the mark of validity which is tied to the legislative provisions is essentially conditioned by notions (with a mark of validity) concerning the competence of the public authorities, see Knud Illum, *Lov og Ret* [Law and Justice] (1945), 82–83.

* Translator's note: Here Ross is referring specifically to the post-World War II prosecutions of those Danish citizens who had collaborated with the German occupants.

[2] For further details, see Knud Illum, *Lov og Ret* [Law and Justice] (1945), 53 f., 103, 118 *et seq.*

[3] This is of course a stylized pattern which does not entirely cover the individual writer's views.

[4] See notes 1 and 2.

[5] Knud Illum, *Lov og Ret* [Law and Justice] (1945), 63, 118.

not to the individual. It must be assumed that it is possible, at least within certain limits, to define scientifically valid Danish law as an externally given, supra-individual phenomenon, not merely as a subjective attitude which can be measured in a Gallup poll among law professors. If there is a fairly good basis for the assumption that a certain rule will underlie the decisions of the national courts, then that rule is scientifically valid Danish law in a juridico-scientific sense, and in so far as this assertion is concerned, it is wholly irrelevant what Professor Illum's (or anybody else's) legal consciousness amounts to.[6]

Behaviouristic realism finds the reality of law in legal proceedings, specifically in [119] the enforcement through the courts. A norm is scientifically valid if it can be assumed that it will serve as a basis for future judicial decisions. The real content of the assertions of legal science about valid law are thus predictions about the behaviour of the judges. According to this view, the fact that such norms are consistent with the prevailing legal consciousness is something derived and secondary—it is a normal, but not essential condition for the exercise of coercion. The contrast to the ideological theory can be emphasized in the following way. While the ideological theory defines the scientific validity of the law in such a way that one feels obliged to say that *the law is applied because it is scientifically valid*, the behaviouristic theory defines the concept in such a way that one feels obliged to say that *the law is scientifically valid because it is applied.*[7]

Similar views have played an important part in American realism dating back to Oliver Wendell Holmes, the famous judge who, as early as 1897, formulated the frequently quoted aphorism: 'The prophecies of what the Courts will do in fact, and nothing more pretentious, are what I mean by the law.'[8] As far as the [120]

[6] On this issue, cf. Theodor Geigers interpretation and critique of Illum's theory of consciousness, *Vorstudien zu einer Soziologie des Rechts* [Preliminary Studies on the Sociology of Law] (1947), 325 f.

[7] Please observe that the two phrases in italics do not express any disagreement concerning the factual context: they merely indicate that the expression 'being scientifically valid' is defined differently in the two statements.

[8] 'The Path of the Law', 10 *Harvard Law Review* (1897), 457 f., reprinted in *Collected Papers* (1920). Holmes's line of thought was pursued by John Chipman Gray (*The Nature and Sources of the Law* 1909), who defined law as 'the rules which the courts . . . lay down for the determination of legal rights and duties', and expressly declared that 'the law of a great nation means the opinions of half-a-dozen old gentlemen, some of them, conceivably, of very limited intelligence', since 'if half-a-dozen old gentlemen form the highest tribunal of a country, then no rule or principle which they refuse to follow is law in that country', *op. cit.*, 84 and 125. Thereupon, this line of thought was carried to its extreme logical conclusion by Jerome Frank (*Law and the Modern Mind*, 1930)—namely, that law does not consist of rules at all, but is nothing but the sum total of all individual decisions. 'We may now venture a rough definition of law from the point of view of the average man: For any particular lay person, the law, with respect to any particular set of facts, is a decision of a court with respect to those facts as far as that decision affects that particular person. Until a court has passed on those facts no law on that subject is yet in existence. Prior to such a decision, the only law available is the opinion of lawyers as to the law relating to that person and to those facts. Such opinion is not actually law but only a guess as to what a court will decide—Law then, as to any given situation is either (a) actual law, i. e. specific past decision as to that situation, or (b) probable law, i. e. a guess as to a specific future situation', *op. cit.*, 46. Benjamin Cardozo, a great name in the US Supreme Court, reacts against the extravagances of realism but accepts its fundamental tenet: 'I find lying around loose, and ready to be embodied into a judgment according to some process of selection to be practised by a judge, a vast conglomeration of principles and rules and customs and usages and moralities. If these are so established as to justify a prediction with reasonable certainty

Nordic region is concerned, similar views were recently adopted by Ingemar Hedenius,[9] Henry Ussing,[10] and Theodor Geiger.[11]

From the preceding discussion in this section, it will have emerged that a purely behaviouristic interpretation of the concept of scientific validity is not feasible because it is impossible to predict the behaviour of the judge by a purely external observation of customary regularity. The law is more than an internalized, habitual order, cf. § 8 above.

Therefore, a tenable interpretation of the scientific validity of the law is only possible (as I have tried to explain in the present chapter) through a *synthesis of ideological and behaviouristic views.*[12] This view is behaviouristic in so far as it aims to find coherence and predictability in the externally observable, verbal behaviour of the judge. It is ideological in so far as the coherence referred to is a coherent whole of meaning and motivation which is possible only on the hypothesis that the judge, in his inner thoughts, is governed and motivated by a normative ideology with a certain kind of content.

that they will have the backing of the court in the event that their authority is challenged, I say that they are law', *Selected Writings* (1947), 18.

A more detailed account, as well as criticism of Gray and Frank can be found in my book *Towards a Realistic Jurisprudence* (1946), 59 f.

[9] *Om rätt och moral* [On Law and Morality] (1941), 16 f.

[10] *Retsstridighed* [On Unlawfulness] (1949), 8 f.

[11] *Vorstudien zu einer Soziologie des Rechts* [Preliminary Studies on the Sociology of Law] (1947), 157 f. Geiger's conception of 'valid law' is, however, rooted in the premises and habitual views of a sociologist and thus inadequate in view of specifically legal problems. On this issue, see my article 'Om begrebet "gældende ret" hos Theodor Geiger' [On the concept of 'valid law' in Theodor Geiger], *Tidsskrift for Retsvitenskap* 1950, 242–72.

[12] This version of realism is not affected by Jansson's well-founded criticism of the naive identification of law and application of law, see Jan-Magnus Jansson, *Hans Kelsens statsteori mot bakgrunden av hans rättsfilosofiska åskådning* [Hans Kelsen's Theory of the State Against the Background of his System of Legal Philosophy] (1950), 274–82.

CHAPTER III [121]

The Sources of Law

§ 15. The Doctrine of the Sources of Law and the Concept 'Source of Law'

In the previous chapter we arrived at the conclusion that the real content of the assertion of legal science that

$$A = (D) \text{ is scientifically valid Danish law}$$

is a prediction to the effect that D, under certain conditions, will serve as a basis for judicial decisions in future lawsuits.

Experience has shown that such predictions are indeed possible within certain limits, although the degree of probability with which they can be made may vary.

If Danish law merely consisted of a small number of unalterable norms (as do the rules of chess), then predictability must simply be assumed to depend on the fact that these norms are always present and active in the mind of the judge.

This is not the case, however. Danish law does not only consist of an enormous variety of norms, it is also subject to an ongoing development process. Therefore, the judge has to search in each individual case for the norm of conduct he needs as a basis for his decision. Since prediction is nevertheless possible, it must have to do with the fact that the mental process through which the judge arrives at a stage where he can base his decision on one rule rather than another does not [122] take place in a capricious and arbitrary way (varying from judge Peter to judge Paul), but is determined by attitudes and notions—by a common normative ideology which is present and operative in a uniform way within the minds of Danish judges when acting in their vocation as judges. It is true that we cannot directly observe what takes place within the judge's mind, but we can make hypotheses thereon, and their value can be tested exactly because they enable us to make predictions.

This ideology is the subject of the theory of the sources of law. It forms part of scientifically valid Danish law and consists of directives. These directives are not directly concerned with how a certain dispute should be resolved; however, they point out to the judge how he should proceed in order to discover the directive or directives which are decisive in resolving the dispute.

It stands to reason that this ideology can only be found in the actual behaviour of the courts. It is the basis for the predictions of legal science concerning the way in which the courts will react in the future. The only conceivable basis for these predictions is to make a study of how the courts actually have behaved until now. *The ideology of the sources of law is the ideology which in fact animates the courts, and the theory of the sources of law is the doctrine of the way in which the courts in fact behave.* Starting from certain assumptions, it would be possible to develop directives on how the judges ought to proceed when selecting the norms of conduct on which to base their decisions. It stands to reason, however, that unless such directives are identical with those which are actually followed by the courts, they are completely valueless as bases for predictions concerning the future behaviour of the courts, that is, for establishing what is scientifically valid law. Any attempt to arrive at a doctrine of the sources of law which is normative in the sense that it sets up directives on how the courts ought to behave, instead of stating and describing those directives which are actually followed by the courts, is doomed to fail—that is, in so far as it is presented as scientifically valid law and not merely as a project for a different, and better, law of the land. Like any other theory of scientifically valid law, the theory of the sources of law is *norm-descriptive, not norm-expressive*: it is a theory about norms, not a theory in norms.

Traditionally, this theory is called 'the doctrine of the sources of law', because we are used to thinking that the ideology we are discussing consists of directives to the judge, ordering him to apply the rules which have been created according to certain methods of procedure. From there, it is only a short step to conceiving of such a method of procedure as a source. What comes to light in a certain way, what gushes forth from a certain procedure, this is the law the judge has to apply. This idea fits in well with the rules of statutory law. They are, indeed, defined as being created in a legislative process, and it is perfectly natural to call legislation the 'source' of all law existing in the form of legal rules. If there existed an additional number of other methods of procedure for creating law in parallel with legislation, it would be perfectly correct to speak of a correspond-
[123] ing number of sources of law. This, however, is not really the case (as will be shown below). If one should wish to mention (apart from legislation) precedent, custom, and the nature of the matter as sources of law, then it must be emphasized that these do not indicate three further methods of procedure for the creation of law, supplying the judge with a finished product in the same way legislation does. Metaphorically speaking, one might say that whereas legislation

delivers a finished, ready-to-use product, precedent and custom are only capable of delivering half-finished products which must be completed by the judge himself, and that 'the nature of the matter' produces nothing except certain raw materials, out of which the judge himself has to create the rule he needs.

Under these circumstances it is both problematic and precarious to put forward a concept of 'legal source' comprising such varied factors as legislation, custom, precedent, and the nature of the matter. In any case, one has to emphasize that the expression 'source of law' does not designate a method of procedure for the production of legal rules. This characteristic applies only to legislation. If we insist on formulating a concept of 'source of law' (something which is not necessary for describing the ideology we are speaking of), then this concept must be defined rather vaguely, so that the term 'sources of law' can be understood to mean *the sum total of the factors exercising influence* on the judge's formulation of the rule on which he bases his decision; adding the qualification that this influence with regard to the various sources can vary considerably, ranging from cases where the source provides the judge with a ready-made legal rule which he only has to take over, to cases where the source offers the judge nothing but certain inspiring ideas from which he himself has to formulate the rule he needs.

Since the ideology of the sources of law is part of scientifically valid law, varying from one legal system to another, it is a task for the doctrinal study of law to provide a description of it. As mentioned above, this task can only be accomplished through a detailed study of the manner in which the courts of a country actually proceed in their search for the norms on which to base their decisions. The task for general legal theory can only consist in stating and characterizing certain *general types* of sources of law, which experience tells us are found in all well-developed legal systems.

Various approaches suggest themselves as a basis for a generalizing typology of this kind. Thus, for example, it would be possible to characterize the various types of sources according to the predominant role they have played at different stages of legal development. From this point of view, precedent and 'the nature of the matter' may be characterized as two types of sources which have always played an important role, corresponding to the ideas of formal and substantive justice; and custom and legislation as two types of sources whose role has varied greatly, custom being the predominant source in primitive law and legislation in modern law.

In this book, however, another view will provide a basis for the description, [124]
namely, the degree of objectification possessed by the various types of sources. By saying so I mean the degree to which the sources provide the judge with a ready formulated legal rule; or conversely, the degree to which they merely provide him with material which only after an active cooperation on his part is formed into a rule.

Accordingly, our classification is as follows:

(1) the *completely objectivized* type of source: authoritative formulations (legislation in its widest sense);
(2) the *partially objectivized* types of source: custom and precedent; and
(3) the *non-objectivized*, 'free' type of source: 'the nature of the matter'.

§ 16. *Legislation*

The most important source of law in modern Continental Europe is undoubtedly the law which has been laid down by public authorities. Judges feel, in fact, very much bound by announcements of the legislative power, and, according to the official, ideological doctrine, enacted law possesses absolute binding force. It is nevertheless the case that the courts, overtly or covertly, disregard statutory rules which do not square with the prevailing substantive legal consciousness.[1] For judges, too, there is a limit to the span between institutional and substantive legal consciousness (§ 11 at note 5). Especially among older statutory rules it happens that they sink into oblivion, so to speak, because they no longer harmonize with altered conditions and views. We say that the rule has lapsed through *desuetudo*.

From a historical perspective, the coming into being of a legislature is a curious phenomenon (§ 18), and many years were to pass before the authority of the law achieved general recognition. Allen[2] mentions that, as late as in fourteenth-century England, it was not uncommon for judges to refuse, flatly, to apply statutory law. Ideologically supported by the doctrine of natural law, a struggle for law-creating supremacy[3] arose between common law and Parliament. In *Bonham's Case* (1610),[4] Chief Justice Coke defended the right of common-law [125] judges to declare an Act of Parliament null and void. After the Revolution of 1688, however, the absolute supremacy of Parliament was recognized.[5] Blackstone (1765) might still give lip service to the natural-law doctrine that no law is valid if it contradicts the principles of natural law; in practice, however, he recognized the absolute and unfettered competence of Parliament.[6]

Statute law is 'enacted' law (gesetzt = Gesetz = statute), that is, it has been created through a decision made by certain human beings and thus presupposes competence norms which indicate under what conditions this enactment may take place. To develop these competence norms is a task for the doctrinal study of the sources of law. The general theory of the sources of law must limit itself to bringing to light certain characteristic features of enacted law.

[1] See, e.g., Jean Cruet, *La vie du droit et l'impuissance des lois* [The Life of the Law and the Impotence of Statutes] (1908).

[2] *Law in the Making* (4th edn, 1946), 365 f.

[3] See also W. Friedmann, *Legal Theory* (2nd edn, 1949), 50 f.

[4] 'It appears in our books that in many cases the common law will control Acts of Parliament and sometimes judge them to be utterly void, for when an Act of Parliament is against common right or reason or repugnant or impossible to be performed the common law will control it and adjudge such Act to be void' (1610), 8, Co. C. P., 114 a.

[5] See, however, *Goshen v Stonington* (1822), 4 Conn., 209, 225, where Hosmer, J. still questions the omnicompetence of Parliament; see Julius Stone, *The Province and Function of Law* (1946/50), 226.

[6] Blackstone, *Commentaries on the Laws of England* (1765–1769), vol. II, 41–43.

The umbrella term for all enactment by virtue of a competence is legislation, and all enacted law is called statutory law, or in short: the law. Thus, the law comprises the constitution, the law in a narrower sense, ordinances, statutory orders, by-laws, regulations, instructions, private contracts, unilateral private statements, and whatever else has been formulated authoritatively in the field of law. In the terminology of constitutional law, however, the terms 'legislation' and 'law' are reserved for the type of enactment which takes place at a certain level, as well as for its result. In general terms, this level can be described as the highest level where extensive enactment takes place—enactment which in no small degree only consists of the enactment of competence norms.[7]

[126] The condition for a rule to be formulated authoritatively can generally be expressed as follows: namely, that the rule has been *enacted by an authority, and within that authority's sphere of (substantive) competence.*[8]

This means:

(a) in the first place ('enacted by an authority') that the formulated rule has come into being in conformity with a prescribed *method of procedure*, according to which the individual stages of the process have been carried out by precisely those human actors who are qualified to do so (formal competence). For example, to say that a certain rule is statutory law is shorthand for saying that the rule has come into being in conformity with the method of procedure—namely through legislation—according to §§ 16, 23, 24, 43, 51, 52, 60, etc. of the Danish Constitution; where, in turn, it is assumed that the role which in these rules is ascribed to 'Parliament' and to 'the King,'* respectively, is carried out by precisely those human beings who—partly according to the Electoral Law, partly according to the

* In the Danish Constitution of 1920, 'the King' frequently stands for 'the Government'.

[7] With regard to legislation, the law at the higher levels appears mainly in the form of competence norms (constitutional law), and the law at the lower levels mainly as concretizing implementation regulations within the framework of given statutory laws (administrative decrees). Thus, the law is a hierarchy, presupposing a certain type of structure in the gradual enactment of the law—a historically conditioned structure which, of course, does not possess any kind of necessity. Nowadays, there is a tendency to obliterate this type of structure. On the one hand, for example, in some of the US federal states, there is extensive legislation in constitutional form; on the other, extensive legislative power quite frequently seems to be delegated to the government and the administration. Nothing prevents us from envisaging a legal system where the enactment of substantive law is evenly spread over a number of levels. The law in the form of a hierarchy will then have disappeared, cf. Alf Ross, *Theorie der Rechtsquellen* [Theory of the Sources of Law] (1929), ch. XV, 2.

[8] In this text, the term 'competence' carries different meanings. When I am speaking of 'competence norms' or 'norms warranting a certain competence', the term stands for the quintessence of all the conditions for a valid enactment of a certain type, thus comprising both formal directions on the method of procedure and substantive restrictions. Here, the term refers only to the substantive conditions. Both meanings differ from the meaning currently used in administrative law, according to which 'competence' only refers to certain conditions in connection with the method of procedure, namely, those one must meet in order to qualify as an actor in the law-creating process.

Act of Succession—are qualified as Members of Parliament and as King, respectively. Of course, it is not always the case that the prescribed method of procedure is this complicated. For example, if it is a question of a verbal administrative statement, the procedure is quite simple. As previously mentioned (§ 10), it may happen that a procedural violation does not lead to invalidity, only to liability, and that there may even exist procedural rules—such as, for example, § 51 of the Constitution—whose infringement does not lead to either invalidity or liability.

(b) In the second place, it means that the legal norm, come into being in this way, as to content falls *within the competence of the respective authority*, with the area of competence of said authority understood as representing the sum total of all other limits of validity of the decision. As mentioned previously (§ 10), it may happen that a norm of conduct makes a certain exercise of competence obligatory, in the sense that the opposite behaviour leads to liability but not to invalidity.

The competence to enact laws is usually not limited to a single authority but, rather, extends over a hierarchy consisting of partly superior and subordinate, partly coordinate instances. Thus, the Constitution comprises competence norms which constitute partly the legislative power, and partly the power of the Crown, which can be seen as directly stemming from the Constitution, that is, the royal prerogative. However, part of the law created by statute consists of new competence norms which, for example, constitute the King's competence to issue royal decrees, and the competence of private contracting parties to determine rights through contracts. However, these legal formations may also consist of new competence norms, and so on. In this way, a highly complex system of competence authorities arises at various levels. [127]
An authority whose competence is determined by norms which have been created by another authority is located at a lower level in relation to the latter. Two authorities whose respective competence has been created by the same superior authority are said to be located at the same level, or coordinate.

If we call the authority in question A_1, then A_1 is constituted by a set of (formal and substantive) rules of competence of this kind. If we call these rules C_1, then C_1, as such, must either have been authoritatively enacted by a superior authority, A_2, or not have been enacted by A_2. Had they been enacted by A_2, then A_2 must have been constituted by C_2 which, in turn, must either have been authoritatively enacted by A_3 or not have been enacted by A_3. Since the series of authorities cannot be infinite, it necessarily follows that *ultimately, the highest competence norms must be of a non-posited, merely presupposed nature.* This line of thought can be illustrated by the following figure:

A_3 constituted by C_3 < (either enacted authoritatively by A_4)
or not " " " "

|

A_2 constituted by C_2 < either enacted authoritatively by A_3
(or not " " " ")

|

A_1 constituted by C_1 < either enacted authoritatively by A_2
(or not " " " ")

This figure means, then, that A_3 is the highest authority and must, therefore, necessarily be constituted through competence norms which have not been enacted by any authority but are merely given as a presupposed ideology.

Further, it is worth noting that the norms constituting an authority A and A's competence are, at the same time, norms which determine how law created by A can be amended. The constituent norms determine the conditions for the validity of the subordinate norm and thus refer equally to the norm's enactment and its cessation due to an amendment. And conversely: the rules formulated as rules of change concerning law created by A are, at the same time, norms which constitute A. For example, the rules of the Constitution governing the legislature are, at the same time, rules on the amendment of statutes (namely, through another statute). And vice versa: the rules in § 94 of the Danish Constitution, governing the special procedure for amending the Constitution, are, at the same time, rules which establish a constituent authority, as distinct from a legislative authority.

Let us return to the figure above. We have seen that a certain authority is the highest authority, and that the norms constituting this authority thus cannot have been enacted by any other authority, but must have been given as a merely presupposed ideology. The fact that this ideology has not been enacted by any authority means that there is no superior norm to determine the conditions for [128] its valid enactment and amendment. From a legal point of view, then, it is not possible to say anything about how the presupposed, supreme constituent ideology might be changed. Yet changes there are, and they can have come about through revolution as well as through evolution. In both cases, however, the phenomenon of the change is a purely social psychological fact beyond any legal procedure.

In Danish law, the highest authority is the constituent authority, constituted through the rules of § 94 of the Danish Constitution. These rules embody the supreme ideological assumption which, as such, has not been laid down by any authority and cannot be amended by any other authority. Any amendment of § 94 which, in fact, succeeds in establishing itself in the general consciousness is an a-legal fact, not a legal enactment according to an institutionalized procedure.

Of course, I am well aware that as to this point, some people raise the objection that all the leading politicians in the country do, in fact, act on the assumption that § 94 can legally be amended, and amended only in a certain procedure, namely, the procedure indicated in § 94 itself. Of course, I accept this view as a social psychological fact which will exert great influence on the actual course of political life, but this fact is no reason to modify the logical analysis above. There is only one possible way of challenging the reasoning expressed in the above figure. It could be maintained that a certain authority, for example A_3, can be constituted through norms enacted by itself, which amounts to saying that it is possible for a norm to determine the conditions for its own enactment, including the way in which it can be amended. A 'reflexivity' of this kind, however—and this is a generally recognized view among logicians—is a logical impossibility. A sentence cannot refer to itself.[9] It would be possible to adduce proof thereof, but this would lead us too far. However, it will surely be admitted, I believe, that the legislature cannot be conceived of as being constituted by law, and that a statute cannot state the conditions for its own amendment. The rules for this must necessarily lie at a level one stage higher than the statute. If this is admitted vis-à-vis the statute, however, then the same must be admitted vis-à-vis the Constitution. Similarly to the statute, the Constitution cannot state the conditions for its own amendment. Thus, § 94 of the Constitution is not in itself the Constitution, but consists of presupposed norms at a higher level. These, in turn, cannot state the conditions for their own amendment, either. If such conditions existed, they would be located at a still higher level. There are no such conditions, however. § 94 is not enacted law, but presupposed law.

Moreover, it might be maintained that if § 94 of the Constitution is actually amended through a procedure in conformity with its own rules, then it is [129]
possible to consider the new '§ 94' as having been derived from the old one; or as valid because it has derived from the old one. Any such derivation presupposes the validity of the higher norm and thus its continued existence. Consequently, it is impossible to establish, through derivation, a new norm which conflicts with the basis of derivation. It will be easier to understand this if we consider less complicated cases than the rules of § 94 of the Constitution.

If an absolute monarch grants a 'free constitution', the legal significance of this act might be interpreted in two different ways (depending on circumstances). The new constitution can be seen as granted and scientifically valid by virtue of the absolute power of the monarch, who thus continues to be the supreme authority. Thus, the old basic norm is still scientifically valid, and the new order

[9] Notwithstanding the recognized unanimity prevalent among logicians, K. Grue-Sørensen, *Studier over Refleksivitet* [Inquiries into Reflexivity] (1950), 101 f., claims that this is possible. His argumentation is neither deep nor convincing, and, as far as I know, his peculiar views have not attracted any followers.

can be revoked at any time and by the same absolute power that has granted it. There has been no change in the ultimate presupposition of the system—in its fundamental ideology. The situation in Denmark in 1831, when the constitution of the corporative state was introduced, must doubtlessly be interpreted in this way, and presumably also the situation in the German states after the introduction of the corporative constitutions (forcefully imposed at the beginning of the nineteenth century).

In certain circumstances, however, it may be intended that the King should not be able to revoke the new constitution. In that case, one cannot regard the new constitution as deriving from the absolute power of the King, even if it has been granted by an absolute monarch. In a deductive inference, the conclusion must not contain anything which contradicts the premises. The idea of a king handing over his sovereign power to the people as if it were a physical object is grounded in purely magical ideas of sovereignty.

Thus, the 'new constitution' is either derived from the old one—and if so, it is not really a new constitution, since the absolute power of the King remains unchanged; or, the new constitution has replaced the previous one—and in that case, it cannot be derived from it. Which of these two interpretations is adequate under the given historic circumstances does not depend on legal-logical considerations, but solely on the prevailing political ideology.

The same applies to the case of the highest presupposed norm requiring a majority of, say, 60 per cent for amending the constitution. If a majority of 60 per cent decides that a majority of 70 per cent will be required in the future, then the new norm (that is, if it should prevail) cannot be regarded as having derived from the old one. For in this case, it must be possible to change the new basic norm by the same manner in which it was created—by a majority of 60 per cent—and thus the original norm requiring a 60 per cent majority would still be the highest norm.

The same applies to the more complicated rules of § 94 of the Constitution.

As mentioned before, I do not mean to deny the social psychological fact that a new '§ 94' will be carried into effect more easily if it is adopted in conformity with the rules of § 94 of the Constitution.

The outcome can be summarized as follows. Every system of enacted law is
[130] necessarily grounded in a basic norm, which constitutes the supreme authority but is not itself enacted by any authority. It exists only as a political ideology, which is a precondition for the system. Any amendment of enacted law by established procedures is only possible within the system whose identity is determined by the basic norm. Every change of the latter, that is, every transition from one system to another, is an extra-systematic phenomenon—a factual, social psychological change within the prevailing political ideology, which

cannot be described as the enactment of law by means of a procedure. At the same time, it is recognized as a social psychological fact that § 94 of the Constitution can hardly be considered as amended unless this happens in the course of a process which appears as if amended within a legal procedure determined by § 94. Political forces are actually dominated by ideas which cannot be expressed rationally but only in magical terms: the procedure laid down in § 94 is the magical act which alone can untie the bonds tied by the very paragraph. This reasoning comes with perhaps one reservation: if it should prove unworkable to amend § 94 in conformity with its own rules, it might be possible to fall back upon an even more fundamental ideology for legitimizing an amendment—namely, the right of the Danish people to form a constitution for themselves at any time.[10]

In his work *The Age of Jackson* (1946), 410, Arthur M. Schlesinger recounts an interesting, albeit unsuccessful attempt to resort to the fundamental constituent power of the people. In the federal state of Rhode Island whose constitution, compared to that of the other federal states, was of a very conservative nature, there arose around 1840, under the leadership of Thomas Wilson Dorr, a popular movement demanding extension of the franchise and other liberal constitutional reforms. Since the conservative government insisted on its exclusive rights, Dorr resorted to the means of appealing to the sovereign power of the people, as being the foundation of all government. In 1841, this strategy resulted in two rival constituent assemblies: one summoned in haste by the government in order to soothe public feeling, and a second one which did not stem from any lawful procedure, but grounded its legitimacy directly in the 'constituent power' of the people. On this basis, two constitutions were seen to evolve. The popular constitution received overwhelming support in a referendum, whereupon Dorr formed a government with himself as governor. However, neither of the two governments was disposed to yield voluntarily. In 1842, the situation escalated into armed rebellion where Dorr drew the short [131]
straw. He fled the state while hundreds of his supporters were imprisoned. When he secretly tried to return the following year, he was immediately caught and brought before the court, where he was sentenced to life imprisonment and penal servitude. In spite of the fiasco of the whole initiative it had strengthened the liberal movement. As early as 1845 Dorr was released from prison, and in 1854 his sentence was quashed.

[10] In their essential features, these views on constitutional amendment can already be found in my book *Theorie der Rechtsquellen* [Theory of the Sources of Law] (1929), ch. XIV, 4. On the basis of these views, I am criticizing those of Jan-Magnus Jansson, *Hans Kelsens statsteori mot bakgrunden av hans rättsfilosofiska åskådning* [Hans Kelsen's Theory of the State against the Background of his System of Legal Philosophy] (1950), 359–60.

§ 17. Precedent

It may be safely assumed that precedents, that is, previous judicial decisions, have always played a very important part in deciding an ongoing lawsuit. The fact that in an earlier case of a similar nature a certain rule was chosen as a basis for decision-making, is a strong motive for the judge to base his present decision on the same rule. Apart from the fact that this saves him time, trouble, and responsibility, this motive is closely tied to the idea of formal justice—something which always seems to have been considered an essential element in the exercise of legal authority: namely, the demand that like cases be treated alike, or that each actual decision be based upon a general rule (see § 68 below for further details).

On the other hand, it is obvious that there may be good reasons to break with former practices. This is especially the case in times of changing social conditions, when there are areas of law where legislation has not yet intervened and brought the law up to date. To attach too much importance to precedent under these circumstances would be regarded as formalism—as an overestimation of the demands of formal justice, at the expense of substantive 'justice'.

As pointed out in § 15, the theory of the sources of law is concerned with the factors that actually influence the behaviour of the judge, because these alone can help us predict his future reactions. Therefore, what is important for the doctrine of the sources of law is solely the motivating role of precedent, not the official doctrine as to whether the judge is permitted to take precedents into account and, if so, whether or not he is 'bound' by them. This doctrine has been subject to considerable variation at different times and in different societies.

In connection with large-scale codifications, the legislator (vainly hoping that his achievement would be preserved thereby) has often issued prohibitions against interpretations of the law and the practice of the courts (building upon these interpretations) as a source of law. As early as Roman times, Justinian
[132] prohibited ruling according to precedent (*non exemplis, sed legibus judicandum est*).[1] Similar prohibitions can be found in the Prussian Civil Code (*Allgemeines Landrecht*) of 1794. Also here in Denmark, after the promulgation of King Christian V's Danish Law [*Danske Lov*], attorneys were forbidden from citing precedents in the Supreme Court.[2] This prohibition was rescinded by Struensee[*] in 1771.[3] Naturally, such drastic prohibitions proved wholly

* Editor's note: Johan Friedrich Struensee (1737–1772) was a German doctor who became the physician of King Christian VII. In 1771 he was appointed Privy Cabinet Minister and enjoyed practically unlimited powers.

1 *Codex Justinianus*, Codex 7, 45, 13.

2 See Andreas Højer, *Juridisk Collegium over Processen* [Lecture on Procedure] (1742), 14.

3 That is, by not reiterating the prohibition in the Supreme Court Instruction of Dec. 7, 1771.

ineffective, and the predominant view on the Continent held that in the interests of legal certainty, the previous decisions of superior courts, in particular the Supreme Court, should be shown considerable respect, but that they—in contrast to statute law—did not possess formally binding force.

Anglo-Saxon doctrine is diametrically opposed to this view.[4] As early as the thirteenth century, the practice of citing previous cases became a general custom, and in his famous *Note Book*, Bracton collected 2,000 legal cases—no doubt for practical use. Initially, however, there was no intention that the judge should be bound by them. The doctrine evolved gradually, taking shape in the seventeenth and eighteenth centuries. However, the lack of a clear court hierarchy as well as the state of the written judgments prevented the doctrine from becoming fully developed before these deficiencies were remedied (in the course of the nineteenth century). Nowadays, the doctrine generally recognized as the doctrine of *stare decisis* can be summarized as follows:

(1) Every court is bound by the decisions of higher courts, and the House of Lords as well as the Court of Appeal are bound by their own decisions.*
(2) Every relevant decision pronounced by a court is a strong argument, entitled to be taken into serious consideration.
(3) A decision is only binding with respect to the *ratio decidendi* of the case.
(4) A precedent does not become obsolete, but very old precedents are usually not applicable to circumstances of modern life.

It is difficult to establish to what extent the Anglo-American doctrine of the 'binding force' of precedent corresponds to English and American judges in their decision-making actually attaching greater importance to precedent than their colleagues on the Continent. You cannot take this for granted by any means.

On the one hand, it is a fact that Anglo-Saxon judges, unhampered by the doctrine of *stare decisis*, widely disregard precedents that are no longer in harmony with altered circumstances. The best proof for that is the fact that the *common law*, developed through the practice of the courts, is no longer the same as it was a hundred years ago. In fact, the common law has adapted, and [133]
is continually adapting. The doctrine of *stare decisis* does not rule this out. What is decisive in assessing this doctrine is not the ideological question of whether or not precedents actually possess 'binding force'; rather, it is a question of whether the doctrine offers criteria sufficiently objective for speaking of a genuine restraint upon the judge's discretion in allowing himself to be motivated by

* Editor's note: the reader is reminded that Ross wrote these lines before the establishment in 2009 of the Supreme Court of the United Kingdom.

[4] See C. K. Allen, *Law in the Making* (1946), 151 f.

previous judicial decisions. And this question must be answered in the negative, especially for the following two reasons.

(a) In the first place, a precedent is considered binding (as mentioned previously) only with respect to the *ratio decidendi*[5] forming the basis of the decision. The *ratio decidendi* is a general legal rule presumed to support the actual decision. When searching for the leading principle, however, the judge is not bound by the possible pronouncements thereon issued by the judge who decided the previous case, but is regarded as entitled to interpret the decision according to his lights.[6] However, it stands to reason that an actual decision might be taken as relating to a large diversity of general rules, depending on which of the accompanying circumstances are considered material. An American author[7] has adduced the following example. Imagine a court's decision according to which a father, who had persuaded his daughter to break her promise of marriage, was not liable to pay any compensation to her former fiancé. This decision might be grounded in a diversity of general rules—for example:

- fathers have a right to induce their daughters to break marriage promises;
- parents have a right to do this;
- parents have a right to do this with regard to daughters as well as sons;
- all persons have a right to do this;
- fathers (parents, all persons) have a right to persuade their daughters (children, all persons) to break any kind of promise, etc., etc.

The combinations are innumerable, depending on the aspects (intent, age, time, place, etc.) deemed relevant. Even though many of these possible interpretations may appear absurd and seemingly transcend anything a
[134] judge might ever think of submitting, it cannot be denied that the judge thereby enjoys considerable freedom to interpret the *ratio decidendi* in such a way that a cited precedent will not stand in the way of the decision which he—for other motives—really wants to make.

Many difficulties arise in any attempt to discover what are the material facts. Thus in Donoghue v. Stevenson[8] *it was decided that a manufacturer*

[5] See C. K. Allen, *op. cit.,* 227 f.; G. W. Paton, *A Text-Book of Jurisprudence* (1946), 159–61.

[6] 'Where case law is considered, and there is no statute, he (the judge) is not bound by the statement of the rule of law made by the prior judge even in the controlling case. The statement is mere dictum, and this means that the judge in the present case may find irrelevant the existence or absence of facts which prior judges thought important. It is not what the prior judge intended that is of any importance; rather it is what the present judge, attempting to see the law as a fairly consistent whole, thinks should be the determining classification', Edward H. Levi, *An Introduction to Legal Reasoning* (1949), 2.

'Any case is an authoritative precedent only for a judge who, as a result of his own reflection, decides that it is authoritative,' Jerome Frank, *Courts on Trial* (1949), 279.

[7] H. Oliphant, 'A Return to Stare Decises' [*sic*], 14 *American Bar Association Journal* (1928), 71 *et seq.*, 159 *et seq.*

[8] (1932) AC 562.

of ginger beer owed a duty of care to the consumer to prevent the remains of decomposed snails from causing gastric trouble. It would have seemed absurd to confine the ratio to ginger beer. But was the rule limited to foodstuffs? Or to things likely to result in danger to life, limb, or health? Was it material that there was no possibility of intermediate examination by the retailer? Or was it enough that the res would reach the consumer subject to the same defect, there being no commercial probability of intermediate examination? Many decisions have been necessary to work out the real meaning of the doctrine. Professor Goodhart suggests that a fact is material unless it is expressly or impliedly held immaterial, but the difficulty is to discover what is implied. In truth we frequently cannot discover for what a case is an authority unless we consider it in relation to prior and subsequent cases. One case, so to speak, plots a point on the graph of tort, but to draw the curve of the law we need a series of points.[9]

(b) In the second place, even though the judge does not want to dispute the *ratio decidendi* of a precedent, he has the possibility to *distinguish*, as they say, the case before him from the earlier one. After all, factual circumstances are never absolutely identical. The judge estimates which of them are relevant, and he can disregard a cited precedent by maintaining that the case before him differs from the earlier one in this or that respect, and in such a way that he is not bound by the precedent.

As a consequence of the above, the doctrine of *stare decisis* is really nothing but an illusion. It is an ideology which is upheld in order to veil, vis-à-vis oneself as well as others, the free, law-creative function of the judge, and to convey the impression that he only applies already existing law that can be determined by virtue of a set of objective rules as given in *stare decisis*.[10]

On the other hand, it is a fact that Continental judges allow themselves to be [135] highly influenced by earlier decisions and only rarely and reluctantly depart from accepted practice, regardless of the circumstance that precedent is not supposed to possess 'binding force'. But here, too, it is difficult to discover what actually happens, partly because precedent is rarely cited in the judge's reasoning, partly because a new conception of law often will not appear as a frankly admitted *overruling* of former practice. If an ideology similar to the Anglo-American ideology has not prevailed on the Continent, it is presumably owing

[9] Quotation from G. W. Paton, *A Text-Book of Jurisprudence* (1946), 160.

[10] Although Allen adheres to the traditional doctrine that the judge is bound by precedents, he admits that it is up to the judge to decide whether or not he is bound under the given circumstances. 'We say that he is bound by the decisions of higher Courts; and so he undoubtedly is. But the superior Court does not impose fetters upon him; he places the fetters on his own hands. He has to decide whether the case cited to him is truly apposite to the circumstances in question and whether it accurately embodies the principle which he is seeking. The humblest judicial officer has to decide for himself whether he is or is not bound, in the particular circumstances, by any given decision of the House of Lords.' C. K. Allen, *Law in the Making* (4th edn, 1946), 247–48.

to the fact that on the Continent legislation plays a far more important role as a source of law. The need to envisage the judge as being bound by a previously laid down and objectively determinable law is met, here, by the doctrine of the absolute 'binding force' of law.

Under these circumstances, one must admit that there is no foundation for a direct comparison of the two systems as regards the part actually played by precedent, as a motivating factor in judicial practice. The only certainty is the ideology that has been avowed, but this ideology tells us nothing about the real situation.

On the other hand, one might point out various factual circumstances which can explain (and explain much better than the promulgated ideology) the difference between the two systems, and which can explain why precedent and legislation have to play different roles within these systems.

First and foremost, there is the role traditionally played by the academic jurist (legal science) and systematic legislation in the historical development of the law. It is precisely at this point that the fundamental difference between the two systems can be found. In the Continental legal tradition, the law is largely an academic product and thus bears a corresponding stamp of academic thinking, with its yearning for systematic analysis and rationality. Firmly grounded in the legal tradition (which naturally constitutes the historical *a priori* of legal science) and in rational considerations, one tries to arrive at general, guiding principles and to systematize the legal material to that effect. Without any academic tradition—without the part played by the law professors from the times of the glossators until the present day—the Continental codifications, whether large-scale or minor, would be unthinkable. In England, on the other hand, it was the legal practitioner in the shape of the judge who would leave his stamp on the development of the law, which consequently developed along the lines of an experimental method. Slowly and gropingly, one tentatively pushes one's
[136] way from one case to another, in order to arrive gradually (as the outcome of a series of decisions which converge, so to speak, upon a guiding idea) at formulating a 'doctrine' as an expression of general principles of law appertaining to the legal field in question. It was in modern times that there first arose a tendency to systematize and generalize the legal material developed in this way. In view of the overwhelming number of precedents which in America simply threatened to burst the libraries, one has resorted to producing a series of *restatements*, that is, codifications in the European style but without official authority. These restatements are the result of collectively produced, extensive scholarly work. Scientific systematizations are playing an ever-increasing role in England as well. Maybe the next stage in the development will be an authoritative codification through legislation. Thereby, the real difference between Continental and Anglo-American law will vanish—in spite of the fact that the doctrine of *stare decisis* continues to exist undisturbed.

It is understandable that the idea of precedents as 'authoritative' sources of law should have had its natural soil in a system where the law has developed through the practice of the courts, legislation playing a subordinate role. But as I said before, it is by no means certain that this corresponds to a proportionally greater bindingness vis-à-vis earlier decisions. On the contrary: one might guess that the Continental judge does not feel as responsible for the development of the law as does his Anglo-American colleague but, rather, tends to leave all attempts at reform to legislation, at least in those spheres of law which are traditionally subject to legislative intervention. This might have the effect that he—contrary to the official ideology— will actually be less inclined to depart from precedent.

Further, the way in which decisions are traditionally drawn up has an important influence on the actual weight attached to precedent. English judgments are remarkable for their broad discussions of the legal views the sentence is based upon. According to the official doctrine, such reasonings are not binding when it comes to interpreting the *ratio decidendi* of the judgment, but they are nevertheless of great consequence. Actually, they offer a wealth of material for guiding a later judge. Continental practice follows very different patterns. However, in so far as there is a tendency to draw up the motivation of the sentence in terms as concrete and non-committal as possible (as is done in Denmark, for example), then the necessary consequence will be that the sentences will to a corresponding degree lose the ability to serve as guiding precedents.

Another factor is the quantity and accessibility of the precedents. Regular recourse to precedent as the basis of the procedure presupposes a whole machinery of analytical registers with excerpts from judicial decisions—a machinery on a scale unknown in Continental Europe. [137]

§ 18. Custom

It is a well-known sociological phenomenon that the life of primitive people is regulated by custom, down to the smallest detail. There are customary norms for hunting, fishing or waging war, for sharing booty, for sexual relations, social intercourse, good manners, the performance of magical and religious ceremonies, etc., etc. Custom is a mode of conduct which is generally followed and experienced as 'binding', and whose infringement arouses reactions in the form of the tribe's disapproval. Originally, these reactions stem from the group as a whole and can assume an immense variety of forms—anything from killing and various forms of physical punishment and expulsion from the tribe, down to the expression of public scorn and ridicule (the singing of diatribes, and the like).[1]

> *As Abraham Tucker observed, 'it is a constant argument among the common people, that a thing must be done, and ought to be done, because it always has been done.' Children show respect for the customary, and so do savages. 'If you ask a Kaffir why he does so and so, he will answer—"How can I tell? It has always been done by our forefathers".' The only reason which the Eskimo can give for some of their present customs, to which they adhere from fear of ill report among their people, is that 'the old Innuits did so, and therefore they must'. In the behaviour of the Aleut, who 'is bashful if caught doing anything unusual among his people', and in the average European's dread of appearing singular, we recognize the influence of the same force of habit.*[2]

Even among very primitive people there is sometimes a chieftain, a group of elders, a council of priests, or some sort of tribunal which, in case of doubt, decides whether sanctions should be applied.[3] This might be seen as the first germ of a 'public authority'. From this, a stable and organized judiciary has been gradually developed, followed by special bodies whose task consists in legislating and carrying out the decisions by means of physical force. In this way, a legal machinery has gradually evolved, as well as a system of public authorities claiming to have a monopoly on the exercise of force. Thus, *law and custom have gradually differentiated themselves*—on the one hand, the norms which are upheld through an organized exercise of force and, on the other, the norms which are merely upheld through spontaneous reactions of a non-violent nature (contempt, ridicule, etc.).

[1] For examples, see Edward Westermarck, *The Origin and Development of the Moral Ideas*, vol. I (1924), 170 f.
[2] Edward Westermarck, *op. cit.*, 159.
[3] *Op. cit.*, 173.

Judicial power always seems to have preceded legislative power. Originally, the judges adjudicated according to the traditional rules of custom. In the course of time and with new situations arising, the judges gave their 'finding' on what was right, that is, the traditional rules were adapted and further developed in the spirit of tradition and under pressure from growing demands. Through the practice of the courts, a tradition of legal notions was gradually formulated and fixated; this tradition was vivid in the consciousness of people—or at least in the consciousness of those who were specifically learned in the law. In the Nordic region, this tradition went under the name of 'the law'. However, this had nothing to do with the modern idea that the law has been created by a lawmaker.[4] [138]

As far as primitive law is concerned, then, the problem is not whether custom is a source of law, and why. Custom is the natural starting point. From the perspective of historical evolution, on the other hand, the rise of legislative power is a big problem: how could the ideology arise and become consolidated that certain persons had authority to issue new norms—norms which were accepted as 'valid'[5] by the judiciary and the people? This problem turns on the origin of political ideology. It is a task for the sociology of law, not for the philosophy of law, to deal with it. We take the rise of legislative power to be an accepted fact.

It may be assumed that originally, legislation consisted to a large extent of codified law already in force. Only gradually did it become an instrument of social policy for the deliberate and purposive regulation of community life. While custom originally determined the law, the law, in the course of time, showed an ever-stronger tendency to determine custom. It is understandable, however, that the legislator's power of influencing the development of the law was limited. When the gap between the law and legal notions that had been passed down from generation to generation became too wide, the law—unable to entice the legal consciousness to follow—became a mere dead letter.

As the law became more fixated through legislation and the practice of the courts, custom as a source of law came to play a progressively lesser role. Nowadays, custom is of only minor importance, but sometimes courts still resort to norms derived from an actual customary pattern of behaviour.

At this point a problem arises which has played, and is still playing, a certain role in the history of legal philosophy which is out of all proportion when compared with the role played by custom (at least within modern legal communities), for it is obvious that not every custom can be regarded as a source of

[4] Cf. Poul Joh. Jørgensen, *Dansk Retshistorie* [Danish Legal History] (1940), 16.

[5] 'American Indians sometimes say: "In the old days, there were no fights about hunting grounds or fishing territories. There was no law then, so everybody did what was right!" The phrasing makes it clear that in their old life they did not think of themselves as submitted to a social control imposed upon them from without', Ruth Benedict, *Patterns of Culture* (New York: Mentor Books, 1946), 233.

[139] law. Only *legal custom* is a source of law, they say, and legal custom is characterized by a particular, subjective aspect based on experience; an aspect which, in theory, goes under the name of *opinio necessitatis sive obligationis*—that is, a feeling of being bound, or a conviction that the behaviour demanded by custom is (legally) binding, too.

This explanation is hardly tenable, however. Every custom—even the custom that prompts me to appear in suitable attire—is felt to be binding in itself, and patterns of behaviour which defy custom are experienced as something which is resented. It is precisely because of this feeling and this reaction that custom is distinct from mere habit, from convention, and from use. The specific conviction which is said to characterize legal custom cannot be a conviction that the courts will use it as a basis for their decisions, either. After all, a conviction like this must be justified by the custom in question clearly distinguishing itself from other customs. There must be something that justifies that the conviction has arisen in regard to this particular custom, not in regard to any other custom. The conviction of the legal character of the custom must necessarily derive from an objective criterion, and can no more define legal custom than we can define lead as the substance which is usually regarded as lead.

Rather, the explanation must be sought pursuant to our schematic outline above of the historical development of the law. Originally, all matters of life were equally subjected to an unorganized regulation through custom. However, the gradual differentiation of a legal order based on the use of physical force has led to a division in those matters of life. Many areas of life were subjected to regulation through law, whereas other areas, where the means of physical coercion were not thought necessary, were left to convention, the corresponding sanctions being limited to non-violent means of exerting pressure. *A legal custom is simply a custom in an area of life which is subject to legal regulation.* This theory explains, firstly, why the judge has a good reason to take precisely these customs into consideration; and, secondly, why this behaviour on the part of the judge is anticipated by those who practise the custom. At the same time, the *opinio necessitatis* characterizing every custom is bound up with the awareness that some kind of disapproving reaction must be expected by those who violate the custom. If it is a question of a matter of life subject to regulation through law, this awareness has taken the form that those who behave in defiance of social norms must expect legal sanctions if the matter is brought before the courts. Thus, the general feeling of being bound (*opinio necessitatis*) is combined in this field with an expectation or an assumption which may well be called a conviction of law.

A certain Norwegian decision concerns a case where the owner of a small farm in Trysil claimed that according to a local custom in those parts, smallholders
[140] had the right to collect dead wood in forests belonging to someone else. Such a

custom was not found to exist, but if this had been so, it would have been a clear case of a legal custom because property relations are governed by law.[6]

The timber industry has developed the custom that payment made within thirty days from the invoice date shall be regarded as cash payment. This is a legal custom because the issue of prompt payment is subject to regulation by law. It is the same with other kinds of trade usage concerning commercial relationships.

On the other hand, the custom prompting me to wear my gown at the annual academic celebration of the university is not a legal custom, since matters of dress (within the limits of decency) are not usually governed by law. (A distinct *opinio necessitatis sive obligationis* is nevertheless bound up with this custom!) In exceptional cases, however, where the matter of dress is governed by law (as is the case with uniforms), legal customs may arise within this particular sphere—such as, for example, with respect to Act no. 140, dated 30 March 1940 (now expired) concerning the prohibition on wearing uniforms.

Within a well-developed legal system where the differentiation between law and convention may be considered as brought to completion, there is usually no doubt which customs can be regarded as sources of law. What can be doubtful—especially with respect to commercial practice, for instance—is the issue of whether or not a custom exists, that is, an order by which people feel bound, and whose violation generally earns disapproval; or whether there merely exists a habit without any normative character, conditioned by technical expediency or other external circumstances. Surely most of us switch on the light when it gets dark and put on warm clothing when the weather is cold, but we do this without feeling bound by a custom, and nobody acting differently would meet with social disapproval. However, the distinction between custom and habit is not always clear. It can be difficult to decide, for example, whether regularly given discounts, certain services or similar benefits are merely *ex gratia* payments, that is, usual methods of competition, or whether they constitute a custom.

On the other hand, this explanation of the distinction between legal custom and other types of custom does not apply to undeveloped legal systems, since it is not possible to draw a sharp line between the areas of life regulated by law and those which are not. However, this must simply be taken to mean that under these circumstances, one cannot draw a sharp line between legal custom and other types of custom, either. The situation is still under development, and it is precisely a task for the judge (and the legislator) to decide which customs are to be transformed into law and which not. This still applies to the greater

[6] *Retstidende* [Legal News] 1918 II, 261, mentioned in P. Augdahl, *Forelesninger over Rettskilder* [Lectures on the Sources of Law] (1949), 238.

part of international law. There, part of custom is still of an unspecified nature,
[141] which is to say that it is difficult to decide whether it will be accepted as law or merely considered as part of the *comitas gentium*. Many customs in diplomatic practice as well as customs which have to do with the signs of respect vis-à-vis another state are of this kind, and only future case law or codification will be able to decide the issue.

Let us return to the modern state. From what has been said above, it will emerge that a legal custom is an indication of the fact that otherwise duly promulgated law is, in certain situations, actually not observed by larger or smaller sections of the population. A certain area of life may be subjected to regulation by law, but in certain other respects, the people nonetheless follow a norm that departs from it. General property rights may, for example, be overridden by a (local) custom which authorizes the appropriation of dead wood in a forest belonging to someone else. It is easy to see that such a state of affairs can motivate the judge, when making his decision, to take this custom into account. A decision made on this basis will best agree with the attitudes and expectations of the parties in the case and will, therefore, be felt to be right and proper. It will strengthen confidence in the courts as well as legal certainty, such as it is experienced by the layman; that is, the feeling that the decision is in line with the expectations of the common sense of justice.[7] On the other hand, it may also happen that, in the judge's view, the custom in question contradicts fundamental legal principles in such a way that he refuses to accept it.

The essential aspect of custom—the aspect that explains why the judge takes account of it—is *the psychological moment*, the feeling of being bound, or the validity with which the customary behaviour is experienced and which (since it is about an area of life subject to regulation by law) might well be called legal consciousness. The outward pattern of behaviour, on the other hand, is only important as a conclusive outward sign and a proof that such an attitude, in fact, exists, with such earnestness and strength that it is capable of prevailing, effectively, among a certain group of people. Seen in this light, the judge has no reason to demand that the custom shall have been observed for a certain length of time, as long as the existing circumstances afford sufficient grounds for holding that a legal conviction of a certain stability has come to prevail. When the demands placed upon the outward pattern of behaviour and the time factor have lessened, custom as a source of law leads imperceptibly to situations where the judge is motivated by another legal conception in the community, even though it may not have found expression in any custom.

> *If this is the case, however, one has to examine whether a prevalent pattern of behaviour and the lapse of time really are factors as important for the*

[7] Legal certainty, in the professional sense of the term, means the certainty (degree of probability) with which the expert jurist can precalculate the reactions of the court.

development of law as is assumed by the doctrine of legal custom as a source of law. And the answer must surely be in the negative. The Royal Decree dated March 21st, 1800, included the prohibition of strikes and lockouts which, of course, was held to be part of scientifically valid law. As far as we know, the provision has never been applied by the courts, and long before strikes and lockouts were provided with a legal basis by the law of the Permanent Court of Arbitration in 1910, the prohibition (which never had been formally repealed) was assumed to have become extinct due to desuetude. According to the general conception of legal custom, it would then have been the frequent occurrence of strikes during the seventies and eighties [i.e., the 1870s and 1880s] in combination with the passivity of the authorities, which was the reason for the provision being dropped. Reality tells another tale, however. As far as we know, in 1851 there was an opportunity to apply the provision for the first time, namely in connection with a strike among bricklayers. The authorities arrested three journeymen but had to release them again, due to the pressure of public opinion. Also, the authorities abstained from bringing a charge against the men. After this episode, the validity of the provision was no longer relied on.[8] [142]

As far as customs in connection with contracts are concerned, the courts are usually not at all interested in their age. In the journal Retstidende *[Legal News] 1919, 819, there is a striking example. A fishing-boat, which under extremely precarious conditions had taken in tow a colleague's boat with engine trouble and pulled it out of the ice-covered sea, was denied salvage money in conformity with 'a custom observed in the polar seas, according to which taking in tow was frequently done as a service among friends, neither party assuming or expecting any remuneration'. The cited passage is taken from the reasonings of the maritime court in Tromsø; any more detailed information about this custom was not available to the Supreme Court. Above all, there was no information about the age of this custom. The custom was nevertheless considered relevant—albeit contrary to the law (only to a non-mandatory law, to be sure).*

If a custom exists that taking a vessel in tow in ice-covered seas is done gratuitously, then it stands to reason that this custom is deemed relevant irrespective of age, if the skipper of the towing vessel knew about it and yet did not indicate any reservation to the contrary. The circumstance that skippers in the polar seas would know about such a custom as soon as it arose would naturally be the main rule, outweighing everything else. In the present case, the skipper duly asserted that he was ignorant of the custom. There is no reason, though, to pay attention to this assertion. If 'ignorance of the law' must be clearly proven, the proof will almost always fail; and if

[8] Knud Illum, *Lov og Ret* [Law and Justice] (1945), 109–10.

> *the opposite must be clearly proven, this will turn out to be just as impossible. Thus, a rule ascribing relevance to ignorance would here*
[143] *amount to an extraordinarily strong temptation for the skipper to lie and deny a knowledge he actually possessed.*[9]

Similar to the English doctrine of precedent, the traditional doctrine of customary law purports to establish the objective conditions under which the judge is bound by custom. From the times of the evolution of this doctrine in Roman-canonist theory, from the twelfth to the sixteenth century (the glossators) down to the present day, the details of the formulation of these conditions have certainly varied somewhat, but the underlying idea has always been the same, namely, that it is possible to lay down *objective criteria* for determining when a custom is 'binding'. According to Danish doctrine, the usual requirement is that the custom has been practised 'generally, continually, for a long time, and in the firm conviction that one was legally obligated to do so (*ex opinione obligationis*)'.[10] With respect to English law, Allen formulates the conditions as follows.[11] Custom:

(1) shall be *immemorial*, that is, it shall have existed since 1189. If the custom has existed for a long time, it is presumed to have existed since that date;
(2) shall have been practised continually;
(3) shall have been practised *peaceably* and *nec clam nec precario*;
(4) shall have been practised on the basis of *opinione necessitatis*;
(5) shall have a definite content; and
(6) shall be *reasonable*, which *inter alia* implies that it must not contradict the fundamental principles of Common Law and Statute Law.

According to Allen, it is the judge's duty to declare the custom valid law if it can be proven that these conditions have been fulfilled. Also this doctrine is an ideology, whose function is the concealing of the freedom and law-creating activity of the judge. It is obvious that the conditions under (4) and (6) in particular are of such a kind as to allow the judge a very wide scope for exercising judicial discretion.

However, in one particular area it was evident that the traditional, mechanical doctrine of customary law would fail. Customs within contractual relationships—especially commercial customs, the so-called trade usages—usually do not meet the demands of a legal custom. Moreover, they are frequently not very old.

[9] Per Augdahl, *Forelesninger over Rettskilder* [Lectures on the Sources of Law] (1949), 229–30.

[10] Viggo Bentzon, *Retskilderne* [The Sources of Law] (1900-1907), 84, cf. Goos, *Forelæsninger over den almindelige Retslære* [Lectures on the General Study of Law], vol. I (1885), 119 f.; A. W. Scheel, *Privatrettens almindelige Deel* [The General Part of Private Law] (1865), 1564 f.

[11] C. K. Allen, *Law in the Making* (4th edn, 1946), 127 f.

Nonetheless it is imperative, and a general legal practice as well, to take them into account when establishing the legal relationship of the parties. This circumstance has compelled the prevailing theory to offer a construction which is theoretically untenable and has led to unacceptable practical consequences.[12] [144]

To avoid the problem, this theory teaches that trade usages are not part of legal custom; that they are not objective law at all[13]—merely tools for contract interpreting and gap filling.[14]

This theory is untenable because it assumes that the tools used for contract interpretation and gap filling cannot, in themselves, be scientifically valid law. This is obviously not correct. Conversely, one has to deprive all declaratory legal rules—a large part of the Sale of Goods Act, for example—of the character of scientifically valid law; a conclusion which the authors of this theory do not wish to draw.

In addition, attempts have been made to draw various practical conclusions from this idea of the fundamental distinction between legal custom and trade usage.

First, it has been argued that whereas the judge is bound by legal custom, he is not bound by trade usage, thus being able to accept or reject it according to his own discretionary assessment, whether it deserves the approbation of the legal order.[15] It emerges from the preceding pages that it is impossible to make such a distinction, because the judge will always refuse to accept a custom which contradicts fundamental legal principles. At best, it can be said that the judge will disregard a recently formed trade usage he disapproves of with greater speed and fewer scruples than he would break with a time-honoured custom. It is obvious, however, that the boundary is rather vague and unable to motivate any fundamental distinction between legal custom and trade usage.

Secondly, it has been argued that trade usage can be considered only in so far as the parties to the legal relationship have any knowledge of it, whereas legal custom and declaratory legal rules (such as objective law) are scientifically valid without this underlying condition. Although it is not totally irrelevant that the

[12] In connection with the following, cf. Per Augdahl, *Forelesninger over Rettskilder* [Lectures on the Sources of Law] (1949), 251 f. and Henry Ussing, *Aftaler paa Formuerettens Omraade* [Contracts in the Field of Property Law], § 39, V, with references.

[13] Cf. § 20 below, where it is mentioned that according to traditional theory, legal custom is most frequently seen as objectively valid law in itself.

[14] It seems that the theory was first put forward by Laband in Levin Goldschmidt's *Zeitschrift für das gesamte Handelsrecht* [Journal of Commercial Law] Vol. 17 (1893), 466 f. It has been accepted (in a somewhat unusual variant) by, e.g., Ragnar Knoph, *Rettslige Standarder* [Legal Standards] (1939), 12–13; Julius Lassen, *Haandbog i Obligationsrettens almindelige Del* [Handbook on the Law of Obligation—General Part] § 39, II, 1; L. A. Grundtvig, *Om Reklamation i formueretsforhold* [On Complaints in Matters Pertaining to Property] (1903), 47 f.

[15] Thus, e.g., R. Knoph, 'Nogen Ord om Dommerens Stilling til Kutymen' [A few words on the judge's views on trade usage], *UfR* 1923 B, 177 f., 190.

parties know about a certain trade usage (or custom), this position is not recognized, neither in practice nor by the prevailing theory.[16] The significance that may be ascribed to the parties' knowledge of the custom is not tied to the age of the custom.

Finally, in so far as one differentiates procedurally between *factum* and *jus*, one
[145] has arrived at the conclusion that legal custom shall be treated according to the rules on *jus* and trade usage according to the rules on *factum*. A procedural differentiation of this kind may appear in two relationships—partly with respect to appeal, partly with respect to evidence. Without entering more closely into these rather complicated issues, I shall content myself with merely observing that not even in this respect is there any reason to draw a distinction between legal custom and trade usage.

[16] See Henry Ussing, *Aftaler paa Formuerettens Omraade* [Contracts in the Field of Property Law], § 39, V, at note 81, with references.

§ 19. *Cultural Tradition ('The Nature of the Matter')*

In the previous section, we discussed how law, having originally emerged from tribal customs, was eventually fixated through decisions of courts and through legislation. Law created in this way is called positive law—a term which indicates that the law exists in the form of objectively fixated norms. Positivization is most noticeable in enacted law, that is, in law which has found authoritative verbal formulation by statute. However, case law also possesses a high degree of positivity (even without any clear verbal formulation), provided that there is an established practice of long standing.

Enacted law is of course no arbitrary *fiat* issued by the legislator. His power is a power over men's minds, rooted in the institutional legal consciousness (§ 11). However, there is a limit to the gap between loyal respect for statute law and the perception of substantive validity, embedded in the people's traditional customs and the cultural tradition behind these customs.

Popular custom is not the ultimate source but is, as such, the manifestation of an even deeper well. In every people, there is a common *cultural tradition* animating all manifest forms of that people's life—its customs and its legal, religious, and social institutions. It is hard to find the appropriate words to describe the nature of this tradition. We usually speak of a set of evaluations, but this expression is misleading in so far as it suggests systematically formulated objectives and principles of action. It is much more likely that there exists, in the shape of myths, religion, poetry, philosophy, and art, a spirit which expresses an attitude to life, which is an intimate combination of what can be discerned, in an abstract analysis, as evaluations (attitudes, cf. § 70) and a theoretical worldview, respectively, including a more or less primitive social theory. It would be highly misleading, however, to transfer this abstraction to reality, and to conceive of a cultural tradition as being composed partly of evaluating attitudes, partly of a theoretical conception of reality. *Myths* are beliefs about the creation of the world and its nature; about the power of the gods and their lives; about the [146]
origin of the people and their history, destiny, and mission; about the fight between good and evil; about the origin of life and its meaning; and about the lot of mankind in relation to the gods and to nature. *Religion*, *philosophy*, *poetry*, and *art* are in various forms concerned with the same subjects. And all of them are in equal measure expressions of ideals, of practical and evaluating attitudes to life, and of theoretical beliefs held to be true. The concept of 'belief' contains precisely this duality. Belief is a theoretical conviction whose chief function is to allow an evaluating attitude to life to express itself. The attempt to draw a distinction between non-evaluating knowledge and an evaluating attitude, which is the guiding principle of science, is a late product, accomplished within a

particular cultural sphere cultivated by a small group of specialists, and frequently without much success.

This cultural tradition is not unalterable. The driving force in its development would seem to be an insight of a more or less scientific kind, slowly evolving out of experience. This conditions, on the one hand, a change of technology in all matters of life—methods of production, methods of warfare, political and administrative methods, and so forth; and, on the other hand, it conditions a critical revision of fundamental myth; and both of them influence cultural traditions.

I have drawn attention to these basic facts (which are better and more thoroughly described in sociological studies of culture[1]) in order to make it clear how unrealistic the narrower juridical positivism is—in its zeal to limit the law to positivized norms, and believing that the activity of the judge merely consists in mechanically applying them. Positivized norms can be compared to crystals which have sedimented in a saturated solution and continue to be sustained by that solution, and which would be broken down if they were put in a different fluid. Also, we might compare them to plants that die because they have been taken away from the nourishing soil from which they have grown. Legal norms cannot be understood in isolation from the cultural milieu that has given birth to them; nor can any other objective manifestation of culture. The law is tied to our language as a carrier of meaning, and the meaning that attaches to the words of the law is in a thousand ways conditioned by tacit assumptions along the lines of those beliefs and prejudices, aspirations, objectives, and evaluations which are embedded in our cultural tradition, surrounding legislator and judge alike.

The fact that the judge, in pursuance of his vocation, is under the influence of our cultural tradition, is simply the result of his being a human being made up of flesh and blood and not an automaton; or, rather, of his being not merely a biological, but also a cultural phenomenon. He looks upon his activity as a
[147] societal task. He wants to arrive at a decision that shall not be the fortuitous result of a mechanical manipulation of facts and paragraphs, but something that has purpose and meaning, something that is 'valid'. Cultural tradition becomes important here, mainly because it represents the spirit in which the judge reads and interprets the law. (This side of the matter will be followed up in more detail in the subsequent chapter on interpretation.) However, our cultural tradition can also function as a direct 'source of law', that is to say, it may constitute the basic material inspiring the judge to formulate the rule on which he bases his decision.

[1] See, e.g., Ruth Benedict, *Patterns of Culture* (1934). On the concept of myth, see R. M. MacIver, *The Web of Government* (1947), 3f., cf. 447 f.

Sometimes, a situation will arise where the judge, among the positivized sources, cannot find the rule that might serve as the basis for his decision. In this situation, he can always acquit the defendant on the basis that 'there is no legal ground' for the claim of the plaintiff. This would be the most likely outcome if A, for example, brought an action against his neighbour B so as to obtain an order against him to remove a statue which B has put up in his garden, the poor artistic quality of the statue being an eyesore to A, who could see it from his windows. It is not certain, however, that the outcome would be the same if A were to claim that B should be ordered to halt his noisy or malodorous activities. Circumstances may be such that a negative outcome might appear unsatisfactory to the judge, since the result would not conform to an evaluation of the situation that was done in harmony with the attitudes and views which are embedded in the traditional legal and cultural tradition, and which determine the judge's emotional reaction to the case put before him. He cannot approve of dismissing the plaintiff with the pronouncement that 'there is no authority' for his claim. The non-existence of any legal ground is felt as a defect, as a shortcoming in legislation, as a 'gap' in the law, to be filled in by the judge. He will do so in the following way: making a decision (which he can approve of) in the case immediately before him, he will, at the same time, attempt to justify his decision by emphasizing those points in the real subject matter which seem relevant to him. Thus, inspired by the fundamental ideas of our legal and cultural tradition, the judge will formulate—tentatively, so to speak—a general legal rule. Through a number of decisions concerning similar circumstances the outlines will gradually become fixed, and a judge-made law of precedent will come into being.

Thus paving the way for new law, the judge may either allow himself to be guided directly by his sense of justice or try to rationalize his reaction through an analysis of policy considerations on the basis of a legal-sociological calculation of the effects, which one general rule or the other may be supposed to have. Also in the latter case, however, the decision will stem from an evaluating deliberation, based upon the assumptions inherent in our legal and cultural tradition. What we call 'policy considerations' is a fusion of a conception of reality and an evaluating attitude; for details, cf. § 83 below.

However, it must be assumed that in most cases lack of time will prevent the [148]
judge from entering more deeply into theoretical studies of the social conditions which are implied in the question of law he has to decide. Left to his own resources, the judge, in the main, has to trust his instinct. In this respect, however, it is possible that doctrine may provide practice with valuable support: in *de sententia ferenda* reasonings, it is precisely a task for doctrine to collect and systematize those insights into, and evaluations of, social facts and contexts which might be of value to the further development of the law through case law.

Thus, positivism must be rejected because of this lack of understanding vis-à-vis the influence exerted by the cultural atmosphere over the application of law, and because of the view that there are no sources apart from the positivized ones. On the other hand, one must just as firmly reject the current anti-positivist attitude which interprets the supra-positive basis of the positivized norms in metaphysical terms, that is, as natural law, grounded in *a priori* reasoning. At this juncture, it will suffice to refer to § 13 and to Chapter XI. The term 'positivism' is ambiguous. It can mean both 'what is building on experience' and 'what has formally been enacted'. The reaction against positivism (which seems to be a dominant feature of modern legal philosophy) is well founded with respect to the latter meaning but not to the former. A realistic doctrine of the sources of law builds on experience, but recognizes that not all law is positive in the sense of having been 'formally enacted'.

In the traditional Danish terminology concerning the sources of law, the source implying that the judge should allow himself to be motivated by our cultural tradition (possibly together with a legal-sociological analysis of the contexts of the case) is called 'the nature of the matter' ['*forholdets natur*']. This expression is undoubtedly encumbered by natural law. However, as soon as we have realized the true nature of the circumstances in question, there is actually no reason to make objections against it.

§ 20. *The Various Sources in relation to 'Scientifically Valid Law' and Legal Practice*

Usually it is assumed as a matter of course that any duly promulgated statute is scientifically valid law in itself, that is, valid independently of subsequent application by the courts. On the other hand, there are probably very few people who think that what may be derived from 'the nature of the matter' thereby should acquire the nature of scientifically valid law. In that case, it is only recognition through the courts which endows the product of the source with [149] this nature. With respect to custom, opinion has been sharply divided. The traditional, mechanical doctrine of customary law assumes that custom, if it fulfils the requirements for recognition as a legal custom, is law in itself, in the same way as a statute is law. Others, however, think that custom does not become law unless it is formulated authoritatively and recognized by the courts.[1] Through this recognition custom acquires a new status—something merely factual has been transformed into scientifically valid law. When it comes to precedent, the issue does not arise in Continental law, since precedents are not recognized as a legal source proper (in the metaphysical sense) on the Continent. In Anglo-American law, by contrast, one surely assumes in general that precedents are scientifically valid in themselves.

These issues are usually treated according to the following pattern: to what extent is law already created through the source itself (through legislation, through custom, through precedent, through the nature of the matter), and to what extent is law created by the judge?

Hopefully, it is easy to understand—in light of our analysis of the concept 'scientifically valid law' (§§ 8–10)—that what is discussed here in substantial terms as if it were a question of creating a material product, concerns in reality the *degree of probability* with which the motivating influence of a source upon the judge can be predicted.

Considering legislation as law means that we can predict, consistently and with a degree of probability bordering on certainty, that it will be accepted by the judge. Conversely, the propositions derived from 'the nature of the matter' are not directly considered as law in themselves, because here we can do no more than guess how the courts will react. The controversy concerning the metamorphosis of custom into law reflects the fact that in spite of objective

[1] After Austin, this is the prevailing doctrine in English theory. In France, the same view is held by Lambert, and in Germany, by a small minority of writers, cf. the overview of the literature on customary law in Alf Ross, *Theorie der Rechtsquellen* [Theory of the Sources of Law] (1929), 435 f.

elements to support a prognosis, there is, at the same time, also considerable scope for the judge's discretion to decide whether to accept or reject the custom.

It must be emphasized that it is, here, a question of difference in degree. According to circumstances, even a statute may be disregarded by the judge. This view prompted Gray to deny that the statute, as such, is law. According to Gray, it is only a motivating factor, only an attempt to create law, and we do not know what the outcome of the attempt will be until we know whether the courts will accept the statute and how they will interpret it. Therefore, Gray maintained that law consists only of the rules applied by the courts, and that hence all law is judge-made law.[2] On closer inspection, however, this view is quite inconsistent. Precisely what rules are 'applied in practice' emerges from previous court decisions. This means, then, that Gray refers to precedents as the
[150] source which creates law in itself. As I see it, however, the point of view taken by Gray towards the statute as a source can just as well be applied to precedents as a source. These, too, are nothing but motivating factors, and we do not know for certain how they will influence future legal decisions. In short, if a rule is to be recognized as scientifically valid law only under the condition that one can say with certainty that the courts will apply it in future, then no rule can ever be recognized as scientifically valid law. This conclusion was drawn by Jerome Frank as well as other American realists when they pointed out that law does not consist of rules but, rather, of the sum total of actual judicial decisions.

[2] John Chipman Gray, *The Nature and Sources of the Law* (1909), 84, 125 *et passim*, cf. § 14 note 8 above, and Alf Ross, *Towards a Realistic Jurisprudence* (1946), 59 *et seq.*

§ 21. *The Doctrine of the Sources of Law*

In the preceding section, we characterized various types of sources of law which—as experience has shown—can be found in all well-developed legal systems; indeed, a proper task for a general theory of the sources of law. It is a task for the doctrine of the sources of law, as part of the doctrinal study of law, to provide a more detailed description of each of the sources and their relative importance within a specific legal system.

Such a description is of particular importance when it comes to *legislation* (in the widest sense) as a source. In all modern legal systems, there is a well-developed set of norms concerning the various modes of procedure for the laying down of formulated law (procedural rules for the constitution, for legislation, for ordinances, for contracts, etc.); norms concerning the reciprocal relation between the various levels of enacted law, the promulgation and coming into force of statutes, the delegation of legislative power, invalidity, judicial review, and so on. All of these topics are elements within the doctrine of the sources of law, even if they are not normally collected systematically under this heading, but are part of constitutional law, administrative law, and contract law.

On the other hand, it is hardly possible to develop in a similar manner a doctrine of the sources of law with respect to *non-posited law*, since it emerges from the aforesaid that with regard to custom, precedent, and 'the nature of the matter', one cannot indicate objective conditions for their motivating influence. Common attempts to set forth such conditions are, in reality, mere ideological [151] rationalizations, purporting to maintain the fiction that the judge only applies objectively existing law. In this respect, therefore, the doctrine of the sources of law must restrict itself to pointing out the more or less important role that is actually played by various sources within a given legal system.

Circumstances may vary considerably in this respect. While legislation is definitely predominant in Continental law, Anglo-American law continues to be primarily based upon precedent, although there is a growing tendency to systematize and perhaps even codify the case law. In primitive law, custom is the primary source (as it still is in international law), albeit with a growing tendency towards stabilization through precedents as well as codification. 'The nature of the matter'—that is, that production of law which, without any objectification, directly reaches back to basic cultural attitudes, evaluations, and objectives—manifests itself especially in the period immediately following a revolutionary upheaval. Until the victors have succeeded in revising and recasting the enacted law in the spirit of the revolution, the judge will be required to let himself be inspired directly, and as much as possible, by the social mythology and philosophy of the new regime. After the Bolshevik revolution, the philosophy of Marx and 'the revolutionary consciousness of the working class' would play the part of supreme source of law, in the same manner as was done by the Führer ideology and Hitler's 'Mein Kampf' in Germany after the Nazi revolution. As the situation gradually stabilizes and reverts back to normal, this tendency yields to greater respect vis-à-vis enacted law.

§ 22. Confrontation

As has been pointed out in § 15, a realistic doctrine of the sources of law must be a doctrine concerning the ideology which actually animates the courts and motivates them in their search for the norms to be taken as the basis of their decisions. Therefore, this ideology must be discovered by studying the actual pattern of behaviour of the courts.

It is generally believed, however, that the doctrine of the sources of law is *normative, not descriptive* (or to put it more precisely: norm-expressive, not norm-descriptive). The presumed purpose of the doctrine is to prescribe, for the judge, how he is in duty bound to act—not, to describe how he, in fact, does act. But what kind of duty is this, and from what kind of binding norms is it derived?

It seems unlikely that the duty referred to should be meant as a (mere) moral [152] duty: in that case, the doctrine of the sources of law would turn into moral philosophy, and its contents would become a matter of conscience. This cannot be right.

It seems equally unlikely, however, to conceive of the duty as a legal duty for the judge in the same sense as, for example, a debtor is duty bound to pay his debts, or a citizen to obey the Penal Code. For a legal duty like that would, as such, have to stem from a legal rule which, in turn, derives from a legal source. In order to determine what is a source of law, we should thus have to presuppose a knowledge of the sources of law, something which obviously constitutes a vicious circle. This circle becomes clearly visible when the doctrine of the sources of law nonetheless from time to time is further developed, through the interpretation of positive provisions—such as, for example, the Swiss Civil Code, Article 1, or Article 38 of the Statute of the International Court of Justice.[1] In those instances, it is assumed that enacted law and treaty law, respectively, are binding upon the courts, and this is precisely a constituent part of the doctrine of the sources of law which is supposed to be derived from the provisions in question.

In principle, the same applies to the situation (and sometimes this happens) where the doctrine of the sources of law has developed, not on the basis of statute but with the support of what is called 'the nature of the matter', that is

[1] Thus, e.g., Max Gmür, *Die Anwendung des Rechts nach Art. 1 des schweizerischen Zivilgesetzbuches* [The Application of the Law Pursuant to Article 1 of the Swiss Civil Code] (1908); Erich Danz, *Einführung in die Rechtssprechung* [Introduction to the Administration of Justice] (1912); and Géza Kiss, 'Gesetzesauslegung und "ungeschriebenes Recht"' [Statutory interpretation and 'unwritten law'], *Iherings Jahrbücher* vol. 58 (1911), and 'Theorie der Rechtsquellen in der anglo-amerikanischen Literatur' [Theory of the sources of law in Anglo-American legal literature], *Archiv für bürgerliches Recht*, vol. 39 (1913); for details, see Alf Ross, *Theorie der Rechtsquellen* [Theory of the Sources of Law] (1929), 321–22 incl. note 14. The method commonly used in presentations of the sources of international law is the positive-law method.

to say, on a basis of free evaluations as to what method of procedure can be recommended as being the most expedient in view of various considerations.[2] Furthermore, it should be noted that however interesting and well founded those evaluative recommendations may be, they are nonetheless totally irrelevant to establishing what is scientifically valid law if the courts do not, in fact, act in accordance with those views. An example taken from modern Nordic theory is Per Augdahl, who declares that he means to develop rules which, in his view, provide the courts with the best guidelines for dealing with enacted law, custom, precedent, and so on.[3] Very well, then: now we know professor Augdahl's view on these matters. However—and with all due respect to him—this view, as such, does not tell us how the Norwegian courts look upon these issues, and we must be clear about that on this basis, the whole work is useless to someone who wants to establish what is scientifically valid Norwegian law, in the sense of being able to predict the reactions of the courts. Not surprisingly, however, a more detailed study of Augdahl's work reveals that his
[153] evaluations of what is right and proper have a strong tendency to adapt to the views actually prevalent in Norwegian practice. Why does Augdahl consider enacted law, but not precedent (for example) as the principal source of law? There is no discussion on the relative merits of different systems, but the author has evidently accepted the situation in Norway—as opposed to that in England—as a fact. In this way, Augdahl's account is nevertheless useful as a Norwegian doctrine of the sources of law, that is, in so far as it is in reality, and contrary to his own methodological manifesto, a description of the actual pattern of behaviour of the Norwegian courts.

However, the normative doctrine of the sources of law often refers neither to a duty of positive law nor to a duty based on 'the nature of the matter'. In accordance with the presuppositions of idealistic jurisprudence, the idea is that *the law itself possesses an inherent, supra-empirical validity or binding force, and the source of law is precisely the factor which this validity depends on.* That something is a source of law, and that it is the duty of the judge to apply it is, therefore, one and the same thing. There is thus no presupposition of any norm, distinct from the source of law itself, which would obligate the judge to follow the source. The duty of the judge is merely another expression of the idea that the law itself—that is, independently from any physical sanctions—possesses 'binding force' or supra-empirical validity.

If this line of thought is pursued, a plurality of sources of law is an impossibility.[4] The unity of the concept of law would be destroyed if one were to assume, on

[2] A typical case is Philipp Heck, *Gesetzesauslegung und Interessenjurisprudenz* [Statutory Interpretation and the Jurisprudence of Interests] (1914); for details, see Alf Ross, *Theorie der Rechtsquellen* [Theory of the Sources of Law] (1929), ch. XIII, 2 (with several examples).

[3] Per Augdahl, *Forelesninger over Rettskilder* [Lectures on the Sources of Law] (1949), 34 cf. 22.

[4] 'Whenever the plurality of the sources of law is at issue, then it is this difference between the sources of the valid legal norms' contents which ought to be kept in mind. It does not only have a natural, linguistic basis, but

the one hand, that statutory law is 'valid' because it has been enacted by an authority with the power to command and, on the other, that custom is 'binding' because it emerges from the legal consciousness of the subjects. According to one's conception of the 'validity' of the law, there has to be a single source of the binding force, and all other sources must be regarded as derivative in relation to it.

The traditional doctrine of the sources of law consists chiefly in such speculations, namely, as to whence the different sources derive their 'binding force'; what, in the last analysis, is the *supreme source* of all 'legal validity'; and, consequently, what conclusions as to the strength of the various sources can be drawn from this—whether, for example, a custom can abrogate a statute, whether free creation of law can take place not only *praeter legem*, but also *contra legem*, etc. All this is both futile and speculative. In the following, I shall—very briefly—give an account of some of the prevailing system models.

(a) On the Continent, the *positivist* doctrine was predominant (probably due to the influence of absolutism). According to this doctrine, there is in every community a sovereign will, which is the supreme source of all legal validity. The expression of this will, the enacted law, is, therefore, the supreme source [154] of law. Apart from that, usually only custom is recognized, and the reason for the binding force of custom is sought in the recognition—express or tacit, special or general—of the legislator.[5] During the age of absolutism, such views were prevalent in Denmark as well. Moreover, Ørsted also wished to recognize 'the legal system which has formed itself through the natural sense of justice, through common sense, the needs of civil society, the nature of legal matters, and popular *mores*'. Instead of grounding the validity of the system in the tacit consent of the legislator, he preferred to say that the system 'exists in and by itself, as long as no particular law ordains a deviation'.[6] Goos returned to the former attitude. The authority of society is the source of all validity, and custom and 'the nature of the matter' are grounded in the recognition through this authority.[7] The practice of the courts is of great factual importance but without any binding force.[8] There has always been unanimity of opinion that custom can only obtain the force of law *praeter legem*, not *contra legem*—a dogma still embraced by Vinding Kruse.[9]

the concept requires it as well. For if we inquire after the source of the assumed validity, there cannot, in reality, exist any plurality of sources—only a single source, namely, the authority of society', C. Goos, *Forelæsninger over den almindelige Retslære* [Lectures on the General Study of Law] I (1885), 89.

[5] On the so-called *Gestattungstheorie* [Theory of Permission], see Alf Ross, *Theorie der Rechtsquellen* [Theory of the Sources of Law] (1929), 430 *et seq*.

[6] A. S. Ørsted, *Haandbog over den danske og norske Lovkyndighed* [Compendium on Danish and Norwegian Knowledge of the Law], I (1822), 90, 108–09.

[7] C. Goos, *Forelæsninger over den almindelige Retslære* [Lectures on the General Study of Law] I (1885), 89, 194–05, 119, 121, 124 *et passim*.

[8] C. Goos, *op.cit.*, 140. Thus, any approval through the authority of society is not assumed here, which is explained by the law-enforcing organs having no mandate to enact law.

[9] *Retslæren* [Jurisprudence] I (1943), 152.

(b) In contrast to this positivist theory is *natural law* theory. According to this theory, the validity of the law emanates from the idea of law (or the idea of justice) as an *a priori* principle of reason. Therefore, the enacted law possesses binding force only to the extent to which it is a realization, or an attempt at a realization, of the idea of law. Frequently, however, there are but few practical advantages because it is assumed—with or without any construction of a social contract—that natural law demands obedience to the established authority of society, the law.[10] The inadequacy of the written law is strongly emphasized, however, and 'scientific' deductions from the idea of law are turned into an important and independent source alongside the enacted law.[11]

(c) The *romantic or historical school* of law can be regarded as a version of natural law, with the difference that natural law is not assumed to be derived from abstract principles of reason but, rather, from the idea of law manifesting itself in history and in the national life of the people (§§ 61 and 86). Custom and the legal convictions manifesting themselves in custom are, therefore, the supreme source of law. The law is not a supreme act of will; it is merely an attempt to clarify the law as it lives in the consciousness of the people—in particular in that of the legal profession. Knud Illum
[155] held similar views: according to him, 'the only possible criterion for the existence of a legal precept is the confrontation with the general legal consciousness'.[12]

Viggo Bentzon, whose work *Retskilderne* [The Sources of Law] (1900–1907) has been a landmark contribution to the realistic view which the present work is based upon, has a special place in the Danish theory of legal sources.

In spite of being formulated normatively, Bentzon's theory of the sources of law is, in fact, purely analytical and descriptive. The binding force of the theory of the sources of law, he says, 'has to do with something customary: it *is* the scientifically valid fundamental principle of legal life *because* it is integrated in our previous legal practice'. Thus, Bentzon refers to the practice of the courts as the ultimate foundation, and the whole of his theory of the sources of law is nothing but an analysis of the ideology actually prevailing in the Danish courts. Therefore, it is hardly relevant whether the outcome is presented normatively or descriptively.[13]

[10] Cf. § 66 below.

[11] A typical example is Geny's theory of the sources of law; on this issue, see Alf Ross, *Theorie der Rechtsquellen* [Theory of the Sources of Law] (1929), ch. III, 5–7.

[12] *Lov og Ret* [Law and Justice] (1945), 53, cf. § 14 notes 2 and 5 above.

[13] For details of Bentzon's theory of the sources of law, see Alf Ross, *Virkelighed og Gyldighed i Retslæren* [Reality and Validity in Jurisprudence] (1934), ch. VII, 6.

CHAPTER IV [156]

Legal Method (Interpretation)

§ 23. Method and Methodology

In Chapter II, it has been explained how doctrinal propositions about scientifically valid law according to the pattern

A = (D) is scientifically valid Danish law

can be understood as predictions (of varying probability) to the effect that the courts, under certain conditions, will use D as a basis for their decisions. Subsequently, in Chapter III, the part played by the ideology of the sources of law in relation to these predictions has been explained.

The doctrinal study of law, however, is not limited to sentences following the above-mentioned pattern. Typically, it contains *inter alia* sentences concerning the interpretation of D, that is, of the norms regarded as scientifically valid law. For the time being, we can say that these interpretational statements purport to define more precisely the meaning of the directive, by indicating more specifically under what circumstances it is to be applied and how, in that case, the judge is to behave. For example, if someone claims that the word 'citizens' in § 74 of the Danish Constitution must be interpreted as including both Danish nationals and other nationals, then this is a claim that the judge, whenever applying § 74, should not attach any importance to the question of whether or not a person claiming the right to form congregations for the worship of God is a Danish national.

The question that arises here is: can such statements concerning interpretation [157] be understood as theoretical statements, that is, as assertions as to what is 'scientifically valid interpretation'—by analogy with assertions as to what is 'scientifically valid law'? If this should prove to be the case, then these statements, too, must be understood (according to their real content) as predictions, to the effect that such an interpretation will be adhered to by the courts when the rule in question is used as a basis for the judicial decision in a specific case.

The basis of such a prediction may consist in precedents, where the courts have taken a stand on the problem of interpretation that has been under discussion. In that case, the statement concerning interpretation enjoys the same status as statements about scientifically valid law.

When precedent does not provide any guidance, the question arises whether it is possible, by studying legal practice, to discover certain principles—a certain ideology—which, in fact, guide the courts when they apply general rules to specific subject matters. If this is possible, then it is also possible to understand the doctrinal statements concerning interpretation, which are building thereon, as assertions concerning 'scientifically valid interpretation', that is to say, as predictions as to how the rule will be applied by the courts. However, as long as the contributions of the doctrinal study of law do not claim to be based upon 'scientifically valid' principles of interpretation, they belong to the realm of legal politics, not legal science.

Our task, then, is to analyse the practice of the courts when it comes to discovering principles or rules which actually guide the courts in that stage of their activity when they are supposed to arrive from a general rule to a concrete decision. This activity is called *legal method* or—if formulated law (statute law) is applied—*interpretation.*

In anticipation of the subsequent analysis, it should be noted here that it is not possible to formulate an ideology of method with even remotely the same precision as an ideology of the sources of law (especially the part concerning enacted law). It is not possible to lay down fixed rules. One does not get any further than what may be called a *style of method* or *style of interpretation.* Consequently, assertions concerning scientifically valid interpretation have a very low degree of certainty. We are moving within the area mentioned in § 9, where juridico-theoretical assertions are merging with directives of legal policy. Hence it is understandable that many jurists do not regard their doctrinal interpretation as theoretical statements as to how the courts will exercise their legal authority but, rather, as advice or instructions to the judge on how he should do this. Nevertheless, there is no doubt that even a jurist whose intentions are of a legal and political nature will allow himself (consciously or unconsciously) to be guided by that style of method or spirit of method which is actually 'scientifically valid' in the courts. If he does not do so, his interpretations will have no chance of finding a sympathetic ear in the courts. On the other hand, the more his political interpretation is influenced by the spirit and style animating the method of the courts, the greater is the chance that the courts will allow themselves to be influenced by his advice; in other words: his interpretation will make itself a 'true' one and may, contrary to his
[158] intention, also be understood as a prediction of how the courts will, in fact, apply the law. The interpretation of scientifically valid law demonstrates indeed

most clearly that in the last analysis, the science of law and legal politics cannot be separated.

Similarly to the doctrine of the sources of law, a *methodology* meant to serve as a guide to doctrinal interpretation—and this regardless of whether it is understood as scientific or as political—must be a doctrine of how the courts actually set about applying valid law in specific situations. The methodology must be *descriptive, not normative* (norm-descriptive, not norm-expressive). Of course, there is nothing to prevent us from setting up, for some reason or other, directives concerning the manner in which the courts ought to proceed when applying the law. In that case, however, one should understand that such a normative methodology would be a scheme for a different state of the law, and would not be of any value as a guideline, neither to doctrinal interpretation nor to the practitioner's calculations as to how a legal dispute will be decided by the courts.

Furthermore, similarly to the doctrine of the sources of law, methodology falls into a *doctrinal part and a general part.* Doctrinal methodology investigates the method used by the courts of a specific legal system, and constitutes part of the doctrinal study of law. There is no universal method, just as there is no universal ideology of the sources of law. General methodology can only aim to explain certain factual presuppositions concerning problems of method, and to place and characterize various existing styles of method and interpretation within the framework of a general typology.

There is an intimate connection between the ideology of the sources of law and method, and therefore it is understandable that doctrinal methodology must assume a highly different character within different systems. Thus, for example, problems of method will turn out differently within a system like the English system, where precedent constitutes the predominant source of law, compared with a system where the predominant source is legislation.

In the first named instance, the judge is not faced with an authoritative formulation of a general rule of law. Therefore, the problem of method is the problem of how the judge derives a general rule from existing precedents and then applies it to the case before him. The situation is complicated by the fact that the general rule often changes from one case to the next. This change depends on whether the judge, when considering similarities and differences between the case before him and the precedent, finds that the relevant facts can be classified under the same concepts as those presupposed in the precedent, or whether he finds that a distinction must be made with the aid of another, or more specified, concept formulation (classification). In the latter case, this means that the general rule has assumed a different or more nuanced content. At the commencement of a series of precedents, the content of the presupposed general rule will often be found to be extraordinarily vague. As yet, there is no established 'doctrine'. Therefore, the task facing the judge does [159] not so much consist in applying a general rule to a specific case, as in deciding whether the case before him differs from the precedent in such a way that there are grounds for making a different decision. In such a system, 'legal reasoning' (legal method) is 'reasoning by example', and the technique of argumentation that is employed according to this method purports to point out the similarities and differences between the cases and to explain whether the differences are relevant.[1]

In the second instance, on the other hand—that is to say, within a system where legislation is the predominant source of law—method chiefly assumes the character of an interpretation of the authoritative text. Here, attention is focused upon the relation between a given linguistic formulation and a specific complex of facts, and the technique of argumentation employed by this method purports to discover the meaning of the statute and to explain whether the given facts are covered by the meaning or not.

The latter pattern is typical of the problems of method within Continental legal systems, and the contributions towards a general methodology provided in this chapter will be restricted to statutory interpretation.[2]

[1] For details, see Edward H. Levi's excellent description in his work *An Introduction to Legal Reasoning* (1949).

[2] 'Statutory interpretation' refers here exclusively to statutes in the narrower sense (formal law, ordinances, etc.). Private, one-sided or two-sided, non-mandatory statements (wills, contracts, etc.) present special problems of interpretation which are not discussed here.

§ 24. Semantic Foundations[1]

All interpretation of enacted law begins with a text, that is, with a linguistic formulation in writing. If the scrawl of black lines and dots of which the text of a statute physically consists is able to influence the judge in the way it does, then this is obviously because it has a meaning which has nothing to do with the actual physical substance: rather, the meaning is ascribed to the substance [160] by the individual who—from certain preconditions—visually perceives these signs and characters. They are functioning as *symbols*, that is, they 'stand for', or 'point to', something other than themselves.

There are a great many things in life which have a symbolic function among the members of a certain group. The badges worn by officers indicate their rank; an emblem worn on the lapel indicates that the wearer is a member of a certain association. The Royal Emblem is a symbol of patriotism, the hammer and sickle is a symbol of a certain political conviction. The eagle over the main entrance of the university is a symbol of academic aspirations; chemists have agreed that H shall mean hydrogen, that O shall mean oxygen, and so on. Postmen, soldiers, policemen, scouts, priests, kings, and a host of others wear garments or decorations symbolizing their occupation, dignity, or rank. Everywhere—in primitive as well as highly civilized societies—we come across a variety of different symbols.

We can distinguish between *signs* and symbols. The fact that the earth is moist I take as a sign that it must have rained recently; I take thunder as a sign of lightning; I take a child's tears as a sign that something unpleasant has happened to him, and so on. The difference between sign and symbol lies in the fact that a sign is 'natural' whereas a symbol is something 'artificial'—it has been produced by human beings. More precisely: I understand what the sign refers to, but only thanks to my knowledge of nature and my awareness of the relations between phenomena. It is because I am counting upon, in virtue of my experience, that A and B usually occur together, that I take A (the moisture of the earth, the thunder, the child's tears) as a sign of B (the rain, the lightning, the unpleasant experience). On the other hand, it is not possible to understand, on the same basis, that a red uniform means that the wearer is a postman, or that a crown is

[1] Recent years have seen the development of a scientific sub-discipline called 'general semantics'. This sub-discipline is concerned with language as a means of expression and communication, with its importance for action and knowledge, with the symbolic function and emotional value of words, and with other related problems. There is quite an extensive body of literature on the subject. For a popular introduction, see S. I. Hayakawa, *Language in Thought and Action* (1949). Among the better known works can also be mentioned C. K. Ogden and I. A. Richards, *The Meaning of Meaning* (8th edn, 1946); C. Morris, *Signs, Language and Behavior* (1946); A. Korzybski, *Science and Sanity* (2nd edn, 1941); M. Black, *Language and Philosophy* (1949); C. L. Stevenson, *Ethics and Language* (1944); Arne Næss, *Interpretation and Preciseness*, I–V (1947–1951); Stephen Ullmann, *Words and their Use* (1951).

a symbol of royal dignity. These things are not connected in a natural way, but are chained together in an arbitrary manner by human beings: the red uniform could just as well have been made the symbol of royal dignity, and the crown the symbol of the post office. For a person in possession of the requisite knowledge, a red light alternating with green and amber at an intersection is a sign that there must be an electric installation and a mechanical device, regularly switching the lights on and off. However, that the red light also is a symbol of a crossing restriction issued by the police has to do with a certain convention which just as easily could have ascribed a different meaning to these colours. *All symbols are conventional*, that is, the connection between the symbol and what it symbolizes is brought about by human beings, through agreement or usage (custom).[2]

[161] Among the existing symbol systems, language is the highest developed, the most efficacious, and the most complicated system. Language can manifest itself in a series of forms, perceived either auditorily or visually (speech and writing). Also with regard to these forms, it is obvious that the meaning assigned to them is conventional. Of course, there was nothing to prevent the Danish word 'kat' [i.e., cat] from being used as a name for the four-legged domestic animal saying 'bow-wow', and the word 'hund' [i.e., dog] as a name for the animal saying 'meow'. The meaning assigned to linguistic symbols is determined by the customs of the speech community as to the circumstances under which it is thought proper to utter certain noises. We who have grown up with the customs of the Danish speech community are trained to the effect that we think it proper to say: 'Se, der er en kat!' ['Look, there is a cat!'] when the meowing domestic animal appears, but we think that the same utterance is out of place when it is used about the barking animal.

The conventional character of linguistic symbols can be described in more detail with the help of the pattern we have used in connection with the coherence of meaning of the game of chess and the law. Accordingly, we must distinguish between the phenomena of language and the norms of language as two abstract sides of the same coin. The linguistic phenomena (spoken and written utterances) acquire their specific meaning only by being interpreted in relation to the normative ideology that prevails within the speech community in question. This ideology, in turn, emerges from the linguistic phenomena themselves: it is the ideology which is followed efficaciously and, therefore, enables us to comprehend our simple effusions (oral or written) as meaningful utterances, bound together within an interpersonal and coherent whole of meaning and motivation.

[2] Many delusions and pseudo-problems of metaphysical philosophy have to do with the belief that words represent objectively given concepts or ideas, the meaning of which it is the task for philosophy to discover and define. Taking this view (which goes back to Plato's theory of forms) as a starting-point, philosophers keep asking what 'truth', 'beauty', 'goodness', and the like *really are*, and they believe that they are able to establish this in *true definitions*. Traditional philosophy of law has seen it as its chief task to arrive at a definition of 'the concept of law' according to this pattern.

The linguistic customs or norms that are constitutive of the symbolic function of language can only be discovered by studying the manner in which people express themselves. By *utterance* I mean the smallest linguistic unit that is the carrier of independent meaning (an atom of meaning). 'Look, there is a cat!' is an utterance. It is in its entirety a carrier of meaning. Linguistic communication between human beings takes place by means of such unified wholes, and consequently they must be our starting point for studying the symbolic function of language.

It is important to emphasize this because, otherwise, it is easy to fall victim to a misunderstanding, namely, that the meaning of an utterance is a compound of the meanings of the individual words contained within the utterance. The individual words do not have any independent meaning, however: they only have a meaning abstracted from the utterances in which they occur. It is meaningless to say 'cat' and nothing else. This is no utterance—unless, indeed, the circumstances are such (I am sniffing and looking searchingly around, for example) that the expression can be interpreted as a radically simplified form of an utterance, such as: 'Surely there is a cat around here.'

Although it is the utterance in its entirety that is the carrier of meaning, the individual words making up the utterance have their peculiar function when [162] bringing about this meaning. Let us consider the following sentence: 'This house is red.' If I replace the word 'house' with the word 'table', the meaning will change. If I replace the word 'red' with the word 'green' the meaning will also change—but in a different way. This shows that the two words have their own peculiar function of meaning within the unified whole of meaning.

What does the word 'table' mean in Danish? This question can only be answered by studying a large number of utterances in which the word occurs. This is indeed the procedure adopted for compiling a dictionary: there, a large amount of material is collected, consisting of exemplifying utterances within which the word is used. In each individual utterance it will emerge, from the context, what the word is referring to. With each individual reference being registered, there will then emerge a reference area corresponding to the word. This reference area can be compared to a target: around the centre there will be a density of spots, each marking a hit of the reference, while the density will decrease towards the periphery. The semantic reference of the word has a solid core, so to speak, where application is common and certain, as well as a hazy outer circle of uncertainty, where the word is less frequently applied, until eventually it is uncertain whether or not the word can be applied at all. I have no hesitation in calling the piece of furniture at which I sit and write, a table. I also use the word for objects of similar shape but of smaller size—such as, for example, a nursery table, or a table in a doll's house. But is there not a limit as to how small things may be? In other instances, it seems to be the function rather than the form that determines the linguistic usage. 'Shall we put up the table?' I ask my fellow passenger in the railway compartment, thereby referring to a drop-leaf hanging from the wall. Normally, I would not describe a chest as a table, but if I have put a cloth on it (for want of something better) and arranged the plates and glasses, I may as well say that 'the table is laid'. Can an operating table be called a table, or may only the compound word as such be used to denote it?

Therefore, there is no point in asking what a table 'really is'.[3] If I am doubtful in certain cases whether something is a table or not, this doubt does not express any lack of knowledge and insight into the 'nature' of the object; it simply expresses that I am uncertain whether it would conform to Danish usage to use the word 'table' as a name for the object in question. This hesitation, in turn, has to do with the fact that the word can be used in this manner in certain utterances under certain circumstances, but not in other utterances and under other circumstances. We have seen, for example, that under certain circumstances, I can describe a chest as a table, whereas it is obvious that I would not normally do so.

[163] These remarks about the word 'table' also apply to all words used in everyday language. It is true of them all that their meaning is vague, or that their reference area is indeterminate, consisting of a core of obvious applications which, imperceptibly, merge into a circle of indeterminacy. This circle of indeterminacy covers possible uses of the word which are atypical and subject to special conditions.

The abstract reference area which can be ascribed to a word lexicographically indicates the possible scope of application of the word, abstracted from the utterances and situations in which the word occurs. In the individual utterance, this area is not evoked in its entirety; only larger or smaller parts of it are evoked. In the utterance 'The table is laid', the word 'table' has a potential reference area which is narrower than the area as such, but wider than in the utterance: 'Cabinet-maker Petersen makes tables and chairs.' In the first case, the word can cover, for example, a marble table, or a flat stone on the grass, but it cannot do this in the second case. Moreover, if we take into account the situation in which the utterance is made, the area is further reduced and will perhaps only comprise a single object. This is the case when the utterance, 'The table is laid', is seen within the context of the situation in which it is made (that is, if there is no doubt whatsoever what kind of table is meant).

Most words have more than one reference area, each of them following the pattern: core + circle of indeterminacy. Such words are called ambiguous. In colloquial Danish language, this applies for example to the word *bor(d)*.*

* Translator's note: In Danish, the word 'bord' means 'table,' and the word 'bor' means 'drill'. These two words are pronounced the same way, the *d* in 'bord' being silent.

[3] Cf. note 2 above.

In the previous sections, we have discussed the *meaning* of a word as well as its *reference* (the object to which the word refers) (connotation and denotation). It might be useful to specify these terms. It is said that the meaning of a word is the same as the notions we are connecting with that word, whereas 'reference' is the object corresponding to, or fulfilling, these notions. Obviously, however, it is not possible to observe, directly, how people are visualizing a certain word—for example, the word 'table'. All I can do is ask questions, and the answer I shall get will be expressed in . . . other words. I will be told, for example, that a table is visualized as a kind of free-standing article of daily use, consisting of a horizontal slab propped up in one way or the other, and designed to support things at a height suited to sitting or standing human beings. However, it is easy to see that this explanation does not cover all situations. It is simply not possible to arrive at an adequate definition: just as words do not have any definite reference areas, they do not have any definite meaning. Whenever we are confronted with an isolated word, we are actually at a loss to understand what it means. Not until the word is functioning as part of a coherent whole of meaning—the coherence of the words in an utterance, the coherence of the utterances themselves within a given context and with other facts in a given situation—not until then does it acquire meaning, in virtue of its functioning within a whole of meaning. If we then try to specify the meaning by substituting the word with another word, we say that we establish the meaning of the word. If we, on the other hand, try to specify the meaning by taking [164]
a stand on whether certain real or imagined facts are covered by the meaning, we say that we thereby establish what is denoted by the word. By way of illustration, we can point out that the doctrinal interpretation of a legal text purports to establish the meaning of the words, and the judge's decision purports to confirm or deny whether they denote a fact presented to him.

The previous reflections can be summed up in the following tenets (applying to everyday language):

(1) The possible meaning of every word is vague, and its possible reference area is indeterminate.

(2) Most words are ambiguous.

(3) The meaning and reference of a word are determined more precisely when the word is seen as an integral part of a definite utterance.

(4) The meaning of an utterance, and thus the meaning and reference of the words contained in it, is determined more precisely when the utterance is seen within the wider context in which it is made. This wider context can be either linguistic (the con-text strictly speaking) or non-linguistic (the situation).

From (3) and (4) we can deduce the following generalization: *The meaning (reference) of a word is a function of the coherent whole—utterance, context, situation—in which the word occurs.*[4] Let us now, in view of analysing more closely the role of the context, look at a few examples.

The Danish word 'bakke' can refer to a certain landscape formation [a hill] as well as to a certain article of daily use [a tray]. In the utterance: 'The waiter entered with a *bakke*' it seems clear that the word is used in the latter sense. But why? It would not be correct to say that the utterance would lack meaning if the word were interpreted as a scenic hill, for the meaning of an utterance is in no way tied to what can be imagined as realized, or as existing in reality (for example: 'With his outstretched arm he lifted a 1,000-ton weight'). It is more likely that we spontaneously opt for the interpretation mentioned above, because only this interpretation seems to endow the utterance with a *proper* or *reasonable* meaning. Therefore, our point of departure is the hypothesis that the utterance has a reasonable meaning, a meaning which it can be assumed would be uttered by a reasonable person under certain circumstances. From the perspective of this hypothesis, the spontaneous interpretation seems obvious, but it is not the only interpretation. It is possible to imagine circumstances—for example, when the utterance makes part of a conversation concerning the production of a play—where the word means that the waiter entered with a piece of scenery decoration representing a hill.

[165] The same applies to the coherent whole of context and situation. In the utterance: 'The waiter entered with a *bor(d)*', it is still unclear in which sense the word 'bor(d)' is used.* If the information now goes on telling us that those present sat down at the table for playing bridge, we have no doubts that the word designates a table [*bord*] and not a drill [*bor*]. Once again, it would appear, because we think that interpreting the word as referring to a carpentry tool would not make any reasonable or, on certain hypotheses, probable, sense at all.

From that, we have learned the lesson that the part played by the coherent whole in determining the meaning consists in providing a basis for deciding which of several interpretations—each of them possible according to linguistic usage—is (on certain hypotheses) most probable. *Wider contextual interpretation thus operates with a basis of interpretation beyond linquistic usage, and with interpretation data beyond the used words.* Wider contextual interpretation operates with all the facts, all the hypotheses, and all the experience that can throw light on what a certain person in a given situation intended to communicate. It

* See translator's note at p. 134 above.

[4] Paul Diderichsen strongly emphasizes this in his work 'Sprog og livssyn' [Language and worldview] (*Mennesket i Tiden* vol. VIII, 1952). He says the following (21): 'The first thing one must remember is that the meaning of language is always determined by context or situation, and determined to an extent almost inconceivable to the naive user of language.'

is a study of circumstantial evidence, reminiscent of the work of a detective investigating a crime.

Starting from this premise, it must be established what, under the circumstances, is to be included in the context proper and the situation. The context stretches just as far as one dares to assume that the one utterance has been formulated with the other one in mind, and that the author wanted both utterances to apply at the same time. It is often optimistically assumed that this is the case with all utterances within a given scientist's collected works. However, if an author's earlier or later works are taken as interpretation data, one should take into consideration that in the meantime, the author's views, his terminology, and his style may have changed. In the doctrinal study of law, it is common to consider utterances within one and the same statute (decree, contract, etc.) as forming part of the same context. If earlier as well as more recent statutory provisions are also taken into consideration, similar reservations must be made. All the facts that can provide an indication of the author's intention are included in the situation. According to circumstances, one can find here the author's political persuasion, his philosophical stance, the audience to which he addresses his statements, the presumed intention behind these statements, accompanying gestures, facial expression, emphasis, etc., alongside the entire factual, physical, and social situation of life that has conditioned the utterance.

The activity purporting to explain in more detail the meaning of an utterance is called *interpretation*. This word is also used for denoting the result of this activity. Interpretation can take two forms. It can be done in such a manner that the meaning of an utterance is defined more clearly with the help of a paraphrase, that is, by using other words or utterances whose meaning is less vague; or it can be done in such a manner that when it comes to a definitely experienced, concrete set of facts, it can be decided with a 'yes', a 'no', or a 'perhaps', whether or not this set of facts constitutes a reference corresponding to the utterance. If we, for [166]
example, consider the utterance: 'When hydrochloric acid is combined with zinc, hydrogen is released', an interpretation of the former type will purport to explain more fully in words what is to be understood by some of the expressions. We might point out, for example, that 'is combined' means that the zinc is submerged into the acid, but not, for example, that a piece of zinc and a bottle of hydrochloric acid are wrapped up in a piece of paper. An interpretation of the second type will purport to decide whether a certain factual course of events 'fulfils' the meaning of the utterance, so as to confirm that we are concerned with the facts the utterance is referring to. The first type of interpretation is called *interpretation by meaning*, whereas the second type is called *interpretation by reference*.

The guiding principle governing all interpretation is the principle of *the primary function of the unified whole and the wider context, namely to determine the meaning of the utterance*. The starting point for all comprehension is the utterance as a whole, as experienced by the recipient in a given situation. From this, reflective interpretation can move partly towards an analysis of the elements of the utterance (that is, the individual words and their syntactical connection), partly towards an analysis of the context within which the utterance occurs and of the situation in which it has been made (provided that the latter is distinct from the situation at the time of the experience).

With regard to the former—that is, when it comes to the meaning of individual words—it is important to realize that the meaning of an utterance is not put together piece by piece, like a mosaic, from the meaning of the individual elements of the words, but that the meaning which in the analysis can be ascribed to the individual elements is always a function of the unified whole in which they occur. In Denmark, it is widely held that the starting point for statutory interpretation may be, or must be, the ordinary meaning of the words as warranted by Danish usage. This is an illusion. There is no such meaning. Only the context and the desire to find 'good' or 'reasonable' meaning in relation to a given situation determine the meaning of the individual words. However, the function of the context is frequently so 'natural' as to escape notice. If the entrance to a cattle show carries the sign: 'Entrance for animal keepers only', no one would imagine that the sign implies admission for keepers carrying head lice or germs, or for keepers who brought their canary birds with them. This is so obvious that it is easy to overlook the fact that the word 'animal' here is given a reasonable interpretation conditioned by situation and purpose, which is far more specific than a definition of the meaning of the word according to Danish usage. Of course, the word might include the phenomena mentioned here in other contexts and situations.

With regard to the latter—that is, when it comes to the significance of the context and the non-experienced situation in which the utterance occurred—the situation is somewhat different. This kind of context, an external one, is not the primary context. It is experienced successively rather than simultaneously. When I am reading a book, it is not true that I do not associate any meaning
[167] with the first sentence until I have read the whole book. And yet, the context is co-determinative. My comprehension of the first few pages of the book has often changed by the time I have finished the book and started reading it again. A curious 'interpretative vibration' takes place. My understanding of the first few sentences is co-determinative for the understanding of the subsequent ones. However, the coherent whole thus evolving may have repercussions on my understanding of the individual utterances where, again, it is possible that my holistic view will undergo changes, and so on. Something like that may make itself felt with regard to the significance of the situation in which the utterance occurred.

In everyday language, the coherent whole and the wider context are the most important factors in determining the meaning. However, they are not the only factors. The meaning of words is relative or dependent on quite a different level as well, a level which might be called a *synonymic* or *systematic* level. This means that the meaning of a word is defined more precisely if it is compared with other words which can occupy the same place in a sentence, and which indicate a more comprehensive 'semantic field'—for example, the adjectival scale *red hot, hot, warm, tepid, cool, cold, ice-cold*, etc. By comparing a certain word with related or contrasting words, the relative position of the word within a semantic field is being determined. For example, the meaning of the word 'intent' in a given utterance is more precisely defined by figuring out what other expressions might be inserted in the same place in the utterance, and then determining the relative position occupied by 'intent' within the field of meaning thus established (*accident, negligence, gross negligence, purpose, intent, premeditation*, etc.). In everyday language, however, it is never a question of sharp or absolute lines of demarcation, and this method to determine the meaning can therefore never oust and replace context and situation as a basis for interpretation. On the other hand, scientific language is characterized by a tendency to cultivate systematic concept formation and thus becomes independent from the context and situation. However, it is only in the highest forms of scientific language, in the symbols of logic and mathematics, that this effort has fully succeeded. Since most legal directives are couched in the terminology of everyday language, context and situation are the basic tools for juristic interpretation, and the synonymic-systematic method plays only the same (and more modest) role as in any other non-scientific linguistic usage.[5]

It happens frequently that neither kind of interpretation will lead to an unambiguous and definite outcome. Let us consider the following examples, taken from the Norwegian philosopher Arne Næss.[6] Some students asserted that more than 25 per cent of the candidates, who in a certain year had attempted to pass an exam in philosophy at the University of Oslo, had failed. If we, in this assertion, focus on the part saying: 'More than 25 per cent of the candidates failed', this can be interpreted at least in the following ways:

Theme: 'More than 25 per cent of the candidates failed.' [168]

Interpretation 1: 'More than 25 per cent of those candidates who entered for the examination did not obtain pass marks.'

Interpretation 2: 'More than 25 per cent of those candidates who actually took the examination, did not obtain pass marks.' (Some candidates did not turn up because of illness, etc.)

[5] The reflections in this paragraph are taken from Paul Diderichsen, 'Sprog og livssyn' [Language and worldview] (*Mennesket i Tiden* vol. VIII, 1952), 24 f.

[6] Arne Næss, *Interpretation and Preciseness*, vol. I (1947), 51.

Interpretation 3: 'More than 25 per cent of those candidates who actually took the examination and did not, immediately after reading the assignment, leave the examination hall, did not obtain pass marks.' (Some candidates mean to try, but give up immediately if the questions seem too difficult.)

Interpretation 4: 'More than 25 per cent of those candidates who attempted to answer the questions did not... etc.'

Interpretation 5: 'More than 25 per cent of those candidates who handed in their exam papers did not... etc.'

Which one of these possible meanings covered the assertion of the students in question? How to interpret their utterance? It is quite possible that this question cannot be answered at all, and for two reasons: first, because it is possible that an interpretation based on context and situation will not lead to any result (just as a detective may be unable to find decisive evidence with respect to the identity of the murderer); secondly, because it is possible that the negative result is due to the fact that the original speaker did not realize what, exactly, he did mean. This will become apparent when he is being questioned, because he may admit that the various possibilities had not occurred to him, and consequently that he had not committed himself to any of them. In this situation, the detective is unable to solve the murder case—for the simple reason that no murder has been committed. Following Næss, we say in such a case that the theme for interpretation possesses less *determinacy of intention* or *depth of intention* than do the possible interpretations.

Indeterminacy of intention does not necessarily have to be assessed as the original speaker's fault. Presumably, a certain degree of indeterminacy is inevitable under any circumstances, since it is certainly possible, in every case, to devise ever more subtle definitions. The practical purpose of an utterance determines the appropriate degree of determinacy of intention. It does make sense to tell a motorist that the distance from Copenhagen to Roskilde is 30 kilometres. And certainly, the intention can be deepened by interpretative precision (from what point in Copenhagen to what point in Roskilde, and so on), so that the distance can be given in millimetres; in practice, however, it would be pointless to do so in the given situation.

If for one reason or other (that is to say, either because no conclusive evidence can be found, or because the intention is not deep enough) it is not possible to
[169] proceed with the interpretation beyond a certain point that leaves open a number of possibilities, then the interpreter must give up. If he nevertheless opts for a particular possibility, then this step is not the next step in an interpretation but, rather, a decision motivated by considerations other than the desire to

grasp the meaning of an utterance. This can happen especially in the interpretation of directives. If it has been decided, for example, that in the case of more than 25 per cent of the candidates failing in the philosophy examination, the vice chancellor of the university shall take certain steps, then the vice chancellor might find himself in a situation where he is obliged to opt for one of the possible, further specifying interpretations. (It is not absolutely necessary, because frequently the outcome is certain, that is, independent of the type of interpretation.) In that case, the vice chancellor makes a decision that transcends the interpretation of the directive.

Frequently one distinguishes between the so-called *subjective and objective interpretation*, in the sense that the former purports to discover the intended meaning, that is, the idea that inspired the original speaker, and which he wished to communicate, while the latter purports to establish the meaning that has been communicated, that is, the meaning that lies in the communication as such, regarded as an objective fact. A literary or scientific work, for example, can either be interpreted by trying to arrive at what the author really thought and meant; or it can be regarded as an objective intellectual manifestation, detached from its source, which one tries to interpret in the sense it must convey to the individual reading it. Similarly, a promise can either be interpreted with regard to what the promisor really meant to express (even if he has expressed himself badly); or with regard to the perception which his words may have elicited in the recipient.

Taken that way, that is, as an absolute contrast between intention and communication, between what is meant and what is said, the distinction is untenable. On the one hand, the intention—a phenomenon of consciousness within the author's mind—is basically inaccessible. What we mean is, in reality, the interpretation we arrive at when taking into account, not merely the linguistic utterance, but all the relevant interpretation data—the context and the situation, including the author's political and philosophical views, the declared and presumed purpose in making the utterance, and so on. We can even question him, and his answer will furnish us with further interpretation data. On the other hand, the communication itself has no definite objective meaning, but the perception it elicits in other people varies with the interpretation data which the recipient takes into account.

Therefore, the reason for the contrast between subjective and objective interpretation cannot be found in the contrast between the purposes of the interpretation (the intended meaning as opposed to the communicated meaning). All interpretation begins with communication and attempts to arrive at intention. The difference has to do with the interpretation data that has been taken into consideration. Subjective interpretation makes use of any circum- [170]
stances that can shed light on the meaning, in particular all personal and factual

circumstances related to the coming into being of the utterance and its pronouncement. Objective interpretation, on the other hand, restricts the relevant data to those which can be discerned by the recipient in a situation in which he experiences the utterance. The significance of the difference reaches its climax when the situation of experience differs from the situation in which the utterance was made. In the case of an older literary work, for example, a subjective interpretation will delve into the basic cultural views of the period as well as into the author's life story, in hopes of finding clues to an understanding of the work; whereas an objective interpretation will ignore all this and try to understand the work from its 'immanent' idea content. However, this does not mean that objective interpretation is purely linguistic. From the following sections, it will emerge that the belief in a 'literal interpretation' is an illusion. The interpretation will always depend upon other factors, in particular upon conjectures about the 'idea,' the 'intention', or the 'purpose' associated with the work. The very awareness of dealing with either a work of poetry, a scientific work, a statute or the like, is of vital importance. Objective interpretation merely declines to seek out information about the author's intention by studying how the work came into being. Hereby an objective interpretation—contrary to what the terminology might lead one to believe—acquires a colouring of greater vagueness and arbitrariness than a subjective interpretation. An 'objective' interpretation of poetical works such as Goethe's 'Faust' or Shakespeare's 'Hamlet' tends towards becoming 'subjective' in the sense that it turns into an expression of what different periods of time have read into these works.

An objective interpretation may turn into an ideal construction contrary to the author's intention. The various interpretations of Kant, for example, do not really purport to ascertain what Kant 'really meant', and his own answer, if one could interrogate him, would not be decisive in determining which interpretation is 'the right one'. These interpretations have the character of a rational reconstruction of the original speaker's work, and possess greater intentional depth than the work itself. They are based upon an ideal of logical consistency within the system which transcends the factual, and they are oriented towards a hypothetical, ideal meaning, rather than towards Kant's meaning *qua* historico-psychological fact. This rational reconstruction, however, can be accomplished in more ways than one, depending on what is regarded as the system's essential point. Therefore, interpretations of this kind constitute an evaluative and creative activity, transcending the bounds of an interpretation
[171] proper (in the sense in which the term is understood here).

§ 25. Problems of Interpretation I: Syntactic Problems

The guiding principle of all interpretation, as stated in § 24, is that of the primary, meaning-determining function of the coherent whole and the wider context of the utterances of any text or entity. This must be borne in mind when proceeding to distinguish between different groups of problems connected with interpretation: syntactic problems, problems of logic, and semantic problems (in a narrower sense). We must remember that we are speaking of analytical abstractions, and that the isolated problems of interpretation we have discussed so far are, in reality, always experienced as organic links within a coherent whole of meaning, experienced simultaneously or successively.

A few examples will soon make us realize that the meaning of an utterance depends on the word order and on the way in which individual words are connected. In our inquiry into the meaning of an utterance, the problems associated with the connection between the words within the sentence structure are called *syntactic problems of interpretation*.

As will emerge from the examples adduced below, the situation with regard to syntactic problems is the same as that concerning semantic problems: in the same way as words have no definite reference in themselves, the syntactic forms of linkage have no unique meaning-determining function. Here, too, 'natural' understanding is conditioned by factors other than linguistic ones, namely by the wish to find a 'good' and 'sensible' meaning in conformity with what is reasonable to assume, considering the context and the situation.

As far as is known, the syntactic problems of interpretation have not yet been the subject of a systematic presentation and analysis.[1] Nor does the present account pretend to be anything of the sort. My only aim here is to provide an understanding of problems of this nature by offering examples. Apart from that, systematic studies within this field would certainly prove valuable for statutory interpretation, especially for legislative drafting.

(a) *Adjectival (relative) clauses and parts of the main clauses to which they refer*

(1a) An attempt was made to find a solution *that* would satisfy everyone.

(1b) An attempt was made to find a solution *which*, however, was not successful.

[1] Erik Rehling, *Skriftlig form* [Written Form] (1948), especially chs. 8 and 9, contains very interesting material. However, this material has not been analysed and systematized according to any theory of interpretation.

(2a) Nobody can be appointed a civil servant *who* is not a Danish national (§ 17 of the Danish Constitution).

(2b) No foreign national can be appointed to an office *which* is in the gift of the King.*

These examples show that there are no syntactic rules specifying which part of
[172] the main clause the relative clause is referring to. Still, one has little doubt about the above-mentioned situations because there is only one reading that makes any sense. In other situations, however, the meaning may be ambiguous. If we say, for example:

(3) Incitement to a crime *which* has been committed abroad is not included,

then it is doubtful whether it is the incitement or the crime itself that has been committed abroad. In this case the interpretation must be based upon data other than those which are linguistic, especially upon information concerning the objective of the rule. If the interpreter lets his own assessment as to which meaning yields the best results be the decisive one, he exceeds the bounds of an interpretation proper (§ 24).

(b) *The question of whether adjectival clauses and parts of main clauses refer to two or more basic words in the main clause*

(4a) Books and magazines *which* contain indecent pictures must not be imported.

(4b) Officers and privates *who* have been conscripted for more than six months are entitled to extra provisions.

(5a) *Young* men and women *who* have passed the entrance examination can be appointed.

(5b) *Young* men and women *who* have served in the Women's Army Corps can be appointed.

(6a) The King may take the initiative to introduce proposals *for* legislation and other measures in Parliament (§ 23 of the Constitution).

(6b) The Council deals with proposals *for* legislation and other matters of importance.

* Editor's note: The point Ross is trying to make here does not translate well into English. In Danish, the relative pronouns that he is using are the same in both 1a and 1b (i.e. 'der'), and in both 2a and 2b (i.e. 'som') respectively. However, in English, these relative pronouns translate differently, i.e. into 'that' and 'which' (1a and 1b respectively), and into 'who' and 'which' (2a and 2b respectively). An example that would be closer to Ross's intention would be the following:

(1a*) The theft of the book that I read took place on Monday.

(1b*) The theft of the book that I committed took place on Monday.

These examples show that there are no fixed rules that can tell us whether an adjective ('young' in (5 a) and (5 b)), a relative pronoun, or a preposition links to a single basic word or to several basic words. In these instances, the meaning is already fairly clear in light of the demand for a 'reasonable' meaning. In example (4a), however, the presumed purpose of the legislator or the interpreter's own evaluation will be of consequence; and in (4b) it will matter if it emerges from the context whether it is possible for officers to be 'conscripted'. In other instances, there can be serious doubts. Thus, for example, when § 61 Danish Civil Service Act states:

(7) When an official, who is entitled to a pension, is dismissed on the grounds of misconduct or malpractices *which*, without leading to a loss of pension rights according to § 60, diminish the respect and confidence demanded by his position, it shall be decided, according to the requirements of the Budget or the Law on Supplementary Grants, whether he shall receive a pension and, if so, of what size.

It is not clear whether the relative clause refers only to 'malpractices' or to 'mis- [173] conduct' as well, and only a comprehensive and coherent analysis of the legal rules concerning the dismissal of officials without application as well as of the pension rules can provide a basis for an (evaluative) interpretation.[2]

(c) *Demonstrative and relative pronouns*

(8a) The king summons an ordinary parliament annually and decides when to end the session. *This*, however, cannot take place until, in pursuance of § 48 of the Constitution, legal warrant has been obtained for the collection of taxes and the defrayal of government expenses (§ 19 of the Constitution).

(8b) The Speaker calls a meeting and encloses a copy of his report. *This*, however, cannot take place until the treasurer has presented his accounts.

(9a) Should one of the Houses be dissolved when Parliament is in session, the meetings of the other House shall be postponed until Parliament reassembles. *This* must take place within two months after the dissolution (§ 22 of the Constitution).

(9b) Should the capacity of the Speaker be called into doubt, the chairman adjourns the meeting until the council has made a decision. *This* must be done even if the Speaker declares himself willing to resign.

(10a) Ministers may be impeached by the King or Parliament for *their* maladministration of office. (§ 14 of the Constitution).

[2] On this issue, see Poul Andersen, *Dansk Forvaltningsret* [Danish Administrative Law] (2nd edn, 1946), 234.

(10b) The teachers gave John and Peter a present for *their* birthday. (It emerges from the context that they were twins).

At first, when perusing the quotations from the constitutional provisions, there does not seem to be any doubt about what the italicized words are referring to. The constructed counterparts demonstrate, however, that from a purely syntactical point of view, they may be understood in more than one way, and that the 'natural reading' is, in reality, not only determined by what can be read, but also by an estimation of what 'reasonably' can be presumed to be the meaning. This estimation, however, does not always lead to certainty. Thus, for example, difficult problems of interpretation have arisen with regard to the expression 'such a trade licence' in the Danish Trade Law nr. 138, dated 28 April 1931,[3] and the expression 'the same obligation' in the Statute of the International Court of Justice, Art. 36, section 2.[4]

[174] (d) *Modifying, excepting, and conditioning parts of a clause*

From a purely syntactical point of view, it will frequently be open to doubt as to which basic word the modifying, excepting, or conditioning parts of a clause are referring to. In such cases punctuation may be important.

(11) In the performance of their duties, the judges shall be governed solely by the law. They shall not be dismissed except by judgment, nor shall they be transferred against their will, except in cases in which a rearrangement of the courts of justice is made. (§ 71 of the Constitution).

It does not emerge from the sentence structure of this formulation whether the exception with regard to the rearrangements of the courts applies only to the rule that judges shall not be transferred against their will, or also to the rule that they shall not be dismissed except by judgment. The decisive factor is the comma after the word 'will'. It is an indication that the inserted 'nor shall they be transferred against their will' stands in apposition to (is parallel with) the first part of the sentence, and that the exception relates equally to both situations. If the comma were omitted, the converse reading would be the natural one.

The importance of punctuation is strikingly emphasized by the Berlin Protocols, dated 6 October 1945, whose sole content was to replace a semicolon with a comma! 'Crimes against humanity' was defined as follows in Art. 6 of the Charter of the International Military Tribunal, in pursuance of the London Agreement signed 8 August 1945:

[3] On this issue, see Poul Andersen, *Næringsretten I Hovedtræk* [Trade Law Outline] (3rd edn, 1944), 71 and H. D. in *UfR* 1952, 20.

[4] See Hans Kelsen, *The Law of the United Nations* (1950), 526.

(12) Crimes against humanity: namely murder, extermination, enslavement, deportation, and other inhumane acts committed against any civilian population, before or after the war; or persecutions on political, racial or religious grounds in execution of or in connection with any crime within the jurisdiction of the Tribunal, whether or not in violation of the domestic law of the country where perpetrated.

In the aforementioned protocols, the semicolon after the word 'war' was replaced by a comma. Thereby, the jurisdiction of the Tribunal was substantially circumscribed, since the condition that the criminal act should have been committed in connection with one of the crimes within the jurisdiction of the Tribunal was now to apply to all cases of crimes against humanity, not merely to the group (persecutions) mentioned after the original semicolon. The adjustment was hardly prompted by altered intentions, however; it was merely an indication that the syntactic function of the semicolon had not been observed before.

(13a) The King can postpone the ordinary sessions of Parliament for a given time, but without the consent of Parliament not for more than two months, nor more than once per year until the next ordinary session (§ 21 of the Constitution). [175]

(13b) The King can postpone the ordinary sessions of Parliament for a given time, but without the consent of Parliament not for more than two months, and during the following ten years not more than once per year until the next ordinary session.

With regard to the a-formulation, there seems to be no doubt that 'without the consent of Parliament' refers to both the postponement for more than two months and the postponement more than once per year. From a purely logical perspective, the qualifying part of the sentence (inserted into the b-formulation with regard to the latter case) does not appear to make any difference at all in this respect. Yet, our linguistic perception naturally leans towards suggesting that the words 'without the consent of parliament' now merely refer to the first part of the clause, and that afterwards—during the following ten years—the King, even with the consent of Parliament, cannot postpone the sessions more than once a year. This example shows how the syntactic function of a part of the clause can change with nuances in the sentence structure.

The various groups of examples adduced above (and there are many more) are probably sufficient to confirm the assertion that syntactic connectives do not have an unequivocal function, and that, consequently, syntactic problems must be solved on a basis of something other than purely linguistic interpretation data. In this respect, they are similar to semantic problems. On the other hand, however, they differ from these in the following respect: whereas the vagueness

in the meaning of the words cannot be remedied even in principle, careful (and possibly troublesome) linguistic drafting may reduce syntactic problems to problems that can doubtlessly be solved through common sense—for example, that the word 'their' in (10a) refers to 'the ministers' and not to 'the King or Parliament'. Genuinely doubtful syntactic problems of interpretation—as contained, for example, in § 61 Danish Civil Service Act, in § 3 Trade Law, and in Art. 36 of the Statute of the International Court of Justice—might have been avoided through more diligent drafting. When a certain text is called clear or unambiguous, then this (strictly speaking) can only refer to its being interpreted syntactically. Semantically, a text is always fraught with the inevitable vagueness of the meaning of words and is, in this sense, never clear or unambiguous. There is something else that must not be confused with this, namely, that there may be practical situations where there is clarity in the sense that
[176] there are no doubts that the reference is determined by the text.

§ 26. Problems of Interpretation II: Logical Problems

Logical problems of interpretation are problems concerned with the relation of an utterance to other utterances in a given context. Contradiction, redundancy, and assumptions are particularly important among these problems.

(A) Contradiction

Two norms are said to contradict each other if incompatible legal consequences are tied to the same factual conditions.

Two norms can contradict each other in three different ways.

(1) *Total-total* contradiction: This means that neither of the norms can under any circumstances be applied without conflicting with the other norm. If the conditioning facts of each norm are symbolized by a circle, then a contradiction of this kind exists when the two circles are coextensive.

(2) *Total-partial* contradiction: This means that one of the two norms cannot be applied under any circumstances without conflicting with the other norm, whereas that other norm has a wider field of application where it does not conflict with the first norm. A contradiction of this kind exists when one of the circles is within the other circle.

(3) *Partial-partial* contradiction: This means that each of the two norms has a field of application where it conflicts with the other norm, but that each of them also has a wider field of application where no conflict arises. A contradiction of this kind exists when the two circles intersect.

To simplify our language, we can also use the following terminology without any possibility of misunderstanding:

(1) *Total* contradiction, or *absolute incompatibility.*

(2) *Total-partial* contradiction, or *contradiction between a general rule and a special rule.* The terms 'general' and 'special' rules are correlative. A rule is special in relation to another rule, if its conditional fact is a special case of the conditional fact of the other rule. If this is indicated by F (a, b, c), that is, a fact defined by the signs a, b, c, then the conditioning fact of the special rule is F (a, b, c, m, n). For example, if there is a rule stipulating that foreigners do not have the right to fish in the territorial waters of Denmark; and if there is another rule stipulating that foreigners, who have been domiciled here for two years, do have such a right, then the first rule is general in relation to the second rule, and the second rule is special in relation to the first rule.

[177] Sometimes (in the Criminal Code, for example) one applies a presentation technique that consists in dividing the code into a general part and a special part. This distinction must not be confused with the distinction between general and special rules (defined as above). On the contrary: the rules included in the general part are frequently special in relation to the rules included in the special part. For example, the rule in § 16 (on diminished responsibility) must be understood as an exception in relation to each of the sections in the special part, because, in regard to a certain subgroup of murderers, thieves, swindlers, etc., it warrants the deviating rule that they are exempt from punishment. In other cases, the rules included in the general part appear as supplementary provisions (concerning, for example, sentencing, different types of punishment, etc.) with respect to individual prescriptions of punishment included in the special part. The rules included in the general part are 'general' in a sense other than established above, namely, in the sense that they are common exceptions from, or additions to, the prescriptions of punishment included in the special part.

(3) *Partial* contradiction, or *norm conflict.* When assessing contradictions, the relationship between the statutes containing the conflicting norms is an important factor. A distinction must be drawn between contradictions within the same statute and contradictions between older and more recent statutes; and with regard to the latter case, depending on whether the two statutes are located on the same level or on different levels (§ 16 of the Danish Constitution).

I. *Total* contradictions are seldom found *in one and the same statute.* See, however, § 36 of the Danish Constitution 1920, where it is stipulated, in the first subsection, that the number of the members of the First Chamber must not exceed seventy-eight, while it contains, in the second subsection, detailed regulations for the members' election and distribution which make it clear that all in all, the number of members to be elected is seventy-nine. There are no general rules how to solve an absolute incompatibility between two norms. According to circumstances, the decision will depend on an interpretation based on data other than textual, or on discretion.

Nor does the relationship between *general and special rules* often give rise to interpretational doubts. Just as in spoken language, a special rule is frequently connected with a general rule by syntactic links ('however', 'unless', 'with the exception of', and the like), thus indicating that the general rule shall only apply with the limitation imposed by the special rule. In that case, there is no genuine contradiction at all but, rather, a linguistic form of expression which can be paraphrased as a single rule. Instead of the double version: 'Foreigners have no right to fish in the territorial waters of Denmark. However, those foreigners who have been domiciled in Denmark for two years, have such a right', one may just as well use the single form: 'Foreigners who have been domiciled in Denmark for two years, and only such foreigners, have the right to fish in the territorial waters of Denmark.'

Moreover, there is a general and established convention in statute drafting that the syntactic connecting links can be omitted without the meaning being altered. The special rule still limits the general rule. Frequently, the general rule [178]
is contained in one section, whereas the exceptions are contained in another section (or in several other sections). Thus, § 21 of the Age of Majority Act says unconditionally that both parents jointly exercise parental authority over legitimate children, while §§ 22–24 set up various rules for special situations where parental authority is given to either of the parents. To say that this is a simple linguistic interpretation with an implied syntactic conjunction; or that this is a positive rule of interpretation which can be called *lex specialis* (within the same statute), is a matter of opinion.

On the other hand, problems of interpretation will frequently arise in connection with a norm conflict within the same statute. There are no general rules to solve them: the decision must rely either on data other than textual, or on discretion. By way of example, one might adduce the relationship between articles 51 and 53 of the Charter of the United Nations. According to art. 53, no enforcement action shall be taken under regional arrangements or by regional agencies without the authorization of the Security Council (and one must remember that as a consequence of the veto rule, such an authorization will be obtained only if there is unanimity among the permanent members of the Council). According to art. 51, however, nothing in the Charter shall impair the inherent right of individual or collective self-defence if an armed attack occurs, and defence actions of this kind are not dependent on authorization. These two rules are conflicting and, consequently, the problem arises which of them shall yield if, according to a regional arrangement, one wants to enforce coercive measures of the nature of collective self-defence against an armed attack. This problem (which has figured prominently in the debate concerning the Atlantic Pact) cannot be solved by any linguistic interpretation or logical construction. The answer must depend on information on the genesis of the Charter or on an evaluation of the political desirability of one particular interpretation.

II. In the relationship between *different statutes*, it is often thought that contradictions of whatever kind must be resolved in accordance with two simple conventional rules of interpretation, known as *lex posterior* and *lex superior*, respectively.

Lex posterior means that of two statutes situated on the same level, a subsequent statute prevails over an earlier one. It is undoubtedly a basic legal principle (albeit not expressly formulated) that the legislator can repeal an earlier statute, and that he can also do this by issuing a new regulation which conflicts with, and replaces, the previous one. It is not correct, however, to elevate this principle to the rank of an absolute axiom. Experience shows that it is far from being invariably followed: indeed, it is set aside if interpretation or evaluation speak conclusively in favour of the opposite outcome. Therefore, the *lex posterior* principle can merely be characterized as one important consideration (among [179] others) when interpreting. Moreover, the force of the principle varies somewhat in different situations of contradiction.

(1) In cases of absolute incompatibility, it is hardly possible to conceive of considerations weighty enough to justify a departure from the *lex posterior* principle.

(2a) The same applies to cases of a total-partial contradiction when the subsequent rule is a special rule. Here, the *lex posterior* principle operates in conjunction with the *lex specialis* principle.

(2b) In the case of a contradiction between an earlier special rule and a subsequent general rule, the *lex specialis* principle can (according to circumstances) prevail over the *lex posterior* principle. For example, let us imagine an earlier statute, comprising a general rule to which, in subsequent legislation, various exceptions were made for particular situations. Later on, the earlier general rule was replaced by a more recent one in which the exceptions are not mentioned. In such a situation, it would depend on other data and evaluations whether or not the earlier exceptions were to be regarded as still scientifically valid.

(2c) The same applies to situations where the earlier rule is 'general' in the sense of comprising common exceptions from, or additions to, a group of rules. For example, if in subsequent special legislation (which primarily concerns other matters of life) penalty provisions and damages provisions are given, it can be reasonable to assume (according to the circumstances) that these, in spite of their being formulated without any reservation, must be limited according to earlier legislation which comprises 'general' rules on the conditions for, and shaping of, punishment and compensation.[1] For if these (as shown) are really special in relation to the single rules, then this is only a new result of the *lex specialis* principle. The same

[1] According to § 2 of the Penal Code, the 'general' provisions in chapters 1–11 apply *ceteris paribus* to all criminal offences. There is no doubt that it is the purpose of the paragraph that the general provisions shall also apply to future special legislation, since the latter does not expressly exclude their being applied. This purpose is in conflict with *lex posterior* as an absolute principle. For according to this principle, § 2 of the Penal Code must yield to each subsequent provision contradicting the paragraph, not only when subsequent law expressly repudiates the rule in § 2. § 2 of the Penal Code is an interesting example of legislation with the intention of (limited) precedence over subsequent law, in contradistinction to an absolute *lex posterior* principle. One might say that the legislator rises here above the present and identifies himself with 'Danish law' as a continuous tradition.

applies to subsequent rules on individual contractual relationships in relation to earlier 'general' rules on the validity of contracts, on the coming of age, etc.

(3) In the case of norm conflict, the *lex posterior* principle certainly supports the assumption that the more recent rule will take precedence over the earlier one, but that does not apply unconditionally. Here, as elsewhere, it [180] must be asserted—in subjective terms—that the *lex posterior* principle only applies if the 'legislator' has 'willed' the superseding of the earlier law. However, it may also be intended to incorporate the new rule harmoniously, as a supplement, into already existing law. The decision as to whether the first or the second possibility applies will, as usual, depend on evidence other than textual, or on discretion.

Lex superior means that in a conflict between legal rules of different rank, the rule at the higher level will take precedence over the rule at the lower level—irrespective of conflict type and chronological order: the Constitution takes precedence over ordinary legislation, which takes precedence over ordinances, etc.

Legal experience shows, however, that this principle cannot raise the claim of absolute validity, either. Firstly, the primacy of the constitution is contingent on the courts having competence to review the substantive constitutionality of ordinary legislation. Nay, even if the courts do have such competence they will, in fact, often shrink from stating conflicts and invalidity. In such cases, they are likely to uphold the *lex superior* principle formally, but they will refuse to recognize any conflict whose existence they would have acknowledged in other circumstances. Secondly, the legislative organ at the higher level may authorize the subordinate organ to issue rules with derogatory force vis-à-vis the norms at the level directly above. Thus, for example, ordinary legislation may authorize the King to issue ordinances which can repeal or modify valid law,[2] or authorize private individuals to enter into agreements in conflict with declaratory law. The possibility that the courts may deviate from the *lex superior* principle even without express authority cannot be excluded.

(B) Redundancy

Redundancy occurs when a norm gives rise to a legal effect which, under the same factual conditions, is authorized by another norm. One of the norms is then superfluous, as it were. In everyday speech, it is not unusual to embellish one's utterances with redundancies ('Now don't tell me lies—say how it really was!'). On the other hand, in the drafting of statutes (where more care is needed)

[2] See Alf Ross and Ernst Andersen, *Dansk Statsforfatningsret* II [Constitutional Law in Denmark II] (1948), 142.

one usually strives to avoid saying more than what is necessary. One might say that there is a presumption that the law does not contain redundancies, and an apparent overlap of two norms is, therefore, a motive to interpret one or the other of the two norms in such a way that the apparent redundancy disappears. An unconditional principle of interpretation to the effect that redundancies
[181] must not be allowed cannot be acknowledged, however. One must make allowance for certain eventualities—such as, for example, that the draftsman did not observe the overlap (especially in cases of redundancy in relation to a previous norm); or that one has wished, on historical grounds, to emphasize a particular view (for example: the prohibition in § 25 of the Constitution against provisional laws at variance with the Constitution); or that one has wished to provide a general survey (especially for the benefit of the less experienced reader) and to put forth, in a coherent way, what otherwise would have been discovered by comparing different regulations (*ex tuto* statements).

Actually, the doctrine of redundancy could be developed according to the pattern applied to contradiction; however, this would not be particularly interesting. The important thing is to point out that there is no technical solution for redundancy, either, and that the decision must be based on various considerations, including the general presumption that redundancy does not exist.

(C) Presuppositions

If I say to a child holding an apple in his hand, 'Give me that apple you have stolen', if the child has not in fact stolen the apple, then my directive has no realizable meaning. Whether the child in this situation chooses to hand over the apple or to keep it depends on motives and ideas that have nothing to do with a wish to comply with the directive. Something similar happens when a legal provision gives expression to factual or legal presuppositions which are incorrect or defective. The ensuing problems cannot, therefore, be solved through linguistic interpretation, but must be decided on the basis of other interpretation data, or at discretion.

A mistake of fact occurs, for example, when a statute refers to a harmless substance as a poison, prohibits fishing within an area which is (now) dry land, regulates navigation on a river which is not (any longer) navigable, or directs the administration to consult an organization which does not (any longer) exist. A mistake of law occurs when a legal rule gives expression to incorrect or defective presuppositions as to what is valid law, or concerning specific legal conditions, for example, that the age of majority in Denmark is twenty years, that women do not have the right to vote, or that a certain local area belongs to a different municipality than it actually does. Such gross inaccuracies are not likely to occur, of course. On the other hand, less flagrant discrepancies occur easily, especially when a statute refers to other statutes which, in turn, have been superseded by still other statutes, and when one has forgotten to update the reference.

Problems of interpretation may arise from mistakes of fact as well as mistakes of law, and they cannot be solved by any mechanically operating rule. Here, too, it is a question of harmonization with subjective interpretation data, common sense, and discretion. There may be an issue of either upholding the rule irrespective of its incorrect or defective presupposition, or of regarding it as no longer existing. In [182] the case of a mistake of law, the question arises whether the presupposition can be understood as authorizing a legal formation in conformity with its content.[3]

Reconsidering what has been said so far about norm conflicts, it is obvious that there are indeed no established principles concerning technical problem-solving. All types of logical problems of interpretation are logical in the sense that they are assessed through a logical analysis of the legal materials. On the other hand, they are by no means logical in the sense that they can be solved through logic, or by using mechanically operating principles of interpretation. *Lex specialis*, *lex posterior*, and *lex superior* are not axioms, but considerations of relative weight which, in interpretation, work together with other considerations—especially with an estimate of what kind of harmonization of the conflict would best conform to common sense, to the demands of a sense of justice, or to presumed social objectives.

[3] Per Augdahl, *Forelesninger over retskilder* [Lectures on the Sources of Law] (1949), 159, has submitted a few illustrative examples to point out the impossibility of laying down a general rule. Distinct from these are 'spurious conclusions e contrario' concerning situations where the meaning of the law is expressed indirectly or implicitly, see § 30.

§ 27. Problems of Interpretation III: Semantic Problems

The semantic problems of interpretation are those concerning the meaning of a legal provision, with particular regard to the sense or semantic reference of individual words.

On this issue, one can for the most part refer to § 24. In particular, it must be remembered that most words are ambiguous and that all words are vague, that is, their field of reference (or fields of reference) is (are) indefinite, consisting of a core and an outer circle of uncertainty; and that the precise meaning of a word in a specific situation is always a function of the unified whole, namely, of the utterance itself, the context, and the situation.

It is, therefore, erroneous to believe that semantic interpretation starts with ascertaining the meaning of the individual words and arrives at the meaning of the utterance by adding them together. The starting point is the utterance as a whole and the situation that has been experienced, and the issue of the meaning of an individual word is always the issue of its meaning precisely in this context. In the Danish language, the word 'house' can be used to designate a great variety of objects. There are dwelling-houses, the house on the back of a snail, inkpots, pencil boxes,* hen houses, the houses of royal families, etc. Under certain circumstances, an old shoe or a bottle can serve as a house (for example, [183] if a family of mice has settled there). However, in connection with planning and building regulations or preservation regulations we are perfectly aware—from the very start, and without even thinking about it—that the greater number of these possibilities is ruled out as being quite unreasonable.

Therefore, it is also erroneous to believe that a text can be so clear that any interpretational doubts simply cannot arise.[1] As discussed in § 26, this can be the case with respect to syntax (with the proviso of a certain minimum of common sense, *qua* precondition for understanding), but not with respect to semantics. As soon as we jump from the realm of words to the realm of things, we are confronted with a fundamentally insuperable uncertainty.[2] What we are

* Translator's note: The Danish words for inkpots [*blækhuse*] and pencil boxes [*penalhuse*] literally translate as 'ink-houses' and 'pencil-houses', respectively.

[1] This view is widespread, however. By way of example, one can adduce a provision contained in the draft of the Code Civil of the year VII: 'Quand une loi est claire, il ne faut pas en éluder le texte sous prétext d'en respecter l'esprit.' ['When a law is clear, we must not evade the text under the pretext of respecting the spirit.'] In this connection, Henri Lévy-Bruhl says the following in his work 'Les sources, les méthodes, les instruments de travail' [Sources, Methods, Tools] (1951), 283: 'si la loi est claire, son interpretation est inutile, voire dangereuse.' ['if the law is clear, it is useless, even dangerous, to interpret it.'] The International Court has repeatedly declared that 'les travaux préparatoires ne sauraient etre invoqués pour interpréter un text qui est, en lui meme, suffisament clair' ['the preparatory work cannot be adduced to interpret a text which is in itself sufficiently clear.'], Sér. A/B no. 47, 249 and no. 50, 378.

[2] Possibly with a caveat concerning individual designations (names) and numerals.

thinking of when erroneously speaking of semantically unequivocal utterances are clear, that is, obvious cases of reference; that is to say, situations where there is no doubt that an actual state of affairs meets (corresponds to) the meaning of the utterance.

Thus, semantic interpretation is not a mechanical process, either. Except in obvious cases of reference, the judge is forced to make a choice and adopt a certain position which is justified by something other than respect for the letter of the law. And even if the reference itself should be obvious, the judge, if he should deem it necessary (cf. § 30), will always have the possibility of legitimizing a deviating decision by applying a suitable argumentation technique.

§ 28. *Interpretation and Legal Practice*

The preceding sections included examples of various problems of interpretation, such as are usually presented to judges and other organs exercising legal authority.

In the following, we shall deal with the question of how these problems are solved in the exercise of legal authority.

However, by saying so I do not mean to suggest how these problems *ought to* be solved. As explained in more detail below (§ 31), current theories of interpretation
[184] are normative, that is, they purport to set up directives on how the law ought to be interpreted in the exercise of legal authority. In so far as they are deduced from preconceived ideas about 'the nature of the law', 'the concept of law', 'the purpose of the exercise of legal authority' and the like, they have the character of dogmatic postulates. In so far as they are based upon reality, from a perspective of social advantages and inconveniences weighed in relation to certain presupposed values, they have the character of legal political suggestions or recommendations to the judge. In both cases—except when they reflect (more or less incidentally) the method actually followed by the courts—they are equally useless for an understanding of positive law and the possibility of predicting future legal decisions.

The task before us is *analytical-descriptive*, that is, we intend to describe how interpretation is actually practised. As mentioned in § 23, a more thorough analysis must be left to the doctrinal study of a specific legal system. The task of a general methodology can only consist in explaining the general factors which operate in every exercise of legal authority and determine the framework of a *general typology* for characterizing the varieties in the style of method and interpretation that actually exists. Moreover, such an investigation into the real character of the task of interpretation and the various considerations surrounding it is a necessary prerequisite for a rational, legal political, and methodological discussion. Without insight into the very exercise of legal authority, we lack the basis necessary to arrive at well-founded, legal political desiderata as to the manner in which legal authority ought to be exercised.

Above all, one must be perfectly clear about the kind of activity the judge engages in when he faces the task of interpreting and applying the law to a specific case before him.

The task of the judge is an issue of *practical action*—this must be our point of departure. The judge must come to a decision on whether or not coercion shall be exercised against the defendant (the accused party). Certainly, the knowledge of various circumstances (the facts of the case, the substance of the legal rules, etc.) is important in decision-making, and the exercise of legal authority is so far dependent on theoretical processes. However, this does not alter the fact that the exercise of legal authority, albeit prepared by theoretical processes, is by its very nature, and definitively, a decision—an act of will.

Like all other deliberate decisions (for details, see § 70), this decision, too, must emerge from a state of consciousness consisting of two components: partly a motivating attitude (or several of them) which gives the activity a direction towards a goal; partly certain operational views, that is, a theoretical insight which directs the activity towards this goal. (To illustrate this point: my decision to take an umbrella with me when I go out stems from a desire to avoid getting wet as a driving motive, in connection with the operational view that it probably will rain, and that an umbrella is a device suited to protecting me from getting wet.)

The older positivist-mechanical theory of the function of the exercise of legal [185] authority gave a very simple picture of these components. The motivating attitude was assumed to be (or assumed that it ought to be) law-abidingness, that is, an attitude of respect and compliance with valid law (conceived of as the will of the legislator). The operational views were assumed to consist of (or assumed that they ought to consist of) an insight into the true meaning of the law, in conjunction with the available facts. It can hardly be said that the meaning of the law is always clear: frequently, the meaning must be discovered through interpretation. Interpretation, however, is basically a theoretical and empirical task. It may be that the meaning cannot be established with any certainty, and consequently there is room for discretion for him who exercises legal authority as to what, in the given circumstances, must be presumed to be the most likely outcome. However, the same uncertainty characterizes so many other problems of knowledge and it does not affect the theoretical character of interpretation.

Thus, this picture of the exercise of legal authority does not allow the judge to evaluate and take a stand vis-à-vis different interpretations. The judge is an automaton. Since his law-abidingness seems to be taken for granted, his function is limited to purely rational cognition: to grasp the meaning of the law and to compare the law's description of legal facts with the facts in the case before him.

This picture bears no resemblance to reality.

It is misleading for the very reason that interpretation in the sense of empirical description (as we have seen in § 24) frequently does not lead to any result. The inevitable vagueness of words and the inevitable limitation of intentional depth often make it impossible to establish whether or not the case in question is covered by the meaning of the law. There is nothing unclear about the case in question. It is possible to specify reasonably well the intention or the meaning of the words in such a way that the facts of the case are covered by the law. However, it is also possible, and just as reasonable, to understand the law in such a way that the case falls outside the law's frame of reference. Descriptive interpretation proper must give up, but the judge cannot give up. He must make his choice, and this choice, no matter which choice, will originate in an evaluative deliberation. In this sense, his interpretation of the law is *constructive*, not merely descriptive, and it presupposes some other motive than that of following a certain directive.

However, the picture is false in yet another way, because it is based on untenable psychological views on the activity of the judge. The judge is a human being like everybody else. The decision he makes is underpinned by his entire personality. Even if obedience to the law (formal legal consciousness) is deeply rooted in the judge's mind as a professional and moral attitude, it is nonetheless a fiction that obedience to the law should be the sole driving force. The judge is not an automaton, mechanically transforming statute articles plus facts into decisions. He is a human being who wants to fulfil his social task by making decisions which he feels to be 'correct' in the spirit of our legal and cultural tradition.
[186] His respect for the law is not absolute, and obedience to the law is not his only motive. To him, the law is not a magic formula but, rather, a manifestation of the ideals, attitudes, objectives, or evaluations which we have called cultural tradition (§ 19). Under the label 'substantive legal consciousness', this tradition is alive in the mind of the judge and creates there a motive which may conflict with the demand of formal legal consciousness for obedience to the law. His criticism can be directed against the decision in a specific case—a decision which is felt to be inequitable in spite of the fact that the rule itself is considered equitable; or it can be directed against the rule itself. Criticism can appear in the judge's consciousness as a spontaneous emotional reaction; or emerge as the result of a conscious analysis of the effects of the decision or of the law, measured in relation to presupposed considerations and objectives ('policy considerations'; thus far, then, his critical attitude is co-determined by legal-sociological views). These attitudes will at any rate work together in the mind of the judge as a motivating factor in his decision. The judge will understand and interpret the statute as far as possible in light of his substantive legal consciousness, so that he is able to accept his decision not merely as 'correct', but also as 'just' or 'societal'. If the tension between the formal and substantive legal consciousness exceeds a certain limit, the judge may even disregard the outcome of descriptive statutory interpretation. Then, his constructive interpretation is not merely a specification, but a correction of the outcome reached by a purely descriptive interpretation of the law.

Thus, one can say that the exercise of legal authority is *the resultant in a parallelogram of forces, where the dominant vectors are the formal and the substantive legal consciousness, respectively*. The decision that is made is determined by the combined effort of theoretical statutory interpretation and the evaluating attitude of the legal consciousness.[1] It would not be correct to restrict this evaluating activity to the comparatively rare occasions when it manifests itself as a deviation from the outcome of descriptive statutory interpretation. The substantive legal consciousness is active in all decisions. If the judge in the majority of cases holds on to a decision within the scope of descriptive statutory interpretation, it is a sign that his legal consciousness could approve of the decision, or that his legal consciousness at any rate did not find it contradicting the 'just', or the socially desirable, to such an extent that he deemed it necessary, as a last resort, to try to free himself from the bonds of the law. If the judge had found the decision unacceptable by virtue of the moral, legal, and political postulates of his legal consciousness, he would have been able, through suitable argumentation, to find a different and better solution.

Thus, although the exercise of legal authority is widely different from statutory interpretation in the proper, descriptive sense,[2] it is nevertheless quite common to use this term (interpretation) to designate the whole activity leading the judge to his decision, that is, including his evaluating views informed by directing attitudes outside the law. This linguistic usage has to do with a desire to conceal the active, deliberative function and keep up the appearance that the law, and nothing but the law, determines the outcome. Therefore, the judge does not openly admit that he has set aside the law. Through a certain technique of argumentation which has developed as a traditional element in the administration of the law, he makes it look as if his decision, through legal interpretation, could be deduced by means of various inferences (for details, see below § 30). [187]

As a result of the above, it can be stated that the exercise of legal authority is more than mere intellectual activity. It is rooted in the judge's entire personality, in his formal and substantive legal consciousness, as well as his rational views. It is constructive and deliberative interpretation as well as descriptive interpretation, aimed at the reading of specific interpretation data. It is at the same time knowledge and evaluation, passiveness and activity.

In order to arrive at a true understanding of the judge's function, it is important to emphasize the two-fold nature of his exercise of legal authority. At the same time, however, it must be admitted that the distinction between his cognizing

[1] This does not mean that the two factors appear, in the consciousness, as independent motives and considerations which thereupon are weighed against each other. This might possibly occur, but more likely they will more or less amalgamate, so that the judge spontaneously interprets the law in light of his own sense of justice and his social evaluations.

[2] This has already been realized by Ørsted: he distinguishes between interpretation proper and inferences of consequences in the spirit of legislation, see *Haandbog over den danske og norske Lovkyndighed* [Compendium on Danish and Norwegian Knowledge of the Law], vol. I (1822), 292–93. Even Bentzon, *Retskilderne* [The Sources of Law] (1900–1907), 184–85, distinguishes between (receptive) interpretation and (productive) gap-filling.

functions and his evaluating functions is an artificial one, in so far as these practically merge, thus rendering it impossible to specify where one ends and the other begins. This is due to the fact that for the judge himself, as well as for others, it is problematic or even impossible to distinguish between, on the one hand, those evaluations which are the judge's own, and thus are expressions of his active deliberation; and, on the other hand, those evaluations which are ascribed to the legislator, and thus are a datum for purely descriptive interpretation. As pointed out in § 24, the meaning-determining function of the context lies in the very fact that it provides a basis for what the author can *reasonably* have meant in the given situation. Similarly, all proper legal interpretation includes presumptions concerning the social considerations and evaluations which must be assumed to have motivated the legislator. If the judge now—rightly or wrongly—identifies his own evaluations with those of the legislator, then the distinction in his mind between passive-descriptive and active-deliberative interpretation will vanish. Indeed, one might draw a parallel between this situation and what has been said earlier (on pages 59–61 *et seq.*) about the blurred boundary between legal-doctrinal intention and legal policy considerations in [188] the theory of law. It follows that the boundary is fairly blurred between (a) those cases in which the judge believes that there are certain reference points—either in the law itself, or within its legislative history—which prove that his interpretation conforms to the legislator's intention; (b) those cases in which the judge—rightly or wrongly, and without his being aware of it—identifies his own pragmatic attitudes with those of the legislator; and finally (c) those cases in which it is clear to the judge that he is interpreting the law in the light of ideas which cannot be ascribed to the legislator—ideas which even may contradict the latter's intentions.

In the preceding section, the general factors common to every exercise of legal authority were established: on the one hand, an activity which comprehends or understands in a purely rational way, aiming at expounding given data; on the other, an evaluative and deliberative activity which, in itself, may be co-determined by legal-sociological ideas (policy considerations). Within this framework, however, various *types as to style of interpretation* can be distinguished, depending on the force with which each of these factors makes itself felt, as well as on the data which in interpretation proper, descriptive interpretation, is conventionally taken into consideration.

(a) According to the degree of freedom with which the judge permits himself to interpret, re-interpret, or even correct the directives of the law in light of the demands of substantive legal consciousness and social exigencies, we can distinguish between a (relatively) *free* and a (relatively) *bound style of interpretation*. However, it is difficult to decide whether the difference in style is really as big as it may seem at first sight. It may be that the difference, at least to some extent, is not so much a difference in the freedom that the judge takes advantage of, as in the bluntness with which this freedom is acknowledged.

Around the middle of the last century, a distinctly bound style of interpretation had developed in France and Germany. In conformity with the spirit of a strictly positivistic theory of the sources of law, an attempt was made to make it appear that a legal decision could always be derived from the law with the aid of linguistic interpretation and logical methods of inference, or that it could be constructed through deduction from presupposed legal concepts ('conceptual jurisprudence').[3] At the turn of the twentieth century, a strong opposition arose against this in both countries: in France, this opposition went by the name of 'le combat pour la méthode', and in Germany by the name of 'die Freirechtsbewegung'.[4] The traditional method was labelled 'rule worship', 'stickler for the letter of the law', and 'formalistic construction of concepts',[5] and the opposition demanded that the judge should have more freedom to draw his inspiration [189] from life, practical needs, and interests. This demand became amalgamated with natural law ideas of a 'natural law', discovered scientifically on a philosophical or sociological basis in order to supplement the positive law ('la libre recherche scientifique', 'das freie Recht'). It is not easy to decide to what extent this movement was an expression of a genuinely legal and political demand for a new spirit in the exercise of legal authority, and to what extent it was merely a legal-theoretical reckoning with the then current formalistic fictions of interpretation.[6] Here in Denmark, there was no corresponding 'battle of methods', but slowly and steadily, there seems to have arisen a tendency towards a freer style of interpretation.

(b) Another difference in the style of interpretation has to do with the extent to which data other than the wording of the law are used as a basis for interpretation proper, that is, for the activity that purports to establish the meaning of the law as neutrally as possible. In § 24 we mentioned the difference between so-called subjective and objective interpretation, and in conformity therewith, we can distinguish, in statutory interpretation,

[3] For details, see Alf Ross, *Theorie der Rechtsquellen* [Theory of the Sources of Law] (1929), ch. II, 3 and VI, 6.

[4] For details, see *op. cit.*, ch. III, 4–9 and ch. VII with a comprehensive bibliography.

[5] A typical example is the following caricature of the positivistic conception of the judge: 'This high-ranking official with academic record is sitting in his cell, armed only with a calculating machine (albeit with one of the best kind, to be sure). The only piece of furniture in the cell is a green table, on which the Code of Law [*das staatliche Gesetzbuch*] is placed. You may put any case before him—a real case or a fictitious one: he will be able, duty-bound, to establish with absolute exactness the decision predetermined by the legislator, through purely logical operations and a secret technique, intelligible only to himself.' Gnaeus Flavius, *Der Kampf um die Rechtswissenschaft* [The Battle for Legal Science] (1906), 7.

[6] By way of expressing, rather excessively, the ideas of the Free Law Movement, it is customary to mention *Magnaud*, who, in the last decade of the nineteenth century, had been appointed as President of the tribunal at Chateau-Thierry. Because of his decisions (which showed great humanity, but only little respect for the letter of the law) he acquired the nickname 'le bon juge' ['the good judge']. Cf. H. Leyret, *Les Jugements du président Magnaud* [The Judgments of President Magnaud] (1900).

between a *subjective and objective style of interpretation*. A completely objective style of interpretation (that is, understood as an interpretation that is exclusively founded upon the wording of the statute) is unthinkable. The judge's understanding of the law will always be influenced by a number of situation factors and their connection with the rest of the legal materials. He will never be able to avoid taking into account that the text before him is not a piece of prose fiction or a scientific work, but a law, that is, a tool for political management, emanating from conflicting interests and ideas and aiming at certain social objectives. The judge's understanding of the meaning of the law will always depend upon his understanding of the law's social motives and purposes. What distinguishes a subjective from an objective style of interpretation is, in reality, only their respective attitude about the issue of whether or not the *travaux préparatoires* are to be considered as interpretation data in order to throw light on the purpose of the law and on the details of its meaning.

The distinction between subjective and objective interpretation does not coincide with that between bound and free interpretation. The former concerns the manner in which the interpretation proper comes into being; the latter concerns the degree of freedom with which the judge reacts to the outcome of this interpretation. There is nonetheless a connection between them, however. Precisely because objective interpretation rejects certain
[190] interpretation data (the *travaux préparatoires*) and keeps only to the text in question, it will frequently lead to somewhat vaguer results than does subjective interpretation, thereby providing a larger scope for the judge's discretion. In a certain sense, then, objective interpretation is more subjective than subjective interpretation.

The interpretational importance of the *travaux préparatoires* lies in the circumstance that they may contain information concerning 'the legislator's' intention with the legislation in question, the general considerations and evaluations underlying it, or a deeper insight into the formulation of individual rules.

However, in what sense are the *travaux préparatoires* able to give information about 'the legislator's' intentions? If the legislator were a single individual who did all the legislative work himself, then there would be no problem. In reality, however, there is no single legislator, and the laws are largely worked out by persons who are not part of the legislature. Thus, for example, the *travaux préparatoires* are worked out by the administration, or by specialists. What is decisive for a law's coming into being as a law is solely the fact that there has been a decisive vote in Parliament where a bill in its final form has obtained the requisite number of votes. Thus, the actual 'will of the legislator' lies ultimately with those members of the House who have voted for the bill. But how can the *travaux préparatoires* give any information about the attitudes held by these persons who possibly did not even know about the submitted bill but merely—as a matter of routine—voted in favour of it?

The answer to this question can be found in something purely conventional. Indeed, the importance of the *travaux préparatoires* is owing to sheer convention. If their importance has been established, however, then this convention furnishes a basis for the reasonable conclusion that the passivity of the voting members can be seen as an expression of approval of the views set forth in the legislative material. For precisely because of this convention, the voting members have a motive to study the *travaux préparatoires*, knowing that if they do not dissociate themselves from them it will be interpreted as approval. Also, one might say that what is put to the vote is not merely the legislative text but, rather, the text in the light of the accompanying motives and other parts of the legislative material.

According to these views, various circumstances will have an impact on the weight attached to different types of *travaux préparatoires*. Their importance will depend on the extent to which the draft has been amended in the course of the readings in Parliament. Naturally, there is no new legislative material to a draft that has been amended. The better drawn up a draft is—especially if it is drawn up by a commission of experts—the greater will be the weight attached to the accompanying *travaux préparatoires*. With regard to the prevailing importance of committee work for the qualified debating of a bill, one generally attaches greater weight to statements in a committee report than to statements made in the House. In Denmark important issues concerning the scope and understanding of a basic formulation have even found a solution through an authoritative [191]
committee decision.[7]

It cannot be denied that subjective statutory interpretation entails a considerable amount of uncertainty. It dissolves, as it were, the very concepts of the law and makes it difficult for the citizens to know what rules they should obey. This circumstance, together with the English judges' traditional aversion and jealousy vis-à-vis statutory law (which is regarded as an intrusion into the territory of common law) would explain why English jurisprudence only to a very limited extent permits them to use the *travaux préparatoires* for statutory interpretation. Reports of parliamentary debates are not admissible as documentation of the statute's objective ('the policy of a statute'), and a report of a Royal Commission can only be used as a documentation of the state of the law previous to the passing of the

[7] See, e.g., the report submitted by a parliamentary committee dated 14 February 1947, concerning the meaning of the expression 'unreasonable prices', as found in § 8 Act on Prices etc., nr. 472 of Nov. 28, 1942, *Rigsdagstidende* [Parliament News] 1946/47, supplement B, column 2552, cf. supplement A, column 2661–62 and 2665–66.

statute. Therefore, English judges are forced to form their opinions of the statute's objective solely on the basis of the statute itself.[8]

On the Continent, on the other hand, the *travaux préparatoires* are usually acknowledged as interpretation data.[9] Of course this does not mean that the *travaux préparatoires* are 'binding' upon the judge; only, that they are, in the interpretation proper, one element among others which additionally may overlap with opposing free considerations and evaluations. The freer the interpretation, the easier it is for the judge to ignore even clear statements in the *travaux préparatoires*. Therefore, the supreme importance of the latter lies in their being determining factors in the choice between alternatives among which none is clearly preferred by the judge as being the practically most valuable one.

The *travaux préparatoires* will naturally become less important as the statute gets older. Subjective statutory interpretation will then assume the character of *legal-historical interpretation*. In spite of certain dogmatic ideas concerning 'the will of the legislator' endowing the law with its 'force', it is practically inevitable that the judge will offer resistance towards being ruled by the dead, if the conditions of present-day life and the evaluations represented by us suggest that we interpret the law in a spirit other than the
[192] original legislator's.[10] This view is particularly important for the interpretation of constitutions, which frequently remain unaltered in their original and venerable form, while the preconditions for political life are subject to the law of development. It is a well-known phenomenon that in such a case, an extensive 'Verfassungswandlung'[11] or 'reinterpretation'[12] can take place without any formal amendment to the constitution.

[8] See, e.g., G. W. Paton, *A Text-Book of Jurisprudence* (1946), 191; W. Friedmann, *Legal Theory* (2nd edn, 1949), 282; C. K. Allen, *Law in the Making* (4th edn, 1946), 404 *et seq.*

[9] Concerning Norwegian law, the book by Jon Vislie, *Lovmotivers Betydning for Lovfortolkningen* [The Importance of Legislative Material in Statutory Interpretation] (1932) provides some interesting information. Methodologically, it is a traditional normative work.

[10] Ballot-Beaupré, president of the Cour de Cassation, expressed this view in a striking way on the occasion of the centenary of the Code Civil in 1905, by using the following, much-quoted words: '(The judge) should not get involved in an obstinate search for what was, a hundred years ago, the idea of the authors of the Code; he should ask himself what this idea would be if the same article were formulated by them today: he should understand that, considering all the changes which, over the course of a century, have taken place in morality, in the institutions, and in the economic and social conditions of France, justice and reason demand a liberal adaptation of the text to the realities and needs of modern life.'

[11] Georg Jellinek, *Verfassungsänderung und Verfassungswandlung* [Constitutional Amendment and Constitutional Transformation] (1906).

[12] Ernst Andersen, *Forfatning og Sædvane* [Constitution and Custom] (1947).

§ 29. Pragmatic Factors in Interpretation and their Results

In §§ 24 and 27, it was emphasized that all interpretation starts from the utterance as a whole, together with the context and the situation in which it occurs. Therefore, it is erroneous to believe that the starting point consists of individual words, understood according to their natural linguistic meaning. This linguistic meaning is extremely wide, but as soon as the word occurs in a given context its field of reference is restricted. Take the word 'house', for example: what does this word not cover purely linguistically! When appearing in the Building Code, however, most of these possibilities are automatically excluded (§ 27).

It has also been pointed out that the meaning-determining function of the context lies in the fact that the context offers a basis for conclusions as to what the author may *reasonably* have meant. When it comes to interpreting statutes (and other practical directives), this view takes a particular turn. In this context, 'reasonable' does not mean 'theoretically probable'; rather, it means *practically reasonable*. The interpretation is here built upon the assumption that the legislator wished to lay down something which in its practical effects would harmonize with the objectives, evaluations, or attitudes by which he was presumably swayed.

By *pragmatic factors* in the exercise of legal authority, I mean all the co-determining considerations based upon an evaluation of the practical reasonableness of the result, judged in relation to certain presupposed evaluations. The pragmatic factors hereby contrast with the purely linguistic ones (the individual words, the joining of words, the context together with the parlance). In this context, one does not consider whether the operative evaluation is ascribed to the legislator himself, so that it is a question of a proper, descriptive interpretation; or whether it is a result of a critical attitude on the part of the judge, so that it is a question of a constructive interpretation in the name of the sense of justice.

Thus, pragmatic factors assert themselves everywhere the result of interpretation deviates from what a merely linguistic interpretation—blind towards all practical [193]
evaluation—would lead to. They assert themselves much more than is generally assumed. As a rule, one puts the 'point zero', in relation to which the pragmatic or teleological interpretation is measured, at the point of 'the natural linguistic understanding in conformity with the customary meaning of the words'. As mentioned previously, however, this meaning is in reality to a great extent (albeit more or less unconsciously) co-determined by the practical reasonableness and fairness of the result. With respect to § 14 of the Constitution, there is no doubt that the word 'their' refers to 'the ministers'; from a purely linguistic and syntactical point of view, however, this understanding is not an obvious one.

When § 49 paragraph 3 of the Constitution states that each House appoints '15 members' to form a committee, it is obvious that this means 15 members of the respective House and not, for example, 15 members of a sports club. The word 'citizenship' in § 50 of the Constitution means, of course, 'Danish citizenship', and when § 56 of the Constitution states that no Member of Parliament can be 'charged' ['*tiltales*'],[*] no one would think for a moment that this means that he must not be spoken to. This is so obvious that we must make an effort to see that it might be at all possible to understand the legal rule in question in any other sense than the 'obvious' one. It is nonetheless true that in these and innumerable similar cases, the interpretation is not solely determined by 'the meaning of the words according to common linguistic usage'. It is beyond dispute that in the Danish language, the above-mentioned words can quite easily be used with the invented 'unnatural' meanings. When these meanings are so 'unnatural' within the given context that one must make an effort to discern them, then this is due to pragmatic considerations. The outcome will be so obviously awkward and unreasonable that this possibility simply does not occur to us.

Therefore, we can assert that interpretation does not have any independent linguistic starting point, but that it is *from the very beginning co-determined by pragmatic considerations* in the shape of 'common sense'.

However, let us disregard this in the following and, in conformity with common understanding, move point zero upwards to what is called 'natural linguistic interpretation' and which is, in reality, pragmatic interpretation which has excluded the obviously unreasonable.

At that level we find 'higher' pragmatic considerations, expressing themselves in conscious deliberations concerning the consequences which one or the other interpretation will lead to, together with an evaluation of these consequences in relation to presupposed attitudes (considerations) and a weighing between these different evaluations and considerations—in short, what is usually called argumentation on the basis of policy considerations. Thus far, there is no fundamental difference between legal political argumentation *de lege ferenda* and *de sententia ferenda*. The difference lies solely in the ties with which the statutory wording restricts the legal practitioner's freedom of action.

[194] It is not really feasible to enumerate or classify the possible evaluations in pragmatic interpretation. It may not only be a question of particular, predicted social effects, but also of more general considerations as to the legal-technical perspicacity of the interpretation, or as to its harmonious fit with the legal system and the cultural ideas on which the system is building. Here, attention is

* Translator's note: The Danish verb 'at tiltale' can mean either of these two things to address someone, or to charge someone (with an offence).

drawn solely to the negative view, namely, that pragmatic interpretation cannot be identified with interpretation from the perspective of the *purpose* of the law, and consequently that the current term *teleological interpretation* is misleading in being too restricted. For more than one reason.

First, even if the purpose of an activity can be pinned down more or less precisely, this is not the only guideline for carrying out this activity. For we never pursue a single purpose to the exclusion of all other considerations. For example, if the purpose of building a bridge is to provide better communication facilities between two provinces, the construction of the bridge is not exclusively determined by this purpose or this consideration. In itself, the purpose simply demands that the bridge be made as effective as possible. However, this demand must be weighed against conflicting considerations or be coordinated with neutral ones—such as, for example, production cost, interference with shipping, aesthetics, military and political considerations, local interests, etc., etc. The purpose indicates the intended effect. However, unwelcome effects and various side effects on different levels must be taken into consideration as well as guidelines for displaying the activity. The same applies to the activity which consists in legislating and carrying out laws in the exercise of legal authority. Here, too, it is impossible to keep one's eyes rigidly fixed on the isolated *ratio* of the individual legal rule, and more comprehensive evaluating approaches must be adopted.

Secondly, it is frequently impossible to establish—even approximately—the exact purpose of a legal rule. On a subjective basis, one might obtain information about the effects intended by the legislator.[1] But what happens if the *travaux préparatoires* are silent on this matter, or if objective principles of interpretation are used? Which of the predictable effects shall be chosen as the purpose of the rule? In a situation like this, 'the purpose of the rule' is not something that is found but, rather, a construction—a mere label we affix to our evaluations.[2]

[1] Sometimes the legal text itself contains information concerning the purpose; see, e.g., § 41 of the Danish Promissory Notes Act.

[2] In his work *Är den juridiska doktrinen en teknik eller en vetenskap?* [Is the Doctrinal Study of Law a Technique or a Science?] (1951), 21 f., especially at 29, Per Olof Ekelöf suggested a method of how to 'determine' the purpose of a legal rule. The method amounts to the following. The legal rule, as such, is seen as a means for achieving the purpose which these means are meant to serve. To this end, not every possible application can receive consideration. One must adhere to applications which are both clear and typical, which means that there are no circumstances pointing at either restrictive or extensive interpretation. In my view, this kind of reasoning is definitely untenable. First, since both restrictive and extensive interpretation are justified precisely through purposive considerations, it is impossible to indicate a typical field of application before one has formed an opinion of 'the purpose' of the rule. This is circular reasoning (an issue touched upon by Ekelöf himself). Secondly, from the use of a certain means one cannot draw conclusions concerning the purpose which these means shall serve. Just like other measures, a legal rule has chains of effects in manifold directions. Which of these effects are intended? Ekelöf admits that, naturally, not all of them can receive consideration. 'Only those which are part of the overall result, realized through harmonious cooperation between the rule in question and other rules of valid [*gällande rätt*] law, is of importance *qua* purpose of the rule.' However, this criterion merely tells me that the assessment of what is assumed to be the purpose of the law must depend upon a comprehensive evaluation in the spirit of the legal system. Provided that there is no subjective indication, the purpose of the law cannot be determined objectively; rather, it is the result of an evaluation.

[195] Finally, it is frequently impossible to ascribe any purpose to a law. Purposive considerations chiefly belong in areas where the modern legislator intervenes technically and administratively in the life of the community, through various regulations and measures for political purposes (in the narrower sense): economic legislation; business legislation for the regulation of production and trade; social welfare legislation; legislation dealing with building and fire inspection; health legislation, etc. On the other hand, when it is about legal rules concerning our central legal institutions, deeply rooted in our cultural tradition, then it is frequently impossible to ascribe any purpose to them. For example, what is the purpose of marriage laws and divorce laws, of the laws on property and the laws on inheritance? What is the purpose of permitting intestate succession in five classes? Anything that could be said about that is either so trivial or so contrived that as a benchmark, it is practically useless. The purpose of divorce laws is to show people the proper way to get a divorce, etc. An altogether different issue is the following, however. When a certain institution—such as, for example, the institution of marriage—is taken as given in its entirety, then an individual, integral rule can be judged according to the extent to which it fits with the institutional whole. But as mentioned before, this is something completely different from purposive considerations.

Therefore, we maintain that, similarly to legal and political considerations *de lege ferenda*, pragmatic interpretation is evaluation that includes a great variety of considerations; and that adaptation to the purpose of the law (the intended effect) is only one consideration among many others, and has therefore to be weighed against, and made to harmonize with, other active considerations. If one still prefers to speak of teleological interpretation (and not, as I do, of pragmatic interpretation), it must be emphasized that *telos* does not refer to the isolated purpose of the individual legal rule, that is, to the effect that is directly aimed at; but that it refers *pars pro toto* to all applicable considerations and evaluations.

In the following, I shall turn to the effects of (higher) pragmatic considerations measured in relation to the results of 'natural linguistic meaning' (which, as mentioned previously, as such already contains a considerable amount of pragmatic reason). There are only three possibilities: pragmatic considerations imply
[196] either specifying, restricting, or extending the rule's 'natural' field of application. Accordingly, the correct terms are specifying interpretation, restrictive interpretation, and extensive interpretation.

(a) *Specifying interpretation* occurs when pragmatic considerations are decisive for the choice between several interpretations, all possible and reasonable within 'natural linguistic interpretation'. The choice may refer both to syntactic and to logical and semantic interpretational doubts and, as regards the latter, to doubts concerning ambiguity as well as vagueness.

Example: The word 'property' in § 80 of the Constitution can be reasonably understood both in a narrower sense (comprising full right of disposal over an object) and in a wider sense (as being synonymous with property right). Pragmatic considerations are decisive in choosing the wider meaning. Hereby, a possible meaning of § 80 is being specified.

Augdahl adduces an amusing example of an audacious, pragmatic, specifying interpretation. During the war between Norway and England, an Order of 1807 proclaimed that *inter alia* 'saddles and 'tømmer' [i.e., reins]' were to be considered contraband of war (which may be seized as war prize). A neutral vessel bound for England and laden with balks, masts, rafters, etc., was captured by a Norwegian privateer and taken to Kristiansand, where it was brought before the local prize court. Was the cargo a proper prize of war? The Norwegian word *tømmer* is ambiguous. It can mean both *timber* and a *piece of riding equipment* [namely reins]. The textual context within the Order suggests of course the latter meaning, and the prize court accordingly released the vessel. On appeal, however, the High Court of Admiralty found that the ship was a prize of war. It was a naval war and Norway had nothing to fear from the English cavalry, whereas masts and rafters were indispensable to the British fleet. Against this background, it could not be assumed that the word 'tømmer' was referring to riding equipment.[3]

(b) The term *restrictive interpretation* is used when pragmatic considerations exclude the application of a rule in cases which, according to 'a natural linguistic interpretation', doubtless fall under the rule's scope of application. We can distinguish two sub-categories:

(1) *Restrictive purposive interpretation* occurs when the restriction is due to the motivation that, in certain cases, the application of the rule is superfluous (useless) for achieving the purpose of the law. [197]

Example 1: Pursuant to § 78 of the Constitution, any person who is taken into custody shall be brought before a judge within twenty-four hours. When the purpose of § 78 is presumed to consist in guaranteeing the security of the citizens against any deprivation of liberty that lasts more than a negligible period of time, it is unnecessary to bring the person taken into custody before a court when the police are willing to release him before the twenty-four hours have run out. The provision is thus interpreted restrictively.

Example 2: Pursuant to § 71 of the Constitution, judges can usually only be dismissed by judgment. Legislation lays down the requirements for legal capacity. If there is a condition for retirement among these to

[3] Per Augdahl, *Forelesninger over Rettskilder* [Lectures on the Sources of Law] (Oslo 1949), 174.

the effect that judges shall be dismissed when they have reached a certain age, it will be superfluous in such a case (considering the purpose of the provision—namely, to safeguard the independence of the judiciary) to apply the provision concerning dismissal by judgment. The age of a judge is such a well-known fact that there cannot be any danger in letting the administration attend to the dismissal.

However, also within this context one must bear in mind that a consideration focusing only on the purpose (on the intended effect) does not exhaust all possible pragmatic considerations. In particular, one ought to be attentive to the circumstance that positive effects apart from those that were directly aimed at may indicate that a certain rule ought to be applied, quite irrespective of the fact that from a mere purposive consideration, such a measure would be superfluous.

(2) *Restrictive interpretation of exceptions* is the term used when the restriction is motivated by opposite considerations, despite the fact that the case itself is covered by the purpose of the provision. If the opposite considerations have found expression in other overlapping statutory rules, this interpretation turns into a norm conflict (§ 26).

It is often difficult to illustrate this type of interpretation with the help of clear examples, because the courts are usually unwilling to admit openly that they are limiting the province of the law but, rather, choose the phrase that it cannot be assumed to be 'the purpose of the law' or 'the intent of the legislator' to affect a case such as the one before them. As mentioned earlier, these 'teleological' expressions are used as a cover for any kind of pragmatic considerations. Anything the judge himself thinks good and right, he politely ascribes to the real or hypothetical will of the legislator.

Sometimes the legislator himself is aware that a rule is too broad without, however, being able to say more precisely where to draw the line. In such a case he will content himself with a hint to the judge that the rule should be interpreted restrictively, because he leaves it to legal practice to
[198] discover the considerations and circumstances determining the demarcation. The word 'unlawful' can be used for this purpose. When §§ 28 and 29 of the Contracts Act mention a declaration of intent that has unlawfully been elicited through violence or the use of other kinds of force, then this expresses that no kind of force will be taken into account. Similarly, not every exploitation of somebody else's mistake for one's own benefit is regarded as fraud or deceit. However, here it is also difficult to draw a demarcation line, and § 279 of the Penal Code evades this problem by speaking of 'unlawful' exploitation. Even without any such pointer, however, the judge will frequently have occasion to interpret a rule restrictively because of conflicting considerations.

Moreover, we often speak of restrictive interpretation when a legal provision is restricted through an implicit reservation for certain general rules or principles, be they authorized by law or not. Examples include when the special rules of the Penal Code are interpreted with a number of general reservations (self-defence, necessity, legitimate law enforcement, *negotiorum gestio*, utility etc.), or when legal provisions concerning special contractual relationships are interpreted with a reservation for the general principles of the law of obligation. However, in these cases where the judge is confronted with restricted considerations as part of valid law, it would be preferable to speak of a norm conflict.[4]

(c) The term *extensive interpretation* is used when pragmatic considerations result in the application of the rule to situations which, seen in the light of 'natural linguistic interpretation', clearly fall outside its frame of reference.

On the face of it, one might be inclined to think that extensive interpretation is symmetrically similar to restrictive interpretation, and that it therefore shows analogous forms. Upon further reflection, however, it appears that this is not the case. On the basis of purposive considerations, there is often a great deal of certainty that a legal reaction in certain cases is not necessary to realize the purpose, and that a restrictive interpretation is therefore indicated. On the other hand, it will rarely happen that an extensive interpretation is necessary for a legal rule to achieve its presumed purpose. In this situation, one must consider the possibility that the restriction was owing to conflicting considerations. It requires a more detailed investigation and is an expression of a far more radical evaluation of the legal rule to maintain that such considerations do not apply, and that the rule therefore ought to be extended. Also, restrictive interpretation referring to conflicting considerations appears largely as a matter of course. There is no parallel to this in extensive interpretation. This disparity between the two types of interpretation is reflected in common legal usage in the following way: while restrictive interpretation is denoted by precisely this expression, extensive [199]
interpretation is mostly called *argument by analogy*—an expression which indicates that it is a question of a more complicated process than restrictive interpretation. Further, 'analogy' is often conceived of as a new, independent legal source beside the law. It is impossible to point out any fundamental difference between mere extensive interpretation and argument by analogy. The former expression is used in connection with more modest extensions, in particular if there are special indications that a word is used with a wider aim than is covered by its normal linguistic meaning.

The problematic underlying extensive interpretation (the argument by analogy) may be described in the following way. If a rule according to its

[4] Cf. Viggo Bentzon, *Retskilderne* [The Sources of Law] (1900–1907), 339 *et seq.*

'natural linguistic meaning' applies to sphere (a), its extension to sphere (b) presupposes (1) that a legal evaluation according to the purposes and ideas that are presumed to have determined the rule, is in favour of applying it also to sphere (b). Such an evaluation can be especially based on the view that the rule is a casuistic formulation, an unfinished, sporadic revelation of a more general point of view. And (2) that there is no difference between (a) and (b) which, according to other legal evaluations and ideas, could justify a different treatment of the two cases. If, for example, older statutory provisions employ words such as 'he' and 'man', it might be argued that the differentiation between men and women within the legal sphere in question is no longer based upon the ideas which govern modern law, and that these provisions, therefore, should be extended to women by analogy.

In traditional interpretation theory, these two evaluations find their expression in the comprised formula 'the similarity of causes'. Moreover, one usually adds that it is a condition for an argument by analogy from (a) to (b) that (b) is not yet determined by statute. This is not respected in practice, however, nor does the requirement seem well founded. It must be assumed that the relation between the analogical rule and an existing statutory rule covering the same case will be judged like other instances of conflicting norms. Thus, for example, there will be nothing to prevent the extension by analogy of a rule of exception, despite the fact that the case is covered by the general (earlier) rule.

(d) There are no further possibilities besides those mentioned under (a), (b) and (c). Compared with 'natural reading', an interpretation is either specifying, restrictive, or extensive. The type of interpretation known as *argument a contrario* is not a further variant of higher pragmatic interpretation: either it is merely a part of the 'natural reading', or it is an expression that extension by analogy has been rejected.[5]

[200] For those cases where a meaning according to linguistic custom is expressed indirectly but nevertheless unambiguously, we may use the term *spurious arguments a contrario*. If we say: 'Ten candidates sat the examination, of whom one passed', then, obviously, the meaning is that the other nine candidates have failed. It would be fanciful to maintain that the utterance as such merely says that one has passed at any rate, and that the utterance therefore does not exclude the possibility that perhaps others have passed as well. The same mode of expression is frequently found in legal language. When, for example, § 6 of the Constitution rules that the King shall be of age when he has completed his eighteenth year, this means indubitably that he is under age until then. When it is said in various other sections that the King cannot do this or that without the consent of Parliament,

[5] This idea has not been expressed previously. Without this idea, however, it is very hard to explain what, exactly, an argument *a contrario* amounts to. Thus, for example, Per Augdahl's account of it in his work *Forelesninger over Rettskilder* [Lectures on the Sources of Law] (1949), 160 *et seq.* seems unclear to me.

it is hereby unequivocally said that he can do these things with the consent of Parliament. When § 4 of the Companies Act says that there must be no less than three founders, nobody will doubt that three founders are sufficient. In these and a great many similar cases, 'the argument *a contrario*' is merely a part of the general linguistic interpretation and cannot claim the attention of the doctrine of higher pragmatic interpretation—which is precisely the interpretation which goes beyond the natural-linguistic interpretation.

An argument a contrario proper, on the other hand—that is, an argument which goes beyond a general linguistic interpretation—is not a genuine argument. It merely implies that a legal rule is applied with the limitation which, to a certain extent, emerges from its content, since one thereby rejects the possibility of extensive interpretation by analogy with respect to that limitation. Let me clarify this by looking at some examples. § 29 of the Contracts Act says that a declaration of intent that has unlawfully been elicited by compulsion, is not binding on the person thus compelled, if the person to whom the declaration was addressed has himself used compulsion, or has realized, or ought to have realized, that the declaration has been elicited unlawfully through coercion by a third party. We usually say that we can infer *a contrario* from this that, as a rule, a declaration of intent is binding if the recipient has acted in good faith. Since § 29 occurs as an exception from the general rule of the binding force of promises, the 'inference' only means that the exception expressed in § 29 is adhered to with the limitation that the addressee of the promise is acting in bad faith, thereby rejecting the possibility of extending the rule by analogy, so as to include cases of good faith as well. Similarly, if we conclude from the rules in §§ 29 and 30 of the Danish Promissory Notes Act, saying that the debtor in certain cases is released from paying to the transferor, that the debtor (as a rule) is not released from paying to third persons other than the transferor. This only means that one adheres to §§ 29–30 with the given limitation and resorts to the general rule that a debtor is not released by paying other persons than the creditors. §§ 42–44 of the Danish Marriage Act I contain rules concerning those cases where marriage can be dissolved. [201]
From this, one can presumably 'infer' *a contrario* that a marriage cannot be dissolved in other cases—not, for example, if the marriage has been concluded in defiance of conditions as to age. However, this only means that one rejects extension by analogy concerning the cases where marriage can be dissolved. In connection with the general view that marriage cannot be dissolved unless there is a legal ground for it, this rejection leads to the aforementioned result.

In systematic statutory documents like those mentioned above, an 'argument *a contrario*' is based on the presumption that the statute has been so thoroughly thought through that its provisions with regard to exceptions, conditions, etc. may be regarded as exhaustive. However, it may also be that the opposite is indicated, either in the statute itself or in the accompanying commentaries. § 15 of the Danish Promissory Notes Act lists a number of objections as forfeitable, but we cannot conclude from this that all other objections are non-forfeitable. This emerges partly from the *travaux préparatoires*, partly from the statute itself, which, in its § 17, includes a contradictory description of a number of non-forfeitable objections. This means that one has decided to waive an exhaustive enumeration, thereby explicitly leaving the door open for any of the groups being extended by analogy.

The habitual approach to this problem is the following. In a given situation, one has the choice between inferring by analogy and inferring *a contrario* from a statutory provision. From what has been said above, it will emerge that, in reality, the choice lies between undertaking and not undertaking an extensive interpretation by analogy.

§ 30. Pragmatic Factors and Argumentation Technique

It is only rarely that the constructive part played by the judge in the exercise of legal authority, when defining more precisely, or correcting, the directive of the law (as discussed in the previous section), is actually manifest. Usually, the judge does not say: the law has more or less abandoned me, but for certain practical reasons, I make this decision within the framework of the law—or even by transgressing it. On the contrary: the judge, by employing an *argumentation technique*, usually tries to make it look as if the decision he makes can be discovered objectively and rationally by studying the given data and is, therefore, covered by 'the meaning of the law' or by 'the intention of the legislator'. Thus, he tries—for his own benefit, or at least for the benefit of his surroundings—to preserve the picture (discussed in § 28) of the exercise of legal authority as solely determined by the motive of respect for the law, combined with rational insight [202] into the meaning of the law or the will of the legislator.[1]

When the combined factors—the formal and the substantive legal consciousness combined with notions of the wording of the law, its purpose, its effects, etc.—have worked together in the judge's mind and prompted him to make a certain decision, then a sham legitimation is constructed which, to a larger or smaller extent, differs from what in reality has determined the judge's decision.

If the judge is satisfied with applying the law in clear reference cases, he keeps to the literal wording of the statute, possibly combined with a rejection of a conceivable repression or restriction of it by the application by analogy of other legal rules (argument *a contrario*). On the other hand, if the judge desires to make a decision which lies within the ambiguous sphere of the rule (specifying interpretation), or which even goes against the 'natural linguistic meaning' (interpretation by restriction or by extension), he seeks support for the desired result wherever he can find it. If the *travaux préparatoires* can offer support, they are cited, otherwise they are tacitly ignored. A norm conflict leaves the judge much freedom and offers wide possibilities for 'justifying' a desired result, not least when there is also an overlap with extensions by analogy concerning other

[1] The following remarks made by Justice Bernard Botein, *Trial Judge* (1952), 52, illustrate the constructive function of the judge and, at the same time, the fiction that the judge after all merely moves within the limits of the law:

'A judge first searches the facts, then searches the law, and lastly searches his soul. If all three inquiries lead in the same direction, his task will be easy, but if they diverge, he cannot straddle for any appreciable distance.

Laws are not made to be broken by judges, but in sensitive hands, they have a certain tensile tolerance for yielding to meet an individual situation. The law will snap back when pressed too far by an insensitive judge who lays violent hands upon it. It can be twisted out of shape by an impetuous judge.

The judge who has come of age will shape the law within the range of its tolerance, to fit the contours of the particular case. The precise, meticulous judge will miss the contours through the unyielding severity of his plumb line.'

legal rules. Moreover, restrictive interpretation can be achieved by constructing 'the meaning of the law' or 'the intention of the legislator' out of considerations of the presumable purpose of the law. Extensive interpretations are supported by the circumstance that the conditions for an argument by analogy are satisfied. If the judge cannot think of any other possibility, he will resort to mere postulates as to what is, or could be, the legislator's intention, simply presuming that the legislator must naturally have meant and wished what is regarded as well-founded and desirable by the judge himself.

The secret of this argumentation technique lies in the fact that there is no criterion that indicates when to use what 'rule of interpretation', or what 'method of inference'. When are pronouncements in the *travaux préparatoires* decisive? [203] When there are no considerations sufficiently weighty for disregarding them![2] When to infer by analogy, and when *a contrario*? To a certain extent, this choice can be motivated by the interpretation data available. As mentioned earlier, the systematic character of a statute, possibly in connection with some pronouncements in the *travaux préparatoires*, can thus be a very strong, almost compelling, reason for rejecting extension by analogy. Apart from that, there is no external criterion indicating when to use argument by analogy and when to use 'argument *a contrario*'. Pursuant to § 3 section 1 no. 2 of the Danish Tax Law, the staff at embassies of foreign countries are exempt from paying taxes, no distinction being made between Danish and non-Danish nationals. On the other hand, the last sentence of the same section states expressly, with regard to consulate officials, that exemption from paying taxes applies exclusively to non-Danish nationals. On this basis, the High Court of Eastern Denmark[3] concluded *a contrario* that this restriction did not apply to embassy staff, implying that the court has refused to apply, by analogy, the rule concerning consulate officials to the embassy staff. However, if the court had wished to achieve the opposite result it might have argued that, presumably, it was owing to an oversight that citizenship is not mentioned as a restriction with respect to the embassy staff, and that the rule in § 3 section 1, last sentence concerning the consulate officials should be applied by analogy to the embassy staff, since there is no reason why the two cases should be treated differently. While it is a matter of course (according to a classic example) that the prohibition against, for example, letting dogs travel on trams must be interpreted by analogy (or *a fortiori*) with reference to apes, bears, or other equally annoying animals, this is due to a legal evaluation of the result in relation to the policy considerations underlying the prohibition. However, if another solution is preferred, it would be equally possible (according to circumstances) to infer *a contrario*—for example, if the prohibition is

[2] See, e.g., *UfR* 1952, 735: Two judges interpreted § 4 of the Danish Vacation Law with regard to the *travaux préparatoires* of the law, while seven judges abstained from doing so because they ascribed greater weight to the (under the circumstances justified) requirement for unequivocal statutory authority.

[3] *UfR* 1952, 28.

motivated by the risk of spreading canine diseases. Should we infer *a contrario* or by analogy from a prohibition against walking around in a bathing suit, when it comes to walking around in one's birthday suit? The decision will doubtlessly depend on whether the prohibition was put up in a nudist camp or on the terrace of a missionary hostel.

All this is rather technical: it is one of the tools which any trained lawyer handles with skill. He has to know how to justify, in an acceptable way, the solution he finds 'just' or socially desirable, in conformity with the postulates of his convictions of law and justice. However, one must not get dazzled. It would be a mistake [204] to think that this technique—these 'methods of interpretation' for manipulating the wording of the law—are the driving factors. Barring a few exceptions (certain arguments *a contrario*, cf. this §), these methods are so cleverly arranged that they never impose themselves, but can be chosen according to need. It is not the methods that determine the conclusion: it is the conclusion that determines the methods. One chooses what one needs. However, the evaluation by the legal consciousness is always the driving power, while the methods merely serve to 'cover' the result. Otherwise it would be curious, would it not, that until now, one has never yet heard of an argument by analogy imposing itself even if one deems the conclusion deplorable.[4]

An interesting socio-psychological problem in itself is why one should wish to conceal what really happens in exercising legal authority. Now is not the time to approach this problem. We must content ourselves with stating that the urge to pretend that the exercise of legal authority is a simple deduction from objectively given legal rules, without any evaluations given by the judge, seems to be a universal phenomenon.

There is probably no reason to regard this fictionalization in the exercise of legal authority as a misfortune, whether or not the judge himself believes that the sham argumentation expresses what actually determines his decision. Without thorough socio-psychological investigations, one dare not even deny the possibility that it may have beneficial societal effects.

That this concealment of the truth is not compatible with science is a totally different matter altogether.

In the case of a description *de lege lata* (such as the description of the present state of the law that has evolved through practice, invoking a constructive 'interpretation' of certain legal provisions), the actual justification of what is scientifically valid law must be sought precisely in this practice, not in the interpreting of sham arguments which practice has made use of by way of legitimation. Good

[4] With respect to American law, the same view is emphasized and convincingly illustrated by Torstein Eckhoff, *Rettsvesen og rettsvittenskap i U.S.A.* [Legal System and Legal Science in the USA] (1953), 139, 153 f., 194 and 199 f.

examples to illustrate this are the regulations concerning negotiability before the Danish Promissory Notes Act came into being. The fact was that there was no legislation concerning this issue, but that the courts, under pressure from the exigencies of life, gradually developed a well-constructed practice concerning the forfeiture of rights to, and objections to, bonds and other negotiable documents. In England, under the same circumstances one would have spoken of a doctrine of negotiability, grounded in a number of precedents. Here in Denmark, one pretended that this very complicated set of legal rules was authorized by an interpretation of two rather short, specific provisions in § 2
[205] Regulation Febr. 9th, 1798 and in § 1 Regulation July 28th, 1841, at the end of the document. This interpretation was a sheer cascade of fireworks consisting of conjuring tricks with varying arguments by analogy, complete and partial arguments *a contrario*, and deductions from general principles. Of course, one might have masterfully tampered with the two short regulations and arrived at a diametrically opposed result—if one had thought that it conformed to the needs of practical life. It is really incredible that this jiggery-pokery should have been taken seriously by legal science. The only reasonable thing to do would have been to describe the rules that had developed through the practice of the courts, and then possibly to add in a footnote that in conformity with current Danish argumentation technique, one had attempted to legitimize these rules through interpreting the two regulations in a certain way. One did the opposite, however: in all seriousness, one referred to the scrawl as a legal authority and put the precedents in footnotes.[5]

This also applies to considerations *de sententia ferenda*. The task of doctrine is to clarify assumed evaluative attitudes, to give an account of the considerations, and to analyse social facts and contexts in order to provide the courts with instructive material for their law-creating function through constructive interpretation. This is honest and straightforward. When the power behind the law-creating activity of the courts is precisely the sense of justice and the policy considerations underpinning them, it must be assumed that this method of procedure is effective. Nor is there anything wrong if doctrine, in order to relieve the courts, indicates how to turn the argumentation by means of sham legitimation. It is a misrepresentation, however, if doctrine attempts to justify its recommendations, or simply pass them off as scientifically valid law, by setting up one or the other (more or less stilted) interpretive argumentation.

[5] Pursuant to § 46 of the Constitution, no taxes shall be imposed, altered, or repealed except by law. It has been asserted that historically, 'law' ['*lov*'] meant general law, as opposed to the Budget. Nevertheless, in practice tax and tariff laws are regularly altered through a note attached to the Budget. Ernst Andersen (Alf Ross and Ernst Andersen, *Dansk Statsforfatningsret* II [Constitutional Law in Denmark II] (1948), 111–12) believes that even if the historical meaning is retained, § 46 can be interpreted in such a way that this practice does not contradict the Constitution. It is assumed that § 46 purports to protect the interests of the Upper House of the Danish Parliament [*landstinget*]; that the House, by passing a licensing law of a financial content, has renounced this protection, and that § 46 is consequently not applicable. Can anyone believe that this interpretation would have been invented if it did not purport to legitimize the present practice?

A typical example of this type of argumentation is Vinding Kruse's nicely turned interpretation of King Christian V's Danish Law [Danske Lov], 6-17-5, in view of providing legitimacy for a recommendation to the courts to recognize extinguishment in favour of *bona fide* purchasers in the open market at a sale of chattels.[6]

In both cases, the interpretation manoeuvres show symptoms of pettifoggery [206] which have no place in honest science. A lawyer should not acquire a reputation for interpreting the law in the same way as the devil reads the Bible. This is lawyerly rhetoric, not law [*jura*]. Probity and realism require us to put our cards on the table, and this means that we honestly give an account of practice (*de lege lata*) and legal political *desiderata* (*de sententia ferenda*) without basing either upon an unworthy interpretation technique, the function of which is to make others (or oneself) believe in an illusory legal basis.

[6] See Vinding Kruse, *Ejendomsrettens Overgang* [Ownership Transition] (1924), 114; cf. Alf Ross, *Ejendomsret og Ejendomsovergang* [Ownership and the Transfer of Ownership] (1935), 117.

§ 31. Confrontation

Similar to the traditional theory of the sources of law, the traditional methodology is constructed, not as an analytical-descriptive theory expounding how legal practice, in particular legal interpretation, is actually done, but as a dogmatic-normative doctrine stating how the law ought to be administered, how the law ought to be interpreted. These dogmatic postulates are developed, more or less consciously, by deduction from preconceived ideas of 'the concept of law', 'the nature of law', and 'the task of the exercise of legal authority', and are formulated as assertions concerning the 'purpose' of interpretation. From these postulates a number of deductions regarding general principles of interpretation or more concrete rules of interpretation are made. In general, it can be said that these constructions are irrelevant to an understanding of scientifically valid law or to the prediction of future legal decisions unless they reflect, more or less incidentally, the method actually practised by the courts; and that their relative truth value is limited in so far as they attempt to force the various interpretational considerations into one single 'purpose'.

There is of course a close connection between the theory of the sources of law and methodology. A *positivist* theory of the sources of law, intent on deriving the validity of all law from a supreme, powerful, sovereign will (§ 22), is in parallel with a theory of interpretation, which sees the task of interpreting the law from the perspective of the inner coherence of the given legal material, and without involving legal principles, purposes, or evaluations outside the law. A number of 'logical methods of inference' have been developed, which helps in deducing the meaning that is contained in legislation beyond what is directly expressed. These methods of conclusion are often developed through so-called conceptual construction. The possible legal effects are believed to be determined by a limited number of given concepts, presupposed by the legal order, and a legal case is
[207] decided by classifying the case under one of the recognized concepts, whereupon the solution is deduced from the legal effects contained in this concept.[1]

[1] By way of illustration we can mention the Norwegian jurist F. Hagerup, who, in a programmatic article ('Nogle Ord om den nyere Retsvidenskabs Karakter' [A few words on the nature of modern legal science], *Tidsskrift for Retsvitenskap* 1888) polemicizes against a trend 'which numbers highly talented and energetic adherents especially among Danish lawyers', and which 'has so to speak revived the method of deducing the legal rules from external principles—not, however—as does natural law—from abstract postulates of reason but, rather, from certain general, economic or ethical, principles (the interests of commerce, the principle of public utility, the principle of conservatism, the principle of veracity, etc.)'. According to Hagerup, these purposes outside the law are irrelevant, both to the doctrinal study of law and to legal practice. 'The basis for all doctrinal study of law . . . can only be the valid legal rules themselves.' It is *the internal coherence of the legal material itself* (i.e., excepting the practical purposes or interests which condition the law, but lie outside the legal rules themselves) which it is the task of the construction to show, and which yields the only valid principle as a basis for the application of law (op. cit., 19–20. The expressions used here as well as the emphases are Hagerup's own).

In contrast to the above, there are the theories of method of the '*Freirechtsschule*'. They correspond to the idealistic theories of law, according to which the validity of the law is derived from an idea, a principle or a purpose inherent in law (the idea of justice, people's legal beliefs, the principle of solidarity, the principle of public utility, etc.), and according to which the law is only regarded as a more or less successful attempt to realize this idea. Accordingly, the task of statutory interpretation is defined as 'thinking the law to its fruition', in conformity with the principle immanent in the law. Depending on the assumed basic attitude towards the nature of law, the theories of method and interpretation of the *Freirechtsschule* can have the appearance of *natural law*, or show *sociological* or *historico-psychological* signs. In modern times, in particular, it has been customary to refer to considerations of social purposes and balancing of interests as guidelines for free legal interpretation.[2]

The theories of the *Freirechtsschule* get nearer to the truth than the positivist theories. Underneath the dogmatic-normative garb, there is a correct understanding of the fact that the exercise of legal authority is different from a logical derivation from positive norms. The positivist theories conceal the judge's legal-political activity. Just as the chess player is motivated, not only by the norms of chess but also by the purposes of the game and by insight into its theory, the judge, too, is motivated by social objectives and operative views on legal-sociological contexts. As has been mentioned in § 29, the part played by free considerations can vary with the style of interpretation, but they can never be completely excluded. The 'immanent logic' employed by the positivist theories is an illusion. The 'legal basis' immanent in the legal rule itself cannot be separated from the practical purposes lying outside the rule, nor can the 'formal [208]
consequence' be separated from an evaluating adjustment of the rules in relation to assumed evaluations and purposes.

Within the theory of interpretation in the narrower sense, there is usually a distinction between the so-called *subjective and objective theories*. According to the former, the purpose of interpretation is to discover the will of the legislator. According to the latter, however, the law is regarded as an objective manifestation of the mind which, once born, 'lives a life of its own' and must be understood solely on the basis of what emerges from it. The external communication—'the words,' not the 'will' behind them—constitutes what is legally binding and, thus, the object of any interpretation.

As has been mentioned in § 24, this distinction is false. Actually it concerns the interpretation data which are taken into consideration. What distinguishes the

On positivist theory of the sources of law and positivist theory of interpretation, see further Alf Ross, *Theorie der Rechtsquellen* [Theory of the Sources of Law] (1929), ch. III, 3 and ch. VI, 6; on conceptual jurisprudence, see Ross, *Virkelighed og Gyldighed i Retslæren* [Reality and Validity in Jurisprudence] (1934), ch. VII, 7.

[2] For further information, see Alf Ross, *Theorie der Rechtsquellen* [Theory of the Sources of Law] (1929), ch. III, 4–9 and ch. VII with comprehensive reference information.

subjective theory from the objective theory is the question of what importance attaches to the *travaux préparatoires*, and this question of course cannot be answered on a basis of metaphysical ideas as to whether the 'binding force' of the law springs from 'the will' or 'the word'. One might ponder the advantages and disadvantages of either theory, but when it comes to a current legal system, it is a factual question whether the courts traditionally follow a subjective or an objective style of interpretation, cf. § 29.

Between the end of the eighteenth and the beginning of the nineteenth centuries, the theory of interpretation, or hermeneutics, played an important part in theory. In conformity with the metaphysics of the will taken over from Roman law, and in harmony with the political ideology of absolute monarchies, the predominant view was purely subjectivist. This applies also to Ørsted, who taught that even an unambiguous linguistic interpretation has to give way when it is certain that the legislator has meant something different than the linguistic interpretation suggests.[3] Not until the second half of the nineteenth century did an objective theory appear, with writers like Thöl, Binding, and Kohler. In Denmark, this theory is represented by Goos, who believed that he could prove, through deduction from the legal concepts, that the true meaning of the law and the purpose of interpretation is not the meaning which 'the legislator has intended the law to have' but, rather, 'the meaning which the notification of the law can evoke in him who receives it in his consciousness'.[4] This view is also endorsed by Vinding Kruse, according to whom it is 'a common law of life' that 'the words of a declaration of intent, such as they must be understood naturally, according to common usage, must apply with regard to the law as a major rule—not the hidden will of the utterer of the declaration of intent, nor a wish or an expectation on the part of the receiver. Thus, the very words of the statute or the ordinance, understood objectively according to common linguistic
[209] usage, constitute the standards for the citizens' decisions; not the *travaux préparatoires*, showing that the legislator meant something different from what the clear words of the law are saying.'[5]

It will emerge from this chapter that both the objective principle of interpretation and the subjective principle are dogmatic constructions. The fact is that the Danish courts do not follow one single principle, but that both the *travaux préparatoires* and 'the natural linguistic meaning' are powerful factors in the exercise of legal authority, together with overarching pragmatic interpretive considerations. It is impossible to create a rule saying that 'the will of the legislator' takes precedence over the words of the law; nor is it possible to do the reverse—namely, to create a rule saying that the words of the law take precedence over

[3] A. S. Ørsted, *Haandbog over den danske og norske Lovkyndighed.* [Compendium on Danish and Norwegian Knowledge of the Law], (1882), 355 cf. 292.
[4] [Goos], *Indledning til den danske Strafferet* [Introduction to Danish Penal Law] (1875), 160 f.
[5] Vinding Kruse, *Retslæren* I [Jurisprudence] (1943), 193–94.

the 'will'. As has been mentioned in § 29, the weight that can be ascribed to pronouncements in the *travaux préparatoires* and other kinds of legislative material varies according to circumstances, and in most cases, *freirechtliche* evaluations will be the decisive factor in the choice between subjective and objective interpretation.

In the current literature, Bentzon's theory of interpretation occupies an exceptional position. He opposed all attempts at developing an 'ideal' (normative) theory of interpretation, deduced from the concepts of law and the application of law or derived from 'the nature of the matter', and he maintained that the task must consist in discovering, analytically-descriptively, the principles followed (maybe unconsciously) by Danish practice ('true' Danish theory of interpretation).[6] Also, he realized that interpretation depends on a discretionary weighing up of a number of considerations and, consequently, that it is not possible to set up proper rules concerning the methods of procedure: the utmost a theory can do is to give expression to the most important tendencies that have dominated practice. These considerations frequently overlap, and it has been the fault of the theories until now that they have failed to appreciate this and wanted to discover a single formula for the aim of interpretation.[7] Bentzon's theory of interpretation was surprisingly realistic, and the viewpoints discussed in this chapter proceed along the course pursued by Bentzon.

6 Viggo Bentzon, *Retskilderne* [The Sources of Law] (1900–1907), 195 *et seq.*, 202.
7 *Op. cit.*, 205–07.

[210] CHAPTER V

The Legal Modalities

§ 32. The Terminology of Legal Language

As explained above in § 7, legal norms must be interpreted as directives to the judge, telling him how to decide a certain case; that is to say, as interpreted from a juridico-scientific perspective which is directed at stating what is scientifically valid law. However, it is very rare for the law (the Penal Law, for example) to be framed linguistically according to this pattern. Usually the law addresses citizens directly, prescribing how they should behave towards each other, and in such a way that the directive to the judge emerges indirectly.

However, directives to citizens are not formulated as typical regulations either, telling them how they should behave in certain situations. At this point, we encounter the curious circumstance that the law is frequently not expressed in colloquial directional terms, that is, in terms directly expressing a call to action (an order, a desire, a suggestion, etc.). Instead, the law seems to contain a description of a mechanism through which various events (facts or human actions) produce a number of invisible effects which are called 'duty', 'claim', 'ability', 'validity', etc. The law often expresses itself as another reality existed beyond the world of time and space—a world of 'legal relationships' determined by forces which have been released through 'law-creating' ('law-amending' and 'law-dissolving') facts in accordance with the respective provisions of the law. For example, the law says that certain facts are 'binding' upon a person or 'obligate'
[211] a person, and that other facts have 'exonerating effects'; that certain facts create a 'right' for a person—a right which can be altered or extinguished by virtue of other facts, and either possess 'validity' or 'yield' in relation to other person's 'right'. In the case of a sale, for example, the law expresses itself as if the agreement produced a 'legal relationship' between the parties, consisting of a set of 'claims' and 'duties' for each of them. By virtue of other events, these effects develop dynamically. If the seller does not deliver on time, for example, the buyer becomes 'able to' cancel the contract and claim damages, which is to say that henceforth, certain actions on his part have the 'effect' that his own 'duty to pay' is 'extinguished', whereas the seller's 'duty to deliver' is transformed into

a 'duty' to pay a certain sum of money. In a similar way, a number of other, subsequent events (impossibility, performance, bankruptcy, etc., etc.) may intervene and create 'effects' through which the 'legal relationship' between the parties is subject to change. If the legal relationship has not been 'annulled' previously, it can ultimately be realized in a judgment and its enforcement and thus vanish into thin air.

Thus, the law appears to consist of theoretical statements (assertions) concerning an invisible world of peculiar qualities—of legal relationships—which are created and evolve as the effects of a particular 'force of law' within certain facts. As explained in § 2, however, we cannot possibly take this mode of expression seriously. It is absurd to say that some invisible effects arise when we enter into a sales contract. Whatever the explanation of how this terminology has arisen—and this is not an issue I shall discuss here—it is clear that the real meaning and function attaching to the law is not theoretical, but practical. The apparently theoretical statements of the law are, in reality, meant as directives to influence the behaviour of human beings—citizens and judges alike.

Yet conversely, the peculiar mode of expression we have mentioned just now is a fact, compelling us to investigate the words and phrases used by the law in a directive function. Specifically, we have to disentangle the mutual relationship between the different phrases and find out if a fairly stable and unambiguous terminology has evolved. On the basis of an analysis of the legal materials, we can distinguish between the following groups of expressions.

(1) Expressions of duty and synonyms

Expressions in which we are told that person A under certain conditions *has a duty* or *is obligated* to act in a certain way, occur very frequently. That A *shall*, *must*, or *has to* act in a certain way, or that *it is incumbent on A* to act in a certain way, are expressions used synonymously.

These expressions—in line with common linguistic usage, and reflecting the citizens' attitude of respect and obedience vis-à-vis the legislator's authority—are suited to motivate the citizens to behave accordingly. This effect is enhanced [212] through an appeal to self-interest, since the same expressions also motivate the judge: if A does not comply with his duty (and if certain other conditions are fulfilled), then the judge will be motivated to adjudicate so that certain unpleasant sanctions against A will be carried out.

It is the latter effect that interests the jurist. When he is studying the law in order to establish what is scientifically valid law, then—as we have seen—this means exactly that he tries to form a well-founded opinion about the judge's possible reaction. It is of vital importance to him to be able to anticipate societal reaction in case the directive of the law is not obeyed. His expert knowledge in this particular field amounts to an insight into how the judge is likely to be motivated by the law, and the task that is expected of him consists of conveying the possibilities so that people may adjust their behaviour accordingly, and in the best way possible.

However, it becomes apparent that the reaction that can be expected if A does not comply with what the law has called his duty is not always of the same kind.

(a) In some situations, A will risk being sentenced.

(b) In other situations, A will risk a judgment providing for enforcement, that is, a judgment ordering A to fulfil his duty. This judgment is the basis of executive measures. These measures imply—that is, if A continuously fails to fulfil his duty—either that the desired result[1] will be achieved by means of physical force, or that A will be prevailed on to fulfil his duty through coercion.[2] This will occur, for example, when A's duty consists of paying a certain sum of money to another person, and also—at least in most cases—when A's duty amounts to the delivery of individual or generic goods.

(c) In yet another situation—for example, if A has a duty to accomplish certain individual work tasks, or in a case whereby there are certain obstacles preventing fulfilment of his duty—A will hardly be ordered to fulfil his duty but, rather, to pay *damages* instead (*performance interest*).

(d) It is also the case, however, that the law states that a certain behaviour is A's duty without any of the above-mentioned effects arising. Pursuant to § 51 of the Danish Sale of Goods Act, the buyer in a non-consumer contract has a duty to inspect the goods, and pursuant to §§ 26, 27, 31, 32 and 52, both the seller and the buyer have a duty of notification. In these cases, sentences, judgments providing for enforcement, or orders to pay damages are
[213] not possible. The legal effect tied to the non-compliance with these duties does not pose a risk of A himself being sentenced, but implies a curtailment of his own legal position, that is, a risk of not being able to achieve a judgment against the other party. In these cases, the fulfilment of the duty is a *condition* for gaining or retaining certain legal advantages.

From a juridico-ideological perspective, there is a radical difference between, on the one hand, the situations in (a), (b), and (c) and, on the other, the situation in (d). In the former situations, the legal reaction is also experienced as a social and moral resentment of A's pattern of behaviour, intended to prompt him as well as others (in other situations) to fulfil their duty. A's contrary behaviour to

[1] The bailiff will deprive him of the object he meant to deliver, for example, or of his belongings which, if sold at auction, can realize the sum of money that he owes.

[2] He will be ordered to pay day-fines, for example, or a sentence will be imposed on him.

this is therefore called unlawful. In the latter situation there is no such thing. The fact that the buyer does not examine the goods, or that he does not announce that he means to invoke a fault, is only an omission in so far as he thereby harms his own interests. Any experience of social disapprobation is not involved here, and the buyer's behaviour is not called unlawful.

(2) Expressions of claim and synonyms

In legislation, expressions such as: B *has a claim for*, B *can claim* or B *can demand* are used in close correlation with the expressions of duty mentioned under (1). Thus, B's claim (against A) is *the counterpart to A's duty* (towards B). These two things are two sides of the same coin, and it does not matter if you say, for example, that A has a duty to pay damages to B (§ 24 of the Danish Sale of Goods Act), or that B has a claim for damages against A (§ 30 of the Danish Sale of Goods Act).

As far as I know, however, this applies only to the cases mentioned under (1)(b) and (1)(c), that is, to those cases where A can be found guilty, and for which a private prosecution brought by B is a precondition. Therefore, it can hardly be said that someone has a claim against others not to be killed by them, or that the seller has a claim against the buyer to examine the object of purchase.

(3) Expressions of right and synonyms

In legal terminology, expressions such as: A *has a right to* and A *is entitled to* are used in very different senses.

(a) In many cases, this means the negation of the notion that A has a duty to behave in a way which is contradictorily opposite to the one indicated, and that he is consequently *permitted* to act as indicated, or that he is free to act or not. For example, when § 39 of the Danish Sale of Goods Act states that the seller, under the given circumstances, has the right to retain the goods or to prevent them being handed over to the buyer's estate, this means that he has no duty to deliver the goods or to let them be handed over to the buyer's estate. Thus, he is permitted to do as he pleases, whether this be retaining the goods or handing them over. Further examples of this can be [214] found in several sections of the Constitution, which state what citizens 'have a right to' do, or 'are entitled to' do; meanwhile, the Danish Trade Law states what trade licences 'entitle to'. There are many more such instances to be found besides these.

Similarly to the expression 'claim to', the expression 'a right to' corresponds to a relationship of duty. The difference lies in the fact that while A's 'claim to' is the counterpart of B's duty, A's 'right to' is *the negation of A's duty vis-à-vis the contradictorily opposite behaviour.*

When the legislator has occasion to express himself negatively, it is often because the pronouncement includes a further specification of, or an exception from, a presupposed general rule. Thus, the rule in § 39 of the Danish Sale of Goods Act appears as an exception from the general rules on delivery and tradition in §§ 14–16; the constitutional rules appear as a restriction of the general competence of the legislative power; and the rules of the Danish Trade Law appear as exceptions from an assumed general prohibition against engaging in such trade as is covered by the law.

That A is *not entitled* to a certain matter—such as, for example, subletting—implies, *qua* negation of a negation, that A has a duty to behave in a contradictorily opposite way, that is, that he is in duty bound not to sublet.

Frequently, the word 'may' is used synonymously with the expression 'a right to'; thus, § 29 of the Danish Trade Law stating when, for example, personal applications 'may' take place; or §§ 55–57 of the Danish Rent Act nr. 251, dated June 14, 1951, mentioning a diverse range of things which the tenants 'may' not do.

(b) Perhaps just as frequently, the expression 'a right to' ('entitled to') is used synonymously with the expression '*claim to*'. When § 57 of the Danish Sale of Goods Act states, for example, that the seller under the given circumstances is not 'entitled' to regain the goods, then this does not mean, of course, that he is acting in breach of duty if he receives the goods; rather, it means that he cannot claim to regain it. Further examples include: when § 3 of the Danish Trade Law establishes who has 'a right to' apply for a trade licence; and when §§ 60–62 of the Danish Rent Act mention various measures which the lodger has 'a right to' implement; with many more instances besides.

(c) Finally, the expression 'A has a right to' is often used *synonymously* with the *expressions* (mentioned under *(4)* below) *establishing a power or a competence* for A. Thus, for example, when § 42 of the Danish Sale of Goods Act states that the seller is 'entitled to' rescind the contract, or when § 70 of the Constitution states that the courts are 'entitled to' decide any question relating to the scope of the executive's authority.

(4) Expressions of power, competence, authority, ability, and synonyms

As has been mentioned in § 7, the legal norms can be divided into two groups according to their *prima facie* content: norms of conduct; and norms of competence (or procedural norms). [215] The former are norms prescribing a certain behaviour, and these norms have been discussed under points (1)–(3) above. The latter are norms creating a competence (power, authority) to do something; this, in turn, means that they are directives concerning the issue that directives, which are created in conformity with a given mode of procedure, shall be understood as norms of conduct. One might say that competence is an 'ability', derived from the competence norm, to create law through linguistic announcements—law which is in conformity with the content of the announcement.

The legislator hardly ever makes use of the specific terms 'power' and 'competence' in these situations. Usually the law uses expressions such as *can*, *has a right to*, *is entitled to*, or *is authorized to*. Thus, there are many constitutional provisions which state what the King 'can' dispose of; many laws which mention what kind of administrative acts 'can' be carried out by the different administrative authorities, 'authorize' the King or others to issue certain ordinances, or state under what conditions private citizens 'can' make binding legal arrangements (to avoid a purchase, to give notice of termination, to transfer, to bequeath, etc.).

§ 33. *Criticism of the Terminology of Legal Language*

From the survey in the previous section, it will have emerged that the terminology used in legal language suffers from high imprecision. All expressions that have been used are *ambiguous*, and even if how a certain expression must be understood usually emerges from the context, the ambiguity may well give rise to doubts. Thus, when the Act on Wheat from the harvest of 1950, nr. 240 of 27 May, 1950, states that on delivery, the farmer is *entitled* to a price exceeding the latest published commodity price by 5 Danish Crowns, it is not immediately clear whether this means that the farmer is *permitted* to get this price, or whether he can *claim to* get it.

	can mean or be reduced to:
'A is in duty bound to ...' 'A has a duty to...' and the like.	1) that A can be sentenced 2) that A can be ordered specific performance 3) that A can be ordered to pay damages. 4) that compliance is a precondition for gaining or retaining certain legal advantages to A.
'A has a right to...' 'A is entitled to...' and the like.	1) that it is at A's discretion to... 2) that A has a claim to... 3) that A has the competence to...[1]
'A must...' 'A may...'	1) that A is in duty bound to...[2] 2) that it is at A's discretion to...[3] 3) that it is a precondition for gaining or retaining certain advantages, that A...[4]

[1] Examples of all three readings can be found in the preceding section under (3).

[2] E.g. § 2 subsection 2 of the Danish Promissory Notes Act: 'If one of the joint debtors obviously cannot pay, or if his place of residence is unknown, then the others *must* sort out their respective part of the outstanding sum.'

[3] E.g. § 29 of the Danish Trade Law: 'Personal inquiries...for receiving orders *may*...only be directed to...'; see also § 31.

[4] E.g. § 36 of the Danish Trade Law: 'Those wishing to peddle, cf. § 40, *may*...submit an application.'

This ambiguity is inherent in the expressions of duty, and since other expressions can be reduced to these, they are consequently ambiguous, too. What is more, the very reduction is frequently ambiguous. Opposite, you will find a schematic survey of the ambiguity in some modal expressions. [216]

Another fundamental defect in regard to the usefulness of the terminology for describing the legal reactions can be found in its *burdensome ideological load.* The latter manifests itself in the use of the concept of duty. When the law states that A has a duty to behave in a certain way, this usually means (that is, excepting the situations mentioned above on page 188, under (d)) that A can either be sentenced, or be ordered specific performance, or be ordered to pay damages. However, the relationship between 'duty' and these types of reaction is not clear; for conversely, we cannot say that reactions of this kind are conditioned by a breach of a duty. Liability for damages is not necessarily conditioned by A's having behaved in a way which the law calls contrary to duty. For example, if A has made a promise to pay a certain sum—a promise which it was already impossible for him to fulfil at the time of entering into the agreement—then A, according to circumstances (even if he should have been excusably ignorant of this impossibility), will be ordered to pay damages; but it can hardly be said that he was in duty bound to perform according to his promise.[5] The situation is similar in the case of strict liability for dangerous activities. Irrespective of any liability for damages, we would not speak, here, of any violation of duty; rather, the dangerous activity is considered lawful. [217]

As mentioned above, this absence of a clear relationship between duty and legal reaction has to do with the ideological function of the concept of duty. This concept is only used when the conditioned reaction is experienced as an expression of societal disapproval. In the cases mentioned above, the reaction is not experienced in this way, and consequently we do not speak of any violation of duty.

There is no doubt that this ideological function is valuable in legal life. The idea of duty functions as a motive to act lawfully—not for fear of sanctions, but because of a non-interested attitude of respect for the law. This ideological, motive-creating function is an extremely important factor in legal life. It endows the law with 'sacredness' or 'validity', and no social order could be constructed without it. It is quite another thing, however, that ideological contingency hardly turns the concept of duty and other concepts of modality deriving from it into tools suited for a juridico-scientific description of scientifically valid law. In contrast to legislation, it is not a task for legal science to influence the citizens ideologically, but, rather, to describe the legal reactions to be expected under certain circumstances. And it is obvious that the concept of

[5] Cf. Henry Ussing, *Dansk Obligationsret, Almindelig Del* [Danish Law of Obligation, General Part], § 4, II (1946), *in fine* and, e.g., § 59 of the Danish Sale of Goods Act.

duty is not really qualified for the task. On the one hand, a statement saying that A is in duty bound to behave in a certain way, does not clearly indicate what kind of legal reactions may be expected if he violates this duty. On the other hand, reactions of the same kind which are typically connected with breaches of duty may occur just as well without being conditioned by such breaches.

Therefore, we must conclude that it would be desirable if juridico-scientific accounts could definitely rid themselves of the concept of duty. Instead of operating with this inadequate term, it would be more appropriate simply to pay attention to the juridico-functional connection between conditioning facts and conditioned reactions. Carrying out this project would be difficult, however. The conceptual framework that has been passed down from generation to generation and the difficulty involved in freeing oneself from ideological viewpoints are a great hindrance.[6]

[6] It is only fair to note that all things considered, Henry Ussing has been successful in presenting the Law of Contract and Tort according to this pattern. Instead of making the debtor's 'duty to pay' and the creditor's 'claim' the basis of the presentation (as is usually done), Ussing—consistently focusing on describing the connection between conditioning facts and conditioned possibilities of reaction—has proceeded radically and made the concept of 'correct performance' the starting point of a purely juridico-functional description of the debtor's legal position under various circumstances.

§ 34. An Improved Terminology [218]

Since a terminology of duty, of claim, etc., is indispensable to legal language and can hardly be eliminated from legal science, the question arises whether it might not be possible to improve its usage. From the account in § 32 it emerges that the various expressions of modality are connected reciprocally as correlates or contradictories; accordingly, our task must be to develop, in a systematic way, a set of logically derivable modalities and to reserve a specific term for each of them. Whatever one may think about the feasibility of implementing such a terminology in practice, the investigation as such will be of great value, namely as an analysis that will open our eyes to the various modalities and the relationship between them. The terminology to be used will, perhaps, be less of a decisive factor than the awareness of the various relations it refers to.

Below, a terminology is suggested which proceeds from the system worked out by the American jurist Hohfeld.[1] The internal coherence of this terminology can be symbolized in the following diagram:*

Norms of conduct

(1)	duty A–B (C)	~	claim B–A (C)
	↕		↕
(2)	liberty A–B (C)	~	no-claim B–A (C)
(3)	claim A–B (C)	~	duty B–A (C)
	↕		↕
(4)	no-claim A–B (C)	~	liberty B–A (C)

* Editor's note: In spite of thus proceeding from Hohfeld's system, in the 1958 English translation of *On Law and Justice* Ross deliberately chose to deviate from Hohfeld's specific terminology regarding the various *relata* in his system of fundamental legal concepts. On this point, this translation follows the distinct terminology suggested by Ross in 1958. This is done, first of all, because Ross, unlike Hohfeld, deliberately shied away from using the word *right* because, as stated in § 35 below, he did not want to feed the widespread notion that all 'legal relations can be analysed into the correlative concepts duty and right'. Instead of *right* he therefore opted for the term *claim*. Second, the terminology applied in the first English translation is continuous with the terminology applied in the larger framework of Ross's legal theory, notably with regard to the fundamental and important distinction between norms of conduct and norms of competence. Third, even if Hohfeld's terminology may be more familiar to some readers, Ross's terminology has also exerted some independent influence, notably through his later work *Directives and Norms* (1968), where it is reapplied with a few minor changes (i.e. *duty* is replaced by *obligation*, and *liberty* by *permission*).

[1] W. N. Hohfeld, *Fundamental Legal Conceptions as Applied in Judicial Legal Reasoning and Other Essays* (1923).

Norms of competence

(5)	subjection A–B (F)	~	competence B–A (F)
	↕		↕
(6)	immunity A–B (F)	~	disability B–A (F)
(7)	competence A–B (F)	~	subjection B–A (F)
	↕		↕
(8)	disability A–B (F)	~	immunity B–A (F)

[219] In the diagram above, the sign ~ indicates that the *relata* thus connected are correlates (read: 'corresponds to' or 'is equivalent to'); the double arrow indicates that the *relata* thus connected are contradictorily opposed to each other (the expressions negate themselves reciprocally). The formula *duty A–B (C)* is read: A has a duty towards B to exhibit conduct C, etc. The formula *subjection A–B (F)* is read: A is subjected to B's dispositions [norm-creating acts] within the field F, etc.

We can see that in this way, eight modalities evolve, namely: *duty*, *liberty*, *claim*, *no-claim*, *subjection*, *immunity*, *competence*, and *disability*. (Please observe that the ambiguous expression 'a right to' has disappeared.) Of these eight modalities, the first four and the last four, respectively, are logically reducible to each other. Furthermore, since A's subjection to B means that A's legal position expressed in terms of duty, claim, etc. is determined according to B's dispositions, the last four modalities can be reduced to the first four modalities. Thus, it follows that all eight modalities can be reduced to expressions of duty. If this concept is defined, then all of them are defined.

To obtain a better understanding of the diagram I would like to mention the following.

Re the correlative pair duty–claim

The value of the modality system as a whole depends on establishing a fairly precise definition of the term *duty*. For this reason, at least the meaning mentioned above on page 188 under (d), according to which 'duty' indicates a behaviour as a precondition for gaining or retaining certain legal advantages, must be kept out of the concept. The right and proper thing to do would be to apply the term 'duty' only to situations in which the person concerned (under certain specified conditions) can be sentenced, be ordered special performance, or be ordered to pay damages. A definition of this kind, however, would be incompatible with the traditional ideological function of the term. Therefore, if we cherish the hope that we can influence linguistic usage, we are forced to limit this term to those situations in which the legal reaction is experienced as a societal disapproval, and where the judgment is experienced as a motive to fulfil one's duty. Henceforth, then, we shall not speak of a duty in situations of excusable impossibility, for example, or in situations of objective liability.

Expressions of duty can be re-written as *prescriptions* and *prohibitions* according to the following rules. That an act is prescribed means that there is a duty to perform it; that an act is prohibited, means that there is a duty not to perform it:

$$\text{duty}(C) = \text{prescription}(C),$$

$$\text{duty}(\text{no-}C) = \text{prohibition}(C),$$

resulting in:

$$\text{prescription}(C) = \text{prohibition}(\text{no-}C),$$

$$\text{prohibition}(C) = \text{prescription}(\text{no-}C).$$

To A's duty corresponds B's opposite *claim*. That B has a claim against A means, [220] then, that B is able to set the legal machinery in motion for obtaining a judgment against A; or that B's prosecution is a necessary condition for thus adjudicating A. If A's legal position has been fully described, the condition for filing a lawsuit is already stated, and thus there is no new information contained in the correlative statement concerning B's claim.

Usually the person who has the power to file a lawsuit is also the person directly interested in A's duty-bound behaviour. If A has promised B 100 Danish Kroner, then B is both the directly interested person and the person who has the power to file a lawsuit. However, it may happen that the two parts do not go hand in hand. For example, A may promise B to pay 100 kroner to C. If it can be assumed (according to the circumstances) that B, and B alone, can file a lawsuit, then it will best fit in with common linguistic usage to say that B, and B alone, has a claim against A, and the definition above has been formulated in accordance with this. B, the claim holder, is called *the party entitled to bring an action*, and C, the directly[2] interested person, is called *the interested party*.

Thus, B having a claim against A, as such, merely expresses the fact that B's prosecution is a necessary condition for a judgment against A. This relationship can also be expressed by saying that B has the *power* to prosecute, thereby implying that B, by means of a certain behaviour, is able to trigger certain legal effects he wishes to bring about. Another problem is whether B is free to

[2] B, too, must be assumed to have an interest in A paying up, but his interest is an indirect one, that is, it is an interest in C's interest being considered, cf. Alf Ross, *Virkelighed og Gyldighed i Retslæren* [Reality and Validity in Jurisprudence] (1934), ch. IX, 2.

prosecute or not (as he may think fit), or whether he is subjected to a legal obligation in this respect. Usually B is free to decide whether or not to prosecute. His claim is thus combined with the liberty to enforce it or not, because the very purpose of the law in endowing B with a claim is to provide him with an instrument for protecting his own interests. Should the situation arise where B does not have this liberty, it is doubtful whether one can speak of a claim at all. Therefore, the question arises whether the liberty to prosecute should not, perhaps, be included in the definition of 'claim'.

This question is important when a prosecution is brought by the authorities as an official act (which is normal in criminal proceedings). The public prosecutor does not have the liberty to prosecute or not, according to his own judgment: rather, he is legally obligated to exercise his power in conformity with directions laid down by the law. Public prosecution differs so fundamentally from private prosecution that I find it right and proper to highlight this by reserving the term 'claim' for those situations in which *the power to prosecute is combined with the liberty to exercise this power in one's own interests.*

[221] It follows that those duties which are enforced only through public prosecution in criminal cases are *absolute* duties, that is, no opposing claim corresponds to them, neither on the part of the person whose interests have been violated, nor on the part of the authorities.

Re the correlative pair liberty—no-claim

If an action is not prohibited, it is *permitted*:

$$\text{permission}(C) = \text{no-prohibition}(C) = \text{no-duty}(\text{no-}C)$$

If an action is neither prohibited nor prescribed, it is *free*:

$$\begin{aligned}\text{Liberty}(C) &= \text{no-prohibition}(C) + \text{no-prescription}(C)\\ &= \text{no-duty}(\text{no-}C) + \text{no-duty}(C)\end{aligned}$$

Thus, the permitted action and the free action have in common that they are not prohibited. The difference between them is that a permitted action can be prescribed (I am permitted to fulfil my duty), whereas a free action cannot be prescribed.

It follows from this definition that if C is free, then no-C is free, too. Both formulae state the same thing, namely, that there is no duty, either towards C or towards no-C.

To say that an action is free is the same as saying that it falls outside the ambit of legal regulations. It is a legally *indifferent* action. Neither its performance nor its non-performance result in legal reactions.[3]

[3] It follows from the definitions above that the negation of duty A–B (C) is, in fact, a permission A–B (no-C) and not, as indicated in the modality diagram, a liberty A–B (C). For we have:

To say that I have the liberty to go out in the woods, to walk down the street, to smoke a cigar, or to wear a red tie means, then, that I am not in duty bound [222] either to do or not to do these things; nor that others (B or others in relation to whom my freedom avails) have any claim whatsoever against me.

It is impossible to enumerate the liberties a person is entitled to, since the realm of liberty is defined negatively, namely, as comprising everything which is not subject to legal regulations.

The fact that we nonetheless frequently mention particular liberties has to do with that they appear as exceptions; either the liberty pertains to a particular person only, or it certainly pertains to all, but appears as an exception to an otherwise accepted, general rule. In the former case, we speak of a *special liberty* or *privilege*; in the latter, we speak of a *public liberty*.

It is the privilege of the owner of a property to walk on his land. He is free to do so, and at the same time he has a claim towards all other persons to keep off. According to the Danish Nature Conservation Act, there is a public liberty for people to walk by the water's edge over private land. The so-called 'harmless easement' is a public liberty as well.

Another reason for mentioning particular liberties may be the fact that the Constitution grants the citizens various spheres of liberty—spheres protected from legislative intervention (freedom of religion, freedom of the press, and so forth).

When a liberty is common to all people (as is usually the case), its value to the individual may be problematic. After all, my own liberty merely entails that others have no claim against me, that is, no legal obstacles can be put in my way to prevent me from enjoying my liberty. On the other hand, *this liberty does not include any claim against others to provide me with the actual opportunity to act as*

duty A–B (C)
= prescription A–B (C), from which the negation
no-prescription A–B (C)
= no-prohibition A–B (no-C)
= permission A–B (no-C)
For example: The negation of
A has a duty to pay 100 kroner to B
= *A is permitted to refrain from paying B 100 kroner.*
This is narrower than:
A is free to pay B 100 kroner,
for the latter also includes the meaning:
A is permitted to pay B 100 kroner.

If I have nonetheless chosen to set up liberty (C) and not permission (no-C) as the negation of duty (C), it is because of the following argument. If C is not chosen arbitrarily, but as a position that can be conceived, in practice, as a legal duty, then it is practically out of the question for no-C to be a legal duty. Therefore, the negation of duty A–B (C) not only means that A is permitted to do no-C, but also to do C; i.e. that A has liberty to do (C). Accordingly, it is practically justified to say that the negation of A's duty to pay B 100 kroner is not only that he is permitted not to do this, but that he is free to do it or not to do it.

I please. I am free to sit on a bench in Ørsted Park [Ørstedsparken]. However, this liberty is of no use to me if the bench is occupied by other people—after all, I have no claim against them to give up their seat to me. If the liberty of one individual cannot be reconciled with the liberty of another individual, struggle and power will decide who shall prevail. However, a certain amount of regulation concerning this struggle, and thereby some protection to him who was the first to arrive, often follows as a reflection of other claims which limit the means of ousting another person. If I am sitting on the bench, for example, I certainly have no claim against others to let me sit there. But I have a claim against these others that they shall not attack my person, and this entails, *qua* reflection, that I cannot be (legally) driven away from the bench by force.

In business life there is a large amount of freedom to operate in the market in the fight for customers. No one has a claim that others shall leave his customers alone. But here, too, the competition laws and the legal order as such draw a limit with regard to the means to be employed in the competitive struggle.

Liberalism is that political ideology which demands a maximum of freedom for the citizen and a minimum of regulation concerning the matters of life. [223] Totalitarian ideologies, by contrast, seek to minimize the individuals' spheres of liberty.

Re the correlative pair subjection–competence

Competence is a special case of power. *Power* exists as soon as a person is able to trigger certain legal effects which he desires to produce.[4] A creditor has the power to commence proceedings or to suspend the limitation period of the claim, and parents have the power to permit or not to permit their children of a certain age to get married. *Competence is a power of disposal*, and it exists when the triggering act consists of a dispositive statement, that is, a statement which usually (that is, barring particular reasons for invalidity) produces legal effects which correspond to the content of the statement.[5]

A dispositive statement is a directive,[6] often formulated as an apparently theoretical statement concerning the existence of duties and claims. Laws, promises, and wills are examples of dispositive statements.

The borderline between competence and other kinds of power is not clear-cut. There is a sliding scale of transition from those situations in which the disposition contains a detailed description of the legal relationship that is created (a law, a detailed contract, or a collective agreement); through situations in which the

[4] Ussing frequently uses the term power; see, e.g., his book *Dansk Obligationsret. General part* [Danish Law of Obligation. General Part] (3rd edn, 1946), 282, 374, 443; and his work *Aftaler paa Formuerettens Omraade* [Contracts in the Field of Property Law] (3rd edn, 1950), 285.

[5] On the use of the term competence, cf. § 16 note 8.

[6] For further information, see § 52.

disposition is almost limited to filling in a blank line in a series of legal effects which, according to type, are otherwise fixed in legislation (for example, a sales agreement limited to stating article and price, whereas the relationship between the parties is regulated by the standard norms of the Danish Sale of Goods Act); to still other situations, where the disposition is limited to a formulaic statement which admits of no individual variation and whose effects are exhaustively laid down by the law (thus, for example, when the buyer announces that he 'cancels the contract'). To say that the notification of the cancellation of the contract is a dispositive statement which has effect according to its content, or to consider the notification of cancellation as an act which releases legal effects determined by legislation, is a matter of opinion, for the effects of the notification are standardized and brought about automatically—just as if a button had been pressed. If it comes to that, one might just as well have decided that a sale is being cancelled by sending a postcard with three crosses written on it to the other contracting party.

As a main rule, private citizens only have competence to make dispositions which are binding upon themselves, whereas public authorities have compe- [224] tence to bind other persons as well (§ 46). If a private citizen has the power to make binding dispositions for another person, this power is frequently based on a previous disposition made by that other person. Thus, an offer endows the recipient with the power to bind the offeror through his acceptance, and authorization endows an agent with the power to bind the principal.

The problem whether the individual who possesses power is free to exercise this power as he pleases, or whether he has an obligation to exercise it according to certain guidelines, is distinct from the power-(competence) relationship as such. An agent's authorization, for example, may be narrower than his legitimation. In this case, the exercise of power within the delimited area will be unlawful in relation to the principal. A similar rule applies to power relationships governed by public law. Power is not assigned to public authorities to be exercised as they choose, but according to expressly stated rules or assumed general principles. Here, too, it is frequently possible to distinguish between their legitimation and their authorization, in so far as overstepping the norms does not entail invalidity, only liability.

Subjection is the correlate of power (competence). Linguistically it may be slightly problematic to operate with this term, since it has decidedly 'unfavourable' characteristics, but it is meant to cover the opposite of favourable dispositions as well. Citizens are 'subjected' to the power of the legislator, heirs to the power of the testator, offerors to the power of the recipient, the successor to the power of the transferor, and so forth—and all this irrespective of whether the disposition in question is binding upon the subjected person or gives rise to any claims for him.

Re the correlative pair immunity–disability

The views applicable to these negative modalities are analogous to those concerning the pair liberty—no-claim. Being negative terms, they cover everything not subject to legal regulation of power, and in so far as it is not possible to mention specific immunity relationships. Everyone enjoys immunity from everyone else, provided that the other person is not endowed with power in relation to the first one. If we nevertheless still operate with specific 'immunity rights', it is because they occur as exceptions. Thus, we say that foreign ambassadors enjoy immunity from the jurisdiction of the courts. Similarly, we may say that citizens enjoy immunity from the legislature in so far as the latter's competence is constitutionally limited.

§ 35. Confrontation [225]

Until now, the legal modalities have only marginally been an object of scientific study. Generally, it is assumed that 'legal relations' can be analysed into the correlative concepts of duty and right. This assumption is quite unsatisfactory, however.

In the first place, one has not realized that in reality, the analysis is about the directive content of the legal language—about the way in which conditioning facts and legal reaction are tied together legally-functionally; instead, one has looked upon duty and rights as a sort of metaphysical matter or spiritual forces, arising *qua* consequences of certain facts and, in turn, causing the legal effects which manifest themselves in law enforcement. This substantial approach, which still largely prevails in Continental and Anglo-American legal thinking, has in several respects resulted in unfortunate consequences in solving practical legal problems.[1]

Secondly—as will emerge from what has been said above—the analysis is far too superficial. One often fails to realize how the term 'right' conceals such heterogeneous matters as claims, liberty, power (competence), and immunity, and duty is not differentiated from the rest of the passive modalities. This inadequate theoretical analysis is responsible for the confusion that characterizes legal language (as shown in § 33)—the language of legislation as well as that of the doctrinal study of law.

Finally, it is a mistake to introduce 'right' as the counterpart of 'duty'. As will be explained more in detail in the following chapter, the concept of rights is a systematic concept in which a number of legal rules are conceived as united. This concept comprises a notion of a complex totality of legal effects, each of which may be expressed in the customary modalities. The right of ownership, for example, comprises a whole set of claims, liberties, competences, and immunities. Certainly, we have seen that expressions such as 'right to' and 'entitled to' occur as modal expressions. However, 'right' as an umbrella term for right of ownership, lien right, claim rights, etc., is not a legal modality through which the individual legal rule is expressed; on the contrary, it is a higher-level construct—it is the systematic unity of a set of legal rules.

[1] For further information on this issue, see Alf Ross, *Virkelighed og Gyldighed i Retslæren* [Reality and Validity in Jurisprudence] (1943), ch. IX, 6 and *Ejendomsret og Ejendomsovergang* [Ownership and Ownership Transition] (1935), ch. I.

To the best of my knowledge, it was the American Wesley Newcomb Hohfeld who was first to investigate the legal modalities (*Fundamental Legal Concepts*, 1923).[2]

The present account has largely been inspired by Hohfeld, especially with [226] regard to the idea that the various modalities are interconnected through the logical relationships of contradiction and correlation. My own position concerning this matter is somewhat different, however. Hohfeld makes no attempt to interpret the modalities juridico-functionally, and he does not realize that, in reality, it is a question of directive phrases informed by ideology.

[2] This work was published posthumously. The author's original treatise was published in *Yale Law Journal* 23 (1913), 16. On Hohfeld's analysis and the discussion initiated by this analysis in the USA, see Torstein Eckhoff, *Rettsvesen og rettsvitenskap i U. S. A.* [Legal System and Legal Science in the USA] (1953), 288 *et seq.*

CHAPTER VI [227]

The Concept of Rights

§ 36. *The Concept of Rights as a Technical Tool of Presentation*

In the preceding chapter, it was explained how the legal language makes use of a number of ideologically coloured modal expressions: duty, claim, etc.[1] To all appearances, the law consists of theoretical statements on how these modalities arise as effects, caused by certain facts. It was also explained, however, that in reality, the apparently theoretical statements of the law are meant as directives. If we ignore the ideological undertones of these expressions—undertones which aim directly at prompting citizens to behave in a certain way—then their proper legal meaning can be reduced to directives to the judge, namely how he shall adjudicate under the given conditions. Thus, it is always possible to restate the sentences of the law in the formula:

$$D\left(\text{if F, then C}\right),$$

that is, as a directive to the judge that he shall adjudicate C [legal consequence], if F [conditioning fact] exists.

If the task of legal science were limited to a description of all scientifically valid legal rules, nothing would prevent us from being content with formulae of this kind. Thus, we might imagine a juridico-scientific description purporting to present, as scientifically valid law, a number of directives—something like the following examples:

D_1 (if a person has purchased a certain object lawfully, a judgment of restitu- [228] tion shall be given in favour of the purchaser against other persons retaining the object in their possession);

D_2 (if a person has inherited a certain object, a judgment for damages shall be given in favour of the heir against other persons who have damaged the object out of negligence);

[1] [General remark to § 36:] On this issue, see further Alf Ross, 'Tû-tû,' in *Festskrift til Henry Ussing* [A Tribute to Henry Ussing] (1951), 468–84. [English translation in *Harvard Law Review*, vol. 70, Issue 5, March 1957, 812–25].

On Law and Justice. Alf Ross. © Alf Ross (original Danish, 1953), Jakob v. H. Holtermann (editor, introduction), Uta Bindreiter (translation). Published 2019 by Oxford University Press.

D_3 (if a person has acquired a certain object by prescription and raised a loan which is not repaid on time, the borrower shall be given a judgment for performance on the basis of the object);

D_4 (if a person has created a certain object and bequeathed it to another person, a judgment shall be given in favour of the legatee against the testator's estate for surrendering the object);

D_5 (if a person under certain circumstances has taken possession of a certain object which subsequently is appropriated by another person, the latter shall be punished for theft);

D_6 (if a person has purchased a certain object, and if this object is subsequently appropriated by another person, the latter shall be punished for theft);

and so on and so forth. Please note that in each case, the formulation may of course be far more complicated than in the above examples.

An account along these lines would be rather intricate and confusing, however. Also, it is a task for legal science to *systematize the legal rules*, that is, to provide a description of the law which is as simple and clear as possible. This can be achieved by employing the following *presentation technique*.

Surveying a large number of legal rules according to the pattern above, we shall find that it is possible to single out a certain complex totality which can be presented in the following way:

$$
\begin{array}{ccccc}
F_1\text{–}C_1 & F_2\text{–}C_1 & F_3\text{–}C_1 & \ldots\ldots\ldots\ldots & F_p\text{–}C_1 \\
F_1\text{–}C_2 & F_2\text{–}C_2 & F_3\text{–}C_2 & \ldots\ldots\ldots\ldots & F_p\text{–}C_2 \\
F_1\text{–}C_3 & F_2\text{–}C_3 & F_3\text{–}C_3 & \ldots\ldots\ldots\ldots & F_p\text{–}C_3 \\
\vdots & \vdots & \vdots & & \vdots \\
F_1\text{–}C_n & F_2\text{–}C_n & F_3\text{–}C_n & \ldots\ldots\ldots\ldots & Fp\text{–}Cn
\end{array}
$$

(Please read: The conditioning fact F_1 is connected with the legal consequence C_1, etc.), which means that each individual fact out of a certain complex totality of conditioning facts (F_1–Fp) is connected with each individual legal consequence of a given totality of legal consequences (C_1–Cn); or that it is true of each individual F that it is connected with the same complex totality of legal consequences (C_1+C_2...+Cn), or that a *cumulative plurality of legal consequences is connected with a disjunctive plurality of conditioning facts.*

[229] In the figure below, these n X p singular legal rules can now be described in a simpler and more convenient way:

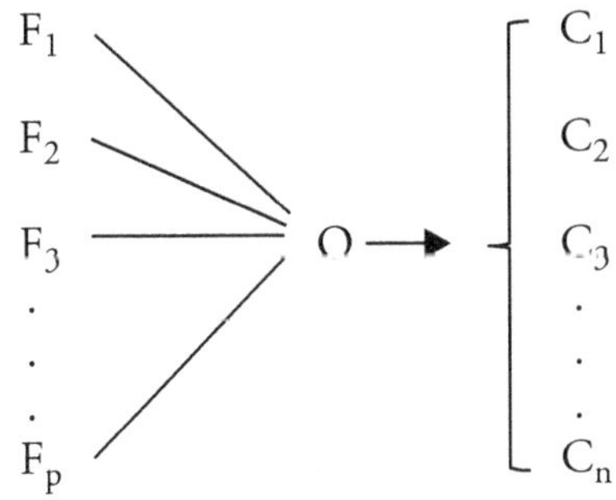

where 'O' (ownership) does not really stand for anything but the systematic connection that F_1 as well as F_2, F_3... Fp entail the totality of legal consequences C_1, C_2, C_3... Cn. Technically, this is expressed by stating in one set of rules the facts which 'create ownership', and in another set of rules the legal consequences 'entailed by ownership'.

Now we can see that the word 'ownership' inserted between the conditioning facts and the conditioned consequences is, in reality, a rather empty word, a word without any semantic reference whatsoever which merely serves as a technical tool of presentation. We are talking as if 'ownership' were a causal link between F and C, an effect caused or 'created' by every F and which, in turn, is the cause of a totality of legal consequences. For example, we say:

(1) If A has lawfully purchased a thing (F_2), ownership of this thing will arise thereby.
(2) If A has ownership of a thing, he can (*inter alia*) recover it (C_1).

It is clear, however, that (1) + (2) is merely a rephrasing of one of the presupposed norms (F_2–C_1), namely, that purchase as a conditioning fact entails the possibility of recovery as a legal consequence. The very idea that something should have been 'created' between purchase and access to recovery which can be called 'ownership' is nonsense. Nothing is being 'created' because A and B exchange a few remarks which are legally interpreted as a sales contract. What happens is that the judge is now prepared to take this fact into account and give judgment in favour of the purchaser, should the latter bring an action for recovery.

What has been described above is a simple example of intellectual systematics. One would expect it to be the task of legal science to undertake this simplifying process, but this task has largely been anticipated by pre-scientific thinking. The fundamental concepts of rights—for example, the concept of ownership—have not been created by legal science, but have come down from our general legal imagination. And it is quite another thing that people in general have only the haziest ideas about the facts which 'create ownership' and the 'effects' which are the 'consequences of ownership'. In principle, however, the pre-scientific concept of rights is constructed in the same way as the scien- [230]
tific concept. It expresses the connection between certain facts (purchase,

inheritance, etc.) and certain experiences of legal and moral 'claims' and 'powers'. I shall return to this matter in the following.

The function of the concept of rights can be illustrated in diverse contexts.

In an abstract presentation of scientifically valid law, the function of the concept of rights is the same as described above. The word 'right', as such, has no semantic reference whatsoever. The sentences in which the concept occurs can be rewritten into sentences which, without using the concept, indicate the connection (established through the directives of the law) between conditioning facts and conditioned consequences. A juridico-scientific sentence like the following, for example: 'Right of ownership is created through adverse possession, pursuant to the following rules...', can thus be rewritten as: 'Adverse possession (to be described in more detail in the following) is one of those facts which entail the totality of the consequences set out below, in the chapter on the legal effects of ownership.'

In strict conformity with the above, the concept of rights is used in the counsels' argumentation before the courts, as well as in the reasoning behind the decisions. This type of argumentation purports to justify a certain judicial decision by referring to the facts in the present case as well as the legal consequences tied to these according to valid law. A counsel will argue, for example, that through the sales contract concluded on a certain day, his client had become the owner of a car, and that his client consequently must be able now to demand a judgment for delivery against the vendor. Here, too, the inserted ownership can be omitted. What the counsel in reality maintains is (1) that a valid sales contract has been concluded; and (2) that according to valid law, this fact entails, *qua* legal consequence, that the judge shall give judgment for delivery.

Finally, the concept of rights is used in contexts which are not—or at least not apparently—about describing, or referring to, legal rules, but where the statement in which the concept occurs seems to be purely factual and descriptive; for example, when it is reported that A is the owner of a certain thing; or when the law describes the individual upon whom, as the owner of real property, it is incumbent to clear snow.

Before explaining the actual state of things in these situations, I would like to remind you that when describing persons, objects, or situations, it is common practice to mention, alongside purely factual qualities and situations, others that are conditioned by the law. A passport, for example, contains not only information concerning the holder's age and hair colour, but also concerning his nationality and marital status. Now, when describing a certain person, what does it actually mean to say that this person is 'married'? The assertion seems to refer to the actual fact that this person, at a certain time, has contracted a

marriage which has not been dissolved since. 'Contracting a marriage', however, is not something which is purely factual. Just as there is no spatial moving of an object which, in itself, is a chess move, neither is there any factual event which, in itself, constitutes 'contracting a marriage'. As has been mentioned in [231]
§ 3, both parts acquire their specific meaning only by interpreting a factual occurrence in relation to a prevailing ideology—the norms of chess or the norms of law. The assertion that a person has 'contracted a marriage' includes an assertion about scientifically valid law, namely that the event referred to is, according to scientifically valid law, 'marriage-creating', which, in turn, means that it entails a certain complex totality of legal consequences. In everyday language, we usually do not have a clear and comprehensive notion of exactly what these consequences are, but we do know, for instance, that they include that the respective person cannot contract another marriage while the first one is still valid. Thus, the statement that a certain person is 'married' refers to a double state of affairs: partly to what is purely factual, partly to what is legal (which, in the last analysis, is something factual as well, of course)—that this event according to scientifically valid law entails a set of legal effects about which we have more or less vague ideas.

The seemingly purely descriptive uses of the concept of rights can be understood in a similar way. The statement that A has the right of ownership to a certain thing, refers not only to the purely factual circumstance that A has either purchased the thing, inherited it, acquired a right by prescription, etc.; it also refers to the legal circumstance that, according to scientifically valid law, these events entail a certain totality of specifically legal consequences. Statements of this type function in everyday language in this way, even though the notion of the respective legal consequences is extremely vague, of course.

Consequently, we can state that it applies to all the contexts we have considered that statements on rights are working fairly well when they describe scientifically valid law or its application to specific situations. At the same time, however, it must be maintained that *the concept of rights has no semantic reference whatever.* It does not designate any phenomenon of any kind which inserts itself between conditioning facts and conditioned consequences, but is solely a means through which it is possible to visualize—more or less accurately—the content of a set of legal rules, namely, those rules which connect a certain disjunctive plurality of conditioning facts with a certain cumulative plurality of legal consequences.

Not to forget: the same presentation technique can often be employed successfully without, however, being connected with the idea of an intervening right. In international law, for example, one set of rules may state which area is included in a certain state, as its territory. That this area has the character of 'territory' is in itself without any meaning. The meaning arises only in connection with another set of rules, expressing what legal consequences are tied to an area's character of 'territory'. In this situation, too, it would be possible to describe the legal relationships without using the intermediate concept (territory), but there is no denying that the description would turn out rather complicated and confusing.

Sometimes we think that the intermediate link which 'is created' is not an indi-
[232] vidual right but, rather, a complex legal relationship of rights and duties: thus we distinguish, in family law, between the conditions for the contracting of marriage and the legal effects of marriage; in constitutional law, between the acquisition of citizenship and the legal effects of nationality; in administrative law, between the creation of civil servant status and its legal effects. In these and similar situations, we usually speak of the creation of a *status* (marital status, nationality status, status of civil servant).

Yet, whatever we are imagining—the reality is the same, namely, a technique which is of the greatest possible importance if we are to achieve clarity around a complex set of legal rules.

§ 37. *The Typical Rights Situation*

The concept of rights is a technical tool of presentation. However, this tells us nothing about those situations in which the concept is employed. After all, we have seen that the same technique can also be used without this concept. Therefore, our task must be to clarify under what conditions the concept of rights is applied. In answering this question, it must be emphasized that the task is not one of deciding when a right 'really exists', for 'right' does not designate a phenomenon that exists under specific conditions. It is quite possible to give an account of scientifically valid law without using the concept of rights at all. Therefore, our task can only be to clarify the characteristics of those legal situations in the presentation of which the terminology of rights is usually employed. On the face of it, it is by no means certain that common usage is consistent and adheres to a specific criterion. However, if the concept is to be profitably employed in legal science, it is necessary to define more precisely its sphere of application. The present section is dedicated to the typical rights situation. In the next section, we shall examine how the concept is applied in certain atypical situations.

(a) The starting point of our analysis must be the view that the concept of rights is used to express that side of a legal situation which is *favourable* in relation to the typical interests of a certain individual. A legal situation which is advantageous to A can be disadvantageous to B or to others. Thus, the concept of rights implies that the law is seen in a certain perspective, namely in that of the privileged individual.

The word right is often used indiscriminately, namely, in expressions such as 'to have a right (permission) to', 'to be entitled to', and the like, in order to [233]
indicate an advantage which merely consists in a person being free to pursue a certain course of action, and which simply means that this course of action falls outside legal regulations (§ 34). This usage is inappropriate. As a tool in legal science, the concept of rights must be able to indicate a specific legal content. Mere liberties differ most distinctly from situations in which the advantage enjoyed by a person is the result of regulation with this in mind. Therefore, mere liberties must be separated from the concept of rights.

(b) Let us take the next step now: the advantage to a specific person which the concept of rights is referring to must appear as though it results from legal regulation. Since the law always acts restrictively, this means that a right is always the *counterpart of a duty*,[1] that is, a restriction on the freedom of

[1] The use of the word duty in this context is misleading in so far as it is of no importance in the description of a rights situation whether or not the reactions (for example, mandatory payment of damages which can be used by the privileged individual) express social disapproval, cf. § 34. If the word is used at all, it is used simply because there is no word in our language that would express the same thing in an ideology-free way.

action of others. The duties of others can imply an advantage to A, and in two ways: either by obligating another person to perform a positive action in which A is normally interested—for example, paying him a sum of money, or doing some work for him (rights of claim); or by obligating all persons except A to forbear from a certain course of action—for example, from disposing of an object (rights of disposal). In the latter case, A's freedom becomes a special freedom, or privilege. He is guaranteed a certain sphere of action which is reserved for him alone. Ownership is an example *par excellence*. The owner's right of disposal of the object he owns is a privilege, a reserved sphere, because he is free to dispose of the object while all the others, at the same time, are forbidden from doing so.

These situations are not always regarded as rights situations, however. If B has promised A to pay a sum of money to C, for example (provided that only A can enforce the claim), then there arises, *qua* counterpart to B's duty, an advantage to C—but we would not say in such a case that a right for C has been created.

(c) Let us take one more step now. The concept of rights presupposes that the rights holder also has a *claim* on the obligated party, that is, that he is *free to assert his right by filing a lawsuit*. At the same time, it is presupposed that no other individual is empowered to file a lawsuit. Just as the owner's right of disposal is an exclusive right, a privilege, his power to file a lawsuit is an exclusive power.

A new aspect of the function of the concept of rights is thereby emphasized. This aspect expresses a legal situation which entails not only an advantageous position for the right holder which can be enjoyed passively: it also expresses an absolute power to maintain—or give up—this position at one's discretion. Naturally, this power does not consist of any mystical
[234] force with which the legal order has endowed the subject of the right; this power only means that the legal machinery and the compelling forces developed by it are set in motion at the instigation of the rights holder. His filing a suit has the same effect as pressing a button: the legal machinery is thereby set a-going.

(d) In common legal usage, the concept of rights is undoubtedly used in a number of situations as described under (a)–(c). In the most typical situations, however—namely, in situations concerning well-developed property rights—there is a further element to be added. There, the right comprises one more power, namely, power *qua* competence, or *power of disposal* of the right,[2] at the same time as the right holder enjoys immunity

[2] In my book *Virkelighed og Gyldighed i Retslæren* [Reality and Validity in Jurisprudence] (1934), ch. IX, 4, cf. 218–20, I emphasized that the competence to dispose of something concerns one's legal position as such, that is, the freedom to use and enjoy something and the power to file a lawsuit. The reason for this was a thought I still believe to be correct, namely, that it would lead to logical problems to speak of a competence

against other persons' dispositions (exclusive competence). This means that the right holder has the power, through targeted dispositive pronouncements[3] (in particular, through declarations of transfer and through wills), to evoke the legal effect that another person, indicated in the pronouncement, succeeds to the right.

(e) To sum up, we can say that the concept of rights is typically used to indicate situations where the legal order has wished to guarantee an individual freedom and power—within a specified area—to act as he chooses when looking to his own interests. The concept of rights indicates *the individual's autonomous self-assertion.*

This does not mean unbridled individualism, of course, nor does it stand in contradiction to the social character of all law. It only means that precisely out of societal considerations, it is considered desirable that the individual be given the possibility to act freely (within certain bounds, of course). It has become a popular slogan to say that, nowadays, ownership has become a social function. There is a grain of truth in it, of course: nowadays, the freedom surrounding the owner's expansion is far more circumscribed by societal considerations than was the case under the nineteenth-century regime of extreme individualism. However, the phrase is apt to disguise the fact that the right of ownership, with its restricted content, still has the function of promoting the autonomy of the individual. This autonomy has been circumscribed, but even circumscribed autonomy is autonomy still—not a social function.

It is necessary to emphasize this, because one should separate from the [235]
concept of rights such liberties and powers which are expressly not given to the autonomous safeguarding of personal interests but, *qua* social function, to the safeguarding of social interests. In communal life, individual persons are frequently endowed with a privileged freedom of action and the power to safeguard the interests of others, or of common interests. In a family, for example, the parents have the liberty to chastise their children, and they have the power to determine their lives in various ways. Still more frequently, various persons in public life are endowed with a special freedom of action and a special power to make legally binding arrangements for others. In these and similar situations, however, liberties and powers have not been given to those persons for the autonomous safeguarding of

referring to itself. On the other hand, O. K. Magnusson is right (*Naboretlige Studier* [Inquiries into the Law relating to Adjoining Properties] (1950), 52–53) when he points out that the disposition of the right holder means that the competence to dispose of something passes to the transferee as well. I leave the question open.

[3] In my book *Virkelighed og Gyldighed i Retslæren* [Reality and Validity in Jurisprudence] (1934), ch. IX, 4, I included under the heading 'competence' the succession that takes place in debt enforcement and the succession to property apart from dispositions *mortis causa*. I regard this now as an inappropriate extension of the concept of competence, which ought to be reserved for those cases in which the legal ground of the succession consists of a dispositive statement.

their own interests, but as a social function. This is not only a moral ideology: it has its juridico-functional expression in control—not merely the control of the legal boundaries, but also of the spirit in which those functions are exercised (guardian inspections, misuse of power, etc.). Therefore, situations of this type should be kept outside the concept of rights. Current linguistic usage is ambiguous, but there is nonetheless a clear tendency to speak of *authority* in such situations, not of a right (parental authority, public authority). In the interest of clarity, this terminological distinction should be consistently adhered to[4] (§ 46).

[4] French legal theory sometimes uses the terminology *droits à fin égoiste* and *droits-fonction*; see, e.g., Jean Dabin, *Le droit subjectif* [Subjective Law] (1952), 217.

§ 38. *Rights as Substance*

We have seen that the concept of rights is merely a technical tool of presentation. Nevertheless, we usually express ourselves as if a right were something which inserts itself between facts and legal consequence—something which 'is being created' and, in turn, causes various consequences. A purchase is said to create a right of ownership for the purchaser, and this right of ownership has the effect that he can claim recovery.

This mode of expression is harmless as long as we are aware of the true context; else it may exert power over our minds which might lead us astray. If linguistic usage leads us to reason as if 'the right itself' were distinct from its 'effects', then we have a typical example of what is called, in logic, a *hypostasis*, that is, a scheme of thought according to which we insert, 'besides' or 'behind' certain functional contexts, a new reality, or substance, as a 'bearer' of, or cause for, [236] these contexts. This power of the language over the mind possibly originates in a tradition which goes back to primitive magical thinking.[1]

In my view, it cannot be denied that a tendency towards hypostasizing a right into a substance in this way actually makes itself felt in the thoughts of both the learned and the unlearned. Hardly anyone can entirely disclaim associating, with the concept of rights, more or less vague ideas of a power of a non-sensuous nature, a kind of inner will which endows the concept with 'validity' and power in relation to the opposing wills of others. This power manifests itself in, but is at the same time distinct from, those coercive measures—sentences and their enforcement—through which the right holder's factual and visible control is effectuated.

Even children show this tendency. A child quickly learns that he 'owns' certain things he calls 'his', and he perceives that usually certain practical advantages are connected with it. At the same time, however, the 'owning' itself is something which interests the child just as much as do the practical advantages, and which is conceived of as distinct from them. Until my children had reached the age of ten, I was able to come to an arrangement with them—without much difficulty and to our mutual satisfaction—that they should 'have' certain flowers in the garden; reserving for myself at the same time complete control over what should be done with them.

There is no doubt but that the adult learns to understand the real functions of owning much better, and that he will not in the same way be fobbed off with a

[1] In his book *Der römische Obligationsbegriff* [The Notion of Obligation in Roman Law] (1927), Axel Hägerström has adduced weighty arguments in support of the magical origin of legal notions in Roman law. Modern research in sociology and history of religion points in the same direction. On this issue, see Alf Ross, *Virkelighed og Gyldighed i Retslæren* [Reality and Validity in Jurisprudence] (1934), ch. XI, 2–5.

single word. Nevertheless, there obviously persists a tendency to regard a right as an independent reality, distinct from its functional context. This tendency even permeates scientific disciplines. Hidden metaphysical ideas reveal themselves there in various ways in pseudo-problems, fictions, and delusions which may also have an unfortunate influence on the solution of practical legal questions.

The metaphysical notion of law as a spiritual force comprises two views, namely: (a) that a right is always a unified property, necessarily existing within a specific subject; and (b) that this subject must be a being endowed with intellect or reason, that is, a human being or an organization of human beings. Both views are likely to lead us astray.

(a) To regard a right as a *single generic property*, necessarily existing within a specific subject, does no harm in the typical situations described in the
[237] preceding section. In these cases, the various functions included in the legal situation all relate to the same subject. Usually it is one and the same person (1) for the benefit of whom other persons' freedom of action is restricted; (2) who can assert his right by filing a lawsuit; and (3) who can use and enjoy the right. One and the same person is both *interested party*, *the party entitled to bring an action*, and *the person endowed with the right of disposal*. Therefore, it is not confusing to conceive of these different functions as being the results or effects of 'the very right' *qua* unified property within this *principal subject*.

Situations in which the various functions do not relate to the same subject are different states of matter, however.[2] And in fact, this happens very often. A unified property conceived within the substantial concept of rights is actually nowhere to be found in these cases, and the very thought of it must necessarily lead to pseudo-problems and fictions.

In situations concerning minors, for example, the minor is the subject of interest, and the guardian is the party entitled to bring an action as well as the party invested with the right of disposal. Nevertheless, we are in the habit of viewing this relationship as if 'the right' pertained to the minor, that is, the subject of interest. In the case of a false third-party agreement, on the other hand, the promisee—and, at the same time, the party entitled to bring an action and the person invested with the right of disposal—is regarded as the possessor of the 'right'. Apparently, the varying constructions are conditioned by a difference in the power ascribed to the acting

[2] As far as is known, it was Bekker with his work 'Zur Lehre vom Rechtssubjekt' [On the Doctrine of the Legal Subject], *Jahrbücher für die Dogmatik*, Bd. XII (1873), 1 f., who was the first author to point out the splitting up of the right, so that different functions (enjoyment and management) are separate and distributed among different hands. Later on, this view was further developed by R. Demogue, *Les Notions Fondamentales du Droit Privé* [Fundamental Concepts of Private Law] (1911), 325 f., and the present account has been especially inspired by this author. Also Alexander Nékám, *The Personality Concept of the Legal Entity* (1938), 21 f., has strongly emphasized this view; however, he reserves the term 'subject of the right' for the interested party and calls the administrating party 'administrator of a right'. Moreover, all three authors turn sharply against the dogma that only human beings can hold the position of subject of rights.

subject. Whereas the promisee can exercise his power of bringing an action as well as his power of disposition and control as he pleases in his own interest, the power of the guardian is an authority which is exercised in the interests of the minor, and exercised under control.

In other situations, the split between, on the one hand, an interest in using and enjoying, and, on the other hand, active management is even more pronounced.[3] In this context, it is possible that individuals may hold the position of either the using and enjoying subject or the managing subject with reference to a certain property change from time to time because they are selected according to a special set of rules. This happens in various associations and foundations where there are rules, through by-laws or instruments of foundation, determining how the board of directors shall work, and how the using and enjoying subjects shall be selected. In this [238] situation, the assumption (included in the substantial concept of rights) that the right is a unified property pertaining to a specific, tangible subject is altogether inadequate. Who owns the Carlsberg Foundation, the tennis courts of the Copenhagen Ball Club, or The Master Builders' Widows of Lyngby Foundation? In order to maintain the substantial notion we must resort to fictitious constructions. In Continental law one usually succeeds by simply inventing a unified subject where none exists. The so-called *legal person*[4] is introduced, *qua* subject of the right. In English law, *the construction of* trusts[5] is often used in similar cases. Both *the trustee* (the controlling subject) and the *cestui que trust* (the using and enjoying subject) are conceived as endowed with ownership—the former with *legal ownership*, the latter with *equitable ownership*. This double ownership comes closer to the truth in so far as it indicates that, in a certain sense, each party can be called the subject of the right. However, instead of speaking of double

[3] There is a sliding scale of transition between those cases in which the construction with the guardian is used and those where the juristic person is employed; on this issue, see Alf Ross, *Virkelighed og Gyldighed i Retslæren* [Reality and Validity in Jurisprudence] (1934), 196. See also Hjalmar Karlgren, *Ändamålsbestämmelse och stiftelse* [Provisions on the Purpose of a Foundation] (1951) and C. J. Arnholm 'Noen bemerkninger om "Ändamålsbestämmelse och Stiftelse"' [A few comments on 'Provisions and the purpose of a foundation'] in *TfR* 1952, 258 f.

[4] There is extensive literature on the question whether the legal person is a reality, that is, a natural organism equipped with its own will, a living whole which is distinct from the individuals participating in a collective—in the same way as the individual exists as an independent whole which is more than the sum total of the cells making up the individual organism; or whether the juristic person is only a *fiction* employed by the legislator when he wishes, on practical grounds, to treat a collective as an individual legal person. Leaving aside the question whether this debate can be ascribed any meaning when considered within the framework of sociology, it must be asserted that in a juristic analysis, it certainly involves a metaphysical pseudo-problem. For a juristic analysis it is decisive to show that the legal situations under consideration here are definitely not analogous to the typical individual rights situation, but show a totally different and complicated structure. 'Treating a collectivity as an individual legal person' is not possible. There is simply no principal subject in these situations, and consequently any discussion about the nature of this subject is pointless. Once this is understood, there is of course nothing to prevent us from further using the firmly established terminology and speaking of legal persons as rights subjects.

[5] On this issue, see Torstein Eckhoff, *Rettsvesen og rettsvitenskap i U. S. A.* [Legal System and Legal Science in the USA] (1953), 39 f.

ownership, it would be more accurate to say that in those situations there simply exists no ownership in the ordinary sense. The fact is that in these cases, the functions which we conceive as united within the typical concept of ownership are separate and divided among different persons, neither of whom holds a position that is identical with the typical owner's position.

Other atypical situations arise in connection with succession to the position of rights subject. Transfer of ownership[6] is a typical example. When A transfers ownership to B, the question arises at which moment [239] exactly B will have the legal status of an owner vis-à-vis the rest of the world. This 'vis-à-vis the rest of the world' can be broken down into a number of legal problems concerning the transferee's relations to various groups of 'third parties'. It is not necessary that one and the same fact should be decisive for B's legal position in these various relationships. For practical reasons, it may be preferable to have different crucial criteria. Therefore, both the legal doctrinal and the legal political analysis must be analyses of relationships. When the legal positions in the various relationships have been established, it will be a mere terminological question without any real content at exactly which moment ownership will be said to have passed from A to B.

In Scandinavian legal science (especially thanks to Torp's pioneering work), this problem is mostly[7] treated in conformity with the functional-relative views mentioned above. In other law systems, by contrast, the problem is still affected by the metaphysical assumptions of the substantial concept of rights. The transfer of ownership is conceived as a substantial phenomenon from which the various legal effects derive. This entails, firstly, that the transfer is regarded as a phenomenon which basically occurs directly between the parties, and from which the position of the parties in relation to third parties derive as consequences; and, secondly, that the transfer is conceived to be absolute, that is, to have effect against all third parties by virtue of one and the same fact. Any real debate concerning a relativistic account of the problems surrounding the transfer of ownership is thus precluded.[8]

(b) The metaphysical idea of a right as a *moral-spiritual force* leads to the dogmatic postulate that *only human beings* (and legal persons) can be the subject of rights.[9]

6 On this issue, see the more detailed account in my book *Ejendomsret og Ejendomsovergang* [Ownership and the Transfer of Ownership] (1935), ch. I.

7 However, for some reminiscences of a substantial approach see *loc. cit.*, 21 *et seq.*

8 See *loc. cit.*, 18–21 and ch. VII. From Henry Ussing's interesting account of the discussions at the 7th International Private Law Conference in The Hague in 1951, see *NTIRJG* 1952, 114–15, it emerges that this is still the prevailing view in foreign law.

9 This dogma—regarded by most people as a self-evident truth—apparently derives from a moral and metaphysical idea of the human being as the centre of the universe and the purpose of all things. It is often combined with the equally untenable dogmatic assertion that *every* human being is a legal person; see, e.g., Carl Goos, *Forelæsninger over den almindelige Retslære* [Lectures on the General Study of Law], vol. I (1885), 181 and Jean Dabin, *Le droit subjectif* [Subjective Law] (1952), 116. For a criticism of the dogma, see the authors mentioned in note 2.

Naturally, only human beings are able to carry out the activity that is necessary in order to function as a party entitled to bring an action and invested with the right of disposal. On the other hand, there is nothing to prevent scientifically valid law from recognizing that things other than a certain human interest can be taken care of through a right.

Thus, legacies left for the benefit of *animals* are often accepted, and these legacies are then administered according to rules that are identical with [240] those governing the legacies left for the benefit of human beings. There is no sound reason to deny that in such a case, the animal is the interested party and—according to ordinary linguistic usage[10]—the holder of the 'right'. It would be dogmatic and unrealistic *Begriffsjurisprudenz* to construe the animal's enjoyment of the legacy as a mere reflection of a right of the board, limited by instructions, and to draw certain conclusions concerning the legal position in various respects; for example, in the event of the executor's bankruptcy, or with regard to taxation.[11]

The same applies if it is accepted that legacies can be left for a specific, *objective purpose*—for the maintenance of a monument, for example. It is one thing that the testator is given the very power to leave such legacies—as well as the power to leave other legacies—in order to look after his own interests; the fact that in the legal situation established through such a legacy—in contrast to other kinds of legacies—there is no enjoying interest, is quite another thing. Perhaps we could say in these situations that the objective purpose adopts the position of interested party, and characterize the property as 'purposive property' (*Zweckvermögen*).

[10] Cf. p. 216 above.

[11] In the Danish paper *Politiken* [Politics] 24 August 1952, there is a report on an American lady who bequeathed a sum of 50,000 dollars to her surviving dog. This caused the ensuing dispute over the issue of whether the dog should pay taxes on this amount.

On the issue of penalties for *animal cruelty* and the frequent misinterpretation of these rules, see Alf Ross, *Virkelighed og Gyldighed i Retslæren* [Reality and Validity in Jurisprudence], 198–99.

§ 39. Structure of the Right

The concept of rights is used to describe legal situations. Within this concept, we can distinguish certain elements which make up the structure of a right. These elements are the following.

(a) The *subject* of the right. On this issue, see the two preceding sections from which it emerges that we must distinguish between the position as subject in different relations, in particular as subject of interest, of proceedings and of disposition, respectively. In typical situations, these subjects merge into a single principal subject. In atypical situations, on the other hand, they are separate from each other and distributed among different parties.

(b) The *content* of the right. In a wider sense, the content of the right comprises both the right holder's claim against others (concerning a given, positively or negatively determined, course of action) and his power to [241] enforce these claims by instituting proceedings and by his right of disposal. However, since the power to institute proceedings and the power of disposal are accessories to the content of the primary claim and are, thus, constant elements to be found in different rights, it is appropriate to restrict the concept of content so as to concern only those specific claim-contents through which one right distinguishes itself from another right.

Since the right is the counterpart of other persons' duty (§ 37 (b)), the *specific* content of the right is a restriction upon other persons' freedom of action, or the opposing claim of the rights holder. Thus, the content of the right of claim is the debtor's duty of performance or the creditor's claim for performance. The content of the right of ownership is the owner's claim that others shall refrain from disposing of a certain object, etc. In more informal language, and as far as the rights of disposal are concerned, the term '(specific) content of a right' is used to designate the rights holder's privileged freedom of action, which is the intended, factual economic outcome of his legal claim. We say, for example, that the content of the right of ownership consists of the owner's freedom to dispose of his chattels as he pleases (within certain bounds).

(c) The *object* of the right. With respect to the rights of disposal it seems natural—since their content is always defined as a limited or unlimited disposal of an object—to call that object the object of the right. Thus, the object is only one element of the complete definition of the content. But since one can have rights with varying content of disposal but concerning one and the same thing, and on the other hand rights with the same content of disposal but concerning different things, it is natural to separate *in abstracto* the object of the right from the content of the right. The specific content of the different types of rights of disposal (the right of ownership and the limited rights *in rem*) is determined through the content that has been abstracted from the object.

What has been said above does not apply to claim rights.

(d) *Protection* of the right. Since a claim is legally-functionally identical with the possibility of obtaining a judgment against the obligated party, the *procedural* (or *static*) protection of the right is merely stating another side of its content. There is no claim without the sanction applied by the machinery of law. It cannot be ruled out, however, that one and the same claim may be sanctioned by different legal reactions (judgments providing for a penalty, for performance, for restitution, for damages); therefore, it is justified to distinguish *in abstracto* between the content of a right and its procedural protection.

The *dynamic* protection of a right is distinct from its procedural protection—or, as I prefer to call it—static protection. Dynamic protection concerns legal problems which only arise in connection with the transfer of rights or other forms of succession; that is, in connection with the dynamics of the rights. It is not clear, however, what exactly 'protection' means in this context.

When A has sold an object to B—and considering, in isolation, merely a given set of facts and a given set of legal rules—then there exist the neces- [242] sary and sufficient conditions for B's succeeding to A's position; merely considering, in isolation, a given set of facts and a given set of legal rules, though. For if A has sold the object to C as well; or if A's creditor D levies execution against it, then there exist—likewise, merely considering in isolation a given set of facts in connection with the same set (or another isolated set) of legal rules—the necessary and sufficient conditions for C's and D's respective succession to A's position. In this case we speak of a collision of rights. This expression is misleading, however, for it is obvious that B and C (D) cannot both have a right, so that these rights could collide. The legal order must include more extensive rules, containing an adjustment of the two isolated ways of looking at things, so that either B or C (D) has a right to the object. Thus, there is no collision of rights, but a collision of isolated considerations. From a holistic perspective there is no collision: either B or C (D) is the sole rights holder.

In these situations, then, the problem of protection rests upon the circumstance that, for technical reasons, the rules of the legal order are formulated in sets which, considered in isolation, regulate the transfer of rights in relation to certain facts. These isolated sets necessarily presuppose other supplementary rules, regulating the 'collision of rights' which occurs when the individual set of rules is used in temporary isolation. These

[243] supplementary rules are the rules governing the dynamic protection of the acquirer of the right.

Now we can see that there is a crucial difference in meaning with respect to the word 'protection' in these two situations.

Static protection concerns the means of exerting pressure which can be applied against violations of the right. These means of exerting pressure can be effective to a greater or lesser degree, depending on the conditions under which infringement is punished, on the magnitude of the penalty, and on the conditions under which the rights holder can obtain a judgment providing for enforcement (vindication) or at least a judgment for damages. The more effective the sanctions, the better the protection of the right, that is, the higher the probability that the rights holder will in fact achieve undisturbed economic enjoyment of certain things which the legal order wishes to assign to him. It is obvious that this protection can never be absolute.

Dynamic protection, on the other hand, has nothing to do with sanctions. Here, the assurance in question is not an assurance that the legal rules (norms of conduct) are actually obeyed, but an assurance that, considered holistically, the acquirer of a right really will succeed to the legal position of his predecessor. In this situation, then, protection does not mean protection of an existing legal position, but protection of an acquirer's expectation of being placed into such a position. According to circumstances, this protection can be absolute, since the legal order under certain conditions precludes any possibility of further discussion of the legal position as the result of a succession.

It emerges from the above discussion that whereas static protection concerns the relationship between substantive law (norms of conduct) and procedural law, dynamic protection concerns problems within substantive law.

It is an age-old problem whether there exists a natural or necessary connection between the content of a right and its dynamic protection. This problem will be addressed in the following chapter, dealing with rights *in rem* and obligatory rights.

(e) The structural elements indicated under the above headings constitute the basis for a juridico-scientific division of rights into different types. Divisions based on the content of the right are especially important. It would lead us too far into current legal doctrine to pursue the question of a systematics of rights. Only one important issue will be taken up in the following chapter.

§ 40. Confrontation

In modern times,[1] a *critique of the concept of rights* which is basically related to the views expressed in this book, has been put forward by Duguit[2] in France and by Lundstedt[3] in Sweden. These authors also emphasize the metaphysical burden that has been handed down to the concept of rights: in their view, the very idea of a right as substance, as a spiritual power or force caused by certain facts, is nonsense; the only demonstrable reality in so-called situations of right consists of the function of the legal machinery. According to scientifically valid law, an individual can, under certain conditions, set the legal machinery in motion by filing a lawsuit, with the effect that public power is being exercised in his favour. He can achieve a sentence and its enforcement. Thereby, an advantageous position is created for him—an opportunity for action in the shape of an economic benefit. And that is all.

As far as one can see, this is quite correct. However, instead of taking one more [244] step and asking what are the typical features of these situations, and how the concept of rights might be analysed and shaped in order to serve as a tool for describing them (as has been attempted in the preceding pages), these authors give a peculiar twist to their critique by saying that *rights do not exist*, and that anyone mentioning rights consequently talks nonsense about something that does not exist.

Duguit's argument to prove the 'non-existence' of subjective rights is fairly simple. To begin with, it is established that the term subjective right can only mean a certain power inherent in a given individual's will; a power to assert itself, as such, against other wills, that is, a superiority or supremacy inherent in the will in relation to other, subordinate wills. Then, it is asserted that, in reality, there is no such immanent difference in quality between the wills themselves. And in conclusion: consequently, there are no subjective rights!

It is evident that this way of thinking is grounded in the curiously naive idea that a word has an inherent meaning which cannot be changed. The whole 'argumentation' depends on the opinion that Duguit, from the outset, is adamant

[1] It should be noted that criticism similar to that addressed by Duguit and Lundstedt had already been largely forestalled by Bentham; see, for example, *The Works of Jeremy Bentham* (1838–1843), Vol. I, 248, 358, 361, in Vol. II, 497 *et seq.*, and especially his work *The Limits of Jurisprudence Defined* (first published in 1945), 57 *et seq.*

[2] See, in particular, Léon Duguit, *Traité de droit constitutionel* [Treatise on Constitutional Law] Vol. I (3rd edn, 1927); cf. Alf Ross, *Virkelighed og Gyldighed i Retslæren* [Reality and Validity in Jurisprudence] (1934), ch. X, 3 and Jean Dabin, *Le droit subjectif* [Subjective Law] (1952), 5 f.

[3] See, e.g., Vilhelm Lundstedt, *Obligationsbegreppet* D. 1 [The Concept of Obligation, Part One], 1 (1930) and the detailed account and critique in my book *Virkelighed og Gyldighed i Retslæren* [Reality and Validity in Jurisprudence] (1934), ch. X, 4.

that the term 'subjective right' *cannot* mean anything except something meaningless, in order to announce, later on, as a radically new truth that this meaningless something does not exist!

Lundstedt, too, believes in the inherent meaning of the word. He maintains that rights do not exist conceptually, but he nevertheless admits that there are certain realities behind the concept, and that he sees no reason why the word 'right' should not be used, for the sake of brevity, as a mere designation for these realities. One might think that Lundstedt thereby means to create a new concept of rights, exclusively determined by exactly these realities. This is definitely not the case, however. Although the word—for lack of anything better—may be employed to designate certain realities, these cannot logically be 'classified' as rights; which, of course, must mean that they are not rights!

In the abstract, this naive linguistic mysticism may be regarded as something of a curiosity. It is not harmless, however.

First, it offends against something in the ethics of science, to the detriment of understanding, cooperation, and progress. A stubborn wish to impute absurdities to other people; a lack of ability, or of will, to understand that also other people may use (more or less consciously elaborated and consistently) the expression 'right' as a word to designate certain legal realities; all this is pathological egocentricity which impedes the mutual understanding which the scientific community is based upon.

Secondly, and most importantly, because an attitude such as Duguit's and Lundstedt's easily leads to neglecting the most important aspect of the matter, namely, a thorough analysis of those situations which are commonly called
[245] rights situations, and of the use which legal science actually makes of the concept of rights in order to describe those situations. It is typical that neither Duguit nor Lundstedt appreciate the value of the concept of rights as a technical tool of presentation, nor the various functional relations that can be distinguished in rights situations. Undauntedly, they proceed with the idea of the unity of the concept, although exactly this idea is the most tangible manifestation of the metaphysical ideas that underpin the concept of rights.

This also explains why both Duguit's and Lundstedt's concept formation is sociological rather than legal. The economic advantage, the real opportunity for action or the 'protected position' these authors are speaking of, obviously constitute the practical consequence of a certain legal situation, not the legal situation as such.[4] As a legal concept, however, the concept of rights must be analysed and conceived as a tool to describe a legal content, a legal situation—not its economic consequences.

[4] Ingemar Hedenius, *Om rätt och moral* [On Law and Morality] (1941), 104 and Per Olof Ekelöf, 'Juridisk slutledning och terminology' [Legal inferences and terminology], *TfR* 1945, 266–67, hold the same view.

Less pretentious, but much more productive in connection with a juridico-philosophical analysis has been the discussion in the Nordic countries on the concept of rights and the function of this concept in the field of legal science as well as in practical juristic argumentation.[5]

The *traditional discussion* on the concept of rights has moved to a level, which—if the basic attitude defended in this book is correct—must be rejected as metaphysical and ideologically infected. The problem has been to determine 'the essence' of the right. On the one hand, there is Ihering's well-known theory,[6] according to which the essence of a right is the *legally protected interest.* On the other hand, there is Windscheid's theory, similarly well known, according to which the essence of a right is a *power of will* (considering the right holder's possession in fact and the right to file a lawsuit) or a *rule of will* (considering his ability to dispose of things). The debate between these two theories never seems [246]
to cease. Against the theory of interests, the argument is advanced that there can be situations where interests are distinct from the right—for example, when property is encumbered with charges to the advantage of others, or in cases of false third-party agreements. Altogether, it is difficult, according to Ihering's theory, to distinguish between the right itself and its reflexive effects to the advantage of others. Against the will theory, on the other hand, the argument is advanced that individuals who have no will, or no rational will (human embryos, children, demented persons), can nevertheless be the subjects of rights. Many authors in the modern era have chosen a middle way and assume a certain combination of interest and will as the essence of a subjective right.[7]

This discussion is futile. If it is correct that the concept of rights in no way corresponds to any reality arising between the conditioning facts and the conditioned consequence, then it does not make sense to discuss whether the very essence of a right is interest, will, or something else. Concealed behind the

[5] Per Olof Ekelöf, 'Juridisk slutledning och terminologi' [Legal inferences and terminology], *TfR* 1945, 211 f.; Ivar Strahl, 'Till frågan om rättighetsbegreppet' [On the issue of the concept of rights], *TfR* 1946, 204–10; Per Olof Ekelöf, 'Till frågan om rättighetsbegreppet' [On the issue of the concept of rights], *TfR* 1946, 309–13; Ivar Strahl, 'Till frågan om rättighetsbegreppet' [On the issue of the concept of rights], *TfR* 1947, 481–514; Per Olof Ekelöf, 'Om begagnandet av termen rättighet inom juridiken' [On the use of the term right in the law], in *Svensk Juristtidnings Festschrift för Birger Ekeberg* [Swedish Law Journal, Tribute to Birger Ekeberg] (1950), 151–77; Ross, 'Tû-tû,' in *Festskrift til Henry Ussing* [A Tribute to Henry Ussing] (1951), 468–84; [English translation in *Harvard Law Review*, vol. 70, Issue 5, March 1957, 812–25]; Anders Wedberg, 'Some Problems in the Logical Analysis of Legal Science', *Theoria* (1951) 246–75; Per Olof Ekelöf, 'Är termen rättighet ett syntaktisk hjälpmedel utan mening?' [Is the term right a syntactic tool devoid of meaning?], *Skrifter tillägnade Vilhelm Lundstedt* [Papers dedicated to Vilhelm Lundstedt] (1952), 546–59.

[6] Ihering's theory is described in his work *Geist des römischen Rechts auf den verschiedenen Stufen seiner Entwiklung* [The spirit of the Roman Law at the various stages of its development], vols. III and IV, slightly varying with the different editions of the work. Windscheid's doctrine is described in his work *Lehrbuch des Pandektenrechts* [Textbook of the Law of Pandects], vol. I, also slightly varying with the different editions. See further Alf Ross, *Virkelighed og Gyldighed i Retslæren* [Reality and Validity in Jurisprudence] (1934), ch. XIII, 3 and Jean Dabin, *Le droit subjectif* [Subjective Law] (1952), 56 *et seq.*

[7] See Alf Ross, *Virkelighed og Gyldighed i Retslæren* [Reality and Validity in Jurisprudence] (1934), 176 and Jean Dabin, *Le droit subjectif* [Subjective Law] (1952), 72 f.

various ideas of a substantial essence are different elements in the typical rights situation: the factual advantage, determined by the restriction of others' freedom of action, the power to prosecute, and the competence of disposition. The apparently insurmountable difficulties which each of the theories has to struggle with simply result from the fact that the integral functions in the typical rights situations are split up among different subjects in the atypical situations.

The pioneers with respect to a deeper analysis of the concept of rights have been, not so much the above-mentioned authors who deny the existence of subjective rights but, rather, others who realized that the right covers different, mutually independent functions—in particular, the functions of use and enjoyment. Within this context, the names Demogue, Nékám and Bekker deserve to be mentioned.[8]

[8] See § 38 note 2.

CHAPTER VII [247]

The Theory of Rights *In Rem* and Rights *In Personam*

§ 41. Doctrine and Problems

In property law, we have distinguished—from time immemorial—between two main groups of rights: rights *in rem* and rights *in personam* (whereto a third group is frequently added nowadays, namely, a group called intellectual property rights).*

The doctrine concerning this distinction can be framed in various ways as regards details. Its unchanging core,[1] however, consists of a necessary, or at least natural, connection between the content of a right and its protection. It is assumed that the division of property rights according to their content corresponds to the division of protection. The rights which according to their content are rights *in rem* (by which is usually understood that they authorize a direct use and enjoyment over a thing) are provided with protection *in rem* (by which is usually understood that the rights holder can recover the thing against anyone who has taken possession of it without title, that he is a secured creditor in the bankrupt estate of the transferor, and that he has priority over later acquirers of the thing). The rights which according to their content are *in personam* (by which is usually understood that they consist in a claim against a person to render performance) are provided with protection *in personam* (by [248] which is usually understood that they can only be enforced against the debtor: the rights holder has no right of recovery, he is not a secured creditor in the bankrupt estate of the debtor, and he must give way to later *bona fide* acquirers).

Depending on how the distinction according to content and difference in protection is defined in more detail, the doctrine of rights *in rem* and rights *in*

* Translator's note: In common law systems, *intellectual property rights* is a perfectly natural subset of rights *in rem*.

[1] Moreover, it is assumed that the distinction is significant in several other respects as well and is, therefore, essential for the division of property law into two main branches, namely the law of things and the law of obligations. This issue will be discussed below in § 48.

personam will assume a different character. If we ignore this for the moment, the common idea-content of the doctrine can be expressed in the following sentences:

(1) A right *in rem* is a right which, according to its content, is a right over a thing and, therefore, equipped with protection *in rem.*

(2) A right *in personam* is a right which, according to its content, is of an obligatory nature and, therefore, equipped with obligatory protection.

This terminology is not very felicitous, however, because the expressions 'rights *in rem*' and 'rights *in personam*' refer equally to the content of the right and its protection, which may cause confusion if the expression is used with reference sometimes to the one and sometimes to the other.

Therefore, it is preferable to use different expressions for the distinction according to content and for the distinction according to difference in protection, respectively. If we introduce the expressions 'right of disposal' and 'right of claim' with regard to the former, then the essence of the doctrine can be expressed in the following sentences:

(1) According to the content of the property rights, we can make a distinction between rights of disposal and rights of claim.

(2) According to the principles of the protection of a right, we can make a distinction between protection *in rem* and protection *in personam*; and

(3) There exists a (necessary or natural) connection between these two distinctions, in the sense that a right of disposal is (normally) equipped with protection *in rem* and a right of claim with protection *in personam.*

We can now offer a framework for analysis and critique:

re (1): Are the common distinctions between right of disposal and right of claim tenable? (§ 42)

re (2): Are the common distinctions between protection *in rem* and protection *in personam* tenable? (§ 43)

re (3) Can the two above-named distinctions be endowed with such a meaning that there exists a (necessary or natural) connection between them? (§ 44)

In short: the following inquiry purports to demonstrate that the first two questions must be answered in the negative and the third one in the affirmative. This means that even if the way in which the two distinctions have been made, and the way in which one has imagined the connection between them, are untenable, one nonetheless has had something important in mind which prompts investigation.

The doctrinal position[2] is, broadly speaking, as follows: [249]

(a) The prevailing doctrine determines the fundamental distinction between the right of disposal and the right of claim by stating that the former is a right *directly over an object*, the latter a right *against a person*. The right of disposal is that right which, without being based on a legal relationship with any other person, immediately endows the rights holder with direct control or power over a thing—power to use and enjoy the thing, either in every respect (ownership), or in certain, more defined respects (limited rights *in rem*); all of this, however, within the general limits of the law. The right of claim is that right against a person which originates in a legal relationship between two given persons, and which corresponds to a duty for that person to render performance to the rights holder, in virtue of that same legal relationship.

From this difference within the innermost essence of rights there follows a difference in their legal effects: since the right *in rem* is a right over things as such and not against any other person, it applies to all persons—or applies absolutely—to both acquirers and creditors. It is, as the French say, equipped with *droit de suite* and *droit de préférence*. When judgment is given against the other party, it is not because of any obligations this party has, but is merely a symptom of the negative fact that the other party has no right which he could oppose to the plaintiff's right of disposal. This right is in itself strong enough to uphold the claim for a sentence and its enforcement. Even if the expression is still used sometimes that a third party is bound not to interfere with the exercise of legal authority, it is nevertheless expressly emphasized that this 'being bound' is merely a result of the right of disposal, not a part of its essence. Conversely: since the right of claim is a right against a certain person who is bound accordingly, it applies solely to him, or is relative. It lacks *suite* and *préférence*. In this case, the judgment against the debtor rests on his obligation towards the creditor, not merely on the latter's right and the former's non-existent right.

(b) There is widespread *criticism* of the way in which the concept of '*right of disposal*' is defined by the prevailing doctrine.

Since all law in the last analysis is a regulation of the behaviour of human beings towards each other, the right of disposal—or so the argument runs—cannot be defined as a direct power, or control, over a thing. For example, the power which ownership bestows upon the owner, is a power over other persons in so far as the owner can demand—and to a great extent enforce, through the means of coercion appertaining to the legal order—that these other persons do not disturb his actual use of the thing.

[2] For further information, see the comprehensive exposition in my book *Virkelighed og Gyldighed i Retslæren* [Reality and Validity in Jurisprudence] (1934), ch. XI.

Legally, ownership consists merely of the claims which the owner can [250] enforce against other persons, or of the corresponding duties on the part of others to abstain from disturbing the owner's possession. Accordingly, the right of disposal is defined as a *universal and negative obligation to abstain.*

Just as much as the right of claim, the right of disposal thus expresses an interpersonal legal relation. The difference lies in the structure and content of the legal relationship. In one situation, the obligation applies to only one (or several) specific persons, and its content can be defined both positively and negatively. In the other situation, the obligation applies to all, and its content is defined negatively, namely as a duty not to interfere with someone else's disposal.

From the universal character of the right of disposal it follows that it is available against everyone.

We shall see that this criticism does not affect the fundamental distinction between rights of disposal and rights of claim, nor the prevailing view that there is an intimate connection between the content and the protection of a right. One might say that it merely aims at a formulation of the purpose of the prevailing view that would be more tenable from a juridico-philosophical perspective.

(c) The *criticism* put forth in Nordic, especially Danish, theory[3] is still more radical, for it is directed towards *the very assumption that there is a connection* between the content of a right and its protection.

It all began with the circumstance that various authors, working in former times, noticed situations in which a right certainly amounts to a possession according to its content, but nevertheless does not need to be endowed with protection *in rem.* The legal situation of the tenant was pointed out, for example. Whereas the tenant enjoys protection *in rem* (King Christian V's Danish Law [Danske Lov], 6-17-5) according to Danish law, this was not the case according to Roman law. The same applies to the person who (previous to the Registration of Property Act) had purchased real property on the basis of a sales contract and perhaps even taken possession of the property. As far as the transfer of movables is concerned, there was no agreement as to the exact moment that the purchaser acquired protection *in rem*; it was generally assumed, though, that this issue required more than a mere sales agreement. In any case, however, the content of the purchaser's right seems to amount to the same thing, namely, to give him control over the object.

At first, an attempt was made to uphold the traditional doctrine by simply denying that the content consisted in a right of disposal if the right was not

[3] For further information, see *op. cit.*, ch. XI, 10.

protected *in rem*. The right of disposal, or claim of disposal, would, thus, not be an expression of a real right, but merely a reflection of the legal protection of a claim.

In the long run, there was no disguising the fact that this recourse was merely a haphazard construction, a play upon words to preserve a postulate. Therefore, more modern authors drew the inevitable conclusion, namely, that there was no necessary connection between the content of a right and its protection. This does not mean, however, that one denied every connection. It was admitted [251] that pure claim rights, that is, claims to specific services, never enjoy protection *in rem*. As far as claims to individually specified things are concerned, there is no room for a distinction on the basis of whether the law, according to its content, amounts to a right of disposal or to a claim. There is no real basis for such a distinction, and any attempt to make it will result in metaphysical ideas about whether 'the law itself', as a mystical substance, has evaporated or not. From a juridico-functional perspective, this way of thinking results in attaching decisive importance to the words used by the transferor—words which do not have any real meaning but work like magical incantations (declaration of transfer *contra* promise). From a legal political perspective, however, it is not advisable to let legal protection depend on party autonomy. Exactly when protection *in rem* occurs ought to be prescribed by the legislator. In these situations, the protection of the right has nothing to do with the content of the right. It is the same before and after the occurrence of those facts which lead to effects *in rem* (for example, registration, transfer of ownership, payment). All one can say is that individually specified rights have a chance of achieving protection *in rem*.[4]

[4] This rendition of an idea that was first put forward by Carl Ussing ('Løsøres Overdragelse' [The transfer of movables], *Tidsskrift for Rettsvidenskap* 1890, 181 *et seq.*, especially 184–89) and, later on, embraced by Ernst Møller (*Forudsætninger* [Presumptions] (1894), 126–30) and Vinding Kruse (*Ejendomsretten* [The Right of Property] (3rd edn, 1951) 165 *et seq.*), is somewhat stylized and has been adapted to my own mode of expression. It should be particularly noted that Vinding Kruse's exposition is puffed up as if it were a radical novelty, whereas in reality, and on closer inspection, it does not contain any important findings compared to Carl Ussing's theory.

§ 42. The Distinction between Right of Disposal and Right of Claim

The criticism just accounted for gives us a glimpse (albeit just a glimpse) of the circumstance that the distinction between the right of disposal (as the right to use and enjoy a thing) and the right of claim (as the right against a person to render performance), apparently so simple, is nevertheless untenable. To be sure, the distinction is not problematic in the case of generically defined claims. It does not seem to be difficult to distinguish between the ownership of a cow and a claim against B for 100 Danish Crowns. Things are different, however, if the claim concerns individually specified things.

On the one hand, there is no reason why a right authorizing the rights holder to dispose of a thing, at present or in the future, should not exist under such [252] circumstances that the legal enjoyment presupposes cooperation, on the basis of a certain behaviour, on the part of another person. This is the case, for example, with restricted rights of disposal; for there, the owner is placed in a position of an exceptional relationship of duty vis-à-vis the holder of the restricted right. In the case of a tenant's usufruct, for example, it is irrelevant whether one chooses to define its content as an actual, immediate use and enjoyment (which must be respected by everyone, including the owner) or as a claim against the owner to surrender the usufruct to the tenant and see to it that it is constantly at the disposal of the latter.

Nor is there any reason why a claim against a person should not, according to its content, obligate the debtor to hand over, or continue to allow his creditor, the use and enjoyment of a thing, and thus, to that extent, constitute a right of disposal. It is the same thing, merely viewed from the other side. This ambiguity typically appears in connection with the sale and purchase of movables until they are actually handed over. In view of the real situation, it seems irrelevant whether we say that the purchaser's right is a right of disposal, and that his claim for the surrender of the things can be compared with an owner's claim for the delivery of his property against the person who is in possession of it with a provisional right only (until the date of delivery); or whether we say that the purchaser's right is a right of claim against the vendor for the surrender of the things.

These difficulties arise simply because the *distinction is skewed*, that is, the two concepts are not formed on the same *fundamentum divisionis*.

'Right of disposal' is a sociologically oriented concept; that is to say, it defines a legal situation in relation to the real economic effect, to the real utilization of a benefit—the practical consequence of the fact that certain legal rules are actually upheld in a legal machinery.

The right of claim, on the other hand, is a purely legal concept, that is to say, it expresses solely the legal position in a certain legal situation (the claim of the creditor, the duty of the debtor) and disregards the real economic advantage resulting from the enforcement of the law (the creditor's prospect of receiving payment).

Now, if the debtor's duty of performance precisely consists of procuring, or continuing to permit, the creditor the use and enjoyment of a thing, the two concepts overlap, and it is not possible to draw a distinction between them.

If a meaningful distinction shall be drawn, it must be based solely and consistently (a) on the real, intended effect; or (b) on the legal claims and duties at which this effect is aimed.

(a) Every right—and we recall that the present discussion is limited to proprietary rights only—intends, from the real economic perspective, to give the rights holder the use and enjoyment of specified objects, simply because it is not possible to use and enjoy anything but specified objects: this cow, these sacks of corn, these banknotes. Thus, for example, a generically [253] defined claim for 100 sacks of corn aims at giving (some time) the creditor the use and enjoyment of 100 specified sacks of corn, to be delivered to him by the debtor. That the claim is generically determined thus only means that matters have not yet progressed to a point where it would be possible, at the present stage, to point out the 100 sacks.

It follows that on a *real economic* basis, it is not possible to draw a distinction between rights of disposal and no-rights of disposal (rights of claim). Seen from this point of view, all rights are rights of disposal.

However, a distinction can be made between:

(α) rights whose objects of disposal can be pointed out *right now*, depending on, whether they are

(α 1) rights authorizing the actual use and enjoyment of a specific object, such as ownership, usufruct; or

(α 2) rights authorizing a future use and enjoyment (either conditioned, or determined for a limited period of time) of an (already) determined object; for example, the purchaser's right to a specific cow he has bought; and

(β) Rights whose object of disposal can *not yet* be pointed out; such as, for example, A's right if B has promised him to deliver, at a later date, 100 sacks of corn, or to pay him 100 Crowns.

Or, putting it briefly:

(α) Rights over, or to, an (already) *individually determined* object: and

(β) Rights to a (for the time being) *generically determined* performance.

As far as rights under (β) are concerned, their object cannot be pointed out until certain later events have taken place (binding individualization, delivery, executive steps).

Of course, we may hold on to traditional linguistic usage and go on calling α-rights 'rights of disposal' and β-rights 'rights of claim'—provided we bear in mind that the latter also aim at establishing a real economic use and enjoyment. We shall discover that it is the characteristic of the rights of claim to represent a preliminary stage of the rights of disposal. Sooner or later, every right of claim (not dissolved) turns into a right of disposal. A legal situation which, at a certain moment, is characterized as a right of claim will—due to later events—develop into a situation characterized as a right of disposal.

(b) From a purely juridico-functional perspective, every right consists of the
[254] legal claims which the rights holder can assert by filing a lawsuit. Usually we speak of the existence of a claim, even though not all conditions necessary for taking legal action are given. For example, we say that A has a claim against B as soon as B has promised A to pay him 100 Crowns in 14 days, even though A cannot take immediate steps in this situation; not before B fails to pay his debt on the due date. In this case, however, it is possible to indicate, at the very outset, the mode of behaviour that will bring about the actual power to prosecute, namely, that B does not pay his debt within 14 days. Therefore, it is possible to ascribe a specific content to A's claim and B's corresponding duty. In other cases this is not possible. If we say, for example, that the owner has a claim that others should not disturb his possession, it is still rather uncertain what future acts will bring about A's actual power to prosecute. It may happen that B appropriates the thing by stealing it; or that C sets fire to it; or that D damages it by colliding with it; or that E borrows it and happens to lose it; or that the thing accidentally comes into F's possession, whereupon F refuses to hand it over, etc., etc. Obviously, the owner's claim is, as yet, fairly indeterminate, both with regard to the person against whom the claim is directed and with regard to the act that conditions the lawsuit in question. The claim expresses merely a preliminary fundamental condition for a lawsuit: only later events will give a specific content to the claim.

We can express this by distinguishing between *mature* and *immature* claims: the former designate legal situations where either the rights holder is actually able to take legal action, or it is at least possible to indicate, specifically, the mode of behaviour that will bring this about; whereas the latter designate legal situations where a fundamental condition for taking legal action certainly exists but where, as yet, it is only with considerable vagueness that one can indicate the mode of behaviour which will bring about the actual power to take legal action.

On this basis, we can put forward the definition that 'rights of disposal' shall designate rights with immature claims only, and that 'rights of claim' shall designate rights consisting of mature claims.[1]

Please observe that this definition of rights of disposal and rights of claim in a functional sense does not coincide with the definition of these expressions, given under (a), in an economic sense. For example: in the real economic sense, the right of the purchaser to a specific thing that he has bought as well as the limited rights *in rem* (the tenant's usufruct, etc.), are rights of disposal. In a functional sense, however, the situation is of a mixed nature. In the direct relationship with the purchaser and the vendor, respectively, there exist mature claims and, thus, a right of claim; but in so [255] far as the purchase and the tenancy agreement, respectively, can serve as a basis for immature claims because of the fact that the legal situation has been disturbed, then the position of the rights holder must be characterized as a right of disposal.[2]

Thus, all this lack of clarity pervading these and similar situations can be explained as simply resulting from the fact that one has worked with a distorted distinction, mixing up real economic and legal functional criteria.

It emerges, from what has been discussed under (a) and (b), that the distinction between rights of disposal and rights of claim (in both senses appertaining to this pair of concepts) is closely connected with something *dynamic*—with a legal situation developing over time. A right of claim (in the real economic sense) develops into a right of disposal; and according to circumstances, a right of disposal (in a functional sense) can mature into a right of claim.

[1] In his inaugural lecture, 'Formuerettens grundbegreber' [The fundamental concepts of property law], *Tidsskrift for Rettsvidenskap* 1951, 239, W. E. v. Eyben discusses a similar definition of the two concepts.

[2] Of course, it is inconvenient to work with two different sets of definitions concerning the pair of concepts right of disposal–right of claim. However, both notions are so deeply ingrained in connection with these expressions that it would hardly be right to create a new terminology. In case it should not emerge from the context, one should therefore clearly indicate in which sense the terms are used.

§ 43. *The Distinction between Protection* In Rem *and Protection* In Personam

In general, protection *in rem* suggests (1) a power to recover a thing from anyone in possession of it without a valid title; and (2) a legal position that has priority in relation to various groups of 'third parties', in particular the successors and creditors of the predecessor, especially the bankruptcy estate.

This definition of 'protection *in rem*' actually conceals various legal problems, each of them reaching beyond the definition.

In conformity with the statements in § 39, a distinction must be made between static and dynamic protection.

Static protection concerns those legal remedies through which the legal order attempts to influence the behaviour of human beings in such a way that the intended economic effect is realized. Access to legal recovery is one of these remedies. Penal sanctions, claims for damages, claims for unjust enrichment and prohibitions also figure among the legal remedies through which the legal order attempts to secure a certain factual position to a given person.

[256] *Dynamic protection*, on the other hand, concerns problems in connection with succession in rights. If the necessary conditions for a valid succession from A to B are given, it may well be the case that B's right, notwithstanding its validity in relation to his predecessor, is not efficacious vis-à-vis certain third parties. This is so because, at the same time, the necessary conditions for a valid succession to the advantage of others can be given. Succession occurs in three main forms: transfer; appropriation by creditor; and inheritance. The conditions for valid succession in each of these forms are expressed in relatively independent rules. If there are several successions—of the same type, or of different types—with respect to the same right, so that several persons, considered independently, can make a claim for succession, then a set of higher rules is needed to settle this conflict; that is, to decide which of the competing successors, from a final, comprehensive perspective, shall succeed to the position of the right. These rules are called the rules of dynamic protection.

The problem of dynamic protection is, thus, concerned with the reciprocal relation between several successors and can therefore be perceived, not only from the position of a transferee in relation to other transferees or creditors or heirs, but just as well from the position of a creditor or an heir.

Questions of dynamic protection arise not only in the case of succession to rights of disposal, but also in the case of succession to claims. In both cases, the problems are fairly analogous.

Thus, the distinction between protection *in rem* and protection *in personam* is more complex than commonly assumed. The qualified protection suggested by the term 'protection *in rem*' means something essentially different, since it aims at static or dynamic protection, respectively, and since the problems are in both respects more extensive than current accounts indicate and must be dealt with in a wider context. But is there any foundation at all for making this distinction, and if so, what is the connection between the distinction and the content of the right? These questions will be discussed in the following section.

§ 44. The Connection between Content and Protection

(a) As far as *static protection* is concerned, one might reasonably ask whether there is a necessary or a natural connection between the content of a right
[257] and its protection. For protection in this sense is something which appertains to the individual right, and therefore, it is—on the face of it—not inconceivable that the protection may vary with the content, cf. § 39.

That there is no good reason why rights of claim should not have static protection in the same way as rights of disposal is quite another matter. Where the legal order aims at the real effect that A, who has a claim against B, shall achieve a performance from B, it would only be half the battle if it furnished him only with remedies against B and not against others, who, by their behaviour, are causing the non-fulfilment of the claim. The claim itself cannot be asserted against anyone except the debtor, of course. The duty of a third party can never be a duty of performance, but it can be a duty to *respect the obligation according to its content*. That there is an actual need for such a protection is particularly manifest in those cases where a third party, through a certain behaviour, is able to extinguish the creditor's right—for example, by transferring a negotiable debt instrument with extinctive effect, by demanding a debt with discharging effect on the debtor, or by causing an impossibility which extinguishes the debtor's obligation. However, the same also applies when a third party, without extinguishing the creditor's right, damages his interests by bringing about, or taking an active part in bringing about, the claim not being properly fulfilled—for example, by causing an impossibility, or by demanding a debt under such circumstances that the debtor is not released.

In modern constitutions, such legal protection is, in fact, also granted to the creditor—to a greater or lesser degree.[1] The elder Romanist doctrine, according to which rights of claim can only be violated by the debtor and therefore do not enjoy protection against others, is a purely doctrinal construction, drawn from the distinction between rights '*in personam*' and rights '*in rem*'.

Just as with the rights of disposal, the remedies which can be employed against third parties may notably consist of penalties, claims for damages, unjust enrichment claims, as well as prohibitions (interim or permanent injunction). A claim analogous to the claim for recovery exists, if exercising the claim rights of others entails demands for repayment, unqualified by bad faith on the part of the third party.

[1] For details, see Carl Ussing, *Dansk Obligationsret. Almindelig Del* [The Danish Law of Obligations. General Part] (3rd edn, 1946), § 47, and Alf Ross, *Virkelighed og Gyldighed i Retslæren* [Reality and Validity in Jurisprudence] (1934), 301–05.

If the term 'right of claim' is understood functionally and, thus, includes demands for individually determined performance—for example, the purchaser's claim against the vendor for the object he has bought—then there is no good reason to make the purchaser's static protection against a third [258]
party dependent on his having achieved dynamic protection '*in rem*' in relation to other successors.[2]

Therefore, we must conclude that there is *neither a necessary nor a practical and natural connection between the content of a right and its static protection*; on the contrary, it is justified that claim rights are granted protection against interfering acts on the part of third parties, on essentially the same principles as those applying to the rights of disposal.

(b) With respect to *dynamic protection*, on the other hand, it may be asserted that it is impossible *ab initio* that there should be any connection between content and protection, to the effect that certain rights are endowed with protection '*in rem*', but others only with protection '*in personam*'. This is simply due to the fact that the rules governing dynamic protection concern a conflict between several successions (each of them being valid in itself), and consequently can be *conditioned by the type of the conflict, not by the type of right*. The notion that a right is 'endowed' with a specific kind of dynamic protection is, thus, erroneous.

This does not mean that there is no connection at all between, on the one hand, the distinction between rights of disposal and rights of claim and, on the other, the rules governing dynamic protection. However, this connection must necessarily be brought about by the possible types of conflict. If the two kinds of rights are symbolized by the letters 'a' and 'b', then three types of conflict are possible, namely (a–a), (b–b), and (a–b), and the question arises whether different principles apply to dynamic protection in these three cases.

In fact, they do so. This does not mean that there is any logical necessity for it, nor does it mean that these issues have been settled the same way in all legal systems. However, it may be said that in all modern constitutional legal systems—indeed in all legal systems based upon a monetary economy[3]—the view prevails that these three types of conflict are treated according to different principles—which, of course, does not preclude that

[2] The access of the purchaser to legal proceedings against a third party does not imply that the vendor, in turn, is precluded from doing so. As long as there is an unsettled disagreement between purchaser and vendor, each party has an interest in the object not being withheld from the area of the disagreement, and each of them should, as representing 'the interests of the disagreement', be able to bring about independently legal action against third parties, provided that the other party is given the opportunity to intervene in order to take care of his own interests. For details, see Alf Ross, *Ejendomsret og Ejendomsovergang* [Ownership and the Transfer of Ownership] (1935), Ch. IV, 2 and 3.

[3] In my book *Virkelighed og Gyldighed i Retslæren* [Reality and Validity in Jurisprudence] (1934), Ch. XII, 4, there are some reference points in order to show that the distinction between individually and generically determined performance is universally found in legal history.

in individual cases, there may be considerable deviations as to the way in which these principles are implemented in more detail. However, the great similarity in respect of their basic features justifies the view that there is a natural connection between the type of conflict—determined by the
[259] division of the rights according to their content into rights of disposal and rights of claim in an economic sense; that is, defined as rights over, or to, individually specified objects and rights to generically defined performances—and the principles governing dynamic protection.

The principles can roughly be described as follows:

Conflict No.1: Right of disposal v. right of disposal (a–a): the principle of priority

This means that the conflict is resolved on the basis of temporal priority: the right that was created first takes precedence over the right that was created subsequently. On legal technical grounds, the principle undergoes modification in the rules governing registration, good faith acquisition through possession, the extinction of rights to instruments of debt, etc.

Conflict No. 2: Right of claim v. right of claim (b–b): the principle of competition

If a debtor first creates a right of claim to the advantage of A and then another one to the advantage of B, then this means—or, at least, could mean—that A's chances of achieving performance have diminished. Several creditors in relation to the same debtor always means a conflict of interests, at least potentially. The situation is analogous to that of double sale, and on the face of it, there is no reason why a solution according to the principle of priority should not be possible, namely to the effect that the first creditor should have a claim for performance before later creditors. However, all modern legal systems are based on another principle, namely, the principle of competition.

According to this principle, the creditors must compete for performance irrespective of the date of their claims. Normally, the competition is free, that is, a creditor does not enjoy protection against another creditor. Each of them can pursue the debtor in any way he likes, without regard to the existence and priorities of the others. The competition is restricted only under certain circumstances, namely, when the conflict of interests has become urgent, or threatens to become urgent, because all claims cannot be fulfilled. At this point, bankruptcy proceedings commence, that is, restricted competition, where all creditors are granted reciprocal protection, so that they all must submit to an equally proportionate reduction of the performance of their claims, out of the available assets, but regardless of when the claim arose.

Legally and technically, this principle is modified by the rules on invalidation. Further modifications occur through the acknowledgement of preferential claims, that is, claims which—with due consideration of the situation in which they have arisen[4]—enjoy priority over simple creditors.

Conflict No. 3: right of disposal v. right of claim (a–b): the principle of preference [260]

This means that the right of disposal has precedence over the right of claim, irrespective of when the conflicting rights have been created: the holder of the right of disposal is a secured creditor in the debtor's bankruptcy estate.

On legal technical grounds, this principle is modified by the rules on invalidation, registration, etc.

From what has been said above, it emerges that there are not two kinds of dynamic protection ('*in rem*' and '*in personam*') tied to two kinds of rights but, rather, three kinds of principles of protection tied to three kinds of conflict. However, it is not difficult to see how the idea of two kinds of protection could arise. The truth is that the two kinds of rights do not belong to the same types of conflict. While the right of disposal (a) belongs under No. 1 (a–a) and No. 3 (a–b), the right of claim belongs under No. 2 (b–b) and No. 3 (a–b). A superficial glance might suggest that they are protected according to different principles, directly determined by the content of the right. The real situation can be described as follows:

Protection *in rem* = protection according to
- principle of priority in the collision a–a
- principle of preference in the collision a–b

Obligatory protection = protection according to
- principle of competition in the collision b–b
- principle of preference in the collision a–b

Thus, while neither of the two terms is an expression for a homogeneous principle, both are partly an expression for the same principle (the principle of preference) as seen from a different angle.

As long as we are clear about this, there is no reason why we should not continue using the established terms.

[4] Vinding Kruse, *Ejendomsretten* [The Right of Property] (3rd edn, 1951), 173 cf. 1359 *et seq.* misleadingly compares the position of preferential creditors with the protection according to the principles of priority and preference which goes with the right of disposal. Thereby, he is wrongly led to think that everything one owns and will come to own, on the one side, and preferential claims on the other, are legal creations of one and the same kind. Thus, one overlooks the fact that preferential creditors do not enjoy any protection against dispositions or appropriations made before personal insolvency, and that they have to give precedence to secured creditors in the bankruptcy estate.

[261] CHAPTER VIII

The Legal System

§ 45. *Traditional and Rational Systematics*

The task of the doctrinal study of law is to present an account of scientifically valid law. The accomplishing of this task presupposes that the account follows a certain system, that is, that a plan exists for the order and context in which the individual parts of the legal material are presented.

The value of the system will show on several fronts. In the first place, the system is a precondition for a certain clarity and simplicity, without which it would be impossible to find one's way in the immensely detailed legal material. Just as a library would hardly be of use to us if the books were not arranged and catalogued according to a certain system, a casual and aimless account of scientifically valid law would be inadequate as a source of knowledge to anyone asking for information on a particular issue. We need some kind of principle if we do not want to get lost in a chaotic mess. Moreover, the system serves as a basis for the division of labour which, at least in our days, is necessary for mastering the legal material. In this respect, the system manifests itself as a division of legal science into various fields or disciplines, studied by their respective specialists and reflected in corresponding professorships at scientific institutions of higher education. Last but not least: when built upon essential or relevant criteria, systematization is of heuristic value to the scientific analysis as such and to the legal material. Systematic development is well suited for posing interesting
[262] questions and opening our eyes to similarities and differences which otherwise might have gone unnoticed. For example, the discussion on the extent to which intellectual property law pertains to property law has had a stimulating effect on an in-depth analysis of the nature of intellectual property law. Apart from that, systematics go hand in hand with a fruitful generalization. By grouping homogeneous legal relationships in a certain discipline and abstracting the peculiarities of individual relationships from them, one attempts to sort out the common problems and present, in a general part, the legal rules which are common to the area in question. On an even higher level of abstraction, there are principles and ideas which express the prevailing values within the legal area in

question, and which—without being considered legal rules proper—play an important part in legal interpretation. 'The spirit' in property law is different from that in family law, the spirit in labour law is different from that in the law of obligations, etc.

A systematic division of the legal material can be achieved on the basis of various considerations and criteria. There is no 'true' or 'correct' system as such, but a division of the system can be regarded as more or less right and proper. Nor is there even a common point of view, according to which the suitability could be judged unambiguously. From a purely scientific perspective, one is inclined to emphasize internal criteria, that is, criteria connected with fundamental features of the structure or content of the legal rules and, thereby, with the fundamental concepts of legal science. From a purely practical perspective, on the other hand, one is inclined to look out for external criteria, that is, criteria which subsume the legal rules in accordance with their application in certain typical areas of life. The traditional divisions are characterized by a blend of both considerations. In litigation, for example, one adduces legal rules which are highly varying in nature, seen from an internal perspective. The unifying point of view is a practical one, namely, the fact that the rules are concerned with legal relationships manifested directly before the judge. In family law, proprietary rules and rules pertaining to the law of persons are unified from the point of view that they are concerned with family life. These circumstances will be examined more closely in the following.

In considerations concerning systematic appropriateness the established tradition itself is a weighty factor. Just as one cannot create a new system of concepts from scratch, but only adjust, reinterpret, and refine the concepts handed down to us, one cannot create new legal systematics from scratch. It would be idle to attempt it. Deliberations concerning rational systematics are nevertheless not without interest. They may be able to arouse a deeper understanding of those considerations and criteria which, more or less unclear and covered by other factors, are concealed behind traditional systematics; and thereby, in turn, create a basis for such an adjusting reform of the system as lies within the realms of possibility.

The prevailing systematization[1] (characterizing Continental law, in particular) [263] has its roots in Roman law. The Romans divided the entire legal material into public law and private law, and the latter, in turn, into the law of persons, the law of things, and procedural law (litigation). Generally speaking, this system prevailed until the beginning of the nineteenth century: then, German legal science added important nuances to it, thereby creating the grouping that is common today. The distinction between public law and private law is retained as the fundamental division. *Constitutional and administrative law, criminal law*

[1] For further information, see Fredrik Stang, *Innledning til Formueretten* [Introduction to Property Law] (3rd edn, 1935), § 10 with references.

and *procedural law* are parts of *public law*, but there is no general part introducing this group of disciplines. At the head of private law, on the other hand, there is a part entitled *private law: general part*, dealing with certain features common to all private aspects of legal relationships. In recent times, however, this topic seems to have gone out of fashion and been partially substituted with a general study of law. Within the field of private law, a gradual differentiation has taken place. The law of things has been divided into the law of things, which concerns the direct rights of disposal of things, and the law of obligations, which concerns claims against a person and otherwise goes further than claims for things or performances *in rem*. The law of things and the law of obligations often appear under a common heading, namely *property law*. Furthermore, private law includes the *law of persons*, *family law*, and *inheritance law*. The classical repertoire is thus exhausted. Modern times have witnessed the development of legal areas which were unknown to the Romans, and which were difficult to integrate into the established model. This development concerns the legal protection granted to artists, authors, inventors or other originators to enjoy the fruits of their labour, as well as various rights protecting trademarks in business competition. These legal creations are sometimes bracketed together under the headings *intellectual property law*, *immaterial law*, or the like.

In the following, it will be my task to examine to what extent this traditional way of dividing up topics is determined by, or can be adjusted to, rational and internal criteria.

§ 46. *The Division between Public Law and Private Law*

As a social and institutional order for the exercise of force (cf. §§ 7 and 11), the law invariably presupposes a set of public authorities. This must be seen as the basis for arriving at a rational definition of the concept *public law.*

Authority is a special competence—competence as a social function. That is to say, the competence is bestowed upon the competent person for taking care, not of his own interests, but of the interests of society. Seen from a juridico-functional perspective, this social function is manifest, partly with regard to the exercise of the competence, partly with regard to its content. [264]

With regard to the exercise of the competence: while individual competence can be exercised at will, the exercise of social competence is a duty, a public office in the widest sense, just as there are duties, more or less precise, concerning the manner in which the competence is exercised. These duties are accompanied by sanctions and measures of control for correcting wrongful exercise of competence. (These duties and this control must not be confused with the problem of overstepping the limits of the competence and the consequent voidness.)

With regard to the content of the competence: while individual competence is autonomous, that is, limited to the power of binding oneself or others (provided they consent), authority is heteronomous, that is, it is the power to bind others even without their consent.

This difference between individual-discretionary-autonomous competence and social-in-duty-bound-heteronomous competence can be expressed briefly by saying that the former competence is ascribed to the subject in its capacity as an individual, and the latter competence is ascribed to the subject in its capacity as an organ for a society.

An authority is *public* when it serves the comprehensive sovereign community we call a state (including its subordinate parts—for example, the municipalities). An authority is private, by contrast, when it rests with the parents within the family and the organs of various kinds of societies and associations.

Accordingly, public law can be defined as *the law concerning the legal position of public authorities: their appointment, competence, and duties.*

Therefore, public law solely consists of norms of competence and the appertaining norms of conduct, that is, concerning the exercise of competence.

Every norm of competence defines a legal act, that is, indicates a method of procedure to determine valid law. Herein, we can distinguish the description of partly the simple or compound acting organ (personal competence), partly the formal procedure (procedural competence), partly the limitation in the content which, in this way, can be posited as law (substantive competence). Accordingly, the main theme of public law is a description of the constitution of the state organs; of the procedure in which their power is exercised; and of the substantive limits of their power. In addition, there are rules on whether and how one can check whether a transgression of competence has occurred (voidness).

The norms of competence are accompanied by more or less precise norms of conduct, prescribing certain duties of the organs in connection with the exercise of their public authority. For example, it may happen that an administra-
[265] tive organ is required to consult with certain persons before coming to a decision. If transgressing this requirement does not result in voidness, there is no transgression of competence, merely a duty the violation of which may result in liability on the part of the organ. Apart from prescriptions of this kind a general standard applies, namely, that all public authority shall be exercised in the spirit of the community on a basis of 'objective', 'public' evaluations ('the principle of equality', the doctrine of the misuse of power).

At least in a state like ours, it is the case that public law, in principle,[1] must fall into three main categories which deal with legislative acts, administrative acts, and judicial acts, respectively. The general part of public law must contain a general account of public persons (state and municipalities) and official acts (which, to be sure, is not very much).

The theory of public authorities, or of the organization of state power, is a well-defined area, characterized by the essential, internal criterion expressed in the concept of authority. Defined in this way, the concept of public law acquires a clear meaning. However, the concept loses consistency if it is extended to include a number of other areas of law which are traditionally called public law areas.[2]

First, there is *criminal law*. In so far as the duties enforced through penalty provisions are duties concerning the exercise of public authority, criminal law is a part of public law as previously defined. Leaving aside this fact, however, criminal law ties sanctions to norms of conduct directed towards private persons. It protects ownership, honour, life, and liberty, and this legal protection is an integral component of the legal consequences constituting the corresponding rights to property, honour, life, and liberty. In this way, criminal law is comparable to the law of torts (which, as yet, has not been classified by anyone under

[1] For an overview of the organization of the state apparatus and the inner coherence of the various branches of state government and state powers, it is presumably most expedient to abide by tradition and gather the fundamental rules governing the organization of the state apparatus in a common discipline, namely constitutional law; the latter includes a detailed description of the legislative act, while more detailed rules as well as the administrative act and the judicial act are classified as administrative law and procedural law, respectively.

[2] The following observations are mostly in line with the critical account given by Hans Kelsen, *General Theory of Law and State* (1945), 201 *et seq.*

public law). The only thing that typically distinguishes punishment from compensation is the fact that *prosecution is usually public*, that is, an official function of a public authority. This shows that there is normally such a strong public interest in matters sanctioned through punishment that the power to prosecute cannot be left to the discretion of the victim. However, it is clear that the public character of criminal law (understood in this sense) is rather different from the sense in which the rules governing the organization of state power are public. Furthermore, it is clear that from the same perspective—the dominance of public interest—all mandatory statutory provisions abolishing private autonomy [266] might be called provisions of public law, whereby the concept will lose all firmness and all correlation with the common division into branches.

Secondly, there is a large body of law which is generally called public law and is included in what is called *special administrative law*—such as, for example, social welfare law and social insurance law, the laws concerning taxes and dues, labour law, laws relating to agriculture, shipping, and fisheries, trade law, import and export control laws, laws governing prices, traffic laws and road laws, building regulations and regulations concerning the fire-fighting service, health law, currency law, time regulations, laws on weights and measures, etc. That these laws are classified as public law is owing to various considerations, the most important one being that the legal position of the individual is largely not determined directly by statutory law (general rules of law), but presupposes an intervening, concrete administrative act in the form of a permission, a licence, a dispensation, an approval, or an order. These areas of life are thereby characterized by a *one-sided, authoritative, and concrete legislation and adjudication by the authorities*, in contrast to an enactment *via* private party autonomy.

This criterion is not sufficient in all situations, however. Several laws belonging to the above-named categories—such as, for example, stamp duties acts and acts concerning several other taxes, traffic, and safety at work—either do not require any concretizing administrative act at all, or only do so in certain particular relations. What makes us consider them as governed by public law is either the circumstance that they are only enforced by *public prosecution*; or the circumstance that they concern *payments to the Treasury*. But irrespective of whether the apparent character of public law in these areas is justified in this situation or another, it must be admitted that the character of public law that is at stake here is something rather different from the organizational law in connection with public authorities.

Finally, as far as *procedural law* is concerned—excepting those parts of it which concern the organization and competence of the courts—it is still more difficult to understand from which perspective this area of law is considered to belong to public law. Large parts of procedural law—such as, for example, the rules of evidence and the substantive rules for the division of an estate—cannot be distinguished from what is otherwise regarded as private law. As far as the very rules on court procedure are concerned, the notion of their character of public law seems to stem from the dim idea that a legal relationship with the authorities is established through them. The fact is that the observance of these prescriptions is a further condition (in addition to substantive legal facts) for obtaining a sentence and its enforcement. These prescriptions are tied to the substantive rules on the underlying legal relationship, and there is no reason to consider them as public law any more than this underlying legal relationship.

The great uncertainty and lack of consistency pervading the prevailing ideas [267] about public law has probably to do with the fact that the concept 'public law' is actually construed negatively—as a repository for all law that is not private law. Thereby, the latter concept is implicitly defined by the criterion that it is law which can be enforced in disputes between private individuals. However, if public law is defined thus negatively and comprehensively, it does not, as we have seen, constitute a homogenous sphere. Conversely, if public law is confined to the law governing the organization and exercise of public authority, and if private law is defined negatively in relation to it, the concept of private law will be lacking in both consistency and meaning.

Thus, the concept of private law as well as that of public law can be defined in such a way that each of them has a precise meaning. The concepts are not jointly exhaustive, however; rather, the relation between them can, for instance, be compared to that between the concepts 'canary' and 'elephant' in a classification of animals.

A common view is that public law lacks uniformity, and actually corresponds to a class of animals defined as all those animals which are not canaries. This is borne out by the observation that a general part of public law does not exist, and probably cannot be imagined as existing.

If we, in order to give consistency to the concepts, choose to take the two expressions in their respective tenable meaning—*viz.*, public law = the law concerning the status of public authorities; and private law = the law that can be enforced in disputes between private individuals—then the problem arises that the terms 'private' and 'public' suggest an exhaustive division of the field which does not exist. Thus, if we retain this terminology (and it may be difficult to get rid of it), it must be strongly emphasized that these two terms do not imply a fundamental division of the material of the law in its entirety.

All the attempts that have been made to define the distinction between private law and public law as constituting such a fundamental division have consequently proved to be indefensible, cf. § 50.

§ 47. *The Division between Substantive Law and Procedural Law*

A norm of competence determines the method of laying down legal directives. On the face of it, a norm of competence is not in itself a directive: it does not prescribe a certain mode of conduct as a duty. It is a pattern of action but not in the same sense as a norm of conduct: a norm of competence merely indicates the pattern that must be followed in order to bring about valid directives. A norm of competence, as such, does not say that the competent person is in duty bound to exercise his competence.

Therefore, norms of competence cannot be directly 'enforced' by the courts or [268] other organs exercising legal authority. Only norms of conduct can be directly 'enforced'. In a lawsuit, norms of competence can only be of indirect importance, namely, as constituting the premises for the issue of whether or not a valid norm of conduct exists.

These introductory remarks are meant to emphasize that what follows *refers exclusively to norms of conduct*,[1] these being the only norms that can be directly 'applied' or 'maintained' by the courts.

In § 7 it has been explained that all norms of conduct are, in fact, directed to the judge (and other organs exercising legal authority). They are directives to the judge concerning the conditions under which he shall order the exercise of physical force against a person. The actual legal norm—for example, § 28 of the Danish Bill of Exchange Act—is a directive to the judge to order (under certain conditions) the exercise of force in order to enforce payment against the person who has accepted a bill of exchange but failed to meet it on the day of payment. The apparent directive to the acceptor to meet the bill on the day of payment is merely a reflex of the directive to the judge, combined with an ideological appeal to the citizens' respect for law and justice.

However, § 28 of the Danish Bill of Exchange Act is only a fragment of a norm of conduct. The complete directive to the judge and the executive concerning the exercise of force on the grounds of the acceptance of a bill of exchange is

[1] The distinction (to be explained in the following pages) between substantive law, sanction law, and procedural law applies, therefore, to norms of conduct in both public law (laying down the exercise of public authority as a duty) and non-public law. In the field of public law, however, one does not usually follow this technique of presentation and take it as a basis for a corresponding division of disciplines. The rules governing the duties and responsibilities of ministers as well as impeachment proceedings are thus presented together in constitutional law, and the rules governing the duties of civil servants, their responsibilities, and the procedural regulations connected with them, are presented together in administrative law. In so far as they are authorized by the Criminal Code, the sanctions are partly presented in criminal law. *Therefore, the following aims exclusively at non-public law.*

actually far more complicated than would appear from this section. In the first place, the conditions for obtaining a judgment against the acceptor are not indicated exhaustively by indicating a certain mode of conduct on the part of the 'obligated' party, i.e. the acceptor of the bill (acceptance + non-payment on the day of payment). It is further required that the drawer of the bill shall, in accordance with certain regulations, bring an action against the acceptor, in the course of which he shall be able to prove, in more detail, both his own title and the fact that the bill was not successfully presented for payment (protesting the bill). Secondly, further regulations are required concerning the kind of coercive measures that shall be carried out when all conditions are fulfilled, that is, more specific rules as to what the judgment shall be, and how it can be executed. In the above-mentioned case these questions are straightforward. In other cases,
[269] however, where the law also speaks of a person's duty to pursue a certain course of conduct, the content and the execution of the judgment are governed by completely different rules. This manifests itself if one compares cases where a person, in virtue of a statute or other legal rule, is said to be obligated:

to pay a sum of money;

to deliver 100 sacks of flour;

to deliver the cow Lotte;

to paint a portrait;

to remain faithful to his spouse.

According to circumstances, the judgment may be about performance (or prohibition, respectively), punishment, or damages, and the more specific rules governing the enforcement of the judgment will vary accordingly.

This shows clearly that it would be an immensely complicated matter to present one single norm of conduct in its entirety. However, the specific conditions governing legal proceedings (proof and other procedural measures) as well as the more detailed rules concerning the content of the judgment and its enforcement are to a large extent the same for various norms of conduct within certain groups. *For reasons of presentation technique, it was decided to split the complete norm of conduct into fragments and collect those of the same kind to be treated in separate disciplines.* As far as the economy of presentation is concerned, huge advantages are gained thereby. On the other hand, however, there may be a certain danger with this method of procedure, namely, if one should forget that what hereafter is called a legal rule, generally is merely a fragment of a legal norm, and consequently acquires its full meaning first by being considered together with other rules which, considered individually, are of a fragmentary character, too.

The division here can be described as follows (at present, in somewhat imprecise terms). In one division, we are told what we must and must not do; in a second division, we are told what legal sanctions we expose ourselves to if we act contrarily; and in a third division, we are told how these sanctions are determined on and executed. Below, the division will be described more accurately. First of all, it is worthy of note that the division is not carried out consistently in all fields of law, but can vary with the peculiarities of the legal material, or with arbitrary traditions. Generally speaking, we use the following distinctions:

(1) One division, known as *substantive* or *primary law*, states the necessary but insufficient fundamental condition for exercising a coercive sanction against a person, namely, a certain outward behaviour on the part of that person. Usually this condition is stated indirectly by characterizing a certain behaviour as a duty,[2] implying that the contradictorily opposite behaviour is a [270] necessary but insufficient condition for imposing a sanction. For example, when § 28 of the Danish Bill of Exchange Act states that the acceptor has a duty to pay the bill on the day of payment, this means that the contrary behaviour is the preliminary condition for a judgment against A and the exercise of force.

A rule of substantive law is merely a fragment, of course. At present, we do not know what other conditions are required for a judgment, nor the nature of the coercive measures which in such a case can be applied against a person who behaves contrarily to the substantive law. But nevertheless, the very presentation of the substantive law is highly important. Even if we do not know what will happen in case of its being violated, we do know that a person who does not violate these rules is on the safe side: it is impossible that his conduct should give rise to legal reactions.

Substantive law, in turn, is divided into a series of disciplines, determined by the areas of life it is concerned with, cf. the next section.

(2) A second division, which can be called *sanction law* or *secondary law*, states the different sanctions that can be applied through a judgment against a person who has violated a rule of substantive law, as well as the more precise conditions concerning the circumstances of the responsible person—however, apart from his outer behaviour, contrary to duty—under which the different sanctions can be applied. Thus, *the law of torts* mostly presupposes primary rules concerning undutiful behaviour (determined *inter alia* through the rules concerning the distribution of property) and determines, on this basis, further conditions for liability (attribution, accountability, etc.) as well as further rules on the extent of liability (the adequacy principle), etc.

[2] As mentioned in §§ 32 and 33 above, the duty terminology is connected with the ideological function to express societal disapproval of behaviour that conditions a sanction. The appeal to the citizens' formal sense of justice, to their respect for law and justice, gives rise to a disinterested motive to act lawfully; a motive that goes hand in hand with the interested motive derived from the fear of a sanction. It is not every situation, however, where the sanction is conditioned by this disapproval. The sanction may also refer to behaviour which is not coloured ideologically as being unlawful or undutiful. In these situations, then, substantive law cannot avail itself of the duty terminology but must be presented as rules regulating the liability for lawful acts.

To a certain extent, the same also applies to *criminal law*.

This distinction between substantive law and sanction law is not a clear one, however; nor is it made consistently. Frequently, it is determined directly—that is, without any preceding norm establishing a duty—that certain actions shall entail damages or punishment. The rules concerning contractual damages are usually presented as closely connected with the rules of substantive law concerning individual contractual relationships. On the other hand, both tort law and criminal law contain important parts of
[271] substantive law, in so far as the sanction rule does not refer to substantive norms stated elsewhere. The prescriptions of the Criminal Code concerning murder and crimes of violence, for example, are not referring to rules of substantive law stated elsewhere and informing us of the citizens' duties with respect to other people's personal integrity.

Traditionally, the sanction expressed in the form of a judgment providing for enforcement (prohibition) is not treated in a *law of performance* parallel to the law of torts and criminal law but, rather, in connection with the law of obligations.

To sum up, we can say that the distinction between substantive law and sanction law is anything but consistent (which would hardly be desirable, for that matter). This explains why according to the traditional view, frequently no distinction is made between substantive law and sanction law, whereas tort law and criminal law fall under substantive law.

(3) A third division, finally, known as *procedural law* or *tertiary law*, deals with further conditions (apart from the circumstances surrounding the responsible individual) which must be fulfilled in order to render and enforce the judgment. These conditions concern the procedure to be followed in order to establish and enforce liability—among these especially the rules on prosecution, proof, and the handling of cases by courts and executive organs.

As far as *the relationship between substantive law and the law of procedure* is concerned, we are often inclined to regard the rules of procedure as something subsidiary, in the sense that they purport to promote the realization of substantive law, that is, lead to the mediate effect that human beings act lawfully as much as possible; and to the immediate effect that in cases of unlawful action, sanctions are carried out effectively. This is basically correct, and any criticism denying it overshoots the mark, cf. § 50. The view becomes incorrect only if it is further tied to the idea that substantive law is primary law and independent of procedural law, in the sense that its content can be determined exclusively from considerations of social objectives; whereupon it is necessary to construct the procedural rules as tools for realizing the substantive law as well as possible. This is not correct, because when creating substantive law, one cannot omit to take into consideration the degree to which it is technically possible to realize it through procedural law (juridico-technical considerations). Thus, even if the realization of substantive law is the purpose of the law of procedure, this purpose does not allow itself to be determined without considering the means necessary for its being fulfilled. Therefore, legal-political considerations must focus on the cooperation between substantive law and procedural law, in order to examine how they can promote, precisely through their interaction, previously decided social objectives in the best possible way. Current legal-political thought corresponds well with this line of thought.

[272]

§ 48. Distinctions within Substantive Law

The distinctions hitherto mentioned—namely, the distinction between public and non-public law and the distinction between substantive law and the law of procedure—are based on criteria given by the very nature of law as rules on the exercise of force through public authorities; they are, therefore, distinctions of universal validity, or distinctions necessary in the sense that they can be made with reference to any well-developed legal system whatsoever, irrespective of content and socio-cultural preconditions. In every well-developed legal system there must be a public authority organization for the purpose of (laying down and) exercising law by force and, in addition, there must be rules on the method to be employed in order to set the apparatus of coercion in motion. The concepts 'public law' and 'procedural law' are thereby given.

If we turn to *the divisions within substantive law*, we notice that the situation is different. These divisions are grounded in the differences within the content of the law, determined through the areas of life it regulates and are, therefore, not universally valid. The concept 'property law' would have no meaning if we could envisage a society with a strictly communist economy, and, at any rate, it would not have the same meaning in a society with a non-monetary economy. The concept 'family law' would be devoid of meaning in a society without the institution of the family. Roman law did not grant artists, writers, and inventors any protection for their work, and consequently was not acquainted with the concept 'intellectual property law'. Competition law is tied to the presumption of business based on private capitalism and has, therefore, no meaning in a socialist society, etc., etc.

If the traditional divisions of substantive law are basically a common feature of modern legal systems in Western culture, it is because they are grounded in certain fundamental cultural phenomena and legal institutions, conditioned by these phenomena, which these societies have in common. Even if the distinctions within substantive law are not universally valid, they are nonetheless *typical* for these legal systems.

The areas of life and their regulation are so varied and motley that there can be no question of any exhaustive systematic division of substantive law. It is more a question of an *out-differentiating topography* than of a differentiating systematization; that is, without any common *fundamentum divisionis* one calls attention to a number of areas of the law, each of them marked by certain characteristics—in the same way as in geography, where we can highlight different landscapes, continents, or islands which, taken individually, form a natural, integral whole yet with distinctive features, as it were. Among the topographic parts of substantive law, the following parts ought to be emphasized:

(a) *Property law*

Property law concerns proprietary rights. This concept is often conceived as defined by the circumstance that the right represents to the rights holder an economic advantage, or a benefit possessing exchange value. This way of looking at things is methodologically wrong. Exchange value is a sociologico-economic concept, indicating that a benefit (a right) qualifies as an object of exchange. It is not certain, however, that the legal order recognizes that all rights which possess exchange value in this sense are negotiable rights. For legal systematics, the decisive factor must be those legal principles which apply to the negotiability of the right, not the real economic possibility of negotiating. Economic value or exchange value can, at best, be something that characterizes proprietary rights; they cannot be the factor that defines the concept. [273]

(A casual remark: Originally, in the Danish word for 'property'—'*formue*'—there is nothing that would indicate economic value either. Similarly to the German word '*Vermögen*', the Danish word '*formue*' indicates ability, capacity, strength, power, or that which falls within the range of a person's ability, etc. Thus, when used in connection with legal relationships, '*formue*' points precisely at the competence or power connected with certain rights.)

It is the *replaceability of the subject* or—as one might say—the *negotiability of the right* (in a broad sense) that characterizes proprietary rights. According to the typical content of legal systems from the times of Roman law to the present day, negotiation can occur in the following three principal forms:

(1) *transfer*, that is, as a result of the rights holder's dispositions;

(2) *debt enforcement*, that is, as a result of legal action conditioned by the rights holder's non-fulfilment of his abstract obligations, especially his debts; and

(3) *inheritance*, that is, as a result of the rights holder's death (with or without disposition *mortis causa*).

A person's property is the totality of his personal proprietary rights; that is to say: the negotiable rights, or the rights that can be transferred, serve as a basis for a credit and are handed down by inheritance.

It is assumed that these three forms of negotiation hang together. This is usually the case. In so far as there are rights whose negotiability deviates more or less from this standard, these rights must be called atypical proprietary rights, or rights of a mixed property-related and personal character. What is most appropriate must depend on an estimation under the given circumstances: to present them as deviations in the field of property law, or

to move them to other disciplines. Examples could include the right to private letters and other items without exchange value, which certainly may be transferred and handed down by inheritance, but cannot be the subject of debt enforcement; and intellectual property rights, the negoti-
[274] ability of which is restricted in all three directions on the basis of personal considerations. With respect to pension claims and similar rights with a highly restricted negotiability—they can function as credit documents within narrower limits—it seems obvious that they must not be included in property law.

Thus, proprietary rights are defined by their negotiability. The question thereupon arises *whether there exists a typical connection between the negotiability of the right and the content of the right*. And, indeed, there is such a connection. Pure proprietary rights are typically identical with *those rights which purport to establish, for the rights holder, a specific control over physical things external to us*, irrespective of whether the object is determined individually or (for the time being) *in abstracto*. Proprietary rights thus comprise both rights of disposal and rights of claim in the economic sense, cf. § 42 above, under (a). In other words, the law of property may, therefore, also be called *the law of things*.

Thus, not all claims fall under the law of property; typically, only claims for generically defined performances *in rem* do so. For example, a claim to a work performance is normally not negotiable.

It appears that an appropriate, systematic classification of the problems of property law must follow these lines:

First of all, one must distinguish between a static part, comprising the direct content of the rights, that is, the duties and claims they consist of; and a dynamic part, concerning the rules that govern their negotiability.

In *static property law*, there is reason to distinguish between rights of disposal and rights of claim in the economic sense. *The law of things* comprises the direct rights of disposal; that is, the right of property, and the restricted rights *in rem*; with regard to the latter, both the immature claims against the outside world in general and the mature claims against the owner (functionally appertaining to the law of obligations, cf. § 42 under (b)). *The law of obligations*[1] comprises the claims to generically defined performances *in rem*.

In *dynamic property law*, we must distinguish between the rules governing transfer, debt enforcement, and inheritance, respectively, since they are followed—in the shape of a general part—by a presentation of the collision

[1] On the issue of a rational division of the law of obligations, see Knut Rohde, 'Till frågan om förmögenhetsrättens systematik' [On the classification of property law], *Festskrift tillägnad Birger Ekeberg* [A Tribute to Birger Ekeberg] (1950), 438.

norms applicable in the case of conflict between transferees, creditors, and heirs (dynamic protection, cf. § 39).

With respect to the doctrine of conveyancing, we must again distinguish between the transfer of ownership (or restricted right *in rem*) concerning movables, ownership (or restricted right *in rem*) concerning real property, and the transfer of claims.

Prevalent legal systematics matches this model only slightly and is extremely inconsistent in several respects.

With respect to the rules of negotiation, the rules of inheritance can [275] be found in the law of succession, and the rules governing debt enforcement can be found partly in the law of procedure, partly in the law of obligations. The rules governing transfer are divided in such a way that the transfer of ownership (and of the restricted right *in rem*) of movables and real estate is treated in the law of things, whereas the transfer of claims is dealt with in the law of obligations. The circumstance that dynamic property law is thus distributed over four different disciplines, traditionally tied to different professorial chairs, has probably contributed to the fact that these problems have never been really dealt with systematically through a general account of the principles of collision.

As far as the division of static property law is concerned, the criterion mentioned above is not adhered to consistently. Whereas mature claims, that is, claims against the owner which are functionally appertaining to the law of obligation, would normally be classified under the law of things (with respect to mortgage and easement, for example), the corresponding dispute in connection with the rent of things is referred to the law of obligations. This difference in treatment is quite arbitrary.

While important parts of dynamic property law have been moved to other disciplines (as mentioned earlier), the law of obligations, on the other hand, encroaches in its present shape beyond the domain of property law by including claims for work performances.

Apart from *general or individual property law*, which applies to individuals considered in light of their individual existence, there are special variants of property law, framed with particular reference to matters connected with property law in certain joint relationships; such as *marital property law*, which is treated in family law, and *property law concerning companies*, which is treated in company law.

(b) *The law governing services, or labour law (in the widest sense of the term)*

All *claims not related to property* fall under this heading; that is to say, all claims which do not purport to provide the rights owner with the use and enjoyment of an external object (proprietary services), irrespective of whether the immediate basis of the claim is a contract, an administrative act, or a law. Among the subgroups, we can mention the claim to the use and enjoyment (specified and time-limited) of another person's labour (hiring of labour) and the claim to achieve a certain output (hiring of production facilities in the widest sense of the term); *inter alia* attending to a legal matter, a transport, a contract, dental treatment, etc. These claims differ fundamentally from proprietary claims by being largely non-negotiable. Moreover, the rules governing their fulfilment and enforcement differ from the rules of property law in several respects. Therefore, it is justified to separate labour law from the law of things. This division corresponds to that in economics, between the production of goods and the production of services.

There is no marital labour law. However, one can distinguish between *individual* and *collective labour law*. The latter deals with the conditions of
[276] employment (of whatever kind) which are regulated by collective agreements concluded between the employers' association and the trade unions; the former deals with all the other conditions of employment.

Even more than in property law, the freedom of contract in labour law (individual freedom as well as collective freedom) is restricted by mandatory statutory provisions, such as can be found in the laws concerning industrial safety, or in the laws concerning paid holidays, the relationship between master and assistant, apprentices, officials, etc.

(c) *The law of persons*

The law of persons does not include all personal rights in the sense of non-negotiable rights. This purely negative criterion is not sufficient to sustain a general classification.[2] However, there may be a reason for separating and gathering, under the law of persons,[3] the rights that are given as a protection for the individual's physical and psychological personality, for his moral and intellectual interests—but only if these rights are not so amalgamated with other complexes of the law that it would be impractical to detach them (elements related to personality form an integral part of intellectual property law, competition law, etc.).

Under this area of the law falls first and foremost the protection of an individual's physical integrity, of his freedom of movement and sexual freedom, of his honour and reputation, as well as of different aspects of his emotional life (his feeling of decency, his religious feelings). The rights thus warranted belong to the traditional realm of the law of persons, and the corresponding prescriptions of punishment to the standard part of the Criminal Code.

In addition to this, various legal formations have developed recently, purporting to provide a more extensive protection of personality rights: the

[2] Cf. O. A. Borum, *Personretten* [The Law of Persons] (1942), § 2.

[3] Cf. Ragnar Knoph, *Oversikt over Norges rett* [Overview of Norwegian Law] (1934), § 13; Carl Jacob Arnholm, *Forelesninger over Norsk personrett* [Lectures on the Norwegian Law of Persons] (1947), 88 *et seq.*

right to privacy, the right to one's name, the right to one's own image. As yet, the situation in these areas remains rather vague.[4]

Apart from the usual, *individual law of personality*, one may set up specific variants referring to family life and social life. *Personality law relating to family law* includes above all the duties of parents towards their children, with reference to the latters' physical and spiritual development, their health, their education, as well as their moral and religious upbringing. *Social personality law* includes various provisions in the law governing associations, especially concerning the protection of the honour, name, and characteristics of collective units.

As an independent discipline, personality law is still rather undeveloped [277] but, in the recent past, it has been increasingly recognized, as such, on a programmatic level.

(d) *Business law*

Commercial life might still be said to rest, at least formally, on the liberal doctrine of free trade (§ 81 of the Danish Constitution). Nowadays, however, this principle is gravely undermined. A multi-sided set of prescriptions for the regulation of commercial life has developed, and it would be appropriate to gather and treat them systematically under the label business law. The movement which for more than a generation has led us further and further away from classical liberalism is rooted in several leading ideas. From the point of view of commercial policy, the reason for the restrictions is, in part, the insight that unrestrained freedom tends to abolish—through anti-competitive agreements—precisely the free competition that is meant to legitimize the freedom of trade. Antitrust laws combating price agreements and the forming of monopolies thus purport to combat the abuse of freedom. To some extent, however, economic-political regulation purports to conform to social or socialist views on the necessity of control over, or at least systematic management of, commercial life in the interest of the community. Alongside these more general economic-political views, the development is characterized by a tendency to raise the level of morality in business life by restricting the means that may be employed in competition with regard to the relationship obtaining between the tradespeople themselves as well as that with their customers. Finally, legal development has been characterized by an increasing tendency to secure exclusive rights for the protection of efforts made.

[4] Cf. Carl Jacob Arnholm, 'En dom om personlighetsværn' [A judgment concerning personality protection], *TfR* 1950, 390 *et seq.* (In its judgment concerning the well-known case of 'the murder of the police inspector', the district court made the following pronouncement: 'The law assumes accordingly that there is, in Norwegian law, a personality protection through law, apart from the special statutory rules in this area, but that the extent of this protection through law is not clear.') See also Ragnar Knoph, *op. cit.*, Alf Ross 'Privatlivets fred' [The sanctity of private life], in *TfR* 1932, 317–19 and Gösta Eberstein, *Om skydd för individualiteten* [On the protection of individuality] (1940).

Thus, we are confronted with a motley set of legal rules—and yet, very little has been done, either in legislation or in theory, towards achieving a systematic account of these matters. The scientific treatment of the problems of business law is not in any reasonable proportion to the great practical importance of this area of the law.

The economic and political provisions are partly tied to a system according to which the pursuit of a trade is conditioned by a licence (trade law); partly they can be found in a number of permanent laws on closing time, industrial safety, price agreements, etc., as well as in a large number of more or less temporary laws and administrative ordinances concerning import and export, measures in connection with foreign currencies, and a vast number of various regulations concerning production and sales volume.

Competition law is centred around the Danish Competition Act which, however—through the so-called big and little general clause[5]*—has left
[278] the more detailed legal formations to be developed through practice; which, in turn, has also developed important rules of competition law concerning boycott, the obligation to enter into a contract, etc.[6] Also, rules of competition law are scattered throughout other laws—such as, for example, § 38 of the Danish Contracts Act (concerning (non-) competition clauses) and § 29 of the Danish Trade Law (on the booking of orders).

There are special rules concerning trademarks, business names, and other *company trademarks* as well as *intellectual property rights* (copyright, performers' rights, invention rights, design rights, and exclusive rights to photographs). These rules can be seen as special ramifications of competition law. The reality behind it is that, in many respects, they must be interpreted in conformity with general principles of competition law. However, these areas of the law can be distinguished from the rest of competition law due to the fact that there, an *exclusive* right to pursue a certain course of action is established for the individual. Therefore, we speak of exclusive commercial rights. Thereby, they become similar to exclusive rights of disposal *in rem*, and this circumstance has misled us to construct them as a right of ownership whose subject is not a physical thing but an immaterial object—the intellectual output *qua* idea (the artistic or literary work, the invention). Except for the fact that it is impossible to ascribe legal political weight in interpretation or legislation to such a construction—to any construction—it is more misleading than guiding. This has to do with the fact that while it is obvious what it means to have full control over an object, it is anything but clear what the equivalent with respect to intellectual production implies. Actually, it is impossible to have control over an intellectual production *qua*

* Translator's note: Den store og lille generalklausul.

[5] Promulgation nr. 80 of 31 March 1937, of the Danish Unfair Competition Law, §§ 15 and 9.

[6] Cf. Vinding Kruse, *Retslæren* [Jurisprudence], Vol. II (1943), 713–29, and Bernt Hjejle, 'Kontraheringspligt' [Obligation to enter into contract], *Festskrift til Henry Ussing* [A Tribute to Henry Ussing] (1951), 150.

idea in the same way as one can have control over a plot of land or a car. A more detailed analysis will show that what is simply called disposing of an author's or artist's intellectual output means, in reality, disposing of the substantive preconditions for experiencing the work. Thus, the exclusive right of the author mainly consists in an exclusive right to produce copies of the work and to present it in public. In addition to this, various other claims vis-à-vis the author may be under discussion; in particular, the claim to limit the owner's usual proprietary disposal of a copy of the work (prohibition of deterioration, destruction, lending, exhibition of the work, etc.). And of course, one might think of still more comprehensive rights for the author; for example, positive claims to be able to use and enjoy specimens of the work in the possession of other persons for exhibition purposes, or the like. However, one is not informed as to exactly which of these conceivable possibilities are included, or not included, in the author's right, by calling this right 'the uninhibited use and enjoyment of his intellectual work as such'. Of course, we can use this formula as a label if we want to, as soon as it has been established through some other channel what, exactly, the copyright consists of. But the formula in itself cannot be used to indicate the contents [279] of the right. It is an expression of a superficial analogy, which is well suited to disguise the fundamental difference in situation and whose true *raison d'être* can be found in the fact that in less responsible hands it can serve, in virtue of its vagueness and emotional appeal, as a banner and pseudo-theoretical argument for certain legal-political claims, apparently deduced from the 'nature' of the copyright *qua* proprietary right. This construction is both bad theory and dishonest policy.[7]

(e) *Public service law*

The fields of law hitherto mentioned are basically dominated by the idea of individual autonomy; that is, it is assumed that all areas of life are, in the main, shaped by the development of individual initiative, so that the task of the law is basically limited to creating the proper legal framework, and

[7] Cf. Alf Ross, 'Ophavsrettens Grundbegreber' [The fundamental concepts of intellectual property law], *TfR* 1946, 321 *et seq.* (336 *et seq.*); Ragnar Knoph, 'Felles Nordisk åndsverkslovgivning?' [Common Nordic legislation on intellectual products?] in *TfR* 1937, 133 *et seq.* and *Aandsretten* [Intellectual Property Law] (1936) § 62; Gösta Eberstein, 'Immaterialrätten och dess underarter' [Intellectual property law and its subdivisions], in *TfR* 1937, 81 *et seq.* and 'Replik om polemik och systematik' [A reply on the issue of polemics and systematics], in *TfR* 1938, 40 *et seq.* as well as 'Om författarrättens och konstnärsrättens föremål' [On the subject of copyright law and the law relating to artists' rights], in *NIR* (1946), 1 *et seq.*; Östen Undén, 'Några systematiska spörsmål' [Some systemic problems], in *TfR* 1937, 419 *et seq.*; Hartvig Jacobsen, *Ophavsretten* [Intellectual Property Law] (1941), 324 *et seq.*; Erik Hedfeldt 'Om upphovsmannarättens föremål' [On the subject matter of copyright law] in *TfR* 1952, 152 *et seq.*; Vinding Kruse, *Ejendomsretsspørgsmål* [Some Problems in Connection with Property Law] (1934), 41 *et seq.* and *Ejendomsretten* [The Right of Property], Vol. I (3rd edn, 1951), 92 *et seq.* and 450 *et seq.*; Torben Lund, *Billedkunsten i retlig Belysning* [Pictorial Art in a Legal Perspective] (1944), 326 *et seq.* and O. K. Magnussen, *Naboretlige Studier* [Studies in the Law Regulating Neighbouring Rights] (1950), 35–49.

to restricting as well as regulating this autonomy in accordance with general societal interests.

Now we shall turn to a field of law where this point of view does not hold. In modern society, there are very large areas of life where one tries to attend to common interests through *public services*; that is, services which are carried out, or at least directed or inspected, as official tasks by public administrative authorities. Specifically, it is a question of the army, schools and other educational establishments, the Church, social welfare institutions, tax authorities, transport and road authorities, building and fire services, the public health department and the authorities for coinage, weights, and measures.

As explained in § 46 above, it is misleading to describe these areas as public law areas, in the same sense as constitutional law and administrative law are public law areas. The law governing these matters certainly includes, to a greater or lesser extent, norms concerning the competences and duties of administrative authorities, but here, it is essentially a question of norms of conduct creating duties for private individuals. What is peculiar is simply the fact that these norms of conduct *are not based upon the idea of individual autonomy but, rather, impose duties on the individual, and that this has been laid down either directly, through mandatory statutory provisions, or indirectly, through intervening administrative acts; that is to say, laid down unilaterally by public authorities*. Therefore, there is no reason to class under public law the rules of tax law, for example, or the rules concerning military service. It is not a question of public competence norms in the first
[280] place but, rather, of duties imposed on the private individual, to the effect that the concrete establishing of the content of the duty takes place through an intervening administrative act (assessment, levying).

Concerning these areas, then, we must distinguish between *public administrative law proper*, which concerns the competences and duties of administrative authorities—for example, administrative tax law governing the levying of taxes—and *substantive law*, which concerns the citizens' duties—for example, substantive tax law, substantive conscription law, etc. Of course, this does not preclude that, for practical reasons, we might find it right and proper to present the two sets of rules together.

The areas of law we are discussing here are characterized by their frequently being the subject of rapidly changing legislative measures, adjusted to the political, economic, and cultural situation of the period in question. Fiscal legislation, for example, must be continuously adapted to varying financial demands and the economic policy of the state; the levying of conscripts must be adjusted to the situation of the country relating to foreign affairs; health legislation must be adapted to new requirements and methods concerning hygiene, etc. These areas are not part of what is called, in England, '*the lawyer's law*'. Due to their strong dependence on politics and changing social conditions, they have not been subjected to a thorough scientific treatment to the same extent as the more 'juristic' areas of law. In spite of the fluctuation, there is in several of the aforementioned fields (tax law, for example) a strong tendency to separate some essential parts fairly consistently.

(f) *The general part of substantive law*

The topographical parts of substantive law, mentioned under (a)–(e), do not claim to be exhaustive; however, they are the most important distinctive formations within the area of substantive law. Alongside the special disciplines of substantive law, there is finally room for the general part of substantive law. In common with the whole area, the doctrine of private legal entities (the law of persons) can be treated here as well as the doctrine of private legal acts.

The first division must essentially comprise what is now being treated, in *the law of persons*, in a disorderly mixture together with parts of personality law; that is, partly different individual status relationships, cf. § 36, partly juristic persons. There is always something discretionary in deciding which personal status relationships to present and involve in the law of persons. Viewed in this light, there is nothing that prevents the description of a status that is determined through the quality of being a baker. It would be reasonable to limit the status to relationships which are conditioned by general personal qualities and of fundamental importance to the person's legal capacity and autonomy; in particular, different age levels, mental illness, incapacitation, disappearance, character (penalty), and citizenship. There are no rational grounds whatsoever for the last-named status relationship being traditionally treated in constitutional law—a position which obviously has to do with a rather dim and untenable view, namely, the view that 'the people of the state' is part of the concept of the state.

The second division of the general part includes an account of various [281]
private dispositions: promise, order, will—and specifically, contract theory.

Supplement to § 48.

It is not necessary to create new sections in order to mention the distinctions within the fields of sanction law and procedural law. There is very little to say about them.

Tort law and *criminal law* are firmly established and deal with clearly delimited problems. These fields of law could be complemented with a corresponding account of the general preconditions for other sanctions (judgment providing for enforcement or prohibition, and injunction and detention as provisional legal remedies).

Procedural law as it is currently presented is a conglomerate of public law, substantive law, and procedural law proper.

§ 49. Summary

From what has been said above, it will have emerged that the traditional division is not based upon consistent systematics but, rather, upon a blend of inner criteria, determined by the structural or substantial peculiarities of the very particular relationship; and of outer criteria, determined through the relevance of the rules to certain typical areas of life. Thus, family law and procedural law, in particular, have evolved around family relationships and the administration of the law, respectively—regardless of the fact that these disciplines, judged from inner criteria, are actually a compound of heterogeneous elements.

The classical, fundamental division of the law into public law and private law is untenable. If the concept of public law has any firm basis, its task must be limited to governing the organization and competences of public authorities. However, gathering the rest of the law under the concept of 'private law', as a result, is pointless. There is no common denominator to this field of law, apart from the negative quality of falling outside of the concept of public law.

The second classical major distinction between legislation and enforcement of the law, between substantive and procedural law, is meaningful only with respect to norms of conduct, and this means, primarily, with respect to non-[282] public law.[1] By adding sanction law, this distinction can develop into a tripartition. In substantive law, only a typological differentiation of distinctive parts of the law is possible.

The systematics emerging from this basis is presented in the following overview:

A. Public law

- I. Public law: General part (?)
  - a. Public persons (the state, municipalities)
  - b. The official act
- II. Public law: Special part
  - a. Constitutional law, with focus on the legislative act
  - b. Administrative law
  - c. Judicial law (organization and competence of the courts)

B. Non-public law

- I. Substantive law

[1] Cf. § 47 note 1.

a. Substantive law: General part
  1. The law of persons
  2. The private legal act, especially
    α) Contract law
    β) Law of wills and succession
b. The topographical parts of substantive law
  1. Property law
    α. Individual property law
      † Individual property law: General part (dynamic property law)
        * General collision norms
        ** Transfer, especially of movables, real property and claims
        *** Debt enforcement
        **** Inheritance
      †† Individual property law: Special part
        * The law of things
        ** The law of obligations
    β. Property law relating to the family
    γ. Property law relating to companies
  2. Labour law
    α. Individual labour law
    β. Collective labour law [283]
  3. Personality law
    α. Individual personality law
    β. Personality law relating to the family
    γ. Personality law relating to companies
  4. Business law
    α. Business law (relating to business politics)
    β. Competition law
    γ. Exclusive commercial rights *
      † Trade mark rights
      †† Intellectual property rights
        * Artists' rights and copyright
        ** Patent rights and design rights
        *** The right to photographs

5. Public measures law

6. , 7. …(?)

II. Sanction law

a. Tort law

b. Criminal law

c. The law providing for performance (judgments providing for performance [opfyldelse] or prohibition)

d. Prohibition law and the law governing detention.

III. Procedural law

a. Civil proceedings

b. Criminal proceedings

It is worth noting that the rubrics of the individual academic disciplines must not be taken in their traditional sense but, rather, should be understood in line with the position taken in the previous sections.

* Translator's note: Today this would be called, in Danish, *Immaterialretten.*

§ 50. Confrontation [284]

Over the course of time, various attempts have been made to achieve a comprehensive, systematic division of the whole legal material and of legal science into corresponding disciplines.[1] Mostly, however, the discussion has centred around two fundamental divisions, namely, the division between public and private law and that between substantive and procedural law.

Notwithstanding Hans Kelsen's criticism,[2] which basically corresponds to the points of view presented in § 46, the prevailing opinion is that *the distinction between public law and private law* is the corner-stone of legal systematics, although there is wide disagreement on how to make this division and why it is important.

The diverse theories on the subject can basically be divided into two main groups, usually called interest theories and subject theories, respectively.

According to the *interest theories*, the fundamental difference between private law and public law lies in the purpose of the legal rules, that is, the human interests the rules are designed to protect. Accordingly, public law is defined as that part of the law which is determined, totally or predominantly, with regard to public interest, to societal interest; whereas private law is the law that has been laid down specifically in order to protect the private interests of a single individual.

This theory must be rejected, however. Apart from the difficulties of defining precisely what is meant by private and public interest, respectively—here, one resorts to the terms that ought to be defined—it is impossible, in 'private law', to ignore such interests which are commonly considered public interests; or, conversely, to ignore private interests in 'public law' (in the usual sense of that term).

Individual ownership has always been regarded as being eminently 'private'. Nowadays, however, nobody calls into question that the right of ownership is not bestowed upon the individual merely for the satisfaction of his individual interests, but depends very much on social conditions and restrictions. All the so-called mandatory or non-derogable legal rules are likewise expressions of what is called public interest. Moreover, just think of the innumerable passages in civil law where a certain provision is justified by general social considerations.

[1] See, e.g., Vinding Kruse, *Retslæren* [Jurisprudence], Vol. I (1943), 30 *et seq.*; John Salmond, *Jurisprudence* (10th edn, 1947), Appendix III; W. Burckhardt, *Einführung in die Rechtswissenschaft* [Introduction to Jurisprudence] (1939), 136 *et seq.*; and Hans Nawiasky, *Allgemeine Rechtslehre als System der rechtlichen Grundbegriffe* [General Theory of Law, as a System of Fundamental Legal Concepts] (1949), 227 *et seq.*

[2] See *General Theory of Law and State* (1945), 201 *et seq.*

[285] On the whole, one can say that the content and maintenance of the whole legal order is a public matter of the highest rank. Conversely, when social welfare legislation (classified as public law) warrants the claim of certain persons to receive social security, it cannot be denied that this provision has come about pre-eminently in order to satisfy certain individual interests.

To sum up, we can say that it is impossible to divide the law into two parts, on the grounds that the law protects primarily private or public interests, for in reality, these interests are not coordinated, opposite purposes of the law but merely expressions of two different ways of looking at one and the same thing. Considered as a general system, every part of the law—regulations concerning ownership as well as legislation covering stamp duties and welfare legislation—is based upon public interest. In specific cases, however, every general system must express itself in individual rights and duties. From the perspective of concrete legal relationships, then, any part of the law—both welfare legislation, stamp law, and property law—concerns individual interests.

According to the *subject theories*, the distinction between private and public law is determined by the subjects of the legal relationship that has been created through the legal rule in question. According to this theory, private law concerns legal relationships where both parties are private persons; public law, on the other hand, concerns relationships where at least one of the parties is a public person, that is, the state, a municipality, or another institution or person endowed with public power.

Here, however, one encounters the difficulty that the state, like other persons, can enter into agreements concerning purchase, hire, etc., and that these legal relationships are undoubtedly governed by the rules of private law. One usually resorts to considering only those legal relationships in which the parties involved are not coequal and which, consequently, are governed by rules which are fundamentally distinct from the rules of private law, which presuppose legal relationships between parties placed on an equal footing.

To this, it must be objected that the very idea of non-private law concerning legal relationships between the public authorities and the citizens is unclear and indefensible. In what sense have the rules governing legislative power anything to do with a legal relationship concerning citizens? Or the criminal law, which is distinct from tort law solely through public proceedings? Or the rules governing proof and burden of proof? Or the substantive rules for the division of an estate? It will have emerged from what has been said above that, considering the various parts of the so-called public law, there are, in reality, different peculiarities that condition the idea of their public character. The idea of an 'unequal legal relationship' has merit in the field of so-called special administrative law, where the legal position of citizens presupposes an intervening administrative act, but is otherwise without any basis.

From the explanation in § 47, it emerges that the distinction between substantive and procedural law has nothing to do with metaphysical ideas, but is understood as a purely technical tool of presentation. At the same time, the [286] reader has been warned against making the mistake of forgetting that the substantive law is merely a fragment that has meaning only in connection with the law of procedure and execution and thus conceive of the duties, claims, and rights, laid down in substantive law, as something that possesses validity in itself—quite independently and isolated from the rules of procedural law concerning legal proceedings, evidence, the sentence, and the enforcement of the sentence. This misinterpretation would mean a relapse into magical and metaphysical ideas about the law as a spiritually valid order, through the commands of which 'duties' and 'claims' are created, as ideal and spiritual attributes or forces, valid in themselves; that is to say, independent from the coercion exercised by the legal machinery, which alone extends outer protection to them. Even in cases where this protection should fail for one reason or another, the duty or claim, as ideal validity, would thereby remain unchallenged.

Metaphysical ideas of this kind manifest themselves in the natural law doctrine of innate rights; rights which it is the task of positive law to protect. And it has to be admitted, I think, that similar ideas are lurking behind the legal positivist distinction between substantive and procedural law.

In so far as Lundstedt's criticism[3] of the distinction relates to what has been said above, it is justified. As is usually the case, however, Lundstedt overshoots the mark, because, at the same time, he is blind to the fact that the distinction, correctly interpreted, expresses a fundamental juridico-ideological reality, namely (as has been explained in § 47) the division of the norm of conduct in its entirety, justified on the grounds of presentation technique.

With regard to Lundstedt, one must raise the specific objection that there is no reason for him to see a proof of metaphysical reasoning in the circumstance that, in the course of customary juristic argumentation before the court, it is asserted that A (according to substantive law) has acquired ownership of a thing (for example, by purchase) as a basis for certain legal consequences (for example, claims of vindication).[4] According to Lundstedt, mixing up cause and effect is the same thing as putting things upside down. The fact is, he says, that A has ownership because he can vindicate (claim damages, etc.), and not the other way round. This argument (in Lundstedt's view, inverted) gives in his eyes proof of the fact that by 'property right' (substantive law), we must mean a metaphysical substance, independent of real legal functional contexts.

[3] See, e.g., *Grundlinier i skadeståndsrätten. Senare delen. Strikt ansvar* [The Basic Features of Tort Law. Part Two. Strict Liability], Vol. I (1944), 535 *et seq.*, cf. 519; *Obligationsbegreppet.* D.1 [The Concept of Obligation. Part One] (1929), 58 *et seq.*, 71 *et seq.* and 122 *et seq.*

[4] *Grundlinier i skadeståndsrätten* [The Basic Features of Tort Law] (see note 3), 524; *Obligationsbegreppet* [The Concept of Obligation] (see note 3), 86.

The errors in this captivating reasoning stem from mixing up legal-doctrinal and legal-sociological points of view. From a legal-sociological perspective, concerned with factual phenomena and their causal relationship, it is correct that [287] A's 'ownership' in the sense of real 'risk-free opportunities for action', or his 'secure position', is the result of the legal system actually upheld; specifically, of A's factual possibility to claim recovery, to claim damages, etc. However, this is definitely not what a lawyer is talking about when he justifies his client's claim of vindication by mentioning that his client has acquired 'the property right' to the objects by purchase. *He is not talking about the legal-sociological facts of cause and effect, but about the legal-doctrinal motivations of an assertion; that is to say, he is referring to the contents of an ideology* (a system of rules) which must be assumed to motivate the decision of the judge.[5] According to the contents of this system of rules, the judge shall render a judgment concerning a claim of surrender in favour of the purchaser of the object, and this is exactly what the lawyer will achieve within the judge's consciousness, so as to motivate him towards a decision that is favourable to his client. It has been explained, in § 36, that legal-doctrinal argumentation takes the form that the purchase that has taken place is said to generate a 'property right' which, in turn, generates a claim for recovery, but that 'property right,' thus inserted between fact and consequence, is a completely empty word whose sole function is to serve as a technical tool of presentation. Consequently, it has nothing to do with the 'risk-free opportunities for action' Lundstedt is talking about, and there is no awkward or implied metaphysics in justifying a claim for recovery within the framework of an existing 'property right'.

Further, it can be pointed out—as has been done by Illum and Geiger[6] – that the separation of substantive law from procedural law expresses an *ideological reality*. It may be that a creditor is unable to prove his claim. One of the conditions for him to start the legal machinery is thus missing, and thus far he has no

[5] To the best of my knowledge, this is now the view embraced by Karl Olivecrona. After referring to Lundstedt's definition of legal duty as the factual situation of coercion in which the debtor finds himself, Olivecrona continues:

> 'This [the factual situation of coercion] is conditioned by the creditor's possibilities to adduce evidence, etc. All this must be included if the situation is to be described as it objectively exists. It is perfectly legitimate to make an abstraction, however. One feels the need to employ a concept concerning the conduct which a person, *according to the thought content* of the rules applying to individual conduct, has to observe, so that certain other rules (concerning the conduct of judicial and executive authorities) should not be applicable to him. What is called duty in this sense is *not an objectively existing situation*. Rather, it is a question of *the content of certain merely imagined patterns of behaviour, contained in the legal rules*, which are regarded, with reference to their applicability, in certain *hypothetical* circumstances.' (*Penningen i civilrättens system* [The Monetary Unit in Civil Law Systems], Skrifter tillägnade Vilhelm Lundstedt [Writings dedicated to Vilhelm Lundstedt], *SvJT*, 37, 7–9 (1952), 675 note 3, my italics).

Thus shifting the problem from a legal-sociological to a legal-doctrinal level, as expressed here, must logically lead to Olivecrona's distancing himself, not only from Lundstedt's concept of obligation, but also from his exaggerated criticism of the distinction between substantive law and procedural law, his concept of a right, etc.

[6] Knud Illum, *Lov og Ret* [Law and Justice] (1945), 185; Theodor Geiger, *Vorstudien zu einer Soziologie des Rechts* [Preliminary Studies on the Sociology of Law] (1947), 185.

legal claim, and the debtor has no legal obligation to pay. Nevertheless, it is not completely meaningless to state that according to substantive law, the debtor is [288] in duty bound to fulfil the obligation he has entered into. Irrespective of the factual possibility of exercising coercion, the rule of statutory law itself, by virtue of formal legal consciousness, will create an urge to act 'duty-bound'. The legal order impacts on people—not only by employing intimidation and coercion, but also by unselfish attitudes of respect for law and justice; that is, by an ideology of validity. But of course it must be admitted that the duty we are speaking of here is of another kind than legal duty proper. According to the general definition of law (§ 7), this term ought to be reserved for a behaviour to which a sanction is applied through coercion. Thus, in a legal sense, the duties comprised in substantive law are merely conditional duties; *viz.*, conditioned by the circumstance that all other conditions that are stipulated for the exercise of coercion are fulfilled. It is merely in an ideological sense that these duties are unconditional.

In § 49 above, *the concept of property right* has been defined through the negotiability of the right, and it has been pointed out that exactly this juridico-functional quality, not the real economic exchange value of the goods, must be the decisive factor in legal systematics. This coincides with the views put forward by Vinding Kruse.* Unfortunately, however, this author—paying much attention to the economic sense of the word 'property' [*formue*]—holds that the same idea must be expressed by abolishing the concept 'property law' ['*formueret*'] and instead speak of 'property law' ['*ejendomsret*'].[7] In doing so, he has entangled himself in difficulties which are not merely of a terminological kind but have led to complete intellectual and conceptual confusion.

It is terminologically obvious that the term 'property law' ['*ejendomsret*'] is an extremely unfortunate choice for a superordinate concept covering all kinds of negotiable rights (in Vinding Kruse's terminology: rights endowed with 'powers 2–4'). For at the same time, 'property right' is meant to denote one of these, distinct from the right of use and enjoyment, easement, the right of claim etc.[8] Thus, one has to operate with a single term that is used in two different senses, relating to each other in the same way as superordinate and subordinate concepts. Had the author only kept the two terms (covered by a single word) strictly apart, there would only have been a certain clumsiness with respect to

* Editor's note: The following discussion depends upon the distinction, in Danish, between two words which both translate into 'property' in English, namely, *formue* and *ejendom* (and correspondingly 'right of property' translates into *formueret* and *ejendomsret*, respectively). In order for the patient reader to follow Ross's somewhat polemic and not terribly rewarding discussion of his former teacher Vinding Kruse's position on the concept of property, we shall, in the remainder of this paragraph, indicate in brackets which of the two Ross is referring to.

7 Vinding Kruse, *Ejendomsretten* [The Right of Property] (3rd edn, 1951), 201.

8 The confusion is increased by the fact that 'right of property' ['*ejendomsret*'] is meant to indicate, at the same time, one of the two disciplines of property law in the broad sense. Since Vinding Kruse holds that the right of claim is a right of property [*ejendomsret*], it is actually rather odd that he acknowledges the existence of a law of obligations beside a law of property [*ejendomsretten*] (in the narrow sense of a discipline).

presentation technique. However, in Vinding Kruse's world of ideas, the two terms melt into one single term, and this results in a state of genuine confusion.

It is quite plain that *the circumstance that a legal position is negotiable*—which is to say that B, according to certain rules, can succeed to A's position—*does not, in itself, say anything about the content of this position apart from its being negoti-*
[289] *able*. This content—called, by Vinding Kruse, 'inner control' or 'power 1'—can from an economic point of view consist in having access to complete control over a thing, to limited control over a thing, or to a claim to generic performance, and accordingly there exists a right of property [*ejendomsret*] (understood in the usual sense of the word), a limited right *in rem*, or a right of claim, respectively. In Vinding Kruse's work, the fusion between right of property [*ejendomsret*] in the sense of a negotiable right (right of property [*formueret*]) and in the sense of a specific, extensive right of free disposal now leads to the *less than reasonable assertion that all negotiable rights, according to their main content, aim at the same thing*, namely extensive factual possession according to the pattern of ordinary property law. In order to accomplish this absurdity, the author is compelled to seek the object of this factual possession in—the right itself! Thus, the right of claim becomes a right of property [*ejendomsret*] (understood in the usual sense of the term) concerning the claim, and the limited right *in rem* becomes a full right of disposal over the limited right of disposal. Powers 1–4—*inter alia* power 1 = complete factual disposal—is to be had in these cases over power 1 in the sense of right of claim, or limited right *in rem*.[9] Vinding

[9] 'This is the state of things: The content of property law [*ejendomsrettens*], *the powers 1–4 are the same also with respect to partial rights of property* as with respect to direct rights of property [*ejendomsret*]. However, *the benefit* is simply a different one with regard to the partial or limited rights of property [*ejendomsrettigheder*]—not, as with the direct right of property [*ejendomsret*] which, at the same time, includes powers under 1 minus the powers of those who are partial rights holders, but it is a *simple power* (or simple powers) under 1'; Vinding Kruse, *Ejendomsretten* [The Right of Property] (3rd edn, 1951), 143 (V. K.'s italics). Here, the author says explicitly:

(a) that direct right of property [*ejendomsret*] (right of property in the usual sense of the word) consists of powers 1–4 over power 1 minus the powers of those partial rights holders. Power 1 is, then, a complete factual disposition of complete factual disposition minus the disposition that is set apart to others. Or, in other words: right of property [*ejendomsret*] (in the usual sense of the word) is right of property [*ejendomsret*] of right of property [*ejendomsret*]!
(b) that restricted rights of property [*ejendomsrettigheder*] (and the same must apply to the right of claim) consist of powers 1–4 over one single power, set apart to others by Power 1. Power 1 of easement is, thus, complete factual disposition over the restricted disposition of the holder of the right of easement; power 1 of the right of claim is complete factual disposition over the disposition connected to the claim (which, by the way, does not exist). Or in other words: easement is a right of property [*ejendomsret*] to easement, and the right of claim is a right of property [*ejendomsret*] to a right of claim.

From what has been said above, the following emerges with abundant clarity: while in reality the right of property [*ejendomsretten*] (in the usual sense of the term), easement, and claim have negotiability ('powers 2–4') in common but, on the other hand, are distinct with regard to the content of the primary law, they are construed, by Vinding Kruse, as property right [*ejendomsret*] to right of property [*ejendomsret*], easement and claim, respectively; which should prove that the content of the primary law (power 1) is the same in all these cases. It stands to reason that the construction 'a power to factual disposal over a power to factual disposal' is sheer nonsense, and that a 'property right [*ejendomsret*] to right of property [*ejendomsret*], easement and claims, respectively', based upon this, is totally devoid of meaning. It is embarrassing that such nonsense on stilts has been taken seriously by Nordic jurists—at least for a time.

Kruse's exertions in striving to detect a meaning in *the construction of complete factual disposal over a restricted disposal or a claim*[10] have been unavailing. A claim is a claim—it is not a property right [*ejendomsret*] to a claim. A limited [290]
right *in rem* is a limited right *in rem*—it is not a property right [*ejendomsret*] to a limited right *in rem*. In Vinding Kruse's work, even the right of property [*ejendomsret*] (understood in the usual sense of the word) becomes a property right [*ejendomsret*] to a right of property [*ejendomsret*].[11] The entire train of thought is a tangle of logical absurdities. Other writers have dedicated an exorbitant amount of brain work to the task of unravelling all the particulars of Vinding Kruse's views.[12]

Obviously, the gliding in Vinding Kruse's train of thought has to do with the vague linguistic usage frequently employed by him (as well as by others), according to which one speaks of the transfer of things (movables, real property, etc.). What is transferred is the right to the objects, of course. Since even claims and limited rights *in rem* can be transferred, this particular usage entails that the claim or the limited right *in rem* are classed as things—and, thus, classed as what is the subject of property law [*ejendomsret*].

This meaningless construction: property right [*ejendomsret*] to a right, together with the construction of intellectual property rights as property rights over an intellectual production and the so-called doctrine of spiritual property right [*ejendomsret*], constitutes the foundation of Vinding Kruse's reaction against the 'materialistic' notion of the law of property [*ejendomsretten*] as a law of things and of his theory that the subject of property law can be a limited section of the inner world in the same way as of the outer world.[13] The foundation is indefensible with regard to all three branches. On the issue of the copyright *qua* property right to an intellectual production, see the criticism in § 48 note 7 above. 'Spiritual' property right [*ejendomsret*]—as O. K. Magnussen[14] has shown—is not a new form of ownership concerning a 'spiritual' object, but merely an expression of the circumstance that ordinary ownership not only satisfies physical needs, but also 'spiritual' needs, first and foremost through the sentimental value within objects. Thus, the distinction between material—intellectual—spiritual property right [*ejendomsret*] cannot be sustained. We can safely omit both intellectual and spiritual issues. The subject of the right of property [*ejendomsrettens*] (and of other rights of property [*formuerettigheders*]) are physical objects—things, and nothing else. Property law [*formueretten*] is the law of things.

[10] On this issue, see Henry Ussing, *Dansk Obligationsret. Almindelig Del* [The Danish Law of Obligations. General Part] (3rd edn, 1946), § 1.

[11] See note 9 above.

[12] The interested reader (with plenty of time on his hands) is referred to Alf Ross, *Virkelighed og Gyldighed i Retslæren* [Reality and Validity in Jurisprudence] (1934), ch. X, 1; Henry Ussing in note 9 *op. cit.* and O. K. Magnussen, *Naboretlige Studier* [Studies in the Law Regulating Neighbouring Rights] (1950), 50–65.

[13] *Ejendomsretten* [The Right of Property] (3rd edn, 1951), 196.

[14] *Naboretlige Studier* [Studies in the Law Regulating Neighbouring Rights] (1950), 49–50.

Just as there is no reason to dismiss the concept property law [*formueret*], there is no reason to abandon the term law of things as denoting one of the two disciplines of property law [*formuerettens*]. Introducing the term property law [*ejendomsret*] as denoting simultaneously both (1) property law [*formueretten*]; (2) one of the latter's two disciplines (the law of things); and (3) one of the rights of property [*formueretlige*] was an uncommonly unlucky device.

CHAPTER IX [291]

Operative Facts

§ 51. Terminology and Distinctions

As stated in § 25, any legal directive can be expressed in the formula:

If F, then C,

where F stands for a subject matter (factual circumstances, legal facts) and C for a legal consequence which indicates, directly or indirectly, how the judge shall judge. This means that the basis of all exercise of legal authority consists of certain conditioning facts whose existence the judge (or other law-applying organ) regards as proven. It depends upon the content of the applicable legal norms what facts within the boundless diversity of existence are relevant to a certain decision.

The complex totality of all facts that can be of relevance to a decision according to scientifically valid law is called *operative facts*.

Usually a plurality of facts is operative in one and the same case, even if individual facts enjoy a special status. In a case of manslaughter, for example, it is not only the very act of killing that is relevant: a number of attendant circumstances will have to be considered as well. In particular, one would have to investigate whether there are sufficient grounds for exemption from punishment, for absolute discharge, or for a sentence reduction. Similarly, in cases where a legally enforceable promise is advanced, the very fact that a promise has [292] been made is not the only fact that matters. In addition to this, different attending circumstances, positive or negative, must be taken into consideration as being decisive for the validity of the promise (majority, mistake, coercion, fraud, etc.). Nevertheless, both manslaughter and promise enjoy a special status. They constitute the facts which justify and condition the specific legal consequence in question (punishment for manslaughter and legal consequence in conformity with the content of the promise, respectively), while the attendant circumstances merely condition, modify or exclude the coming into force of the specific legal effect.

The above examples explain that among the operative facts, we can distinguish between those which are of specific relevance and those which are merely of conditioning (modifying, excluding) relevance. The former are also called *law-creating facts*.

Since a law-creating fact, as such, is usually not sufficient to give rise to its specific legal consequence, it follows that it is not possible to define a certain law-creating fact as the fact that effectively produces a specific legal effect. For example, if we were to define a promise as a communication, that entails the promisor being obligated in conformity with the content of the communication, then we would debar ourselves from the possibility of speaking of invalid promises, and we would actually have confused, in our definition, the promise itself and the attendant, conditioning circumstances. A specific law-creating fact must be defined as that fact which, as a rule—that is, *unless there are special exclusionary reasons*—gives rise to the specific legal effect.

The law can turn almost any subject matter between heaven and earth into an operative fact, provided it can be described in terms of everyday language. It is pointless to attempt a systematic classification. Only some distinctions and views of relevance shall be emphasized.

Operative facts are usually defined *in general terms*, that is, by abstract, conceptual characteristics. However, they can also be defined individually, that is, by name (personal name, place name) or by some other individualizing criterion that points at an object in its specific existence. Individualizing statements of place occur frequently ('in this country', 'in Copenhagen', etc.), but apart from judgments and administrative acts, individualizing personal details are rare.[1]

Some operative facts are described as *conditions*, including the *qualities* of persons or things, while others are described as *events*, that is, as changes to an [293] existing condition. A condition can be defined in relation to a certain point in time (for example, the criminal's state of mind at the moment of crime), or to a certain period of time (for example, permanent residence in this country, or the possession of an object over a number of years). In principle, particulars as to a current condition can always be reduced to particulars as to occurrences, *viz.*, partly those establishing the condition, partly those terminating it. The statement that a person is more than twenty-five years old can thus be reduced to the fact that he was born more than twenty-five years ago plus the negative fact that, since then, he has not died. These circumstances are of relevance to the definition of the concept 'retroactive legislation'.

[1] At any rate, a legal consequence must relate to a conditioning factual circumstance. There cannot be any 'rights conferred directly by the law'. For example, if a certain individual is granted, by statute, citizenship, pension rights or the like, the conditioning fact is this individual's existence at the time of the statute's coming into force, and possibly his continued existence until certain later points of time.

Some operative facts are *purely factual* (for example, birth, death, fire, collision at sea), others are *legal and factual*, which means that they are defined relative to valid law. As stated in § 36 above, the characterization of a person as 'married' or as the 'owner' of a certain property has reference to certain facts (the contracting of a marriage, the purchase or other acquisition of the property) which are legally qualified in so far as they have been defined as those facts which, according to valid law, entail the embodiment of the legal effects which constitute 'marriage' and 'ownership', respectively. According to this technique of formulation, legal rule R_1 describes its operative facts, not directly, but by reference to the subject matters that are operative in relation to certain other legal rules R_2, R_3, etc. For example, when the tax law makes tax computation dependent on whether or not the taxpayer is married, it could, instead—albeit in a complicated way—have directly stated those facts which, according to the law on the contracting and dissolution of marriage, are decisive as to whether a marriage does or does not exist. This is a widely used technique of formulation. It exists everywhere where the language of the law, in describing operative facts, employs terms such as 'creditor', 'debtor', 'pawnee', 'nationality', 'purchase', 'transfer', etc., etc. The same applies where a term has reference, not to a formal legal rule, but to a legal standard. That a person has acted negligently, for example, is not a purely factual statement, but has reference to a presupposed standard with respect to the course of action which, in the given situation, can be expected from a reasonable man. This distinction between purely factual and legal-factual operative facts is of relevance, *inter alia*, to the doctrine of preliminary decisions and the interpretation of the distinction between 'law' and 'fact' which legislation occasionally builds upon.[2]

Among the operative facts that have the character of events, there is an important distinction between *occurrences* and *human acts*, because in connection with the latter, there often arise certain problems of the same kind concerning accountability and attribution as circumstances which condition the coming into force of the legal consequence.

In the category of human acts, a further distinction can be drawn between *factual acts* and *acts in law*. The latter are also called *legal acts*, *transactions*, or *dispositions*: they consist of linguistic communications whose specific legal effect is determined, more or less exhaustively, in conformity with the content of the communication itself, and which consequently are suitable instruments for conscious human activity specifically aimed at creating new law. [294]

Every legal act (transaction) is the effect of a competence, cf. § 34. However, there is a profound difference between the competence of public authorities,

[2] See, e.g., the appeal to the Danish Supreme Court in criminal cases, § 966 section 2 and § 945 section 2 of the Danish Administration of Justice Act; on this issue, cf. Stephan Hurwitz, *Den danske Strafferetspleje* [Criminal Procedure in Denmark] (2nd edn, 1949), 560 *et seq.*

which is exercised for the protection of the interests of a community and is based on the idea of authority, and the competence of private persons, which is exercised for the protection of private interests and is based on the idea of autonomy, cf. § 46. Therefore, there is no point in presenting all legal acts under one heading. We must distinguish between public legal acts and private transactions. Within the category of public legal acts, in turn, we must distinguish between legislative acts, government acts, administrative acts, and judicial acts. Neither do these acts have sufficient things in common so as to warrant a joint presentation, but the individual types must be referred to special treatment in the respective parts of public law. Therefore, the account given here (§§ 52 and 53) is restricted to *the private transaction.*

In the category 'factual human acts', the *act contrary to duty* (the *unlawful act*) has traditionally played a special role in theory. Therefore, it will be made the subject of a special mention (§ 54).

§ 52. The Private Disposition

A private disposition is traditionally defined[1] (with variations) as a private declaration of will entailing legal effects in conformity with its content.[2] In view of the phenomena we have in mind, this definition is inadequate in several respects.

(1) As already mentioned in the preceding section, a specific law-creating fact cannot be defined as the fact that *entails* the specific legal effect. If 'disposition' is defined according to this pattern, we are debarred from speaking of [295] invalid dispositions and confuse the conditioning circumstances with the specific conditioning fact itself. This is inappropriate and not clear. Therefore, the definition must be corrected on this point, to the effect that it is sufficient if the communication *as a rule*—that is, *unless there are special grounds of invalidity*—entails the specific legal effect.[3]

(2) In the definition above, the specific legal effect is defined as a *legal effect in conformity with the content of the declaration*. This may very well apply, for example, to a contract which regulates in detail the legal relationship between the parties, but it is less appropriate in other situations also covered by the concept. The majority of contracts—for example, a normal brief sales contract or rental agreement—merely offer an extremely scanty framework for the legal relationship which must be filled with flesh and blood, taken from the non-mandatory legal rules that govern the legal relationship in question. Thus, the legal effect that comes into force is only with regard to certain basic features defined by the content of the disposition/transaction. The same thing shows even more clearly in 'truncated' communications, quite similar to stereotype forms, the legal effect of which is entirely standardized in legislation. Just to name a few examples: notices of withdrawal, notices of a lack of conformity, default notices, letters of resignation, applications for set-off, receipts, certain procedural notices, etc. In these situations, the legal order places a sort of keyboard at the disposal of private persons: you may choose to press a keyboard key, or you may choose

[1] For further information, see Carl Jacob Arnholm, 'Omkring rettshandelsteorien' [On the theory of legal transaction], *TfR* 1948, 376 *et seq.*

[2] [General remark to § 52:] Until recently, the expression *legal transaction* [in Danish: retshandel] has dominated in Nordic legal theory. I can fully join Carl Jacob Arnholm in his criticism of the expression, put forth in the interesting and inspiring article, *op. cit.*, 368 *et seq.*

[3] In the same vein: Julius Lassen, *Lærebog i Romersk Privatret* [Textbook on Roman Private Law] (3rd edn, 1924), 118; Henry Ussing, *Aftaler paa Formuerettens Omraade* [Contracts in the Field of Property Law] (1950), § 1.II; Knud Illum, *Forelæsninger over almindelig Formueret ved det Økonomiske Fakultet ved Aarhus Universitet* [Lectures on General Property Law, held at the Faculty of Economics of Aarhus University] (1939), 30. F. Stang, on the other hand—*Innledning til Formueretten* [Introduction to Property Law] (3rd edn, 1935), 210—defines the disposition/transaction by its actual legal effect.

not to do so. Herein lies the autonomy of the individual. However, the legal effect that is produced is stereotypically determined by the legal order itself. It is of course arguable whether such 'truncated' communications ought to be included in the concept of disposition. However, since they function as tools for the autonomous formation of legal relationships by the parties (in the same way as do the more articulate communications); and since they are treated legally according to the same rules with regard to the conditions for their validity, etc., the most appropriate thing to do would be to include them in the concept of disposition. In that case, however, it is necessary to modify the definition. The specific legal effect must not be defined as a 'legal effect in conformity with the content of the communication', but as *a typically autonomous legal effect*, that is, a legal effect which a party frequently can be interested in producing, *qua* integral part of its autonomous shaping of his legal relationships.

(3) According to the definition above, the operative fact, which (normally) entails the specific legal effect, is defined as a *declaration of will*. This is a highly ambiguous and mystical concept.

To begin with, it is not clear what is meant, in this context, by the
[296] expression *declaration*. It seems that it can be understood in two different ways, namely: either as a piece of information or news concerning a factual circumstance—in the present case, the will of the person who makes the declaration; or in such a way that the disposition—similarly to an exclamation or a suggestive command—is a spontaneous, direct expression of an emotional-volitional state of mind on the part of the person making the declaration. Neither of these two ways, however, seems to apply to the present situations.

The first possibility (supported by Vinding Kruse[4]) must definitely be rejected. A promise is not a piece of information that imparts knowledge. A person who promises another person to pay 100 Danish Crowns on 1 January does not mean to send a message concerning a matter of fact, or to express an assertion. If this were the case, it would be possible to characterize promises as either true or false, just like other assertions. Furthermore, it is obvious that the legal order does not treat promises from the perspective usually applied to messages.

The second possibility does not hold water, either. A direct expression of emotion and volition may exist, if the person who makes the promise simultaneously—in pathetic expressions and deeply moved—protests and swears that he means to act in keeping with his promise. This is not a typical case, however. A person who buys a half-crown's worth of carrots in an everyday manner does not display any emotional-volitional passions.

[4] *Retslæren* [Jurisprudence], Vol. I (1943), 183–84.

In addition, it is not clear what, exactly, is the *will* that is announced, or manifested, in the dispositive statement. If it is a question of a promise, then this will can be understood psychologically, as an intention concerning the individual's own future course of action. But what if it is a question of a prescription, that is to say, a disposition concerning the recipient's course of action? What does it mean to say that it is my 'will' that another person shall act in a certain way? My intentions or decisions can only be directed towards my own conduct and the consequences that are brought about by it. Therefore, I can only 'will' another person's course of action in so far as I am in a position to bring it about by my own actions. Now, if the prescription—for reasons beyond my control—is able to motivate the other person, then I can, to that extent, 'will' his action—just as I can 'will' his death by firing a pistol at him. But for this reason, the prescription is no more a declaration of will than is the pistol shot. It is quite another matter that in both situations, one can infer from my behaviour that I have 'willed' a specific result, achieved through my own course of action.

As a matter of fact, all this talk about will and declaration of will has nothing whatsoever to do with a psychological description of what is happening when a disposition is made. Just like the general theory of scientifically valid law as an expression of the will of the state,[5] the theory of the [297] disposition as a declaration of will, or an expression of will, is rooted in purely metaphysical ideas of the will as a magically creative power. Just as the Word of God has created light, the will creates 'the law', that is, rights and duties, envisaged as a kind of spiritual attribute or substance.

The current mode of expression is not merely a terminological relic of a bygone age: it has also proved capable of giving rise to dogmatic postulates and misleading theories in connection with practical legal problems. Certainly, 'the dogma of the will' as an 'explanation' of the 'binding force' of a promise and a solution to the problem of delusion in the law seems to have outlived itself these days. But as for assessing the boundary between binding statements and mere information, suggestions, requests etc., we have not yet got rid of the idea that the crux of the matter is, whether or not any expression of will has taken place. But more of this later.

It goes without saying that volitional aspects are important in the making of legal dispositions, but they are important in a way that is different from what the doctrine of the disposition as a declaration of will expresses. To the judicial decision—just as to other human acts (the act of killing, for example)—it is of relevance whether or not the act has been performed *with volition and intent*. Normally, a person who makes a disposition—he enters into an agreement, for example—does so volitionally, in the sense

[5] Cf. Karl Olivecrona, *Lagen och staten* [On Law and the State] (1940), 21 *et seq.* and 'Viljan bakom rätten' ['The will behind the law'], *StvT* 1947, 1 *et seq.*

that it is his will to enter into the agreement and to produce the effects which the agreement entails according to the legal order. If there should exist any abnormalities in this respect concerning either his general mental health (accountability), or his volitional attitude towards the act of disposition, or his conceptual views on the contents of the act (attribution), then problems will arise concerning the validity of the disposition. The utterer's will and ideas are part of the operative facts of conditioning relevance.

But then what, exactly, is the content and meaning of a dispositive statement, if not a declaration of will? Does it have representative or expressive meaning? Is it an assertion, an exclamation, or a directive (cf. § 2)?

We have seen that the statement cannot be interpreted as an *assertion* concerning the psychological state of the utterer—his 'will'. It is clearly not a prophecy either, a prediction of what will happen in the future.

Nor is it an *exclamation.*

Is it a *directive*? If we study a lengthy contract, this characterization does not seem entirely misleading. Expressed in the current modalities of the legal language (claim, duty, power, subjection), we find here patterns of action which, should the need arise, can serve as a benchmark, both for the parties concerned and for the judge. It must be emphasized, however, that the directive meaning is conditioned by the existence of a legal order—by that rule of valid law which endows private dispositions with validity
[298] and 'binding force', that is, which motivates the judge to take them as a basis for his decision. In abstraction, the dispositive statement is merely a directive formula, a fantasy statement of the same kind as a draft bill, or a sentence I am jotting down on a piece of paper without intending to make an assertion.

The matter is presented even more clearly if we consider the 'truncated' dispositive statements, or the formula 'I promise...' If it has been agreed that in order to gain admittance to a secret night club one must mumble a meaningless word, then this word, *in itself*, is and will remain meaningless in spite of the fact that it functions as a directive to the doorman *by virtue of this agreement.* The situation is exactly the same with the promise-statement, for example. In itself—that is, abstracted from the legal order—the expression 'I promise...' is without any meaning whatsoever. One might just as well say 'abracadabra' by way of trigger word. But by virtue of the effect that the legal order attaches to the formulaic word, it functions as a directive to the judge and can be used by private parties as an appropriate tool for exercising their autonomy.

The knowledge that a dispositive statement in itself is not an expression of a will is important when dealing with borderline cases between binding dispositions and non-binding statements of various types. It is often difficult to establish this borderline. The problem arises in connection with various communications in the form of information, invitations (in particular when making an offer), requests, feelers before a definitive agreement, casual statements, and drafts. In such cases, it may be doubtful whether or not the borderline between a non-binding announcement and a binding disposition has been transgressed.

The point of departure when dealing with these problems has hitherto been the question of whether the communication expresses a dispositive intent on the part of the utterer, a will, or a decision to be bound.

This is putting the cart before the horse. A properly executed promise is not in itself an expression of will, decision, or intent. Simply because the legal order endows the promise with 'binding force', we can usually take for granted that the individual who makes use of this tool does so because he wants to bring about the legal effect attached to the promise—just as one can normally take for granted that a person firing a revolver at another person does so with the intent to take the other person's life. Thus, the situation is contrary to what is generally assumed: if a certain type of statement is traditionally binding, we can normally take for granted that the act of pronouncing it indicates dispositive intent.

Our task, then, is to set a limit where a bargain is a bargain, guided by what is right and proper, and supported by conventional views. This approach is corroborated by the way in which the borderline is drawn. It is generally assumed, for example, that price lists distributed on a large scale are merely an invitation to make an offer, whereas a window display of [299] priced goods is regarded as a binding offer to sell the goods in question, or at least other goods of a similar kind.[6] If this rule is not considered well known it is impossible to arrive at the conclusion (*via* psychological analysis) that the one announcement, but not the other, is borne by the will to be bound. But if the rule is once made and a matter of general knowledge, it follows that a display of priced goods can be taken as a sign of a will to be bound; not, however, the distribution of price lists. It is the same with the other borderline cases. With all of them, the point of departure is the conventional view. Where no such conventional view exists, or where it is unstable, a decision must be made with respect to a further elaboration of the convention.

(4) When the disposition is defined as a declaration of will, it is presupposed that it appears in the form of a *statement*, that is, a linguistic communication.

This expression must not be understood too narrowly in the present context. Here, 'language' does not only cover ordinary language, but other symbols as well—symbols which help us to express ourselves so as to be understood by other people. Thus, it is clear that a nod can be just as binding as a spoken 'yes'.

[6] Henry Ussing, *Aftaler paa Formuerettens Omraade* [Contracts in the Field of Property Law] (1950), § 5, II, 3.

One might inquire whether we should not take one more step and let the concept of disposition also include certain *acts* which do not have the character of linguistic communications. On the face of it, there is, of course, nothing to prevent the legal order from attaching, to certain factual acts, the same typically autonomous legal effects as are attached to dispositive statements. Indeed, it is a well-known fact that, to a certain extent, such a thing actually happens. Example: if a person unlawfully appropriates a book that has been sent to him on approval, or a box of cigars lying on the tobacconist's counter, then these acts entail a duty to pay, not only compensation but also damages. Thus, appropriation is regarded as a disposition and not as a tortious act. The situation is the same with respect to passivity in certain situations (in particular, omission to lodge a complaint) and to certain acts of payment.[7]

From our basic attitude towards the nature of the disposition, it follows that in neither of these situations can the decision over which acts should entail the effects of the disposition be justified by reference to whether or not the act (omission) expresses dispositive intent. For example: it is a purely conventional question whether or not passivity towards the person who makes me an offer shall entail that I am bound. If it has been established that passivity (in this or any other situation) produces the same effect as the disposition, then we may on this basis (but not otherwise) understand passivity as an indication of a corresponding intent.

However, these situations—going under the name of quasi-contracts
[300] (*quasi-dispositions*)—are normally not included in the concept of disposition proper. In view of the fact that they present various peculiarities, this is only right and proper.

If we combine the views expressed under (1)–(4), we arrive at the following definition of private disposition. It is a *statement which usually—that is, unless there are special grounds for invalidity—produces typically autonomous legal effects*, that is, legal effects which the individual who makes the disposition is typically interested in producing. If the statement contains a designation thereof, these effects will be determined, partly according to these designations, partly through supplementary statutory rules. If the statement merely consists of certain formulaic words, the legal effect is exhaustively determined by the law.

[7] For more information, see Henry Ussing, *op. cit.*, § 37.

§ 53. Promise, Order, and Authorization

In relation to the two principal forms of legal modalities, duty and power, the subgroups of a disposition are defined by means of the following figure:

Dispositions entailing

	for the individual who makes the disposition	*for others*
duty	promise	order
power	?	authorization

A promise (in the narrower sense) is a statement purporting to *obligate the promisor himself.* That an obligation exists means (§ 34) that the promisee has the possibility to obtain a judgment providing for enforcement or performance interest. In order to speak of a binding promise, however, it is not necessary that one can actually enforce the promise by filing a lawsuit. A promise is said to be binding, even if such a possibility is conditioned by certain future circumstances—such as non-performance within a given time—provided that this possibility does not depend on the promisor's will. Thus, the promise is *binding* if there is an actual or independently conditioned right to compulsory performance. It follows that the promise is not binding (1) if—owing to special circumstances—it was *invalid* when it was made, which implies that the right to compulsory performance is precluded; and (2) if the promise is [301] *revocable*, which means that the promisor has the power to preclude the possibility of compulsory performance.

Thus, a valid promise is binding from the moment it has become irrevocable. Thenceforth there exists an independently conditioned right to enforce a promise by filing a lawsuit. Should it happen, later on, that proceedings are precluded—because of a subsequent impossibility of performance, for example—then the promise is said to become *ineffective*. Also, subsequent performance entails ineffectiveness. This mode of speech may seem a little strained, but it is nonetheless logical. Precisely because a promise has worked in conformity with its real economic intent, its specifically legal effect disappears. A promise does not become effective as a directive to the judge because it has become effective as a derived guiding principle for the behaviour of the promisor.

The term 'promise' is not usually defined thus narrowly. Rather, it is extended to include all dispositions that *lay a burden* on the promisor.[1] Apart from the previously mentioned, personally binding dispositions (promises in the narrower sense), the term also covers *transfers*, that is, dispositions purporting to convey a right to another person, and *waivers*, purporting to relinquish a right totally or partially (promises in the wider sense). It is right and proper to include these phenomena in the concept of promise, for, in many respects, the rules applying to them are the very same rules as those applying to promises in the narrower sense. On the other hand, it should be noted that promises in the wider sense differ from promises proper with respect to an important point: in connection with promises in the wider sense, there is no act of performance on the part of the promisor. As a result, using everyday language and speaking of promises is not really appropriate in these situations. Thus, it seems odd (as has been pointed out by Arnholm) to speak of a promise when I give a beggar a penny, or when I refuse a sales offer.[2]

Orders are dispositions purporting to *obligate* the addressee (or another person) or, in a wider sense, *to lay a burden on him* by extinguishing, totally or partially, a right belonging to him.

[302] As a main rule, private persons cannot bind other persons by means of an order. Obviously, a private individual cannot, in this way, normally have power over other private individuals. Usually such power is solely vested in public authorities. Therefore, an order presupposes a special basis. The basis for A ordering B is frequently the fact that B has authorized A to issue orders. Thus, B's duty originates in his own autonomy. Such authorization may be embedded in the offer of the promisor, enabling the recipient to bind the promisor by accepting—which, then, in effect is an order. Similarly, the principal authorizing the agent is the basis of the agent's power to obligate the principal by dispositions with a third party.

A relationship analogous to authorization exists when an order is issued as a condition for acquiring a right. Difficult questions may arise in connection

[1] See Henry Ussing, *Aftaler paa Formuerettens Omraade* [Contracts in the Field of Property Law] (1950), § 2, especially § 2, III.

[2] *Almindelig Avtalerett* [General Law of Contracts] (1949), 63. For the reasons stated above, it seems to me that it would be more expedient to restrict the concept of promise so as to cover only personally binding dispositions; and, thus, to detach from the concept transfers, waivers, and wills, cf. the text at the end of this section. The current concept formation has probably to do with the Scandinavian theorists' criticism of the Romanist theory of promise and the legal transaction concerning transfer as two separate acts; see, e.g., Vinding Kruse, *Ejendomsretten* [The Right of Property], Vol. II (1951), 809 *et seq.*, 988 *et seq.* It is undoubtedly correct to say that this theory is misleading. But even though it were admitted that transfers normally take place in one single act, there is nothing that prevents our dividing it analytically into two conceptual elements. Furthermore, it must be admitted, in my view, that there may be situations where we actually have to distinguish between a promise to transfer, and the transfer itself as being two different acts.

with the condition becoming known and the effect of the condition vis-à-vis subsequent acquirers.[3]

Without special authorization, general legal power relations between A and B can be the basis of an order. Thus, for example, parents and school authorities can, within certain limits, issue orders to the children in their care. The same applies to the relationship between employer and employee within the framework of the employment contract.

Finally, it happens that the legal order, without establishing a general power relation, endows a person with the power to dictate to others in some respects. This is less exceptional than one is inclined to think at first. In situations where the legal order has endowed a person with an exclusionary right of disposal, it would not really be thought odd if this right were restricted, to the effect that a contrary disposal of other people were excluded only on condition that there existed a corresponding prohibition on the part of the rights holder. Example: this technique is used in §§ 14 and 15 of the Law on Copyright, pursuant to which certain acts do not constitute a breach of copyright unless the author has expressly forbidden reproduction. Similarly, it would not be unreasonable to think that walking over somebody else's property was unlawful only in so far as the owner had forbidden such passage.

In addition, there are orders occurring as secondary dispositions within the framework of a primary legal relationship. Examples of these orders are letters of resignation, notices of cancellation, and declarations of set-off.[4]

Authorizations are dispositions purporting to ascribe to *the addressee* (or another person) *a power*, in particular *a competence.*

Due to an inadequate analysis of the legal modalities, it has hitherto been difficult to identify this type of disposition. Ussing, for example, always works with a division of the dispositions in relation to property (promise and order) but observes nonetheless that there are 'declarations of will' which cannot be called either promises or orders.[5] [303]

Competence is the ability (power) to make dispositions. As a rule, A can only authorize B to make dispositions which are onerous to A himself.

The most common example of an authorization is 'power of attorney'. A transfer usually also includes a transfer of the competence to dispose of the right.

[3] On the prohibition of sales of goods below list price and of the lending of books, see Vinding Kruse, *Ejendomsretten* [The Right of Property] (1951), Vol. II. 1258–60 and 1263–64.

[4] The term 'secondary legal relationship' was coined by Vinding Kruse, in *TfR* 1919, 192 *et seq.*, cf. *Ejendomsretten* [The Right of Property], Vol. II (1951), 793 and *Retslæren* [Jurisprudence], Vol. I (1943), 230.

[5] *Aftaler paa Formuerettens Område* [Contracts in the Field of Property Law] (1950), § 2, I.

Frequently, dispositions occurring in practice are of a compound nature. Thus, offer and transfer are simultaneously promise and authorization; and acceptance, notice of resignation, and declaration for a set-off are simultaneously promise and order.

The last will and testament enjoys special status. Oddly enough, it has traditionally been classified as an order (notice[6]), although it purports to transfer rights to the heirs, not to lay a burden on them (apart from an order as a condition for the acquisition of the right). The view that the last will and testament is an order addressed to the public authorities, or the universal heirs, concerning the state of the heritage is misleading, since it directly transfers the right on the death of the testator. In my opinion, the last will and testament must be a disposition concerning transfer and thus—according to current legal terminology—a promise (in the wider sense), as to which there are special rules concerning the validity of its conditions. The erroneous view has probably arisen due to the circumstance that the last will in itself does not bind the testator in his lifetime. But this circumstance does not affect the nature of the disposition as a transfer. It merely implies that concerning this transfer, there is a special rule of revocability, so that the disposition becomes binding only on the death of the testator. At that moment, his estate will be bound by it.

Moreover, because of the special legal status of the last will and testament, it is only natural to keep it expressly outside the concept of promise and call it a disposition *sui generis* within the group that lays a burden on the individual who makes the disposition.

[6] See, e.g., C. Goos, *Forelæsninger over den almindelige Retslære* [Lectures on the General Study of Law], Vol. I (1885), 226 and Viggo Bentzon, *Almindelig Retslære* [The General Study of Law] (2nd edn, edited by Vinding Kruse, 1938 [1904]), 76.

§ 54. Unlawful Acts [304]

In the two preceding sections, we have discussed the operative facts which consist of (private) legal acts, that is, statements purporting to bring about typically autonomous legal effects. Let us now turn to those operative facts which consist of factual acts, that is, acts which do not have the character of legal acts.

It has already been mentioned that certain factual acts, *viz.* the so-called quasi-dispositions, may entail legal effects in roughly the same way as dispositions.

In the present section, we shall only mention such factual acts as entail legal effects of a totally different type, namely, those which the agent is usually not interested in producing: primarily punishment and damages. Legal effects of this type are called *sanctions*.

It has been mentioned in § 47 that the law, for reasons of presentation technique, is often formulated in such a way that primary norms indicate the pattern of behaviour that is demanded of a person, in the sense that the opposite behaviour (together with further conditions) will entail the carrying into effect of certain sanctions against this person; and that the secondary norms determine in more detail what sanctions shall be applied against the person who has violated primary (substantive) law.

It would seem natural now to call 'contrary to duty' any pattern of behaviour that contradicts the claims of primary law and, consequently, may entail sanctions.

However, it is not always possible to prove that there is a distinction between primary and secondary norms (as is assumed here). The Criminal Code, for example, states simply and straightforwardly that a person who kills another person shall be punished in a certain way; that is to say, without interpolating a primary norm according to which there is a duty not to kill other persons. Nevertheless, interpolating a primary, duty-creating norm does not present a problem in this case.

In other similar cases, however, interpolating a duty as a precondition for a sanction would defy common sense—thus, for instance, when a high-voltage plant is ordered to pay compensation for damages for which the plant was not culpably responsible. In this case, one does not really feel inclined to interpret the damage-reaction as a sanction for breach of a presupposed duty not to establish dangerous installations of this sort. In this and other similar cases, we speak of damage suffered as a result of a lawful act, that is, an act regarded as not violating any duty.

From the perspective of presentation technique alone, there was of course nothing whatsoever to prevent the use of the word 'duty' in these situations too. If one still does not like to do so, however, it is because the word not only has a
[305] presentational-technical function, but is, at the same time, the bearer and mediator of a juridico-ethical ideology of validity, cf. §§ 33 and 34. If a certain behaviour is called 'a duty', this means that the contradictory relationship is outweighed, not only by interests, that is, by the fear of a foreseeable judicial reaction, but also *stigmatically*, that is, by the morally-suggestive influence that emanates from the word duty. The latter can also be expressed by saying that a certain pattern of behaviour is disapproved of, or labelled, as unacceptable. It would mean closing one's eyes to a very important fact among the legal phenomena, if one did not pay attention to this ideological function, but limit what is genuinely legal to the prospect of sanction.

This results in a distinction between reprimanding and non-reprimanding sanctions.

Consider the following definition: *An act*[1] *is called unlawful if its performance contradicts a primary, duty-imposing norm.*

Or: *An act is called unlawful if its performance—pursuant to a secondary norm—will incur a reprimanding sanction.*

These two definitions are identical, because—as we have seen—reprimanding sanctions in secondary norms are tied precisely to those acts which are labelled 'unlawful' in the primary norms.

If we do not give the word 'prohibited' another meaning apart from that an act is contrary to duty in the above-mentioned sense,[2] then we can also put forth this identical, third variant: *An act is called 'unlawful' if it is prohibited.*

From the above, it emerges that it is possible to put forth both of these two sentences:

1. *An act shall incur a reprimanding sanction, if it is unlawful (that is, prohibited in a primary norm);* and
2. *An act is unlawful if it will incur a reprimanding sanction (because it is prohibited in a primary norm).*

The apparent circle[3] expresses that unlawfulness (breach of duty) is a word devoid of semantic reference. In reality, there is neither a logical nor a causal

[1] Both here and in what follows, the word 'act' is short for 'act or omission to act'.

[2] Especially not the meaning that the law consists of commands.

[3] Lundstedt was the first person to point out (and make a big thing of) this seeming circle, cf. Ross, *Virkelighed og Gyldighed i Retslæren* [Reality and Validity in Jurisprudence] (1934), 348, 352 and 366, with references; as well as § 50 and note 3 above.

connection between unlawfulness and sanction. They are solely connected by virtue of a legal rule, and each of the above-mentioned sentences (as has been [306] made clear by the parentheses) expresses this connection alone, namely the fact that according to scientifically valid law, certain acts indicated in primary partial norms shall be succeeded by reprimanding sanctions. Hence, also the concept of unlawfulness can be eliminated by contraction. The two sentences:

1. *Certain acts (determined in primary norms) are called unlawful.*
2. *When an act is called unlawful, it shall incur a reprimanding sanction.*

do not say anything except that

3. *Certain acts (determined in primary norms) shall incur a reprimanding sanction.*

Now, is there any room left for a '*doctrine of unlawfulness*'? The term 'unlawful act' (or 'unlawfulness' as an act's property of being unlawful) is purely formally defined with reference to scientifically valid norms. The value of the concept lies in drawing a distinction within the set of conditioning human acts, corresponding to the distinction between reprimanding and non-reprimanding sanctions in the area of legal consequences. This distinction is important, and of course it is possible to develop a doctrine of unlawfulness where the distinction is made the subject of more detailed studies and considerations. What kind of sanctions can be applied as reprimanding and non-reprimanding sanctions, respectively? Given the circumstances, how does one know what kind of sanction it is? How is it 'made known' to a person ordered to pay damages, whether or not the order is an expression of disapproval? These and similar questions can be asked and dealt with in a way that is meaningful.

However, this type of question was not addressed by what has hitherto been called 'the doctrine of unlawfulness'. This doctrine—or so one believed—was a doctrine purporting to answer, or at least to assist in answering, the following question: what acts (determined according to their content) are unlawful acts in the above-defined (formal) sense?[4]

Since it is obviously assumed that all impermissible (unlawful, prohibited) acts must have a substantive element or characteristic in common, one asks what this [307] *common substantive characteristic* of an unlawful act—which, thus, is also a common objective condition for all reprimanding law enforcement—consists in.

Without always being aware of it, the doctrine of unlawfulness, as commonly understood, operates with a substantive concept of unlawfulness that can be defined in the following way. *Unlawfulness in the substantive sense* is a content-related

[4] 'By saying that an unlawful act is an act that contradicts the law and, consequently, is opposed by the law, one does not give any real characterization whatsoever of such an act. For immediately afterwards, one will ask: Well—but what acts do contradict the law, what kind of acts are they, what is it that actually differentiates these acts from other acts?' Vinding Kruse in *TfR* 1915, 269.

property as part of a description of the objective character of the act, which all formally unlawful acts have in common. Or (identically): substantive unlawfulness is the common objective condition for a reprimanding sanction. In my view, one might add—at any rate, as seen from the original way of thinking—that substantive unlawfulness is the circumstance that 'legitimizes' or 'explains', according to certain views on the 'idea' or 'principle' of the law, that the act is prohibited by law.

Let us attempt now to free ourselves for a moment from the power of the ideas that have come down to us and easily may induce us to go on with problems and a terminology which no longer correspond to our own presuppositions. Does it not, on the face of it, seem highly improbable that such a problem and such a concept formation are at all plausible? Do we really dare to assume, with a mere grain of reasonableness, that all these different acts, counteracted by the legal order with reprimanding sanctions, should have anything in common in their objective description? What—one might ask—could be envisaged as the common denominator in the objective description of acts such as killing another person; omitting to pay one's debts; fraud; violating somebody else's copyright; jeopardizing the security of Parliament; misuse of power when carrying out an administrative act; performing competitive acts in defiance of good faith and fair dealing; excessively harassing one's neighbours with noise or stench; delivering defective goods when fulfilling a sales contract; rape; riding a bicycle after dark without a light; refusing your lodger access to the place he has rented, etc., etc.

On the face of it, the problem may seem hopeless, and at least one might expect that before posing such a problem, one would receive an account of the foundation which can make one believe that there really exists such an objective common denominator, namely, unlawfulness in the substantive sense.

An explanation of how we have been induced to think along these lines can probably be found in the following circumstances (to be examined in more detail later on). Originally, 'the doctrine of unlawfulness' dealt with certain interpretational problems in connection with the rules concerning liability for violation of the personal integrity. Owing to erroneous juridico-philosophical views originating in natural law, these rather common interpretational problems (no different from hundreds of others) were identified with a doctrine of the unlawfulness of the respective violations (in the substantive sense). All of a sudden the wheels were set in motion. A concept had been created, and one [308] believed to have touched upon an essential problem. Words beget more words, and the grinding mill was kept busy. Finally, Ussing turned to the problem of a 'general theory of unlawfulness' without, however, pointing at any result, but also without getting rid of the traditional concepts and problems.

In my opinion, the question: 'what acts, described substantively, are unlawful (in the formal sense, that is, prohibited by the legal order and, therefore, the subject of reprimanding sanctions)?', cannot be answered otherwise than by means of an exhaustive rendition of the whole legal order's rules in that respect.

The question of whether or not a given act is unlawful, is identical to the question of whether scientifically valid law contains a norm that prohibits the performance of this act and, consequently, imposes reprimanding sanctions in the case of a violation of the prohibition.

Simple as this may sound, the judicial decision—as we know only too well—may be rather problematic in practice. The law does not lie before us in a set of formulae, ready to be applied automatically. The administration of justice in its entirety amounts to an interpretation of rules which often only with great difficulty can be deduced from various sources, and in all administration of justice, a decisive role is played, actually or potentially, by evaluations, purposive considerations, ideology and other pragmatic factors (frequently without realizing their social and subjective contingency and using a natural law-coloured, objectivizing denotation, summarized as 'the nature of the matter'.)

Therefore, when deciding whether a given act, or a certain abstract type of act, is unlawful or not, we have arrived at the problems of the sources and the interpretation of the administration of justice, such as they present themselves in all their infinitely differentiated diversity. Naturally, unlawfulness does not present any *specific* problem of interpretation, and what can generally be said about the sources and their interpretation does not, of course, appertain to a 'doctrine of unlawfulness' but to the general theory about legal method.

However, it so happened that Goos noticed a special problem of interpretation and attributed particular importance to it. What he had in mind were the orders—either formulated as statutory law in the Criminal Code, or established by theory in tort doctrine—that prohibit the violation of other persons' external goods, things, and body by physical force; that is, the so-called violation of integrity. These orders are typically formulated as rules concerning causation, or as rules causing, or bringing about, a certain damage. Example: when the Criminal Code says 'to kill another person' (causing his death), or 'to bring about another person's death'.

It is obvious that a conditional interpretation based upon a general conflict of laws (§ 29 at note 4) must entail that such a rule will not be applied in many situations which, as such, fall within the scope of application of the rule according to its words.

To begin with, there are subjective conditions which refer to different mental [309]
states (attribution and accountability).

Then, there may be various objective circumstances which (under certain conditions) legitimize an otherwise impermissible act and consequently, like other reprimanding sanctions, foreclose both penalty and damages in accordance with culpability. These circumstances might properly be called the *special legitimations*, the *special bases of legitimacy*—or the *special circumstances which preclude the normal impermissibility of an action*. Irrespective of whether these circumstances are expressly stated in law, or are warranted by practice and a deep-rooted conception of law: the important thing is that the general rules must be read in light of these provisos. For reasons of formulation technique, they are not included in the formulation of each individual legal rule, but are kept separate and—if I may say so—kept in readiness, just like proofreading marks, to be fastened on to the general rules.

Usually the following items are mentioned.

1. Self-defence.
2. Necessity.
3. Legitimate law enforcement.
4. *Negotiorum gestio.*
5. Consent.

Whether to include more or fewer of these items is a matter of discretion, for usually they can only be applied under certain conditions, and only with respect to certain restrictive rules. With respect to manslaughter, for example, neither No. 2, nor No. 4, nor No. 5 can be used.

Goos discovered that with respect to violations of integrity, a further objective reservation according to the nature of the matter must be made. Not every causation can be considered as creating liability. It is not possible (as was formerly believed) to find a reasonable delimitation solely in the requirement of intention or negligence, if negligence is defined purely subjectively as an insight (or due insight). For since 'insight' may mean the insight that the respective act had properties which are stated as prohibitions in the objective description of the act, one does not arrive at any reasonable delimitation of liability along these lines, given that one lets the objective determination include acts with even the remotest possibility of causing harm.

On the basis of these considerations, Goos developed his theory that an act, in order to count as a foundation of liability, must have potential for damage or
[310] dangerousness which is not completely insignificant; and that, in this case, the act will nevertheless (according to circumstances) be regarded as justifiable (will be legitimate) in view of its utility and necessity in other respects. When judging the justifiability, one must consider first of all the general value of permitting

a certain behaviour, not the concrete usefulness of the individual act, and the judgment must to the greatest possible extent be based on the established, customary views on, how a good and reasonable man who is well acquainted with the areas of life in question, would act in the given situation. If there is no such custom, one must resort to a freer, discretionary weighing of the potential for harm and the utility value of the act.

This theory has no doubt a certain value, at any rate for a theoretical clarification of the relation between objective and subjective elements in the foundation of liability. In the field of criminal law, the theory can be understood as an interpretation, grounded in custom and free evaluations ('the nature of the matter'), which constitutes another conflicting reservation or special legitimation which briefly can be called a 'utility legitimation': irrespective of the fact that there is causation, the act nevertheless does not entail liability, provided that it can be considered legitimate in view of its utility as weighed against its dangerousness. In the law of torts, where there is no general rule for damages fixed by statute, the theory is part of the general rule of culpability, developed in both theory and practice. In both fields of law, the theory is tied to the shaping of the liability rule in connection with the causation of integrity violations.[5]

Still, it is incomprehensible how this particular reservation with reference to the usefulness of the act can be identified with a doctrine of the unlawfulness of the act, and how, in the 'dangerousness and indefensibility' of the act, one can see a genuine, substantial criterion of unlawfulness. 'Dangerousness–indefensibility' is not an independent description of a certain act, but only an abstract factor in defining more closely the description contained in other rules. Of course, not every act which is 'dangerous–indefensible' in relation to certain interests is an unlawful act—only those acts which fall under the prohibition rules of the law. Their content consists primarily in stating what effects must not be brought about, and not in the proviso regarding certain causes. Moreover, the utility legitimation is only one among several general reservations, and one might well ask why it should constitute the criterion of unlawfulness any more than the other reservations.

An explanation of how Goos could arrive at this strange confusion between a special reservation and an act's real, substantive character of unlawfulness must [311] be sought in his relapse into natural law ideas. If one assumes that rights, as such, exist independently of the legal order, and that the latter's task consists merely in delimiting and protecting them, then all law, according to its idea or nature, must consist in a weighing of considerations with regard to the freedom of action and of considerations with regard to the protection of rights.

[5] In my article 'Opgør med Retstridighedslæren' [Against the doctrine of unlawfulness], *TfR* 1951, 205 *et seq.*, especially 215 *et seq.*, I presented Goos's theory as an interpretation of the concept of causation. This was justly criticized by Henry Ussing, 'Til Retsstridighedsdebatten' [On the debate on unlawfulness], *TfR* 1952, 237–39, and the present account has been adjusted accordingly.

Accordingly, Goos puts forth his theory as being based upon 'a weighing of the reasonable demands of two opposing considerations: on the one hand, the demand of such freedom of action as is necessary for achieving the justified purpose of one's life's work; on the other, such a *protection of rights* as is a precondition for true legal certainty.[6]

If the view that the law, according to its nature, consists in delimiting the freedom of action vis-à-vis conflicting rights really is tenable, then it is only logical and natural to regard the law of freedom of action, expressed in the weighing of the consideration of the freedom of action and that of the protection of rights, as the fundamental expression of the command of law, and to consider the dangerousness and indefensibility of the act as determining its substantive unlawfulness. For 'dangerousness–indefensibility' is, then, precisely the common substantive property that characterizes all acts prohibited by the law.

But the assumed conception of the essence of law is fundamentally wrong, of course. Nowadays, there surely is no need to argue for it in more detail. What is more, it even contradicts Goos's own premises. The problem of what rights or benefits are protected through the legal rules concerning freedom of action is referred, by Goos, to legislation.[7] But in legislation, rights are defined—according to Goos himself—exactly as the counterpart to others' duties—and duty implies restricting the freedom of action.[8] Thus, the right as such already implies restricted freedom of action, and consequently the principle of the limits to the freedom of action cannot be determined through considerations of rights protection. Goos overlooks that the problem he deals with under the name of 'the problem of unlawfulness', or 'the problem of freedom of action', cannot be the problem in its entirety but, rather, merely an abstract, partial aspect of that which contains a more detailed definition of the rules of action, presupposed as given.

In principle, it does not make any difference if we, instead of presupposed rights, speak of benefits or interests, and if we conceive of all law as an expression of the weighing of conflicting interests. For the fact is that it is justified
[312] interest alone that is considered for this weighing; for detailed information on this issue, cf. the thorough analysis and criticism I have put forward earlier.[9,10]

6 C. Goos, *Den danske Strafferet II. Den danske Strafferets almindelige Del* [Danish Penal Law II. General Part] (1878), 190 cf. 165, 167, 173; emphasis added. Almost identical statements can be found in his work *Almindelig Retslære I* [General Study of Law I] (1885), 336–37 and 339.

7 *Op. cit.*, 79–80.

8 C. Goos, *Forelæsninger over den almindelige Retslære* [Lectures on the General Study of Law] I, 152.

9 *Virkelighed og Gyldighed i Retslæren* [Reality and Validity in Jurisprudence] (1934), 371; *Kritik der sogenannten praktischen Erkenntnis* [Critique of So-called Practical Knowledge] (1933), 366 *et seq.*

10 By way of modifying the above, it should be noted that one may call into doubt, and with some justice, whether Goos really harboured the views ascribed to him here. Perhaps they rather represent a somewhat one-sided interpretation of certain aspects of his thought. An indication for this interpretation can be found in his

Perhaps one might now think that whatever Goos called his theory is surely of minor importance, as long as the theory itself works. This is not the case, however. The basically erroneous view that one can discover substantive aspects in the objective description of a formally unlawful act (which is the real reason why the act is forbidden) as well as the common objective condition for all law enforcement (reprimanding sanction) has naturally enough proved to be well suited to put our ideas on the wrong track by leading to untenable theories and posing unhelpful problems.

(a) Once the idea has arisen that the dangerousness of the act (compared with its utility) is an expression of its basic, substantive unlawfulness, it is quite understandable that it occurs to us that other specific rules on circumstances which preclude an act's usual unlawfulness are superfluous, because, in principle, they must revert to the general, fundamental condition for unlawfulness. And it was precisely at this point that Goos and his successors, especially Torp, ascribed scientific importance to the Nordic doctrine: this doctrine is capable of providing an elegant, monistic solution to the problems of reservation and of thus prevailing over the non-systematic, *ad hoc* treatment of these problems by German and older Nordic doctrine. For further details, I refer to my book *Reality and Validity in Jurisprudence*, at pp. 358–65. For the present, I content myself with the remark that nowadays, it is generally recognized this was a delusion, and that especially [313] Torp's attempt to generalize away the rule of necessity was likely to betray us into extremely unfortunate practical tendencies.

(b) Goos put forward his theory only with reference to acts violating the integrity of external legal benefits. Of course this has to do with the fact that it is mainly in this field that the concept of causation plays a part concerning the rules of the law. However, one has difficulties in realizing that one occupies oneself with a problem of interpretation that is specific for this field;[11] and if one believes in defining a fundamental concept concerning

defining 'breach of law' as an impairment of a benefit protected by the law through an unlawful act. This is a superfluous reiteration. If there is an impairment of a benefit which is protected by the law in relation to the performed act, then this means *eo ipso* that the act is unlawful. For what else can legal protection mean, but that an act which impinges on a benefit contradicts the law and is, therefore, the reason for liability? Conversely, if we take for granted that an act is unlawful in relation to the benefit, then this implies *eo ipso* that the benefit is protected against the act. This doubling is a clear sign that Goos has regarded the rules on unlawfulness (limitation of the freedom of action) as rules which are independent vis-à-vis previously granted benefits or rights. On the other hand, there are also statements (for example, in Goos's book *Forelæsninger over den almindelige Retslære* [Lectures on the General Study of Law] I (1885), 327, para 1) which indicate that Goos has conceived of the doctrine of unlawfulness merely as a more detailed specification of the restriction of the freedom of action, already indicated by recognizing the benefit as a legal benefit or a right. However, the crucial thing is not what Goos may have meant, or whether it is possible to establish that with any certainty. The crucial thing is that the interpretation given here is the one that is implied in the more recent attempt to generalize the doctrine here towards a general doctrine of substantive unlawfulness.

[11] In the case of tort law: a specific factor in the shaping of the principle of culpability.

substantive unlawfulness, then it must be quite natural to extend the theory so as to apply it to all fields of law.[12] And this is what happened. Jul. Lassen as well as Torp and Stang present their theory of (substantive) unlawfulness as a general chapter which relates to all formally unlawful acts.[13] However, none of them seems even to have considered how the theory might be applied outside the field of integrity violations.

It was Ussing who first addressed the problem of a 'general doctrine of unlawfulness'. Bound by traditional views, he defines 'the unlawful' (in the substantive sense) as the condition (common to all law enforcement) concerning human behaviour to which a legal reaction (of a reprimanding nature)[14] is related. This definition seems to presuppose, *qua* postulate, that there is such a condition that is common to all law enforcement. More probably, the definition is meant to state the problem: if we are able to set up a substantive concept of unlawfulness, then it must have such a content; our task is to examine whether such a common condition can be shown to exist. The outcome of Ussing's investigations seems to be that this is not the case.[15] From that, however, the author has not drawn the conclusion that it is impossible to establish a (general, substantive) concept of unlawfulness.[16]

[314] However, the idea of generalizing the 'doctrine of unlawfulness' is meaningless from the very outset, because this doctrine is actually not a doctrine of unlawfulness (as a substantive hallmark of forbidden acts): rather, it merely concerns a special reservation limiting the liability for causation. Since the acts which are

[12] Presumably, Goos himself did not have the least intention to undertake such a generalization and set up a general concept of substantive unlawfulness. In his work *Forelæsninger over den almindelige Retslære* [Lectures on the General Study of Law] II (1892), 512, he says the following: 'It is mentioned in the doctrine on the various legal relationships, what kind of acts that are unlawful in relation to the various benefits.' One must bear in mind, however, that the general study of law was an account of legal relationships from the perspective of 'the nature of the matter'. It may be assumed that Goos, in an account of positive law, would similarly have referred to legislation; that is to say, he would, in a general way, have answered the question purely formally.

[13] For details, see Ussing, 'Retsstridighed' [Unlawfulness]. In *Festskrift udgivet af Københavns Universitet* [Tribute Published by the University of Copenhagen] (1949), 30.

[14] *Op. cit.*, 38.

[15] *Op. cit.*, 50, 53, 55, 99.

[16] On the issue of Ussings's doctrine of unlawfulness, see my critique in the article 'Opgør med retstridighedslæren' [Against the doctrine of unlawfulness], *TfR* 1951, 205 *et seq.*, and Ussing's reply in 'Til Retsstridighedsdebatten' [On the debate on unlawfulness], *TfR* 1952, 225 *et seq.*

Also Knud Illum ('Nogle korte bemærkninger om begrebet retstridighed' [Some brief remarks on the concept of unlawfulness], *Juristen*, 1951, 177 *et seq.*) has addressed criticism to Ussing which, in its essence, is in line with my own views. With respect to a particular point, however, Illum's criticism seems to me to be misplaced. The fact is that it is mainly based upon the idea that the inapplicability of the substantive concept of unlawfulness is made good, if it can be shown that one (disapproving) sanction—punishment, for example—can be applied under certain conditions where another sanction—damages, for example—cannot be applied. For this shows, according to Illum, that there is no common fundamental condition for all reprimanding sanctions which are postulated in the concept of substantive unlawfulness (*op. cit.*, 178, 181, 182).—This must be a misunderstanding. A certain act is disapproved of by the legal order and is, thus, formally unlawful, provided that it is counteracted by some sort of reprimanding sanction; by damages, for example—but not by punishment. The presupposed common condition must, therefore, mean a common condition for disapproval *by means of one form of sanction or another*. To put it more precisely: unlawfulness means the common *necessary*—not the common *sufficient*—condition for sanction.

repressively counteracted by the legal order (prohibited and formally unlawful acts) *outside the realm of integrity violations* are typically defined, not as certain causations, but as *conduct violations*—this expression formed by analogy with the expression conduct crime—*the so-called doctrine of unlawfulness (doctrine of the reservation of the law) cannot possibly, according to its content, be applied to, or adjusted to, those other fields.*

This is exaggerating, of course. For naturally, the concept of causation is also applied outside the realm of integrity violations. Yet, arguments concerning the natural scope of life—arguments which are typical for the 'doctrine of unlawfulness'—usually do not fit in here. Take the Criminal Code prohibition of causing a rebellion (§ 111) or causing a riot or unruly gathering (§ 133), for example. You will notice immediately that there is no room for customary rules concerning a certain freedom irrespective of any possibility of danger, or for weighing the possibility of danger of a certain behaviour against the latter's general usefulness. We can also say that the same free, pragmatic interpretive considerations do not apply here.

The main point, however, is that in all those situations where the formally unlawful is by no means defined as a certain causation, the current 'doctrine of unlawfulness' does not apply—even if in many situations interpretive problems will of course also arise here, and a general rule will be restricted by virtue of a reasonable evaluation of the purpose of the rule as weighed against other societal considerations. But it is both meaningless and purposeless to attach the label 'doctrine of unlawfulness' to all restrictive interpretations based upon societal evaluations. Their diversity and heterogeneity match those of the rules and the areas of life they are concerned with, as well as the evaluations that are underpinning them. Just look, for example, at the formally unlawful act of not paying one's debts according to the obligations undertaken. What can be the meaning of speaking, within this context, of dangerousness and indefensibility? And what could be the meaning of enquiring into the substantive criterion for [315]
the formal unlawfulness of such an act? Or, let us look at the rules of criminal law. One can see that by far most of them concern conduct crimes where no causation problems occur. Many of them have the character of a crime of danger, capturing acts which expose external legal benefits to considerable danger—for example, by causing a general shortage of drinking water; or by adding hazardous substances to water tanks, water mains, or streams (§ 186); or by adding poison to substances intended for sale or widespread use (§ 187); or by exposing, through sexual intercourse, another person to infection with a venereal disease (§ 256) etc., etc. In these situations, the act is by definition so dangerous that a reservation in connection with a utility legitimation does not come into play. As regards breaches of *preventive laws*, the danger may be more remote, but attention to public order entails nonetheless that there cannot be a discussion about the usefulness and necessity of the act, or about its being defensible

according to 'the rule of life'. Maybe the principle of necessity in individual situations can legitimize a breach of the traffic regulations, but apart from that, there can be no question as to the usefulness and necessity of riding without a bicycle light after dark. In other situations, the act is not forbidden as dangerous—that is, dangerous because it can cause undesired effects—but simply because the act *in itself is considered undesirable*. Bigamy, incest, theft, rape, ignoring the regulations on opening hours, selling coupons, appearing in uniform, exceeding the maximum price, giving false statements before the court, and breaching a thousand other laws and regulations: these are not dangerous acts in the sense that they are forbidden because they are able to cause certain effects distinct from themselves. They are forbidden as being undesirable in themselves.[17] They are conduct crimes, and any weighing of the danger against utility is useless.

It cannot possibly be my task to go over all types of unlawful acts outside the realm of integrity violations, just in order to show that the problem of 'the doctrine of unlawfulness' does not apply to them. It must suffice to have shown by means of the examples and considerations that have been adduced, that this is the case to a very great extent, and that, on the face of it, it is thus less than reasonable to inquire into the possibility of a general 'doctrine of unlawfulness'.

[316] By saying so, I do not mean, of course, that there cannot be situations in which legal rules give rise to problems of interpretation which are at any rate congenial to those treated by the doctrine of unlawfulness. Regardless of the fact that a forbidden act is described without reference to any causation, it is quite conceivable that the legislator was not able to formulate the limit of the freedom of action in the way it must be drawn when allowances are made for all societal considerations—irrespective of whether he himself has been clear about the deficiency of the formulation and given the judge a hint that, for certain reasons, there is occasion for a restrictive interpretation; or whether the judge (this not being the case) has felt the necessity of such an interpretation all the same. This applies to defamation, for example. Acts suited to offend another person's honour are usually forbidden, irrespective of any proof that such an offence has, in fact, occurred. On the other hand, considerations concerning the scope for freedom of expression and criticism suggest that not all such acts should be forbidden. At this point, there arises a problem of interpretation, intimated in § 269 of the Criminal Code and concerning the rules on proof of the truth and

[17] This should not be misunderstood. A prohibition against such acts is usually based upon an evaluation of the effects that would generally arise if the acts in question were permitted. Thus, it is, here, a question of the effects of whether or not a certain prohibition rule exists, and this is quite another thing than the effects of an individual act. The prohibition on extending opening hours beyond a certain time, for example, is based upon certain social considerations as to the effects on working hours etc. this measure would have, if such a freedom existed within this area. However, this is quite another thing than prohibiting a certain act because of its harmful consequences.

the justified safeguarding of a manifest general interest, or of one's own, or others', interest. In the course of such an interpretation, customary points of view and discretionary weighing of the general value of a certain behaviour play a role similar to that in the 'doctrine of unlawfulness'. However, the situations mentioned here differ from integrity violations in so far as no question arises as to any gradation of the dangerousness of the act, or its ability to cause harm. The act is either insulting or it is not insulting. If it is insulting, then the only question is whether it can still be justified out of considerations concerning the interests of freedom of expression.

Similar problems also arise in connection with fraud and other kinds of deceit. Obviously, taking advantage of someone else's mistake cannot always be considered forbidden. To a great extent, competition amounts to making use of specific information, and it is not quite easy to draw the line between ignorance and mistake. Also here one must draw a line which is indicated, by the law, by speaking of 'unlawful exploitation'. When the word 'unlawful' is used by the law in these and similar cases, its only function is to remind the judge that the rule shall not be strictly enforced, *viz.*, enforced according to its wording, but be limited in view of conflicting considerations based upon custom and free evaluations. A reservation concerning unlawfulness is the same as declaring that the act shall be performed in such a way, or under such conditions, that it must be considered unacceptable even if those considerations are taken into account which suggest a certain freedom.

It is, of course, conceivable that a free creation of law based upon societal evaluations will entail that a certain course of action is considered forbidden, irrespective of the fact that it has been pursued within an area in which freedom of action is normally supposed to reign. By way of example, one usually adduces the rules governing the limits for boycott and similar interferences with the freedom of trade, introduced *via* practice. In these situations the terminology [317]
of unlawfulness is also frequently used. But these matters are so different from integrity violations—especially 'the rule of life', that is, custom, is unimportant here, exactly because it is about incorporating new, normative patterns—that the only real similarity with the 'doctrine of unlawfulness' proper seems to consist in the fact that it is about a creation of law based upon free societal evaluations.

In my view, the result of these considerations which throw a sidelight on various areas of the law can be expressed in the following way. The erroneous identification of a specific problem of *caveat* which announces itself when limiting the responsibility for integrity violations (the problem of causation) with a basic description of a substantive criterion of formal unlawfulness, has misled us into believing that one can generalize 'the doctrine of unlawfulness' and posing the (otherwise reasonable) question, what is the common substantive characteristic of all formally unlawful acts. However, such a generalization or such a question is unreasonable from the start. There is no substantive characteristic, common to all formally unlawful acts; and those problems of *caveat* which constitute the real and tenable content of the 'doctrine of unlawfulness', are specific for integrity violations. The word 'unlawful' is sometimes used by the legislator in order to intimate that a rule should be interpreted with certain restrictions; sometimes it is used in legal practice to 'justify' a free creation of law, either in order to restrict a generally worded prohibition rule, or to set up a prohibition rule within a field where formerly freedom of action was supposed to reign. One may add here that this use of the word is likely to conceal a free creation of law: by using this artificial word, incomprehensible to most people,* one makes it look as if one operated with a previously formulated legal rule.

In order to summarize, specify, and supplement the above, let me point out the following.

(a) Until now, legal theory has operated more or less consciously with two different concepts of unlawfulness, a formal concept and a substantive concept. Unlawfulness in the formal sense can be defined in the following way: an act is called unlawful, if the carrying out of this act would contradict a primary, duty-justifying norm; or if its carrying out, pursuant to a secondary norm, would be followed by a reprimanding sanction. The concept has no semantic reference. Its value consists exclusively in emphasizing the distinction between reprimanding and non-reprimanding sanctions and in giving expression to the ethical-legal, evaluative attitude connected with it.

(b) Should we wish to talk about a doctrine of unlawfulness whose subject is unlawfulness in the formal sense, then this must be identical with a doctrine of the difference between reprimanding and non-reprimanding sanctions and their functions in the law working in real life.

[318] (c) Unlawfulness in the substantive sense can be defined as a content-related property—as a component of the description of the objective nature of the act which is shared by all formally unlawful acts; or as a common objective condition for reprimanding sanctions. The concept of unlawfulness is without any subject, because such a common property or condition cannot be proven.

(d) Consequently, it is impossible to provide any doctrine of unlawfulness in the sense of a doctrine of substantive unlawfulness.

(e) What goes under the label of 'Nordic doctrine of unlawfulness' is, in reality, only a way of dealing with certain questions of *caveat* which arise in

* Translator's note: The Danish word for 'unlawful' [retsstridig] is comparatively more technical than its English counterpart.

delimiting the basis of liability, pursuant to rules about the causing of physical harm to persons and things (integrity violations).

(f) We do not deny that, except for its misleading name, this theory has a certain value. Furthermore (and please note the following carefully!) it has not been my task here to enter more closely into the content and formulation of the doctrine and to adopt a critical stance towards it. On this issue, I refer the reader to my earlier account in *Reality and Validity in Jurisprudence*, especially at pp. 373–76, with the proviso that, to a certain degree, I may there have overexposed the tendency towards a concrete weighing of interests. Ussing's work 'Unlawfulness' (already mentioned several times) contains without doubt a number of valuable contributions to a tenable shaping of the 'doctrine of unlawfulness' in the traditional sense.

(g) On the other hand, we maintain that the fundamental misinterpretation of the nature of the 'doctrine of unlawfulness' has had unfortunate effects in two respects. In the first place, it prompts us to make an attempt at generalizing away the other, specific *caveats* for circumstances which exclude the normal impermissibility of an act. Then, it prompts us to make an attempt at generalizing the 'doctrine of unlawfulness' so as to include legal relationships outside the realm of integrity violations, where, however, the same problems of *caveat* usually do not arise. A 'general doctrine of unlawfulness' is not possible.

(h) As far as the concept of 'unlawful' is actually used in legislation and legal practice, it merely indicates that a free creation of law, based upon discretion, is appropriate or has taken place.

(i) In the present account, I did not enter more closely into a juridico-philosophical idea that has played an important part in history, as the driving force behind the creation of the concept of unlawfulness. I am thinking of the role played by the concept in order to 'explain' or 'legitimize' the nature of law enforcement as 'law', that is, as a valid use of force, as distinct from brute force. Since law enforcement is considered justified in the case of a previous violation of the law, it is conceived as a manifestation of the invisible powers of the law, or as a realization of a moral world order; and thus, unlawfulness is seen as the fundamental, morally necessary condition for all law enforcement. In this way, one rids oneself of any responsibility. In different variations, this metaphysics of validity has played a decisive role in con- [319]
nection with the rise and further development of the doctrine of unlawfulness. On this issue, I refer the reader to my account in *Virkelighed og Gyldighed i Retslæren* [Reality and Validity in Jurisprudence].[18]

[18] At p. 322 *et seq.*, 331 *et seq.*, 338, 342, 366 *et seq.*

[320] CHAPTER X

Some Features of the History of Natural Law

§ 55. Greek Popular Belief: Homer and Hesiod

It is not my intention to write a history of natural law.[1] This survey merely purports to underline a few main features of the historical evolution of natural law, in order to promote understanding of what actually characterizes natural law thinking as we know it today. From this standpoint, it may possibly look like excessive thoroughness to begin at the beginning, that is, with primitive Greek popular belief circa 700 BC. The explanation is that the contrast between natural law philosophy and a realistic theory of law on a sociological basis cannot be regarded as a contrast between different scientific theories: in reality, it expresses a much more radical contrast, namely, a contrast between a magical-religious-metaphysical approach to life and its problems and a scientific one. To understand this, it is necessary to go back to the beginnings of civilization, to
[321] show how natural law theory in all its variations has essentially remained the same. Its characteristic features are certain modes of thought and expression which in all its phases—magical, religious, and philosophico-metaphysical—are radically different from scientific ones. There is an unbroken line from the magical-animistic belief of primitive man, over dogmatic theology to the great philosophico-metaphysical systems. The principal idea behind all manifestations of this line of thought is a fear of existence and its powers, and the impulse to seek refuge and safety in something absolute; that is to say, in something that is

[1] [General remark on Chapter X]: For a history of natural law as seen from an orthodox Catholic point of view, see the work of the Thomist Henri Rommen, *Le droit naturel* [Natural Law] (1945). See also W. Friedmann, *Legal Theory* (2nd edn, 1949), 15 *et seq.* and Julius Stone, *The Province and Function of Law* (1946/50), 209 *et seq.* It is worth mentioning that the two last-named books contain highly interesting information about the impact of natural law on legal practice in England and the USA. [In this section and the next, we have used the same English translations of ancient Greek works as used by Ross in his 1958 publication of *On Law and Justice.*] [General remark on § 55:] The account given in this section is mainly based upon C. W. Westrup, *Rettens opståen* [The Origin of Law] (1940); cf. by the same author: *Introduction to Early Roman Law* VII, 1 (1939); Hartvig Frisch, *Magt og Ret i Oldtiden, Dike 1: fra Homer til perserkrigene* (1944); translated into English 1949: Hartvig Frisch, *Might and Right in Antiquity, 'Dike' I: From Homer to the Persian Wars*, transl. by C. C. Martindale (1949); another English publication appeared in 1976 (publisher: Ayer Co. Pub.).

above all vicissitudes of life and all transitoriness and can offer peace and security. Peace and security, that is, not only vis-à-vis the external powers of existence—the uncertainty of life, poverty, and death—but also vis-à-vis fear and doubt within yourself, vis-à-vis the dread of taking responsibility for one's own actions. Therefore, the nature of the absolute is both cosmic and moral—it is both a world order and a moral law.[2]

Such a view of life is rather infantile. The history of science is the history of the liberation of the human spirit from these bonds of fear. The process has not yet finished, however. While the scientific view of life seems to have triumphed with regard to our view of nature, we are still deeply immersed in persisting infantilism with regard to social, moral, and legal issues. The philosophy of natural law is a consequence of this infantilism.

We are able to study the contrast we are speaking of in an eminently instructive way, namely, by tracing the development of Greek thought, from the primitive Greek popular belief as we find it in the work of Homer and Hesiod, down to the great philosophical systems of Plato and Aristotle. Within a span of about 300 years, the seeds of all that would unfold later in more differentiated forms were already germinating. We can observe the development from a primitive magical-mythical conception of law towards a budding scientific and humanistic attitude, most notably manifested within the circle of the Sophists during the years of Athens' greatness in the fifth century BC, during the period between the Persian Wars (490 BC and 480–79 BC) and the end of the Peloponnesian War (404 BC). It is not totally insignificant that this development paralleled that of a primitive clan community towards democracy. But just as political freedom was unable to assert itself, freedom of thought likewise succumbed. The philosophical systems of Plato and Aristotle signalled a fatal reaction. In these two men all forces united to reinforce the diminishing belief in the absolute, in a cosmic and moral world order. Primitive magic and religion were replaced by metaphysical speculation, but the spirit remained the same. And it was exactly this spirit that would continue to characterize subsequent developments for a long time to come. Without difficulty, Christian scholasticism (St. Thomas Aquinas) was able to interpolate a new religious doctrine into Aristotle's [322]
system. To this day, Thomism pervades all Catholic legal philosophy. And even though natural law was de-Christianized in the Protestant world and assumed the form of a rationalist-philosophical metaphysics, it nevertheless remained essentially the same, namely, a belief in the eternal, in validity. We shall now proceed to throw light on the development that has been sketched in very broad lines here.

[2] On philosophy as a substitute for religion, see Victor Kraft, *Einführung in die Philosophie* [Introduction to Philosophy] (1950), 16 *et seq.*

The Ancient Greek, *Homeric* community (eighth century BC) can be assumed to have presented the usual picture of a primitive agricultural people in its tribal stage.[3] The population was divided into a number of small tribes, each of them under its own chieftain or king. The king's 'reign' was not far-reaching, however. His function was mostly restricted to the task of a judge in civil matters and that of a war leader. Furthermore, tribal life was strictly regulated by tradition and custom, embodied in taboos. The ideas of law were of a magical-religious nature, as can be found in other primitive people. The people were ruled by the gods, led by Zeus, but the gods themselves were subject to the power of fate. This cosmic power, which gives to everything its rightful lot, governs nature and humans alike and is in both instances maintained through the punishment of fate. The idea of the laws of nature in the modern sense did not yet exist. Necessity is not causality but, rather, a fate-necessity determined by a powerful will, by guilt, and by punishment. It is said of the sun that he will not overstep his measures; but if he does, the Erinnyes (the goddesses of fate)—the handmaids of Justice—will know how to find him.[4]

Therefore, the nature of law and justice is not a moral one, as we understand 'moral'.[5] A just judgment is simply a judgment which, in conformity with the will of the gods and of fate, allots to everyone his rightful portion. A wise and just king is he who receives divine revelations from Zeus (*themistes*) and takes them as a basis for his decision (*dike*). That is why king Minos of Crete visited Zeus secretly every ninth year.[6] Justice in this sense is a prerequisite of the people's well-being and prosperity. Insubordination vis-à-vis the cosmic order is as usual subject to punishment by the gods and by fate. Zeus is the guardian of the law. His daughter Dike sits at her father's side and tells him of the people's transgressions, which the almighty Zeus then punishes. 'For upon the bounteous earth Zeus has thrice ten thousand spirits, watchers of mortal men, and these keep watch on judgments and deeds of wrong as they roam, clothed in mist, all over the earth.'[7] Through this heavenly army Zeus apportions good fortune and misfortune to the just and unjust. Hesiod (circa seventh [323] century BC) depicts the golden fruit that awaits the people whose king keeps the law of the gods, as well as the disasters that will befall the people if their king recklessly lets himself be enticed to set up violence and arbitrariness against the will of the gods.

[3] Cf. Hartvig Frisch (1944), *op.cit.*, 40 *et seq.*

[4] Heraclitus, Fragment 94, in Hermann Diels, *Die Fragmente der Vorsokratiker: griechisch und deutsch* [Fragments of the Pre-Socratics: Greek and German], 5th edn. (1934–1937).

[5] Cf. C. W. Westrup, *Rettens Opstaaen* [The Origin of Law] (1940), 94.

[6] *Op. cit.*, 81 and 105 *et seq.*

[7] Hesiod, as cited in Hartvig Frisch (1944), *op.cit.* 108; the English translation here is Hugh G. Evelyn-White's, used in the 1958 publication of Alf Ross, *On Law and Justice,* at 229–30 [Hesiod in *Works and Days*, transl. by Hugh G. Evelyn-White in *Hesiod, The Homeric Hymns and Homerica* (1914), at 21].

> *But they who give straight judgments to strangers and to the men of the land, and go not aside from what is just, their city flourishes, and the people prosper in it: Peace, the nurse of children, is abroad in their land, and all-seeing Zeus never decrees cruel war against them. Neither famine nor disaster ever haunt men who do true justice; but light-heartedly they tend the fields which are all their care. The earth bears them victual in plenty, and on the mountains the oak bears acorns upon the top and bees in the midst. Their woolly sheep are laden with fleeces; their women bear children like their parents. They flourish continually with good things, and do not travel on ships, for the grain-giving earth bears them fruit.*
>
> *But for those who practise violence and cruel deeds far-seeing Zeus, the son of Kronos, ordains a punishment. Often even a whole city suffers for a bad man who sins and devises presumptuous deeds, and the son of Kronos lays great troubles upon the people, famine and plague together, so that the men perish away, and their women do not bear children, and their houses become few, through the contriving of Olympian Zeus. And again, at another time, the son of Kronos either destroys their wide army, or their walls, or else makes an end of their ships on the sea.*[8]

This description is merely another illustration of the fact, otherwise well known from the history of religion and the study of culture, that the power of the chieftain in primitive communities originates in magic.[9] The chieftain's task is to ensure, by ritual magic (especially songs, dances, and sacrifices), that it will rain, that the earth will bear fruit, and that the animals will thrive.[10] If the spells do not work and the tribe is afflicted by widespread crop failure, drought, or other disasters, the king is thought to have lost his power and is put to death, to be replaced with another and better one. In the Homeric-Hesiodic world, however, this pattern has undergone the refinement that the magical force which conditions the well-being of the tribe is no longer conceived of as tied to simple magical rituals but, rather, to the king's administration of his judicial power. It is not so much by imploring the gods, but by obeying their revealed will, by realizing the cosmic law, that the king brings blessings to his people. Stripped of metaphysical ideas, this simply signals a belief in the king's task to pronounce judgment in accordance with established custom and usage, and [324] that the prosperity and well-being of the tribe depends on respect for tradition and the established order.

[8] Hesiod, in *Værker og dage* [Works and Days], cited in Hartvig Frisch (1944), *op. cit.*, 107; the English translation here is Hugh G. Evelyn-White's, used in the 1958 publication of Alf Ross, *On Law and Justice*, at 230 [Hesiod in *Works and Days*, transl. by Hugh G. Evelyn-White in *Hesiod, The Homeric Hymns and Homerica* (1914) at 19–21].

[9] See Westrup, *op. cit.*, 68 *et seq.*

[10] Ruth Benedict, *Patterns of Culture* (1946), gives (at 54 *et seq.* and 131 *et seq.*) a highly interesting description of rain magic and agricultural magic among present-day primitive peoples.

It is understandable that proclaiming the laws of fate, punishing the unjust, would acquire a particularly pathetic sound, with a tone of resentment and a clamour for rebellion on the part of the oppressed, at a time when the old established forms of the tribal community were beginning to disintegrate, together with social conflicts and upheavals through which new classes rose to power. Signs of such a disintegration were beginning to be seen during the period between Homer and Hesiod. The Homeric kingdom with its patriarchal idyll had been superseded by an aristocracy of great landowners, who fought for supremacy between themselves and strove to subject the free peasants. The respect for inherited traditions—for justice in the Homeric sense—was on the wane, whereas violence, the law of the jungle, and perjury were the order of the day. Also, there is a recognizable difference between the message of Homer, the court minstrel, and Hesiod, the Boeotian farmer. It seems that for the former, Zeus is more of a protecting and defending preserver of a harmonious order, whereas for Hesiod—filled with indignation and bitterness towards the wickedness of the time—Zeus has become the great criminal judge over the mighty and unjust. While Homer represents the point of view of the ruling class, Hesiod reflects the distrust and indignation of the peasant who, merely intent on living in peace, is witness to the bold arrogance with which the mighty are struggling for power and displaying a total lack of respect for the traditional order of things.

The same pessimism paired with the confidence that sooner or later, punishment will fall on the haughty, we find again in Solon (circa 600 BC). Far too often it seems as if the presumptuous escape punishment. Therefore, Solon stresses the point that Zeus is not like mortal men, who lose their temper over little things. But nothing escapes his watchful eye forever. 'One man payeth his penalty early, another late. If the guilty man himself escape and the fate of the gods come not upon him, it cometh full surely in aftertime: the innocent pay for his offence—his children or his children's children in later generations.'[11]

There were further political upheavals during the period between Solon and Heraclitus (circa 500 BC), that is, in the sixth century BC. Urban growth and the development of a new economy was followed by the rise of a middle class which attempted to divest the aristocracy of their ancient privileges. This period of transition from aristocracy to democracy signals the reign of the tyrants, arisen from the need for a strong government to combat the land-owning nobility—thus, a situation where several things remind us of the period of absolutism, as a bridge in the transition from aristocracy to democracy here in Denmark.

[11] Cited in Hartvig Frisch (1944), *op.cit.*, 194; the English translation here is Ivan M. Linforth's, used in the 1958 publication of Alf Ross, *On Law and Justice*, at 232 [Ivan M. Linforth, *Solon the Athenian* (1919), at 165].

Presumably, it is personal experience of the political ups and downs of the time [325] that is reflected in Heraclitus's discovering the law of change. Until then, philosophers had tried to understand the world as a collection of things, and had inquired into its unchanging elements. The *leitmotif* of Heraclitus's philosophy is that everything is in a constant state of flux. The world is a continuous process of events, not a collection of things. Everything is flowing. 'You cannot step twice into the same river.' At the same time, however, everything—nature as well as man—is subject to a world order created by neither gods nor men, but always was, is, and will be eternally living fire, inflamed according to measure and extinguished according to measure. The quotation above—namely, that the sun will not overstep his measures—goes back to Heraclitus. This universal law is, at the same time, the law of justice, and all human laws are nourished by the one divine law.[12] Thereby, the *motif* of natural law has for the first time been expressed in philosophical terms. Human laws are more than sheer arbitrariness. They are an emanation from a universal law, and are 'nourished' by the very force of destiny that holds sway over all that exists. This is an aristocratic-conservative philosophy of natural law which, at a time when everything handed down through the ages threatened to disintegrate, seeks solace in a new philosophical formulation of the old belief in the ties between human laws and the forces that rule the world.

[12] Cf. Hartvig Frisch (1944) *op.cit.*, 226 *et seq.*

§ 56. The Sophists

In the fifth century BC, during the period between the Persian Wars (490 BC and 480–79 BC) and the defeat of Athens in the Peloponnesian War (404 BC), the Hellenic culture reached its zenith, whilst at the same time democracy had come to prevail in most city-states. This achievement—only a generation or two removed from the primitive magical-animistic ideas still adhered to by Heraclitus—has at all times aroused people's astonishment and admiration. In the fields of art, literature, science, and philosophy, this small-numbered people produced works which were to set an inimitable standard for a long time to come. I shall only dwell on a single, yet very important, aspect of this flourishing cultural era, namely, the emancipation from the traditional magical-religious view of life, the overcoming of the belief in the absolute and eternal in
[326] knowledge and morality, the foundation of a scientific outlook on life, based upon the relativity of all insight, and the development of a new morality along broad humanistic lines—all of which are intimately connected.

This change in thinking was brought about by a group of teachers who were called the *Sophists*,[1] and whose leading figure was Protagoras. In return for a fee, they instructed well-to-do citizens in the art of discourse and argumentation and such skills as were important to anyone wishing to speak in public assemblies or to conduct a trial in court. Indeed, they could almost be described as private professors of rhetoric. From time immemorial, they had had a reputation for immorality and intellectual dishonesty—something which still clings to the word 'sophistry' but is actually misleading: there is a perfectly reasonable explanation if we remember that our knowledge of the tenets of the Sophists is solely drawn from an account that was given by their bitterest opponents, especially Plato. At all times, those who attack absolutist moral doctrine have been branded, by their opponents, as being immoral and dangerous to civilization. It is easy to see that, in this respect, the Sophists did not fare better than the adherents of the Uppsala School of Philosophy and other prevalent schools of thought which have subjected our moral ideas to critical investigation.

Protagoras teaches scepticism—scepticism towards knowledge and scepticism towards morality, summed up in the formula: 'Man is the measure of all things.' It must be kept in mind, however, that the knowledge towards which he was sceptical was the knowledge which had hitherto been the objective of the philosophers, namely, absolute insight into the unchangeable; and that the

[1] In my view, one of the best descriptions and critical evaluations of the Sophists is to be found in George H. Lewes, *The Biographical History of Philosophy from its Origin in Greece Down to the Present Day* (3rd edn, 1867), 105 *et seq.*

morality towards which he was sceptical was the absolute law of divine validity. He realized the futility and vanity in the philosophers' attempts to gain knowledge of the absolute 'essence' of existence and of things, and he taught that all knowledge lies in our sense perception and is, therefore, necessarily relative and individual. Things are as we see them, but human beings see them differently. However, anyone of sound mind sees them in the same way, as do other people of sound mind.

All things considered, this is the position of modern science: the relativity of all science and its dependence on sense perception. Naturally, Protagoras lacked true insight into the method of modern science to create, through mathematical interpretation, an intersubjective control which raises knowledge above individual experience. Thus, his doctrine had to be more radically sceptical than was warranted.

On the other hand, his philosophy contains the very beginnings of a critical groundwork of the objectivity of science. On a charitable reading, his reference to the congruence of the views of sound persons can very well be seen as constituting the germ of a verification theory.

It is much the same in the fields of morality and law. Here, too, man is the [327] measure of all things. There is no eternal universal law, and laws are not of divine origin. They are simply the work of man, based on decisions and power. This does not mean that all laws are equally good. Here, too, the measure must be sought in the congruence of sound persons. Presumably, this induced Protagoras himself to adopt a conservative, conventional attitude in defending the existing order, but the younger Sophists further developed his teachings into a severe critique of the existing social institutions. They saw through the hollowness and deceptiveness of ascribing divinity to laws. In fact, human laws are an expression of the arbitrary power of the rulers. All governments create laws that are of service to themselves, and what serves their own interests they call just. The doctrine of the inherent justice of laws is, thus, nothing but a crafty camouflage of the rule of force. Along these lines, the Sophists provided a first approach to a sociological theory on the relation between law, power, and interest, and on the conflict between social groups.[2]

However, this doctrine of the posited and power-based nature of the laws did by no means imply that the Sophists in general identified law and power, and that they did not recognize, *qua* standard for the good, anything that was not actually upheld by power. Their criticism of the ideology of justice was underpinned by a new humanistic view of life, accompanied by far-reaching revolutionary demands for reforming social and political life. Hippias taught that all

[2] Cf. Hartvig Frisch, *Athenernes Statsforfatning* [The Athenian Constitution] (1941), 94 *et seq.*; K. R. Popper, *The Open Society and its Enemies* (1945), I, 49 *et seq.*

human beings are by nature equal, and that it was through human laws alone that inequality and slavery have been introduced. While the great moralists, Plato and Aristotle, defended the institution of slavery as stemming from the natural inequality of men, it was the 'immoral' Sophists who demanded its abolition and, thereby, also condemned the distinction, so deeply ingrained in the Greek mentality, between Greeks and Barbarians. Lycophron demanded the abolition of nobility, and Phaleas demanded equality concerning the distribution of property and the opportunity, for all citizens, to have access to education. Nay, even the issue of the political equality of men and women was allowed on the agenda.

All these demands for reform were put forward, by the Sophists, as something that is *just according to nature* (*fysis*), in contrast to something that is *just according to the law* (*nomos*).

> *The rules of the law (says the Sophist Antifon) are adventitious, while the rules of nature are inevitable. The rules of the law are created by covenant and not produced by nature, while the rules of nature are exactly the reverse. A man, therefore, who transgresses legal rules, is free from shame and punishment whenever he is unobserved by those who made the covenant, and is subject to shame and punishment only when he is*
> [328] *observed. It is otherwise with transgression of the rules which are innate in nature. If any man strains any of these rules beyond what it can bear, the evil consequences are none the less, if he is entirely unobserved, and none the greater, if he is seen of all men; for the injury that he incurs is not due to men's opinion but to the facts of the case. I put forward reflections on these points because most of what is right according to the law is at variance with nature... And much of what is said here will be found to be at variance with nature. For the parties concerned lay themselves open thereby to more penalty than necessary and have less enjoyment than they could have, and suffer where they could avoid it.*[3]

This raises a topic that should recur in all later instantiations of natural law: the contrast between, on the one hand, the positive law and the historically given institutions and social conventions and, on the other, the demands of nature, independent from human arbitrariness and power. However, there is a distinct difference between the various schools of natural law with respect to their ideas on the mutual relationship between the two spheres, a difference which reflects the political tendency underpinning the construction. The dominant school is *conservative* natural law, such as represented by Heraclitus: the positive law is, in its essence, an emanation or revelation of something that is, by nature, eternally valid. Thereby, it is endowed with binding force, and this alone turns the

[3] Cited in Hartvig Frisch (1941), *op. cit.*, 107–09. The English translation is taken from E. Barker, *Greek Political Theory. Plato and his Predecessors* (1918), at 66–69.

institutional order into a legal order, as opposed to a rule of force. This school of natural law is called conservative, because its practical function is to legitimize the existing institutions through moral-religious sanctity. This contrasts with that philosophy of natural law which is *revolutionary* (or *evolutionary*)—just like the sophistic philosophy, or the corresponding liberalist philosophy of natural law in the eighteenth century. This school emphasizes the discrepancy between the positive law and the law of nature and is called revolutionary, because its political function is to legitimize the revolution of the desired social conditions through the sanctity of a higher validity.

It may seem to contradict Protagorean scepticism (which was the Sophists' point of departure) that they ended up with propounding a law of nature, that is, a moral truth. And strictly speaking so it was. We must bear in mind, however—and this also emerges from the above quotation from Antiphon, for example—that the nature which the Sophists appealed to was not expressing any religious or metaphysical absolutism. Also here, the principle seems to apply that man is the measure of all things, that is, that it is man's factual experiences of pleasure and pain, his factual needs and evaluations, the Sophists are referring to. A natural law of this kind is essentially different from the metaphysical natural law that was to prevail later on, and may on a charitable reading be interpreted as a first attempt at a rational legal politics.

[329]

§ 57. *Aristotle*

Ancient Greek philosophy of enlightenment had achieved a good deal towards emancipation from the traditional magical-religious conception of law.[1]

We have seen that the doctrine of the Sophists contained at least the germ of a sociology of law as well as of a realistic legal policy—areas which might well have been scientifically elaborated. The time was not yet ripe, however. Two of the greatest minds known to mankind, Plato and Aristotle, set out to rebuild what the Sophists had been busy pulling down: namely, the belief in the absolute and the eternal.[2] And it would be these two men—with respect to legal philosophy, especially Aristotle—who would have a decisive influence on subsequent developments up to today.

Any revival of the belief in the Olympic gods and the cosmic law of destiny was out of the question, of course; magic and mythology had vanished, never to return. Instead, magic and religion were replaced by philosophical metaphysics, which is essentially of the same kind but employs more sophisticated tools. Romancing myths and poems were replaced by philosophico-metaphysical speculation, that is, an intellectual activity which, due to its logical-systematic structure, imitates disciplined scientific knowledge but is, in fact, only a new mythology. This is true, because its function—similar to that of mythology and religion—is to give inner peace and edification by believing in the absolute; and because it unfolds, likewise with poetic licence, into assertions about the 'innermost essence' of existence and things. This innermost essence is beyond all control through observation and experience, and, therefore, everyone is at liberty to assert whatever he likes, based on absolute rational insight, on intuition, on a feeling of self-evidence, on transcendental consciousness—or whatever one has decided to call the supposed source of knowledge concerning eternal truths.

Aristotle transferred the animation and personification of nature (animism and mythology), which had characterized earlier Greek thinking, to a philosophical system of thought. Subsequently, this system was treated with great respect, because reading his writings requires some erudition, but still more to see through the primitiveness of his reasoning. He assumed that each individual

[1] [General remark to § 57:] In this section, I present (in more informal terms) a summary of the interpretation of Aristotle which I have put forward, in a more scholarly style, in my book *Kritik der sogenannten praktischen Erkenntnis* [Critique of So-called Practical Knowledge] (1933) ch. VI, 3.

[2] 'The invention of philosophy itself can be interpreted, I think, as a reaction to the breakdown of the closed society and its magical beliefs. It is an attempt to replace the lost magical faith by a rational faith', K. R. Popper, *The Open Society and its Enemies* (1945), I, 165. On the issue of philosophy as a substitute for religion, see also Victor Kraft, *Einführung in die Philosophie* [Introduction to Philosophy] (1950), 16 *et seq.*

thing in itself has some kind of soul (he called it the 'form') which, to start with, determines the 'essence' of things as belonging to a certain class. Thus, for [330]
example, it is the 'essence' of the cat Musse that makes a cat of him. This hidden essence is the reality that lies behind our ordinary concepts, such as the concept of 'cat'. The essence cannot be discovered through comparison and induction from external observations, but can be found and recognized through inner intellectual intuition. It is the province of science to define the essence of things—for example, what it is that turns a cat into a cat—and to establish the characteristics of the essence in a definition.[3] Then, the soul—or the form—of things is also the measure of perfection that is enclosed in them, and towards which they are striving. This ultimate goal of the striving of each thing both is and is not lying within the thing itself. As long as the seed has not developed into a plant, the plant does not exist (as a reality), but exists nevertheless (as a possibility, a potentiality) as a guiding objective, enclosed deep down within the essence of the seed.

Since the good is what we are striving for, the soul of all things likewise determines what is the good for every single thing. A good cat is a cat that manifests its being a cat to perfection. The same applies to human beings. But what is the essence of a human being, what is it that makes a human being a human being? Well: it is that part of the soul which is endowed with reason, as opposed to the sensual part, which we have in common with animals. By doing this, Aristotle has split man into two parts and introduced a distinction that was fundamental to all spiritualistic metaphysics. Man belongs to two worlds. As a sensuous being he is a part of nature, as a rational being he belongs to the realm of morality, validity, and freedom.

Accordingly, the moral task of man is to realize, guided by reason, what his innermost being (in its rational nature, as opposed to its sensuous nature) is striving for. But what is that, then? What norms of action follow from it? Obviously, these metaphysical speculations about the nature of the Good are like empty vessels that can be filled as one likes—and this, in turn, actually means: can be filled with the moral-doctrinal prejudices, aspirations, and ideals that have inspired the constructor as an individual under the influence of his times and surroundings. Aristotle makes no attempt to deduce systematically the content of morality, but contents himself with referring to the respective opinions of sound and good people. Thus, it is ultimately the positive moral consciousness of Aristotle himself and his contemporaries which, as 'natural

[3] The opposite of this metaphysical *essentialism* is scientific, methodological *nominalism*, understanding concepts not as reflections of the 'true nature' of things, but as linguistic tools for the most appropriate description of the phenomena and their causal relations. Essentialism can still be found in well-known, but completely futile and unscientific discussions—such as, for example, the discussion on the issue of whether international law really *is* law, cf. Alf Ross, *Lærebog i Folkeret* [A Textbook of International Law] (1947), § 5. See also K. R. Popper, *The Open Society and its Enemies* (1945), I, 25 *et seq.*

morality', has been clad in the garb of absolute validity by means of metaphysical constructions.

I have given an account of Aristotle's ethics because its leading tenets have been [331] received into Catholic natural law. Aristotle himself did not develop a theory of law with similar thoroughness. He adopted the Sophists' distinction between natural law and positive law, but, once again, the philosophy of natural law was given a conservative and metaphysical twist. The law of nature is law valid in itself and binding upon everyone. It is apprehended by reason. It is true that human laws contain much that is arbitrary or determined by utility considerations—for example, when it has been decided that the ransom for a prisoner shall be a mina, or that a sacrifice shall consist of a goat and not of two sheep. Apart from such 'positivities', however, the laws are based on the law of nature and shall be interpreted in conformity with the latter whenever they are deficient or ambiguous.[4]

[4] Aristotle, *Den nikomakæiske Etik* [Nicomachean Ethics], Book V, Chapter 10 1134 b; *Retorik* [Rhetoric], Book I, Ch. 15 1375 a.

§ 58. *The Stoics and Roman Law*

Among the philosophical schools and trends of the Hellenistic period, stoicism was to become of particular importance to the development of natural law. In the old and the new world, this school of thought became widespread in the centuries immediately preceding the birth of Christ, and due to its humble and religious undertones it was instrumental in introducing Christianity.

Also stoicism refers to reason and the nature of man as the measure of a wise man's actions. But Aristotle's somewhat intricate and colourless line of thought has been replaced with a religious interpretation with an element of mysticism, easier to understand as well as moving. This interpretation was well suited for establishing stoicism not merely as an academic discipline, but also as a philosophy of life, to be disseminated among the educated classes. At the same time, the worship of reason is combined with the ancient Greek idea of fate as a universal cosmic law. Reason is not just individual reason. The latter is but a spark of the eternal, of universal reason or divine reason, reigning over all that exists. The claim to live in *harmony with nature* or in *conformity with reason*, which is the basic tenet of stoicism, thus acquires a strangely equivocal character of its own, a fascinating ambivalence of self-assertion and humility, independence and subjection, freedom and duty. On the one hand, nature is identical with universal reason or the divine will. Accordingly, the moral claim is a claim to be willing to subject oneself entirely to what is divine, to efface oneself by voluntarily subjecting oneself to the omnipotence that rules the world, by willingly becoming one with the universal, with God. On the other hand, nature is also man's own rational nature, and, seen from this angle, morality is a claim to complete freedom and independence, that is, to a life [332]
solely determined by our rational nature, freed from the delusion of the senses. This inner moral freedom alone is what is truly good. Those who chase after sensual pleasures deceive themselves and are slaves. The wise man is a king, that is, he has control over himself and is not dependent on anybody or anything; for no one can rob him of his inner freedom. These two opposed perspectives merge into one, precisely because man, being rational, is himself a spark of the eternal and has a share in the divine. Thus, the law governing us is, at the same time, the law in our inner self. Only those who are God's slaves have achieved absolute freedom.

The Stoics introduced the *concept of duty* into moral and legal philosophy. In classical Greek thought, fate was an external power which bound mankind through punishment, but not in their conscience. Thus, to exceed one's objectives was presumption and folly (*hybris*), but not sin or disobedience. The philosophers had hitherto always steered the problem towards the nature of the good. It was among the Stoics—presumably under the influence of oriental despotism—that the idea first arose that the essence of morality did not lie in the external objectives of the will but, rather, in its conformity with a law that is central to the idea of duty.[1]

Stoicism gave a religious and universalistic touch to natural law. It is not individual reason, but cosmic-divine reason that is the supreme source of law. But universal reason commands us to realize a peaceful social life, while observing the rules inherent in our reasonable nature. When interpreting the latter, the idea of the equality of all human beings increasingly manifested itself to the Stoics. In every human being there is a spark of the eternal, and therefore we are all equal before God. The fundamental command of reason is to respect all other rational beings as ends in themselves, and the ideal of social life is a world state wherein all people are equal and live in harmony with the commands of nature and reason. In such a state, there would be neither private ownership nor slavery. But the folly and wickedness of men have resulted in their living in separate states and according to human laws, which but imperfectly reflect natural justice.

Stoicism also became the philosophy of life of the educated Romans. Cicero popularized Stoicism in a rather dry legal form, disregarding its mystical-pantheistic undertones. Thanks to Cicero, the doctrine of natural law developed into a kind of philosophical introduction to the law which was frequently used by the great jurists of the classical period. Henceforth, a distinction was made between three kinds of law. Firstly, there was *jus civile*, the law applying to Roman citizens and determined by the traditional Roman system of procedure, *legis actiones* and the formulary system. Secondly, there was *jus gentium*, the law common to the Romans and other peoples and thus applied to foreign citizens as well as in the relations between Rome and other powers. Just like the *jus*
[333] *civile*, the *jus gentium* is positive law, a coercive order based on force and administered by the Roman foreign praetor (*praetor peregrinus*). However, the *jus gentium* was less formal and more elastic than the *jus civile*. Under the influence of Stoicism, it was interpreted as being determined, and to a larger extent than the specifically Roman law, by the human nature common to the different peoples, and hence to a larger extent than the *jus civile* an expression of the natural principles of law. Finally, there was the very *jus naturae*, based on the reason inherent in man and identical with the divine reason that applies to all living beings. The *jus naturae* was not a coercive order, though, and it was actually contrary to traditional Roman thought to call such an order 'law'. It merely happened out of respect for the authority of the Greek philosophers. However, a certain connection with Roman ideas could be found in the Roman concept of *aequum et*

[1] Alf Ross, *Kritik der sogenannten praktischen Erkenntnis* [Critique of So-called Practical Knowledge] (1933), ch. VII.

bonum. In the course of time, doctrines of equity (*aequitas*) had developed to temper a strictly ritual law, and those doctrines thus found support in natural law philosophy. This is chiefly borne out by the development towards the informal promise and a freer interpretation of it, less bound by the words that were actually applied, than by the considerations expressed in them.[2]

[2] Cf. Stig Juul, *Grundrids af den romerske Formueret* [Outline of Roman Property Law] (1942), 152–53.

§ 59. Scholasticism and Natural Law (Thomas Aquinas)

It did not pose a problem to the Church Fathers and the scholastic philosophers to interpolate the specifically Christian ideas into the classical natural law tradition.[1] They had only to exchange the vague pantheistic concept of a divine universal reason for the God of Christianity. The Aristotelian distinction between man as a sensuous being and man as a rational being suited the Christian distinction between body and soul, between this world and the Kingdom of God, to perfection. Only, it was more in the spirit of the Gospel to emphasize purity of heart—conscience—rather than rational thinking as the organ through which the voice of God speaks to man. The most important novelty was concerned with two issues. Firstly, natural law acquired a more sophisticated content. While the ancient natural law philosophers stayed with rather vague ideas of an eternal and absolute *lex naturae* and, in fact, attached more weight to asserting the idea as such than attributing a definite systematic content to it, Christianity found a firm, dogmatic foundation in Revelation.
[334] The core of all Christian natural law is the revealed, and in this sense positive, will of God: the Mosaic law and the Gospel. Secondly, the idea of the supremacy of natural law over human law was now realized. Human law acquires its binding force, its validity as law as opposed to a regime of violence, only by virtue of its being derived from divine law, and no human law which fundamentally contradicts natural law has any validity whatsoever. But this did not mean that it was permitted to refuse to comply with every unjust law—for example, a tax regulation according to which the burdens are not distributed fairly. In such a case, the law of nature commands us to put considerations of peace and order above the consideration of one's own right. However, should the positive law decree or permit something that is in direct conflict with one of the fundamental commands of natural law (as taught and interpreted by the Church), then everyone is entitled as well as obligated to rebel against the king and the authorities; for then the law is no longer law, and the king no longer a king, but a tyrant. As we can see, these two issues taken together implied that in an ingenious way, a conservative natural law was combined with a mildly oppositional natural law. In general, law and justice were endowed with religious sacredness, but at the same time, the Church was granted the powers of censorship in defence of certain fundamental principles, especially in support of the papal power in its conflict with secular power.[2] A theory along these lines can already be found in Gratian's decree of the twelfth century. Of course,

[1] [General remark to § 59:] For a more detailed and documented account, see my book *Kritik der sogenannten praktischen Erkenntnis* [Critique of So-called Practical Knowledge], ch. VII, 4.

[2] The political aspects of natural law, especially the doctrines of sovereignty, the social contract and the right of resistance as well as the role played by these theories in political history, are treated more fully in my

once the conflict between Emperor and Pope had subsided, natural law became increasingly conservative.

The final formulation of Catholic natural law was provided by Thomas Aquinas (1226–74), who—with admirable energy and gifted with constructive powers—established the theologico-philosophical system of the Middle Ages in his monumental work *Summa theologica*, the doctrines of which—without any alterations or additions to speak of—are accepted by Catholic legal philosophy to this day.

Thomas's moral and legal philosophy is meticulously based on that of Aristotle (whom he simply calls 'the Philosopher'), of course with the interpolation of the Christian conception of God. Also Thomas's view of the world is animistic. The Good is that towards which everything, alive or lifeless, is striving, in accordance with its divinely created nature and destiny. The Good is reality itself in its own perfection, in accordance with God's idea. In accordance with its own nature, everything strives towards perfection in God, and, therefore, all natural striving is legitimate.

Accordingly, what is good for man is that towards which he strives in accordance with his own nature. This does not mean, of course, that everything actually desired by man is good. The inner truth is only bound up with our innermost, true will that underpins our conscious striving. If only reason would [335] follow the natural insight which God has planted in our hearts, our conscious will, too, would always be directed towards what is truly good. But man's reason may be corrupted and defy the law of nature. In this way, the will is led astray, seeking what seems good although in reality it is not.

What kind of law is it, then, that reason shall follow in order to direct the will towards the truly good? In its perfection, it is the *Eternal Law*, identical with God's sovereign reason, the divine wisdom reigning over the entire creation, over all natural processes and all actions. All other laws receive their force from this law. However, the eternal law in its perfection cannot be apprehended by man. In so far as it can be comprehended by man solely by the light of nature (reason), it is called *natural law*. But natural law is not sufficient for man to reach his divine purpose. Thus, for further guidance, God has through revelation granted man a share in the eternal law, which is the *Divine Law* (the Mosaic law and the Gospel). Finally, there is the *Human Law*, laid down by man with the aid of reason, and necessary for concretely applying the fundamental principles expressed in divine law and in natural law.

book *Hvorfor Demokrati?* [Why Democracy?] (1946), 30 *et seq*. The English translation dates from 1952: Alf Ross, *Why Democracy?* (1952).

The various levels of the laws possess differing degrees of self-evidence.[3] Naturally, the revealed law possesses most self-evidence—especially the Mosaic law, whose second table contains the fundamental commands for human co-existence whose breach fills every human being with natural horror. On the other hand, the principles that are grasped only by the light of reason possess a lesser degree of self-evidence, because reason can be led astray by passions and the sinful nature of man. More remote applications of these principles to the circumstances of life possess the least degree of self-evidence. Thus, for example, the special application of the seventh commandment, in the sense that a deposit must be returned, is only valid as a general rule in most cases. There may be exceptions, according to circumstances. Therefore, the law-giver must be granted considerable freedom when creating positive law. Natural law determines only the framework, and positive law should not only be just, but also useful, that is, it should serve the people's needs. However, needs change with changing ideas, customs, and common practice—indeed with civilization itself, varying in time and place. Therefore, the law must change, too.

Now we can see that although Thomas has given natural law more substance by incorporating the fundamental dogmas of Christian morality (the indissolubility of marriage, for example), he is nonetheless far from an abstract rationalism which seeks to derive, from reason, a solution to every single, concrete problem. His construction admits of sufficient space for a sociologico-realistic legal [336] politics. The same also applies to the Thomism of today. Thus—provided we can ignore the metaphysical and the dogmatic—there are good chances of achieving an understanding between this school of thought and a realistic theory of law.

[3] Cf. Henri Rommen, *Le droit naturel* [Natural Law] (1945), 72 *et seq.*

§ 60. Rationalism

With the impact of theology on human thought gradually waning, even natural law (apart from the traditional Catholic tradition) had to undergo a process of secularization as well.[1] With the seventeenth and eighteenth centuries we are entering the age of rationalism and enlightenment and, at the same time, the heyday of the great systems of natural law. Natural law was to become the seminal practical philosophy of an entire epoch, dominating human thinking not only in the realms of legal science and moral philosophy, but also in those of economics and politics. Natural law divests itself now of its theological garb and claims to appear as pure science, studied according to the mathematical-deductive method, the great discovery of the period. The foundation of this school of thought was laid by the Dutchman Hugo Grotius (*De jure belli ac pacis libri tres*, 1625), but not until the second half of the century did natural law come into full bloom, namely, in the great systems associated with the names Spinoza, Pufendorff, Thomasius, Barbeyrac, Wolff, and others. A markedly political dimension had the natural law of Hobbes, the radical defender of absolutism, as well as the works of John Locke and Rousseau, both of them of vital importance in connection with the foundation of modern democracy. Locke was the ideological founding father of the American revolution, just as Rousseau was the ideological founding father of the French revolution. These two great revolutions signified the triumphant breakthrough of the natural law idea of the liberation/emancipation of the individual, pleading his inalienable right to freedom as well as his inalienable human rights. These rights found their historically well-known expression in the American Declaration of Independence (1776) and the French Declaration of the Rights of Man (1789), adopted as a preamble to the French Constitution of 1791. The committee draft of the Code Napoléon began with the following striking sentence which contains the creed of the revolution in a nutshell:* 'Il existe un droit universel et immuable, source de toutes les lois positives; il n'est que la raison naturelle, en tant qu'elle gouverne tout les hommes.'[2]

* Translator's note: 'There exists a universal and unchangeable law, the source of all positive laws; it is the natural reason ruling all mankind' [this translation has been taken from the 1958 publication of Alf Ross, *On Law and Justice*].

[1] [General remark on § 60:] Kåre Foss, *Ludvig Holbergs Naturrett på idéhistorisk bakgrunn* [Ludvig Holberg's Natural Law, as seen in Light of the History of Ideas] (1934), 177 *et seq.* gives a very instructive and vivid account of natural law in the age of enlightenment; cf. Alf Ross, book review in *TfR* 1936, 478 *et seq.* See also Ross, *Kritik der sogenannten praktischen Erkenntnis* [Critique of So-called Practical Knowledge] (1933), ch. VI, 5.

[2] For details on the significance of natural law for political development from the Reformation until the French Revolution, see Alf Ross, *Hvorfor Demokrati?* [Why Democracy?] (1946), ch. II, 5–8. The English translation dates from 1952: Alf Ross, *Why Democracy* (1952).

[337] The last great name belonging to this period is Kant. Especially towards the end of the period, however, there was a host of lesser known authors and systems. It is hardly an exaggeration to say that eventually it became the fashion for every self-respecting author to work out a system of his own.

As I said before, the primary and most obvious feature of the new natural law was its secular, non-theological character. This had already emerged in Grotius' famous words that the law of nature would still be valid, even if it were assumed—and this would be a horrible crime—that God did not exist (*et si Deus non daretur*). The law of nature would now further develop without any support from theology and Revelation, solely on the basis of human nature.

This is not saying much, however. Also the scholastics had taken human nature as their basis, and it makes little difference to the interpretation of the commands of nature whether God is added or subtracted. What makes the new school of thought special, however, is the new method of deriving natural law from the nature of man. The new, decisive factor is the proud confidence in having discovered an unswerving, scientific method to replace the partly theological, partly empirical patchwork of former times. This is Descartes' *deductive* or *geometrical method*. One had found a way now—or so one believed—to raise philosophy up to the same scientific level as mathematics. All that was needed was to find a firm point of departure within a series of indubitably true (self-evident) axioms.[3] Then the rest would just be logic and deduction—in the same way as the whole of mathematics is nothing but deduction based on a system of axioms. With regard to the realm of legal philosophy, this would mean that by starting from a few principles, apprehended with absolute clarity and self-evidence by reflection on the nature of man, one would be able to deduce a complete legal system. This is the optimistic and proud programme of rationalism.

And it was carried out thoroughly indeed. Starting from the principle of sociability which demands that man, in accordance with his social nature, unites with his fellow men in peaceful and rational social life, one deduced a comprehensive system of legal rules, frequently down to the minutest details.[4] This system was divided into disciplines, similar to the positive law. Thus, natural law came to consist not merely of a few leading ideas or dogmas, but of a detailed legal system with a structure similar to that of positive law. In the systems of natural law we can thus find rules of privity, rules on the conclusion
[338] of contracts and their validity, rules on the acquisition and transfer of property,

[3] As is well known, Descartes took as his starting point the sentence *cogito, ergo sum*.

[4] K. D. A. Röder mentions as elementary violations of the law of nature *inter alia* the following: to enter unbidden; to make journeys troublesome; the stiff leather stocks worn by soldiers. See *Grundzüge des Naturrechts oder der Rechtsphilosophie* [The Main Features of the Law of Nature, or Philosophy of Law] (2nd edn, 1860), II, 82, 91, 98.

on marriage, on inheritance, on the government, etc., etc.—all of them described with an attention to detail that made of natural law a system of the same order of magnitude as positive law.

Related to the issue above is another circumstance which should have far-reaching and fatal importance. As long as natural law was believed to comprise only a few general abstract maxims (as had been the case in all previous philosophy), there could be no danger of conflating natural law and positive law. Even if there should be a connection between them in so far as the positive law derived its validity from the law of nature, it was nonetheless obvious that the law of nature was directed at a different addressee than was positive law. For the law of nature comprised the legal-ethical principles that bound *the lawgiver*, and their observance was a prerequisite of his commands constituting a genuinely binding legal order, not a mere tyranny. The basic idea was that the law, alongside its coercive nature, also possessed a higher moral validity. The law of nature indicates the highest principles that are the source of this validity. Thus, natural law had an ethical or legal-political character, although no basic distinction was made between morality and law since one assumed that it was part of the essence of law to be morally binding as well—binding in conscience. Thus, 'morality' must be understood as an expression of the validity that is common to law and morality in the narrower sense, in contrast to the specific character of the law as a coercive order. On the other hand, there was never a question of considering natural law as rules which directly addressed themselves to the *citizens* and regulated their internal relationships in terms of rights and duties. This is borne out by the fact that natural law has always been spoken of as a natural *law*, never as a set of natural *rights*.

Things are different now. Once one had begun to deduce an entire legal system on a natural law basis, the inevitable consequence was that natural law was seen as a set of rights and duties, directly valid for the citizens in their mutual relationships, in the same way as positive law. From having been a moral discipline, natural law now became a *genuinely legal discipline*. That is to say, instead of the logically not unreasonable idea that positive law was subordinate to certain moral principles that conditioned its morally binding force, one was led to envisage a duplication of the legal system: behind or above factual legal relationships (principally expressed in the category 'rights'), there is another set of rights—namely, natural rights. Accordingly, one arrived at a sharp distinction between law and morality. The concept of right (I add) is inextricably linked with an experience of power, resulting from the possibility of setting the coercive machinery of the state in motion. The concept of right is in essence a concept of positive law. However, since the law of nature was presented under the category of rights as well, it follows that all law, natural law as well as posi- [339]
tive law, is—in contrast to morality—characterized by the coercive power inherent in the concept of right.

In this way, then, one arrived at an unfortunate reduplication of the legal system, at the idea of a genuinely juristic natural law—a system of rights behind, or above, the system of positive rights. Whereas natural law had hitherto been a moral-philosophical doctrine which the jurists could accept or reject without any noticeable effect on the study of positive law as such, the new conceptual apparatus was likely to create confusion, leaving deep traces in juristic thinking to the present day (§ 66).

In the eighteenth century especially, the ideological content of the reform demands of natural law was determined by the demands of the Age of Enlightenment for the liberation of the individual from oppressive state power and from the bonds and privileges left over from the age of feudalism. Using clichés, one might say that the ideology of natural law was individualistic and liberal. The state shall interfere as little as possible in the lives of citizens. Its task shall be largely restricted to safeguarding internal and external peace and protecting private property rights and the freedom of contract. The privileges of the nobility, guild coercion, and other arbitrary encroachments on freedom shall be abolished. This ideology found its most striking expression in Kant, who defined freedom as the original right of man and expressed the supreme law of nature in the well-known formula: A course of action is lawful, if the freedom to pursue it is compatible with the freedom of every other person under a general rule.[5] Apart from the fact that this formula is actually devoid of meaning, its intention is clearly to assert a maximum of freedom, intimating that freedom may be restricted only in its own interest.

[5] Cf. Alf Ross, *Kritik der sogenannten praktischen Erkenntnis* [Critique of So-called Practical Knowledge] (1933), ch. IX, 1.

§ 61. Crypto-Natural Law

It is usually assumed that with the conservative reaction to the upheavals of the French Revolution, natural law has vanished from the intellectual scene—at least for the time being. A brief glance at the prevailing currents of thought in moral and legal philosophy as well as politics during the period of the Restoration and several years afterwards seems to confirm this opinion. No further natural law systems were developed, and the very concept seemed to have disappeared off the face of the earth.

In Germany, a romantic-conservative philosophy of history was flourishing which, in sharp reaction to the abstract speculations of natural law, focused on [340] the historical evolution of social institutions. Savigny and Puchta founded the Historical, or Romantic, School of Jurisprudence. The basic tenet of this school was that law is not created consciously through rational deliberations but, rather, grows blindly-organically—as an expression of the *Volksgeist* and the popular legal consciousness. Custom, not statutory law is, thus, the highest source of law.[1]

In France, Comte laid the foundations of positivism,[2] a school of thought purporting to create a scientific politics, based upon the laws that govern society and the evolution of society (sociology). What is more, after the enactment of the great civil code, the Code Napoléon, in 1804, French jurists naturally enough lost interest in juridico-political demands for reform and, thereby, also in natural law. Their interest turned to positive law now: to the Code and the interpretation of the Code.[3]

In England, finally, we can also find corresponding historical-conservative schools of thought (Burke). Bentham, the founder of utilitarianism, exercised a greater influence, however.[4] Even if Bentham is close to the natural law philosophy of the eighteenth-century with his liberal tendencies and unhistorical, abstract method, he nevertheless was the most fanatic enemy of natural law, and no one has more thoroughly and passionately dismissed the idea of natural rights as an illusion. He wanted to create a moral doctrine which should be based exclusively on the utility of an action as measured against the criterion of the greatest happiness (pleasure) for the greatest

[1] For details on the Historical School of Jurisprudence, see Alf Ross, *Theorie der Rechtsquellen* [Theory of the Sources of Law] (1929), ch. V.

[2] See Alf Ross, *Kritik der sogenannten praktischen Erkenntnis* [Critique of So-called Practical Knowledge] (1933), ch. VI, 6.

[3] Cf. Alf Ross, *Theorie der Rechtsquellen* [Theory of the Sources of Law] (1929), ch. II, 3.

[4] See Alf Ross, *Kritik der sogenannten praktischen Erkenntnis* [Critique of So-called Practical Knowledge] (1933), ch. IV, 1; *Hvorfor Demokrati?* [Why Democracy?] (1946), ch. III, 2.

number. Thanks to the work of the legal philosopher Austin, the founder of the so-called analytical school,[5] Bentham would exercise a decisive influence on English legal thinking.

Yet, the view that natural law belongs to the past is very misleading, at least if the concept is not restricted to include only the rationalist theories of the seventeenth and eighteenth centuries. If instead we understand 'natural law' to include any metaphysical legal theory that is also a legal politics (as we have done here), that is, if it establishes a criterion of the correctness or justice of the law, then the fact is that natural law, even when called by another name, has survived and prospered throughout the nineteenth century. If that century nevertheless regarded itself as hostile to natural law (and that century's natural law, therefore, can be called crypto-natural law) then this is explained by the fact that from the relative closeness of a contemporary perspective, natural law was identified with the trend that had prevailed in the two preceding centuries. [341] Indeed, what one reacted against was not natural law as such but, rather, the *rationalism*, *individualism*, and *liberalism* that had characterized natural law philosophy during the preceding period. Both historicism and positivism are pursuing lines of thought which are familiar from older natural law. Surely, the same cannot justly be said of Bentham's utilitarianism, even though that, too, holds that morality can be derived from the nature of man—from man's striving for happiness or pleasure. We shall see, however, how ideas distinctly based on natural law were transplanted into utilitarianism in the course of its further elaboration in the nineteenth century.

For *historicism*[6] is much more than history. The leading idea of historicism is that history is also a criterion of the Good. The history of mankind gives rise to powers which, in accordance with inner necessity, bring mankind to its destination. Therefore, morality is not devised by any speculation by individual reason, but must be sought in the social and legal institutions seen in their historical development. What exists is also—in its essence—what is good. The judgment of history is also a moral judgment. History is the path of God in the world.

In view of the aforesaid, it is easy to see that this line of thought is a new variant of the Aristotelian-Thomistic doctrine that the Good is identical with the essence of things and is determined by the striving towards a goal, inherent in all things. The only difference is that instead of the individual and human nature, it is now mankind and its history which are introduced as the subject whose being and striving determines the Good.

[5] See Alf Ross, *Theorie der Rechtsquellen* [Theory of the Sources of Law] (1929), ch. IV, 3–6.

[6] On this issue, cf. Alf Ross, *Kritik der sogenannten praktischen Erkenntnis* [Critique of So-called Practical Knowledge] (1933), ch. XII, and *Hvorfor Demokrati?* [Why Democracy?] (1946), 87 and 140.

This train of thought has been developed in many variations, but none of them with more fantastic nonsense than in Hegel's famous philosophy.[7] According to Hegel, the innermost essence of existence is reason—is absolute spirit—and history is a kind of gigantic logical operation, in which reason or God conceive of themselves as participants in a peculiar triadic process. To begin with, a concept or thesis is put forward; this concept or thesis generates its own contradiction; next, they are united in a higher unity, whereupon the game continues. According to Hegel, it was possible to interpret the whole of existence according to this scheme, and to deduce the most amazing results.[8] In the realm of politics, his philosophy resulted in an interpretation of history, according to which the German people are chosen to realize God's ultimate purpose with existence, and the Prussian state of 1821 figures as a model of the true nature of the state. In the realm of moral and legal philosophy, he formulated the following much-quoted phrase: '*Was vernünftig ist, das ist wirklich; und was wirklich ist, das ist vernünftig*'.* Of course, by saying so Hegel did not mean that everything that actually exists must be valid and good. He meant that what is moral cannot be conceived by individual human reason, but is revealed in the his- [342] torical institutions of objective morality: in the family, in the fundamental features of civil society and the state—that is, such as their concept or idea is interpreted, by Hegel, by using the dialectic method.

The Historical School of Jurisprudence did not build upon Hegel but on Schelling.[9] Schelling returned to the ancient idea of fate-necessity and interpreted history as a gigantic drama of fate where the individual thinks that he is acting freely, but is nevertheless inexorably led towards a predestined goal. Applied to the law, this idea resulted in the doctrine that the law develops, with fatal necessity, by blind forces in the depths of the *Volksgeist*. The only thing the legislator can do, in reality, is precisely what the good gardener does, namely, encourage natural growth. All arbitrary interventions are doomed to fail from the beginning. This is the reason why Savigny, in a famous treatise, not merely deprived his own times, but any time, of the mission to legislate.[10]

* Translator's note: In translation, 'What is rational is actual; and what is actual is rational' (translation taken from Hegel, *Elements of the Philosophy of Right*, ed. by Allen W. Wood, transl. by H. B. Nisbet [Cambridge: Cambridge University Press, 1991], at 20; original German title, *Grundlinien der Philosophie des Rechts*, 1820).

[7] Cf. Alf Ross, *Kritik der sogenannten praktischen Erkenntnis* [Critique of So-called Practical Knowledge] (1933), ch. XIII, 4. Moreover, K. R. Popper's critical presentation of Hegel in his work *The Open Society and its Enemies* (1945), II, ch. 12, can be warmly recommended.

[8] See Popper, *op. cit.*, ch. II, 25–26.

[9] See Alf Ross, *Kritik der sogenannten praktischen Erkenntnis* [Critique of So-called Practical Knowledge] (1933), ch. XII, 3.

[10] Cf. Alf Ross, *Theorie der Rechtsquellen* [Theory of the Sources of Law] (1929), ch. V, 2.

The sociology of Comte[11] and the *positive politics* built thereon have close affinities with the Historical School. The laws that Comte thinks he can establish for the different stages of civilization have nothing to do with scientific causality: they are laws of fate—expressions of an inner purposive necessity which, at the same time, determines what is real and possesses value. Therefore, what is political is, on the whole, also what is necessary. However, developments do not always follow the straight line of necessity. There may be deviations in both directions. If the politician is to fulfil his mission; if politics are to be more than an impotent gesture—then politics must be the bringing to fruition of the spontaneous tendencies in development. All man can do is accelerate what is necessary, combat certain inhibitions, and thereby reduce possible deviations from the straight line of necessity.

Much of what has gone by the name of sociology—later on, in France and elsewhere—is not really empirical science but, rather, a metaphysics of natural law, of a kind similar to the one described here.

Mill's book *On Liberty*[12] (1859) is a shining example of how pure natural law ideas, in spite of Bentham's witch-hunt, have crept into later *utilitarianism*. The book purports to establish the principle that determines the right of society or the state to exercise force (moral or legal censure) against the individual. According to this principle, the only purpose that can justify the exercise of coercion is to prevent the individual from harming others. Since 'harm' cannot be identical with every violation of interest, what must be meant is that the freedom of action is limited in view of the conflicting rights of others. Since we [343] are dealing with a guiding principle for legislation, these rights must necessarily be *natural* rights—and saying this, we again find ourselves caught in typical natural law thinking.

This shows even more clearly in Spencer's evolutionary elaboration of utilitarianism.[13] Spencer pointed out that it was impossible ever to calculate all the consequences of an action and their importance for human happiness. Instead, he meant to attach great importance to the issue of whether the action conforms to those rules of life which generally are decisive as to whether the action promotes pleasure or pain. Even if these rules must be derived from experience, the latter—due to the evolution of mankind—has nonetheless accumulated in such a way that it appears, to the individual, as *a priori* evident principles—namely, the principles of justice and equality! Spencer himself—N.B. without any knowledge of Kant's work!—formulated the law of justice in a manner that was closely related to Kant's principle. According to Spencer, everyone is free to

[11] See Alf Ross, *Kritik der sogenannten praktischen Erkenntnis* [Critique of So-called Practical Knowledge] (1933), ch. VI, 6.

[12] See Alf Ross, *Kritik der sogenannten praktischen Erkenntnis* [Critique of So-called Practical Knowledge] (1933), 191.

[13] See Ross, *op. cit.*, ch. V, 6.

do what he desires, provided that he thereby does not encroach upon the equal freedom of other people. Again, this principle makes sense only under the assumption that the 'freedom' of others is defined in terms of natural rights.

In a similar way, the eternal principle of justice was likewise interpolated into Ihering's social utilitarianism.[14] Ihering conceived of society as a new, independent being, and he replaced the sum of individual utilities with the utility of society. The highest aim, determining all morality and law, is the safeguarding of the conditions necessary for the existence of society. And where are these expressed? In the demands of justice! Now, since this assertion can hardly be deduced from experience—frequently, it is put forward precisely by those people who castigate our present society for injustice—it must be seen as a new manifestation of the ancient metaphysical-religious postulate of justice as a cosmic law, guaranteeing that the just, the children of God, will be victorious, and that the virtuous will win the crown of happiness. Cf. Heraclitus above!

One might give many more examples, but these must suffice to show how a metaphysical natural law and an *a priori* ideology of justice continued to flourish in the nineteenth century, disguised in theories which looked upon themselves as being hostile to natural law, and which now and then owned up to a scientific empiricism. What disappeared with the eighteenth century was not natural law, but the rationalist systems of natural law. Due to a change in the political climate, however, the inherent ideology experienced a change in tendency. To an ever-increasing extent, individualism gave way to socially tinged views. People gradually realized that unfettered freedom, especially in the field of contract law, not only brought blessings with it, but also a tendency to make the strong stronger and the weak weaker, and consequently that social provisions and legal regulations can be necessary to establish some sort of balance [344]
and protect the weaker members of society.

[14] *Op. cit.*, ch. V, 7.

§ 62. The Renaissance of Natural Law

In view of the situation described above, it is not surprising that natural law has reappeared at the turn of the twentieth century and steadily gained ground ever since—indeed, to such an extent that it is quite common now to speak of a rebirth of natural law in the twentieth century. The radical upheavals—upheavals not only within the realm of politics but also in that of economics and culture—which characterize this century after two world wars, did presumably have a stimulating effect on the need for something absolute, as an anchorage point, in a world in decay and chaos. It would seem that the brutality of reality has increased our urge to assert the ideals of the law. Already World War I has been very conducive to absolutistic natural law. French idealism was compared and contrasted with the German doctrine of power, and the theory of the idea of law *qua* manifestation of the absolute was used to justify the war aims of the Allied Powers and to increase the power of resistance on the part of the population.[1] In a similar way, Hitler's atrocities must have contributed to the awakening of a general desire to confirm the belief in human rights, just as the German regime of violence in the occupied countries stimulated the urge to emphasize, in absolute terms, the difference between right and might, and the foundation of the law in an absolute idea.

The new law of nature—nowadays the prevailing school of thought within the greater part of legal philosophy—does not constitute a revival of the rationalistic systems of the eighteenth century, however. Rather, the threads of scholasticism have been picked up again. With regard to two points, in particular, modern doctrine differs characteristically from that of the Enlightenment.

In the first place, there is no longer anyone who would think of deducing detailed rules concerning loans, rents, deposits, etc. These pretensions have been given up, and one must content oneself with postulating certain fundamental principles while admitting, at the same time, that their carrying out, in practice, must adapt to the circumstances and pay attention to historical traditions, technical and economic conditions as well as practical needs. It has become a common thing to speak of a natural law of varying content. Generally, certain highest principles or formal criteria are maintained as being eternal and
[345] unalterable. Sometimes relativity is extended even to these, with the effect that one gets close to historico-sociological positivism.

In the second place, the ideological tendency has continued the development that had already made itself felt in the nineteenth century—namely, a

[1] See Alf Ross, *Theorie der Rechtsquellen* [Theory of the Sources of Law] (1929), ch. II, 7.

development shifting away from the liberalism and individualism of the Enlightenment, and directed towards a social and collectivist ideology.

With respect to the philosophico-metaphysical justification of natural law, the twentieth century can hardly be said to have produced constructions of particular originality—irrespective of whether the possible themes are exhausted, or whether the talent for metaphysical thought effusions is on the wane. All the different trends that can be distinguished are extensions, and frequently dilutions, of well-known stylistic elements.

First, there is of course *Neo-Thomism*, which plays a prominent part especially in France.[2] Thomism—deeply rooted in Catholic tradition, the so-called *philosophia perennis*—has existed throughout the ages, untouched by the vagaries of metaphysics. Nowadays, however, Thomism seems to win support also from outside the circle of orthodox Catholics.

Especially in Germany, various *Neo-Kantian* trends have played an important role. The distinction between them is due to the fact that in their interpretation of Kant, they attach importance to different aspects of his philosophy. The distinctions are subtle, and I shall only touch upon them.[3] One school of thought (the Marburg School) maintained Kant's so-called formalism, that is, the idea according to which what is moral is defined through the principle of the autonomy, or the sovereign law-making, of the will: what is decisive is solely the compatibility of the maxim for action with the idea of a universal law. From that, one arrived at the idea of a pure will, solely determined through itself and unaffected by any sensuous desires whatsoever. Upon this basis—which is completely devoid of content, of course, and which can arrive at moral postulates only with the help of conjuring tricks—upon this basis, then, Stammler constructed a law of nature in a formalist garb, a law of nature incredibly hollow and stilted; nevertheless, many regard it as profound. His fundamental postulate is the idea of a society of freely (purely) willing individuals, and therefrom he develops a series of basic principles which concern the just or correct law, and which are definitely tautological.[4] Another school of thought (Friesianism) drew upon Kant's idea that the moral law is given in our consciousness, as a direct 'fact of reason'. Upon this basis Leonard Nelson constructed his theory of justice as an even balance of interests without distinction of persons (§ 69). From Nelson, in turn, emanates the Dutch School, seeking to deduce the fundamental law of justice through an analysis of factual legal [346]

[2] For details on French doctrine of natural law, see Alf Ross, *Theorie der Rechtsquellen* [Theory of the Sources of Law] (1929), ch. II, 3–7 and 3, note 1. On the issue of Neo-Thomism in the USA, see Torstein Eckhoff, *Rettsvesen og rettsvitenskap i U. S. A.* [Legal System and Legal Science in the USA] (1953), 272 *et seq.*

[3] For a fuller account, see my book *Kritik der sogenannten praktischen Erkenntnis* [Critique of So-called Practical Knowledge] (1933), chs. X and XI.

[4] For further information, see W. Friedemann, *Legal Theory* (2nd edn, 1949), 93 *et seq.*; Julius Stone, *The Province and Function of Law* (1946/50), 319 *et seq.*

consciousness, as well as the Danish doctrine of *Rule of Law* which has given rise to the current *Rule of Law Party*.[5]

The nineteenth-century schools propagating a *crypto-natural law* have likewise grown new shoots in the twentieth century. Sociological 'positivism' is carried forward by the Frenchman Duguit. Similarly to Hugo Grotius (§ 60), Duguit seeks to deduce the law (*le droit objectif*) from the fact that man can exist only in community with others—from the fact of solidarity. Although Duguit behaves as if he were the arch-enemy of all metaphysics and all natural law, it is obvious that the solidarity he is working with is an ideal, not a fact, and that his 'droit objectif' is simply another name for 'droit naturel'. In the later phases of his work, metaphysics has become increasingly apparent. In accordance with the German Historical School, the fact of solidarity was re-interpreted as popular legal consciousness, and Duguit finally declared that he was in agreement with Thomas Aquinas in his assumption of a concept of justice as an unchangeable element of human nature.[6]

Hegel had his successors as well. On the one hand, his historicism was watered down to a more relativistic philosophy of culture, where culture in its various phases has usurped the position of absolute reason (Kohler, Pound).[7] On the other hand, Hegel's deification of the state and his extreme nationalism were tailor-made for further development towards a fascist philosophy of law (Binder, del Vecchio).[8]

In addition to these representatives of the somewhat pithier types of natural law, there are many writers who embrace natural law on an eclectic basis, or without worrying too much about philosophical foundations. The prominent French legal philosopher Francois Gény, who combines sociological elements with reminiscences from rationalistic natural law and inspiration from Bergson's mysterious, fashionable philosophy,[9] is an example. However, Gény's extensive work deals less with the philosophical justification of the rational and ideal factors in the law, than with their application in legal science and adjudication.

[5] See Alf Ross, *Kritik der sogenannten praktischen Erkenntnis* [Critique of So-called Practical Knowledge] (1933), ch. XI.

[6] See Alf Ross, *Theorie der Rechtsquellen* [Theory of the Sources of Law] (1929), ch. II, 5; *Kritik der sogenannten praktischen Erkenntnis* [Critique of So-called Practical Knowledge] (1933), ch. V, 5.

[7] Cf. Alf Ross, *Kritik der sogenannten praktischen Erkenntnis* [Critique of So-called Practical Knowledge] (1933), ch. XIII, 6. For information on Kohler, see Julius Stone, *The Province and Function of Law* (1946/50), ch. XIII; for information on Pound, see *op. cit.* , ch. XV.

[8] Cf. Ross, *op. cit.*, ch. XII, 6. For information on Del Vecchio, see Friedmann, *Legal Theory* (2nd edn, 1949), 100 et *seq.*

[9] See Alf Ross, *Theorie der Rechtsquellen* [Theory of the Sources of Law] (1929), 31–33 and 52–63.

CHAPTER XI [347]

Analysis and Critique of the Philosophy of Natural Law

§ 63. *Epistemological Considerations*

A thorough critique of the philosophy of natural law would lead us deeply into the realm of epistemology, and far beyond what can be expected to be done within the scope of a general theory of law.[1] But perhaps a glance at the history of natural law, more than any amount of epistemological argumentation, can help bring out the arbitrariness and gaping emptiness of metaphysical speculation. Strictly speaking, metaphysical assertions cannot be disproved, precisely because they are hovering in a sphere beyond justification and verification. We simply learn to overlook them as something that is unwarranted or is without any function in scientific thought. Has anyone ever proved that it is neither Zeus nor the goddesses of fate who ordain the path of the sun? All we can say is that modern astronomy can manage without this assumption. Similarly, the most effective way to conquer legal metaphysics is simply to create a scientific theory of law, the self-sufficiency of which will make the metaphysical speculations sink into oblivion, along with other myths and legends dating back to the childhood of civilization.

In the outline of the history of natural law (given above), there are two points [348] that catch our eye: the total arbitrariness of the fundamental postulates concerning the nature of existence or of man; and the same arbitrariness of the legal-ethical ideas deduced from this foundation. Natural law seeks the absolute, the eternal—to make something out of the law that would be more than the work of man, and to exempt the legislator from the pains and responsibility of decision-making. The source of this has been sought in a magical law of fate,

[1] In my book *Kritik der sogenannten praktischen Erkenntnis* [Critique of So-called Practical Knowledge] (1933), I have tried to show in more detail that the very idea of practical knowledge (that is, such knowledge as is postulated in current moral and legal philosophy) contains a logical contradiction, and that this contradiction, in turn, is reflected in the two categories where practical knowledge occurs, namely, in the idea of the Good and the idea of duty. The philosophy of natural law is predominantly conceived as falling under the category of the Good. See also § 75 below.

On Law and Justice. Alf Ross. © Alf Ross (original Danish, 1953), Jakob v. H. Holtermann (editor, introduction), Uta Bindreiter (translation). Published 2019 by Oxford University Press.

in the will of God, or in absolute rational insight. However, experience shows that the doctrines one thought could be drawn from these sources, far from being eternal and unchangeable, have changed in accordance with times, places, and people. Clad in the noble garb of natural law, one has over the years defended or fought for every conceivable kind of claim, evidently arising out of a specific situation in life, and determined by economic and political class interests, by the cultural traditions and prejudices of the time as well as its aspirations—in short, by all that is included in what is commonly called 'ideology'.

Does nature prescribe that all men shall be alike, like brothers, or is it a law of nature that the strong shall rule over the weak, and that slavery and class distinctions are, thus, part of God's meaning for life on earth? Both propositions have been asserted with the same force and the same 'right'; for how should anyone be able to make a choice between these absolutes in any other way than by an absolute assertion, raised above all inter-subjective argumentation: it is so, because I know that it is so! The ideology of equality was put forward by the Sophists in the fifth century BC, and by Rousseau in the eighteenth century—in both cases as an expression of the political aspirations of a certain class; likewise, it was put forward by the Stoics and by Christianity, but in these cases on a religious basis and without any political tendencies. Plato, on the other hand, postulated the innate inequality of mankind and defended slavery and a society strictly divided into classes. Aristotle followed in his wake with regard to the natural legitimacy of slavery; and thenceforth, the postulate concerning the natural inequality of men has been the starting-point for many conservative doctrines of natural law as well as for organic or totalitarian theories of state—including our own homely little shoot (of more recent date) from that noble tree.[2]

Haller, a Swiss professor of constitutional law at the beginning of the nineteenth century, maintains that according to the law of nature, the strong shall rule over the weak, the husband over the wife, the father over the child, the leader over his followers, and the teacher over his pupils.[3] Similarly Thomas Dew, an American political theorist from the South, declares that 'it is ordained by nature and by God that he who possesses the greatest abilities and the greatest knowledge and thus greater power, shall govern and control him who is inferior'. On this basis, he defended the institution of slavery in the Southern
[349] States, and others went so far as to maintain that slavery guaranteed the slaves' natural rights. Freedom in the true sense of the word is not the same as lack of restraint. 'Therefore, slavery secures them their natural rights and endows

[2] Vinding Kruse, *Retslæren* [Jurisprudence] (1943), II, 877 *et seq.*

[3] Karl Ludwig von Haller, *Restauration der Staats-Wissenschaft oder Theorie des natürlich-geselligen Zustands der Chimäre des künstlich-bürgerlichen entgegengesezt* [On the Restoration of Political Science, or the theory of the natural condition of Mankind, as opposed to the chimera of artificial and civic conditions] (1816), see Tingsten, *De konservativa idéerna* [The Conservative Ideas](1939), 77 *et seq.*

them with true freedom—to the extent they are capable of receiving it. If the institution of slavery were to be abolished, they would no longer enjoy their natural rights.'[4]

As far as politics is concerned, it is widely known how natural law in combination with the social contract theory could be used, and indeed has been used, to justify any kind of government, from total absolutism (Hobbes) to total democracy (Rousseau). Natural law has lent itself equally to those who were bent on consolidating the existing order (Heraclitus, Aristotle, Thomas Aquinas, etc.) and those who were keen on changing society through revolution (Rousseau).

In the socio-economic area, the natural law of the eighteenth century espoused extreme individualism and liberalism. Inviolability of private ownership and unfettered freedom of contract became the two dogmas which the nineteenth century inherited from natural law, and which were enforced—especially in American case law—so as to overturn a number of laws in the sphere of social welfare. As late as 1922, the United States Supreme Court (in the *Adkins case*)[5] struck down the validity of a law concerning minimum wages for women in the District of Columbia, on the grounds that this law—enacted in order to guarantee the worst paid women a more or less acceptable subsistence level and rescue them from the necessity of semi-prostitution—was an infringement of the natural right of these women to enter into a contract freely. On the other hand, natural law has also been used in order to establish a basis for a morality of solidarity (Grotius, Comte, and other 'sociologists') and even—in Duguit's interpretation—in support of a denial of all individual rights in favour of a system of social welfare services.

Perusing the chapter on family law in natural law systems is always a source of amusement, because the moral prejudices of the times are so clearly reflected in this chapter. For Thomas Aquinas, the indissolubility of marriage ('thou shalt not commit adultery') is, of course, an evident truth of reason. The curious dryness of rationalism is reflected in Kant's definition of marriage as a contract between two persons of the opposite sex, concerning the lifelong mutual possession of their sexual qualities. Sexual intercourse is only permitted in wedlock. If one of the spouses entrusts himself or herself into the hands of another person, the other spouse is entitled, invariably and at all times, to retrieve the runaway just like any other object.[6] According to Bornemann, marriage is 'that sensuous, worldly and spiritual, i.e. universal, all-embracing life partnership between man and woman, which is grounded in the complete submission of the entire undivided personality, the perfect communication between all

[4] Cited in Tingsten, *op. cit.*, 161. [5] (1922), 261 U.S. 525.

[6] Immanuel Kant, *Metaphysik der Sitten*, Metaphysische Anfangsgründe der Rechtslehre [*The Metaphysics of Morals*, Metaphysical first principles of the doctrine of right], (1797), § 25.

[350] worldly and spiritual interests'. He recognizes divorce, but deduces from the definition the spouses' complete community of property.[7]

It would be easy to go on, but let me finish by reminding you that it is no less a personage than St. Paul the Apostle who writes the following in his letter to the Corinthians: 'Judge in yourselves: is it comely that a woman pray unto God uncovered? Doth not even nature itself teach you, that, if a man have long hair, it is a shame unto him? But if a woman have long hair it is a glory to her: for *her* hair is given her for a covering.'[8]

Like a harlot, natural law is at the disposal of everyone. There is no ideology that cannot be defended by invoking the law of nature. And indeed, how could it be otherwise when the ultimate basis for every natural law is to be found in a private (intra-subjective), direct insight, a self-evident contemplation, an intuition. Cannot *my* intuition be just as good as *yours*? Self-evidence as a criterion of truth explains the utterly arbitrary character of metaphysical assertions. It raises them above any form of inter-subjective control and opens the door wide to unbridled fantasy and dogmatism.

Even if the historical variability of natural law is in tune with, and to a high degree supports, the interpretation that metaphysical postulates are mere constructions to underpin emotional attitudes and fulfil certain needs, it must nevertheless be admitted that this variability is no conclusive proof. One might argue that even scientific theories change, and one might agree with Thomas Aquinas and say that reason can be led astray by passions, and that not everything that seems self-evident is necessarily true self-evidence. This, however, raises the difficult question as to the hallmark of true self-evidence, a problem which—or so it would appear—can only be solved by recourse to further self-evidence in the second power and, thus, continuing *ad infinitum*.

A decisive objection[9] to that is that self-evidence cannot be a criterion of truth. What we mean by saying that a certain assertion is true is obviously something quite different from experiencing the assertion with the accompanying feeling of lucidity and certainty. The sentence that self-evidence determines the truth of a judgment thus cannot be held as an analytic truth, that is, as a definition of the meaning of truth. It must be meant synthetically, that is, as an assertion that when self-evidence exists, there exists also what we mean by truth. But how can we be sure that these two parts always go together? A feeling of self-
[351] evidence certainly accompanies many assertions we believe to be true, but there is no reason to think that this feeling could not arise just as well in connection

[7] F. C. Bornemann, *Foredrag over den almindelig Rets- og Statslære* [Lectures on the General Theory of Law and State] (1863), § 51 as compared with §§ 56 and 57.

[8] 1 Corinthians 11: 13–15 [The Official King James Bible].

[9] This is not the only objection, however. See note 1 above, concerning the contradiction within the very concept 'practical knowledge' as well as within the categories 'the Good' and 'duty'.

with untrue assertions, or with sentences which are devoid of any theoretical content whatsoever.

Historical variability is not in itself decisive. The argument that has been put forward is valid independently thereof. Even if it were the case that we all subscribed to the same interpretation of the law of nature; yes—even if it were the case that these ideas forced themselves upon us with the automatism of a law of nature, the criticism would still remain unshaken. If the whole of mankind had visions under the influence of poison, these fantasies would still not be true, as sure as by truth, we do not mean psychological coercion but something different.

§ 64. *Psychological Considerations*

Psychological considerations serve as a supplement to the critique based on grounds of principle. The overall picture becomes clearer as soon as we understand, not only that ethical-metaphysical speculations are empty, but also, why people indulge in them all the same.

Here we need to emphasize two things. One is what the metaphysics of morals has in common with all other kinds of metaphysics. It is the *angst* of the vicissitudes and uncertainties of life, of the transitoriness of all things; or, conversely, the craving for the absolute, for the eternally immutable that defies the law of transience. Within the realm of morality, this means the fear of making choices and decisions. All actions that are not performed automatically confront us with a choice and demand a decision, but all decision-making is burdensome because it entails responsibility. Therefore, we attempt to justify our behaviour with general principles and evaluations and the maxims deduced therefrom. By doing so, however, we are not relieved of the burden of responsibility—it is merely transposed into a responsibility for these points of departure. The metaphysics of morals originates in the fear of this responsibility. We refuse to accept it, maintaining and believing that the highest principles that determine our actions are independent of our own choice and discretion, and that they are given us as an eternal truth grounded in God's will, or as an *a priori* insight of reason. If there is a law, grounded in the substance of existence or in my own rational nature, which dictates to me the 'right' course of action, then I am an obedient link within a greater whole and without any responsibility whatsoever.

The second thing is a characteristic specifically of the metaphysics of morals. The craving for the absolute, which can give us freedom from responsibility and the peace that passeth all understanding, has in the realm of morality the best psychological conditions for being gratified, and for flourishing, in a dogma-
[352] tism difficult to crush by critical thinking. The reason for this is a certain psychological mechanism, implying that in every individual who has been reared to identify himself with society, there develops a set of seemingly blindly imperious impulses, which are experienced in what is called *moral consciousness* or *conscience*. Since these impulses make themselves felt in complete independence of our conscious needs and desires, they are well suited to force upon us, with the strength of an illusion, the view that in our conscience there is a voice or law speaking to us, telling us of a 'validity' or a 'rightness' which is radically different from, and independent of, our physical nature, its instincts and desires. Henceforth, the road is clear for all sorts of metaphysical constructions of the nature of moral validity and the content of the moral law.

But just as the force of an illusion of the senses is dispelled when its object is observed more closely and distinctly, also the mirage of the moral consciousness vanishes when under closer psychological scrutiny. A more detailed account of the psychological mechanism that gives rise to the moral consciousness is outside the scope of what I can embark upon in this book.[1] What is at stake here is merely to make it clear, on the one hand, that the moral consciousness with its mystical pathos is like manna from Heaven to the metaphysically hungry; and, on the other, that the moral consciousness is after all not so mystical as to be inaccessible to scientific explanations on a psychological basis.

What has been said here on the issue of morality and the moral consciousness applies equally to the law and *the legal consciousness*. The law, too, is experienced as something that is validly 'binding', that is, as something I obey—not merely because I am afraid of the external compulsion of the sanction, but also because I respect the inner authority, or validity, of the law.[2] Thus, the legal consciousness—just like the moral consciousness—gives rise to super-empirical interpretations. Natural law and moral philosophy are closely intertwined, irrespective of whether natural law is understood as a part of morality, or as an independent province—coordinate with morality—within the realm of 'ethics'.

[1] For more detailed information, see *Kritik der sogenannten praktischen Erkenntnis* [Critique of So-called Practical Knowledge] (1933), ch. III, 8, ch. VII, 1 and ch. XIII, 1; *Virkelighed og Gyldighed i Retslæren* [Reality and Validity in Jurisprudence] (1934), ch. V, 3.

[2] Cf. *Virkelighed og Gyldighed i Retslæren* [Reality and Validity in Jurisprudence] (1934), ch. V, 3.

§ 65. *Political Considerations*

As mentioned previously, natural law may be conservative, evolutionary, or revolutionary in its political orientation. Its political tendency cannot be put [353] forward as an argument, of course—neither for nor against the theoretical tenability of the doctrine of natural law; but depending on our own political views, it will be decisive for our own actual sympathy or antipathy in relation to the doctrine.

Although all three kinds occur, the function of natural law throughout history has primarily been a *conservative* one, endowing existing power relations with the sacred garb of validity. First and foremost, it is an ideology created by those in power—by statesmen, jurists, and priests—in order to legitimize and reinforce their position of authority.[1]

A natural law which originally was of the revolutionary kind will naturally turn conservative, once the social classes whose interests it asserted have prevailed. The individualistic and liberalistic natural law that led to the American Revolution is an example thereof. The principles of ownership, economic freedom and freedom of contract, which had enabled the tremendous expansion of American society at the beginning of the nineteenth century, became in the latter half of the century a reactionary power which, to the advantage of the possessing class, impeded development towards achieving social levelling and welfare. The United States Supreme Court used its constitutional powers to overrule (through a frequently strained interpretation of the Constitution) the validity of a series of laws which had resulted from the needs of this development, but were in conflict with the natural law principles of freedom.[2] Examples: laws concerning the regulation of working time or the establishment of minimum wages; laws on child labour in mines and factories; laws prohibiting employers from interfering with their employees' membership in trade unions; laws prohibiting the payment of wages in kind; laws restricting the owner's unlimited use and enjoyment of his property. Even a law proposing a modest income tax was declared invalid by the Supreme Court (1895), with the effect that no income tax could be introduced before an appropriate amendment to the Constitution had been adopted as late as 1913.[3] This battle against

[1] This must not be taken literally, that is, as if the ideology had been consciously invented for this purpose. The relationship between ideology and interest is much more subtle than that. On this issue, see T. Geiger, *Sociologi. Grundrids og hovedproblemer* [Sociology. Outline and Main Problems] (1939), 466 *et seq.*

[2] A good description of this is given in Charles Grove Haines, *The Revival of Natural Law Concepts* (1930). See also J. Stone, *The Province and Function of Law* (1946/50), ch. IX; Wolfgang Friedmann, *Legal Theory* (2nd edn, 1949), ch. 9 and Ernst Andersen, *Forfatning og Sædvane* [Constitution and Custom] (1949), 28 *et seq.*

[3] It was Cordell Hull, later US Secretary of State during the Second World War, who from 1907 onwards fought for the introduction of an income tax and finally succeeded in having the necessary constitutional amendment carried through. See Cordell Hull, *The Memoirs of Cordell Hull* (1948), vol. I, 48–50, 58–61, 70–71.

increasingly prevalent social principles in legislation reached its dramatic climax when President Roosevelt, after the great depression of 1929, started his New Deal programme in the thirties. Several laws aiming at the constructive rebuilding of the economy were overruled by the Supreme Court, and the President found that he had no choice but to break the resistance of the Supreme [354]
Court by a sort of 'coup by peers', that is, by appointing a sufficient number of new, progressive judges. In a message to Congress in 1937, the President presented a proposal for a general reform of the court organization; a proposal whose real (albeit veiled) purpose was to achieve the appointment of six new judges of the Supreme Court. The proposal met with violent opposition and was never carried out. For quite some time a growing minority had existed in the Supreme Court, ready to side with the government in its economic policy. This wing carried off the victory now, possibly as a result of the President's threat; no drastic measures were taken, however. Since approximately 1937, the American Supreme Court has accepted the new economic ideology—without, however, changing its views on the court's power of judicial review, or on the principles of constitutional interpretation.[4]

[4] However, see also Ernst Andersen, *Forfatning og Sædvane* [Constitution and Custom] (1947), 40; cf. Alf Ross, book review in *TfR* 1947, 453, and Wolfgang Friedmann, *Legal Theory* (2nd edn, 1949), 59.

§ 66. *Juridico-Theoretical Considerations*

As long as the nature of natural law was merely that of a moral philosophy, purporting to justify positive law and guide the legislator, it was not able to do serious damage to legal thinking proper. Its postulates that law shall be in conformity with man's nature or the principles of justice did not, as such, preclude (as previously mentioned in connection with Thomas Aquinas, § 59) on this basis a realistic treatment of the problems of legal politics, that is, taking account of cultural preconditions, customs, and practical needs. Due to their broad generality, the highest principles could be likened to a roomy cloak, providing a moral garb for the law and not necessarily entailing any limitation to the freedom of thought.

As mentioned in the historical overview above (§ 60), rationalism entailed a decisive change of view in that respect. Rationalism turned natural law from a moral into a genuinely legal discipline. It duplicated the legal system, because it conceived of natural law as a set of natural rights located above, or behind, positive rights. In contrast to merely philosophico-ethical speculations, this
[355] duplication of the legal system was well suited to confuse the concepts and, in a conclusive way, do damage to the juristic analysis and the treatment of juridico-political problems.

As previously noted, the concept of right is inextricably linked to an experience of power, resulting from the possibility of setting the state apparatus of coercion in motion. When natural law, too, was presented under the category of the concept of right, this necessarily entailed that all law, both natural law and positive law, must—in contrast to morality—be characterized by the coercive power inherent in the concept of right. And indeed, this was the prevailing doctrine of natural law philosophy in the eighteenth century.[1]

Whereupon the question arises: What kind of coercion is meant here? Obviously, the actual state apparatus of coercion cannot be meant here, for this is determinative of positive rights. That it is morally allowed to use force cannot be meant, either, for natural law would thereby disintegrate into ethics. It is inherent in the construction itself that the coercion in question can only be the coercion emanating from hidden spiritual powers, an invisible dominion beyond sensuous reality.[2]

[1] See Alf Ross, *Virkelighed og Gyldighed i Retslæren* [Reality and Validity in Jurisprudence] (1934), ch. II, 1–2.

[2] For details, see Ross, *op. cit.*, ch. II, 1–2.

I am not saying that this spiritual mysticism has ever been expressed overtly and clearly. I would like to suggest, however, that it is latently embodied in the very idea. Moreover—and of course this is the pivotal point—I would like to suggest that juristic thinking, under the influence of natural law, has been dragged into a complete confusion of concepts which has impeded our understanding of basic connections, and which becomes clear only if we presuppose previously existing and invisible rights. Here, I am thinking of a widespread and erroneous view concerning the relationship between rights and sanctions. The actual state of things, as we know (§ 36), is that the right is nothing whatsoever but an imagined unity in a complex of legal rules. I am an owner, because there is a set of rules pursuant to which I, owing to certain facts, can claim damages, can recover goods, etc. For the natural law conception, however, the situation is reversed. For example, a claim for damages is justified by my right having been infringed. In principle, damages are a just claim for reparation. In a similar way, all other sanctions are assumed to be conditioned by previous unlawfulness, that is, an infringement of another person's substantive rights.[3] In this way, one has from the outset become involved in a meaningless and circular discussion about the justification of the legal institutions, and precluded oneself from a realistic debate concerning the social function of damages or other legal institutions. Only in recent times, and in Nordic jurisprudence in particular, has one escaped this elusive confusion of concepts. For this achievement, a considerable part of the honour must doubtlessly be ascribed to the Swedish scholar *Lundstedt*, even if his critique of current views has often been curiously exagger- [356] ated and exalted.[4]

In short, one can say that the errors of rationalist, juristic natural law originate in the fact that, unlike earlier, natural law was conceived as belonging under the specific category of positive law, that is, as a certain complex of rights. On the other hand, the criticism frequently put forward nowadays—namely, that the shortcomings of natural law consisted in passing off its own ideal demands as valid law—is misleading. Natural law was typically not revolutionary. It expressly acknowledged that the citizens owe obedience to civic laws, irrespective of whether or not they conformed to natural law. For laws are always valid by virtue of the social contract and the principle of *pacta sunt servanda*.[5] This was

[3] See Alf Ross, *Virkelighed og Gyldighed i Retslæren* [Reality and Validity in Jurisprudence] (1934), ch. XIII, 2.

[4] See, e.g., Ross, *op. cit.*, ch. X, 4 and § 50, note 3 above.

[5] See, e.g., Samuel Pufendorf, *Le droit de la nature et des gens* [Of the Law of Nature and Nations] (translation by Barbeyrac), Book 8, ch. 1, §§ I and II. According to Pufendorf, the relation between natural law and positive law can be described as follows. Due to the weakness and sinfulness of man, natural law is inadequate to safeguard peace. Therefore, people subject themselves in the social contract to a government which has the authority to issue laws and maintain them through force. By virtue of the contract and the natural maxim that agreements must be kept, civic laws obtain their natural validity, that is, they become binding also vis-à-vis God. However, it is the authority of the sovereign that gives them their full force before the civic courts. This applies quite irrespective of their content. Only if civic law does not contain a certain regulation does natural law intervene complementarily. The content of civic laws consists primarily of the fundamental principles of natural law, on whose observation any peaceful coexistence of human beings depends. In the civic codes, however, these prin-

in line with the absolutist political theory and practice of the times. The practical, liberal demands for reform as expressed in the construction of natural law were exclusively intended as a legislative programme. Natural law was reformatory and evolutionist—not revolutionary.[6]

ciples are mixed up with regulations which are given in order to benefit the individual state and, what is more, with a number of formalities concerning the technical implementation of the law. Thus, civic law comprises *natural law (justice), utility, and pure positivities*. Pufendorf, *op. cit.*, Book 1, ch. 6, § XII; Book 2, ch. 3, § XI; Book 7, ch. 1, § XIII; Book 7, ch. 2, § VII; Book 8, ch. 1, §§ I–II. It can be attributed to this fact that politics, as a doctrine on utility, is sharply distinguished from morality (and law) as a doctrine on the valid and the rational; see Book 1, ch. 2, § IV. This distinction also plays an important role in the legal philosophy of our times. In Danish legal literature, it has found expression in F. C. Bornemann, *Foredrag over den almindelige Rets- og Statslære* [Lectures on the General Theory of Law and State] (1863), 42: 'It is true, however, that there is a contrast between a natural, that is, purely rational element, necessitated by reason, and a purely positive element within the law, the positive law. The latter does not only include everything that justly can be considered arbitrary and accidental, but everything that cannot be conceptually deduced from the ideas of legal matters, from their moral importance; that is to say, from everything that merely considers utility and purposiveness.'

[6] At any rate, this applies to natural law *qua* juridico-scientific doctrine. The situation was different with respect to the specifically political theories which acquired a revolutionary content, through reading provisos for certain civic rights and liberties into the social contract (Locke), or through re-interpreting the social contract (Rousseau). And indeed it was Locke who was the ideological father of the American Revolution, just as Rousseau was the ideological father of the French Revolution.

CHAPTER XII [357]

The Idea of Justice

§ 67. *Justice and Natural Law*

In the philosophy of natural law, the doctrine of the idea of justice has always played a prominent role. Throughout its history, natural law has claimed that in our inmost conscience, there is a simple and directly evident idea, the idea of justice—the highest principle of law, as opposed to the highest principle of morality. Justice is the specific idea of law: it is reflected—more or less clearly or distortedly—in all positive laws, and is the internal measure of their correctness.

At the same time, there exists indeed another usage (especially in the realm of older philosophy), according to which justice denotes the highest, all-embracing virtue without distinguishing between law and morality.[1] In this usage, justice is simply an expression of love of the good, or of God. It is in this sense we must understand the Sermon on the Mount when we are told: 'Blessed are they which do hunger and thirst after righteousness:* for they shall be filled.'

As a specific principle of law, justice is concerned with the outer limits and harmonization of conflicting desires, claims, and interests in the social coexistence of a plurality of individuals. Taking the view that all legal problems are problems of distribution, the postulate of justice amounts to a demand for *equality in the distribution or allotment of advantages or burdens*. Justice is equality. As early as the fourth century BC, this idea was formulated by the philosophy of the Pythagoreans, according to whom justice is symbolized by the square [358]
number in which like is united with like, and since then, the idea has been repeatedly adopted and varied in countless formulations.

The benefits or burdens whose distribution is discussed here can vary greatly in kind. Examples include: wages, taxes, our lot in life, property, punishment, individual and social services, or rights and duties as apportioned by the legal

* Translator's note: Matthew 5:6 [The Official King James Bible]. In the Danish Bible, the word used for 'righteousness' is 'justice' [*retfærdighed*].

[1] For further information, see Del Vecchio, *Die Gerechtigkeit* [Justice] (1940), 7 *et seq.*

order in general. In all these instances the following applies: if such a distribution takes place, it shall be an equal distribution.

Our experience seems to confirm that here we have to do with a simple and evident idea endowed with an immense motivating force. An instinctive understanding of the demands of justice seems to exist. Even small children appeal to justice if one child gets a thicker apple slice than the other. It has even been claimed that animals possess an incipient sense of justice.[2] The power of justice is enormous. It strengthens and excites those who fight for a just cause. All wars have been fought in the name of justice by all parties, and the same applies to the political class struggle. On the other hand, perhaps the very fact of the enormous applicability of the principle of justice is apt to suggest suspicions of there being something wrong with an idea which can be invoked in support of any cause. Therefore, let us take a closer look at the demand for equality and see what it actually amounts to.

[2] See Del Vecchio, *Die Gerechtigkeit* [Justice] (1940), with numerous references.

§ 68. Analysis of the Idea of Justice

The first possibility that comes to mind is that the demand for equality be understood as an *absolute* demand, that is, in the sense that everyone, irrespective of individual circumstances, should be precisely in the same position as everyone else (*To each the same*). However, it stands to reason that what is usually[1] meant by justice cannot be such an absolute uniformity. Such a banning of all difference-making would mean that each and every one of us should occupy the same legal position—irrespective of age, irrespective of marital status, irrespective of whether or not one had committed murder, irrespective of whether or not one had entered into a contract, etc., etc. A thing like that could never have been intended, of course.

It cannot be considered an injustice—nay, on the contrary, it must be a demand [359] of justice—that a distinction be made to the effect that benefits and burdens, rights and duties are distributed in view of conditioning circumstances. The legal position of a married couple must be different from that of an unmarried couple; the legal position of grown-ups must be different from that of minors; the legal position of criminals must be different from that of law-abiding persons, because such distinctions are relevant. The demand for equality solely comprises the requirement that no one, neither arbitrarily nor without sufficient reason, shall be subjected to a treatment that differs from the treatment accorded to another person.

Therefore, the demand for equality must be understood in a *relative* sense, that is, as a demand that *like shall be treated alike*. This means that as a precondition for applying the norm of equality, and independent of this norm, there must be criteria that stipulate what must be considered as equal and not equal, respectively. This can also be expressed as follows. The demand for equality, contained in the idea of justice, is not directed at each and every one in an absolute way but, rather, at all members of a certain *class*, established through certain relevant criteria (for example, the class of married couples, of promisors, of murderers, etc.). Thus, before the norm of equality can be applied, there must be criteria that determine whether or not two persons under given circumstances belong to the same class.

Then we can see that the different formulations of justice, set forth by various quarters or in various contexts, comprise—alongside the idea of equality—a

[1] By way of exception, 'justice' can also mean absolute equality, immune to any kind of difference-making: thus, when sometimes death is conceived as an equal fate that affects everyone, without regard to worldly distinctions. Obviously, such an idea lies behind the well-known medieval pictures of Death, dancing with people from all walks of life—with emperor and pope, citizens and beggars.

reference to a certain yardstick of evaluation which is presumed to be used for defining the category to the members of which equality shall be applied. Here are a few examples.[2]

(a) To each according to his merit

This formulation is often used when there is talk about justice in this life, or in life after death. Consequently, the relevant criterion is the individual's moral merits or worth, and the idea is that justice demands proportionality between worth and destiny—in this world or the next.

(b) To each according to his contribution

This formulation is often set forth in political theory—by Marxist socialism, for example, to cover the period of transition preceding the full realization of communism—as the principle of the just wage, or the just share, in the production results when these are distributed. Accordingly, the presupposed assessment criterion lies in the individual's contribution to the social product. Thus, the relation of exchange is conceived as an exchange of contributions between individual and society. However, this formulation is also used by theoreticians who conceive of work and wages on an individualist basis, as an exchange of services between private persons (the Danish theorists of the *Rechtsstaat*, for example).

[360] In its purest form, this principle is applied when wages are defined as piece-rate pay. Payment by the hour is a practical adaptation, based on the average amount of work done per hour.

This formula for justice is invoked when nowadays the claim is raised, frequently by women, of equal pay to men and women for equal work. This expresses precisely the idea that work performance is the relevant criterion determining the class that claims equal treatment. All individuals belonging to this class, women as well as men, thus have a claim to receive equal pay.

(c) To each according to his needs

This is the formula for justice put forth by the communist theory for the fully socialized society. In this society, everyone shall contribute according to his ability and receive according to his needs. The relevant criterion determining the class that demands equal shares is, then, not contribution but need. Those who are ill or weak, or have special needs based on other grounds, shall receive

[2] Cf. (in part) C. Perelman, *De la justice* [On Justice] (1945), 16 *et seq.*

what they need, regardless of the fact that, precisely on these grounds, they will probably contribute less or nothing.

While in modern society, socialist and capitalist alike, the pay as such is chiefly based on the principle of equal pay for equal work, the principle of need is increasingly applied to a number of other social services—in short, to social welfare. The idea behind it is that the unemployed, the sick, the disabled, those who are less gifted by nature, or the family breadwinners have a claim that their needs, resulting from their special position, be taken into account. To a certain extent, the principle of need also influences the pay system proper—for example, through the rules on minimum wages, through wage differentiation between women and men, through family allowances, and the like. Presumably also the civil servants' age additions could be regarded as chiefly based on considerations of need.

(d) From each according to his ability

With respect to the distribution of burdens, this principle of justice is the counterpart of the principle of need with respect to the distribution of benefits. It is typically applied in the assessment of income tax, namely, through the rules on tax-free minimum incomes, progressive tax tables, tax deductions for parents with children, etc.

(e) To each according to rank and station

An aristocratic principle of justice of this kind has frequently been invoked in the defence of class distinctions. It must be remembered that the logical correlate of the demand for equality is the demand for unlike treatment of what is unlike according to the presupposed assessment criterion. Here, the criterion is membership in a certain class, determined by birth, race, colour, creed, lan- [361]
guage, patriotism, ethnic characteristics, social status, etc. On the basis of this principle, it is no more than just that a distinction is made between master and slave, white people and black people, nobleman and peasant, the superior race and the inferior race, colonizer and colonized, orthodox believers and heretics, those who are members of the party and those who are not, etc., etc. Formulations of this kind are typically found in organic or totalitarian theories of state, from Plato until the present day—theories which emphasize the natural inequality of men and the organic or hierarchic construction of society through a plurality of classes, each of them with its own special function within the coherent whole.[3]

[3] See the chapter entitled 'Totalitarian Justice' in K. R. Popper, *The Open Society and its Enemies*, vol. I (1945), 74 *et seq*.

I have adduced these examples, not in order to discuss which formulation of the principle of justice is the 'right' one; I did so in order to illustrate that whilst the formal demand of equality in itself does not say much, the practical content of the demand of justice largely depends on presuppositions beyond the very principle of equality, namely, presuppositions concerning the considerations which determine the categories to which the norm of equality shall be applied. One does not really say anything by claiming that wages shall be paid equally, that taxes shall be assessed equally. These are empty formulae, unless it has also been established by what criteria equality shall be determined. Do we have equal pay for equal contribution, or equal pay for equal needs—or, perhaps, according to other imaginable criteria? Do we have equal taxes for equal incomes, or equal taxes for equal abilities—or, perhaps, according to other imaginable criteria?

Consequently, since we can state that the formulae for justice comprise two elements—namely, the formal demand for equality as such, and a substantive criterion (or possibly several criteria) in order to determine the class to which the norm of equality applies—this is a good opportunity to specify the role played by each of these two elements.

From what has already been said, it emerges that the formal demand for equality by no means precludes making a difference between persons who are situated in different circumstances. The only requirement is that this difference be motivated by the individuals in question being placed in different classes, according to certain relevant criteria. In the very principle of equality, however, there is nothing that would tell us what criteria are the relevant criteria. This question being left unanswered, the demand for equality is reduced to the demand that all difference-making be tied to general criteria (no matter what criteria). However, this is merely a demand that the concrete treatment shall appear as the application of a general rule. For it is precisely as a general rule that we understand a directive of action, whereby a certain course of action is made contingent upon circumstances described with the aid of concepts—and this means with the aid of certain characteristics or criteria.

[362] Thus, *the ideal of equality, as such, refers only to the correct application of a general rule*. Through the general concepts or characteristics contained within the rule, a certain class of persons (or situations) is pointed out, with regard to whom a certain kind of treatment shall be resorted to. The equal treatment of all the individuals within this class is, thus, simply the necessary consequence of the rule being applied correctly.

Justice in this formal sense (as being synonymous with the demand for equality as such, or with being rule-governed) can also be expressed as a *claim to rationality*, in the sense that the treatment given to a person shall be predeterminable by objective criteria, whose meaning has been established through common speech habits within a given speech community. Application in the specific case—within certain elastic limits—is thereby rendered independent of the decision-making subject and assumes the character of supra-subjective objectivity. Thereby, justice will stand in contrast to arbitrariness, that is, the decision which, in a non-predeterminable way, arises from the decision-making subject's spontaneous reaction to the specific situation, determined by his subjective feelings and attitudes. An arbitrary decision is, for example, one determined by the circumstance that the individual in question is my friend, or a person whose appearance repels me; it would be a decision made arbitrarily, because these properties cannot be expressed through objective characteristics, but are subjective in relation to the decision-making subject.

This is exactly what is contained in the first of the two elements of the different formulae for justice, namely, the demand for equality itself. It is clear that this formal demand for regularity, or rationality, cannot be used to justify the claim that a rule of a certain content shall be preferred over another rule. Thus, what gives content and force to the actually efficacious formulae for justice is not the demand for equality as such but, rather, the *presupposed substantive criteria* for what shall be assumed to constitute the class whose members demand equal treatment.

Let us consider the following formula for justice, for example: to each according to his contribution, or equal pay for equal work. The significance of this formula does not lie in the claim for equality (which merely states that a certain rule shall be followed): on the contrary, it lies in the demand that it is the work, and no other criterion, which shall be used in the rule according to which wages are assessed in specific situations. Similarly, the claim that everyone shall be taxed equally merely says that taxes shall be assessed according to general rules, and this claim is fulfilled irrespective of whether the tax is a poll tax (the same tax for everyone), a certain percentage of one's income (same income—same tax), a progressive income tax (same ability to pay taxes—same tax), or a tax according to any criterion whatsoever. The demand for just taxation is without any content, unless a certain substantive criterion for tax computation has been postulated alongside the formal idea of equality.

It is extremely important to pay attention to the aforementioned relation between the two elements of the formulae for justice. For the consequence of [363] this relation is that the *apparent self-evidence* that can attach to the idea of equality, and is felt to endow the formulae for justice with their self-sufficient justification, *by no means covers what actually is the essential element in these formulae*, namely, the substantive postulates of evaluation. It is commonly held that the idea of justice arises out of the innermost nature of our conscience with a peremptory *a priori* necessity. On the other hand, one would hardly assert that within the structure of our mind, there is a self-evident postulate that taxes shall be proportionate to one's ability to pay taxes, or that the pay shall be proportionate to one's work. The value of such rules is evidently not beyond dispute and justification on the basis of their empirical effects and their relation to certain objectives. To present them as demands of justice grounded in an evident idea of equality is a misrepresentation, intended to endow certain interest-governed, practical postulates with the apparent self-evidence that belongs to the idea of equality.

To put it more precisely: the misrepresentation must be described slightly differently. The idea of equality itself does not possess any 'self-evidence' or *a priori* validity. The plain fact of the matter is that it is quite easy to arrive at an agreement that taxation, wage assessment, etc. shall take place according to a general rule, and not arbitrarily—according to mood and whim—on an *ad hoc* basis. One attempts now to appropriate this basic agreement in favour of an interest-governed postulate, saying that a rule of a certain content (concerning which there is no agreement) shall be applied.

Thus, the idea of justice, in itself, is nothing but the idea of a general rule and its correct application to cases under its *aegis*.[4] Therefore, the words 'just' and 'unjust' make sense when used to characterize the *decision* made by a judge. To say that the decision is just means that it has been made in a rule-governed fashion, that is, in conformity with the rule, or the system of rules, that is assumed to be valid. (We return to this issue in § 70.) In a slightly wider sense, these expressions can also be applied to *any other course of action* judged in the light of given rules. 'Justice' denotes the behaviour that is right and proper, and in this sense, any course of action which is in harmony with presupposed legal or moral rules, can be called 'just'.

However—and this is really interesting in this context—the words 'just' and 'unjust' are completely empty if used to characterize *a legal rule or legal order*. For as we have seen, it is impossible to deduce from the formal idea of equality any demand whatsoever with respect to the content of the rule or order. Used in this context, the words are *devoid of all descriptive meaning*. An individual
[364] who claims that a certain rule or order—a certain taxation system, for example—is unjust, does not point at any discernible quality in this system: therefore, he is not justifying his own attitude but merely expressing it emotionally. Individual A says: I am against this rule because it is highly unjust. He ought to say: This rule is highly unjust because I am against it.

Invoking justice is the same thing as banging on the table—*viz.*, an emotional expression which turns one's claim into an absolute postulate; and that is the end of it. This is not the proper way to achieve mutual understanding. It is

[4] This and nothing else lies embodied in the maxim: 'Do not do unto others what you would not have them do unto you.'

impossible to have a discussion with somebody who mobilizes justice, because he says nothing one can argue for or against. His words are persuasion, not argumentation (§ 77). There will be no real dialogue unless we try to ask ourselves what factual circumstances and evaluative attitudes are conditioning our emotional attitude, and then argue accordingly.

As far as the debate on the design of the pay system is concerned, some people hold that pay should be fixed only in proportion to the work done and, thus, be the same for women and men. Of course, this rule can be justified and discussed on the basis of considerations referring to the social consequences of different conceivable wage systems. However, putting forward the demand for equal pay for men and women as a just demand for equality is no justification. Invoking justice merely means providing the demand with a *pathetic foundation which precludes rational argumentation* that might pave the way for a mutual understanding. The ideology of justice leads to implacability and conflict, because, on the one hand, it makes us work ourselves up to the belief that our demand is not merely an expression of a certain interest in conflict with opposing interests, but that it possesses a higher, absolute validity; and on the other, it precludes all rational argumentation and discussion concerning a compromise. The ideology of justice implies a fighting attitude of a biological-emotional kind, to which we work ourselves up in order to defend—implacably and blindly—certain interests.

Since the formal idea of equality, or of justice, is completely empty or neutral in relation to any substantive content, any kind of substantive postulate can be put forward in the name of justice. As I have mentioned earlier, this explains why all wars and social conflicts have been fought in the name of the lofty idea of justice. There is very little chance that the situation will change in the foreseeable future. 'Justice' is a weapon far too effective and ideologically convenient to permit us to hope that statesmen, politicians, and agitators, even if they should have grasped the proper state of affairs, would agree to a disarmament on this point. Besides, most of them may have fallen victim to the deception themselves. It is so easy to believe in illusions which excite the emotions by stimulating the function of the adrenal glands.

It is quite another matter, however, that we, who have made it our task to study [365]
the contributions of science to a rational discussion of political problems, and who have seen through the deception, must firmly deny that in a rational juridico-political argumentation there is room for the ideology of justice.

§ 69. A Few Examples

The analysis of the idea of justice that was presented in the preceding section and was based on a few simple formulae taken from a political ideology, will now be further illustrated through more advanced theories taken from legal philosophy itself.

As will have been gathered from the foregoing, the philosophers who have tried to provide a more theoretical presentation of the idea of justice, as the highest norm for the shaping of positive law, have been working under the pressure of a dilemma. On the one hand, if one wished to preserve the illusion that justice was an *a priori* evident idea, it would be necessary to formulate the principle in a highly abstract way in close connection with the pure idea of equality. By doing so, however, the principle ran the risk of becoming empty of meaning. On the other hand, if one wished to provide the principle with a substantive content, it would be difficult to maintain the illusion of self-evidence. This dilemma was bound to result in the principle being formulated more or less tautologically, or empty of meaning, at the same time as one smuggled in undisclosed dogmatic postulates of a juridico-political nature. In this way, what was empty acquired seeming content, and this content acquired seeming self-evidence.

*(a) suum cuique tribuere, neminem laedere, honeste vivere**

This is the formula through which the Roman jurists gave expression to the principle of natural law, or principle of justice. In later periods, the formula has often been repeated as the quintessence of wisdom. It is not difficult to see that it is sheer delusion, and only gives the impression of being a matter of course because it does not say anything.

'To give each his due' sounds great. Who could deny it? The only problem is that the formula presupposes that I know what is due to each person as his own (that is, as his *right*). The formula is completely empty, then, because it presupposes the state of law it was meant to justify.

The demand to harm no one is a similar case. What does 'harm' mean? It can-
[366] not possibly mean 'not acting in a manner that is detrimental to the interests or wishes of others'. In this sense, the creditor 'harms' the debtor by recovering his debts, the businessman 'harms' another businessman in competition, and society 'harms' the criminal by punishing him. No, 'harm' can only mean that I must not infringe the interests of others *unjustly*, or that I must not violate their *rights*—which makes it clear that there is circular reasoning here as well.

* Translator's note: 'To give each his due, to hurt no one, to live honourably.'

Finally, the same applies to the command to live honestly, where 'honesty' can obviously only mean that our conduct should conform to the letter and spirit of the law.

(b) 'Any action is right, if it can coexist with everyone's freedom in accordance with a universal law'[1] (Kant's formulation which is one of the most famous versions of the highest principle of law)

This idea can also be expressed as follows: the only thing that can justify restrictions on freedom of action is that such restrictions are necessary in consideration of the freedom of action of others, when the same rule shall apply to everyone.

The Kantian formula expresses very well that the demand for equality is identical with the demand for a universal law. But when there is no way of knowing the purpose of the universal law, the criterion is an empty one. For it is possible to imagine any course of action whatsoever being justified by one universal law or another applying to everybody. *A* killing his wife's lover, for example, can be justified on the grounds of a universal law, saying that killing out of jealousy is permitted. *A*'s freedom can, thus, coexist with everyone's freedom in accordance with the same universal law. The fact that for different reasons we do not think that this law is commendable is quite another thing and does not affect the application of Kant's principle. If this principle is to have any meaning and content at all, then the point of departure must be that freedom of action is restricted in view of other people's *rights*—whereby the usual circle manifests itself.[2]

(c) Justice as an equal weighing of interests (Nelson)

According to a widely held view, which reflects the general consciousness among both laymen and jurists undoubtedly better than Kant's formalism, justice means an equal weighing of all interests affected by a certain decision. No one has developed this idea more thoroughly and with greater perspicacity than the German philosopher Leonard Nelson.[3] [367]

[1] Immanuel Kant, *Metaphysik der Sitten*, Einleitung in die Rechtslehre [The Metaphysics of Morals. Introduction to the Doctrine of Right], (1797) § C.

[2] A rule with a content similar to that of Kant's rule is included in the Turkish Constitution of 20 April 1924 (10 January 1945) § 68: 'Every Turk is born free and lives freely. "Freedom" refers to any act that is not detrimental to others. The freedom of an individual (which is his natural right) is limited only by the freedom enjoyed by his fellow citizens. These limits are defined exclusively by the law.' It is precisely the absolute emptiness of such a formula, further guaranteed by the last sentence of § 68, that makes it suitable for use as ideological ornamentation.

[3] Leonard Nelson, *Kritik der praktischen Vernunft* [Critique of Practical Reason] (1917). For a detailed and documented account of Nelson's doctrine, see my *Kritik der sogenannten praktischen Erkenntnis* [Critique of So-called Practical Knowledge] (1933), ch. XI, 2.

Taking his point of departure in the general moral and legal consciousness, Nelson claims that the supreme principle of action that determines my duty shows the following three characteristics:

(1) it sets limits, that is, it does not positively command us to pursue certain goals, but sets a limit to our freedom to pursue those goals towards which we are naturally striving;

(2) this limit consists of the demand that when pursuing our interests, we should also consider the interests of others; and

(3) this consideration is expressed in the demand that the agent shall be equally considerate of all interests affected by his action, without allowing himself to be influenced by the question which of them are his own interests, and which of them are the interests of other people. He shall weigh the interests against each other without regard to persons, or in such a way as if all interests were his own.

These three characteristics are now combined, by Nelson, within the following formulation of the principle of justice: '*Never act in such a way that you cannot approve of your course of action if all the interests affected by it were your own.*'

This principle, which practically turns the agent into a judge in his own case and demands an impartial decision of him, by means of abstraction from the difference between his own interests and those of others, is undeniably most intriguing, and no doubt harmonizes well with many jurists' views on the task of finding the correct legal solution to a conflict of interest. Therefore, Nelson's formula calls for a thorough examination. This I have attempted in one of my earlier works.[4] It would lead us too far to repeat my argumentation in its entirety. Only a few principal points will be taken up once again.

The content of Nelson's principle can be broken down into two elements. First of all, he requests us to perform a thought experiment, namely, to imagine (which in fact is not the case) that all interests affected by an action are the agent's own interests. Then, we shall investigate whether the agent, under this imagined condition, would be able to consent to the action. If this condition is fulfilled, the action is lawful—but not otherwise.

I shall not pay attention to the fact that the thought experiment Nelson
[368] demands of us is not feasible in reality. While I can easily imagine myself wearing somebody else's hat, perfectly conscious that it belongs to someone else, this is not possible with an interest. I am unable to experience an interest and, at the same time, consider it, not as mine, but another person's. An accurate analysis

[4] See the previous note.

will show that whatever meaning we are trying to put into Nelson's thought experiment, it will lead to absurdity and is not feasible.

Therefore, we are obliged to cancel the thought experiment and formulate the claim in such a way that the agent shall balance all affected interests according to their respective weight in and of themselves, and regardless of whether they are his own interests or the interests of other persons.

Accordingly, there are two conclusive objections.

Firstly—and this applies irrespective of the cancellation of the thought experiment—Nelson's principle rests on the presupposition that it is possible in a given situation of action, to dissect a certain number of interests with a definite, delimitable content. Otherwise, it would be meaningless to speak of weighing them against each other. This presupposition is also borne out by common opinion. If a bank fails, for instance, it is possible—or so it is believed—to distinguish in this situation at least the following interests: the interest of the savers in getting back their deposits; the interest of the creditors in the satisfaction of their claims; and the interest of the shareholders in the preservation of the share capital. But if we—naively—by A's 'interest in something' only mean that the existence of this 'something' would be advantageous and satisfactory to A in light of the desires, needs, and inclinations with which nature has endowed him, then there is no reason to limit the interests in the manner indicated. It would indeed be advantageous and satisfactory to the depositors to get back, not merely their deposits, but twice as much or ten times as much, and in so far as they may be said to have any interest therein. There would thus be no measure to anyone's interest; instead, everyone can be said to be infinitely interested in anything that would be advantageous to them. If this sounds somewhat twisted, and if no one would dream of referring to the depositors' interest in getting back more than their deposits, then the reason for it is simply that the concept of interest with which we actually work in juridico-ethical deliberations, is not the naive concept presupposed here as the raw material for a legal evaluation. Nobody would dream of referring to the savers' interest in getting back more than their deposits, since such a claim would seem altogether unreasonable and unjustified. However, this means that *the concept of interest itself is legally qualified.* It does not comprise any desire or claim imaginable, but only those desires and claims which are reasonable or justified. And this, in turn, means that the concept of interest presupposes the existence of a legal order, and that 'weighing of interests' cannot be the principle from which the law is derived.

Thus, when Nelson believes that he can deduce the supreme norm of action, or the principle for all law, from a weighing of previously given interests with a definite, delimitable content, he is wrong. The limitation of interests within a certain measure necessarily presupposes an already existing legal order, to [369] distinguish between justified and unjustified interest claims. This legal order can only be the law of nature, manifesting itself in a set of natural rights. Justified interest originates in a natural right. In this way, even Nelson's principle of justice dissolves into a tautology: justice consists in satisfying *justified* interests.

The second objection concerns the weighing of (the justified) interests. As mentioned previously, the trick of referring to how the agent would act if all affected interests were his own interests does not work. One is obliged to demand a weighing on the basis of the respective weights of the interests themselves, regardless of whose interests they are, and regardless of their motivating force. Nelson himself speaks of a *true or well-conceived* interest, determined through the objective weight of the corresponding benefit. Thus, in reality, the weighing is not a test of strength between the motivating force of different interests, but a weighing of benefits in relation to a presupposed, objective evaluation criterion.

Together, these two objections show that the evidence that Nelson's principle of the equal weighing of interests apparently can claim is a delusion. The actual content of the principle does not lie in the 'equal weighing', but, rather, in the hidden presuppositions concerning the justification and objective value-weight of the interests; which is to say, in substantive postulates of a natural law and value philosophical character, seeking cover under the apparent evidence of the idea of equality. The masquerade of the idea of justice could hardly be staged with greater éclat.

§ 70. *Justice and Positive Law*

As we have seen, the idea of justice and equality resolves itself into the purely formal demand that the specific decision appear as the application of a general rule, no matter what rule. Justice is correct rule application—as opposed to arbitrariness.

The first and important consequence thereof, when it comes to the problem of the relation between the idea of justice and the positive legal order, is that *justice cannot be a juridico-political yardstick*, or an ultimate criterion according to which legal rules can be assessed and one rule preferred over another. Claiming that a certain rule is unjust is, as we have seen, nothing but expressing—blindly, emotionally, and inarticulately—that one reacts against the rule. Branding the rule as unjust provides no real characteristic, no reference to any criterion, no [370] argumentation—in short, it is merely a pathetic way of venting one's aversion to the rule. Therefore, the ideology of justice has no place in a rational discussion on the value of legal rules.

This is not to say that there is no connection between valid law and the idea of justice. In this idea two elements can be singled out: first (a) the claim that there is a rule, or a set of rules, as the basis for a specific decision; then (b) the claim that the specific decision is, in reality, a correct application of this rule-basis to the situation in question. Accordingly, the problem can be formulated in the following two ways:

(a) First, one might ask what role the idea of justice plays in the shaping of positive law, in so far as it is understood as a *claim to rationality* (§ 12 above); that is, as a claim that the norms of the law be shaped through objective criteria, in such a way that the specific decision becomes as independent as possible from the subjective reactions of the judge and, therefore, predictable.

There is no doubt that such a claim is inextricably linked with the nature of the law as a social, institutional order, as opposed to individual ethical phenomena (§ 12). Without a certain *minimum* of rationality (predictability), it would be impossible to speak of a legal order, which presupposes, conceptually, that it is possible to interpret human actions objectively, as a coherent whole of meaning and motivation, and (within certain limits) to predict them (Chapter 1). In a way, the idea of justice, in the sense of rationality or regularity, can be said to be *constitutive* of the concept of law.

Furthermore, formal, objective rationality is also an *ideal* of law, in the sense that a *maximum* thereof conforms to certain general considerations and wishes which—at least in our Western culture—make themselves felt in all legal formation.

To begin with, objective regularity—as opposed to subjective arbitrariness—is experienced as a value in itself. It is precisely this idea which is expressed in the old English motto that society shall be based upon *the rule of law, not the rule of men*. A judge shall not be like the Homeric king who fetches his *themistes* directly from Zeus, or like the Oriental kadi whose decision-making is guided by hidden wisdom. It is precisely this idea which makes us react against a tendency prevalent in totalitarian states—namely, to authorize the judge to disregard all fixed rules and decide according to the 'sound legal consciousness of the people' or 'the interests of the proletariat'—and to call a situation like this a denial of the very idea of law.

This evaluation is probably motivated by the social effects of being rule-governed. From the citizens' point of view, this is the precondition for
[371] security and predictability in the affairs of communal life. From the point of view of the authorities, it is a precondition for guiding citizens' behaviour in the long run—that is, over and above the specific relationship at hand—by internalizing fixed patterns of behaviour.

Objective regularity—formal rationality—is, then, a fundamental idea in all law; it is not the only one, however. Fixed in categories which are determined by objective criteria, the legal rule appears as a formalization of the evaluations appertaining to our cultural tradition. But the formalized rule is never able to express exhaustively all the considerations and circumstances that are relevant according to those evaluations. Therefore, it is unavoidable that the rule, when applied to the individual case, may lead to results which cannot be approved by the common sense of justice as a spontaneous, inarticulate expression of the fundamental evaluations. All law and all exercise of legal authority is, therefore, formally determined through a dialectic conflict between two opposite tendencies. On the one hand, a tendency towards generalization and decision-making with reference to objective criteria, and on the other, a tendency towards individualization and decision-making in light of the subjective estimates and evaluations of the common sense of justice. In short: on the one hand there is the idea of formal justice—on the other, there is the idea of *equity* in the individual case.[1]

Both of these factors make themselves felt in the law working in real life under any circumstances, but their mutual relative weight can vary according to time and place, and between different areas of law.

In the exercise of legal authority, this is expressed in the difference between a bound and a free type of interpretation, cf. § 29 above.

[1] 'The most profound tension within the law—and for precisely this reason also the essentially formal tension within the law—can be called: regularity versus individualization', Viggo Bentzon said in his inspirational treatise *Skøn og Regel* [Discretion and Rule] (1914). In this treatise, Bentzon made—with great delicacy—precisely this tension the subject of his investigation.

In legislation, the contrast manifests itself in the extent to which the rules, due to their own formulation, make room for judicial discretion. This can be done in two different ways. The legislator can either preserve the illusion of laying down a rule, but express it in terms so vague, or by referring to prevailing morality, that the outcome will amount to an extended freedom for the judge or administrative civil servant to exercise their discretion. We speak of legal *standards*[2] in these cases. Or the legislator can simply give up and merely state that the decision will be made at the *discretion* of the judge [372] or administrative civil servant (possibly within certain limits).[3]

From an evolutionary perspective, there seems to have been a development from rigorous formalism towards an ever wider scope for individualizing discretion, both as to legislation and the exercise of legal authority.

The tension in the exercise of legal authority between formalized law and the demands of equity becomes particularly noticeable when it is preceded by a social development without any accompanying legislation that would adjust the legal rules to the changed conditions. In such a case, people will experience a strong desire for decisions which contradict the traditional rules. At first, such decisions will have the nature of equity decisions, precisely because they do not follow given rules but, rather, arise from an intuitive, discretionary assessment of the specific situation in its entirety. In the course of time, formal rationality will prevail once again, however. Through the practice of the courts, a set of considerations formulated according to a new doctrine will establish itself, and future decisions will be made on that basis and lose their character of equity. All throughout history, we repeatedly come across the curious circumstance within this context that this innovative and adjusting activity is being exercised, not by the ordinary courts, but by courts of special jurisdiction, with the consequence that the new law, developed in this manner, is regarded as a separate system of law—the law of equity, as a supplement to ordinary law.

The development of *equity law* in English law is an excellent example.[4] Because of the rigidity and obvious unfairness, under altered social

[2] See especially Ragnar Knoph, *Rettslige Standarder* [Legal Standards] (1939) and Marcel Stati, *Le standard juridique* [The Legal Standard] (1927). For example, the Danish Prices Act, promulgation no 463 of 14 Nov. 1949, § 8, which contains a prohibition against *unreasonable* prices, profits, and trade terms; the Danish Unfair Competition Law, promulgation no 80 of 31 March 1937, § 15, referring to *good business conduct*; § 33 of the Danish Contracts Act (*general honesty*). When the law sometimes demands—as, for example, § 29 of the Danish Contracts Act and § 279 of the Danish Penal Law—that an action, as a condition for a certain legal consequence, shall be performed *unlawfully*, then this means a totally empty poster in order to hide that the legislator has given up and refers the judge to a restrictive interpretation on the basis of custom and free evaluations, cf. pp. 300–1 above.

[3] In the field of private law, typical examples (among many others) are § 63 of the Danish Age of Majority Act and § 25 of the Danish Insurance Contracts Act. In the field of public law, especially administrative law, there are so many discretionary powers that it is futile to adduce examples.

[4] For further information, see C. K. Allen, *Law in the Making* (4th edn, 1946), 322 *et seq.* and Alf Ross, *Theorie der Rechtsquellen* [Theory of the Sources of Law] (1929), 123 *et seq.*, with references; see also Torstein Eckhoff, *Rettsvesen og Rettsvitenskap i U. S. A.* [Legal System and Legal Science in the USA] (1953), 38 *et seq.*

conditions, of the traditional *common law*, it became a common practice at a certain point of time to try to mitigate the results by appealing to the king against decisions which defied the demands of the common sense of justice. For the administration of the law was considered a royal prerogative. In such a case, the king exercised his power *via* the chancellor, who 'was deemed to be the keeper of the royal conscience'. The chancellor was formally obligated to follow the *common law*, but in reality, under the stresses and strains of life, he pursued—guided by equity considerations—an activity of a quite discretionary and creative nature. In the course of time, the chancellor's court (*the Court of Chancery*) was made a permanent institution, and the chancellor's original, discretionary equity decisions were replaced by a regular exercise of legal authority, in conformity with the doctrines that had developed through the practice of the chancellor's court. The chancellor's equity decisions have given rise to criticism in their time. Making use of a grotesque metaphor, it was said that *equity*, according to
[373] the chancellor's conscience, was no better than *equity* according to his foot. 'One Chancellor has a long foot, another a short foot, a third an indifferent foot; it's the same thing in the Chancellor's conscience.' Later on, this criticism no longer applied, and Lord Eldon, one of the most famous English chancellors, was able to pronounce in a judgment: 'I cannot agree that the doctrines of this Court are to be changed with every succeeding judge. Nothing would inflict on me greater pain, in quitting this place, than the recollection that I had done anything to justify the reproach that the equity of this Court varies like the Chancellor's foot.'[5]

A corresponding distinction between law (in the strict sense, *jus strictum*) and equity is unknown here in Denmark. This has partly to do with the more important role of legislation in bringing the law up to date, partly with the greater freedom of interpretation which has characterized the Danish courts, at least in modern times. For a Danish judge, law and equity are not opposites: rather, equity is an integral part of the law.

(b) Secondly, one might ask whether the idea of justice asserts a lien on valid law, understood as a demand that the specific decision shall be a correct application of the norms of valid law.

This question must definitely be answered in the affirmative. Whereas justice, as a norm for the legislator (as a yardstick for the 'correctness' of the law), is merely a chimera, *justice as a norm for the judge* is, on the contrary, *a living and palpable reality*. While the assertion that a certain law is unjust is nothing but a theoretically empty and pathetic expression of the speaker's aversion to this law, the assertion that a certain decision is unjust refers to a real subject matter. It expresses the fact that the decision has not been

[5] *Gee v Pritchard*, 2 Swants, 414. Cited in Thomas Erskine Holland, *The Elements of Jurisprudence* (1880), 74.

made according to the rules, but is owing to a mistake (unjust in the objective sense) or to a conscious deviation from the law (unjust in the subjective sense).

It is especially the latter which corresponds to what in common usage is meant by injustice. To do wrong, or do an injustice, means that an individual, who has the power to make legal decisions allows himself—guided by personal interest, by feelings of friendship for one of the parties, by a desire to please those in power, or by other motives—to deviate from the commands of the law. The word is also used in this sense when § 146 of the Danish Criminal Code mentions that a person with judicial authority is deciding or handling a case unjustly.

A more precise delimitation of the concept is nonetheless problematic. For it is not the case—as has been shown in the theory of interpretation (Ch. IV)—that on the basis of valid law, only one decision can be derived as the correct, or the objectively correct, decision. This applies even in cases where there is a genuine rule, expressed in relatively fixed concepts, and of course it applies—to an even larger extent—when it is a question of standards, or even of a more or less unrestricted discretion. [374] There is always a margin of varying breadth, and no one would call a decision that falls within this margin an unjust decision, not even in the objective sense. We call it a *wrong* decision, by which it is meant that the speaker himself would have concreticized the law in the case before him differently.

But how to determine this margin; what are the 'correct' principles of interpretation, and how much interpretive freedom rests with the judge? Referring[6] to 'specifically legal' motivations, as opposed to considerations of power and interest, does not solve the problem, because a specifically legal evaluation does not exist. The law develops out of the same practical attitudes, interests, power factors, and ideological components that make themselves felt in society, even outside legal affairs. As far as I can see, the question cannot be answered in any other way than by reference to what is typical and normal in actual adjudication. Objectivity is the typical, the normal; subjectivity is the atypical, the abnormal. The decision is objective (just in the objective sense) when it is covered by such interpretive principles and evaluations as are common in legal practice. It is subjective (unjust in the objective sense) when it deviates therefrom. The subjectivity or unjustness expresses precisely that the decision is felt to have arisen from the individuality or subjectivity of one particular judge, in contrast to what is typical of the judiciary as a whole. The decisions pronounced by the famous French judge Magnaud ('le bon juge') were, thus, not

[6] Like Otto Brusiin in his work *Über die Objektivität der Rechtsprechung* [On Objectivity in the Administration of Justice] (1949), 25–26; cf. Alf Ross, book review in *TfR*, 1950, 476.

merely 'incorrect' (like so many other decisions), but arbitrary or unjust in the objective sense. That we do not wish to call this man an unjust judge (unjust in the subjective sense), however, is due to his undoubtedly acting to the best of his belief, guided by a profoundly moral conception of law.[7]

[7] H. Leyret, *Les jugements du president Magnaud* [The Judgments of President Magnaud] (1900); see also Francois Gény, *Méthode d'interprétation et sources en droit positif* [The Method of Interpretation and the Sources of Positive Private Law], II (1919), 278 *et seq.*

§ 71. *Equality Claims as Scientifically Valid Law*

From what has been said in the previous section, it emerges that a demand, *worded in general terms*, to the effect that everyone shall be placed on an equal footing or be treated equally, is an empty demand in so far as it merely means that the treatment accorded to every individual shall follow general rules.[1] If [375] such a demand has been authorized by law it will result in a specific problem of interpretation, namely, whether it must be written off as a mere ideological, but legally empty formulation, or whether it is possible, on a historical basis, to ascribe any particular meaning to it. If such a demand exists in doctrine, it will be a task for the critique to demonstrate its emptiness, and to ask what could possibly have been meant by it.

The situation is different if the demand has been given a *special* content, for example, as a demand for equality for all, irrespective of gender or race. Such a demand is meaningful. It contains a prohibition against the occurrence of criteria determined by a person's gender or race in the general rules concerning his legal position, or against paying attention to them in specific decisions. According to circumstances, of course, specific problems of interpretation may arise concerning the exact scope of the prohibition.

In the following, I shall adduce different examples in order to illustrate problems of this kind.

(a) National constitutions often contain a provision stating that all citizens are *equal before the law*.[2] These provisions seem to be devoid of any independent, plain meaning. To all appearances, they can only mean one of two things:

(1) that the law shall be upheld according to its content, without distinction of persons, against anyone whom it concerns—which is a matter of course and already inherent in the concept of a law;

(2) that the law must not base its rules on distinctions or characteristics which are considered 'partial' or 'unjust' in relation to the respective

[1] [General remark to § 71:] In connection with this section, cf. Poul Andersen's informative article 'Lighedsgrundsætninger i forvaltningsretlig Belysning' [Principles of equality in the light of Administrative Law], *JFT*, 1937, 479 *et seq.*

[2] E.g. the Constitution of Ireland of 1 July 1937, art. 40: 'All citizens shall, as human beings, be held equal before the law;' the Constitution of Czechoslovakia of 9 May 1948, special provision § 1: 'All citizens are equal before the law;' the Constitution of Turkey of 10 January 1945, art. 69: 'All Turks are equal before the law' (W. Brorsen (ed.), *Die Verfassungen der Erde in deutscher Sprache nach dem jeweils neuesten Stande*. Übersetzt und herausgegeben von W. Brorsen [The Constitutions of the World, in the German language translation and up-to-date on recent developments. Translated and edited by W. Brorsen] (1950). Among the Northern constitutions, only the constitution of Finland of 17 July 1919 includes a general norm of equality, namely in § 5: 'Finnish citizens are equal before the law.'

> legal effect. Such a prohibition against 'unjust' laws[3] is devoid of any precise meaning, however, since 'injustice'—which, within this context, can only mean 'injustice' in the substantive sense—is, as we have seen, nothing but a subjective and emotional expression of aversion to a certain order.

Provisions of this type can probably be explained historically and ideologically, namely as a reaction against the former state of the law, when certain sections of the population—for instance the nobility—were granted privileges, in particular privileges concerning jurisdiction (now abolished). It is possible—according to circumstances—to understand these provisions on a
[376] historical basis, as a prohibition against the reintroduction of such privileges.[4] If, on the other hand, the demand for equality is qualified by a reference to fixed criteria according to which discrimination is not allowed,[5] then the provision has a tangible meaning. It precludes the occurrence of such criteria in ordinary legislation.

The Danish Constitution does not include a general principle of equality, but it includes, in § 77, a special prohibition against anybody being deprived, by reason of his creed, of access to the full enjoyment of civic or political rights, or against anybody escaping compliance with any common civic duty.[6] And yet it was thought possible on the basis of this provision to project, into the Constitution, a general principle of equality and, by invoking it, demand that a legislation on the freezing of rent be set aside by the courts as unconstitutional. Irrespective of the fact that there is no basis for projecting a 'principle of equality' into the Constitution—which, according to what has been said previously, must mean a less than substantial prohibition against (substantively) 'unjust' laws—one can rest assured that the Danish courts will decline the adventure to set aside a law, made by King and Parliament, as 'unjust'. The exercise of discretion concerning what is 'right and proper' cannot be separated from political evaluations, and, according to the Danish conception of law, this estimation can rest with Parliament alone. Granting the courts a 'right of judicial review' with reference to the 'justice' of the laws would simply amount to the same thing as making the Danish Supreme Court the highest political authority in Denmark. Such a thing would never be tolerated.

[3] Understood in this sense, the provision has actually nothing to do with equality. This expression is merely used to create an appearance of self-evidence for certain postulates, cf. p. 354 above.

[4] The 14th Amendment to the US Constitution, which promises everyone 'equal protection of the laws', and which was adopted in 1868 after the end of the Civil War, thus had a historical purpose—namely, the equality of the black and white races.

[5] E.g. the Constitution of Italy of 27 Dec. 1947, art. 3: 'All citizens . . . are equal before the law, without regard to gender, race, language, religion, political conviction, and personal and social position'; the Constitution of the USSR of 5 Dec. 1936, art. 123: 'The equality of citizens of the USSR in all areas of economic, national, cultural, social, and political life, regardless of nationality and race, is inviolable law' (W. Brorsen, *op. cit.*).

[6] Cf. also §§ 81 and 90.

(b) An *abstract principle of equality* is set up sometimes, *as a guideline to the administration in the exercise of its discretion*. What has been said under (a) applies here as well. The principle does not contain a substantive norm for the exercise of discretion, but expresses only a formal demand, namely, that the decision shall be made on the basis of general deliberations and considerations, not capriciously or arbitrarily. Whether the administration is bound by considerations on which prior decisions of the same kind have been based—this is another question.[7]

An example of a qualified principle of equality is the Danish Statute No 100 of 4 March 1921, which—with some exceptions—gives to men and women under the same conditions equal access to all official positions and [377] assignments, in state and municipalities, and an equal obligation to undertake civic duties.[8]

(c) An abstract *demand for equality as one of the so-called fundamental rights of states* is often set up in international law doctrine. Since this issue appertains to international law,[9] it should only be noted here that such an abstractly formulated demand certainly is devoid of meaning, but that it is underpinned, partly by a prohibition against discrimination on the basis of the size of the states, partly by rules that have nothing to do with equality or inequality (the principle of unanimity and the rule concerning extraterritoriality).

(d) In the doctrine of *expropriation*, it is a generally received opinion that the borderline between expropriation and seizure of property without compensation is basically determined according to a criterion of equality: the seizure falls outside the scope of § 80 of the Danish Constitution if it affects all properties of the same sort; otherwise, it is a case of expropriation.[10] Within this context, one has also invoked the principle under which all citizens are equal before the law, a principle presumed to be presupposed by the Constitution.[11] However, it is clear that the principle of equality is just as empty within this context as anywhere else. Every law that describes the object of the seizure in general concepts or characteristics affects everyone equally and concerns all property 'of the same sort'. What objects are 'of the same sort', is surely not determined by Nature but, rather, because they have been assigned to the same conceptual category, no matter how this category is defined. The term 'farm' defines a group of objects 'of the

[7] On this issue, cf. Poul Andersen, *op. cit.* (see § 71, note 1) 488 *et seq.*

[8] See Poul Andersen, *Dansk Forvaltningsret* [Administrative Law in Denmark] (1946), 138 *et seq.*

[9] Alf Ross, *Lærebog i Folkeret* [A Textbook of International Law], § 34.

[10] See O. K. Magnussen, *Naboretlige Studier* [Studies in the Law Regulating Neighbouring Rights] (1950), 137, 148.

[11] Vinding Kruse, *Ejendomsretten* [The Right of Property] (3rd edn, 1951), 252.

same sort'. But this applies also to all the other conceptual definitions—such as, for example: 'Farms with thatched roofs', 'farms with thatched roofs and adjoining land of over 2 hectares', 'farms on the island of Fyn [Funen] with thatched roofs and adjoining land of over 2 hectares, the owner of which has been in possession of the farm for more than twenty-five years, and on which there is a mortgage debt of more than 100,000 Danish Crowns'—regardless of whether there is possibly only a single farm that meets the above criteria.

When mentioning that the demand for equality must not be understood in the formal sense, and that the decisive factor is whether the seizure takes place according to distinctive marks which are 'objective', 'reasonable', or 'just', then this simply means that the idea of equality vanishes and is replaced with a reference to what is considered 'just' according to a subjective and emotional view. Such a 'principle' is no genuine principle—rather, it means abandoning any attempt at rational analysis.

CHAPTER XIII [378]

Utilitarianism and the Chimera of Public Utility

§ 72. *The Relation of Utilitarianism to Natural Law*

The central idea of natural law had been that the 'correctness' of positive law depends on its conformity to a model or an ideal, inherent in our nature or our reason.[1] Legal rules are not judged by the societal effects they produce. Considerations of utility are not without importance, to be sure, but they distinguish themselves from the demands of justice. One might say that the aim of the law is inherent in the law itself: namely, to materialize the idea of justice.

However, this does not mean that to each individual, specific legal rule there is, in our reason, a corresponding ideal model. Reason limits itself to setting up a small number of fundamental, evident principles, and the correctness of the specific rule depends on whether it can be regarded as a concretized version, deduced from the highest principles.

In the previous section, we have seen that epistemologically, the philosophy of natural law builds upon a supposedly intellectual intuition, or a feeling of self-evidence, which guarantees the correctness of the highest principles, but is, in reality, nothing but a dogmatic and pathetic expression of the moral and legal consciousness prevailing at the time. We give no further thought to how the latter actually came into being—we do not regard it, from a historical or psychological point of view, as a product of combined factors (including the social and legal order that actually exists), we do not criticize it in light of its social consequences, but accept it with reverence—like an oracle which [379] reveals to man the moral truth, the self-valid law of God (or of Reason) for their actions.

[1] [General remark to § 72:] For a more detailed and documented account, see my *Kritik der sogenannten praktischen Erkenntnis* [Critique of So-called Practical Knowledge] (1933), Ch. IV, 1.

Bentham's utilitarianism signalled the breakthrough of a new approach, which looked upon itself as a revolution in the history of moral thought. In line with Locke's empiricist philosophy, Bentham wished to do away with all notions of innate ideas or *a priori* truths. The moral consciousness is not a revelation of eternal truths—it is merely a catalogue of inherited opinions and prejudices which people have some difficulty in shaking off, because they have been implanted into their minds from their earliest childhood. Instead of elevating, dogmatically and conservatively, the moral sense that actually exists to something that is absolutely valid, a progressive moral theory is intent on reaching the rational principle lying behind the moral sense, and on directing it. This principle is not perceived clearly, but works more or less unconsciously and instinctively. Only by bringing it into full consciousness is it possible to provide a rational justification of morality and to criticize and correct the real moral sense, if it should become stagnant or perverted.

Bentham thought that it must be possible to establish this principle on an empirical basis, by considering the nature of man.[2] All human striving is a striving towards pleasure. Therefore, pleasure is good in itself, and the moral principle of action must mean that one should act so as to procure the greatest degree of pleasure in the world. Thus, the value of an action depends upon the effects produced by it, measured in human pleasure and pain.

However, Bentham's break with the past is not as complete as he himself believed. For deriving morality from the natural striving of man is genuine natural law thinking, which—just to mention one example—has been expressed most concisely by Thomas Aquinas. Moreover, it is clear that Bentham's belief in his own capacity to construct a moral theory upon a purely empirical foundation must be an illusion. On the basis of real psychologico-empirical observation, one would never get beyond a description of how people are actually acting, or would act under certain conditions,[3] and one would never get to morality ('standards of right and wrong'),[4] that is, demands as to how one ought to act.[5] On closer inspection, it becomes clear that Bentham's principle of the greatest possible amount of pleasure cannot be derived from experience, but is the expression of a postulate which can only be justified metaphysically-intuitively.

[2] Bentham begins his major work, *An Introduction to the Principles of Morals and Legislation* (printed 1780, published 1789) with the following words: 'Nature has placed mankind under the governance of two sovereign masters, pain and pleasure. It is for them alone to point out what we ought to do, as well as to determine what we shall do. On the one hand the standard of right and wrong, on the other hand the chain of causes and effects, are fastened to their throne.'

[3] Especially if they had a more correct perception of reality.

[4] See the quotation in note 2.

[5] This view was later strongly emphasized by Moore; see Alf Ross, *Kritik der sogenannten praktischen Erkenntnis* [Critique of So-called Practical Knowledge] (1933), 78.

Bentham takes his point of departure in the view that all human striving is a striving towards pleasure. However, this does not mean that human beings always act egotistically in the usual sense, that is, seek their own advantage regardless of the interests of others. Bentham would by no means deny that man is capable of unegotistical, self-sacrificing, or heroic acts, prompted by sympathy and compassion for others. He merely means that also such acts are basically conditioned by the striving towards man's own pleasure, namely, the pleasure of following his own sympathetic feelings for others. Another point—which Bentham points out under the name of *the self-preference principle*—is that the sympathetic feelings in man are generally extremely weak and powerless in their fight against egotistical forces in the usual sense. In practice, it is almost exclusively these forces which determine the actual course of action. The pleasure people are seeking is, therefore, for the most part their own pleasure, understood in the narrower sense.[6] [380]

Let us now turn to Bentham's highest principle of action. It commands us to act so that the sum total of pleasure in the world is maximized. Thus, I am requested that in judging of an act, I shall completely disregard whether it is a question of my own immediate pleasure or other peoples'. The same weight, then, shall be ascribed to the pleasure of others as to my own, and a course of action which is more advantageous to others than it is detrimental to me is to be preferred over a course of action which is advantageous to me, but detrimental to others.

It stands to reason that such a principle simply cannot be derived from the psychological axiom of pleasure, but is, on the contrary, diametrically opposed to the assertion that people generally act egotistically. Like other ethical principles, this principle has the nature of a supreme demand, or a *specific validity*, in contrast to our sensuous impulses and must, like the postulates of natural law, seek its foundation in the rational nature of man and its justification in intellectual intuition. Actually, the principle comes very close to Nelson's formulation of the principle of justice (§ 69). It commands me to suppress my egotistical inclinations and act without respect of persons, or as I would act if all interests affected by my action were my own interests.

Still, it would be wrong to lump utilitarianism together with natural law. Bentham's criticism of the sense of morality and justice and his claim that an action should be judged according to its real effects are steps towards a realistic theory of permanent value. He was mistaken in thinking that the sense of morality and justice was governed by a single rational principle, according to which the judging of the effects of an action could be reduced to a simple maximization calculus with regard to commensurable quantitative units. Now we shall look into it more closely.

[6] For further information, see Alf Ross, *Kritik der sogenannten praktischen Erkenntnis* [Critique of So-called Practical Knowledge] (1933), ch. V.2.

[381] ## § 73. *Dissonance between the Maximization Principle and our Actual Deliberative Actions*

Even if the utilitarian principle—as shown in the previous section—cannot be derived from experience, but is, like other ethical principles, a metaphysical postulate based on intuition, there was of course nothing to prevent it, in this guise, from revealing something that reflects the manner in which we are actually reasoning about moral and political problems. This is also the case with respect to the basic view that actions must be judged by their consequences. But it is not the case with respect to the manner in which this judgment is thought to be delivered.

The principle of utilitarianism rests in this respect on the assumption that in every practical situation of action, our choice can be reduced to a rational choice between commensurable quantitative factors measured in terms of pleasure. Once you have assumed the premise that pleasure is good in itself, and that the same consideration shall be given to the pleasure of others as to your own, then the choice boils down to a purely rational calculation.

This assumption does not hold good, however. It is an expression of an obviously erroneous psychology. Our needs and desires are qualitatively different and mutually incommensurable. People have the most varied needs—for example, they need food, rest and sleep, occupation, sexual activity, the cultivation of the mind and knowledge, artistic experience and recreation, love and respect, power and social esteem, etc., etc. If it is impossible to meet all my needs, and if I am facing a choice between, say, listening to a symphony and eating a good dinner, then this choice cannot be described as a rational choice between two measurable quantities of pleasure. How to find a measure for the pleasure I am experiencing in either situation? What should be an adequate unit of measurement? The only conceivable criterion for calling the one good 'greater' than the other one seems to be the fact that I actually prefer it. But in that case my assertion, that when faced with a choice between two good things, I choose the greater good, becomes meaningless: for it is called the 'greater' good precisely because I have chosen it.

The assumption of the utilitarians implies a tremendous rationalist distortion of the life of the mind.[1] It reduces the irrational basis of our actions to a single evaluation, namely, that pleasure is preferred to pain, and then makes of everything else a rational calculation of quantities of pleasure and pain. The fact is

[1] This has to do with the erroneous—or rather empirically empty—assertion that all striving is a striving towards pleasure, cf. Alf Ross, *Kritik der sogenannten praktischen Erkenntnis* [Critique of So-called Practical Knowledge] (1933), ch. V.2.

that we are affected by many different needs and considerations, running across each other and fighting each other in an irrational process of motivation. In that way, we are influenced by certain patterns of evaluation and preference, which develop and assume a definite form individually and socially. If we con- [382] sider, say, the deliberations that take place in a legislative assembly, in a municipal council, in a board of directors, in a commission—in short, anywhere where public or private affairs are discussed in order to decide on a certain policy—then we shall see that what actually happens is that a variety of considerations is put forward and weighed, each of them possessing a certain motivating power that appeals to certain wishes or evaluations. These considerations are finally integrated into a conclusion, as an expression of the weight or preference ascribed to the different considerations. This conclusion is in the nature of what we call a decision, that is, an irrational mental act in which all the forces mobilized during the phase of deliberation are permitted to fight it out among themselves, until we—with our whole personality—are reacting with an outcome—namely, the conclusion. This is something totally different from a rational choice between quantitatively determined factors.

In short, we can say that *the incommensurability of human needs precludes quantitative maximization.* Therefore, the utilitarian principle is simply inapplicable with respect to situations of action where a plurality of qualitatively different needs (interests, considerations) compete with each other.

It is obvious that the great majority of moral and political problems are about situations of this kind. However, perhaps this is not necessarily the case with respect to purely economic problems. Since all economic interests can be expressed, at least approximately, in common monetary terms, the commensurability exists that makes it possible to apply the maximization principle.[2] Also, it is probably true that the maximization principle reflects something extremely important in the manner in which economic choices of action are made, when it is about a judgment from the perspective of a single individual as the holder of interests. The businessman, for example, estimates various options of investment and production according to the calculated profit measured in terms of money, and among the various possibilities he will choose that which promises the biggest profit. This is a clear calculation of maximization. On the other hand, the principle is ill-suited to serve as a yardstick when it is a question of socio-economic problems, that is, problems concerned with a plurality of individuals competing with each other. By attributing exclusive weight to the sum total, not to its distribution, one has from the very outset closed one's eyes to all conflicts of interest and prevented oneself from endowing 'distribution' with

[2] This explains the extremely important part played by utilitarianism with respect to economic theory, from the nineteenth century to the present day.

[383] an independent meaning.[3] However, most economic problems of social bearing are precisely problems of distribution, or at least problems with a distributive aspect. The problem of national income, for example, is not merely a question of size, but also of distribution; that is, it is possible that an economic system, which yields a smaller sum total but better distribution, is preferred to a system with a larger sum total but more unequal distribution. The same applies to the problem of the country's supply with certain commodities; of the number of houses available to the population; and to many other problems.

In these and similar cases[4]—that is, provided that a quantitative maximization can be imagined—we can simply say: *The mutual dissonance of interests makes the maximization principle unsuitable for solving social distribution problems.*

[3] However, thanks to the marginal utility theory which, fully developed, is already apparent in Bentham's work and was to become, later on, an essential ingredient in economic value theory, distribution did gain some derived significance. For according to this theory, the equal distribution of external assets will yield the greatest sum of pleasure. But even according to this elaboration of the theory, the distribution of pleasure, as such, remains of no importance whatsoever, cf. Alf Ross, *Kritik der sogenannten praktischen Erkenntnis* [Critique of So-called Practical Knowledge] (1933), 136.

[4] Even outside the sphere of economics, problems or partial problems may arise, which can be formulated in terms of a quantitative calculation of commensurable factors.

§ 74. The Chimera of Public Utility

In recent years[1] it has become quite customary to speak of public utility, of the needs of society and the like, instead of the sum of the pleasure of individuals. By doing so, one attempts to conceal the two fundamental flaws of the utilitarian principle that have been noted in the previous section, without, however, changing anything with respect to the real issue at hand.

Owing to this construction, the similarity with Nelson's principle manifests itself still more clearly. In line with Nelson's reasoning, we are requested to imagine all interests united within a single person. The only difference is that while this person, according to Nelson, is presented as the agent, it is now presented as a supra-individual unity—society.

Now, should there be talk of society as a new, independent being, equipped with needs and interests,[2] then this idea must be rejected as illusory. All human needs are experienced by individuals; everything else is fiction and nebulous talk.

Usually this is not what is meant either. But it is difficult to say what is really meant. Objectively, there is nothing that distinguishes itself from the [384] maximization principle, but the mode of speech is obviously dictated by an uneasy feeling on account of its difficulties, especially the reduction of all values to the commensurable units of pleasure and the quantitative adding and maximizing. Thus, instead of 'pleasure', one speaks—more vaguely—of needs and utility, and instead of 'the greatest possible amount', one speaks, somewhat evasively, of 'the most perfect and harmonious satisfaction', 'the best possible fulfilment', and the like. However, the superlative expressions ('most', 'best') undoubtedly refer to maximization.[3]

Introducing 'public utility' as a guiding principle for the legislator does not make the least difference with respect to the objections that have been raised against the maximization principle.

How should the qualitative incommensurability of needs be overcome by invoking 'public utility'? How to choose between promoting art and science

[1] The previous exposition has kept to utilitarianism in its original form as formulated by Bentham. That way, the lines are drawn more clearly, since the later development of utilitarianism was to a great extent characterized by eclectic tendencies, due to which elements of natural law and idealism blended with purely utilitarian elements. On this issue, cf. Alf Ross, *Kritik der sogenannten praktischen Erkenntnis* [Critique of So-called Practical Knowledge] (1933), ch. V, 5–8.

[2] This is Ihering's view, cf. p. 331 above; Alf Ross, *Kritik der sogenannten praktischen Erkenntnis* [Critique of So-called Practical Knowledge] (1933), ch. V, 7 and Ross, 'Realismen i Retsvidenskaben og Samfundsnyttekimæren' [Realism in legal science and the chimera of public utility], *SvJT* 1932, 324 *et seq.*

[3] On Neo-Benthamism, see Alf Ross, *Kritik der sogenannten praktischen Erkenntnis* [Critique of So-called Practical Knowledge] (1933), 194–95.

and house building? How to sum up freedom, food, houses, and good music? Without such a preliminary summing up, however, it is not possible to determine what, exactly, it is that promotes 'public utility' 'as much as possible'.

The same applies to the dissonance between interests. 'We all', 'one', 'people in general'—or so says Lundstedt,[4] for example—wish for good houses to live in, and he believes that he has found a practical guiding principle for housing legislation in the best possible satisfaction of this need. The deception lies in the general subject designations used by Lundstedt. 'One' does not live in houses at all, but A, B and C do so. 'One' does not strive for good houses, but A strives for a good house for A, B strives for a good house for B, etc. If circumstances do not permit all people's wishes to be fulfilled, then these interests are discordant, competitive. 'Public interest', 'public utility' is the deception that glosses over this discord, simulating a single harmonious interest and corresponding utility.

At the end of the day, utilitarianism and the principle of public utility are—in line with natural law philosophy—a result of the need of conscience for an absolute principle of action, capable of relieving mankind of the anguish of decision. In this version of the metaphysics of morals we can distinguish two components. One of them is the postulate that the interests of others shall carry the same weight as my own. This appeal to the feelings of sympathy is the emotionally and politically active idea in utilitarianism. We can easily see that this postulate is a new dogmatization of the moral and legal consciousness that can find justification only in an intellectual intuition—even though utilitarianism itself pretends to be able to derive the postulate from empirical
[385] experience. The second component is the doctrine that our choices, as soon as the postulate has been accepted, can be described as rational choices between commensurable factors. This is a deception that contradicts two basic facts: the qualitative incommensurability of needs; and the disharmony between interests.

Notwithstanding Max Weber's and Gunnar Myrdal's pioneering criticism (see § 78 below), the idea of a 'correct' economic policy—'correct' as determined by the idea of maximum utility or maximum satisfaction of needs (social welfare)—still plays an important part in economics as well. Since one admits (1) that utility does not lend itself to being measured as a multitude of units ('cardinally'), but by being placed within a scale of preference ('ordinally'); and at the same time (2) that interpersonal comparisons of utility are basically excluded; one must admit that 'public utility', or 'the maximum amount of social welfare', cannot be calculated without introducing more or less subjective and arbitrary 'weighing scales'. According to Zeuthen, for instance, the

[4] For further information, see Alf Ross, 'Realismen i Retsvidenskaben og Samfundsnyttekimæren' [Realism in legal science and the chimera of public utility], *SvJT* 1932, 336 *et seq*.

individual's 'welfare function' includes not only the satisfaction of his own needs, but also his interest in the welfare of others and his moral ideals of the organization of society, etc. In order to measure, summarize, and maximize the welfare function of the individual within a social welfare function, it is necessary to introduce weighing scales, which express the weight one wants to attribute to the welfare of the single individual when calculating social welfare. (In addition, similar weighing scales may be necessary when calculating the individual's welfare function.) This weighing scale is determined subjectively, partly in connection with feelings of sympathy with different groups, partly in connection with estimating the marginal utility of income (that 1 Danish Crown is worth more to the poor man than the rich man). Zeuthen finishes thus: 'From the point of view of common sense, it seems reasonable to include all these considerations in our deliberations and combine them, as reasonably as possible, according to the weight which the evaluator attributes to them. *Using a collective term for all considerations, we might, thus, call the desideratum welfare and explain that the objective is the maximization of welfare*' (my italics).[5]

In my view, it emerges clearly from the above that what Zeuthen does in his social evaluations has got nothing to do with the summarizing and maximizing of quantitative factors. One is confronted with a quantity of incommensurable considerations: the fulfilment of needs, moral ideals, sympathy with various sections of the population, regard for the difference between rich and poor, etc. These considerations cannot be measured, summarized, and maximized, but Zeuthen amuses himself with first attributing to them a fictive 'weight', and thereupon 'saying' that the result he has arrived at is determined by maximizing total welfare. The whole thing is a gigantic fiction meant to keep up the appear- [386] ance of a certain rationalism and objectivity in the weighing of considerations which lead to a political position.

Welfare economics is an expression of the fact that economists, unlike other experts, do not accept the role of *technical advisers* who place their knowledge at the disposition of the agent (*in casu* the politicians in power) in order to guide him with a view to the objectives and attitudes he actually embraces (§ 78), but believe that they can claim the role of *moral sovereign*, proclaiming the *correct* economic policy. From a historical point of view, this is a repercussion of the intimate connection between economics and utilitarian moral philosophy. Even assuming that it would be possible to calculate the 'maximum of social welfare'—how could this presumption for evaluation become relevant as a basis for economic policy? If one does not wish to postulate that it is economic policy which, in fact, motivates those in power—and such a postulate would be a rather arbitrary one—then this precondition for evaluation can

[5] Zeuthen, *Vurderinger og Maalsætninger i Økonomien* [Evaluations and Objectives in Economics] (1952), 51, cf. 11–13 and 41 *et seq.*

only be a *moral postulate*: the goal ought to be maximum welfare, as expressing the principle of justice that gives equal consideration to all human beings.

Moreover, Zeuthen is wavering, unsure of himself. While lecturing on his welfare economics, he approvingly mentions the criticism of Max Weber and Gunnar Myrdal.[6] This is like slapping oneself in the face, for this criticism is precisely based upon two principles which are incompatible with welfare economics, namely (1) that economics shall accept the actually prevailing attitudes of the dominant social classes; and (2) that in this respect, it is a question of efficacious, concrete objectives and attitudes, not of empty abstractions of the 'social welfare' type.[7]

[6] *Op. cit.*, 6.

[7] Gunnar Myrdal, *Vetenskap och politik i nationalekonomien* [Science and Politics in Political Economy] (1930), 276 *et seq.*

CHAPTER XIV [387]

Science and Politics

§ 75. *Knowledge and Action*

The presupposition, express or tacit, for the theories of natural law and utilitarianism that have been discussed in the preceding chapters, has been that the task of legal politics consists in discovering the law that is *correct* or *valid* in itself, and that this task can be solved epistemically, *via* the path of knowledge—at least to the extent that certain general principles can be laid down as guidelines for assessing the correctness of positive law.[1]

Starting from this presupposition, there is no point in further inquiring why the law should be 'correct', that is, satisfy the demand of the idea of justice or of the calculus of pleasure. This demand is absolute and categorical, it arises from an *a priori* insight and cannot be justified any further.

According to this view, the juridico-political norm is *simultaneously insight and demand*. It is insight in so far as it is an expression of a piece of knowledge of the valid principles which the law must follow in order to be 'correct' law; a knowledge which, like other knowledge, claims to be true: this is so, and not otherwise. It is a demand in so far as it is also an expression of a claim against the legislator that he shall follow those principles. The hope that the legislator will, in fact, do so, is solely based on an appeal to his reason or his conscience. Like other human beings, he is naturally equipped with an insight, albeit imperfect, into what is valid. It is an epistemic task to clarify this insight and [388] bring it to full consciousness, in the hope that the legislator will interpret the commands of reason and conscience in that light.

'Correctness' is an *a priori* concept, that is, it cannot be derived from sensory experience, but is something perceived immediately through intellectual intuition. Similarly, the knowledge that gives us insight into what is valid is not a science in the empirical sense, but presupposes a source of knowledge distinct

[1] [General remark to § 75:] On this issue, cf. Alf Ross, *Kritik der sogenannten praktischen Erkenntnis* [Critique of So-called Practical Knowledge] (1933), ch. 1.

from sensory experience. This source of knowledge is precisely the intellectual perception in which we directly apprehend—suddenly and unrestrained by our senses—the nature of existence and the law that governs our actions. Knowledge of this kind is called metaphysical knowledge. Consequently, any legal and moral philosophy aiming at the justification of self-valid norms of human action is metaphysical.

All metaphysics is a flight of fancy, however. There is no tenable knowledge other than scientific knowledge. In §§ 63 and 64 above, I have expressed some critical views on the issue of intuitionism and psychological explanations of the urge for metaphysics.[2] These views do not by any means aspire to be a conclusive argumentation. They have only been adduced in order to create an understanding for my point of view, rather than prove its correctness. Getting involved in a profound discussion on fundamental philosophical problems must fall outside the scope of a juridico-philosophical presentation. Surely, it is permitted to state one's position and point out that it is shared by an important group of modern philosophers as well as professionals interested in philosophy, whose aim it is to guide philosophical thinking according to the same standards concerning critical examination, logical stringency, and emancipation from merely subjective influences—the standards characterizing the long-established sciences, which have already given proof of their effectiveness through word and deed.

However, starting from the premise that there is no knowledge other than empirical knowledge, the problem must arise how it is possible to arrive, on this basis, at a legal politics—that is, at something that has the characteristics of advice, guidance, or instructions to the legislator. If there is no *a priori insight* into absolute 'correctness', on what kind of foundation, then, can we possibly arrive at norms of action? And if there is no absolute 'validity', with what 'right' can we possibly formulate directives for human action? If the legislator is not metaphysically bound in virtue of the *a priori* commands of reason, what motivating force can such directives possibly possess? And if the entire body of scientific knowledge according to its nature is insight into empirical facts and their regular functional connections, how is it possible to produce anything on a scientific basis, apart from purely descriptive statements?

Not all of these problems are peculiar to legal politics: rather, they exist *mutatis*
[389] *mutandis* in all applied or technical sciences, that is, sciences issuing instructions on how to behave under certain conditions. Therefore, it is only right and proper to submit the answer in two parts, first dealing generally with the problem of the relation between knowledge (science) and action (politics), and then investigating the particular problems of legal politics. The first task is dealt with in the current chapter, and the second one in the next chapter.

[2] See also p. 384 below.

Let us imagine for a moment (if possible[3]) a human-like being, equipped with intelligence but without any kind of feelings and passions, without any kind of impulse, striving, love, hatred—or in short, with whatever term one wishes to designate the emotional-voluntaristic components of man's inner life. Such a being must be absolutely apathetic and passive towards its surroundings, and must be kept alive by artificial means. By virtue of its intelligence, this being would be able to perceive and understand reality. But even if we conceive of this being as equipped with the most comprehensive knowledge of facts, the most profound insight into the laws and contexts of existence, no amount of knowledge and insight would ever be able to rouse this individual into activity. Knowledge as such is of no practical interest to a person who is not predisposed to be interested in anything. The knowledge that my life is in danger unless I leave the spot I am standing in will leave me completely cold, uninterested, and passive if I do not wish to protect my life. The knowledge of how to attain all the glories and treasures in the world is devoid of any motivating force in the eyes of an individual who does not wish for these things.

This thought experiment purports to illustrate the absolute difference between *believing* (representing or knowing) and *deliberative* mental acts.[4] The latter are characterized by their polar character, shown in such word pairs as attraction–repulsion, love–hatred, approval–disapproval, sympathy–antipathy, benevolence–aversion, etc. As an umbrella term for these deliberative acts, and without indicating their nature of 'plus' or 'minus', the word *interest* may be employed (although this word in common usage chiefly denotes a positive attitude). Even if the believing and the deliberative acts—or, as we can also say—the beliefs and attitudes appear to be closely connected in mutual interaction, it must be emphasized that they designate original and irreducible forms of mental life, and that all conscious activity must arise from an attitude. Mere belief as such, pure insight or knowledge, is devoid of any motivating force.

This is not to say that our beliefs do not influence our activities—not at all; it [390] only means that this influence must always take place on the basis of an interest (attitude). If a motive for action is given in an attitude, then the activity we display is guided by our intelligent belief as to facts and circumstances. If I am interested in not getting wet, my belief as to the state of the weather will determine how I will dress. If I am interested in doing business with economic profit, my business dispositions will be determined by my beliefs as to where the goods can be bought at the cheapest possible price, how prices will develop, etc. This is so simple that it seems ridiculous to adduce examples at all.

[3] The thought experiment can be conducted *in abstracto* only. In reality, the intelligence function itself is an activity grounded in emotions.

[4] Cf. Franz Brentano, *Psychologie vom empirischen Standpunkt* [Empirical Psychology] (1925), vol. 2. According to Brentano, this distinction expresses the fundamental division of the psychical phenomena.

Accordingly, the function of knowledge in the sphere of action can be described as follows: knowledge can never *motivate* an action, but on the assumption of a given motive (interest, attitude), it can *direct* the activity released.

As a result, the role of knowledge (science) within the sphere of action can never consist in setting up *categorical* or *self-valid norms of action*, that is, norms whose motivating force lies in knowledge itself and is, thus, independent of any subjective attitude or interest. Every motive for action, and likewise every encouragement to action, must necessarily arise from, or appeal to, irrational factors (interests, attitudes). The function of knowledge can only consist in giving directives which are valid *hypothetically* only, that is, under the assumption of a given irrational motive (interest, attitude).

Therefore, the idea of a practical knowledge in an ethical sense—that is, the idea of a knowledge that also in itself is a motive and an expression of a categorical demand—is an impossibility. Knowledge can only be practical in a hypothetical or technical sense, that is, as showing the ways and means for an activity arising from an interest or attitude that is independent of knowledge.

Therefore, all the theories that have hitherto been advanced concerning the deduction of absolutely valid norms of action from empirical facts (the fact of solidarity, for example), or the metaphysical nature of existence or man, are illusory. Absolutely nothing concerning human action can be deduced from sheer facts. Facts in themselves are absolutely indifferent. They become relevant only by having a bearing on interests or attitudes independent of them.

This applies even if we were able (which I do not think we are) to perceive empirically in certain objects a specific quality, which is called their 'value' or their 'goodness'. Also with respect to this knowledge we can state that it is devoid of any independently motivating force, and that it is of practical significance only under the condition that I am interested in 'the valuable' or 'the good'.

Presumably all these theories on absolute norms of action, directly deduced from reality or directly given in our knowledge, can be explained psychologically
[391] (as has been mentioned earlier, cf. § 64), namely, by means of the fact that human beings—in order to escape the responsibility of making decisions and the agony of choosing—in this way try to conceal the circumstance that all norms and demands ultimately depend upon our own decisions and choices, our own attitudes and our own will.

§ 76. Interaction between Belief and Attitude

If we limit the term action to those conscious acts which are the subject of deliberation and discussion, we can say that all action is conditioned by two factors, namely, the beliefs of the agent as well as his attitudes.

By *belief* I mean any assumption concerning the nature of reality which is accepted as true, or at least as probable, by the person harbouring such a belief. It may concern simple facts as well as causal connections; everyday phenomena as well as scientific theories; past, present, and future matters—in short, everything concerning which human beings make more or less well-founded assumptions.

By *attitude* I understand the deliberative mental phenomena as the source (motive) of all conscious activity. They are directed towards an imagined object (a thing, a person, an event, a state of affairs) and occur in bipolar basic types, indicated through conceptual pairs such as the following:

benevolence–aversion
attraction–repulsion
desire–dislike
approval–disapproval
love–hatred
sympathy–antipathy
comfort–discomfort

Attitudes can be experienced in many different forms, depending on the way in which they are part of a wider psychological context. What they have in common is that in all situations, the attitude is an expression of a certain disposition to act. However, this disposition can either be of a more unconditional, well-defined, and immediate nature, or of a more conditional, indefinite, and poten- [392] tial nature. The former applies to those attitudes where a *voluntaristic* element is predominant, as is the case in *purposive consciousness*, clarified through deliberation and decision; and also in the more transitory *affective states with a clear tendency to 'let off steam'* (anger, fear, desire, craving). In these attitudes, the disposition to act is characterized by a clear preparedness to take action. The latter applies to those attitudes where an *emotional* element prevails. Here, too, it may be about relatively clarified and stable attitudes of *love and hatred* for things or persons; or about more transitory and changing attitudes of *longing*, *hope*, and *wishing* for a certain event or circumstance. Even if the disposition to act is less distinct in these attitudes, there is no doubt that even in them, there is a tendency to act in a certain direction, if the opportunity and possibility should occur. The person experiencing love for a certain object wishes it prosperity and well-being; and the person who wishes something is also willing to act (provided it is in his power) in furtherance of his wish being fulfilled. But since it is often uncertain whether an opportunity for action will occur, and since its precise content is often indeterminate, the tendency to act, as mentioned previously, becomes here more indefinite and latent. A special group of attitudes are those in which we, in a choice situation, prefer a good (bad) thing to another. These attitudes are called *attitudes of preference*.

Belief and attitude are the two basic forms of mental phenomena, the theoretical and the practical form. They occur frequently in intimate fusion, with the result that the two components can only be distinguished through an abstracting analysis. A great many linguistic expressions fulfil both functions simultaneously. They are both descriptive and evaluative—they have both *theoretical* and *emotional* (*volitive*) *meaning*, as it were. It is not unusual to use two words in order to describe practically the same object, but with different kinds of emotional charge. (Examples: 'freedom fighters'–'criminal gang'; 'leader'–'dictator'; 'heroic'–'reckless'; 'upholding authority'–'oppressing'; 'champion of liberty and justice'–'rebel'; 'Realpolitik'–'Machiavellism'.) On the other hand, it also happens that the same emotionally charged words are used by different people to designate widely different phenomena. This state of affairs reminds one, for example, of the tactics, well known in Nazi and communist philosophy, to use words with a traditional aureole of values in connection with non-traditional objects, in order to appropriate emotional goodwill.[1] In Hitler's linguistic usage, his dictatorship was the 'true democracy', his police state was the 'true' *Rechtsstaat*, his capitalist economy was the 'true' socialism, and his regimentation was 'true' freedom. [393] Neither has Stalin been inclined to waive the capital of goodwill included in the word 'democracy'. He has called the Soviet Constitution 'the only perfectly democratic constitution in the world', admitting, at the same time, that it 'upholds the regime of the dictatorship of the working classes'.[2] In the publication *Land og Folk*,* the emotionally charged expression 'The will of the people' is regularly used to denote the opinion of a minority of 4 to 5 per cent of the population.

These and many similar facts explain why linguistic studies of emotionally charged words are among the methods of obtaining knowledge of the attitudes that prevail among a certain group.[3]

At a higher level, beliefs and attitudes amalgamate, not only as far as single words are concerned, but also in connection with complex theory constructions. This

* Translator's note: In translation, *Land and People* (a Danish communist daily paper).

1 On the issue of the so-called persuasive definitions, cf. Charles L. Stevenson, *Ethics and Language* (1944), 206 *et seq*.

2 J. Stalin, *Vår teori och praktik* [Our Theory and Practice] (1943), 724–25.

3 For further information, see Stuart Chase, *The Tyranny of Words* [1938; 3rd edn, 1939].

is the case in political programmes and ideologies, in religious systems and views of life.

As mentioned previously, a practical attitude is an irreducible mental phenomenon in the sense that a will to action, or a demand for action, can never be derived from a belief. To an individual who is totally devoid of feeling and will, all the knowledge in the world is devoid of motivating force. Therefore, it is impossible to prove the 'correctness' of an attitude through rational arguments, that is, by referring to facts and using logic.

It is quite another thing (and this is a circumstance of the greatest possible importance to the problems we shall discuss) that there is, in fact—that is, *psychologically and causally—an intimate interplay between beliefs and attitudes.*

It is a well-known fact that our beliefs about the world we are living in do not arise successively, in the course of gradually gathering enough evidence for regarding certain assumptions as true, or at least as probable. On the contrary: the requirement of documentation and critical examination does not appear until late in our mental development. The point of departure is that our beliefs are only to a limited degree subject to the control of experience and criticism: rather, they are born by fear, hope, and desires. We all have a strong tendency to regard as true anything that can subdue our fears, renew our hopes, and flatter our desires. In the primitive world, there hardly seems to be a limit to the freedom of the fantasy world, stimulated by our feelings. But even in the case of those people who have made considerable progress towards the capacity for critical thinking; indeed, even in the case of scientists to whom this capacity should figure as a professional virtue, there is still an unmistakable tendency that their conception of reality is formed and coloured under the pressure of irrational factors. We are ever so much inclined to see what we want to see, and to turn a blind eye to unpleasant things. Nelson is not the only one to employ the trick of turning a blind eye. We only have to look at ourselves in order to know how [394] necessary it is, however honest our intention, to be continually on the watch against blindness, prejudices, misrepresentations, or sheer falsifications.

In that case we speak of *wishful thinking* or *personal prejudice* (*bias*). There is a particularly high risk for it when it is a question of beliefs about social matters—partly because our feelings are rather directed towards the affairs of our fellow man than towards nature, partly because in this realm, there are far fewer possibilities for exact knowledge and effective verification than in the realm of nature.

Conversely, our attitudes are also influenced by the beliefs we are harbouring. We are all inclined to justify our attitudes with certain beliefs. For example, I justify my aversion to dictatorship with the belief that dictatorship leads to the suppression of intellectual and personal freedom, to the elimination of the principle of legal certainty, and to a widespread use of violence. However, there is no logical connection between this belief and my practical attitude, because logic solely concerns the relation between the truth value of belief statements. An attitude has no truth value; it is a fact.

In the same way, A may think that cold baths are good, because in his view, they strengthen the nerves; or B may be a vegetarian, because he thinks that meat is detrimental to your health.

Thus, beliefs and attitudes are interacting with each other, and frequently it is impossible to determine what is primary and what is secondary. We cannot always be certain that the (good) reasons people give for their attitudes really are true reasons. In that case we speak of *rationalization*. For example, it may be the case that the vegetarian really is a vegetarian because he dislikes meat, and that his belief that meat is detrimental to our health is expressing a personal bias, derived from this attitude. It cannot be easy to determine whether the people of the Southern United States hate negroes because they regard them as deceitful, stupid, and sexually depraved, or whether they harbour such beliefs because they hate them. In the same breath, one might mention anti-Semitism and its justification with certain beliefs about the ethical qualities of the Jews.

One can safely assume that attitudes, just like reflexes, ultimately have their basis in the biological nature of the organism, but that they, in the course of the individual's growth and development, are elaborated into a ramified set, conditioned by the beliefs through which they are coupled together—in the same way as conditioned reflexes develop from unconditioned ones. Thus, we can—by analogy—speak of *unconditioned* and *conditioned attitudes*.

Through the beliefs which condition them, conditioned attitudes can be grouped under 'higher', or more general, attitudes. For instance, if I am an advocate of cold baths because I think they are beneficial for one's health; and likewise, if I am a vegetarian for health reasons, then both these attitudes can be regarded as derived or subordinate in relation to a more general positive atti-
[395] tude towards health and the preservation and promotion of health. By justifying one's attitudes vis-à-vis oneself, one can in this way try to 'systematize' or 'harmonize' one's attitudes and overcome those that do not fit into the system. A desire to move in this direction is undoubtedly a characteristic of a development towards what we call character and personality. Nevertheless, it must be emphasized that this is not a question of logical systematization but of practical harmonization, and that this is an ideal which is normally realized only to a small extent. In reality, people's attitudes constitute a far more discordant conglomeration than they are inclined to admit. One must be vigilant vis-à-vis declarations of attitudes of a general and fundamental scope. There is a great risk that they are mere *verbalizations* which do not cover the psychological realities. It is very common to hear people say—*nota bene* in good faith—that

they advocate the principle of equal opportunity, but nevertheless they are opposed to the admission of negroes to higher education; or that they embrace the principle of free competition and, at the same time, oppose measures for ensuring it. Many of those who demand freedom for Loki as well as for Thor* are rather intolerant of Loki in practice.

The higher we climb in the levels of generalization, the more doubtful it becomes whether declared ideals correspond to our real attitudes. If someone tells us that he cannot stand his red-haired neighbour, that he loathes beef and onions, or that he is against a certain legislative proposal on import limitation, there is usually no reason to suspect him of deceiving himself. However, we cannot listen to his remarks with the same confidence if he declares that he is an advocate of democracy, or is in favour of social reforms for the benefit of the entire population.

The unrealistic constructions culminate in the numerous attempts that have been made in the history of philosophy to systematize all attitudes under one single, supreme attitude, expressed in the idea of the absolute good. Thus, for example, when utilitarianism defines pleasure as the intrinsically good, and the greatest amount of pleasure as the purpose of all striving. Assertions concerning such a fundamental attitude from which all other attitudes are said to be derived and conditioned by calculi of pleasure, is an obvious verbalization, without any backing in the psychological realities.

Thus, we can state that in so far as it is important to know people's attitudes in order to understand, predict, or influence human action, *it is the specific and efficacious attitudes, not the verbalized formulations of general content that must be grasped.*

* Editor's note: Ross is here referring to a Danish saying stemming from N. F. S. Grundtvig's book *Nordens Mythologi eller Sindbilled-Sprog* (*Mythology of the North or Symbolic Language*, 1832). Thor is usually our hero whereas Loki is less sympathetic. 'Freedom for Loki as well as for Thor' therefore refers to the principle of non-discrimination in the distribution of civic liberties.

[396] § 77. Practical Disagreement: Argumentation and Persuasion

Throughout this section, I shall talk about two persons, A and B: B finds himself in a given action situation, whereas A is a mere spectator. Moreover, we assume that A is curious to see how B will act, and that there exists a practical disagreement between them, which means that A, if he had to make the decision, would act differently from the way in which B declares that he means to adopt. Starting from these premises, two questions are posed now, namely: first (a) what is it that determines that A and B will act differently in the same situation; and secondly (b), what can A do in order to convert B and make him embrace A's view of the matter (by which I understand precisely the will to act in a certain way in a given situation)? If A succeeds in converting B, practical disagreement has been transformed into practical agreement.

(a) On the basis of the previous analysis, we know that a person's point of view is determined through cooperation between his beliefs and his attitudes. It follows that practical disagreement can always be reduced to one of the following three situations:

(1) *Disagreement in belief, agreement in attitude*

Examples:

A and B agree in their wish to keep Denmark out of the horrors of war. A believes that Denmark's accession to the North Atlantic Treaty will serve this purpose. B believes the opposite. Thus, they are in practical disagreement as to their views on Denmark's accession to the North Atlantic Treaty.

A and B agree in their wish to counteract the dangers of inflation as well as those of unemployment. B believes that a credit squeeze is well suited to that, whereas A thinks that a credit squeeze certainly might have an anti-inflationary effect, but would at the same time lead to unemployment. Therefore, A cannot approve of B's ideas of a credit limitation policy.

(2) *Disagreement (qua conflict) in attitude, agreement in belief*

Examples:

A is an anti-Semite, B a pro-Semite. They agree that discrimination against Jews is disagreeable to them, and that it is detrimental to their well-being. Therefore, A advocates such measures, B does not.

A is categorically against abortion, on religious grounds. B's attitude is that a woman should have the right to make her own decisions about her own body. They agree in believing that a certain legislative proposal purports to permit abortion. Therefore, they take opposite stances on this proposal.

(3) *Disagreement* (*qua divergence*) *in attitude.* [397]

Example:

A and B are travelling together. A is interested in art, but not in sports. B is the opposite. They will be in search of different experiences on their journey.

In this case, A and B are disagreeing in attitude, in so far as the one does not share the attitude of the other. But they do not have conflicting attitudes towards the same subject. In the same situation, they are governed by divergent interests. The beliefs relevant to A (which museums are open, what is on at the theatres, etc.) are, thus, irrelevant to B, and *vice versa*. Therefore, we cannot speak either of agreement or of disagreement in belief. Besides, cases of this type easily slide into type (2). If both A and B are interested in both sports and art, but with a difference in preference, then there exists a conflict of preference attitudes. Such conflicts of preference attitudes are typical of many political conflicts, where the parties agree on the relevant considerations, but disagree on the 'weight' ascribed to them. This is the case, for example, when two parties agree that both military security and social welfare are desirable objectives, but ascribe different weight to them in relation to each other—and consequently take different stances on the issue of the defence budget.

(b) Let us now turn to the question of the possibilities available to A of converting B to his own stance. By way of introduction, it must be emphasized that this is not a question of a logical process, intended to prove the truth of an assertion. A's stance is not an assertion, but a mental fact. Facts as such (that is to say: in contrast to assertions concerning facts) are neither 'true' nor 'false', neither 'correct' nor 'wrong', they can neither be proved nor disproved. But facts can change, and they can change due to human endeavour. All technical activity aims at changing facts in the way desired. However, the relationship between technical measures and their outcome is a factual relation between cause and effect; it is a causal relation—not a logical relation between premise and conclusion.

It follows that *all methods for achieving practical agreement are similar to technical measures, aiming at causally influencing the other party to change his stance*. This applies even if A adduces rational arguments. For the purpose of these is not to prove the truth of an assertion, but to have an impact on the mental facts which consist in the beliefs harboured by B.

We have seen that B's stance in a given situation is determined by the cooperation between certain attitudes and beliefs which are of relevance to the present decision, and which I call *operative beliefs*. According to cir-
[398] cumstances, A's task may consist in either influencing B's operative beliefs (type 1); or his attitudes (type 2); or both (type 3).

But whatever the task—the measure undertaken need not target precisely the point where the result is intended. This is due to the previously mentioned close interaction between an individual's beliefs and his attitudes.

For example, if B is against granting negroes access to higher education because he believes that they do not have sufficient intelligence, I can, of course, directly attack this operative belief by referring to intelligence statistics and other facts. However, there is also the possibility that his belief is a prejudice developed in the course of an emotional dependence upon an attitude of general aversion to negroes, and that I can achieve the same result, or even a better one, by trying to change this attitude.

Conversely, if the task—as in the type 2 cases—consists in changing B's attitude, this might be done not only by direct influence, but also through the *conditioning beliefs*, that is, those beliefs which, without being operative in the given situation, usually have conditioned B's attitude.

Thus, we can say that irrespective of the type of disagreement, there will at any rate—owing to the intimate connection between beliefs and attitudes—be a possibility for measures that aim directly at B's level of belief as well as for measures that aim directly at his level of attitude.

It follows that there is a fundamental distinction between the practicable methods to achieve practical agreement: (1) Rational methods, seeking to influence B's level of belief directly (and thereby—possibly indirectly—also his level of attitude); and (2) Irrational methods, seeking to influence B's level of attitude directly (and thereby—possibly indirectly—also his level of belief).

(1) *Rational methods* are practised in the form of *argumentation*, that is, by putting forth assertions in order to justify a certain point of view. Here, one must bear in mind that the word 'justify' is not used in its logical sense. The function of argumentation is not to convince an opponent of the 'correctness' of a certain point of view (such a concept is devoid of meaning) but, rather, to convert him by changing his operative beliefs or his conditioned attitudes. On these grounds, it is impossible to distinguish between 'valid' and 'invalid' arguments. In a given situation, arguments are simply effective or ineffective, and it is impossible to determine beforehand their respective nature. One must feel one's way on the basis of surmising which beliefs are, in fact, decisive for the point of view that is targeted.

The effectiveness of an argument is not contingent upon the truth of the assertion but, rather, upon being believed by the opponent. It is a well-known fact (which one may honestly regret but cannot deny) that much effective propaganda employs mendacious assertions. Example: if one [399] wishes to awaken or strengthen an attitude of dislike towards the Jews, one does not content oneself with giving emotional expression to this attitude. A far stronger effect is obtained if the emotional propaganda is at the same time buttressed by assertions concerning the Jews' odious and pernicious qualities—for example, that they devour small children at their religious ceremonies, that they are to blame for the calamities that befell the country, that they are ready to cheat on honest people, etc., etc. If a certain *bias* against Jews already exists, it is astonishing how quickly such assertions circulate and have effect in spite of their mendacity.

The individual who uses mendacious argumentation naturally runs the risk that the untruth of the argumentation will be exposed by other people. Of course, the truth value of the argument in itself is subject to the usual theoretical criticism and examination, by means of a documentation of facts, an appeal to experience, and scientific insight. Thus, if it is a question of public affairs, public discussion plays an important part in countering and neutralizing untruthful agitation. When information is unrestrained and there is freedom of speech, truth will often prevail in the long run. It is different in those countries where those in power control the information and communication channels. It is one of the most tragic and disastrous features of our time that under such conditions, there is virtually no limit to the mendacity with which propaganda can be disseminated with the purpose of poisoning the minds of men with hate, in order to turn them into willing tools of the politics of those in power.

The argumentation can employ different tactics, varying especially in the following directions:

(i) With regard to the *function* of the belief in the opponent's point of view, the argumentation can take aim either at beliefs that are assumed to work *operatively*, or at beliefs that are assumed to work *conditionally* upon his attitudes.

Thus, in the first case, one aims at a change of opinion which is able to influence the opponent's stance *directly*. The operative beliefs may be beliefs which are operative either in relation to attitudes which *have already manifested themselves* in B's stance (Example I below); or also in relation to attitudes which, in A's view, exist *latently* in B (Examples II and III). The latter plays an important part in current argumentation. Frequently, one does not merely 'realize' one's attitudes in the deliberations which lead to a certain stance. By adducing new considerations, one's opponent attempts, in the course of the discussion, to appeal to latent attitudes that have not been allowed to take effect. In either case the argumentative assertions can aim at throwing light, either on the *immediate content* of the measure under discussion (Example II), or on the *effects* which this measure must be assumed to give rise to (Examples I and III).

In the latter case—that is, where the argument is directed [400] against the conditioning beliefs—one aims at a change of opinion which is able to influence the opponent's stance *indirectly*, by means of a change in attitude (Examples IV, V, and VI).

(ii) With regard to the *means* that are employed in order to change the opponent's beliefs, the argumentation can either directly attempt to prove the *theoretical truth* of the beliefs one wishes the opponent to accept, by invoking the testimony of experience, the conclusions of science, and the demands of logic (Example I); or, one can indirectly attempt to raise doubts in the opponent's mind by opening his eyes to the possibility that the beliefs he is harbouring very likely can be *explained psychologically as prejudices* influenced by certain attitudes (Example VI). He may thus be roused to critical self-reflection which, in turn, may lead to a revision of his beliefs and thereby to a revision of his stance, irrespective of whether it is about operative or conditional beliefs.

(iii) Finally, argumentation tactics can vary, because the aim is to *break down* given beliefs, or to *adduce* new beliefs, or both.

Here are a few examples (partly inspired by Stevenson):

Example I

B: I am against Denmark's accession to the North Atlantic Treaty. An accession merely increases the risk that Denmark will be drawn into a great power conflict.

A: This is wrong. On the contrary, the Treaty would diminish that risk. (Thereupon A puts forward the usual theoretical argumentation in support of his assertion.)

In this case, A attacks B's operative beliefs concerning the effects of a certain measure. He not only wants to break down B's beliefs, but also add new ones.

Example II

B: I am against the draft proposal for a new tax law. It is better that taxes should go up, rather than that the government should have to take out further loans.

A: That may be true. But did you consider that according to the proposal, important necessities of life are taxed, and the tax-free income is reduced to a minimum?

B: I was not aware of that. I shall have to study the proposal in more detail.

In this argumentation, A defends his stance by throwing further light on the nature of the subject at issue. His assertion aims at providing B with operative beliefs calculated to appeal to latent attitudes within him.

Example III

B: In my view, it is right to resort to a credit squeeze in the present situation. It counteracts the danger of inflation. [401]

A: Possibly—but on the other hand, a credit squeeze will generate unemployment.

B: I see. That puts the issue in a new light.

Here, A adduces a new consideration, that is, he wants to convey to B certain beliefs that appeal to an assumed latent attitude.

Example IV

B: Sexual relations outside marriage are sinful and illicit.

A: Just consider for a moment how you have acquired this attitude. It is a tradition you have adopted from other people who, in turn, have adopted it from others. Originally, this tradition developed against the background of the necessity of giving children a stable social status. In those times, reliable birth control methods were unknown. With the methods available to us today, there is no longer the same connection between sexual relations out of wedlock and illegitimate children. Therefore, we must free ourselves from the power of tradition and consider the issue in a new moral light.

A's argumentation is partly of the same type as in (1) and (3), in so far as he wishes to throw light on the consequences of the issue at stake. The novelty consists in the fact that he, in addition, tries to weaken B's position by making him aware of the psychological and sociological origin of his attitude, in the hope that an understanding of it will be suited—as *conditioning beliefs*—to weaken his faith in the absolute validity of his stance. People who have never seriously thought about the historical contingency of their moral attitudes will be inclined to interpret them in religious-metaphysical terms: it is the voice of God, or the law of nature, speaking to them through their conscience. A direct attack on their religious-metaphysical beliefs will often be futile, on the ground that the epistemological argumentation necessary for this purpose is already so complicated that only very few people are able to understand it. Far better results will be obtained by evading a metaphysical position and keeping one's eyes open for the genealogy of morality. Although this genealogy does not logically disprove metaphysics, it will frequently make it crumble away as a matter of psychological fact. In a previous section (§ 64) I have employed these tactics myself in my critique of natural law, and I shall have further occasion to employ it later on, in discussing the common sense of justice and its role.[1]

[402] *Example V*

B: I support a tightening of the Prices Act. It will reduce the tradesmen's exorbitant profits.

A: I believe that you are wrong about tradespeople in general. After all, they fulfil an important societal function, and most of them are making a rather modest living, etc., etc.

B: Well, perhaps I have not judged them fairly.

In this argumentation, A does not touch on B's operative beliefs about the Prices Act and its effects but, rather, aims his gun at B's beliefs which presumably condition his supposed attitude of a general dislike of tradesmen.

Example VI

B: In my opinion, levying a tax on radio sets is unreasonable. After all, radios promote the dissemination of culture.

A: Tell me, are you not a large shareholder in a radio factory?

B: I am.

A: Ah, well, now I can understand your point of view!

This example shows how A, by pointing at B's interests and hinting at their influence on his point of view, tries to rouse B to a critical self-examination which might lead to a change of position. Even if that should fail, A's argumentation—in a public debate—would be suited to discredit B's stance in the eyes of others.

[1] Please observe that in this book as well as in other publications, I have submitted an epistemological critique of the metaphysics of morals.

(2) The *irrational methods* can be defined as the opposite of rational methods. They comprise all the conversion techniques employing methods other than argumentation (pronouncement of assertions). It is hardly possible to find an established term for the opposite of 'argumentation'. Therefore, I have decided to speak of *persuasion*.

The technique of persuasion is based on the fundamental psychological fact that emotions (a shorthand for emotive and volitive attitudes) can be transmitted just as well as beliefs. However, while the communication of beliefs ('thoughts') is always dependent on the use of a language,[2] the transmission of emotions can also use other vehicles: gestures, deportment, tone of voice, mimicry, actions, etc. And if linguistic expressions are used, they function in a way that is different from that of communicating thoughts. They do not have any symbolic function, they do not refer to any object, but are direct exponents of the experienced emotion. One might also say that they have an emotional load [403] but are devoid of descriptive meaning.

This may sound rather strange *in abstracto*. In reality, however, it merely expresses what is familiar from the experiences of everyday life.

It has previously been pointed out (§ 2) that language is used for other things than expressing beliefs (assertions). Exclamations and imperatives are devoid of descriptive meaning, but expose an emotion and are suited to evoking, through suggestive persuasion, corresponding emotions in other people.

> *Examples: A crowd breaks into cheers or shouts: 'Long live the King!' A speaker is shouted down with: 'Shame!' I yell 'Ouch!' when I burn myself. A man shouts: 'Look out!' A mother says: 'You must not', 'Go on, then!' etc. I exclaim: 'How beautiful!' 'I wish he would come!' etc., etc.*

The emotive function of our language is not limited to sentences which are, grammatically, in the optative mood or the imperative mood (like those quoted above). Many sentences which are, grammatically, in the indicative mood, are also devoid of any descriptive content and have, thus, solely an emotional load. This is obviously the case when I say to a child in a tone of command: 'Now you eat your dinner!' However, the same applies to moral statements as well, irrespective of the fact that many people interpret them as genuine assertions about a moral 'validity' or 'correctness' ('it is your duty to ...'; 'it is unjust to ...'; it is immoral to ...').

There is one more step to take, however. The emotive function of language is not limited to statements which are devoid of any descriptive

2 Ordinary language, the sign language of mathematics, signals, or some other system with symbolic function.

meaning. As mentioned above (p. 386), many words have descriptive meaning and—at the same time—an emotional load. It is particularly important to be clear about this, because this fusion opens the way for a type of persuasion which is insinuated under cover of an apparently rational argumentation. However, the emotional load is rather unstable in these cases, and will largely depend upon emphasis, tone of voice, gesture, and other factors beyond the word itself ('There's a true lady!').

Some words glitter like jewels ('our proud fatherland')—other words have a nasty smell ('plutocratic monopoly capitalist'). There are words of many different degrees of warmth and cold, and with subtle differences of nuance as to value, when it comes to praise and blame, respect and contempt, approval and disapproval, admiration and scorn, love and hatred.[3] All of them are well suited to serve as a means of persuasion, and they are often particularly useful precisely because
[404] the persuasive function merges with the descriptive function. They flow more easily, without the recipient ever discovering that he has been subjected to persuasion.

Metaphors play a special role. Because of their vague descriptive meaning (more intimated than expressed explicitly), they are eminently suitable for suggestive persuasion ('the grey mass of the people'; 'the flock of God'; 'capitalist lackeys'; the title 'father' as denoting a priest). All poetry makes use of metaphors, and their practical persuasive function is particularly perspicuous in hymns and national anthems. Metaphor, melody, and community singing are combining here to produce a powerful emotional stimulant, while the words' narrative content is nearly forgotten.

It is an amusing and rewarding task—as was accomplished by Alfred and Elisabeth Lee in connection with Father Coughlin's radio talks, for example—to analyse a text with reference to the persuasive function of the words.[4] Of course, religious, patriotic, and political speeches are particularly suitable objects for such an analysis. However, it would be a mistake to believe that the function of persuasion is limited to these cases. Any text using ordinary language can hardly avoid—consciously or unconsciously—making use of the emotional value of words.

Persuasion *via* language is a matter of particular importance to our problems, because of its greater or lesser external similarity with rational argumentation.

[3] In his work *Vägen till Klockrike* [English title: *The Road*], Harry Martinson lets the cigar manufacturer Ahlbom philosophize as follows: 'The word "whore" is a very ugly and degrading word, I think. "Harlot" is prettier. The Babylonian harlot. It is more stylish, as you can hear. And if you call her Maya or Aphrodite, it becomes still prettier. "Courtesan" is pretty, too. There is still some beauty in this word. "Whore" is merely censuring and ugly.'

[4] *The Fine Art of Propaganda* (1939), cf. Charles L. Stevenson, *Ethics and Language* (1944), 249 *et seq.*

Moreover—as mentioned already—there are forms of persuasion not tied to language. When somebody cries 'Fire!' in a theatre, the force that creates panic not only lies in the exclamation itself, but also in the tone, the gestures, and the excited actions accompanying the cry. A protest march, a funeral procession, fluttering flags, hoisting a flag, a round of applause, stamping, the peal of the organ, a woman in tears—all these and many other non-linguistic phenomena have, each in their own way, their own function of transmitting emotion, which can be used for persuasive purposes. Religious and national integration largely takes place *via* ceremonies which purport to strengthen and stimulate the emotional solidarity of the group. Similar phenomena are known in brotherhoods and *Burschenschaften* of various kinds. A particularly important form of persuasion lies in the ideological effect that is connected with a factually upheld system of sanctions (the legal order).

However interesting these non-linguistic methods of persuasion are in themselves, I shall not discuss them here any further, since their study is not relevant to the problems we are dealing with.

[405]

§ 78. Science and Politics

After this survey of the methods that can be used to overcome practical disagreement, I shall now turn to the question of the part science can be expected to play within this context. This is the same as the question concerning the possibility of science directing human activity, or the relationship between science and politics (the latter term taken in its widest sense).

The fundamental point of view must be that the task of science can solely consist in serving and guiding rational argumentation, by providing it with scientifically tenable assertions and by critically separating those which do not lend themselves to scientific examination. By contrast, all participation in, or support of, persuasion—irrespective of whether it occurs overtly, by taking a stand on something and giving expression to it, or covertly by using the emotional load of words—must be outside the scope of science.

Since the word 'task' has both descriptive and emotive meaning, however, this statement requires a more detailed and precise explanation.

The statement is first and foremost a *theoretical assertion of a semantic nature*. It says that if we, by science, mean something in the way of systematically developed and methodically tested knowledge, then emotional attitudes and their expression simply fall outside the scope of science. But, of course, this semantic assertion says nothing to the effect that scientists cannot, or must not, give expression to practical attitudes. It merely means that this side of their activity cannot be called science, if this word is taken in the aforementioned sense.

Then, the statement is also intended as an expression of a *moral attitude*, of the scientists' professional ethos, of *the idea of the objectivity, or purity, of science*. It is the claim—raised in the name of honesty—that scientists, if they are concerned with taking a stand on something and giving expression to it, should indicate, as clearly as possible,[1] the borderline between that part of their activity which can claim to possess the authority and objective validity of science and truth, and that part of it which cannot do so.[2] If this distinction is omitted, the scientist usurps to the advantage of his subjective attitudes an authority to which he is not entitled. This is not merely dishonest—in the long run it is also detrimental to the general prestige and authority of science.[3]

[1] It is not possible to draw a perfectly sharp borderline.

[2] By emphasizing here that I am giving expression to an attitude, I believe that I have satisfied the moral requirement in the present case.

[3] The last sentence of this paragraph expresses an assertion that conditions my attitude.

From the same perspective, the aforementioned semantic assertion is being elevated to a moral claim: that part of the scientist's work which is not theoretical [406] in nature should not be called 'science', for by doing that, one is adding to the borderline becoming blurred.

On the other hand, my statement must not be taken in the sense that it presupposed a general moral attitude against the use of irrational methods of persuasion. We simply cannot imagine a human society without persuasion. All upbringing and moral education follow this pattern, and the efficacy of law is largely dependent on its ideological-suggestive power. Judged in the light of humanistic ideals, the rational methods are, as such, neither better nor worse than the irrational methods. Both can be employed equally in the service of Good and Evil. An assessment must depend on the spirit in which they are employed, and on the conditions under which they are carried into effect. *Propaganda* is the odious name for an argumentation that is put forward without respect of the truth; that is to say, with the help of mendacious or distorted assertions, or by withholding essential parts of the truth, and by appealing to those human emotions which, from a humanistic point of view, are least admirable: people's lust for power, their hatred, fear, jealousy, vanity. *Regimentation* is the odious name for a type of persuasion that is pursued without respect for the moral autonomy of man. *Enlightenment*, on the other hand, is an appreciative expression for an argumentation that is put forward with respect for the truth, and the terms *awakening*, *edification*, and *upbringing* are appreciative expressions for an emotional persuasion in harmony with humanistic ideals.

If we disregard the metaphysical-philosophical trends which still believe in the ability of science to perceive an *a priori* 'correctness', we can say that the principle of the purity of science is generally accepted nowadays. If it still provokes lively debates, it is (a) partly because, although it is supported, there is frequently a lack of compliance with the principle in practice; and (b) partly because a disagreement exists concerning the methodological conclusions drawn from the principle.

(a) With regard to the first point, it is a fact that the demand for purity is *far more difficult* to comply with in the social sciences than in the natural sciences. This is, of course, due to the circumstance that the social scientist, much more than the natural scientist, is emotionally engaged in relation to the subject matter of his work. Our strongest emotions are those directed towards matters regarding our fellow men. An individual dealing with these is, therefore, himself part of the subject matter he is engaged in—much more than an individual dealing with natural phenomena. Therefore it is far more difficult to cleanse the social sciences of wishful thinking and ideology. If it were the case that certain mathematicians had a strong preference for circles and others for squares; or that certain physicists had a strong preference for light and others for sound; then it would be conceivable that a corresponding inclination towards ideological bias would make itself felt in these sciences.

These circumstances explain the fact that the social sciences have been, and largely still are, an unattractive blend of science and politics. In the [407] field of constitutional law, Kelsen has been indefatigable in demonstrating that large parts of it are virtually pettifoggery, written in defence of the interests of an existing regime. In a masterly way, Kelsen has laid bare the tricks and misrepresentations with which political attitudes, consciously or unconsciously, disguise themselves as science and, thus, fraudulently attempt to usurp authority in the name of science. The same applies to the prevailing doctrinal study of law, where the outcomes of an interpretation are presented as scientifically correct solutions in virtue of 'the nature of the matter', without being followed by an account of the conditioning subjective attitudes (Vinding Kruse has been a typical representative of this trend in Denmark[4]). In the field of economics, Gunnar Myrdal has revealed in brilliant analyses (in his now classic work *Vetenskap och politik i nationalekonomien* [English translation as *The Political Element in the Development of Economic Theory*]) how political attitudes secretly permeate the fundamental concepts and doctrine of economic theory. The concept of value, the theory of price and interest, ideas of 'public welfare', of the 'harmony of interests', of 'balance', of 'equilibrium', of 'stability'; ideas of 'natural function', 'freedom', 'economic management', and many other elementary parts of theoretical economics comprise concealed attitude components which endow the doctrine with a political tendency, while the doctrine is presented as a scientific-objective description of reality. At a later stage, Myrdal would prove that the situation in the field of sociology was the same.[5]

(b) It is a gratifying sign—a token of greater epistemological insight as well as a livelier respect for the ideal of the purity of science—that in recent times, a powerful reaction has taken place in many quarters within the social sciences against the politicizing quagmire of the theory. Max Weber was the pioneer, and many followed in his footsteps. Precisely this reaction might explain, however, why some scholars have drawn more far-reaching *methodological consequences* from the idea of the purity of science than is necessary or justifiable. For example, in the work of Kelsen, in a group of younger

[4] See, e.g., Vinding Kruse, *Retslæren* I [Jurisprudence I] (1943), 86 *et seq.*; *Erkendelse og Vurdering* [Knowledge and Evaluation] (1942), 288 *et seq.*; on this issue, cf. Alf Ross 'En Retslære fra det 19. Aarhundrede' [A jurisprudence dating from the 19th century], in *TfR* 1945, 284 *et seq.*

[5] Gunnar Myrdal, *An American Dilemma* (1944), 1045 et seq.

Swedish jurists[6] as well as in many prominent American sociologists,[7] we meet the methodological attitude that science should keep strictly to facts and their theoretical explanation and, thus, abstain from any attempt to translate theoretical knowledge into guidelines for practical endeavours. This side of the coin should be left to the politicians. This is the motto: Science is one thing, politics quite another.

In an outstanding way, Gunnar Myrdal has claimed that this idealism of objectivity, in itself sounding so attractive, actually overshoots the mark.[8] [408] For one thing, the ideal demand cannot be realized according to intention; and for another—to the extent it could be realized—it would preclude any fruitful cooperation between theory and practice.

With regard to the first point, Myrdal shows that the ideological danger lies, not so much in the overt formulation of practical conclusions drawn from the theory, as in the hidden attitudes which are implied in the concepts that have been used and in the theoretical activity itself, from the posing of the problem onwards. Scientific concept formation and theory do not arise automatically out of the chaos of facts. They presuppose a selection, dictated by certain interests and by questions demanding answers. The terminology used will chiefly be taken from everyday language and be emotionally loaded. In reality, it is impossible for the social scientist to raise himself above the social environment he is living in and exorcize every emotional *bias* from his mind. The idea of simply 'keeping to the facts' is, thus, an illusion. But neither is it a necessary consequence of the demand of the purity of science. This demand is satisfied as soon as the hidden attitudes are brought to light as *explicit assumptions*. Then, the description acquires a hypothetical-objective character: the practical conclusions are maintained on the condition that one accepts a certain set of attitudes.

Myrdal's second objection possibly carries still greater weight. If science really were to abstain from any transformation of its results into practice, we would envisage something like the following: all theoretical knowledge gathered in a fund, from which the politician himself must take what he needs. Only, more often than not, he will not find it. The specific knowledge that is necessary for solving certain practical problems must be worked out with precisely these problems before you. The theoretical research itself must be organized, planned, and carried out, guided by the lodestar of practice. Otherwise, the practitioner will simply not discover the theoretical beliefs which are operative in relation to his practical attitudes.

6 On this issue, see Per Olof Ekelöf, *Är den juridiska doktrinen en teknik eller en vetenskap?* [Is the Doctrinal Study of Law a Technique or a Science?] (1951), 41 *et seq.*, cf. § 84 below.

7 On this issue, see Gunnar Myrdal, *An American Dilemma* (1944), 1041 *et seq.*

8 *Loc. cit.*, 1041 *et seq.*

Moreover, this state of things—as one might add, continuing Myrdal's line of thought—is already well known from the natural sciences. All the technical, or applied, sciences—agronomy, bridge construction, medical science, etc.—do not merely consist of an appropriate selection and coordination of the results of the basic sciences; rather, they are autonomous branches of science, and their study is organized in view of certain practical wishes. A doctor simply adopting his instructions from an appropriate selection from the basic sciences (chemistry, biology, physiology, etc.) would be inconceivable. Medical science is an autonomous science in the sense that it investigates on its own initiative—albeit in light of the general tenets of the basic sciences—into scientific
[409] facts and contexts, determined according to their operative relevance in relation to the practical attitude that this is a question of preserving and promoting human life and health. Technical nuclear physics is organized in the same way in relation to the practical and purposive attitude that it is desirable to make use of nuclear energy, to construct *inter alia* bombs.

It would not occur to anyone to dispute the scientific purity of the applied natural sciences on those grounds. *The scientist himself does not take a definite stand. The premise of evaluation that governs his research is not his own.* The scientific nuclear technician does not affirm the value of producing nuclear bombs, nor does the medical student affirm the value of preserving and saving human life. His science is purely objective and hypothetical: if these objectives are presupposed, the following insight is operative in relation thereto.

To be sure, the hypothetical premise[9] is the *result* of an attitude and a choice. It is not an *expression* of any attitude, however, and it affects the purity of science just as little as the choice which always has to be made before the scholar sets out to deal with one particular branch of science rather than another.

Moreover, the choice of premise is determined by the wish that the results of applied science shall possess operative value in relation to practical attitudes. Therefore, the scholar simply accepts, hypothetically, *common objectives*. Agronomy is justified by the fact that people work in agriculture and want to achieve the greatest possible economic profit. Engineering is justified by the wish to be able to solve various technical problems, etc. Of course, it would be possible to develop an applied science concerning the construction of glass pyramids. If this has not happened yet, it is of course because no corresponding practical desire has actually made itself felt. Such a science would have no operative relevance.

[9] The use of the word 'premise' must not mislead us into thinking that it is, here, a question of a logical explanation.

Now the question arises whether corresponding methodological points of view can be applied to the social sciences. It would mean that the social scientist in the same impersonal manner *hypothetically accepts the political attitudes that actually exist in the ruling circles of society*; that he, like the technician of the natural sciences, places his insight at the disposal of given objectives, without taking a stand himself.

As a matter of general principle, it is my opinion that this question must be answered in the affirmative—even if there are certain differences, not insignificant in themselves, which have the effect that the widespread dream that one fine day the social sciences will develop into an 'art of social engineering', must remain a dream.

To begin with, this has to do with the fact that while it is possible to [410] ground the applied natural sciences in relatively[10] clear objectives—efficiency in agriculture, constructing a nuclear bomb, bridge building—the same cannot be said for applied social science. There is no corresponding, relatively simple objective in policy making. All attempts to construct such an objective in the form of 'the welfare of society', 'social health' and the like are in vain. The task of politics will always be grounded in a diversity of attitudes which do not constitute a system but, rather, a conglomerate. If one analyses a given situation, one will find a diversity of wishes which reflect not only the interests of different social groups, but also the various wishes and needs within these groups. There is no single 'political need', no single 'political objective' that can be defined and isolated in the same way as the technical objectives are defined and isolated. *The task of politics is always a task of integration, a balancing of incommensurable considerations.* There are problems of maximization and distribution; there are economic considerations, party political considerations, and considerations of military strategy; there are considerations of employment, inflation, trade balance, etc.; there are short-term and long-term considerations, cultural and social *desiderata*, as well as a wish for international security—all of them reflecting a diversity of attitudes which calls for weighing and balancing. Therefore, political conclusions are always in the nature of *decisions, not solutions* (as are solutions to technical problems).

In addition, political attitudes are frequently unclear, uncertain, and wavering. As has been mentioned earlier, our attitudes are conditioned by our beliefs. Now, if the latter are uncertain and faltering (as is the case with

[10] The contrast is not an absolute one. Even the task for applied natural science may be determined by several incommensurable considerations which must be balanced against each other. A radio cannot simultaneously possess both maximum selectivity and maximum sound quality; an engine cannot simultaneously possess both maximum lightness and maximum strength, etc. Nevertheless, the contrast is very important. The irreducible choice, which in a specific situation must be made between different technical possibilities, is usually not of a political nature, but will be accepted by the interested party as an objective solution to his needs.

enormously complicated social contexts), the same will apply to our attitudes. We do not know enough about the complex of reality in order to know what we want. No one thought of making full employment an objective as long as economic crises were considered inevitable natural phenomena.[11] Therefore, theory does not merely play a purely technical role. It is also for theory to *provide guidance concerning the very objectives*; to clarify and specify the political attitudes by correcting and supplementing the conditioning beliefs; or to indicate the objectives which those in power would address if they had a more adequate conception of reality than they actually have.

[411] The above-mentioned differences explain why applied social science must both begin and end otherwise than applied natural science.

It must *begin* otherwise, because its premises are not in the same finished and clarified state as those of applied natural science. Therefore, the first thing that must be done is to study and map the actual political attitudes as expressed in the interests, sympathies, aspirations, and ideology of various influential groups. However, this is merely raw material that has to be processed. One must investigate whether the different objectives are mutually compatible, or whether they require mutual balancing. And one must consider whether they are conditioned by an inadequate conception of reality and, therefore, need correction on the basis of a more complete and correct knowledge. First, when this has been done, the social scientist has reached the point where he can put forward his hypothetical premises—the table of political objectives and considerations governing the direction of his research and practical conclusions. Even if the task that has been described here can ideally be assigned and resolved as an objective, scientific task, it must nonetheless be admitted that it is beset with such enormous difficulties and such uncertainties that, in practice, it is unavoidable that personal attitudes and preferences will play a certain part in working out the table of objectives. The emotional presuppositions of applied social science can hardly be objectivized to the same degree as is the case in the disciplines of natural science. It is difficult to eradicate the social reformer within the practitioner of applied social science.

Perhaps it is even more important to note that applied social science also must *end*, otherwise it can never be rationally conclusive in the same way as applied natural science is rationally conclusive; that is, put forward a clear solution to the problems of action. In this context, I am not thinking of the flaws in the operative beliefs, caused by the present, inadequate state of the social sciences. The point is one of basic principle; it applies even if we should acquire perfect insight into the facts and mechanisms of community life.

[11] Neither on this point is the contrast an absolute one. The practical wish to construct motor cars did not arise until we had some knowledge of engineering.

The decisive factor is *the unavoidable fact of multiple considerations*. It will never be possible to develop technical instructions on how to achieve full employment, in the same way as one can provide instructions on how to produce nuclear bombs. For the practical problem of employment can never be isolated from the general state of the society in which the measures will be carried out. The measures themselves will vary accordingly, and must be evaluated on the basis of the totality of considerations, not merely in proportion to their usefulness in combating unemployment. Even after a most thorough examination of the facts and their contexts, there will always remain a leap—a leap which consists of all considerations being thought over and weighed in a *decision*, that is, in an irrational act. Applied social science will never be able to offer a solution, that is, an instruction that emerges unequivocally from the given objective, combined with technical insight.

Hence there arises the methodological problem of whether the scientific researcher himself shall make this leap, this decision-making weighing, [412] or whether he shall content himself with presenting his calculations and leave it to the men of action to draw the practical conclusion themselves (a highly topical problem in the current debate on legal methodology, cf. § 84 below).

It is obvious that the activity we are discussing here is not a scientific one. From this, however—as previously mentioned—we cannot draw the practical conclusion of the idea of scientific purity that the activity should not be performed by a man of science. Only, it must be clearly indicated that he in this regard is not acting as a representative of science. On the other hand, there is reason to think that, in many situations, the weighing done by the theorist will be of guiding value to the practitioner. For this weighing is done on the basis of his direct and comprehensive knowledge of the relevant facts and their respective contexts. The information about these matters which he imparts to the practitioner will hardly provide the latter with the same understanding of the various considerations and probabilities as is possessed by an individual who is directly familiar with them. Let us consider the corresponding relationship between doctor and patient. If it is a question of medical or surgical treatment, for example, the doctor will give his patient a certain piece of advice, although the weighing of the different considerations *pro et contra* is not a theoretical problem in itself. The doctor's opinion will often be regarded as binding by the patient, because the latter understands that the doctor is better qualified than he is himself to evaluate the options in light of the patient's interests. But of course, the weighing may be so ambiguous that the doctor prefers to inform the patient as fully as possible and thereupon leave the matter to his discretion.

Therefore, I think that it is compatible with the idea of scientific purity and, what is more, right and proper that the theorist performs the irrational

leaps himself and presents the result in the form of an instruction to the practitioner. It is worth noting here that the theorist's instruction can never exempt the practitioner from the final resolution and the final responsibility. To clarify this point I shall return to the example with the doctor's instructions to his patient. The doctor's advice is based upon the common, general attitude regarding the preservation of life and health, combined with his medical insight. For the patient, however, other considerations and circumstances may be co-determining, too. Similarly, the directions given by applied economics are determined on the basis of what is dictated by the economist's insight into economic contexts, whereas it is quite conceivable that the responsible politician will adduce other points of view as well—for example, points of view as to military strategy or party tactics. From a purely economic point of view, a rationalization in retail trade is undoubtedly desirable. A good many politicians are nonetheless against it, because—for ideological reasons, or reasons of party tactics—they see an advantage in preserving a class of small, independent tradesmen ('the smallholders of business'). Bismarck—in spite of good economic arguments—was against free trade because, in his view, it represented a danger to the
[413] state in a time of burgeoning large-scale industry. In Russia, the nationalization of business was carried out, less because of economic than political reasons: in order to promote the cooperative movement in agriculture and, thereby, solidarity in the new state.[12]

These examples can be generalized in the following way. The responsible practitioner, finding himself in a real-life action situation, must take into account all attitudes and all considerations that can be derived from the operative circumstances. His policy-making is *integral* [oriented towards the whole]. The theorist never finds himself *in medias res* in the same way. His hypothetical premises of attitude are stylized and simplified. The operative circumstances he adduces, as well as the considerations conditioned by them, are limited to the visual field appertaining to his discipline. His observations are abstracting, his political conclusions are *differential* [oriented towards differences or distinctions].

This explains why all the experts of the world will never be able to make the politician superfluous. The irreducible task that falls to his lot is the integration of the differential policy of the whole body of experts. The expert, in his professional capacity, is and must be wearing blinkers. The politician should preferably also have eyes in the back of his head. The Platonic idea that the men of science are called to rule the state is based upon the intellectualist delusion that the right action is solely a question of the right knowledge. In the United States of today, this idea lives on in the dream

[12] See Niels Lindberg, *Idealer og Regler i anvendt Økonomik* [Ideals and Rules in Applied Economics] (1951), 181.

that one fine day, the social sciences will have reached such a peak of perfection that social scientists, social technicians, and social mechanics will make our politicians superfluous and rule the state with the same objective effectiveness as is currently done by their colleagues from the natural sciences, when they are building an automobile factory.[13]

[13] As far as the jurist's role as a social technician is concerned, Harold D. Lasswell and Myres S. McDougall are typical and influential representatives of a sanguine rationalism; see their joint work 'Legal Education and Public Policy', in Lasswell, *The Analysis of Political Behaviour* (1947), 21 *et seq.*, and Myres S. McDougall, 'The Law School of the Future', *Yale Law Journal* (1947), 1345.

From the opposite camp, Hans J. Morgenthau, *Scientific Man vs. Power Politics* (1946), has offered sharp criticism of the rationalist belief in the ability of science to solve social problems and to control social life by means of social engineering. I agree with these views, but not with the author's argumentation. For Morgenthau primarily stresses the view that the social sciences are not capable of predicting with any certainty the course of social life, but are limited to estimating probable tendencies (*op. cit.*, 126 *et seq.*, 151). Even if this were correct, it is hardly decisive. Even a probability calculus has operative value for human action. If nothing better can be achieved, one must be satisfied with that. The element of uncertainty can certainly explain that one cannot expect the same outcomes from social technologies as from physical technologies, but it does not explain the fundamental peculiarity of social problems, as distinct from those of applied natural science. As explained in the text above, the decisive difference must be sought in the emotional preconditions. The specifically political element consists in the integration of multiple considerations, apart from all possible insight into causal connections.

[414]

§ 79. Confrontation

For many centuries, political theory has been marching under the banner of philosophical absolutism and rationalism. The problem of political action was regarded as a basically rational problem, and the political debate as basically a debate over which course of action, judged in the light of rational principles, is the *correct* one. This absolutism and rationalism have characterized not only theory, but also practice—not only philosophers, but also politicians, jurists, and laymen. Political ideologies have been proclaimed and accepted as rational truths, and juridico-political argumentation has taken the form of deductions from the eternal truths of justice and natural law.

Hidden under this metaphysical cover, there have probably always lain more or less imperfect deliberations, grounded in an operative conception of reality on an empirical basis. Only in recent times—that is, within the last few generations—have there been serious attempts to endow political debate with scientific status. However, these attempts have been without support from, and methodical basis in, a fundamental theory on the nature, task, and mechanics of practical argumentation.

The theory outlined in this chapter is regarded, by myself, as a first fragmentary attempt in this direction. It is based on the fundamental view that the political debate is not located at the level of logic: it does not endeavour to prove truths. Rather, it is located at the psychologico-technical-causal level: it purports to bring about practical agreement, by influencing an opponent's point of view through argumentation and persuasion. Within this framework rational, argumentative assertions based on common experience or scientific insight play an important role. Their function is not to prove a truth, however, but to convince an opponent, that is, convert him to one's own stance.

There is no new thing under the sun! This fundamental philosophical view implies the revival of a discipline which played an important part in classical antiquity, but has been totally neglected since the days of Descartes: namely *rhetoric*. To the Greeks, rhetoric was much more than a theory of eloquence. As emerges from Aristotle's *Topic* and *Rhetoric*, rhetoric was what might be called *the fine art of persuasion*,[1] a comprehensive theory of the technique of gaining the support of others through a proper influencing of their thoughts and minds. And precisely this, and this alone, is the objective of the practical as well as the theoretical politician. This has nothing to do with cynicism (as the rationalists

[1] I have searched in vain for a Danish word for 'persuasion'.

will have us believe). The technique becomes cynical only if it is exercised without respect for truth and the humanistic ideals of our culture. The task of science is [415] precisely this: to see to it that political argumentation occurs with the greatest possible respect for truth.

Stevenson and Perelman,[2] among others, have contributed to establishing a modern rhetoric.

[2] See Charles L. Stevenson, *Ethics and Language* (1944); Ch. Perelman, 'Réflexions sur la justice' [Reflections on Justice], in *Revue de l'Institut de Sociologie,* no. 2/1951 (Bruxelles); 'Raison éternelle, raison historique' [Eternal reason, historic reason], *Actes du VI Congrés des Sociétés de Philosophie de Langue Francaise* (Strassbourg, 1952), 347; C. Perelman et L. Olbrechts-Tyteca, 'Logique et rhétorique' [Logic and rhetoric], *Revue philosophique* (Paris 1950), 1 *et seq.*

[416] CHAPTER XV

Legal Politics: Province and Task

§ 80. The Line of Demarcation between Legal Politics and Other Politics

From the perspective of an idealistic theory of law, it is not difficult to establish what is the specific task of legal politics, and what distinguishes it from other politics. The objective of the law lies within the law itself: namely, to perfect the idea of justice inherent in the law. Legal politics is the study of how to realize this objective. Due to this specific goal, legal politics differs from welfare politics, cultural politics, and power politics, which are established on the basis of other specific goals—economic, cultural, and political goals. One might also take the view that legal politics is a special branch of cultural politics—namely, a branch classed under the cultural idea that is specific for the law.

By contrast, if one rejects—as we have done—a specific idea of law, endowing the law with an absolute, intrinsic value; and instead regards positive law as a social technique, or as an instrument for any kind of social aim (economic, cultural, political), then the question becomes rather more complicated.

Thus, it seems that we must start from the premise that legal politics is not determined by a specific goal, but by a *specific technology*: it comprises all problems of action which arise out of employing the technology of the law, in particular legislation, in order to achieve certain social goals.

Determined in this way, however, legal politics would acquire a dimension far beyond what is usually regarded as the jurist's legitimate field of activity.

The state budget, taxes, tariffs, duties, and government loans are set, imposed,
[417] and raised by legislation. Problems under these headings would nonetheless in general not be regarded as juridico-political problems, but as problems of financial policy under the responsibility of economists. Similarly, issues concerning the regulation of the relation between social classes (in particular, the regulation of working conditions and insurance, and of poor relief) chiefly belong to social politics, irrespective of the fact that such measures are enforced through

legislation; issues concerning foreign exchange regulation as well as import and export restrictions are trade policy issues; issues concerning prices and arrangements for production and distribution are matters for industrial policy and production policy; issues concerning schools and the church as well as radio broadcasting are cultural policy issues; issues concerning treaties are foreign policy issues; issues concerning military matters are defence policy issues, etc., etc.

Leaving aside purely linguistic formulation problems, it seems only natural that objective guidance in these and other political issues has to be provided by the experts in the different fields: by economists, educational experts, military and foreign policy experts—not by jurists.

Under these circumstances, how do we find room for a specific legal politics that should be the domain of the jurists? Perhaps we feel that such a domain must comprise, for example, contracts, purchase, tort law, insurance matters, registration, marital matters, majority, inheritance, penal legislation, as well as other subjects traditionally regarded as the lawyers' principal areas. However, when one knows for sure that in none of these fields—just like in other fields of law—does the law exist for its own sake, but must be evaluated according to its function in relation to objectives and attitudes outside the law, then it seems that these political problems must also be a task for various kinds of non-legal experts. For instance, is it not the case that tort and insurance law are closely connected with economic problems? Or can a law report on instalment buying be submitted without touching upon the importance of this system with respect to production and sales volume?

It emerges from these reflections that *the peculiarity of legal politics cannot be found in a specific objective* in the same way as, say, medical science, agronomy, or bridge construction are organized in relation to a specific task, whereas the knowledge operative in relation thereto stems from various basic sciences. If legal politics is to be an autonomous discipline, the situation has to be reversed. Its peculiarity must be conditioned by a *specific body of knowledge* that is of relevance as soon as the technique of the law is employed for solving social problems, irrespective of their aim. As far as I can see, this specific body of knowledge can only be found in *juridico-sociological knowledge* of the causal connection between legal regulation and human behaviour, or—to put it differently—of the possibilities of influencing human behaviour by means of the apparatus of legal sanction. *Legal politics is applied legal sociology or legal technology.*

In my opinion, this essential view is able to shed some light on the questions raised above. There are no specifically juridico-political legislative problems, [418]
but all legislative problems have a *juridico-political aspect*. This aspect, however, can play different roles in different problematic situations, with the result that

sometimes it is completely overlooked, whereas at other times, it is regarded as the only aspect of the problem.

If it is about introducing new taxes, for example, or compulsory saving, or an increase in duties or other fiscal measures, our interest is not focused on juridico-technical problems, that is to say, on the first link in the causal chain between regulation and compliance; on the contrary, it is focused on the further effects of such measures in relation to inflation, trade balance, employment, etc. The juridico-political problems are of secondary importance. They remain in the background, or are overlooked. This has to do with the fact that these are questions of temporary, changing short-term objectives—which is to say: questions of politics in a narrower sense.

Conversely, juridico-technical problems dominate if it is about institutions which are deeply rooted in the relatively stable economic structure and ideology of the society, such as property, contracts, and marriage. Precisely because the ideological attitudes and objectives underpinning these institutions are traditionally experienced as almost a matter of course and quite unproblematic—raised above the 'political' (in a narrower sense)—they do not attract attention. They are not debated, and they are hardly consciously experienced. All mental energy is concentrated on juridico-technical questions—how the legal rules should be formulated in order to bring about such human behaviour as best harmonizes with the presupposed aims and attitudes. Here, both the jurist and legal politics find their task. *The problem becomes a juridico-political problem to the extent that it is not political in a narrower sense.*

The contrast is not an absolute one. It is a matter of difference of degree and gradual transition. Even the most temporary and short-lived political measures have juridico-political aspects. In connection with the changing tax legislation and its purely fiscal problems, a whole body of juridico-technical problems is created in the course of time, focused on the immediate juridico-sociological relation between norm and behaviour. A tax law evolves. In the same way a labour law evolves, a social law, etc. On the other hand, even the most essential institutions are not raised above all political development and revaluation. Along with the dynamic evolution of society, society's ideological foundation changes, too. Contract law and property law have undergone radical changes during the period between the zenith of liberalism and modern social welfare law. This development has involved problems and conflicts which extend far beyond the juridico-technical area and well into the long-term social effects of the law, as judged in relation to the conflicting interests of various social groups.

Nor must the contrast be understood to imply that the jurist strictly keeps to juridico-technical problems—to legal politics proper—and leaves all other
[419] questions to the other experts. Often the jurist, engaged in problems *de lege ferenda* in a field of law which is largely of a technical nature, will deal with the

group of problems in its entirety, that is, including those aspects of the matter which presuppose expert knowledge of economic or other non-juridico-sociological contexts. A report on the revision of the law of instalment buying, drawn up by a jurist, for instance, deals extensively with the economic functions of this trade system and the economic structure and customs of the retail business in our country. Thus far, the jurist does not act as an expert in his own right, but borrows his knowledge from elsewhere. There is nothing wrong with that, provided it is done with discretion and tact. However, there is an obvious danger of dilettantism if the jurist, instead of relying on other experts, credits himself with the ability to master problems single-handedly outside his field of expertise. In that case, one ends up—and there are examples—in a juridico-economic-social-political polyhistoricism which, considering that modern science is highly specialized, no individual is able to manage.

The varying role played by expert legal knowledge is reflected in the composition of commissions frequently appointed to submit a report on legislative reforms. In such a situation, the jurist's role is often a twofold one. On the one hand, he is an expert in his speciality, the sociology of law. On the other hand, it is often the jurist who, when all the experts have had their say, undertakes the weighing and balancing of all considerations and arrives at the formulation which best integrates all motivating components. As mentioned earlier, this activity is not of a theoretical but a decision-making nature. Thus far, legal politics is in the nature of an art, a skill, where the value of the outcome is measured against the fact that it is accepted by others, in particular by those in power, as the decision which best harmonizes with all predominant attitudes and operative beliefs. The jurist is professionally trained in this art, and in so far as his task consists of acting as *the experts' umpire*. In practice, this manifests itself in the fact that the chairmanship of a commission composed of experts is often given to a jurist.

Accordingly, legal politics as a real type comprises the following elements: (1) specifically juridico-technical problems of a juridico-sociological nature (legal politics proper, or legal politics as an ideal type); (2) further political problems, closely connected with the former in practice, which—according to their objective nature—really belong to the field of expertise of other experts, and with regard to which the jurist thus acts as a mediating expert; (3) the weighing and decision-making activity as the experts' umpire; and (4) the linguistic formulation of the decision (which, by the way, only with great exertion can be separated from the decision itself) in acceptable legal language, and in due consideration of its fitting harmoniously into the already existing body of law.[1]

[1] A possible fifth juridico-political sphere of activity is mentioned in § 88 below, *in fine*.

[420] *§ 81. Legal Politics* de Lege Ferenda *and* de Sententia Ferenda

Legal politics has hitherto largely been regarded as legislative politics. But law has not been created exclusively by the legislator. As mentioned earlier (Chapter IV), all administration of justice comprises a decision-making or stance-taking moment that transcends a mere intellectual activity. The judicial decision, however, is less free than the legislative decision. The law-applying authority, in particular the judge, feels bound by the wording of statutes and other sources of law. Nevertheless, these always leave room for interpretation, and the concrete legal norm in which the decision results will always be a new creation, in the sense that it is no mere logical derivative of given rules.

Therefore, there is room left for a legal politics—not merely for the guidance of the legislator, but also for the guidance of the law-applying authorities (in particular the judge). It is this legal politics that appears in the interpretive contributions of doctrine. It has been mentioned earlier how juridico-theoretical and juridico-political considerations merge here in a unique way, with the result that doctrinal interpretation, depending on the attitudinal premises that have been adopted, can be understood, both as a juridico-theoretical assertion of how the courts presumably will react, and as juridico-political advice to the judge on how he ought to react. I shall return to this point of view at a later stage.

§ 82. The Theoretical Foundation of Legal Politics

All scientifically founded policy-making (technology) is applied theory, worked out on the basis of certain action situations. It consists in developing such beliefs as are considered operative in relation to presupposed attitudes. Thus, practical medical science is the application of physics, chemistry, biology, physiology as well as other theories to the tasks dictated by the wish to preserve life and health. Hence the question: what theoretical insight is applied in the realm of legal politics?

As far as *legal politics proper* is concerned, it emerges from the aforesaid that the insight applied here is the juridico-sociological knowledge of the causal connection between legal regulation and human behaviour; or, the insight into the issue of how it is possible to influence human behaviour through the function of the legal machinery—which, in turn, is determined by the legal regulations. Thus, it is a matter of questions such as the following. How does the formulation of the rules of damages impact upon the diligence people show in different situations? In [421] this context, what part is played by the access to liability insurance? What is the significance of the rules governing mortgages with regard to the granting of credits and sales volume? How does the instalment system impact upon people's financial dispositions, and to what extent does it invite one to criminal transactions?

When it is stated here that the answer to such questions is theoretically grounded in the sociology of law, this statement must be understood as a statement of general principle. A sociology of law in the form of a systematic science, based upon methodical research, does not, in fact, exist at present, or is at any rate only budding. The knowledge the jurist operates with is obtained from the common experience of life, supplemented with more or less fortuitously gathered statistical information.

This explains why in juridico-political reasoning, we must frequently content ourselves with conjectures and vague estimates instead of exact knowledge. Statements like the following, taken from a report on liability for damages, are typical of the vagueness we frequently must accept even in extremely important juridico-sociological problems.

> *It is quite probable that the introduction of a legal rule to the effect that damages shall be paid by the person who has done harm by irresponsible behaviour contributes to the maintenance of the general attitude that due diligence ought to be exercised with regard to other people.*
>
> *Further, it is conceivable that the measure will entail a dangerous relaxation of ordinary diligence. Even in the present state of the law, where*

> *liability insurance is usually voluntary and therefore not taken out by everyone, many people think that liability insurance entails a relaxation of diligence. Others, however, take the view that liability insurance affects due diligence only to a small extent, and it is not easy to find a way in which to decide who is right.*[1]

Frequently, legal politicians do not exhibit similar honesty and circumspection but, rather, attribute—without ceremony—to vague and generalizing surmises a certainty and argumentative force to which they have no claim. The usual argumentation as to what is demanded on the grounds of 'commercial safety' and many other 'policy considerations' adduced in order to justify legal rules can be mentioned as examples.

To create a scientific sociology of law is an extremely important, but surely a very difficult task. It would have to consist partly of a basic part which would investigate, by abstraction from specific legal systems and specific environ-
[422] ments, the general mechanics of motivation through which the law influences human behaviour; partly of an applied or technical part which, in view of practical problems, would investigate concrete contexts. Individual attempts have been made in this direction, especially in the United States. Until this task is accomplished, the legal politician must content himself with a groping and piecemeal insight, deduced from ordinary experience and professional familiarity with the phenomena of law working in real life.

As far as *legal politics in an extended sense* is concerned, it goes without saying that the jurist must obtain the necessary insight into the branches of science, economics in particular, which in a given situation are of relevance to the calculation of the more far-reaching effects of certain legislative measures. In general, he will be well advised to consult the experts in the respective field, since there are grave risks associated with acquiring information only from books, in a field of expertise different from one's own.

Finally, the *activity of weighing and formulating* is not based on theoretical insight. It is a question of skills that must be practised in training, whereby familiarity with the legal tradition and the given legal material naturally play an important role.

[1] *Nordisk Lovgivning om Erstatningsansvar* [Nordic Legislation on Damage Liability], Report submitted by Henry Ussing (1950), 33, 40.

§ 83. *The Task of Legal Politics: Stating the Premises*

As set forth in the previous chapter, the principle of the purity of science is tied to a methodological requirement, according to which any political work must give an account of the objectives and attitudes that are hypothetically accepted as guidelines for the theoretical investigation and the practical conclusions. And what is more, for the practical instructions to be relevant and effective vis-à-vis those they are addressed to, these emotional premises must be chosen objectively. This means that they must be chosen, not because, or as an expression that, the researcher himself shares these attitudes and accepts these objectives, but because they are actually embraced (or can be assumed to be embraced with increased insight) by those who have the power to act. This is the only way to preserve the objectivity of political science. In principle, the sentences of political science have the following form: if this or that attitude and objective is presupposed, then this or that belief concerning facts and contexts is operative and leads to this or that practical instruction.

Therefore, the *first task* of legal politics must be *to examine the attitudes and objectives that are currently prevalent in influential social groups*, and thereby determinative of the organs that have the formal power to legislate. As previously [423] mentioned, this is not about artificial, generalizing phrases, such as 'public utility' or 'the common weal'; it is about arriving at specific, actually effective attitudes, deriving from the prevailing ideology and common interests, or from the interest component emanating from the conflicting interests of different groups.

One might ask if it is at all possible to arrive in this way at a fairly unambiguous set of attitudinal premises. Will it not be the case that there are just as many sets of attitudes as there are individuals, varying with the mental structure of each individual personality, with his creed and specific interests? The answer lies in the fact that a people would not be a people, and that a society would be inconceivable, if there were no comprehensive body of shared creed and will, ideology and interests. This is what we call *the unity of culture and nation*. This unity is not an absolute one, of course. Within the framework of this body, there is much practical disagreement. The claims of different social groups clash with each other. Opposite ideologies collide. To a great extent, however, these conflicts will be rooted in diverging conceptions of reality (see § 77 above), without indicating any disagreement concerning fundamental attitudes. If the disagreement goes that deep, the citizens do not conceive of themselves as one people (national, religious, political minorities).

The programmatic claim raised here should be viewed with some caution. The socio-psychological facts we are speaking of are not mechanically tangible. They cannot be gathered, described, and catalogued in the same way as the flora and fauna of a country are catalogued. They will always be somewhat blurred. A certain interpretation and stylization—and, thus, an element of subjectivity—is unavoidable.

In the case of issues informed by politics in the narrower sense, the material to be examined will chiefly consist of different political ideologies and programmes, together with an analysis of the various interests of important social groups. As a result, a set of objectives will often emerge in a given situation, which can be said to enjoy overwhelming support from the forces dominating power politics and can, therefore, be stated as attitudinal premises. Other situations may be less clear, and it may be advisable to operate with alternative premises.

In the case of legal politics proper, the premises must be primarily sought in the cultural tradition—in the relatively permanent, ideological community. One of its most important forms of revelation is previous legislation and the entire legal tradition that has come down to us. At the same time, one ought to consider that this tradition may be lagging behind in relation to cultural changes—it may constitute what is called *cultural lag*. The juridico-political problem is always a problem of adjustment. The issue is always an issue concerning a
[424] change in existing conditions, never a radical reshaping of the law from the bottom in mid-air, without any historical preconditions.

The programmatic claim must be approached with caution also in a different sense, namely, in the sense that it cannot be a decisive factor that a juridico-political investigation starts with a formal taking stock of all the attitudes that have been accepted hypothetically. It is often the case, of course, that it is only through the juridico-sociological analysis of the causal connections that we notice the 'considerations' to be taken into account when formulating the legal rules. What is called *a consideration is precisely the organic combination of operative belief and evaluating attitude*. The consideration of 'commercial safety', for example, is an expression of the operative belief that the legal measure in question is effective on that front, and that 'commercial safety' is something desirable and ought to be promoted.

Instead, the decisive factor is the spirit in which the investigation is undertaken; that the researcher is aware that his juridico-political instructions must necessarily be based, not merely on facts ('the nature of things'), but also on presupposed attitudes; that he is aware that these emotional premises must be chosen objectively, not as an expression of his own creed and will. The more the researcher is imbued with this spirit, the easier it will be for him to submit an explicit account of the attitudinal foundation of his political recommendations.

Even taken in this rather cautious sense, however, the existing literature cannot, generally speaking, be said to satisfy the methodological claim. On the one hand, one still meets representatives of the completely naive view that it is scientifically possible to discover, directly from 'the nature of things', the most 'advantageous' solution, that is, the solution which brings about 'the best relation between human beings', or 'the effects most beneficial to mankind',[1] without understanding that all policy making must be rooted in attitudes beyond knowledge. Even if the great majority of Scandinavian writers do not subscribe to this primitive intellectualism, their situation is by no means characterized by the necessary clarity. Presumably the predominant view is that the politicizing jurist, without pausing to ponder his method, spontaneously evaluates the law on the basis of the social attitudes that animate himself, feeling at the same time—more or less consciously—that he is the authoritative expounder of national legal culture. Sometimes, this position is combined with a strong belief in the values of the common sense of justice and of legal tradition. The result is a romantic belief in the oracular function of the jurist, acting as the mouthpiece of the nation's sense of justice. Individual intuition takes the place of analysis, and one's scrutiny does not reach down to the attitudes, interests, and objectives that have dictated the sense of justice. Or perhaps one does look behind the sense of justice, but without getting as deep as the effective, particular, social [425] attitudes. Instead, one clings to the empty concept of 'public utility', as the only and supreme guiding idea. Under the cover of an apparent objectivity, the jurist can then fill this shell with his personal aspirations for social reform. In both cases, the result will be a *legal politics in the shape of an exhortation, not science*, with the jurist appearing as a high priest or a social reformer—not as a social technologist. The motivating attitudes are not introduced hypothetically but assertorically. In the conclusions, there is no room for a conditioning 'if'—they are presented as postulates.

However, there are also several examples of a juridico-political position which is actually quite close to the aim I have described, even if it is not carried out according to the pattern. Thus, we might make use of the following presentation of the problem in Ussing's report on Scandinavian legislation concerning liability for damages:

> *Nowadays, it can hardly be denied that legislation concerning liability for damages must be based, first and foremost, upon practical, societal considerations. The rules of tort law have had—and no doubt will have in future—practical effects which are interesting from a societal point of view. In more than one way, the rules contribute towards increasing the safety of the population. They limit the unfortunate consequences of the harm that has been done, and some of the rules at any rate lead to fewer damages than would otherwise have occurred. The modern state must be interested*

[1] Vinding Kruse, *Retslæren* I [Jurisprudence] (1943), 86 and *Erkendelse og Vurdering* [Knowledge and Evaluation] (1942), 285.

in both. Since ancient times, the state has tried to protect the individual by preventing the injurious behaviour of others. Nowadays, however, states are increasingly interested in trying to repair the harm that has been done. From an economic point of view, this is important in all those cases where damage may entail disturbances in the production area or in other types of economic activity. Today, however, states do not content themselves with being interested in that. They show a much broader interest for the well-being of the population, and in this context, it is of particular significance that people experience a growing need to be protected from the dangers of life. Certainly, states have tried to meet this need (which can be found in many areas) in several ways, namely, by establishing social insurance schemes and fixed rules concerning pension payments to public employees and their surviving dependents. However, the immense growth of the entire insurance system and of the pension system in business life shows by far that the need for safety has not been satisfied through public measures.

When the issue of the content of the compensation rules will be taken up in view of legislation, let it be our first and foremost aim to call attention to, and evaluate, the practical considerations that may be of consequence to the legislator.

[426] Ussing's hint as to what 'the states are interested in nowadays', as seen in the light of typical tendencies in legislation, may be understood as an (albeit somewhat groping) attempt to determine, in an impersonal and objective way, the attitudinal presuppositions of the investigation.

§ 84. The Task of Legal Politics: Formulating Conclusions

Having accounted for the motivating attitudes, *the next step* in a juridico-political inquiry must be to *describe the juridico-sociological facts and contexts operative in relation to the premises.* According to the prevailing methodology, the two steps—as previously stated—frequently merge into one single step when stating the 'considerations'. Moreover, this description and investigation of juridico-sociological matters does not cause any specifically juridico-political problems of method. This part of the investigation is purely theoretical and adheres to the same methodological view that applies to other empirical research of a sociological nature. There is no particular reason for entering into this matter more closely—and the less so, because the juridico-sociological investigations, as previously mentioned, do not, as yet, possess any scientific character to speak of.

The *third and last link* in the juridico-political investigation is *the formulation of conclusions in the form of instructions* to the legislator or the judge.

The word 'conclusion' must not lead us astray. It has been previously (§§ 76 and 78) emphasized that the relation between arguments (operative beliefs) and attitude—just like the relation between both of these and the resultant decision or action—is not a logical relation. What we have got here is a purely factual, mental causal connection. Thus, in principle, the practical instructions imply *indications as to how the legislator (the judge) must, in fact, be assumed to act on the basis of his given attitudes, on the condition that he accepts the operative beliefs that have been put before him.* (Here one must bear in mind that this may include the effect that the arguments that have been advanced may alter certain of the legislator's previous attitudes, conditioned by untenable beliefs.)

But precisely because the relation between argument and conclusion is not a logical one, the third and final link in legal politics *is not of a scientific or theoretical nature*, but is the expression of a personal reaction of a *decision-making* nature. This alogical leap further manifests itself in the fact that the decision typically emerges through the weighing of many different, incommensurable considerations.

The question then arises whether the principle of the purity of science implies [427]
that the legal politician must refrain from making this leap, and content himself with putting forward his argumentation before the legislator and the judge, leaving them to draw the practical conclusion. I have already (§ 78) dealt with this question in general terms and maintained that the principle of the purity of science is not violated if one emphasizes that this part of legal politics is not of a scientific nature. In practice, this is done simply by not presenting the

instructions as the authoritative outcomes of science, as the scientifically discovered law (albeit on the basis of hypothetical attitudinal premises), but merely as counsel, as recommendations—combined with the awareness that it is always possible that another individual, even if he accepts all the arguments that have been put forward and does not put forward new counter-arguments, may nonetheless act in a contrary way, without anyone for that reason having the right to say that he has acted 'wrongly'. He has simply made the irreducible leap in a different way, and weighed the relevant considerations differently. Confronted with that, argumentation comes to a halt. The only thing one can do is to restate one's arguments and find out if the opponent really has completely understood them. If this seems to be the case, nothing further can be done. In addition, I have put forward arguments for the view that it is also desirable that the scientist himself completes the investigation by drawing practical conclusions and formulating them as recommendations.

In the following, I shall mention the traces left by these general problems in the discussion on legal method.

From the principle of the purity of science (in particular the science of law), Hans Kelsen has drawn the conclusion with regard to doctrinal interpretation that the latter must abstain from all evaluation, that is, from all kinds of pragmatic consideration as to the purpose of the legal rules or their politico-ideological foundation.[1] According to Kelsen, it is indeed true that authentic interpretation (by which he understands the interpretation made by the judge or by other authorities empowered to make binding decisions) is motivated by pragmatic considerations. By contrast, the task of the legal scholar is to discover—solely through linguistic, logico-syntactic analysis—the various possible interpretations and to point out their practical consequences. It is, then, for the judge, not for the legal scholar, to make a choice between these possibilities. In this way, science is able to keep to the straight and narrow path. Science prepares the way for a practical-political decision by presenting the results of its logical and juridico-sociological analysis, but it does not take a political stand itself. Otherwise, doctrinal interpretation degenerates into a dogmatism where political postulates are camouflaged under sham scientific objectivity.

[428] In reply to that, it must be pointed out, firstly—as explained in more detail in the theory of interpretation (Ch. IV)—that the idea of a purely logical interpretation, free of all pragmatic elements, is an illusion;[2] and, secondly—as has been discussed immediately above—that the idea of the purity of science

[1] See, e.g., Hans Kelsen, *The Law of the United Nations* (1950), Preface.

[2] In a review of Kelsen, *op. cit.* (*Jus Gentium*, 1950, 250 *et seq.*), I have adduced examples to show how Kelsen, when carrying out his theory of interpretation, cannot avoid resorting to hidden pragmatic presuppositions.

is not violated as long as the borderline between science and politics is clearly indicated.

Kelsen's theory of interpretation aptly illustrates Myrdal's assertion that it is not possible to carry out the idea of the purity of science by methodologically banishing from science all evaluations, all emotional attitudes. We must demand that these be made conscious and brought to light as explicit presuppositions; and—we might add—we must demand that practical conclusions be set forward in the modality of a recommendation, not of a postulate.

In the work of several *younger Swedish jurists* we can find a corresponding methodological attitude (presumably inspired by Kelsen), characterized by a demand to expel all evaluation from the productions of legal science. This position has been refuted in a book by Per Olof Ekelöf,[3] the tendency of which, but not the argumentation, I can endorse.[4] Apart from that, this discussion is no reason for me to express opinions apart from what has already been said in connection with Kelsen.

Finally, I would like to admit that it is not without uneasiness that I have taken this stance in opposition to Kelsen and his Swedish adherents. The idea of the purity of science is the cornerstone of the professional ethos of the man of science. I embrace it warmly myself, and I am always happy when anyone defends it by attacking that fraudulence of science which follows when this idea is not honoured. Nevertheless, I cannot close my eyes to the fact that the methodological demands which these scholars wished to derive from this idea are mistaken. One might say that they are caused by mixing up, on the one hand, what applies to science *qua* idea, and, on the other, what applies to science *qua* profession. No violence is done to the idea by those who, in their professional capacity, pursue both science and policy making, provided that the ideal borderline between them is clearly observed.

[3] *Är den juridiska doktrinen en teknik eller en vetenskap?* [Is the Doctrinal Study of Law a Technique or a Science?] (1951).

[4] The same applies to Illum's views in his work *Lov og Ret* [Law and Justice] (1945), 154 *et seq.*

[429] CHAPTER XVI

The Possibility of Legal Politics: Between Fate and Utopia

§ 85. The Prophets of Fate Deny the Possibility of Legal Politics

Certain conditions must be fulfilled if it shall be meaningful to develop a legal politics that would provide guidance to the legislator, or altogether approach other people with claims or counsel. St. Francis preached to the birds, to be sure, but this is something that most people would probably regard as a futile undertaking. Primitive people believe that their words have power over wind and weather, over the crops of the soil, over life and death (magic). Most people alive today still believe that it is possible, by means of verbal appeals addressed to a supreme being, to influence the course of events here on earth (prayer). Side by side with the highest technical achievements of science, this is still widely practised in modern warfare.

From a scientific point of view, the above examples are expressions of a tremendous exaggeration of the power and scope of words and argumentation. However, the source of the disagreement is the presuppositions concerning the essence of nature, rather than the theory of the necessary conditions for influencing through the power of words. Magical and religious practices are based on the assumption that nature is animated, or governed, by a being endowed with reason and will. The natural sciences have done away with this assumption. Nevertheless, the belief that emotional appeals and rational argumentation have meaning only in relation to persons and not to things—that is, only in relation to beings endowed with reason and will—seems to remain unaltered. Precisely what this means calls for an explanation, though.

[430] Traditional religious-metaphysical philosophy (upon which also idealistic legal theory is based) links the matter with the problem of the metaphysical freedom of the will—its independence, as it were, from the law of causality (indeterminism). In that way, the absolute gulf between the realm of nature or necessity and the realm of morality or freedom is determined. There is no meaning in making

demands on someone whose will is not free. If human acts are determined by necessity, it is useless to talk to people in order to make them act differently compared to how they actually act, and must act.

This belief indicates that the meaning of causality, or necessary connection, has been misunderstood. The belief confuses determinism with fatalism or predestination. It ascribes to determinism a necessity of fate that is alien to a scientific way of thinking, which has nothing to do with 'the inevitable'. The correctness of this statement can best be seen by considering for a moment that the assumption of a necessary causal connection in nature by no means entails that the course of nature is considered inevitable. Actually, all natural technology aims at changing the course of natural events through adequate measures, in conformity with desires and objectives. The necessity of nature is always necessity in retrospect in relation to the conditioning circumstances. By changing these, we change the course of nature. This is inevitable only if the conditioning circumstances lie outside the purview of human beings. Therefore, one can for instance predict an eclipse of the sun without reservation. Otherwise, however, the course of nature can be predicted only on the condition that the conditioning circumstances are not interfered with. Thus, determinism in nature does not prevent goal-directed intervention—on the contrary: it is a necessary precondition for it.[1]

The same applies to social technique—the possibility of purposeful intervention in order to influence the course of social action. Determinism itself does not preclude this but is, on the contrary, a precondition for it. The *necessary precondition* for politics conceived as a technique for influencing society with the aid of rational methods is, therefore, *not an assumption of a free will but, rather, the assumption that rational deliberations and arguments are among the factors determining human action.*

With specific reference to legal politics and its possibilities, the decisive question, therefore, is whether and to what extent the law is created by the legislator's 'will', understood as an expression of a conscious activity determined by rational deliberations and rational arguments—not as a metaphysical free will; or, whether and to what extent the law is created in a process that is independent thereof. On this issue, extremely varying views have been put forward at various times. [431]

A view which has played, and still plays, an important role, and which can be called *historicism*, is based upon metaphysical ideas. Its central thought is that the course of history is determined by a *necessity of fate*. The idea of fate is the

[1] The last statement is not quite correct. Determinism is not a necessary condition for scientific method and prediction; see K. R. Popper, *The Open Society and its Enemies* (1945), II 81. However, it is beyond the scope of the present context to discuss the issue in more detail.

age-old religious-metaphysical idea that events move towards a predetermined goal, with sovereign contempt for anything the actors themselves desire and strive for. Its dramatic-tragic power lies precisely in this contrast between good will and inexorable necessity, toying with man. It was prophesied that Oedipus would kill his father and marry his mother. And this is what happened, in spite of taking all precautionary measures. Fate, the will of the gods, cannot be defied.

The necessity of fate has nothing to do with determinism. The necessity of fate is the inevitable. Deterministic necessity, by contrast, is the foundation of the guiding measures of technology. Figuratively speaking, we might say that while the causes are pushing forward the effects, it is—according to the idea of fate—the predetermined future goal that draws the events towards it. But how to determine the future goal of development, and how can this goal, in turn, determine the present goal in any other way than by being decreed by a divine will, which likewise conducts the course of events towards this goal? Thus, the idea of fate is an expression of a religious metaphysics conflicting with the causality of natural science.

The result is the essentially different nature of the predictions that are made on a scientific basis, and those that are made on the basis of the belief in a necessity of fate. The predictions of science are usually made with the reservation that there are certain conditioning circumstances. Their form is hypothetical: if this or that exists as a starting point, then this or that will follow. Only where the conditioning factors are beyond the purview of human beings can the prediction acquire the unconditional character of a prophecy. We can predict that a solar eclipse will take place in two thousand years, but we cannot predict how a certain disease will progress until tomorrow, because the latter also depends upon our own interventions in the conditioning factors.

In contrast, the predictions of historicism are always in the nature of *prophecies*, that is, predictions of the course of history regardless of, and in spite of, all human efforts. Divine necessity renders all human deliberation, planning, and objectives—in other words: all politics—unavailing. Our belief that we can make any difference is nothing but a dream. While we are dreaming this dream, forces over which we have no control lead us towards our inevitable goal. We are mere puppets. The strings are pulled by a higher power. The sage who has understood that deems it best to bow to the inevitable. Thus, he can ease the labour pains in connection with the present giving birth to the future. He can [432] facilitate development by avoiding useless frictions between the divine will and his own will. In the fullness of time, however, both the fool and the sage will end up where he is destined to end up.

The practical influence of such a belief in fate on human behaviour is curiously ambiguous. In theory, it leads to the denial of all policy making, to complete passivity, or to what is called quietism. In practice, things are otherwise. Speaking psychologically, the postulated goal has of course arisen from certain attitudes in the form of demands, objectives, and aspirations. The belief that this objective will be realized with inevitable necessity creates in its adherents a certainty of victory and ruthless fanaticism that leads to a merciless fight. Argumentation and compromise become meaningless. The inevitability of the goal justifies any means. This is the secret behind the utter intolerance of communism towards any other system.[2]

German romantic philosophy at the beginning of the nineteenth century turned away from the rationalism of the preceding era and indulged in apprehensive interpretations of nature and history, as a revelation of spiritual forces evolving towards a predetermined goal. External-mechanical science on an empirical basis was met with scorn; instead, one desired to understand nature 'from within', as a play of forces or principles evolving in successive stages towards ever higher forms of revelation of the world soul.[3] History, too, was regarded as a revelation of the absolute. Schelling, in his philosophy of history, reverted to the idea of fate. The individual believes that he is acting freely, and yet it is necessity that reigns in history. But this necessity does not mechanically conform to the law of nature but is a providence, a necessity of fate. History is the way of God in the world, where the human species evolves towards its destiny. Schelling also compares history with a drama in which each individual [433] actor plays his part as he thinks fit, but where nonetheless a reasonable result emerges from this perplexing play, because it is one single spirit that inspires all.[4] Hegel was to enlarge upon these ideas. The innermost essence of existence

[2] Because communism builds upon Marx's economic philosophy of fate, cf. § 87 below.

[3] Schelling, for example, when explaining the different levels of inorganic and organic nature, assumed that in invisible or organizing nature, there are three fundamental forces—'gravity' ['*die Schwere*'], 'light' ['*das Licht*'], and 'the band, or common life' ['*das Band oder allgemeine Leben*']. 'Gravity', the lowest of the forces, is not physical gravity but 'the principle of bodiliness' ['*das Prinzip der Leiblichkeit*'] which, in the visible world, creates matter in its different compositions. Now, when light appears—not physical light, but light as 'the principle of the soul' ['*Prinzip der Seele*']—and unites with matter, a new level emerges in the inorganic world: the dynamic process, the animated matter. In rising powers, this unfolds as magnetism, electricity, and chemical processes. The organic world rises above this through the appearance of the third force, the principle of the band, or of life. In this world, the principle of gravity reveals itself as reproduction, that is, food, growth, and propagation—the level of plants and women. 'Irritability'—the level of animals and men—corresponds to the principle of light. Through the principle of life, finally, there arises the highest natural phenomenon—'sensibility', or the level of the human being. Thus, Schelling envisages all of nature as consisting of different levels of development, and constructed by inner, invisible forces which, united, constitute the World Soul. See Schelling, *Ideen zu einer Philosophie der Natur* [Ideas on a Philosophy of Nature] (1797); *Erster Entwurf eines Systems der Naturphilosophie* [First Outline of a System of the Philosophy of Nature] (1799); 'Allgemeine Deduktion des dynamischen Prozesses oder der Kategorien der Physik' [General deduction of the dynamic process, or the categories related to physics], in *Zeitschrift für spekulative Physik* (1800); *Von der Weltseele* [On the World Soul] (1798). In Denmark, Schelling's philosophy of nature was introduced by Henrik Steffens in his work *Indledning til philosophiske Forelæsninger* [Introduction to Lectures in Philosophy] (1803). It is a well-known fact that Steffens was an inspiration to the young Oehlenschläger [Adam Oehlenschläger (1779–1850) was a famous Danish playwright and poet].

[4] An account of Schelling's philosophy of history, documented in more detail, can be found in my work *Theorie der Rechtsquellen* [Theory of the Sources of Law] (1929), Ch. V, 10, and in my work *Kritik der sogenannten praktischen Erkenntnis* [Critique of So-called Practical Knowledge] (1933), Ch. XII, 3. I refer the reader to these works.

is reason, an absolute spirit, and history is a kind of gigantic logical operation in which God, or reason, conceives of himself by means of a dialectic process.[5]

While this nonsense has long since passed into oblivion as far as the natural sciences are concerned—who, nowadays, would characterize an atom as the revelation of a spiritual principle?—it has nonetheless left lasting traces in the social sciences, especially in the philosophy of law. German romanticism gave rise to two theoretical constructions which, each in its own way, elaborated upon the idea of the necessity of fate of history and the impotence of the legislator. The first construction is the so-called Historical School of Jurisprudence, founded by Savigny and Puchta, which upheld traditional spiritual metaphysics. The second is Marx's materialist philosophy of history, which 'turned Hegel upside down' and interpreted the absolute materialistically.

[5] See Alf Ross, *Kritik der sogenannten praktischen Erkenntnis* [Critique of So-called Practical Knowledge] (1933), Ch. XII, 4.

§ 86. The Historical School

The Historical School was a reaction against rationalist natural law and its belief in the power of the legislator to transform society and the law in conformity with the demands of abstract reason.[1] In 1814—in the course of the German national awakening—voices were raised for a German code, as a counterpart to the French code and a symbol of national unity. These ideas were reflected in a pamphlet entitled 'Ueber die Notwendigkeit eines allgemeinen bürgerlichen Rechts für Deutschland' [On the necessity of a common civil law for Germany], composed with much fervour by the Heidelberg jurist Thibaut.

By way of response, in the same year Savigny published his famous work *Vom Beruf unserer Zeit für Gesetzgebung und Rechtswissenschaft* [On the Vocation of our Age for Legislation and Jurisprudence]. In this work, Savigny emphasized the historic-organic growth of the law and its dependence on the spontaneous legal conviction prevailing among the people. As with our language, the law is a product of unconscious, dark forces and is not created through deliberation and wilful decision-making. The legal conviction common to all people is the real source of all law. On an earlier level of development, it is directly reflected [434]
in custom. Later on, in periods of more intense cultural development, a specific profession is seen to emerge—the legal profession, whose task it is to interpret the legal conviction of the people and elaborate it technically. Thus, legal science takes the place of custom as the law's most important form of revelation. The legislator cannot create law through an arbitrary *fiat*. Just as the gardener cares for the growth of a plant, the legislator can further the natural development of the law with the support of science, but he cannot interfere with it. If he fails to understand his mission and attempts wilful interference, his work will be in vain and will be crushed by the force of development. To be an adequate interpretation of the living reality of the law, a codification of the law in a statute book presupposes a highly developed legal science which Savigny did not think his contemporaries possessed. And what is more: by implicitly raising a claim to completeness and finality, any codification would be in conflict with the organic growth of the law and can, therefore, only be justified during periods of cultural decline.

Later, this basic view was theoretically elaborated and systematized by Puchta (*Das Gewohnheitsrecht* [The Customary Law], 1828–37). It was Puchta who coined the term *der Volksgeist*, denoting the spiritual substance that grows within a people and is the original source of all law.

[1] For details, see Alf Ross, *Theorie der Rechtsquellen* [Theory of the Sources of Law] (1929), Ch. V, 2.

On a mere cursory reading, it may seem as if the basic view of the Historical School consisted in empirico-juridico-sociological reflections on the law's dependence on society; a view which—perhaps somewhat exaggerated—emphasizes the restrictions thus placed upon the legislator's ability to create law. On this reading, one would then understand Savigny's talk about the organic growth of the law as referring to observable causal connections, and Puchta's concept of the spirit of the people as an abbreviated term for a causal complex, that is, as expressing the totality of observable ethno-psychological characteristics, influenced by conditioning circumstances (climate, race, tradition, history) and, in turn, influencing the creation of the law.

Providing detailed documentation, I have maintained elsewhere[2] that this interpretation would be wrong. The Historical School must be understood in light of the spiritual climate of the age. It is a legitimate child of German romanticism. The 'organic' has nothing to do with causality according to the law of nature. For romanticism, the 'organic' was always an emotionally loaded term, denoting dark forces which animate all living things and strive towards a certain goal—towards something that is absolute and irreducible, the dark primeval force of life, a law unto itself and lifted above mechanical causality. Similarly, 'the spirit of the people' has nothing to do with Montesquieu's '*ésprit des lois*', it does not reflect a causal complex. It is a spiritual principle, an absolute and irreducible spiritual factor which reveals itself in the life of a people, including legal life, and which evolves in conformity with laws of its own towards its own immanent goal, as an expression of the
[435] divine purpose and mission of that people. Finally, the necessity that puts a stop to the legislator's freedom to create law, does similarly not reflect the coercion of the laws of nature which every technician must submit to, but reflects a necessity of fate, as an expression of the sovereign dynamic of the spirit of the people and the law. The evolution of the law is not determined, but predestined. Savigny's doctrine of the historic mission of the legislator, and the latter's impotence when attempting to disregard it, becomes intelligible solely on this interpretation.

In this context, it is important to bear in mind that the Historical School was not merely a doctrine on the factual genesis of the law, but also a crypto-natural law (§ 61). Historicism is not merely history. Its fundamental idea is that history is also a criterion of the Good. The immanent tendency, or objective, of reality is also the supreme value. The absolute principle evolving in history is also the absolute Good. These ideas, fully reflected in the work of Hegel, are also unmistakeably present in the Historical School. They differ from Hegel's in so far as the absolute is not conceived as a universal reason, but as a national spirit. The *popular conviction of law and justice is, thus, not merely the source from*

[2] Alf Ross, *Theorie der Rechtsquellen* [Theory of the Sources of Law] (1929), Ch. V.

which the law in fact emanates, but also the source of the correctness or validity of the law. Reality is also validity, because its innermost essence is spiritual.[3]

The picture of the Historical School has now been finalized. The Historical School is not merely a legal philosophy of fate, it is also natural law. Its apparently apolitical character conceals a political attitude, characterized by a tendency towards authorizing the law professors to act as leaders of a cautiously reformatory legal development on a historical basis. Popular legal conviction is the supreme source of the law, but legal scholars are the authentic interpreters and mouthpieces of the law, the guardians of the nation's legal culture. The spirit of the people is the Absolute, and the law professor is its prophet. As time went on, this tendency became increasingly historico-conservative. Because of its belief in the intrinsic value of legal tradition, the Historical School naturally inclined more and more towards historico-philological pedantry and formalistic conceptual jurisprudence.

[3] For documentation, see Alf Ross, *Theorie der Rechtsquellen* [Theory of the Sources of Law] (1929), Ch. V, 12.

§ 87. Marx's Economic Historicism

Marx was a disciple of Hegel. However—as has often been said—he turned Hegel's system upside down. That is to say, he made the economic forces the Absolute in the course of events, and he turned the spiritual phenomena into a derivative product.

[436] Marx's socialism is an action programme, with deep emotional roots in humanistic impulses, in his sympathy with the oppressed, and his indignation at the wretched conditions of the working class in England during early industrialism.[1] The programme is not merely a set of technical instructions on how to gain power and acquire advantages so that the roles of the classes are reversed. Socialism is also a fight for justice. The capitalist's acquisition of surplus value is branded as exploitation of the worker. When the social revolution has triumphed, no new exploitation shall substitute the old one; instead, the classless society will arise, with freedom and equal opportunities for everyone.

At the same time, Marx scorned all moralizing. He saw it as his mission to liberate socialism from its sentimental, philanthropical background and thereby transfer it from Utopia to science. He was utterly contemptuous of the 'phrases and illusions handed down from the great revolution' and of the well-meaning plans of idealistic socialists, devised for reforming society.[2] 'Die Arbeiterklasse hat keine Ideale zu erfüllen'[3] ['It is not for the working class to fulfil any ideals']. Scientific socialism must build upon an analysis of social causality and predictions based on non-derogable laws for the development of society.

The elements typically found in historicism are thereby given.[4] Just as Hegel—as well as the Historical School and Comte—Marx is opposed to subjective reason and its *a priori* ideas. The 'rational', the political norm, must be found in objective reality itself, in its immanent tendency of development. From here, there is a path towards a philosophy of history that interprets history as a course of events determined by fate, directed at a predetermined goal.

Marx's socialism is 'scientific' in the same sense in which Comte calls his politics 'positive'. Neither of them has anything to do with science. Marx does not think like a social technologist who makes use of scientific insight as a basis for purposive measures. Rather, Marx thinks like a social prophet, predicting the

[1] See the section on the effect of progress on the status of the working class in Karl Marx, *Das Kapital* [Capital. A Critique of Political Economy].

[2] Karl Marx and Friedrich Engels, *Det kommunistiske Manifest* [The Communist Manifesto] (1848). Danish translation in *Socialismens klassikere* [The Socialist Classics] (Tidens Forlag 1945), 53–54, 56.

[3] Karl Marx, *Der Bürgerkrieg in Frankreich* [The Civil War in France] (3rd edn, 1891) 50.

[4] Cf. K. R. Popper's brilliant analysis of Marx in Vol. 2 of *The Open Society and its Enemies* (1945), especially Chs. 13, 15, and 22.

inevitable which is also the Good. The necessity he operates with is not a scientific-deterministic necessity, but the inevitable necessity of fate. Marx confuses determinism with predestination. He erroneously believes that the possibility of scientific prediction is tied to the assumption that the future exists in the form of a germ within the past, just as if telescoped into the past.

For this reason, Marx's attitude towards politics, the purposive human intervention, is an attitude typically found in historicism: *politics is impotent, a mere delusion*. The course of history is predetermined. All we can do is smooth the path of evolution clear of its worst obstacles. 'When a society has discovered the law of nature that determines its development', Marx says in *Das Kapital*, 'it can neither jump over the natural phases of its development, nor eliminate them with a stroke of the pen. But society can do this much: it can shorten and lessen its birth pangs.'[5] (See Savigny's comparison of the legislator and the gardener, who is able to promote the organic growth of the plant, as well as Comte's view that the politician is able to smooth out small deviations from the curve of development.) [437]

It is a characteristic feature of historicism that it interprets history as proceeding through several phases towards a goal which—strangely enough—was expected to be reached in the nineteenth century, or shortly afterwards. The same applies to Marx. From the golden age of primitive communism, society has developed through a series of class struggles, one exploiting class replacing the other. By now, the development has reached the point where the exploited class (the proletariat) can no longer free itself from the exploiting class (the bourgeoisie) without, at the same time, perpetually liberating society as a whole from exploitation, oppression, and class struggles.[6] Now, or in the near future, when the final social revolution has been accomplished, the classless society will arise, the state will wither away, and the true nature of man will be liberated and delivered.[7] The prehistory of Mankind has come to an end, the Fall of Man is overcome, the millennium is a reality.

> Of course, within the present context we cannot possibly enter more closely into the theories Marx used as a foundation for his philosophy of history and his prophecy. In a schematic outline, we can distinguish between three levels in his train of thought.

[5] As cited in K. R. Popper, *op. cit.*, II, 82.

[6] See Engels's 'Preface' to the German edition of *The Communist Manifesto* (1883), reprinted in the Danish translation mentioned above [in note 2].

[7] In an often-quoted passage, Engels says the following: 'Die eigene Vergesellschaftung der Menschen, die ihnen bisher als von Natur und Geschichte oktroyiert gegenüberstand, wird jetzt ihre eigene freie Tat. Es ist der Sprung der Menschheit aus dem Reich der Notwendigkeit in das Reich der Freiheit' [translation: 'The people's own socialization, which has hitherto been experienced as imposed by nature and history, is now their own free achievement. This is Humanity's leap from the realm of necessity into the realm of freedom'].

(1) The *materialist conception of history* is the doctrine that the key to history, even to the history of ideas, must be sought in man's relation to the material world, in the conditions under which economic production takes place—that is, in man's economic, not spiritual, life. The conditions of production and their development constitute The Absolute in history, in relation to which everything else is derived.

[438] (2) *History as class struggle* is the doctrine of the mechanism through which the conditions of production determine history. Since the human acts which constitute history are directly motivated by interests and ideology, it must be explained how these are derived from the conditions of production. The individual's position in the production process determines his membership in a class. Each class has economic interests which are in conflict with those of other classes. These economic interests, in turn, determine the ideology that is accepted by the class. Morality and law, the 'eternal truths' of philosophy and religion, are merely an 'ideological superstructure', varying with the economic foundation. Economic and ideological class conflicts lead to class struggle. The most important weapons of class warfare are the state and revolution. The state is the instrument through which the ruling class maintains its power over the oppressed. Revolution is the rebellion of the oppressed, intent on seizing state power.

(3) *The revolution of the proletariat and the establishment of the classless socialist society*, that is, the doctrine of the progression of the class struggle. Class warfare progresses towards a definitive goal according to a dialectic scheme. On the one hand, capitalism leads to a continuous wealth accumulation; on the other, it leads to an ever-increasing impoverishment of the proletariat. Therefore, the classes are gradually reduced to two: a small ruling bourgeoisie, and a large impoverished proletariat. When this development has reached its peak, the rising tension between the two classes is discharged in a rebellion of the proletariat, in a social revolution that ends with victory for The Many. After a short transition period (the dictatorship of the proletariat *qua* dialectic counterpart to the dictatorship of the bourgeoisie), the classless society will arise—as the final synthesis of the opposites now dissolved. Since there are no longer any class conflicts and class struggles, the state has become useless. It simply withers away. Man lives in freedom and bliss. History has reached its goal.

The Marxist stand on the issue of the social dependence of the law and the possibility of legal politics is largely identical with that of the Historical School: law is not created arbitrarily, but is a necessary product of unfolding events. In reality, the legislator is powerless. He is the mouthpiece of necessity. This correspondence is simply the consequence of the fact that Marxism and the Historical School are twigs of the same branch—the romantic, historicist philosophy of fate. With respect to a more detailed interpretation of the forces that direct the necessary development of the law, however, the content of the two doctrines greatly differs. To the Historical School, these forces are spiritual, as we have seen: it is the spirit of the people, active in the nation's legal consciousness, that is the source of all law. To Marxism, by contrast, the legal ideas and institutions are only ideological superstructures upon economic interests. There is no 'national' legal consciousness. What goes by this name is the ideology of the ruling class, reflecting its economic interests. The eternal ideas of law and justice are illu- [439] sions. All law is an instrument of power in the hands of the ruling class, aimed at the economic exploitation of the oppressed.

§ 88. The Barriers of Legal Politics and Trends Research

The categorical denial on the part of the philosophers of fate that a legal politics is possible altogether must be rejected. This denial is based on metaphysical ideas about predestination that have nothing to do with scientific determinism. From an empirical perspective, experience offers no basis for the assertion that human deliberation, reason, and will should not be among the factors that determine the course of development.

The philosophy of fate is not merely false. It conditions an ethical-political attitude that defies humanistic ideals. The belief that higher powers, whether spiritual or economic, are governing the course of development, leads to either passivity or blind fanaticism, justifying any crime in order to redeem the inevitable. It kills moral responsibility, grounded in the consciousness that we ourselves are the masters of our fate. The deprecation of reason and will leads to an *idolization of power*—interpreted either conservatively, as reflecting existing society and its traditional institutions (Hegel, Savigny); or revolutionarily, as reflecting the class struggle and the revolution that would lead the proletariat to victory (Marx).

The theories we have discussed are typical results of the metaphysical and anti-rationalist mentality of German romanticism. In addition, they seem to be conditioned negatively by the possibilities of the modern liberal state (indeed very meagre possibilities) of effective control and intervention. In view of powerful economic forces, unleashed by industrialism, and the decline of feudalism, the night-watchman state and the *laissez-faire* policy were presumably a necessity rather than a virtue, or a necessity turned into virtue. Our experiences during the last couple of generations with respect to purposive intervention through legislation have shown, in a thoroughly striking way, that assertions about the impotence of legislation and politics are false. It has become clear that even if the state apparatus is no Aladdin's lamp, it is nonetheless the case that he who is in control of this apparatus commands forces so powerful that he is able, for better or worse, to intervene and firmly guide both the spiritual and the material life of the people towards intended goals. *Today, nobody calls political power impotent.* The very rulers who have followed in Marx's footsteps
[440] and elevated his doctrine to a state religion have demonstrated more potently than others how political power can be used.

With regard to the people's legal and cultural consciousness, we have seen examples of how effective propaganda (Nazi Germany), or propaganda combined with a radical reorganization of the conditions of production (Soviet Russia), was able to bring about profound changes in legal and cultural life—changes that cannot be explained by the tranquil growth of the spirit of the people.

With regard to the relation between economics and politics, there is no longer any doubt that *political power is the fundamental power*. It is political power that ultimately conditions economic power, and not *vice versa*. Marx's conviction that ownership of capital is the ultimate source of all power reflects an uncritical, almost natural law-like respect for ownership as an intrinsically valid, pre-statal power. He failed to see that the power of the owner is merely a reflex of the protection given to him by the state in the form of the police and law courts and is, thus, a derivative of political power; or that it is possible, *via* legislation, to undermine, regulate, and control the actual power of the owner in such a way as to reduce him to a more or less well-paid civil servant.

Nevertheless, both Savigny and Marx have taught us something that will not be forgotten. If their theories are divested of their absolute, dogmatic, metaphysical garb, a relative truth emerges: *the legislator's relative dependence on social forces* that imposes a restriction on his juridico-formal absolute power. If they say that the British Parliament can do anything except transform a man into a woman, then this may be correct if taken as expressing a certain legal ideology, but it is misleading if given a juridico-sociological interpretation. The legislator is not like God whose word creates a world out of nothing. His task consists in motivating people towards a desirable course of action. The source of his power in this respect lies in the political ideology, or myth, that endows him with legal authority. However, apart from this formal attitude of respect for lawful authority, many other social forces are at work in people's minds; among these, the blind, irrational forces arising from tradition, custom, and substantive legal consciousness, as well as the purposive, rational forces arising from economic interests and power relations. Thus, political power is not the only component of force, but merely one of many components of force which are woven together, in mutual dependence, in a web of power centres and power relations.[1] Political leadership is an attempt at integration that allows for some tension in the relation between political power and other social forces. The attempt will fail, however, if the tension increases excessively.

The value of these juridico-sociological views is obvious when contrasted with [441] the *unhistorical, abstract rationalism* of the preceding epoch, typically represented by Bentham.

While romanticism worshipped the dark, instinctive, irrational forces, Bentham completely failed to understand that aspect of human nature which lies beyond reason.[2] His biggest dream was 'a pannomium', a clear, exhaustive, and

[1] Cf. R. M. MacIver, *The Web of Government* (1947).

[2] 'It would', says Leslie Stephen, the best English expert on Bentham, 'be impossible to draw a more striking portrait of the abstract reasoner, whose calculations as to human motives omit all reference to passion, and who fancied that all prejudice can be dispelled by a few acts of logic', *The English Utilitarians* I (1900), 199.

rational codification of existing law,[3] which should put an end to all custom[4] and all interpretation.[5] He never speculated how this verbal construction could possibly be actively incorporated into a people's cultural tradition, existing customs and prejudices. Bentham himself drafted a number of large codifications, covering the fields of civil law, criminal law, procedural law, and constitutional law, and [442] he had a dream that the legislators in the young South American states would put his work into effect.[6] What is more, he planned codifications for Russia, Spain, Morocco, and Bavaria.[7] He once remarked that he would be able to legislate for Hindustan just as easily as for his own parish.[8]

If nowadays all this appears to be extremely naive, to be pure *utopia*—that is, something that does not belong anywhere, but flies freely in the world of fantasy—it is due to our insight into the historical and national contingency of the law, which is the core of Savigny's doctrine.

Marx took one more step. He taught us to look behind the ideology of the common sense of justice; not to consider it dogmatically, as a revelation of eternally valid ideas, but to inquire into the forces that condition and direct

[3] Bentham's enthusiasm for codification must be seen in the light of the state of the law in his times. The English *common law*, which had developed slowly through judge-made law, was still permeated by medieval-feudalistic notions. Overgrown with quaint scholastic distinctions and fictions, and unintelligible to people of common sense, English law in Bentham's times was a perfect wilderness, a motley maze eminently fitted to bend the law and turn the administration of justice into a profitable business for 'Judge and Co'. On this issue, see Leslie Stephen, *The English Utilitarians* I (1900), 278, and John Stuart Mill, *Dissertations and Discussions* I (1859), 368 *et seq*. English inheritance law, for example, is described, by Bentham, in the following way: 'It is so complicated with regard to the descent of property; it admits distinctions so singular; the previous decisions, which serve to regulate it, are so subtilized, that not only is it impossible for simple good sense to presume them, it is also difficult for it to comprehend them. It is a study profound as that of the most abstract sciences: it belongs only to a small number of privileged men: it has been necessary, even for them to subdivide themselves; for no one lawyer pretends to understand the whole. Such has been the fruit of a too superstitious respect for antiquity.' And concerning the common law in general he says the following: 'It is the judges (as we have seen) that make the common law. Do you know how they make it? Just as a man makes laws for his dog. When your dog does anything you want to break him of, you wait till he does it, and then beat him for it. This is the way you make laws for your dog: and this is the way the judges make laws for you and me.' See Bentham, *The Works of Jeremy Bentham*, published by John Bowring (1838–1843) I, 323-24 and V, 235, cf. V, 442 and IX, 8.

[4] See Bentham, *The Works of Jeremy Bentham*, published by John Bowring (1838-1843), vol. I, 326: 'If the obscure system called custom were no longer suffered to exist, and the whole law were reduced to writing—if the laws which concern every individual were collected in one volume, and those which concerned certain classes were in separate collections... Every deviation from them would be sensible, every citizen would be their guardian; there would be no mystery to conceal them—no monopoly in their explanation—no fraud or chicane to elude them', cf. vol. III, 211; vol. V, 439; vol. IV, 503 and others.

[5] Like other rationalist supporters of a codification, Bentham concluded, from the idea of codification, that henceforth the judge should not be allowed to interpret the law. See Bentham, *The Works of Jeremy Bentham*, published by John Bowring (1838–1843), vol. I, 325. Cf. Alf Ross, *Theorie der Rechtsquellen* [Theory of the Sources of Law] (1929), Ch. III, 1, on Montesquieu and the French codification.

[6] On Bentham's plans to create legislation for Mexico and Venezuela, see Bentham, *The Works of Jeremy Bentham*, published by John Bowring (1838–1843), vol. X, 433, 457–58, cf. Leslie Stephen, *The English Utilitarians*, vol. I (1900), 220.

[7] Stephen, *op. cit.*, I, 300. On the issue of Bentham's correspondence with the King of Bavaria, to whom he sent a draft constitution, see Bentham's *The Works of Jeremy Bentham*, published by John Bowring (1838–1843), vol. X, 578 *et seq*.

[8] Bentham, *The Works of Jeremy Bentham*, published by John Bowring (1838–1843), vol. X, 292.

them. Thus far he was in agreement with Bentham (§ 72). But whereas the latter wished to interpret the moral and legal consciousness as the symptoms of a single evident 'principle', Marx sees the directing force in the economic interests of the classes. It is not quite that simple—but if we generalize Marx's view and say that the legal consciousness is derived from underlying interests, we are probably on the right track.

The previous reflections can be summed up as follows. *Legal politics is possible*, because the legislator is not impotent. *The possibilities of legal politics are limited*, because the legislator is not omnipotent, either. The legislator encounters social forces (in particular legal consciousness, economic interests, and power relations) that cannot be invoked by mere words. On the other hand, it is not a question of a permanent and impassable barrier, either. Legal consciousness and economic forces are, to a certain extent, themselves the products of legal development (viewing legislation in its historical continuity). All the different social forces—political ideology, legal consciousness, and economic factors—work together in mutual interaction. Therefore, the barriers must not be taken as permanent dikes embanking a canal. They represent a moment of inertia in reciprocal interaction, and might be compared to the banks of a river, determined by water erosion and sediments and, at the same time, determining the river's course.

This conclusion is consistent with the image of the legislator as a social technician, who attempts to shape social development through the mechanism of the law. With regard to its dependence, *social engineering* is basically in the same position as all other *engineering*; the technical engineer does not have Aladdin's lamp at his disposal, either. He, too, is bound by the resistance of matter, by the forces at work there.

The question arises whether science—sociology—can provide guidance to the [443]
legislator by informing him of the limited possibilities of legal politics in a given situation.

According to what has been said, this information can definitely not consist in a description of permanent, impassable barriers to possibilities. It can only be a question of indicating more elastic and relative limits, determined through the plasticity of the social material.

There, sociological inquiries into evolutionary *tendencies* (*trends*) become important. We have said that the course of history is not determined in advance—it cannot be predicted independent of intervention determined by human insight and will. *Nor can it be predicted scientifically by taking into account these measures*. Insight, at any rate, cannot be calculated beforehand, for if it could, it would already exist in our minds. Thus, for example, Einstein's theory of relativity would have existed as a prediction before Einstein had worked it out. And since our objectives and other attitudes are conditioned by our beliefs, they cannot in general be calculated beforehand, either.[9]

On the other hand, human insight and human attitudes change *continually*. Hence, by starting from the given data and referring to the near future, it is possible to calculate evolutionary tendencies. By that, we mean those courses of events which, according to our knowledge of the starting position and the causal connections, must be regarded as probable, under the condition that no substantial changes occur in the given insight and the given attitudes.

Trend determination must not be confused with external mechanical extrapolation of a curve along its tangent line. The fact that prices have been falling for a time, does not in itself[10] provide a foundation for establishing a tendency towards falling prices, any more than the fact that it has been raining for some time in itself[11] justifies the assumption that it will keep raining. Ordinary thinking often tends not to move away from such a tangent line, extrapolation. Scientific trends research presupposes a profound analysis of the given data, together with a knowledge of the causal connections that determine the course of events. Thus, it is possible that an economist with a knowledge of the theory of business cycles will, on the basis of falling prices over a fairly long period, predict a tendency towards rising prices. At the same time, this example illustrates that all determination of trends is dependent on the absence of substantial changes in the underlying understanding (and how it is therefore always transient in nature). Until a few years ago, economists considered business [444] cycles as inevitable and reckoned therefore with a tendency towards continuous up-and-down movements; nowadays, by contrast—thanks to economists like Myrdal and Keynes—one has the necessary insight to counter oscillations effectively through budget balance and other measures. The tendency which one has reckoned with formerly, and which—as far as the United States is concerned—still seems to be a dogmatic presupposition in Soviet Russian politics, thus no longer holds water thanks to our deepened insight.

Trends research must not be confused with the philosophy of fate. Trends research is relative and empirical, while the philosophy of fate is absolute and metaphysical. Trends research does not impute to itself normative significance in relation to legislation and politics. It merely informs the legislator about the conditions under which his work has to be done; it defines his task and sets certain limits for a possible policy. The task consists in bending the trends into compliance with the legislator's aim. The limits lie in the continuity of development and the element of inertia.

[9] The essential unpredictability of history is a further consequence of the fact that the very prediction is a factor that influences the evolutionary process. On this issue, see § 9 above.

[10] Albeit possibly in combination with a theory of business cycles.

[11] Albeit possibly in combination with a meteorological theory on the periodic nature of the weather.

I cannot say to what extent we are able, at the present stage of development of the social sciences, to establish a trends research that would be a guide for the legislator. The approaches to argumentation in this direction, which actually occur in juridico-political considerations, are based not so much on scientific experience and insight than on vague estimates and impressions. To me, the most important thing has been to call attention to a scientific task, which is possible in principle and which, in so far as it can be realized, will add yet another field of activity to the realm of legal politics (as outlined in § 80 above).

[445] CHAPTER XVII

The Role Played by the 'Sense of Justice' in Legal Politics

§ 89. Attitudes Based upon Needs (Interests)

The word 'interest' can be used in a wider and a narrower sense. The wider sense covers every deliberative act. Understood in this sense, we are 'interested' in every subject towards which we have a positive or negative attitude. On the other hand, when we say that a certain act 'originates in a person's interests', the word is used in a narrower sense. Then, interest denotes a particular class of attitudes, called *attitudes based upon needs*. Their counterparts are attitudes not based upon needs, or *persuaded attitudes*. Among these, *moral attitudes* are of special importance to legal politics. Even if the division is not exhaustive, I shall, in the following, speak of interests (attitudes based upon needs) and moral attitudes as a contrasting pair.

Needs[1] originate in a biological mechanism of self-regulation. Various biological conditions that can be called 'deficiency conditions', as compared to the 'normal' function of the organism, stimulate the organism to an activity which—in any case in combination with certain experiences—are well suited to terminate the deficiency condition and, thus, the activity. Example: through a biological mechanism in which the empty stomach, the secretion of gastric juices etc. play
[446] a part, lack of food will stimulate an animal to restless, searching activity until suitable nourishment is found and consumed. The activating biological stimulus is thereby extinguished, and a state of rest follows. After a while the process begins all over again. Such objects—things, materials, or forms of energy (such as food, air, warmth, and light), or activities, or functions (such as exercise movements or excretory reactions)—that is, objects well suited to extinguish the impulse, we call satisfactors.

[1] Part of the following relies heavily on the description given by Jørgen Jørgensen, *Psykologi paa biologisk Grundlag* [Psychology on a Biological Basis], H. 1–5 (1941–1946), Ch. XIII, 392 *et seq.*

Phenomenologically speaking, needs arise in human beings as conditions of *want*, *discontent*, *a yearning* for something (need in a psychological sense). The activity stimulated by need is experienced as a *striving*, and the extinction of the impulse the activity results in is experienced as a *satisfaction*.

It is unlikely that human beings possess an inborn consciousness as to what objects are suited to satisfy certain needs. The urge is initially blind, the striving is aimless. Little children are restless or cry because they need one thing or the other: food, clean nappies, to get warm or cool, etc. Their impulsive movements have no particular 'direction', however, and there is no reason to assume that little children have any idea at all of what they need. Thanks to help from other people, however, their various needs are satisfied, and as their awareness of their surroundings gradually becomes more articulated, they will be able to recognize the different satisfactors they have been provided with on various occasions. Then, they no longer experience the need as mere discontent, as a blind urge—but, rather, as an urge for precisely this or that definite object: their mother, their bottle, their rattle, etc. Their impulsive striving is no longer aimless, but is a purposeful striving, or craving, for specific satisfactors. Thus, the individual's experiences as to what satisfies his needs turn his blind urge into a discerning one, and his aimless impulsive actions into a conscious striving and purposive behaviour.[2]

If one is conscious of the object of one's need, the experience of the need in its various phases (urge, striving, satisfaction) is in the nature of an attitude towards this object. This attitude is called *interest*.

Usually we distinguish between 'physical' and 'spiritual' needs, or rather between needs that are experienced as more or less distinctly located within the body and needs that are not experienced in this way.

The first group includes the following needs: the need for air, warmth, coolness, water (thirst), food (hunger); diverse needs for excretion, cleansing, sexual activity, and rest.[3]

The second group includes the following needs: the need for stimulation or [447]
entertainment; functional needs; the need for expression and production, for company, for love or care, for security; the need to own and collect; the need to help; the need for destruction, self-assertion, self-respect, justification, knowledge, and harmony.[4]

[2] This paragraph has been taken, in a slightly adapted form, from Jørgen Jørgensen, *op. cit.*, 409–10.

[3] For a detailed description, see Jørgen Jørgensen, *op. cit.*, 465 *et seq*.

[4] For further information, see the table with the subsequent description, Jørgen Jørgensen, *op. cit.*, 472 *et seq*. (The so-called attitude-dependent needs (471–72) are deliberately not included in my overview, because I believe that it is not a question of genuine needs.)

Interest is not necessarily selfish interest or self-interest. The interest grounded in the need to help aims at satisfying the needs of other people. It arises from an urge to help others who are in need, and is backed by feelings of sympathy for them. Unselfish interest is mediate: it refers back to an interest experienced by another person as a direct interest or a self-interest. However, when law or morality speak of a 'weighing of interests', only self-interest is meant.

Individual and collective interests.—All interests are experienced by individuals—we do not know of any other centres of experience—and are, in this sense, individual. To speak of collective interests, or community interests, in the sense of interests entertained or experienced by a group, or by the community, is meaningless.[5] The problem is whether these terms can be ascribed an acceptable meaning in any other way.

Let us imagine two persons, A and B, both locked up in the same prison cell, both anxious to escape. Thus, both of them are interested in escaping. Thus far, their interests can be said to be *coincident*. Furthermore, let us assume that this task can be achieved practically only in cooperation, through combined efforts. Thus, each of them is interested in assisting the other one—not for unselfish reasons, but because the escape of each is contingent upon cooperation which also enables the other one to escape. Thus far, their interests can be said to be *combined*. Finally, let us imagine that each of them feels such an unselfish urge to help each other that they think about the escape, neither as A's escape nor as B's escape, but as their common escape, (A+B)'s escape. '*We* must try to escape', they say. Thus far, their interests can be said to be *common*.

We see that the question of whether coinciding interests also are combined interests solely depends on external circumstances—a factual situation of solidarity that refers A and B to each other, as the necessary instruments for fulfilling their selfish interests. Whether A and B themselves are conscious of the mutual connection of interests is, therefore, solely conditioned by rational insight into the facts underlying the solidarity.

[448] On the other hand, whether the coinciding interests are also experienced as a common interest, depends upon something subjective, namely, whether the parties—*via* sympathetic feelings and unselfish interests—identify themselves with each other or with 'the whole' in such a way that a so-called 'group consciousness' arises within each party. That means that each of them feels as if he were not acting in his own name and his own interest but, rather, as an 'organ' for a whole, for a community. It is not A who arranges A's escape and B who arranges B's escape: rather, it is (A+B) who arranges (A+B)'s escape. It will seem

[5] Such ideas must often be assumed to underlie a concept (not further analysed) of 'societal interests'. This is particularly evident in Ihering's work. On this issue, see Alf Ross, 'Realismen i Retsvidenskaben og Samfundsnyttekimæren' [Realism in legal science and the chimera of public utility], *SvJT* (1932), 324–49, especially 329.

natural, then, to speak of an interest in escaping which is not ascribed to A and B separately, but to the whole (A+B). One must bear in mind, however, that the expression '(A+B)'s interest in escaping' is a phrase that must not be interpreted analogously to the expression 'A's interest in escaping'. For it does not denote an individual interest experienced within a common subject (A+B), but a constellation of individual interests, experienced under the emotional preconditions thus described. *Ascribing an interest to a supra-individual whole (a collective, society) is a metaphorical expression for the individual experience of common interests.*

One might ask whether A can experience the situation as a common interest without B doing the same. It seems certain that A can feel sympathy for B and an unselfish urge to be helpful, without these feelings being reciprocated by B. The experience of identification and fellowship, by contrast, presumably presupposes a certain resonance from the other party.

As previously stated, combined interest (*factual solidarity*) is not identical with common interest (*emotional solidarity*). The fact that insight into mutual dependence can easily condition a common attitude is quite another matter. Combined interests are presumably more easily experienced as common interests than merely as coinciding interests.

What has been said about A and B behind prison walls can be generalized so as to apply also to human coexistence in the fight against nature for life and prosperity. The more the technique of production develops into a highly organized and ramified apparatus, the more obvious it becomes that all of us depend upon each other in factual solidarity. No man is an island unto himself. Capital is dependent upon labour, and labour upon capital. The prosperity of agriculture conditions the welfare of businesses and professions in cities and *vice versa*. A crisis in production in the United States would be ruinous for the European economy, but, on the other hand, the United States also profit from a flourishing Europe. Human interests are extensively connected and are pursued in cooperation, which, in turn, enhances mutual dependence. Also, to a certain extent they are experienced as common interests, ascribed to a collectivity. The corresponding types of social life can be called association and society, respectively.[6]

As already mentioned above, the borderline between these two is grounded in a feeling of sympathy and solidarity, through which the individual identifies himself with the group; therefore, the borderline is unclear. With this proviso, [449]

[6] It was the German sociologist F. Tönnies who coined these terms. However, I use them here in a somewhat different sense than Tönnies does. Moreover, 'society' is also characterized by a community concerning moral attitudes, but, within the present context, there is no need for me to call attention to this aspect of the matter. [Translator's note: Here, Ross seems to be mistaken. The terms Ross uses in Danish [*selskab* and *samfund*, respectively] are not the same pair as those usually used, in Danish [*fællesskab* and *samfund*, respectively], to translate Tönnies's conceptual dichotomy [*Gemeinschaft* and *Gesellschaft*, respectively]].

the company limited by shares, other economic-technical associations, and cooperation between states can be mentioned as examples of forms of coexistence with a predominant character of an association; the nation, the family, the group of friends, and the religious communities can be mentioned as examples of forms of life which are predominantly of a societal character.

It is a theoretical task to point out the actual fact of solidarity, that is, indicate to what extent human interests are mutually combined. To speak of common interests or societal interests means something more. It is not merely an assertion concerning the factual connection of interests, but also a means of persuasion, as reflecting an attitude of common feeling that appeals to the same feeling in other persons. For instance, if I say that saving in a given situation is a common interest or societal interest, I am not only pointing out certain economic relations that connect our interests jointly and severally; I am also appealing to the 'societal spirit', the 'societal feeling'—which, in turn, means: to the sympathetic feelings of togetherness, identity, solidarity, and the unselfish interests connected therewith, struggling against the selfish interests that make the individual seek his own advantage at the expense of 'the whole'.[7]

It is worth noting that the interests of the individual are not combined in their totality with the interests of others. Nor must the situation—with few exceptions[8]—be understood as if there were certain interests which are isolated and others which are combined. Rather, it is the case that *every interest has partly an individual and isolated aspect, partly a societal and combined aspect.* For instance, let us consider interests in possession of, and control over, external objects: in this case, every individual is interested in using and enjoying undisturbed as many objects as possible, and this interest collides with the conflicting interests (of similar content) of other persons. These interests coincide and combine only in so far as all individuals are interested in a general property law, guaranteeing everyone's security with respect to a certain limited use and enjoyment. Thus, while A's property right, seen in its concrete individuality—as his interest in using and enjoying a certain piece of land—is only an individual interest, his own interest (and the interest of everyone else) in a property law that guarantees security of ownership is a *social interest.*[9] It should be noted that this term
[450] is introduced as denoting the interests which usually coincide and are combined in a group within a certain social order. Still further hypostatizing the social interests (in a property law) pursued by A, B, C, etc. into a supra-individual

[7] Duguit's philosophy of law, endeavouring to derive the objective (natural) law from the fact of solidarity, is based—to put it briefly—upon the misrepresentation that solidarity, as a fact, is substituted by solidarity as an emotional attitude and claim, cf. § 62 above.

[8] There are individual needs—such as the need for air and excretion—with no social aspect to them, that is, their satisfaction is never conditioned by cooperation with others.

[9] The use of the singular does not indicate that the interest is ascribed to a single interested party (society), but that many interested parties entertain a similar interest.

interest ascribed to society (property law as a *societal interest*)[10] is, as already stated, a metaphor purporting to appeal to sympathetic feelings and unselfish interests whereby the individual identifies himself with the whole.

It follows that any attempt to make lists of individual and social interests is doomed to fail, if we are thinking of conflicting sets of interests that are independent of each other. We are dealing with two sides of the same coin—the specific and the general. Example: if we, as individual interests, mention A's interest in

- using and enjoying external objects
- personal integrity
- married life and family life
- entering binding agreements

then the corresponding social interests are the interest

- in a general system of ownership
- a general peace order
- a general system of marriage and family life
- a general contract system

For the same reason, it is impossible to make a distinction between the spheres of life dominated by individual interests and those that are dominated by social interests.[11]

Private and public interest.—This distinction is based upon the previous one. If a social interest induces the political societal power to safeguard it through legal regulation, then this interest is called 'public interest'. In this comparison, the individual interest is called 'private interest'. Public interests, we might say, are social interests safeguarded by 'the state', thus reflecting the politically organized organs of societal power. Thus, the social interest in a system of ownership, [451]
in a peace order, in a marriage system, in the defence of the realm, etc., etc.) are public interests. The term is also used for the derived individual-specific interests pursued by public authorities in connection with the safeguarding of public interests, understood in a general sense. Example: if the army wants to establish a shooting range in a certain area as part of its work for national defence, then

[10] Here, the use of the singular expresses that the interest is ascribed—metaphorically—to a single interested party, namely society.

[11] It follows that it is impossible on this basis to make a distinction between private and public law. Seen as a general order, all law safeguards social interests (which, as such, are called public interests, cf. the text immediately below). Seen from the perspective of a specific legal relationship, all law regulates individual interests, cf. § 50 above and Alf Ross, 'Sondringen mellem privat og offentlig Ret. En Forelæsning' [The distinction between private and public law. A lecture], in *TfR* (1936), 109–25, especially 112.

this individual interest is called a public interest, too.[12] For the sake of clarity, however, it is appropriate to reserve the term 'public interest' for the social, general interests (in our example: the defence of the realm) and call the derived, individual interests (in our example: the interests in establishing a shooting range in a certain area) 'interests of the state'.[13]

[12] See, e.g., § 68, subsection 1, nr. 9 The Danish Rent Act nr. 251, 14 June 1951, cf. *UfR* 1951, 934.

[13] The problem of individual, social, private, and public interests has been discussed in the literature, in particular by Ihering and Roscoe Pound (on this issue, see Julius Stone, *The Province and Function of Law* (1946/50), Ch. XI, §§ 3 and 7; Ch. XX, §§ 1–5, cf. Chs. XXI and XXII)—in my view, however, without offering a satisfactory explanation of the terms. On Ihering, see note 5 above. According to Pound, public interests are on the same footing as social interests.

§ 90. *Moral Attitudes*

Not all human actions are interested actions, or actions motivated by a need. This does not merely apply to elementary reflex actions (blinking, sneezing and the like) which occur without knowledge and will, but also to more highly organized forms of action, called acts of will.

The most important examples are *suggested* or *inculcated* actions. It is a fundamental psychological fact that it is possible, under certain circumstances, to transmit attitudes and impulses to action to others with the appropriate means of persuasion. As more fully described in § 77 above, the appropriate means of persuasion can be linguistic (commands, pleas, invitations, and other verbal appeals, emotion-laden words etc.) as well as non-linguistic (tone of voice, facial expression, gesture). Usually both kinds are employed simultaneously. When parents say in an imperious tone: 'Don't touch it!'—or when the sergeant commands his men by shouting: 'Quick march!'—this releases spontaneous impulses not to act, or to act in a certain way. Such impulses do not originate in any need, they do not express any interest on the part of the person who obeys. The disposition towards obedience on the part of the child or the soldier may, how- [452]
ever, originate in a relationship of power and dependence between the parties which, initially, has conditioned an interest on the part of the dependent or the subordinate to obey. Once the disposition is established, that is, when power has become authority, the appeal to an interest motive can be omitted, and obedience will result just the same—not from fear, but spontaneously. The impulse to action occurs automatically and with compelling force, even if it conflicts with vivid interests. The purpose of the military drill, with its apparently meaningless eternal repetition of commands, is precisely to generate a disposition towards blind obedience which is so strong that when it comes to the crunch, it is possible, with a command, to make the soldiers react spontaneously, like automatons, in defiance of the powerful motives of the instinct of self-preservation and fear.

Also, the characteristic attitudes and impulses experienced as *moral* attitudes and impulses are of a *disinterested* character, that is, a character not based on needs. This is particularly apparent[1] if the moral is experienced and interpreted as a duty.[2] The distinctive feature of the experience of duty is precisely the fact that we, in this experience, apprehend an urge—a stimulus—which appears as

[1] In Alf Ross, *Kritik der sogenannten praktischen Erkenntnis* [Critique of So-called Practical Knowledge] (1933), Ch. III, 8, I have explained that the same also applies if the moral is interpreted as the consciousness of value, or as the Good.

[2] A more profound analysis of the experience of duty can be found in Alf Ross, *Kritik der sogenannten praktischen Erkenntnis* [Critique of So-called Practical Knowledge] (1933), Ch. VII, 1 and 2.

a claim completely independent of everything we are told by our desires, inclinations, and interests. The call of duty does not seek justification in utility or advantage, it does not appeal to any interest, but presents itself with absolute independence. Duty need not be in conflict with our 'natural' inclinations, but it appears in its purest form whenever this is the case. If we act duty-bound, duty is then experienced as a coercion or a bond on our 'sensuous' nature, and we feel stirred by a motive that has nothing to do with our needs and interests—a disinterested motive in the form of a pure sense of duty.

Furthermore, it must be assumed that moral attitudes have a social origin, conveyed to the individual through *suggestive persuasion* on the part of his surroundings. What is so peculiar about persuasion giving rise to morality is the fact that it occurs during the first few years of an individual's life. From infancy, the child grows up in a social environment, at first represented by parents, siblings, and playmates, and later on by *Kindergarten* and school. In this environment, the child is incessantly exposed to a bombardment of persuasions conforming to the common cultural tradition of society, the social heritage. These persuasions consist at first of verbal appeals: 'You must not lie!'; 'One must keep one's word!'; 'Swearing is not nice!'; 'Share with your brothers and sisters!'; 'It is cowardly to beat people smaller than yourself', etc., etc. These verbal appeals are underpinned by a number of other means of persuasion, expressing approval and disapproval: praise, blame, punishment, isolation from
[453] the group, withdrawal of love and sympathy, and so on. In this way, as he grows, the child internalizes a comprehensive web of conventional rules of life, covering the most varied matters of life: linguistic rules, rules for games and play, rules for social intercourse and etiquette, and moral rules ('moral' in the narrower sense). These rules are felt to be '*moral*', that is, '*binding*', '*obligatory*' *to the extent they are apt to conflict with the individual's inclination.*[3] Thus, the rules of grammar, for example, are experienced as merely conventional, whereas the prohibition against swearing has acquired a moral colouring.[4] To be sure, the demands for cleanliness, decorum, and politeness may initially have been experienced as moral demands, but gradually, the corresponding behaviour has been inculcated to such a degree of automatism that the child no longer feels any desire to act otherwise.[5] In this way, the rules lose their moral character.

[3] Cf. *op. cit.* (1933), 442 *et seq.*—The transition is a smooth ('gliding') one. To this distinction corresponds—likewise by means of a smooth transition—a difference in the social reaction to the infringement of a norm. The infringement of a typical, conventional norm almost evokes surprise, derision, and reserve. A person wearing the wrong kind of clothes is ridiculous and does not belong to polite society. By contrast, the infringement of a typical moral norm is met by a storm of disapproval which may escalate into resentment, indignation, and abhorrence.

[4] If anyone should feel a wish to conjugate a weak verb as a strong one, then the grammatical norm would also—presumably—seem to him to be morally tinged.

[5] Therefore, the common norms for proper dress are usually felt to be merely conventional. Only exceptionally, when the demand is experienced as a burden that contradicts one's inclination (for example, the demand to appear in cap and gown at the annual commemoration of the foundation of the University), will it acquire the character of a moral duty.

Precisely because it is a question of regular persuasions in typical situations of action, the suggestive factor (parental admonitions etc.) may be withdrawn in the course of time. Then, the moral attitude will be directly coupled to the situation and the corresponding moral rule. A grown person—even a mere adolescent—does not remember anything of the mechanism through which the moral impulses have been inculcated in him. Nevertheless, he experiences this suggested impulse in full force and spontaneity as a power that fetters his inclinations. This circumstance explains the touch of 'inexplicability' that characterizes morality. While it is only 'natural' to satisfy one's needs, there is something incomprehensible in the fact that we do our duty in conflict with our interests. It does not seem that this motive can be ascribed to our 'nature'. Therefore, it stands to reason to interpret the moral impulse as an expression of a specific, transcendent '*validity*', originating in God or the transcendent, rational nature of man, and speaking to us through our conscience.[6]

The contrast between interested and disinterested attitudes and impulses, between interest and morality, is not identical with that between egoism and altruism. It should be recalled that interest can be unselfish as well. The decisive con- [454] trast—at any rate as seen from the perspective that interests us, namely, the problem of agreement and disagreement in practical standpoints of social significance—is that between *rationality and irrationality.* In their original, unconditional form, interests are—as we have seen—an attitude towards a satisfactor (repulsor), that is, an object the acquisition (removal) of which is suited to satisfy a need. The interested attitude towards a rule of action or a social order is a derived, conditioned attitude—conditioned by the belief that the respective rule or order is suited to satisfy certain needs. *Therefore, the standpoint based on interest is always conditioned by certain beliefs, and is thus the subject of justification through a rational argumentation. The moral attitude (the moral sense), on the other hand, is a direct and unconditioned attitude towards a norm of action or a social order. It is irrational in the sense that it is a direct expression of an emotion and inaccessible to justification and argumentation.*

The mutually competing motivating force possessed by each of these two types of attitude varies vastly from person to person, depending on certain conditioning beliefs concerning the nature and origin of the moral sense. According to the way in which the individual reacts to the moral sense, one can distinguish between two main types: the moral-dogmatic; and the moral-sceptical type.

The *moral-dogmatic* position is characterized by a feeling of profound awe *vis-à-vis* our inner voice. No one has surpassed the beauty of Kant's account of the

[6] In metaphysical philosophy, this interpretation has given rise to the dualism between man as a sensuous being, subject to the necessity of the law of causality, and man as a rational being whose will is free. I have never been able to understand how this contrast, on which Kant's practical philosophy balances, can be reconciled.

feeling of profound respect and rapture vis-à-vis the sublime majesty of the moral law. He wrote the famous words: 'Zwei Dinge erfüllen das Gemüt mit immer neuer und zunehmender Bewunderung und Ehrfurcht, je öfter und anhaltender sich das Nachdenken damit beschäftigt: der bestirnte Himmel über mir und das moralische Gesetz in mir.'[7]* This position is naturally based on religious or philosophico-metaphysical beliefs concerning the nature and origin of conscience.[8] Our inner voice is interpreted as the revelation of an absolute *a priori* validity, ascribed to God or to man's rational, transcendental nature, which raises it above the world of necessity.

The *moral-sceptical* position, on the other hand, regards with suspicion all emotional attitudes directly confronting certain norms of action, and demands, as a main rule, that these be justified out of considerations determined by interest. This position is based on the belief that the moral sense is an empirical, mental phenomenon like all the others. The conscience within me is not something incomprehensibly sublime. It tells me nothing about God's will or
[455] the categorical laws of reason—merely about the prejudices implanted in me in the nursery. In the long run these, in turn, are the product of a sociocultural heritage. Moral attitudes originate in social needs. However, on the one hand these have been based on magic, religion, and other delusions concerning physical and social reality; and on the other, social conditions have changed subsequently, so that traditional morality no longer serves the interests which gave rise to it. Therefore, the moral sense cannot claim blind respect. At most, it can be taken as a *prima facie* indication that a certain course of conduct serves certain social interests. It must be our task (provided it is feasible)[9] to re-examine this hypothesis and rationalize our emotional attitude by analysing the problem of action in the light of our interests and an adequate conception of reality.

As is customary in practical issues, it is not possible to discuss or prove the correctness of the very standpoint that is adopted—merely of the conditioning beliefs. In support of his attitude, the moral sceptic can point out that a metaphysical interpretation of the moral consciousness is just as untenable, arbitrary, and fanciful as all other metaphysics (§ 63); he can give a psychological explanation as to why the metaphysical urge is so powerful precisely in the sphere of morality (§ 64); and he can refer to the comprehensive modern works

* Translator's note: 'Two things fill the mind with ever new and increasing admiration and reverence, the more often and more steadily one reflects on them: the starry heavens above me and the moral law within me.' The English translation of this famous passage has been taken from the Cambridge version of Immanuel Kant, *Critique of Practical Reason,* ed. by Mary J. Gregor and with an Introduction by Andrews Reath (Online ISBN: 9780511809576).

[7] Immanuel Kant, *Critik der practischen Vernunft* [Critique of Practical Reason] (1788), last section ('Beschluss' ['Conclusion']).

[8] Kant denied that moral consciousness can be explained historico-psychologically.

[9] Cf. § 92 below.

that have thrown light on the origin and evolution of the sense of morality from a sociological, a historical, and a psychological perspective.[10]

If these arguments are accepted, and if the metaphysical mist is thereby dispersed, the psychological effect will undoubtedly be the erosion of the moral dogmatist's blind awe vis-à-vis the moral consciousness. I simply cannot conceive of an individual who accepts a scientific, that is, relativist, historical, and psychological account of the sense of morality as one empirical phenomenon among others and, at the same time, retain an attitude of submissive respect and absolute obedience to its commands.

[10] See, e.g., Edward Westermarck, *The Origin and Development of the Moral Ideas*, I–II (1924–26).

§ 91. The Role Played by the 'Sense of Justice' and Policy Considerations in Scientific Legal Politics: Three Fundamental Postulates

What has been discussed in the two preceding sections concerning interest and moral sense applies *mutatis mutandis* to policy considerations and the sense of justice, as factors in scientific legal politics.

[456] 'Policy considerations' is a term that expresses exactly the evaluation of legal rules on the basis of rational arguments concerning the rules' actual relevance in relation to presupposed interests.

The sense of justice, on the other hand, is—just like the moral sense—a disinterested and inculcated, immediate attitude of approval or disapproval towards a norm of action. It differs from the moral sense (taken in the narrower sense) by not being concerned with the immediate social life (as does the latter) but, rather, with its social, organized regulation. The sense of justice is directed towards the social order. It takes a stand on problems like the following: should criminals be punished in proportion to their guilt; should abortion be permitted; should women have the same legal status as men; should workers have the right to organize unions; should it be possible to dissolve a marriage through divorce, and under what conditions; what are the content and limits of property law? etc., etc. The sense of justice is, in part, determined by the existing legal order which, in turn, is affected by the sense of justice.

On the basis of the previous discussions, I shall now put forward the following three fundamental postulates for the role played by the sense of justice in scientific legal politics, in competition with policy considerations.

(1) *The sense of justice—understood as the scientific legal politician's own sense of justice—must never be understood as a direct norm, or a measure, for the 'correctness' of a legal rule.*

This postulate hardly needs any further justification. It is obvious that every thought of the sense of justness as a revelation of intrinsically valid principles for the 'correctness' of the law leads us back to the metaphysical views we repeatedly rejected.

(2) *The sense of justice—understood as the sense of justice actually prevalent with those in power—must not be included in the impersonal attitude-preconditions of the scientific legal politician.*

In §§ 78 and 83 above, it has been stipulated as a methodological demand, following from the principle of the purity of science in combination with the wish to influence the legislator, that the social researcher, just like the scientific technologist, must accept, as a hypothesis, the political attitudes that actually exist at the highest level of government. Thence it would seem to follow that he must accept the specific attitudes expressed in the sense of justice, too.

However, one must bear in mind (as has been pointed out in the same context) that the existing attitudes are only raw materials in need of processing, especially from the point of view of whether they are conditioned by an inadequate conception of reality and, thus, need correction in the light of a more adequate scientific insight. This is exactly the case with regard to the sense of justice. The points of view to be applied here are strictly analogous to those which have been put forward in the previous section in connection with moral dogmatism and moral scepticism. Once [457] it is understood that the sense of justice is not a revelation of transcendental validity, of the eternal principles of justice, or of the will of God, but merely one empirical mental fact among others; that it is a historical product, resulting from an interplay of forces, among which powerful group interests, primitive instincts, and traditional magical and religious ideas have played a certain role; and that the sense of justice, even if it changes with changing social conditions,[1] nevertheless (owing to the element of inertia of tradition) often lags behind in relation to the development in social conditions; once all this has been clearly understood, the sense of justice loses its motivating force. One, then, cannot help asking why we, when dealing with our social problems, should let ourselves be dominated by this feeling which irrationally binds us to the past. One is inclined to hold the sense of justice accountable and ask whether its spontaneous reaction can be justified as a kind of accumulated experience passed down through generations, regarding what it is that serves certain social interests. The importance of the sense of justice will only be acknowledged as a *prima facie* indication of social needs, and one will demand, to the highest extent possible, that its unreflecting, irrational attitude be exchanged for a rational analysis of the problem of action, on the basis of given interests and a rational insight into the effects of the law in relation to these.

Let me repeat that this sceptical stance towards the sense of justice expresses a standpoint, not a scientific truth; a standpoint, however, which one is obliged to take once one has understood and accepted the beliefs concerning the nature of the sense of justice which I have propagated, and which can be maintained and defended as scientific truths.

Moreover—and irrespective of, whether or not this sceptical stance against the sense of justice is shared—it can be maintained that an appeal to the sense of justice lies beyond the task of a scientific legal politics. For as

[1] Cf. § 92 below.

previously emphasized (§ 78), this task must consist in serving and guiding rational argumentation, by providing it with scientifically tenable assertions and separating those that cannot be tested scientifically. However, an appeal to the sense of justice—provided that it is regarded as a motivating attitude, not just as a factual circumstance; cf. the third postulate—is not an argument, but a direct means of exerting pressure. An appeal to the sense of justice puts a stop to all argumentation and discussion and can only be met with other kinds of inculcatory pressure, such as emotional expressions of a diverging sense of justice. Rational argumentation becomes possible as soon as the sense of justice is not acknowledged as a motivation in itself, but is tested and justified in the light of policy considerations (interests).

The comparison between policy considerations and appeals[2] to the
[458] sense of justice, frequently to be met with in juridico-political argumentation, is a methodically impossible mixture of rational argumentation and irrational persuasion. The absurdity of this mixture is obscured, because an invisible hand seems to govern it so wisely that an appeal to the sense of justice always coincides with the factual argumentation. But what would the position be like if the two approaches were to lead to conflicting results? There are only two possibilities, both of them unacceptable. Either the first approach must take absolute precedence over the second one—the postulate of the sense of justice over the outcome of policy considerations, or *vice versa*. But in that case it is meaningless from the very start to adduce both sets of views, since one of them is destined to be irrelevant in the conflict with the other. Or, one must undertake a weighing and deliberative balancing, in the same way as different policy considerations are weighed against each other. However, such weighing must appear meaningless and unacceptable from either of the two standpoints, the rational and irrational, because both of them claim sovereign validity. If the sense of justice is embraced, any considerations of interest must be rejected. If a certain course of conduct is emotionally disapproved of as being unlawful in itself, no rational, interest-based views can be attributed any weight against this. Conversely, if one has prepared oneself for a rational evaluation of interests, no emotional approval or disapproval can be attributed any weight which could be weighed against the interests.

In the work of modern authors, we may find that the sense of justice certainly is mentioned in line with factual arguments, but that in reality it does not play any role at all in the author's train of thought, and apparently has been adduced merely as a gesture of respect vis-à-vis traditional ideas.

[2] The situation is different if the sense of justice is taken into consideration as a factual circumstance, cf. the third postulate and the next section.

Ivar Strahl's report on legislative measures in the field of tort law[3] is a good example. The chapter on the author's principal considerations begins with due reverence for the sense of justice. We learn that it is a normal wish on the part of the legislator to find the rules that would lead to solutions which appeal to the sense of justice (which are felt to be just). After having touched upon what the sense of justice demands in the field of tort law, the author mentions that it is combined with difficulties and misgivings to legislate on this basis. The outcome of these deliberations is that emotional reactions certainly have a claim to attention, but that tort law nonetheless should not be formed merely on the basis of an uncritical assessment of what is felt to be just. Thereupon, the author moves on to his proper agenda, namely, a factual, interest-based analysis of the problems of tort law, and in the course of the entire investigation we actually do not hear a single word about the demands of the sense of justice. Having taken his hat [459] off to the sense of justice, the author turns his back on it. Seen in this light, his statement that tort law cannot be formed solely on the basis of the sense of justice is a rather cautious understatement.

Also Ussing acknowledges in his corresponding report[4] that practically only policy considerations can serve as guidelines. After mentioning that older jurists were chiefly interested in emotional evaluations of the justice of the rules of tort law, the author maintains that nowadays one would hardly deny that legislation concerning liability for damages should principally be grounded in practical, societal considerations.

> *However, the results yielded by an evaluation of policy considerations ought to be tested in the light of the sense of justice. If it emerges that they do not coincide with the sense of justice, one begins to suspect that there have been flaws in the weighing, or in the basis of the weighing. And even in those cases where one is convinced of the tenability of the weighing, one has to consider whether it can be expected that the new rule, when implemented, will be able to win round the sense of justice. If this—for one reason or another—is deemed improbable it might be a reason to suspend the reform.*[5]

Even though I cannot really agree with Ussing that a discord between the sense of justice and the results of a factual analysis gives rise to suspicions that the results are deficient, I can have no objection, of course, to the modest methodological conclusion the author draws from it, namely, that one should reconsider one's analysis and weighing. For according to Ussing, it is by no means impossible that this reconsideration has the effect that

[3] Ivar Strahl, 'Förberedande utredning angående lagstiftning på skadeståndsrättens område' [Preparatory investigation concerning legislation in the field of tort law]. *Statens offentliga utredningar* [Official Reports of the Swedish Government] 1950:16.

[4] 'Nordisk lovgivning om Erstatningsansvar' [Nordic legislation on damage liability]. Betænkning afgivet af Henry Ussing [Report submitted by Henry Ussing] (1950).

[5] *Op. cit.*, 33.

one holds on to one's results in defiance of the demands of the sense of justice (the last lines of the quotation concern the sense of justice *qua* factual circumstance, see directly below).

(3) *The sense of justice—understood* qua *sense of justice prevailing among the population—can only be taken into account as a spiritual-climatic circumstance counting among the factors on which the practical feasibility of a legal reform depends.*

Concerning this issue, I can essentially refer to the description in the chapter on the possibility of legal politics. The legislator is not omnipotent, he cannot shape developments arbitrarily. His options are restricted within a certain scope, which is determined *inter alia* by the sense of justice prevailing among the population. The sense of justice represents a resistance, an element of inertia vis-à-vis the legislator's attempts to direct human behaviour and must, therefore, be taken into consideration in his juridico-
[460] sociological calculation as to the factual effect of proposed legislative measures. This is the true core of the teachings of the Historical School.

It is worth noting that, according to this view, the sense of justice is taken into consideration as a factual circumstance, not as a motive; that is, it figures among the operative beliefs which describe juridico-sociological facts and contexts, not among the presupposed, motivating attitudinal premises. Accordingly, it is not the sense of justice, as such, that is respected: rather, it is the behavioural effects (presumably conditioned by the sense of justice) that are taken into consideration.

Even though we must assume that an existing sense of justice is not strong enough to annul the effect of a proposed legislative measure, it can nevertheless—as has been stressed by Ussing in the quotation above—constitute the basis of an argument that speaks against carrying out the reform. For it must be taken into consideration that, under such conditions, legislation may entail reluctance, discontent, and frictions which are inconveniences in themselves and, what is more, can negatively affect general law abidance and respect for the law.

Such views are important for a scientific juridico-political evaluation of acts which, without injuring the interests of others, strongly offend against prevailing moral beliefs and thus give rise to general repugnance, indignation, and condemnation. Especially in former times but even today, acts have often been punished, exclusively, or at any rate predominantly, because they were regarded as sinful—such as various sexual relationships (homosexuality between adults, extra-marital sexual intercourse, or sexual intercourse between even more distant relatives or in-laws, adultery, 'unnatural' practices etc.), heresy, infanticide,[6] and other acts condemned by the

[6] See O. K. Magnussen, 'Er det Retsgode, der krænkes, det samme ved Barnemord og ved Manddrab?' [Is the legally protected interest that is being violated the very same in infanticide and homicide?], in *UfR* 1929 B 193, especially 205.

church. To a moral-dogmatic attitude, the sense of morality itself is a sufficient reason for the punishability of such acts. This standpoint does not lend itself to a discussion. If punishability shall be justified on the grounds of practical, interest-based considerations, it must be done because one wishes to protect the feelings of the indignant citizens[7] and satisfy their urge to persecute those who cause offence. As usual in practical evaluations, [461] the decision must depend on a deliberative weighing of conflicting considerations, in the present case the consideration of other people's freedom of religion and freedom of action. In my opinion (and this is a confession, of course!), moral indignation does not deserve protection in competition with other people's interests. I would like to put forward as a general, commendable rule that no act shall ever be prohibited, let alone punished, when its interference with the interests of others depends entirely on the fact that others condemn it morally. To put it bluntly: people ought to be allowed to perform such acts as do not concern others, regardless of whether those others consider them sinful in themselves. Or: an act should not be prohibited solely on the ground that it is offensive to others.

This is the essence of the principle of tolerance. After severe struggles, the evolution of Western culture tends towards leading this principle to victory. In my view, the emancipation from the yoke of religious and moral intolerance, as reflected in the abolition of a great number of older prohibitions and penalty provisions, is a major step forward towards human happiness. This course should be maintained and continued until it is fully implemented within the field of law as well as in other realms of communal human life.

[7] The situation discussed here, characterized by the fact that the action as such, that is, apart from the moral condemnation, does not concern others, must be distinguished from those cases where the act in itself intervenes in the emotional life of other people. Therefore, offences against public decency, insults, also insults to religious feelings (blasphemy), insulting living or dead persons and similar crimes should not be included in the acts discussed here. This is overlooked by Magnussen, when he (*op. cit.*, 205) compares blasphemy, insults to the dead, and animal cruelty with infanticide. As far as animal cruelty is concerned, it is a misleading, dogmatic construction altogether to consider a human feeling as a subject worthy of protection; on this issue, see Alf Ross, *Virkelighed og Gyldighed i Retslæren* [Reality and Validity in Jurisprudence] (1934), 198–99.

§ 92. The Role Played by the 'Sense of Justice' when Policy Considerations Fail

The contents of the present section refer to the third postulate as described above. Thus, it is presupposed that the sense of justice—understood *qua* sense of justice prevailing among citizens—can only be taken into consideration as a factual circumstance, not as an attitudinal premise or a motive in itself.

It has been mentioned before that, according to circumstances, the sense of justice can constitute resistance, or even an insurmountable barrier, to juridico-political demands for reform based on empirical considerations.

I shall explain here that the sense of justice, as an expression of the internalized and the customary, will play a more decisive role under certain circumstances, namely, when empirical policy considerations fail (for reasons I shall instantly return to). Since every law reform is an intervention in itself, entailing a number of inconveniences in connection with all sorts of changes and readjustments, it must carry the burden of proof concerning its justification. If this proof cannot be produced in argumentation based on facts, the conclusion must be that one holds on to tradition, grounded in the internalized sense of justice.

[462] Arguments based on facts may fail, either because the legal order at a certain point really must be assumed to be totally indifferent towards practical, interest-based considerations; or because we ourselves, with our present insight into social contexts, are in no position anyway to form a well-founded opinion on the social consequences of possible solutions and, therefore, are in no position, either, to make a rationally justified choice between them. What is more, these two situations merge into each other.

Situations of this kind can occur, both with regard to more specific legal systems within a larger entity called a 'legal institution' and with regard to the institutions themselves in their fundamental components. The former is well known. The latter has hardly ever attracted attention.

Nowadays, it is not difficult to justify, on factual grounds, the necessity of traffic regulations. Unlimited freedom in this area would lead to chaos. On the other hand, it is hardly possible to adduce empirical reasons in order to decide whether these regulations should be based on driving on the right-hand side or on the left-hand side of the road. Thus, in this situation, contemplation of common perception—if you like: 'the sense of justice'—is solely decisive. The same applies to other traffic rules. Even if certain policy considerations could be adduced, every change in firmly established traffic habits would be an inconvenience encumbered with a heavy burden of proof.

Something of a more or less analogous kind also applies to other fields of law. With regard to limitation periods, notice periods and other legal deadlines, it is very important that there are clear and well-established rules thereon, whereas it is often difficult to justify why, exactly, they should have the established length of time. The same applies to the provisions relating to the age of majority, to the right to vote, to marriage, etc. In trade relations and other matters of life where interests in clarity and certainty play a dominant role, the fact that a certain rule is valid is often more important than the nature of its content.

In such cases one usually speaks of *pure positivities* within the law. This term expresses precisely what is arbitrary, as opposed to what has been determined through rational deliberations.

Still more notable is the circumstance, pointed out by Illum,[1] that something similar must also be supposed to apply with respect to the basic features of the *fundamental legal institutions* themselves.

The necessity of a system of ownership is, empirically, just as well-founded as the necessity of traffic regulations. However, when the question is raised whether such a system shall be based on private capitalism or on socialism, we lack the necessary insight into how either of these systems affects production, commerce, [463]
human mentality and nature etc., in order to be able, through comparison, to form a well-founded opinion as to which system would be preferable with respect to the given attitudinal premises. There are different views on the subject, yet none of them is supported by science and experience to such an extent that they can claim to be called anything but ideologies.

This is perhaps still more evident with regard to the institution of marriage. As far as I can see, it is not possible to provide a tenable, factual explanation of why monogamy is to be preferred to polygamy or other basic forms of marriage known in other cultures. The conditions for contracting a marriage and, in particular, for its dissolution, have varied widely through all ages, and still vary widely from country to country. Regardless of the fact that these variations correspond to some degree to variations in interests and needs, depending on social conditions, it is hard to believe that this should be the whole explanation, and it should be possible, under the given circumstances, to justify, empirically, which rules on the contraction and dissolution of marriage would best serve the given social interests. What do we really know about the consequences, to the individual or society, of more rigid or more lax marital relationships? In former times, people thought that laxity in marital relationships must result in the general moral decline of society. This has not been confirmed empirically. But are we really able to provide a more tenable explanation of the matter ourselves?

[1] Knud Illum, *Lov og Ret* [Law and Justice] (1945), 162 *et seq.*

Thus, it seems that the fundamental legal institutions do not lend themselves to discussion and empirical justification. The problems they raise are too big and comprehensive for us to have an empirical basis for a comparative assessment of their social consequences. We are fairly able to calculate the effects of a technical implementation of specific systems within the framework of the institution (the importance of the registration system for the mortgage credit system, the importance of expropriation for town planning and other social enterprises, etc.). However, it would appear that the fundamental institutions themselves must be accepted as a *cultural fact*. Within our culture, life has taken this shape. In other places, it has taken another shape. Once shaped by causes we cannot sort out, they are continued by a cultural tradition and maintained by a sense of justice which reflects the fact of the cultural tradition. However, this tradition and this sentiment are not unchangeable, but change over time. It may be tempting to assume, as does the Historical School, that they live their own organic life. In reality, however, they probably change under the impact of experience and needs, yet in a way we cannot control. *The fundamental institutions change along with changed social conditions, possibly through revolutions; but they lie outside the realm of rational politics.*

This explains why the feigned rational considerations through which one has [464] attempted, at different times, to justify the fundamental legal institutions such as they have been shaped according to time and place, are, in reality, mere fictions. They seem to bear the mark of *ad hoc creations*. They have the characteristics of an ideology, that is, a theoretical construction arisen from the need to justify a practical attitude or a programme of action, and adapted accordingly.

> The attempt of the Danish Commission on Inheritance Law to provide the private right of inheritance with a rational justification is a typical example. After first explaining that a private right of inheritance is a necessary condition for private ownership since the opposite system would have the effect that the major part of society's assets would pass to the state, the report goes on to state the following:
>
> *'Since it is the task of inheritance law to see to it that the family fortune, at the demise of one generation, as much as possible will serve the same objective to the next generation as to the first one, it is natural that as a main rule, property passes from the parents on to their children, and from these children, in turn, to their own children. Thus, continuity in the economic activities of society is safeguarded in the very best way if the children, in virtue of their close relationship with their parents, and possibly also through participation in the activity connected with the creation and maintenance of the fortune, are usually best suited to, and best prepared for, taking over and continuing their parents' business.'*[2]

[2] *Udkast til arvelov med tilhørende bemærkninger* [Draft of the Inheritance Act, with comments] (1941), 28.

> This seems to be a genuine *ad hoc* construction—and not a particularly happy one at that. It seems that the report wants to justify the children's right of inheritance by saying that a shoe manufacturer's son must be regarded as particularly well-suited for running a shoe factory, and that he therefore ought to take over his father's business. Surely, things are not as simple as that. On the one hand, the law of inheritance does not preclude the possibility that the children sell the business as quickly as possible and squander all the money away. On the other hand, if the report has been serious about discovering the individual who would be 'best suited to, and best prepared for' taking over and continuing the business of the parents, surely more appropriate selection criteria than kinship might be found.
>
> The truth of the matter is that it is not for any commission on inheritance law either to confirm or to interfere with the fundamental legitimacy of the private right to inherit. This right is simply an elementary component of our cultural and legal tradition—an institution beyond empirical justification and rational legal politics.[3] What nowadays may give rise to fundamental debating and fighting is the issue of heavily curtailing private inheritance through a considerable inheritance tax increase. This issue is so typically political in a narrower sense, however, that it is hardly suitable for an objective analysis, conducted by a commission that is composed exclusively of jurists.

In those areas where empirical policy reasons—or, as I prefer to call them, rational [465] arguments—completely fail, or have but little directive force, *the sense of justice, in turn, will take over the guiding role*. This means that for lack of argument in favour of something else, one simply holds on to the legal and cultural tradition that has come down to us. This is not identical with absolute conservatism. The technical developments in society and the changes in common morality—conditioned partly by technical developments, partly by changes in the conceptions of reality that are of relevance to moral attitudes—make a constant adjustment of the law necessary.

Public debate—at least in a democratic society—is a continuous process through which new impressions, new events, and new insights are continually digested and transformed into public opinion. What happens here is a large-scale interchange of views where one tries to influence one another towards practical agreement, by using both rational arguments and irrational means of exerting pressure. In this interchange of views, public opinion is formed with respect to concrete, time-varying problems, out of which, in turn, the more general sense of morality and justice crystallizes. Just think of the American negro problem.

[3] In a later passage (page 35), the report also says in connection with family inheritance law that it tallies with the current conception of law to such an extent that it does not need any more detailed justification.

How is public opinion formed on this issue? In part, it is a function of the conditions of production. The position of the negro in the industrial North has always differed from that in the plantation states of the South. In part, public opinion emerges slowly through an ongoing debate.[4] The driving force in this debate is ultimately information concerning facts, greater insight into, and understanding of, the nature of the negroes, the conditions under which they live, the role they play in American society. With thousands of experiences the facts, great and small, tell their own tale. Scientific and statistical truths are popularized. Serving as soldiers during the wars, many white people learned more about black people than they had ever done before. Information has to fight against mendacious propaganda, but truth is victorious in the long run. At the same time, one appeals to the latent attitudes concerning freedom and equal chances for all, which constitute a central element of the American creed. In this way, delusions and prejudices are slowly broken down—to be specific: the attitudes conditioned by delusions are broken down.

The task of a legal politics in these areas consists in gently adjusting the law to changed technical and ideological conditions, with the sense of justice as the lodestar. The internal coherence of the legal tradition must be preserved, while one attempts, at the same time, to satisfy new aspirations. Of course, the more
[466] detailed shaping of the directives of the sense of justice into manageable legal rules must be done in compliance with juridico-technical considerations, based upon juridico-sociological knowledge or estimates.

The role played by the traditional conception of law and the prevalent sense of justice in those fields of law where rational argumentation fails, clearly emerges from the previously mentioned report on inheritance law, as compared with, say, the likewise earlier mentioned reports on tort law. Whereas the latter, in reality, took no notice of the sense of justice, the former incessantly falls back upon 'the prevailing conception of law', 'inherited sense of justice', 'customary legal notions' *qua* source of motivation.[5] If one did not take into account the difference (pointed out here) between the respective fields of law, this methodological difference in reasoning must seem odd.

The respect for legal tradition and the sense of justice I have mentioned in these pages explains our traditional view of the lawyer as a professionally conservative person. This view was justified especially in former times, when ideological considerations, based upon either natural law or history, almost reigned supreme. Recently, Illum has one-sidedly emphasized the role of the lawyer as serving as a mouthpiece for national legal culture.[6] In line with what has been said

[4] This means that 'ideas' are *no mere* 'superstructure' over the conditions of production (Marx), but that they also possess their own dynamics, cf. Gunnar Myrdal, *An American Dilemma* (1944), 1032 *et seq.*

[5] *Udkast til arvelov med tilhørende bemærkninger* [Draft of the Inheritance Act, with comments] (1941), 35, 36, 39, 63, 64, 66, 68 *et passim*.

[6] Knud Illum, *Lov og Ret* [Law and Justice] (1945), Ch. XII and VIII.

previously, I submit that the task of the jurist as a scientific legal politician consists in functioning—as far as practicable—as a rational technologist. In fulfilling this role, the jurist is neither conservative nor progressive. Like other technologists, he simply puts his knowledge and skill at the disposal of others—*in casu* at the disposal of those who hold the reins of political power.

Appendices

A. Biographical note on Ross

Alf Ross was born in 1899 in Copenhagen, Denmark. In 1922, Ross finished law studies at the University of Copenhagen with exceptional grades and the very rare distinction *laudabilis et qvidem egregie*. The year after, he married Else-Merete Helweg-Larsen (1903–76) and began a several-year-long study journey which brought him to Austria, France, Germany, and the United Kingdom.

Studying with the formidable Austrian jurist and leading figure of legal positivism Hans Kelsen (1881–1973) was to be a turning point for the young Alf Ross. As the tangible outcome of the study journey, Ross, immediately upon his return to Copenhagen in 1926, handed in the treatise *Theorie der Rechtsquellen* [*Theory of the Sources of Law*] as a *habilitation* in law. Primarily due to resistance from Ross's previous teacher, Professor Frederik Vinding Kruse, this was turned down—an event that was to become the source of lifelong enmity between the two men.

Having recovered from the blow, Ross travelled to Uppsala, Sweden, where he spent 1928–29. In this small university town north of Stockholm, Ross sought out Professor of Practical Philosophy Axel Hägerström (1868–1939), who was a leading figure in the starkly anti-metaphysical empiricist philosophical scene known as the Uppsala School. This movement provided the general philosophical foundations for the school of legal theory which was to become known as Scandinavian legal realism, and to which, besides Ross and Hägerström, Vilhelm Lundstedt (1882–1955) and Karl Olivecrona (1897–1980) were to be the leading figures.

In 1929 Ross resubmitted *Theorie der Rechtsquellen* at Uppsala University as a *habilitation* in philosophy, this time with greater luck. Later the same year, it was published in Leipzig and Vienna in Hans Kelsen's series *Wiener Staat-und Rechtswissenschaftliche Studien*. In 1933 Ross wrote *Kritik der sogenannten praktischen Erkenntnis* [Critique of the So-called Practical Reason] and in 1934 *Virkelighed og Gyldighed i retslæren* [Reality and Validity in Jurisprudence], which was finally accepted as a *habilitation* in law at the University of Copenhagen. In 1935 Ross was employed at his *alma mater*, becoming a full professor in 1938 and staying there until his retirement in 1969, first holding the chair in public international law and later in philosophy of law and constitutional law. In the years from 1959 to 1971 Ross served as a judge on the European Court of Human Rights.

Besides *On Law and Justice*, which was first published in Danish in 1953 (as *Om ret og retfærdighed*), Ross was the author of a long list of books and articles covering a broad spectrum of legal and philosophical subjects, many of which were translated into several languages, including English, German, Italian, Portuguese, and Spanish. Besides the works already mentioned, Ross's most important works include *Lærebog i Folkeret* (1942, published in English as *Textbook in International Law* (1947)); *Towards a Realistic Jurisprudence* (1946, a reworked version of *Virkelighed og Gyldighed i Retslæren*); *Hvorfor Demokrati?* (1946, published in English as *Why Democracy?* (1952)); 'Tû-Tû' (1951, English translation 1957); *Dansk Statsforfatningsret* (1959–60 [Danish Constitutional Law]) and *Directives and Norms* (1968). After his retirement, Ross primarily devoted his time to studies in the philosophy of punishment, resulting, *inter alia*, in the books *Skyld, ansvar, straf* (1970, published in English as *On Guilt, Responsibility, Punishment* (1975)), and *Forbrydelse og straf* (1974 [Crime and Punishment]). Alf Ross died in 1979.*

* Readers who wish to learn more about Alf Ross's eventful life are referred to *Alf Ross—A Life* by Jens Evald (DJØF Publishing, Copenhagen 2014) and to 'Alf Ross 1899–1979: A Biographical Sketch' by Knud Waaben, in the *European Journal of International Law*, Vol. 14, issue 4, 661–76 (2003).

B. Ross's preface to the 1958 English language edition

This study by a Scandinavian author is presented to an Anglo-American public in the hope that it will contribute to the strengthening of the ties between Nordic culture and the great traditions of the Anglo-Saxon world. American initiative and generous sponsorship, especially since the Second World War, have made possible a lively exchange of persons and ideas between the New and the Old World; I have felt that we, on this side of the ocean, have a continuous obligation to contribute all that we can to this communication.

Especially in the field of jurisprudence should the opportunities for a fertile co-operation and mutual stimulation be favourable. Since the work of John Austin and Oliver Wendell Holmes Anglo-American legal thinking has been directed towards a realistic interpretation of law, that is, an interpretation in accordance with the principles of an empirical philosophy. A similar empiricism has, since the days of Anders Sandöe Örsted (1778–1860) and Axel Hägerström (1868–1939), dominated Scandinavian jurisprudence. By this common trend the traditions in both parts of the world have been dissociated from the natural-law doctrines and other ramifications of the idealistic philosophy of law prevalent on the Continent.

The leading idea of this work is to carry, in the field of law, the empirical principles to their ultimate conclusions. From this idea springs the methodological demand that the study of law must follow the traditional patterns of observation and verification which animate all modern empirical science; and the analytical demand that the fundamental legal notions must be interpreted as conceptions of social reality, the behaviour of man in society, and as nothing else. For this reason, I reject the idea of a specific *a priori* 'validity' which raises the law above the world of facts, and reinterpret validity in terms of social facts; I reject the idea of an *a priori* principle of justice as a guide for legislation (legal politics), and discuss the problems of legal politics in a relativistic spirit, that is, in relation to hypothetical values accepted by influential groups in the society; and, finally, I reject the idea that legal cognition constitutes a specific normative cognition, expressed in *ought*-propositions, and interpret legal thinking formally in terms of the same logic as that on which other empirical sciences are based (*is*-propositions).

There are, in my opinion, no definite principles determining the province of jurisprudence—no inner criteria that determine where the doctrinal study of law ends and jurisprudence begins. Tradition and personal inclinations will largely decide the question. For my part I have regarded it important to treat not only problems on a high level of abstraction but also notions and questions with which the student of law is familiar from his work in the classroom, in the courts, or in the halls of legislation. In this way I hope to demonstrate that jurisprudence is not only a beautiful mental activity *per se*, but also an instrument which may benefit any lawyer who wants better to understand what he is doing, and why.

Through the more than thirty years that I have occupied myself with jurisprudential studies I have, of course, received guidance and inspiration from many quarters. Without them the writing of this book would not have been possible. Such debts are easily forgotten and I am not able to make a complete account. But I must mention two scholars who meant more to me than any others: Hans Kelsen, who initiated me in jurisprudence and taught me, above all, the importance of consistency; and Axel Hägerström, who opened my eyes to the emptiness of metaphysical speculations in law and morality.

The Danish edition of this book was published in 1953. The path through translation and editing to my publishers has been long and beset with many obstacles. It could not have been trodden without the untiring assistance of the translator, Mrs. Margaret Dutton, London, and the editor, Mr. Max Knight of the University of California Press. Gratefully I will remember the interest they both took in my work and the diligence and conscientiousness with which they accomplished their job.

Finally, I want to express my gratitude to the two Danish foundations which made the translation economically possible, *Rask-Örsted Fondet* and *Statens almindelige Videnskabsfond.*

Alf Ross.

Copenhagen,
September, 1958.

C. Works referenced by Ross

[The pages and footnote numbers are those of the 2013 2nd Danish edition of *On Law and Justice* (*Om ret og retfærdighed*)]

AHLANDER, Björn [1920–1982]

Är juridiken en vetenskap? [Is the Study of Law a Science?] (Stockholm: Geber, 1950): 74 n. 49, 92 n. 19, 93 n. 20.

Om rätt och rättstillämpning. Studier i juridikens idéhistoria och rättstillämpningens teori [On Law and the Application of Law. Inquiries into the history of ideas with reference to the law and the theory of adjudication] (Stockholm: Almqvist & Wiksell, 1952): 74 n. 49.

ALLEN, Sir Carleton Kemp [1887–1966]

Law in the Making (Oxford: Clarendon Press, 1927): 50 n. 19; 4th edn (Oxford: Clarendon Press, 1946): 98 n. 26, 124 n. 2, 132 n. 14, 133 n. 15, 134 n. 20, 143 n. 31, 191 n. 25, 372 n. 14.

AMOS, Sheldon [1835–1886]

A Systematic View of the Science of Jurisprudence (London: Longmans, Green, and Co., 1872): 48 n. 6.

ANDERSEN, Ernst [1907–2002]

Forfatning og Sædvane. Studier over nogle af Forfatningsrettens Hovedspørgsmaal [Constitution and Custom. Inquiries into some fundamental issues of Constitutional Law] (Copenhagen: G.E.C. Gad, 1947): 192 n. 29, 353 n. 13, 354 n. 15.

ANDERSEN, Poul Alfred [1888–1977]

'Lighedsgrundsætninger i forvaltningsretlig Belysning' [Principles of equality in the light of Administrative Law], 73 *JFT* (1937), 479–97: 374 n. 18, 376 n. 24.

Næringsretten i Hovedtræk. Industri, Haandværk og Handel [Trade Law Outline. Industry, trade and commerce], 3rd edn (Copenhagen: Gyldendalske Boghandel. Nordisk Forlag, 1944): 173 n. 11.

Dansk Forvaltningsret. Almindelige Emner [Danish Administrative Law. General issues], 2nd edn (Copenhagen: Gyldendal, 1946): 173 n. 10, 377 n. 25.

ARISTOTLE [384–322 BC]

Den nikomakæiske Etik [Nicomachean Ethics]: 331 n. 20.

Retorik [Rhetoric]: 331 n. 20.

ARNHOLM, Carl Jacob [1899–1976]

Forelesninger over Norsk personrett [Lectures on the Norwegian Law of Persons] (Oslo: Tanum, 1947): 276 n. 8.

'Omkring rettshandelsteorien' [On the theory of legal transaction], 61 *TfR* (1948), 368–431: 294 n. 3 and 4.

Alminnelig Avtalerett [General Law of Contracts] (Oslo: Tanum, 1949): 301 n. 11.

'En dom om personlighetsværn' [A judgment concerning personality protection], 63 *TfR* (1950), 390–403: 276 n. 9.

'Noen bemerkninger om "Ändamålsbestämmelse och stiftelse"' [A few comments on 'Provisions on the Purpose of a Foundation'], 65 *TfR* (1952), 258–77: 237 n. 8.

'Noen metodologiske betraktninger' [Some reflections on methodology], 37 *SvJT* (1952), 505–23: 93 n. 20.

AUBERT, Johan Vilhelm [1922–1988]

'Om rettsvitenskapens logiske grunnlag' [On the logical foundation of legal science], 56 *TfR* (1943), 174–200: 114.

'Noen problemområder i rettssosiologien' [Problematic issues in the sociology of law], 61 *TfR* (1948), 432–66: 66 n. 34.

'Kriminalisering og moralpåvirkning i den næringsrettslige lovgivning' [Criminalization and moral impact on business law legislation], 39 *Nordisk Tidsskrift for Kriminalvidenskab* [*Nordic Journal of Criminology*] (1951), 120–29: 102 n. 31.

AUBERT, Johan Vilhelm [1922–1988], Torstein Einang Eckhoff [1916–1993], and Knut Ove Sveri [b. 1925]

En lov i søkelyset: sosialpsykologisk undersøkelse av den norske hushjelplov [Spotlight on a Statute: A socio-psychological study of the Norwegian law concerning domestic help] (Oslo: Akademisk forlag, 1952): 69 n. 38.

AUGDAHL, Per Andreas [1889–1978]

Forelesninger over Rettskilder [Lectures on the Sources of Law] (Oslo: Kommisjon hos Universitetets Studentkontor, 1949): 140 n. 26, 143 n. 29, 144 n. 32, 152 n. 43, 182 n. 15, 196 n. 32, 199 n. 34.

BARKER, Sir Ernest [1874–1960]

Greek Political Theory, Plato and his Predecessors (London: Methuen, 1918): 328 n. 16.

BEKKER, Ernst Immanuel [1827–1916]

'Zur Lehre vom Rechtssubjekt. Genuss und Verfügung. Zwecksatzungen, Zweckvermögen und juristische Personen' [On the theory of the legal subject. Enjoyment and disposition. Purposive legislation, special-purpose assets and the legal person], *Jahrbücher für die Dogmatik des heutigen römischen und deutschen Privatrechts* [Yearbooks for Doctrinal Studies in Roman and German Private Law], Vol. XII (Jena: Fischer, 1873): 237 n. 7.

BENEDICT FULTON, Ruth [1887–1948]

Patterns of Culture (Boston, MA: Houghton Mifflin Company, 1934): 146 n. 37.

Patterns of Culture. An analysis of our social structure as related to primitive civilizations (New York: Mentor Books, 1946): 138 n. 25, 323 n. 11.

BENTHAM, Jeremy [1748–1832]

An Introduction to the Principles of Morals and Legislation: printed in the year 1780, and now first published (London: T. Payne, 1789): 379 n. 2.

The Works of Jeremy Bentham, published under the superintendence of his executor, John Bowring, 11 vols. [1838–1843]: 243 n. 17, 441 n. 18, 19 and 20, 442 n. 21, 22 and 23.

The Limits of Jurisprudence Defined. Being Part 2 of An Introduction to the Principles of Morals and Legislation. Now first printed from the author's manuscript, with an introduction by Charles Warren Everett (New York: 1945): 243 n. 17.

BENTZON, Viggo [1861–1937]

Retskilderne til Brug ved Forelæsninger [The Sources of Law. For academic purposes] (Copenhagen: Gad, 1900–1907): 73 n. 43, 143 n. 30, 187 n. 19, 198 n. 33, 209 n. 46 and 47.

Almindelig Retslære [The General Study of Law], 2nd edn, ed. by Vinding Kruse (Copenhagen: Gad, 1938 [1904]): 303 n. 15.

Skøn og Regel [Discretion and Rule] (Copenhagen: Copenhagen University, 1914): 371 n. 11.

BLACK, Max [1909–1988]

Language and Philosophy. Studies in method (Ithaca, NY: Cornell University Press, 1949): 159 n. 3.

BLACKSTONE, Sir William [1723–1780]

Commentaries on the Laws of England, Vol. II (Oxford: Clarendon Press, 1765–1769): 125 n. 60.

BORNEMANN, Frederik Christian [1810–1861]

Foredrag over den almindelige Rets- og Statslære [Lectures on the General Theory of Law and State] (Copenhagen: F. H. Eibe, 1863): 72 n. 41, 350 n. 7, 356 n. 20.

BORUM, Oscar Alfred [1894–1983]

Personretten [The Law of Persons] (Copenhagen: Gad, 1942): 276 n. 7.

BOTEIN, Bernard [1900–1974]

Trial Judge. The candid, behind-the-bench story of Justice Bernard Botein (New York: Simon and Schuster, 1952): 202 n. 35.

BRENTANO, Franz Clemens [1838–1917]

Psychologie vom empirischen Standpunkt. Vol. 2: *Von der Klassifikation der psychischen Phänomene : mit neuen Abhandlungen aus dem Nachlass* [Empirical Psychology. Vol. 2: On the classification of psychical phenomena, with as yet unpublished articles from the author's estate], ed. by Oskar Kraus (Leipzig: Felix Meiner, 1925): 389 n. 4.

BRORSEN, Werner [?]

Die Verfassungen der Erde in deutscher Sprache nach dem jeweils neuesten Stande. Übersetzt und herausgegeben von W. Brorsen [The Constitutions of the World, in the German language and up-to-date on recent developments. Transl. and ed. by W. Brorsen] (Tübingen: Mohr [Paul Siebeck], 1950): 375 n. 19, 376 n. 22.

BRUSIIN, Otto [1906–1973]

Über die Objektivität der Rechtsprechung [On Objectivity in the Administration of Justice] (Helsinki, 1949): 374 n. 16.

BRYCE, James, 1st Viscount Bryce [1838–1922]

Studies in History and Jurisprudence, 2 vols. (Oxford: Clarendon Press, 1901): 50 n. 17.

BURCKHARDT, Walther [1871–1939]

Einführung in die Rechtswissenschaft [Introduction to Jurisprudence] (Zürich: Polygraphischer Verlag, 1939): 284 n. 14.

CAIRNS, Huntingdon [1904–1985]
The Theory of Legal Science (Chapel Hill, NC: The University of North Carolina Press; London: Humphrey Milford, 1941): 51 n. 23.

CARDOZO, Benjamin Nathan [1870–1938]
Selected Writings, ed. by Margaret E. Hall, with a foreword by Edwin W. Patterson (New York: Fallon Publications, 1947): 91 n. 17, 119 n. 51.

CASTBERG, Frede [1893–1977]
Rettsfilosofiske grunnspörsmål [Fundamental Issues in Jurisprudence] (Oslo, 1939): 112 n. 41.

CHASE, Stuart [1888–1985]
The Tyranny of Words (New York: Harcourt, Brace and Company, 1938; 3rd edn, London: Methuen, 1939): 393 n. 7.

CLARK, Edwin Charles [1835–1917]
Practical Jurisprudence. A Comment on Austin (Cambridge: Cambridge University Press, 1883): 49 n. 8.

COHEN, Felix Solomon [1907–1953]
'Transcendental Nonsense and the Functional Approach', 35 *Columbia Law Review* (June 1935) No. 6, 809–49: 91 n. 17.

COSSIO, Carlos S. [1903–1987]
'Egologische Theorie und Reine Rechtslehre' [The theory of egologics and the Pure Theory of Law], *ÖZöR* (1952), 15 *et seq.*: 57 n. 30.
'Jurisprudence and the Sociology of Law', 52 *Columbia Law Review* (1952), 356 *et seq.*: 57 n. 30.

CRUET, Jean [1880–1909]
La vie du droit et l'impuissance des lois [The Life of the Law and the Impotence of Statutes] (Paris: E. Flammarion, 1914): 124 n. 1.

DABIN, Jean [1889–1971]
Le droit subjectif [Subjective Law] (Paris: Dalloz, 1952): 235 n. 5, 239 n. 14, 243 n. 18, 245 n. 23, 246 n. 24.

DANZ, Johann Moritz Erich [1850–1914]
Einführung in die Rechtsprechung. Anleitung für junge Juristen [Introduction to the Administration of Justice. Guidelines for young lawyers] (Jena: G. Fischer, 1912): 152 n. 41.

Del VECCHIO, Giorgio [1878–1970]
Die Gerechtigkeit [Justice] (Basel: Verlag für Recht und Gesellschaft AG, 1940): 357 n. 1, 358 n. 2.

DEMOGUE, René [1872–1938]
Les Notions Fondamentales du Droit privé. Essai critique [Fundamental Concepts of Private Law. A critical essay] (Paris: Librairie nouvelle de droit et de jurisprudence, Arthur Rousseau, 1911): 237 n. 7.

DICKINSON, John Sharpe [1894–1952]
'Legal Rules: Their Function in the Process of Decision', 79(7) *University of Pennsylvania Law Review* (1931), 833–68: 91 n. 17.

DIDERICHSEN, Paul Henrik Krag [1905–1964]
'Sprog og livssyn' [Language and worldview], in P. Bagge, P. Diderichsen, and H. V. Brøndsted, *Videnskab og livssyn* [Science and Worldview] (Copenhagen: Hans Reitzel, 1952; Series: *Mennesket i tiden*, Vol. 8): 164 n. 6, 167 n. 7.

DIELS, Hermann Alexander [1848–1922]
Die Fragmente der Vorsokratiker: griechisch und deutsch [Fragments of the Pre-Socratics: Greek and German], 5th edn (Berlin: Weidmann, 1934–1937): 322 n. 5.

DUGUIT, Léon [1859–1928]
Les transformations générales du droit privé depuis le Code Napoléon [The general transformations of private law since the Napoleonic Code] (Paris: Alcan, 1912): 50 n. 21.
Les transformations du droit public [The Transformations of Public Law] (Paris: Librairie Armand Colin, 1913): 50 n. 21.
Traité de droit constitutionel [Treatise on Constitutional Law], T. 1, 3rd edn (Paris: Fontemoing, 1927): 243 n. 18.

DURKHEIM, Émile [1858–1917]
De la division du travail social [The Division of Labour in Society] (Paris: F. Alcan, 1893): 50 n. 20.

EBERSTEIN, Gösta [1880–1975]
'Immaterialrätten och dess underarter' [Intellectual property law and its subdivisions], 50 *TfR* (1937), 81–90: 279 n. 12.
'Replik om polemik och systematik' [A reply on the issue of polemics and systematics], 51 *TfR* (1938), 40–45: 279 n. 12.
Om skydd för individualiteten: den personliga och den ekonomiska [On the Protection of Individualism: personal and economic] (Stockholm: Norstedt, 1940): 276 n. 9.
'Om författarrättens och konstnärsrättens föremål' [On the subject of copyright law and the law relating to artists' rights], 2 *NIR* (1946) 81–85: 279 n. 12.

ECKHOFF, Torstein Einang [1916–1993]
Rettsvesen og rettsvitenskap i U. S. A. [Legal System and Legal Science in the USA] (Oslo: Akademisk forlag, 1953): 204 n. 38, 225 n. 12, 238 n. 10, 345 n. 46, 372 n. 14.

EHRLICH, Eugen [1862–1922]
Grundlegung der Soziologie des Rechts [Fundamental Principles of the Sociology of Law] (Munich and Leipzig: Duncker & Humblot, 1913): 51 n. 23. [English publication under the title *Fundamental Principles of the Sociology of Law*, transl. by Walter L. Moll, with an introduction by Roscoe Pound (1936); with a new introduction by Klaus A. Ziegert (New Brunswick: Transaction Publishers, 2002)].

EKELÖF, Per Olof [1906–1990]
Straffet, skadeståndet och vitet. En studie över de rättsliga sanktionernas verkningssätt [Punishment, Damages, and Penalty. An investigation into the effect of legal sanctions] (Uppsala: Lundequist, 1942): 74 n. 49.

'Juridisk slutledning och terminologi' [Legal inference and terminology], 58 *TfR* (1945), 211–72: 245 n. 20 and 21.

'Till frågan om rättighetsbegreppet. En replik av professor Per Olof Ekelöf, Uppsala' [On the issue of the concept of rights. A reply on the part of professor Per Olof Ekelöf, Uppsala], 59 *TfR* (1946), 309–13: 245 n. 21.

'Om begagnandet av termen rättighet inom juridiken' [On the use of the term right in the law], in *Festskrift tillägnad Birger Ekeberg* [Tribute to Birger Ekeberg], ed. by *SvJT* (Stockholm, 1950), 151–77: 245 n. 21.

Är den juridiska doktrinen en teknik eller en vetenskap? [Is the Doctrinal Study of Law a Technique or a Science?] (Lund: Gleerup, 1951): 74 n. 49, 93 n. 20, 194 n. 31, 407 n. 17, 428 n. 6.

'Är termen rättighet ett syntaktisk hjälpmedel utan mening?' [Is the term right a syntactic tool devoid of meaning?], in *Skrifter tillägnade Vilhelm Lundstedt* [Papers dedicated to Vilhelm Lundstedt], 37 *SvJT*, issues 7–9 (1952), 546–59: 245 n. 21.

ENGELS, Friedrich [1820–1895]

Preface to the German edition (1883) of K. Marx and F. Engels, *Det kommunistiske Manifest* [The Communist Manifesto] (1945 [1848]): 437 n. 14 and 15.

EYBEN, William Edler von [1912–2000]

'Formuerettens grundbegreber' [The fundamental concepts of property law], 64 *TfR* (1951), 232–50: 254 n. 5.

FOSS, Kåre [1895–1967]

Ludvig Holbergs Naturrett på idéhistorisk bakgrunn [Ludvig Holberg's natural law as seen in light of the history of ideas] (Oslo: Gylendal, 1934): 336 n. 26.

FRANK, Jerome [1889–1957]

Law and the Modern Mind (New York: Brentano's, 1930): 91 n. 17, 119 n. 51, 150 n. 40.

'What Courts do in Fact', 26 *Illinois Law Review* (1932) 645 *et seq.*: 91 n. 17.

Courts on Trial: Myth and reality in American justice (Princeton, NY: Princeton University Press, 1949): 90 n. 16, 91 n. 17, 133 n. 16.

FRIEDMANN, Wolfgang Gaston [1907–1972]

Legal Theory, 2nd edn (London: Stevens & Sons, 1949): 124 n. 3, 191 n. 25, 320 n. 1, 345 n. 48, 346 n. 52, 353 n. 13, 354 n. 15.

FRISCH, Hartvig Marcus [1893–1950]

Athenernes statsforfatning. En filologisk-historisk analyse af pseudo-Xenofons skrift De re publica atheniensium [The Athenian Constitution. A philologico-historical analysis of pseudo-Xenophon's work *De re publica atheniensium*] (Copenhagen: Nyt Nordisk Forl./Busck, 1941): 327 n. 15, 328 n. 16.

Magt og Ret i Oldtiden. Dike 1: fra Homer til perserkrigene [Might and Right in Antiquity, Dike I: From Homer to the Persian Wars] (Copenhagen: Fremand, 1944): 320 n. 2, 322 n. 4 and 8, 323 n. 9, 324 n. 12, 325 n. 13. [English publication under the title *Might and Right in Antiquity, 'Dike' I: From Homer to the Persian Wars*, transl. by C. C. Martindale (Copenhagen: Gyldendalske Boghandel, 1949)].

FULLER, Lon Luvois [1902–1978]

'American Legal Realism', in 76 *Proceedings of the American Philosophical Society*, (1936), 191–235: 91 n. 17. [Originally published in 82 *University of Pennsylvania Law Review* 429 (1934)].

GEIGER, Theodor Julius [1891–1952]

Sociologi. Grundrids og hovedproblemer [Sociology. Outline and main problems] (Copenhagen: Nyt Nordisk forlag Arnold Busck, 1939): 353 n. 12.

Debat med Uppsala om Moral og Ret [Debate with Uppsala about Morality and Law] (Lund: Gleerup, 1946): 109 n. 40.

'Svar til Professor Alf Ross' [Reply to Professor Alf Ross], 28 *Juristen* (1946), 309–319: 109 n. 40.

Vorstudien zu einer Soziologie des Rechts [Preliminary Studies on the Sociology of Law] (Aarhus: Universitetsforlaget, 1947): 104 n. 34, 118 n. 94, 120 n. 54, 287 n. 19.

GÉNY, Francois [1861–1959]

Méthode d'interprétation et sources en droit privé positif. Essai critique, II [The Method of Interpretation and the Sources of Positive Private Law. A critical essay]: 2nd revised and updated edition (Paris: Librerairie Générale du Droit & de Jurisprudence, 1919): 374 n. 17.

GMÜR, Max [1871–1923]

Die Anwendung des Rechts nach Art. 1 des schweizerischen Zivilgesetzbuches [The Application of the Law according to Article 1 of the Swiss Civil Code] (Bern: Stämpfli & Cie, 1908): 152 n. 41.

GNAEUS FLAVIUS—see KANTOROWICZ, Hermann Ulrich

GOLDSCHMIDT, Verner [1916–1982]

'Retssociologiens praktiske Muligheder' [The practical possibilities of legal sociology], *UfR* (1952), B 261: 69 n. 38.

GOOS, Carl [1835–1917]

Indledning til den danske Strafferet [Introduction to Danish Penal Law] (Copenhagen: Gyldendal, 1875): 208 n. 44.

Den danske Strafferet II. Den danske Strafferets almindelige Del [Danish Penal Law II. General Part]

(1878): 311 n. 21.

Forelæsninger over den almindelige Retslære. 1, *Almindelig Del* [Lectures on the General Study of Law. 1, General Part] (1885): 72 n. 42, 104 n. 35, 143 n. 30, 153 n. 44, 154 n. 47 and 48, 239 n. 14, 303 n. 15, 311 n. 21, 22 and 23, 312 n. 25.

Forelæsninger over den almindelige Retslære. 2 [Lectures on the General Study of Law. 2] (1892): 313 n. 27.

GRAY, John Chipman [1839–1915]

The Nature and Sources of the Law (New York: The Columbia University Press, 1909): 49 n. 11, 119 n. 51, 149 n. 39.

GRUE-SØRENSEN, Knud [1904–1992]

Studier over refleksivitet. En filosofisk avhandling [Inquiries into Reflexivity. A philosophical treatise] (Copenhagen: J. H. Schultz, 1950): 70 n. 39, 128 n. 9.

GRUNDTVIG, Ludvig August [1868–1913]

Om Reklamation i formueretsforhold. Med særligt hensyn til køb og salg [On Complaints in Matters Pertaining to Property. With particular reference to buying and selling] (Köbenhavn: Salmonsen, 1903): 144 n. 34.

GURVITCH, Georges [1894–1965]

Sociology of Law (New York: Philosophical Library, 1942): 51 n. 23.

HAGERUP, George Francis [1853–1921]

'Nogle Ord om den nyere Retsvidenskabs Karakter' [A few words on the nature of modern legal science], 1 *TfR* (1888), 1–58: 207 n. 41.

HAINES, Charles Grove [1879–1948]

The Revival of Natural Law Concepts. A Study of the Establishment and of the Interpretation of Limits on Legislatures with special reference to the Development of certain phases of American Constitutional Law (Cambridge, MA: Harvard University Press, 1930; London: Humphrey Milford, Oxford University Press, 1930): 353 n. 13.

HALLER, Karl Ludwig von [1768–1854]

Restauration der Staats-Wissenschaft oder Theorie des natürlich-geselligen Zustands der Chimäre des künstlich-bürgerlichen entgegengesezt [On the Restoration of Political Science, or the theory of the natural condition of Mankind, as opposed to the chimera of artificial and civic conditions] (Winterthur: Steiner, 1816): 348 n. 3.

HAYAKAWA, Samuel Ichiyé [1906–1992]

Language in Thought and Action (New York: Harcourt, Brace, 1949): 159 n. 3.

HEARN, William Edward [1826–1888]

The Theory of Legal Duties and Rights (Melbourne: J. Ferres, 1883): 49 n. 9.

HECK, Philipp Nicolai von [1858–1943]

Gesetzesauslegung und Interessenjurisprudenz [Statutory Interpretation and the Jurisprudence of Interests], in 112 *Archiv für die civilistische Praxis* (1914): 152 n. 42.

HEDENIUS, Per Arvid Ingemar [1908–1982]

Om rätt och moral [On Law and Morality] (Stockholm: Tiden, 1941): 74 n. 49, 120 n. 52, 245 n. 20. [Reprinted Stockholm: Wahlström & Widstrand, 1963, 2nd edn, 1965].

HEDFELDT, Erik [1908–1986]

'Om upphovsmannarättens föremål' [On the subject matter of copyright law], 65 *TfR* (1952), 152–61: 279 n. 12.

HEGEL, Georg Wilhelm Friedrich [1770–1831]

Elements of the Philosophy of Right, ed. Allen H. Wood, translated by H. B. Nisbet (Cambridge: Cambridge University Press, 1991) [original title in German, *Grundlinien der Philosophie des Rechts*, 1820]: 341.

HERACLITUS [active *c.* 500 BC]

Fragment 94, in Hermann Diels, *Die Fragmente der Vorsokratiker: griechisch und deutsch* [Fragments of the Pre-Socratics: Greek and German], 5th edn (Berlin: Weidmann, 1934–1937): 322 n. 5.

HESIOD [born *c.* 700 BC]

Værker og dage [Works and Days], in H. Frisch, *Magt og Ret i Oldtiden* [Might and Right in Antiquity] (Copenhagen: Fremand, 1944): 323 n. 9.

HJEJLE, Bernt Ruben Hansen [1901–1994]
'Kontraheringspligt' [On obligation to contract], in *Festskrift til Henry Ussing* [A Tribute to Henry Ussing] (Copenhagen, 1951), 150–64: 278 n. 11.

HOHFELD, Wesley Newcomb [1879–1918]
'Some Fundamental Legal Conceptions as Applied in Judicial Reasoning', 23 *Yale Law Journal* 16 (1913), 28–59: 225 n. 12.
Fundamental Legal Conceptions as applied in judicial legal reasoning and other legal essays (New Haven, CT: Yale University Press, 1923): 218 n. 5.

HOLLAND, Thomas Erskine, Sir [1835–1926]
The Elements of Jurisprudence (Oxford: Clarendon Press, 1880): 48 n. 7, 373 n. 15.

HOLMES, Oliver Wendell, Jr. [1841–1935]
'The Path of the Law', 10 *Harvard Law Review* (1897) 457; repr. in Holmes, *Collected Legal Papers* (New York: Harcourt, Brace and Howe, 1920): 119 n. 51.

The HOLY BIBLE
1 Corinthians 11:13–15 [The Official King James Bible]: 350 n. 8.
Matthew 5:6 [The Official King James Bible]: 357 n.*).

HORVÁTH, Barna [1896–1973]
Rechtssoziologie. Probleme der Gesellschaftslehre und Geschichtslehre des Rechts [Sociology of Law. Issues concerning the social ethics and the history of law (Berlin-Grunewald: Verlag für Staatswissenschaften und Geschichte, 1934): 51 n. 23.

HULL, Cordell [1871–1955]
The Memoirs of Cordell Hull, Vol. 1 (New York: MacMillan, 1948): 353 n. 14.

HULT, Wendel Phillips Adalrik [1895–1960]
'Lagens bokstav och lagens andemening' [The letter and spirit of the law], 37 *SvJT* (1952), 579–608: 94 n. 21.

HURWITZ, Stephan Moritz [1901–1981]
Den danske Strafferetspleje [Criminal Procedure in Denmark], 2nd edn (Copenhagen: Gad, 1949): 293 n. 2.

HÄGERSTRÖM, Axel Anders Teodor [1868–1939]
Till frågan om den objektiva rättens begrepp. 1, *Viljeteorien* [On the Concept of Objective Law. 1, The Will Theory] (Uppsala: Akademiska bokhandeln, 1917): 74 n. 49.
Der römische Obligationsbegriff im Lichte der allgemeinen römischen Rechtsanschauung. 1 [The Roman Notion of Obligation in the Light of the General Roman View of Law. 1] (Uppsala: Almqvist & Wiksell, 1927): 74 n. 49, 236 n. 6.

HØJER, Andreas [1690–1739]
Juridisk Collegium over Processen, saaledes som den bruges I Dannemark og Norge, confereret med den, som bruges i Förstendommene og Tydskland; holden af Andreas Højer. Samlet og til Trykken befordret ved Hans Hagerup [Lecture on procedure as practised in Denmark and Norway, compared with the procedure practised in the Duchies and in Germany; lecture held by Andreas Højer. Collected and handed over to the printer by Hans Hagerup] (Kjøbenhavn, 1742): 132 n. 12.

IHERING, Rudolph von [1818–1892]

Geist des römischen Rechts auf den verschiedenen Stufen seiner Entwicklung [The Spirit of the Roman Law at the Various Stages of its Development], 4 vols. (Leipzig: Breitkopf und Härtel, 1883–1894): 245 n. 22.

ILLUM, Knud Mynster [1906–1983]

Forelæsninger over almindelig Formueret ved det Økonomiske Fakultet ved Aarhus Universitet [Lectures on General Property Law, held at the Faculty of Economics of Aarhus University], 2nd edn (Aarhus: Univ. forl. i Aarhus, 1939): 295 n. 5.

Lov og Ret [Law and Justice] (Copenhagen: Nyt Nordisk Forlag, 1945): 96 n. 23, 117 n. 44, 118 n. 45 and 48, 142 n. 28, 155 n. 52, 287 n. 19, 428 n. 7, 462 n. 31, 466 n. 36.

'Nogle korte bemærkninger om begrebet retsstridighed' [Some brief remarks on the concept of unlawfulness], *Juristen* (1951), 177–85: 313 n. 31.

JACOBSEN, J. Hartvig [1892–1952]

Ophavsretten: forfatter- og konstnerretten, national ret [Intellectual Property Law: Copyright and performers' rights, national law (Copenhagen: Gyldendal, 1941): 279 n. 12.

JANSSON, Jan-Magnus [1922–2003]

Hans Kelsens statsteori mot bakgrunden av hans rättsfilosofiska åskådning [Hans Kelsen's theory of the state against the background of his system of legal philosophy] (Helsinki: Societas Scientiarum Fennica, 1950): 112 n. 42, 120 n. 55, 130 n. 10.

JELLINEK, Georg [1851–1911]

Verfassungsänderung und Verfassungswandlung. Eine staatsrechtlich-politische Abhandlung [Constitutional Amendment and Constitutional Transformation. A constitutional political treatise] (Berlin: Häring, 1906): 192 n. 28.

JUSTINIAN I. [483–565]

Codex Justinianus: 132 n. 11.

JUUL, Stig [1907–1969]

Grundrids af den romerske Formueret [Outline of Roman Property Law] (Kjøbenhavn: Nyt Nordisk Forlag, 1942): 333 n. 22.

JØRGENSEN, Jørgen [1894–1969]

Psykologi paa biologisk Grundlag [Psychology on a Biological Basis]. H. 1–5 (Copenhagen 1941–1946): 53 n. 25, 445 n. 1, 446 n. 2 and 3, 447 n. 4.

JØRGENSEN, Poul Johannes [1873–1947]

Dansk Retshistorie. Retskildernes og Forfatningsretens Historie indtil sidste Halvdel af det 17. Aarhundrede [Danish Legal History. The history of the sources of law and of constitutional law until the second half of the 17th century] (Copenhagen: Gads forl., 1940): 138 n. 24.

KAILA, Eino [1890–1958]

Den mänskliga kunskapen: vad den är och vad den icke är [Human Knowledge: What it is and what it is not], transl. by G. H. von Wright (Helsingfors: Söderström, 1939; Stockholm: Natur och Kultur, 1939): 87 n. 14.

KANT, Immanuel [1724–1804]
Critik der practischen Vernunft [Critique of Practical Reason] (Riga: Johann Friedrich Hartknoch, 1788): 454 n. 20.
Metaphysik der Sitten [The Metaphysics of Morals], 3rd edn (Leipzig: Meiner, 1919): 349 n. 6, 366 n. 7.

KANTOROWICZ, Hermann Ulrich [Gnaeus Flavius] [1877–1940]
Der Kampf um die Rechtswissenschaft [The Battle for Legal Science] (Heidelberg: Carl Winter's, 1906): 189 n. 22.

KARLGREN, Gustaf Hjalmar Teodor [1897–1978]
Ändamålsbestemmelse och stiftelse [Provisions on the Purpose of a Foundation] (Lund 1951): 237 n. 8.

KELSEN, Hans [1881–1973]
Allgemeine Staatslehre [General Constitutional Theory] (Berlin: Julius Springer, 1925): 100 n. 27.
Reine Rechtslehre. Einleitung in die rechtswissenschaftliche Problematik (Leipzig: Franz Deuticke, 1934): 49 n. 15, 57 n. 30 [English publication under the title *Introduction to the Problems of Legal Theory*, transl. by B. L. Paulson and S. L. Paulson (Oxford: Clarendon Press, 1992)].
General Theory of Law and State, transl. by Anders Wedberg (Cambridge, MA: Harvard University Press, 1945): 49 n. 15, 57 n. 30, 265 n. 3, 284 n. 15.
The Law of the United Nations. A critical analysis of its fundamental problems (London: Stevens & Sons, 1950): 173 n. 12, 427 n. 4.

KISS, Géza [1882–1970]
'Gesetzesauslegung und "ungeschriebenes Recht": Kritische Beiträge zur Theorie der Rechtsquellen' [Statutory interpretation and 'unwritten law': Critical contributions to the theory of the sources of law], in *Iherings Jahrbücher für die Dogmatik des bürgerlichen Rechts* [Ihering's yearbook for the doctrine of civil law] (Jena 1897–1943), Vol. 58, NF Vol. 22 (Jena: Gustav Fischer, 1911), 413–486: 152 n. 41.
'Theorie der Rechtsquellen in der anglo-amerikanischen Literatur' [Theory of the sources of law in Anglo-American legal literature], in *Archiv für bürgerliches Recht* (Berlin: C. Heymann, 1889–1919) Vol. 39 (1913): 152 n. 41.

KNOPH, Ragnar Johan Gyth [1894–1938]
'Nogen Ord om Dommerens Stilling til Kutymen' [A few words on the judge's views on trade usage], *UfR* (1923) B: 144 n. 35.
Oversikt over Norges rett [Overview of Norwegian Law] (Oslo, 1934): 276 n. 8 and 9.
Åndsretten [Intellectual Property Law] (Oslo: Nationaltrykkeriet, 1936): 279 n. 12.
'Felles Nordisk åndsverkslovgivning?' [Common Nordic legislation on intellectual products?], 50 *TfR* (1937), 133–157: 279 n. 12.
Rettslige Standarder. Særlig grunnlovens § 97 [Legal standards. In particular § 97 of the Constitution [of Norway]] (Oslo, 1939): 144 n. 34, 371 n. 12.

KORZYBSKI, Alfred Habdank Skarbek [1879–1950]
Science and Sanity. An introduction to non-Aristotelian systems and general semantics, 2nd edn (Lancaster, PA and New York: Science Press, 1941): 159 n. 3.

KRAFT, Victor [1880–1975]

Einführung in die Philosophie: Philosophie, Weltanschauung, Wissenschaft [Introduction to Philosophy: Philosophy, *Weltanschauung*, Science] (Vienna: Springer, 1950): 87 n. 14, 321 n. 3, 329 n. 18.

KRUSE, Frederik Vinding—see VINDING KRUSE, Frederik

KUNZ, Josef Laurenz [1890–1970]

'Zur Problematik der Rechtsphilosophie um die Mitte des zwanzigsten Jahrhunderts' [On the problematics of legal philosophy in the mid-20th century], *ÖZöR* (1951), 1–26: 48 n. 1, 75 n. 51.

LASSEN, Julius [1847–1923]

Haandbog i Obligationsretten: almindelig del [Textbook on the Law of Obligations—General Part]; 3rd, partly revised edn (Copenhagen, 1917–1920): 144 n. 34.

'Afskedsforelæsning' [Farewell Lecture], *UfR* (1918) B. 17: 95 n. 22.

Lærebog i romersk Privatret [Handbook on Roman Private Law], 3rd edn (Copenhagen: Gad, 1924): 295 n. 5.

LASSWELL, Harold Dwight [1902–1978] and McDOUGAL, Myres S. [1906–1998]

'Legal Education and Public Policy', in Harold D. Lasswell, *The Analysis of Political Behaviour: An empirical approach* (London: Routledge and Kegan Paul, 1947): 413 n. 24.

LEE, Alfred McClung [1906–1992] and LEE, Elizabeth Briant [1908–1999]

The Fine Art of Propaganda. A study of Father Coughlin's speeches, ed. by Alfred McClung Lee & Elisabeth Briant Lee (New York: Harcourt, Bruce and Company, 1939): 404 n. 11.

LEVI, Edward Hirsch [1911–2000]

An Introduction to Legal Reasoning (Chicago, IL: The University of Chicago, 1949): 133 n. 16, 159 n. 1.

LÉVY-BRUHL, Henri [1884–1964]

'Les sources, les méthodes, les instruments de travail' [Sources, methods, and tools], in Léon Julliot de la Morandière (ed.), *Introduction à l'étude du droit* [Introduction to the Study of Law], t. 1 (Paris: Rousseau, 1951): 183 n. 16.

LEWES, George Henry [1817–1878]

The Biographical History of Philosophy from its Origin in Greece down to the Present Day, 3rd edn (London, 1867): 326 n. 14.

LEYRET, Henry [1864–1944]

Les Jugements du président Magnaud, réunis et commentés [The judgments of President Magnaud, collected and commented] (Paris: P.-V. Stock, 1900): 189 n. 23, 374 n. 17.

LINDBERG, Niels Tornøe [1904–1971]

Idealer og Regler i anvendt økonomik [Ideals and Rules in Applied Economics] (Kjøbenhavn: Arnold Busck, 1951): 413 n. 23.

LLEWELLYN, Karl Nickerson [1893–1962]

'A Realistic Jurisprudence—the Next Step', 30 *Columbia Law Review* (1930), 431 *et seq.*: 91 n. 17.

'Some Realism about Realism: Responding to Dean Pound', 44 *Harvard Law Review* (1931): 114

LUND, Arne Torben [1902–1970]
Billedkunsten i retlig Belysning. En fremstilling af den åndelige ejendomsret til kunstværker, arkitektur, kunstindustri, fotografier og mønstre [Pictorial Art in a Legal Perspective. A presentation of intellectual property law concerning works of art, architecture, art industry, photographs, and designs] (Copenhagen: Gad, 1944): 279 n. 12.

LUNDSTEDT, Anders Vilhelm [1882–1955]
Föreläsningar över valda delar av obligationsrätten [Lectures on Selected Parts of the Law of Obligation], Vols. I–IV (Uppsala: Norblad, 1920–1948): 74 n. 49.
Superstition or Rationality in Action for Peace? Arguments against founding a world peace on the common sense of justice: a criticism of jurisprudence [London: Longmans, Green, and Co., 1925): 74 n. 49.
Obligationsbegreppet. D.1, *Fakta och fiktioner* [The Concept of Obligation. Part One, Facts and fictions] (Uppsala: Norblad, 1929): 286 n. 16 and 17.
Obligationsbegreppet. D.2, H.1, *Den i förra delen hävdade åskådningen ytterligare konfronterad med jurisprudensens läror* [The Concept of Obligation. Part Two, H.1, The views maintained in Part One being measured still further against the doctrines of jurisprudence] (Uppsala: Norblad, 1930): 243 n. 19.
Grundlinjer i skadeståndsrätten. Senare delen. Strikt ansvar [The Basic Features of Tort Law. Part Two, Strict liability], Vol. I (1944): 286 n. 16 and 17.

MacIVER, Robert Morrison [1882–1970]
The Web of Government (New York: Macmillan, 1947): 104 n. 34, 146 n. 37, 440 n. 16.

MAGNUSSEN, O. K. [1881–1973]
'Er det Retsgode, der krænkes, det samme ved Barnemord og ved Manddrab?' [Is the legally protected interest that is being violated the very same in infanticide and homicide?], *UfR* (1929) B 193: 460 n. 29 and 30.
Naboretlige Studier [Studies in the Law Regulating Neighbouring Rights] (Copenhagen: G.E.C. Gad, 1950): 234 n. 3, 279 n. 12, 289 n. 23, 290 n. 25 and 27, 377 n. 27.

MAINE, Sir Henry James Sumner [1822–1888]
Ancient Law. Its connection with the early history of society, and its relation to modern ideas (London: John Murray, 1861): 50 n. 16.
Lectures on the Early History of Institutions (London: John Murray, 1875): 50 n. 16.

MARKBY, Sir William [1829–1914]
Elements of Law. Considered with Reference to Principles of General Jurisprudence (Oxford: Clarendon Press, 1871): 48 n. 5.

MARTINSON, Harry Edmund [1904–1978]
Vägen till Klockrike [The Road to Klockrike] (Stockholm: Bonnier, 1948; new edn, 1951): 403 n. 10. [English publication under the title *The Road*, transl. by M. A. Michael (London: Cape, 1955)].

MARX, Karl Heinrich [1818–1883]
Das Kapital. Kritik der politischen Oekonomie [Capital. A Critique of Political Economy] (Hamburg: Otto Meissner, 1867): 436 n. 9. [English publication under the title *Capital. A critique of political economy*, 2 vols., transl. from the third German edition (1883) by Samuel Moore and Edward Aveling, ed. by Friedrich Engels (London: Lawrence & Wishart, 1954)].

Der Bürgerkrieg in Frankreich. Adresse des Generalrats der Internationalen Arbeiterassoziation [The Civil War in France. Address of the General Council of the International Workingmen's Association (London, 1871)]; 3rd German edn (Berlin: Verlag der Expedition des 'Vorwärts' [T. Glocke], 1891): 436 n. 11.

MARX, Karl [1818–1883] and ENGELS, Friedrich [1820–1895]
Det kommunistiske Manifest [The Communist Manifesto] [1848]. [The volume contains Engels's preface to the German edition 1883]. Danish translation in *Socialismens klassikere* 1 (Copenhagen: Tidens Forlag, 1945): 436 n. 10.

McDOUGAL, Myres Smith [1906–1998]
'The Law School of the Future: From Legal Realism to Policy Science in the World Community', 56 *Yale Law Journal* 1345 (1947): 413 n. 24.

MILL, John Stuart [1806–1873]
Dissertations and Discussions Political, Philosophical and Historical, Vol. I (London: 1859–1875): 441 n. 18.
On Liberty (London: John W. Parker and Son, West Strand, 1859): 342

MORGENTHAU, Hans Joachim [1904–1980]
Scientific Man vs. Power Politics (Chicago, IL: University of Chicago Press, 1946): 413 n. 24.

MORRIS, Charles William [1901–1979]
Signs, Language and Behavior (New York: Prentice-Hall, 1946): 159 n. 3.

MYRDAL, Gunnar [1898–1987]
Vetenskap och politik i nationalekonomien [English translation as *The Political Element in the Development of Economic Theory*] (Stockholm: Norstedt, 1930): 386 n. 17.
An American Dilemma. The Negroe problem and modern democracy, 2 vols. (New York, 1944): 407 n. 16 and 18, 408 n. 19, 465 n. 34.

MØLLER, Ernst Johannes [1860–1916]
Forudsætninger. Bidrag til Belysning af Principerne for Retshandlers Afhængighed af Fyldestgörelsen av Parternes Forudsætninger [Presumptions. A contribution to highlight the principles governing the dependence of legal transactions on the realization of the presumptions of the parties] (Copenhagen: Gad, 1894): 251 n. 4.

NAWIASKY, Hans [1880–1961]
Allgemeine Rechtslehre als System der rechtlichen Grundbegriffe [General Theory of Law as a system of fundamental legal concepts], 2nd, revised and augmented edn (Einsiedeln: Benziger & Co., AG, 1948): 284 n. 14.

NÉKÁM, Alexander [1905–1982]
The Personality Conception of the Legal Entity (Cambridge, MA: Harvard University Press, 1938): 237 n. 7. [Repr. 1972].

NELSON, Leonard [1882–1927]
Kritik der praktischen Vernunft [Critique of Practical Reason] (Leipzig: Verlag Veit & Comp., 1917): 367 n. 9.

NÆSS, Arne Dekke Eide [1912–2009]
Interpretation and Preciseness, Vols. I–V (Oslo: Universitetets studentkontor, 1947–1951): 159 n. 3, 167 n. 8.

OFSTAD, Harald Frithjof Seiersted [1920–1994]
'Om deskriptive definisjoner af begrepet "rettsregel". En sammenligning mellom Hans Kelsen's og Alf Ross's definisjoner' [On descriptive definitions of the concept legal rule. Comparing Hans Kelsen's and Alf Ross's definitions], 65 *TfR* (1952), 38–83: 76 n. 1.

OGDEN, Charles Kay [1889–1957] and RICHARDS, Ivor Armstrong [1893–1979]
The Meaning of Meaning. A study of the influence of language upon thought and of the science of symbolism. With supplementary essays by B. Malinowski and F. G. Crookshank, 8th edn (London: Kegan Paul, 1946): 159 n. 3.

OLIPHANT, Herman [1884–1939]
'A Return to Stare Decises [*sic*]', 14 *American Bar Association Journal* (1928): 133 n. 17.

OLIVECRONA, Karl [1897–1980]
Om lagen och staten [On Law and the State] (Copenhagen: Ejnar Munksgaard, 1940): 55 n. 27, 74 n. 49, 100 n. 27, 102 n. 29, 117 n. 44, 296 n. 7. [English publication under the title *Law as Fact* (Copenhagen: Munksgaard, 1939)].
Lagens imperativ [The Imperative of the Law] (Lund: Gleerup, 1942): 55 n. 27.
'Viljan bakom rätten' [The will behind the law], 50 *StvT* (N. F. 29) (1947), 1–32: 104 n. 34, 296 n. 7.
'Penningen i civilrättens system' [The monetary unit in civil law systems], in *Skrifter tillägnade Vilhelm Lundstedt* [Writings dedicated to Vilhelm Lundstedt], 37 *SvJT*, Issues 7–9 (1952), 675–684: 287 n. 18.

ØRSTED, Anders Sandøe [1778–1860]
Eunomia, eller Samling af Afhandlinger henhørende till Moral-philosophien, Statsphilosophien og den Dansk-Norske Lovkyndighed. D.1 [Eunomia, or A Collection of Treatises on Moral Philosophy, Political Philosophy, and Danish-Norwegian Knowledge of the Law] (Kjøbenhavn: Seidelin, 1815): 72 n. 40.
Haandbog over den danske og norske Lovkyndighed. Med stadigt Hensyn til Hr. Etatsraad og Professor Hurtigkarls Lærebog. Vol. 1 [Compendium on Danish and Norwegian Knowledge of the Law. In perfect compliance with the textbook provided by Councillor of State, Professor Hurtigkarl] (Kjøbenhavn: Soldin, 1822): 154 n. 46, 187 n. 19, 208 n. 43.

PATON, Sir George Whitecross [1902–1985]
A Text-Book of Jurisprudence (Oxford: Clarendon Press, 1946): 49 n. 12, 133 n. 15, 134 n. 19, 191 n. 25.

PERELMAN, Chaïm [1912–1984]
De la justice [On Justice] (Brussels: Office de Publicité, 1945): 359 n. 4.
'Réflexions sur la justice' [Reflections on justice], *Revue de l'Institut de Sociologie*, no. 2/1951 (Brussels): 415 n. 25.
'Raison éternelle, raison historique' [Eternal reason, historic reason]. *Actes du VI Congrés des Sociétés de Philosophie de Langue Francaise* [Proceedings from the 6th conference of the Societies of philosophy in the French language] (Strasbourg, 1952): 415 n. 25.

PERELMAN, Chaïm [1912–1984] and OLBRECHTS-TYTECA, Lucie [1899–1987]
'Logique et rhétorique' [Logic and rhetoric], 140 *Revue philosophique* (Paris 1950), 1–35: 415 n. 25.

POPPER, Sir Karl Raimund [1902–1994]

The Open Society and its Enemies, Vol. I: *The spell of Plato* (London: Routledge, 1945): 327 n. 15, 329 n. 18, 330 n. 19, 361 n. 5; Vol. II: *The High Tide of Prophecy: Hegel, Marx, and the aftermath* (London: Routledge, 1945): 341 n. 37 and 38, 436 n. 12, 437 n. 13.

POUND, Nathan Roscoe [1870–1964]

'Scope and Purpose of Sociological Jurisprudence', 3 pts., 24 *Harvard Law Review* (1911), 140–68: 51 n. 22 [the other two parts are in 25 *Harvard Law Review* (1911–1912)].

Interpretations of Legal History (New York: Macmillan co., 1923): 51 n. 22.

Social Control through Law (New Haven, CT: Yale University Press, 1942): 51 n. 22.

Outlines of Lectures on Jurisprudence, 5th edn (Cambridge, MA: Harvard University Press, 1943): 51 n. 22.

PUCHTA, Georg Friedrich [1798–1846]

Das Gewohnheitsrecht [Customary Law] (Erlangen: Palm, 1828–1837): 434.

PUFENDORF, Samuel von [1632–1694]

Le droit de la nature et des gens, ou le système général des principes les plus importants de la morale, de la jurisprudence, et de la politique [The Law of Nature and Nations, or, A general system of the most important principles of morality, jurisprudence, and politics], transl. from the Latin by Jean Barbeyrac 1732 [new, revised and augmented edn London: Jean Nours, 1740]: 356 n. 20.

RADBRUCH, Gustav [1878–1949]

Vorschule der Rechtsphilosophie [Introduction to Legal Philosophy] (Willsbach u. Heidelberg: Scherer, 1947): 79 n. 4.

REHLING, Erik Johan Gerhard [1890–1978]

Skriftlig form. Fremstillingens vanskeligheder [Written Form. The problems of presentation] (Copenhagen: Schultz, 1948): 171 n. 9.

RENNER, Karl [1870–1950]

The Institutions of Private Law and their Social Functions, ed., with an introduction and notes, by O. Kahn-Freund (London, 1949): 68 n. 37. [Repr. 1976].

ROGUIN, Ernest [1851–1939]

La science juridique pure [The Pure Legal Science], 3 vols. (Paris: Librairie générale de droit et de jurisprudence, 1923): 49 n. 14.

ROHDE, Knut [1909–1999]

'Till frågan om förmögenhetsrättens systematik' [On the classification of property law], in *Festskrift tillägnad Birger Ekeberg* [A Tribute to Birger Ekeberg], ed. by *SvJT* (Stockholm, 1950): 274 n. 6.

ROMMEN, Heinrich Albert [1897–1967]

Le droit naturel: Histoire, doctrine [Natural Law: History and doctrine] (Paris: Egloff, 1945): 320 n. 1, 335 n. 25.

ROSS, Alf Niels Christian [1899–1979]

Theorie der Rechtsquellen. Ein Beitrag zur Theorie des positive Rechts auf Grundlage dogmenhistorischer Untersuchungen [Theory of the Sources of Law. A contribution to the theory of positive law based on historico-doctrinal studies] (Leipzig: Deuticke, 1929): 44 n. 1, 48 n. 4, 98 n. 26, 112 n. 42, 125 n. 7, 130 n. 10, 149 n. 38, 152 n. 41 and 42, 154 n. 45 and 51, 188 n. 20 and 21, 207 n. 41 and 42, 340 n. 31, 33 and 35, 342 n. 40, 344 n. 45, 345 n. 46, 346 n. 50 and 53, 372 n. 14, 433 n. 4 and 6, 434 n. 7, 435 n. 8, 441 n. 20.

'Privatlivets Fred' [The sanctity of private life], 45 *TfR*, new series XI (1932), 317–19: 276 n. 9.

'Realismen i Retsvidenskaben og Samfundsnyttekimæren' [Realism in legal science and the chimera of public utility], 17 *SvJT* (1932), 324–49: 44 n. 1, 383 n. 12, 384 n. 14, 447 n. 5.

Kritik der sogenannten praktischen Erkenntnis. Zugleich Prolegomena zu einer Kritik der Rechtswissenschaft [Critique of the So-called Practical Knowledge; likewise, the prolegomena to a critique of legal science]. Transl. of the Danish manuscript into German by Hans Winkler and Gunnar Leistikow (Copenhagen: Levin og Munksgaard, 1933): 44 n. 1, 312 n. 24, 329 n. 17, 332 n. 21, 333 n. 23, 336 n. 26, 339 n. 30, 340 n. 32 and 34, 341 n. 36 and 37, 342 n. 39, 41 and 42, 343 n. 43 and 44, 345 n. 47, 346 n. 49, 50, 51 and 52, 347 n. 1, 352 n. 10, 367 n. 9, 378 n. 1, 379 n. 5, 380 n. 6, 381 n. 7, 382 n. 9, 383 n. 11 and 12, 384 n. 13, 387 n. 1, 433 n. 4 and 5, 452 n. 14 and 15, 453 n. 16.

'Samfundsnytteprincippet. Gensvar til Professor Lundstedt' [The principle of public utility. A reply to Professor Lundstedt], 18 *SvJT* (1933), 115–20: 44 n. 1.

Virkelighed og Gyldighed i Retslæren. En Kritik af den teoretiske Retsvidenskabs Grundbegreber [Reality and Validity in Jurisprudence. A critique of the fundamental concepts of theoretical legal science] (Copenhagen: Levin & Munksgaard, 1934): 44 n. 1, 72 n. 40, 41 and 42, 73 n. 44, 76 n. 1, 85 n. 12 and 13, 103 n. 33, 104 n. 35, 109 n. 40, 111 n. 41, 112 n. 42, 116 n. 43, 155 n. 53, 207 n. 41, 220 n. 6, 225 n. 11, 234 n. 3 and 4, 236 n. 6, 237 n. 8, 240 n. 16, 243 n. 18 and 19, 245 n. 23, 246 n. 24, 249 n. 2, 250 n. 3, 257 n. 7, 258 n. 9, 290 n. 25, 305 n. 18, 312 n. 24, 319 n. 33, 352 n. 10 and 11, 355 n. 16, 17 and 18, 356 n. 19, 460 n. 30.

Ejendomsret og Ejendomsovergang. Med særligt Henblik paa dansk Retspraksis [Ownership and the Transfer of Ownership. With particular reference to Danish legal practice] (Copenhagen: Levin & Munksgaard, 1935): 44 n. 1, 205 n. 40, 225 n. 11, 238 n. 11, 239 n. 12 and 13, 258 n. 8.

Book review of Kåre Foss, *Ludvig Holbergs naturrett på idehistorisk bakgrunn* [Ludvig Holberg's natural law, as seen in light of the history of ideas] (Oslo: Universitetsforlaget, 1934), 49 *TfR*, new series XV (1936), 478–506: 336 n. 26.

'Den rene Retslæres 25-Aars Jubilæum. Anm. af H. Kelsen: Reine Rechtslehre' [The 25th Anniversary of the Pure Theory of Law. Review of H. Kelsen, Pure Theory of Law], 49 *TfR*, new series XV (1936), 304–31: 44 n. 1, 49 n. 15, 56 n. 28, 57 n. 30, 76 n. 1. [Translated into English by Henrik Palmer Olsen and published in 31(2) *Oxford Journal of Legal Studies* (2011), 243–72, at 243–64].

'Sondringen mellem privat og offentlig Ret. En Forelæsning' [The distinction between private and public law. A lecture], 49 *TfR*, new series XV (1936), 109–25: 44 n. 1, 450 n. 11.

'Rettens Grundproblemer. Betragtninger i anledning af to Nordiske Bøger' [The fundamental problems of law. Some reflections occasioned by two Nordic publications], 53 *TfR* (1940), 281–98: 44 n. 1.

'Vinding Kruses Bidrag til Retskildelæren' [Vinding Kruse's contribution to the doctrine of the sources of law], *UfR* (1940) B 149 *et seq.*: 44 n. 1.

'Imperatives and Logic', 7 *Theoria* (1941), 53–71: 44 n. 1.

Lærebog i Folkeret. Almindelig del [A Textbook of International Law. General Part] (Copenhagen: Munksgaard, 1942; 3rd edn 1951): 83 n. 9, 330 n. 19, 377 n. 26. [Published in English under the title *A Textbook of International Law. General Part* (London: Longmans, Green, 1974)].

'En Retslære fra det 19. Aarhundrede' [A jurisprudence dating from the 19th century], 58 *TfR* (1945), 273–92: 73 n. 46, 407 n. 15.

'Ophavsrettens Grundbegreber' [The fundamental concepts of intellectual property law], 58 *TfR* (1945), 321–53: 44 n. 1, 279 n. 12.

Hvorfor Demokrati? [Why Democracy?] (Copenhagen: Munksgaard, 1946): 103 n. 32, 334 n. 24, 336 n. 27, 340 n. 34, 341 n. 36. [English publication under the title *Why Democracy?* (Cambridge, MA: Harvard University Press, 1952)].

'Sociolog som Retsfilosof. Theodor Geiger: Debat med Uppsala om Moral og Ret' [A sociologist as a legal philosopher. Theodor Geiger: A debate with Uppsala on the issue of morality and law], 28 *Juristen* (1946), 259–69: 44 n. 1.

'Replik til Professor Geiger' [A reply to Professor Geiger], 28 *Juristen* (1946), 319–24: 109 n. 40.

Towards a Realistic Jurisprudence. A criticism of the dualism in law (Copenhagen: Munksgaard, 1946): 44 n. 1, 56 n. 28, 119 n. 51, 149 n. 39, 150 n. 40.

Book Review of Ernst Andersen, *Forfatning og Sædvane. Studier over nogle af Forfatningsrettens Hovedspørgsmaal* [Constitution and Custom. Inquiries into some of the major problems of Constitutional Law] (Copenhagen 1947, 152 pp.), 60 *TfR* (1947), 447–56: 354 n. 15.

Book Review of Otto Brusiin, *Über die Objektivität der Rechtsprechung* [On Objectivity in the Administration of Justice] (Helsinki 1949, 122 pp.), 63 *TfR* (1950), 473–78: 374 n. 16.

Book Review of Theodor Geiger, *Vorstudien zu einer Soziologie des Rechts* [Preliminary Studies on the Sociology of Law] (Aarhus: Universitetsforlaget, 1947, 347 pp.), 63 *TfR* (1950), 215–24: 74 n. 48, 77 n. 2, 104 n. 34.

'Om Begrebet "gældende Ret" hos Theodor Geiger' [On the concept 'valid law' in the work of Theodor Geiger], 63 *TfR* (1950), 242–72: 44 n. 1, 74 n. 48, 77 n. 2, 104 n. 34, 120 n. 54, 374 n. 16.

Book Review of Hans Kelsen, *The Law of the United Nations. A Critical Analysis of its Fundamental Problems*' (London: Stevens & Sons Ltd., 1950), *Jus Gentium* [ed. by Alf Ross] Vol. II (1951), 250–55: 428 n. 5.

'Opgør med Retstridighedslæren' [Against the doctrine of unlawfulness], 64 *TfR* (1951), 205–31: 44 n. 1, 310 n. 20, 313 n. 31.

'Tû-tû', in *Festskrift til Henry Ussing* [A Tribute to Henry Ussing] (1951), 468–84: 44 n. 1, 227 n. 1, 245 n. 21. [English translation in 70 *Harvard Law Review* (1957) 5, 812–25].

ROSS, Alf [1899–1979] and ANDERSEN, Ernst [1907–2002]

Dansk Statsforfatningsret II [Constitutional Law in Denmark II] (Copenhagen: Munksgaard, 1948): 180 n. 14, 205 n. 39.

RUSSELL, Bertrand Arthur William [1872–1970]

Power. A New Social Analysis (London: Allen & Unwin Ltd., 1938): 105 n. 36.

RÖDER, Karl David August [1806–1879]

Grundzüge des Naturrechts oder der Rechtsfilosofie [The Main Features of the Law of Nature, or of Philosophy of Law], Vol. II, 2nd edn (Leipzig, 1863): 337 n. 29.

SALMOND, John William, Sir [1862–1924]
Jurisprudence: or the Theory of the Law (London: Stevens & Haynes, 1902): 11 n.10; 10th edn (1947): 284 n. 14.

SCHEEL, Anton Wilhelm [1799–1879]
Privatrettens almindelige Deel, fremstillet efter den danske Lovgivning [Private Law. General Part, presented according to the Danish legislation] (Copenhagen: Reitzel, 1865): 143 n. 30.

SCHELLING, Friedrich Wilhelm Joseph von [1775–1854]
Ideen zu einer Philosophie der Natur [Ideas on a Philosophy of Nature] (Jena and Leipzig: Breitkopf und Härtel, 1797): 432 n. 3. [Published in English under the title *Ideas for a Philosophy of Nature as Introduction to the Study of this Science* (1797; 2nd edn, 1803) (Cambridge: Cambridge University Press, 1988)].
Von der Weltseele. Eine Hypothese der höheren Physik zur Erklärung des allgemeinen Organismus [On the World-Soul. A hypothesis of higher physics in order to explain the general organism] (Hamburg: F. Perthes, 1798): 432 n. 3.
Erster Entwurf eines Systems der Naturphilosophie. Zum Behuf seiner Vorlesungen [First Outline of a System of the Philosophy of Nature, for the purpose of instruction] (Jena and Leipzig: Christian Ernst Gabler, 1799): 432 n. 3. [Published in English under the title *First Outline of a System of the Philosophy of Nature,* translated, introduced, and annotated by Keith R. Peterson (Albany, NY: State University of New York Press, 2004)].
'Allgemeine Deduktion des dynamischen Prozesses oder der Kategorien der Physik' [General deduction of the dynamic process, or the categories related to physics], in *Zeitschrift für spekulative Physik*, Vol. I (Jena and Leipzig: Christian Ernst Gabler, 1800): 432 n. 3.

SCHLESINGER, Arthur M. [1888–1965]
The Age of Jackson, (Boston, MA: Little, Brown, 1946): 130.

SCHMIDT, Folke [1909–1980]
'Komparativt rättsstudium' [Comparative legal studies], 64 *TfR* (1951), 473–83: 67 n. 36.

SOMLÓ, Felix [1873–1920]
Juristische Grundlehre [The Basic Features of the Study of Law] (Leipzig: Meiner, 1917): 49 n. 13, 74 n. 50.

STALIN, Iosif Vissarionovitch Dzjugasjvili [1879–1953]
Vår teori och praktik [Our Theory and Practice] (Stockholm: Arbetarkultur, 1943): 393 n. 6.

STANG, Fredrik [1867–1941]
Innledning til Formueretten [Introduction to Property Law], 3rd edn (Oslo: Aschehoug, 1935): 263 n. 1, 295 n. 5.

STATI, Marcel O. [?]
Le standard juridique [The Legal Standard] (Paris: Librairie de jurisprudence ancienne et moderne, E. Duchemin *et al.*, 1927): 371 n. 12.

STEFFENS, Henrik [1773–1845]
Indledning til philosophiske Forelæsninger [Introduction to Lectures in Philosophy] (Copenhagen, 1803): 432 n. 3.

STEPHEN, Sir Leslie [1832–1904]
The English Utilitarians, Vol. 1 (London: Duckworth, 1900): 441 n. 17 and 18, 442 n. 21 and 22.

STEVENSON, Charles Leslie [1908–1979]
Ethics and Language (New Haven, CT: Yale University Press, 1944): 79 n. 5, 159 n. 3, 392 n. 5, 404 n. 11, 415 n. 25.

STONE, Julius [1907–1985]
The Province and Function of Law: Law as logic, justice and social control. A study in jurisprudence; second printing (Sydney: Maitland, 1950 [1946]): 75 n. 51, 125 n. 5, 320 n. 1, 345 n. 48, 346 n. 51, 353 n. 13, 451 n. 13.

STRAHL, Ivar [1899–1987]
'Till frågan om rättighetsbegreppet' [On the issue of the concept of rights], 59 *TfR* (1946), 204–10: 245 n. 21.
'Till frågan om rättighetsbegreppet' [On the issue of the concept of rights], 60 *TfR* (1947), 481–514: 245 n. 21.
Förberedande utredning angående lagstiftning på skadeståndsrättens område [Preparatory Investigation concerning Legislation in the Field of Tort Law], Statens offentlige utredningar [SOU] [Official Reports of the Swedish Government] 1950:16 (Stockholm 1950): 458 n. 26.

TIMASHEFF, Nicholas Sergeyevitch [1886–1970]
An Introduction to the Sociology of Law (Cambridge, MA: Harvard University Press, 1939): 51 n. 23.

TINGSTEN, Herbert Lars Gustaf [1896–1973]
De konservativa idéerna [The Conservative Ideas] (Stockholm: Bonnier, 1939): 348 n. 3, 349 n. 4.

TROLLE, Jørgen [1905–1985]
Syv Maaneder uden Politi [Seven Months without Police Force] (Copenhagen: Nyt Nordisk Forlag, 1945): 101 n. 28.

TÖNNIES, Ferdinand [1855–1936]
Gemeinschaft und Gesellschaft. Abhandlung des Communismus und des Socialismus als empirischer Culturformen [Community and Society. Treatise on Communism and Socialism as Empirical Patterns of Culture] (Leipzig: Fues's Verlag, 1887): 448 n. 6. [Published in English under the title *Community and Society* (New York: Harper & Row, 1957)].

ULLMANN, Stephen [1914–1976]
Words and their Use (New York: Philosophical Library, Inc., 1951): 159 n. 3.

UNDÉN, Bo *Östen* [1886–1974]
'Några systematiska spörsmål' [Some systemic problems], 50 *TfR* (1937), 419–22: 279 n. 12.

USSING, Carl Theodor [1857–1934]
'Løsøres Overdragelse' [The transfer of movables], 3 *TfR* (1890), 181 *et seq.*: 251 n. 4.

USSING, Henry Blom [1886–1954]
Dansk Obligationsret. Almindelig Del [The Danish Law of Obligations. General Part], 3rd edn (Copenhagen: Gad, 1946): 216 n. 3, 223 n. 8, 257 n. 7, 289 n. 23, 290 n. 25.

Dansk Obligationsret. Speciel Del, 2, Enkelte Kontrakter [The Danish Law of Obligations. Special part, 2, Individual contracts], 2nd edn (Copenhagen: Gad, 1946): 52, 56–7.

'Retstridighed. Strejflys over nordisk Retslære' [Unlawfulness. Sidelights on Nordic jurisprudence], in *Festskrift udgivet af Københavns Universitet* [Tribute published by the University of Copenhagen] (Copenhagen 1949): 120 n. 53, 313 n. 28, 29, 30 and 31.

Aftaler paa Formuerettens Omraade [Contracts in the Field of Property Law], 3rd edn (Copenhagen: Gads forl., 1950): 144 n. 32 and 36, 223 n. 8, 295 n. 5, 299 n. 8 and 9, 301 n. 10, 303 n. 14.

Nordisk Lovgivning om Erstatningsansvar [Nordic Legislation on Damage Liability]. Betænkning afgivet af Henry Ussing [Report submitted by Henry Ussing] (Copenhagen: J.H. Schultz, 1950): 421 n. 2, 459 n. 27 and 28.

'Redegørelse for forhandlingerne på den 7. internationale privatrets-konference Haag 1951' [Report of the conference proceedings at the 7th Hague conference on Private International Law at the Hague in 1951], *NTIRJG* (1952), 114–15: 239 n. 13.

'Til Retstridighedsdebatten' [On the debate on unlawfulness], 65 *TfR* (1952), 225–51: 310 n. 20, 313 n. 31.

Enkelte kontrakter, see *Dansk Obligationsret. Speciel Del, 2, Enkelte Kontrakter.*

VINDING KRUSE, Frederik [1880–1963; alternatively: KRUSE, Frederik Vinding]

'Til Problemet om Erstatningsansvar uden Skyld' [On the issue of liability without fault], 28 *TfR* (1915), 265–96: 306 n. 19.

'Til Livsforsikringsretten. Problemet om Tredjemandsretshandlen' [Concerning life insurance law. The problem of third-party agreements], 32 *TfR* (1919), 175–238: 302 n. 13.

Ejendomsrettens Overgang [Ownership Transition] (Christiania: Det Mallingske Bogtrykkeri, 1924): 205 n. 40.

Ejendomsretsspørgsmål [Some Problems in Connection with Property Law] (Copenhagen: Nyt Nordisk Forlag—Arnold Busck, 1934): 279 n. 12.

Erkendelse og Vurdering. Erkendelselærens og Etikkens Grundproblem [Knowledge and Evaluation. The fundamental problems of epistemology and ethics] (Copenhagen: Nyt Nordisk Forlag—Arnold Busck, 1942): 407 n. 15, 424 n. 3.

Retslæren [Jurisprudence], 2 vols. (Copenhagen: Nyt Nordisk Forlag, 1943–1963): 73 n. 45, 154 n. 49, 209 n. 45, 278 n. 11, 484 n. 14, 296 n. 6, 302 n. 13, 348 n. 2, 407 n. 15, 424 n. 3.

Ejendomsretten [The Right of Property], 3 vols., 3rd edn (Copenhagen: Gad, 1951): 251 n. 4, 259 n. 10, 279 n. 12, 288 n. 20, 289 n. 22, 290 n. 26, 301 n. 11, 302 n. 12 and 13, 377 n. 28.—[Volume I of this work—translated from the Danish by P.T. Federspiel—was published in English in 1939 (Oxford: Oxford University Press, 1939), and volume II—translated from the Danish by David Philip—in 1953 (Oxford: Oxford University Press, 1953)].

VINOGRADOFF, Paul Gavrilovitch, Sir [1854–1925]

Historical Jurisprudence (London: Oxford University Press, 1923): 50 n. 18.

VISLIE, Jon Asbjørn [1896–1945]

Lovmotivers betydning for lovfortolkningen [The Importance of Legislative Material in Statutory Interpretation] (Oslo: Olaf Norlis Forlag, 1932): 191 n. 26.

WEDBERG, Anders [1913–1978]

'Some Problems in the Logical Analysis of Legal Science', 17 *Theoria* (1951), 246–75: 245 n. 21.

WESTERMARCK, Edward Alexander [1862–1939]

The Origin and Development of the Moral Ideas, Vol. I, 2nd edn (1924 [1906]): 137 n. 21, 22 and 23; Vols. I–II, 2nd edn (1924–26 [1906–1908]): 455 n. 23.

WESTRUP, Carl Wium [1874–1958]

Introduction to Early Roman law: Comparative sociological studies, 4 parts (Copenhagen: Levin & Munksgaard/ London: Humphrey Milford, Oxford University Press, 1934–1954): 74 n. 47, 320 n. 2.

Rettens Opstaaen [The Origin of Law] (Copenhagen: Einaar Munksgaard, 1940): 74 n. 47, 320 n. 2, 322 n. 6 and 7, 323 n. 10.

WINDSCHEID, Bernhard [1817–1892]

Lehrbuch des Pandektenrechts [Textbook of the Law of Pandects], 3 vols., 10th edn, revised by Theodor Kipp (Frankfurt am Main: Rütten & Loening, 1906): 245 n. 23.

von WRIGHT, Georg Henrik [1916–2003]

Den logiska empirismen: en huvudriktning i modern filosofi [Logical Empiricism: A predominant movement in modern philosophy] (Helsingfors: Söderström, 1943; Stockholm: Natur och kultur, 1943): 87 n. 14.

ZEUTHEN, Frederik Ludvig Bang [1888–1959]

Vurderinger og Maalsætninger i økonomien: I velfærds-teoretisk belysning [Evaluations and Objectives in Economics: In light of welfare theory] (Copenhagen: Universitetets Statistiske Laboratorium, 1952): 385 n. 15, 386 n. 16.

ZWEIG, Stefan [1881–1942]

Schachnovelle [The Royal Game] (Stockholm: Bermann-Fischer, 1943 [Buenos Aires 1942]): 60 n. 31.

Index of Names

For the benefit of digital users, indexed terms that span two pages (e.g., 52–3) may, on occasion, appear on only one of those pages.

Subject Index

For the benefit of digital users, indexed terms that span two pages (e.g., 52–3) may, on occasion, appear on only one of those pages.

The manufacturer's authorised representative in the EU for product safety is Oxford University Press España S.A. of el Parque Empresarial San Fernando de Henares, Avenida de Castilla, 2 – 28830 Madrid (www.oup.es/en or product.safety@oup.com). OUP España S.A. also acts as importer into Spain of products made by the manufacturer.

www.ingramcontent.com/pod-product-compliance
Lightning Source LLC
Chambersburg PA
CBHW070925140926
51335CB00087B/183
* 9 7 8 0 1 9 8 7 1 6 1 0 5 *